**McGRAW-HILL
BOOK COMPANY**
New York
St. Louis
San Francisco
Auckland
Düsseldorf
Johannesburg
Kuala Lumpur
London
Mexico
Montreal
New Delhi
Panama
Paris
São Paulo
Singapore
Sydney
Tokyo
Toronto

BILLY E. GILLETT, Ph.D.

*Professor of Computer Science
University of Missouri-Rolla*

Introduction to Operations Research

A COMPUTER–ORIENTED ALGORITHMIC APPROACH

This book was set in Times Roman by Hemisphere Publishing Corporation.
The editors were B. J. Clark and M. E. Margolies;
the cover was done by Pencils Portfolio, Inc.
The production supervisor was Leroy A. Young.
The drawings were done by ANCO Technical Services.
Kingsport Press, Inc., was printer and binder.

Library of Congress Cataloging in Publication Data

Gillett, Billy E
    Introduction to operations research.

    (McGraw-Hill series in industrial engineering and
management science)
    1. Operations research. I. Title.
T57.6.G56   001.4'24   75-29238
ISBN 0-07-023245-8

**INTRODUCTION TO
OPERATIONS
RESEARCH**
A COMPUTER–ORIENTED
ALGORITHMIC APPROACH

7 8 9 0 K P K P 8 3

To my wife,
CLARA,
and children,
DANNY, KRIS, and LAURA

CONTENTS

PREFACE

It was not until the advent of computers that operations research (OR) made its impact on our society. Although theoretical results had been worked out for the solution of many types of problems earlier, quite often they could not be applied to "real" problems because of the amount of calculation involved. Today the computer is the core of every operations research group; however, very little has been done to fulfill the need for computer-oriented textbooks in operations research. Thus, the motivation for *this* textbook.

A computer-oriented approach is used throughout this book to acquaint those interested in problem solving with the important methods of operations research in a way that they can start solving realistic problems immediately. This approach is especially appealing because of the role the computer plays in the problem-solving process. The general approach throughout is:

1 Formulation of the problem to be solved
2 Construction of a model of the problem
3 Development of a method to solve the model
4 Presentation of a concise computer-oriented algorithm to solve the model
5 Presentation of a FORTRAN computer program for the algorithm

The development of most of the methods of solution is preceded by one or more illustrative examples, many with computer solutions. Parts 1–3 above help the reader learn about the types of problems that can be solved by a particular method and how to model the problem for solution. Part 4, which is written to cover the method in general, is a detailed step-by-step procedure that can be easily programmed for the computer. Then finally, part 5 gives the reader an opportunity to solve a large variety of problems and to emphasize the analysis of the results, thus enhancing the reader's problem-solving ability.

This book is designed to serve as an introductory OR textbook for undergraduates interested in problem solving, as a textbook for a short course in computer-oriented methods, and as a handbook of optimization methods and computer programs for the practitioner. It is meant as a survey of the important methods of operations research integrating the computer and the methods. It can equally serve the practitioner, the student who plans to study operations research in depth, or the student who only desires an appreciation of the general area of operations research.

The text is divided into two parts. Part I covers deterministic models and methods of solution, while Part II covers probabilistic models and methods of solution.

Each part is independent of the other. The deterministic methods are presented first so that the reader who is unfamiliar with probability can become acquainted with the general computer-oriented algorithmic approach first. The chapter on probability theory is not intended as a comprehensive coverage of the subject. Rather, it presents only the essential elements of probability that are required throughout the remaining chapters in Part II.

Since computer programming has become an essential tool in most academic programs and is taught on the majority of campuses, a basic knowledge of FORTRAN programming is assumed throughout the book. A multitude of introductory programming texts is available to those who are deficient in this area. The only mathematical background assumed is a first course in calculus.

This book differs from other texts in the area in its overall computer-oriented approach. In addition, many of the latest OR methods from the literature are presented in easy to understand algorithmic form suitable for programming.

Many of the algorithms are also followed by a useful FORTRAN program that has been run on an IBM 370/168 computer. The processing time for each example problem is for the IBM 370/168. A description of how to modify the storage requirements to meet the needs of users with a limited amount of storage is given.

All computer programs are available from the author for a fee to cover reproduction, handling, and mailing.

ACKNOWLEDGMENTS

I am deeply indebted to Sister Joseph Kieran McAdams for her dedicated devotion during the preparation of this textbook. My sincere thanks go out to her for the many, many days she spent above and beyond the call of duty reading and rereading the manuscript, writing many of the computer programs, checking out all of the programs in the text in minute detail, and helping in the preparation of the solutions manual. Her suggestions and comments were extremely helpful. Words of thanks are only a token of my true appreciation for all she has done to make this textbook possible.

Questions, suggestions, and comments from hundreds of students during the past 11 years have been extremely valuable. My appreciation is extended to Professors F. Garnett Walters, Howard Pyron, and C. Y. Ho for using preliminary versions of the book in their classes. A special thanks goes to Professor Thomas B. Baird for reading the inventory chapters and offering valuable suggestions.

Finally, my family has been inspirational in their understanding, patience, and encouragements during the many long days and nights that were devoted to this project.

BILLY E. GILLETT

**INTRODUCTION TO
OPERATIONS
RESEARCH**
A COMPUTER–ORIENTED
ALGORITHMIC APPROACH

1
INTRODUCTION

1.1 THE BEGINNING AND PROGRESS OF OPERATIONS RESEARCH

Any problem that requires a positive decision to be made can be classified as an operations research (OR) type problem. However, the approach used in decision making has changed considerably over the years. Although OR problems have existed since the creation of man, it was not until World War II that the name *operations research* was coined and the scientific approach of modern OR came into being. The name probably came from a program undertaken by Great Britain during World War II, "research in military operations," thus operations research. It was during the early part of the war that Great Britain brought together a group of specialists from a number of areas to work on the military defense of their country. The work of this first OR group involved, among other things, studies to determine the best use of airpower and the newly invented radar. Because of the success of OR in military operations, it quickly spread to all phases of industry and government. By 1951, OR had taken its place as a distinct science in the United States. Trefethen [11] gives an excellent history of OR since its beginning.

As big business emerged after World War II, many businesses became so diversified and complex that top management quickly lost control of the business as a whole. This prompted a division of management. Further divisions evolved until finally each department or division was interested only in its own welfare without regard for the other areas of the business. This drastically constrained the potential overall effectiveness. Consequently, OR groups, which consisted of specialists from several areas, were formed to assist management in optimizing the overall effectiveness of the business, while recognizing the importance of separate functional units within the business.

Churchman, Ackoff, and Arnoff [2] point out that

> The systems approach to problems does not mean that the most generally formulated problem must be solved in one research project. However desirable this may be, it is seldom possible to realize it in practice. In practice, parts of the total problem are usually solved in sequence.

The methods presented herein are applicable to the well-defined subproblems that are solved in sequence. The emphasis throughout this book is on learning computer-oriented OR methods that are applicable to a large number of problems, rather than on learning the overall systems approach to solving very large problems.

Churchman, Ackoff, and Arnoff [2], as well as Hillier and Lieberman [5], discuss in detail the six standard phases of an OR project, namely:

1 Formulating the problem
2 Constructing a mathematical model to represent the system under study
3 Deriving a solution from the model
4 Testing the model and the solution derived from it
5 Establishing controls over the solution
6 Putting the solution to work: implementation

However, the nature of this text dictates that we concentrate primarily on phases 1, 2, and 3. This in no way is meant to minimize the importance of the other necessary phases of every OR project, but our emphasis is on the methods used to derive an optimal solution for a given mathematical model of a problem.

Of course, the concurrent development of the digital computer is credited with the rapid progress of OR in this country. For example, the simplex method of linear programming was developed in 1947 by George B. Dantzig, but it lay dormant with respect to realistic problems until the mid- to late 1950s when the computer, with its high speed and large storage capacity, became commonplace in many universities and businesses, as well as in government agencies. Since that time, the computer has assisted the development and/or implementation of most of the OR methods in use today. It is clear to most that OR is vitally dependent upon the computer, for without it OR would be reduced to a theoretical science rather than the ever-expanding field that it is. It is because of the computer's essential and vital role in OR that we have merged the two in this textbook.

1.2 CLASSIFICATION OF PROBLEMS IN OPERATIONS RESEARCH

Although there is no single classification of problems that are candidates for solution by methods of operations research, most problems fall into one of the following categories:

1 Sequencing
2 Allocation
3 Routing
4 Replacement
5 Inventory
6 Queueing
7 Competitive
8 Search

Mathematical models have been constructed for each of these categories, and methods for solving the models are available in many cases.

Sequencing problems involve placing items in a certain sequence or order for service. For example, in a job shop, N jobs requiring different amounts of time on different machines must each be processed on M machines in the same order with no passing between machines. How should the jobs be ordered for processing to minimize the total time to process all of the jobs on all of the machines? The solution is quite simple for the two-machine problem and for a special case of the three-machine problem, but is several magnitudes more difficult for the general M-machine problem.

Allocation problems involve the allocation of resources to activities in such a way that some measure of effectiveness is optimized. For example, if the measure of effectiveness can be represented as a linear function of several variables subject to a number of linear constraints involving the variables, then the allocation problem is classified as a *linear programming problem*. Likewise, if the resource is people who can each perform any one of several jobs, possibly in different amounts of time, and the measure of effectiveness is the total time to perform all of the jobs when one and only one person is "allocated" to each job, then the problem is classified as an *assignment problem*. Suppose person A takes 2 min to perform job 1 and 4 min to perform job 2. Likewise, suppose person B takes 3 and 2 min to perform jobs 1 and 2, respectively. Which person should be assigned to each job to minimize the total time to perform both jobs? Obviously, by inspection or enumeration, person A should perform job 1 and person B should perform job 2 for a total effectiveness of 3. Suppose further that three people and three jobs are involved with the corresponding times given by

	Job		
Person	1	2	3
A	2	6	3
B	8	4	9
C	5	7	8

Which person should perform each job? If we enumerate all possible assignments, we have

	Assignments					
	A:1	A:1	A:2	A:2	A:3	A:3
	B:2	B:3	B:1	B:3	B:1	B:2
Total	C:3	C:2	C:3	C:1	C:2	C:1
effectiveness:	14	18	22	20	18	12

Thus, the minimum total effectiveness (time) is 12 units and is obtained by assigning person A to job 3, B to job 2, and C to job 1. These are trivial problems, but suppose 20 people are available to perform 20 jobs. What is the minimum time to perform all jobs? How long do you suppose it would take our fastest computer to find the solution by enumeration? If you guessed thousands of years, you guessed correctly, for there are

$$20! = 20 \cdot 19 \cdot 18 \cdot \ldots \cdot 1 \approx 2.433 \times 10^{18}$$

different assignments to be checked. Obviously, some other means of solution must be used.

Routing problems involve finding the optimal route from an origin to a destination when a number of possible routes are available. The classical traveling salesman problem is an example. A salesman wishes to visit each of N cities once and only once before returning to his home office. In what order should he visit the cities to minimize the overall distance traveled? This problem arises as a subproblem of the *vehicle dispatch or delivery problem.* Once a set of distinct locations have been assigned to a certain truck route in the delivery problem, in what order should the locations be visited to minimize the total distance traveled?

Replacement problems occur when one must decide the optimal time to replace equipment that deteriorates or fails immediately. When, if ever, should an automobile be replaced with a new one? This is a problem faced by most of us today. Of course, we each have our own measure of effectiveness, so there would not be a single optimal answer for everyone even if each automobile gave exactly the same service. Much depends on the purpose of the car, the role prestige plays in our lives, how fast we drive, etc. Another type of replacement problem involves equipment that works perfectly until it fails, such as a light bulb or an intricate computer component. What is the optimal replacement policy for this type of equipment?

The problem of deciding how much of a certain product to hold in inventory is one of real concern. If a customer requests a certain quantity of the product but it is not available, this could mean a lost sale. On the other hand, if an excess of the product is carried in inventory, the many costs associated with inventory may be unacceptable. Hence, the *inventory problem* is to determine the level of inventory that will optimize some measure of effectiveness.

Queueing problems plague us from the time we rise in the morning until we retire at night. Wait for the bathroom, wait for breakfast, wait at stoplights, wait for the computer, wait, wait, wait; that's the story of our lives. Any problem that involves waiting for service is classified as a *queueing or waiting-line problem*. The OR literature is bulging with solutions for many types of queueing models; however, most realistic queueing problems are so complex and the components so interrelated that simulation is a vital technique in this general area.

Competitive problems arise when two or more people are competing for a precious resource. The resource may range from an opponent's king in chess to a larger share of the market in business. Quite often a competitive problem involves bidding for a contract to perform a service or to obtain some type of privilege. A number of different types of bidding procedures are used, but in each case competition is involved. Formal models of realistic problems in this area are scarce; however, the underlying concepts of the decision-making process are worthy of some study.

Search problems differ from the other types of problems we have discussed in that they all involve searching for information that is necessary to make a decision. Some examples are:

Searching the ocean for enemy ships
Auditing books for errors
Exploring for valuable natural resources, such as oil, copper, or coal
Retrieving information from computer storage
Shopping for a new suit

In each case, the objective is to minimize the costs associated with collecting and analyzing data to reduce decision errors and to minimize the costs associated with the decision errors themselves. We will see later that statistical decision theory provides a basis for solving many search problems.

1.3 MATHEMATICAL MODELING IN OPERATIONS RESEARCH

Suppose we want an optimal solution of a given problem. To get at the solution, it is usually more meaningful and convenient to write out the problem in mathematical terms. This mathematical description or representation of the problem is called a *mathematical model* of the problem. Generally, it is easier to get a "handle" on the model and solve it rather than the problem in its original nonmathematical form. If a mathematical model of a given problem can be solved either analytically or numerically, the solution can then be applied to the original problem. If the mathematical model is a good representation of the problem, the solution of the model will be a good solution of the problem. On the other hand, even an exact solution of a poor model will not be a good solution of the problem.

Many problems can be represented by a number of different models, but one model is usually more appropriate than others. To this end, a number of unique models with appropriate methods of solution have become well known during the past 25 years. For example, linear programming models, dynamic programming models, inventory models, and queueing models have solutions readily available. Thus, if a given problem can be modeled as (put into the mathematical form of) a certain type of linear programming model, the method of solution is immediately available. The object of any OR project is to determine the most appropriate mathematical model for the problem at hand, and either use available methods to solve the model or develop new methods of solution.

It may be that a mathematical model of a given problem cannot be constructed. On the other hand, it may be possible to construct a mathematical model, but exact methods for solving the model may not be readily available or may not be amenable for computer solution because of the large amount of computer storage or time required. Consequently, an alternative in this situation is to use an intuitive or heuristic approach to the solution. This approach has been used successfully to solve problems directly without formulating a mathematical model. It has also been used to provide approximate and/or exact solutions of many mathematical models of problems. Quite often heuristic methods provide exact, or at least adequate, solutions of problems much faster than numerical methods that are used to solve an appropriate model of the given problem. For example, one type of problem involving the allocation of resources to activities may be formulated as an integer linear programming model; however, a heuristic method called the *Hungarian method* provides the solution of the problem much faster in most cases.

Finally, if a problem is so complex that it cannot be modeled adequately for solution by one of the available methods or if it cannot be solved adequately with a heuristic method, then the problem solver usually resorts to simulation. Of course, simulation is not the answer to all problems; nevertheless, it does have a great deal of merit in studying large, complex systems where the components are highly interrelated. We will discuss the positive and negative aspects of simulation in Chapter 14.

It is our purpose to present computer-oriented algorithms for most of the methods used to solve the well-known mathematical models, as well as algorithms for important heuristic methods. In most cases, a computer program for the algorithm is presented so the reader can be exposed to the solution and analysis of a large variety of problems to enhance his problem-solving ability. A number of up-to-date methods from the literature are also presented in easy-to-grasp algorithmic form.

SELECTED BIBLIOGRAPHY

1 Ackoff, Russell L., and Maurice W. Sasieni: "Fundamentals of Operations Research," John Wiley & Sons, Inc., New York, N.Y., 1968.
2 Churchman, Charles W., Russell L. Ackoff, and L. Arnoff: "Introduction to Operations Research," John Wiley & Sons, Inc., New York, N.Y., 1957.

3 Cooper, Leon, and David Steinberg: "Introduction to Methods of Optimization," W. B. Saunders, Philadelphia, Pa., 1970.

4 Gaver, Donald P., and G. L. Thompson: "Programming and Probability Models in Operations Research," Brooks/Cole Publishing Co., Monterey, Calif., 1973.

5 Hillier, Frederick S., and Gerald J. Lieberman: "Operations Research," 2d ed., Holden-Day, Inc., San Francisco, Calif., 1974.

6 Levin, Richard I., and Charles A. Kirkpatrick: "Quantitative Approaches to Management," 3d ed., McGraw-Hill Book Company, New York, N.Y., 1975.

7 Sasieni, Maurice, A. Yaspan, and L. Friedman: "Operations Research: Methods and Problems," John Wiley & Sons, Inc., New York, N.Y., 1959.

8 Shamblin, James E., and G. T. Stevens, Jr.: "Operations Research, A Fundamental Approach," McGraw-Hill Book Company, New York, N.Y., 1974.

9 Taha, H. A.: "Operations Research, An Introduction," Macmillan, Inc., New York, N.Y., 1971.

10 Thierauf, Robert J., and Robert C. Klekamp: "Decision Making Through Operations Research," 2d ed., John Wiley & Sons, Inc., New York, N.Y., 1975.

11 Trefethen, F. N.: A History of Operations Research, in Joseph F. McCloskey and F. Trefethen (eds.), "Operations Research for Management," The Johns Hopkins University Press, Baltimore, Md., 1954.

12 Wagner, Harvey M.: "Principles of Operations Research," 2d ed., Prentice-Hall, Inc., Englewood Cliffs, N.J., 1975.

PART ONE

Deterministic Operations Research Models

2

DYNAMIC PROGRAMMING

2.1 INTRODUCTION

Dynamic programming is a mathematical technique that is applicable to many types of problems. It has been used to solve problems in areas such as allocation, cargo loading, replacement, sequencing, scheduling, and inventory. However, dynamic programming is an "approach" to the solution of problems rather than a single algorithm that can be used to solve all of these types of problems. Thus, a separate algorithm is needed for each type of problem. Many problems fall into the general category of allocation problems, so a single dynamic programming algorithm could be used to solve problems such as investing in securities, allocating money for advertising, or assigning men to jobs. On the other hand, a different algorithm or formulation of equations would be needed to solve an equipment replacement problem.

The dynamic programming approach involves the optimization of multistage decision processes. That is, it basically divides a given problem into stages or subproblems and then solves the subproblems sequentially until the initial problem is finally solved. The heart of the dynamic programming approach is the *principle of optimality* set forth by Bellman [2]. It states that

> An optimal policy has the property that whatever the initial state and initial decision are, the remaining decisions must constitute an optimal policy with regard to the state resulting from the first decision.

This principle of optimality is an extremely powerful concept and should become more meaningful to the reader as the dynamic programming algorithms are developed for the examples in Section 2.2.

Although dynamic programming can be used to determine the optimal solution for a large variety of problems, it is by no means the most efficient method to use in all cases. Experience and ingenuity are the guiding factors in determining when to use dynamic programming. In addition, there are a number of problems for which dynamic programming algorithms have been developed, but because of time and storage limitations of present-day computers, only the very small problems can be solved. One example is the traveling salesman problem formulated in Chapter 5. Dynamic programming can be used to solve the 10-, 15-, and 25-city problems but is out of the question for large problems involving 50 or more cities.

Several examples are presented in Section 2.2 to illustrate the underlying concepts of dynamic programming for a particular type of problem. In each example a detailed step-by-step development of the solution using the concept of dynamic programming is followed by a concise dynamic programming algorithm and the corresponding computer program to solve the problem. Our first problem deals with the allocation of money to investment programs.

2.2 INVESTMENT PROBLEM

Consider the general problem of allocating a fixed amount of resource (money) to a number of activities (investment programs) in such a way that the total return is maximized. More specifically, for simplicity, suppose only 8 units of money are available for allocation in unit amounts to three investment programs. The return function for each program is tabulated in Table 2.1. The function $g_i(x)$ represents the return from investing x units of money in the ith investment program ($i = 1, 2, 3$).

The return from each program is independent of the allocation to the other programs. For example, $g_2(5) = 70$ is the return from investing 5 units in program 2 regardless of how the remaining 3 units are allocated to the other two programs.

The other assumptions needed to apply dynamic programming are:

1 The returns from all programs can be measured in a common unit. Note that the unit of measure for x need not be the same as the unit of measure for the

Table 2.1 RETURN FUNCTIONS, $g_i(x)$

x	0	1	2	3	4	5	6	7	8
$g_1(x)$	0	5	15	40	80	90	95	98	100
$g_2(x)$	0	5	15	40	60	70	73	74	75
$g_3(x)$	0	4	26	40	45	50	51	52	53

returns. It may be that each unit of x represents \$5, and the returns may be in actual dollar amounts.

2 The total return is the sum of the individual returns.

With these assumptions, the problem can be embedded in a more general problem that can be solved sequentially in stages. Each stage is a subproblem which, when solved, provides information for the next stage. The solution to the subproblem at the final stage is also the solution to the original problem. This is basically the dynamic programming approach to the solution of the problem. We will now use this principle to determine how many units of money should be allocated to each investment program to maximize the total return.

Step 1

Assume for a moment that program 3 is the only investment program available to invest in. Since $g_3(x)$, the return function for program 3, is an increasing function of the amount invested x, we should invest the entire 8 units in program 3. The return on our investment would, of course, be

$$f_3(8) = g_3(8) = 53$$

and the amount invested to obtain this return is

$$d_3(8) = 8$$

where $f_3(8)$ is the optimal return from program 3 when 8 units are invested in it.

Step 2

Now, let

$$f_3(x) = g_3(x) \qquad x = 0, 1, 2, \ldots, 7$$

be the optimal return from program 3 when x units are invested in it, and let

$$d_3(x) = x \qquad x = 0, 1, 2, \ldots, 7$$

be the optimal amount to invest in program 3. This appears rather trivial, and it is; nevertheless, it is essential to establish the optimal return from program 3 when it is the only program in order to develop the final dynamic programming solution. (See Table 2.2.)

Step 3

Assume now that programs 2 and 3 are the only programs available, and the entire 8 units are available to invest in these two programs. Since both return functions are

Table 2.2 RESULTS FROM STEPS 1 AND 2

x	0	1	2	3	4	5	6	7	8
$f_3(x)$	0	4	26	40	45	50	51	52	53
$d_3(x)$	0	1	2	3	4	5	6	7	8

increasing functions of the amount invested, the entire amount should be invested. The question, then, is how many units should be allocated to each program? We already know the optimal return from program 3 for any amount invested in it, so it is just a matter of examining each of the sums for the maximum return:

$$g_2(0) + f_3(8) = 53 \qquad g_2(5) + f_3(3) = 110$$
$$g_2(1) + f_3(7) = 57 \qquad g_2(6) + f_3(2) = 99$$
$$g_2(2) + f_3(6) = 66 \qquad g_2(7) + f_3(1) = 78$$
$$g_2(3) + f_3(5) = 90 \qquad g_2(8) + f_3(0) = 75$$
$$g_2(4) + f_3(4) = 105$$

This maximum return from programs 2 and 3 when 8 units are available is denoted by $f_2(8)$. That is,

$$f_2(8) = \max_{z = 0, 1, 2, \ldots, 8} [g_2(z) + f_3(8 - z)]$$

The optimal amount to invest in program 2 is denoted by $d_2(8)$ and is necessarily the value of z that yields $f_2(8)$. In this case,

$$f_2(8) = g_2(5) + f_3(3) = 110$$
$$d_2(8) = 5$$

Step 4

We retain the assumption that programs 2 and 3 are the only programs available to invest in, but now assume that only x units are available to invest in these programs $(x = 0, 1, \ldots, 7)$. For each value of x we calculate the optimal return from these programs when x units are available; namely,

$$f_2(x) = \max_{z = 0, 1, \ldots, x} [g_2(z) + f_3(x - z)]$$

The amount to invest in program 2 is

$$d_2(x) = \text{value of } z \text{ that yields } f_2(x)$$

We would calculate $f_2(x)$ and $d_2(x)$ for $x = 0, 1, 2, \ldots, 7$. These values are:

$$x = 0 \qquad f_2(0) = \max_{z = 0} [g_2(z) + f_3(0 - z)]$$
$$= g_2(0) + f_3(0)$$
$$= 0$$
$$d_2(0) = 0$$

$$x = 1 \qquad f_2(1) = \max_{z = 0, 1} [g_2(z) + f_3(1 - z)]$$

$$= \max \begin{bmatrix} g_2(0) + f_3(1) \\ g_2(1) + f_3(0) \end{bmatrix}$$

$$= \max \begin{pmatrix} 0 + 4 \\ 5 + 0 \end{pmatrix}$$

$$= 5$$

$$d_2(1) = 1$$

This says that if one unit of resource is available to invest in programs 2 and 3, the optimal policy is to invest it in program 2 for a total return of 5.

$$x = 2 \quad f_2(2) = \max_{z = 0, 1, 2} [g_2(z) + f_3(2 - z)]$$

$$= \max \begin{bmatrix} g_2(0) + f_3(2) \\ g_2(1) + f_3(1) \\ g_2(2) + f_3(0) \end{bmatrix}$$

$$= \max \begin{pmatrix} 0 + 26 \\ 5 + 4 \\ 15 + 0 \end{pmatrix}$$

$$= 26$$

$$d_2(2) = 0$$

If 2 units are available for programs 2 and 3, the optimal policy is to invest 0 units in program 2 and 2 units in program 3 for a total return of 26.

Remember that we are solving a whole class of subproblems that will eventually lead to the solution of the original problem. Also keep in mind that we need to know the optimal policy for programs 2 and 3 for every amount of money available up to and including 8 units, so regardless of how many units (up through 8) are invested in program 1, we know immediately the corresponding optimal policy for the remaining two programs. This will be illustrated in step 5. For

$$x = 3 \quad f_2(3) = \max_{z = 0, 1, 2, 3} [g_2(z) + f_3(3 - z)]$$

$$= \max \begin{bmatrix} g_2(0) + f_3(3) \\ g_2(1) + f_3(2) \\ g_2(2) + f_3(1) \\ g_2(3) + f_3(0) \end{bmatrix}$$

$$= 40$$
$$d_2(3) = 0 \quad \text{or} \quad 3$$

If we are interested in *an* optimal solution rather than all optimal solutions, we need only retain $d_2(3) = 0$ or $d_2(3) = 3$ and not both. The values $f_2(x)$ and $d_2(x)$ for $x = 4$, 5, 6 are found in a fashion similar to that above. The complete results from steps 1-4 are given in Table 2.3.

Step 5

The final stage is the same as the original problem. How should 8 units of money be invested in the three investment programs? It now becomes a matter of examining the results of investing z units in program 1 and $8 - z$ units optimally in programs 2 and 3 for $z = 0, 1, \ldots, 8$. That is, $f_1(8)$ is the maximum of the quantities

$$g_1(0) + f_2(8) = 110 \qquad g_1(5) + f_2(3) = 130$$
$$g_1(1) + f_2(7) = 105 \qquad g_1(6) + f_2(2) = 121$$
$$g_1(2) + f_2(6) = 101 \qquad g_1(7) + f_2(1) = 103$$
$$g_1(3) + f_2(5) = 110 \qquad g_1(8) + f_2(0) = 100$$
$$g_1(4) + f_2(4) = 140$$

namely,

$$f_1(8) = g_1(4) + f_2(4) = 140$$
$$d_1(8) = 4$$

Note that $f_1(8)$ is the optimal return when 8 units are invested optimally in the three available programs, and $d_1(8)$ is the optimal amount to invest in program 1. Since $d_1(8) = 4$, this leaves 4 units to invest optimally in programs 2 and 3. But we can get this directly from Table 2.3. Recall that $d_2(4) = 4$ represents the optimal amount to invest in program 2 when just programs 2 and 3 are available. This leaves 0 units to invest in program 3. Thus the optimal allocation of money to the three investment programs is:

$$d_1(8) = 4 \text{ units in program 1} \qquad d_3(0) = 0 \text{ units in program 3}$$
$$d_2(4) = 4 \text{ units in program 2}$$

Table 2.3 RESULTS FROM STEPS 1-4

x	0	1	2	3	4	5	6	7	8
$f_3(x)$	0	4	26	40	45	50	51	52	53
$d_3(x)$	0	1	2	3	4	5	6	7	8
$f_2(x)$	0	5	26	40	60	70	86	100	110
$d_2(x)$	0	1	0	0	4	5	4	4	5

Table 2.4 RESULTS FROM STEPS 1-5

x	0	1	2	3	4	5	6	7	8
$f_3(x)$	0	4	26	40	45	50	51	52	53
$d_3(x)$	0	1	2	3	4	5	6	7	8
$f_2(x)$	0	5	26	40	60	70	86	100	110
$d_2(x)$	0	1	0	0	4	5	4	4	5
$f_1(x)$	0	5	26	40	80	90	106	120	140
$d_1(x)$	0	0	0	0	4	5	4	4	4

for a total maximum return of

$$f_1(8) = 140$$

Note that we can check this by examining the sum of the return functions when the corresponding optimal amounts are invested in them.

$$g_1(4) + g_2(4) + g_3(0) = 80 + 60 + 0 = 140$$

Table 2.4 gives the results for any initial amount of money available up through 8 units. For example, if 6 units are available for investment in the three programs, the optimal allocation of these 6 units is:

$$d_1(6) \quad = 4$$
$$d_2(6 - 4) = d_2(2) = 0$$
$$d_3(2 - 0) = d_3(2) = 2$$

for a total return of

$$f_1(6) = 106$$

In arriving at an optimal solution of the initial problem, we have solved a whole class of problems. Keep in mind that this was a very simplified problem to illustrate the dynamic programming technique.

In summary, the dynamic programming functional equations for the investment problem are

$$f_3(x) = g_3(x)$$
$$d_3(x) = x \qquad x = 0, 1, \ldots, 8$$

$$f_i(x) = \max_{z = 0, 1, \ldots, x} [g_i(z) + f_{i+1}(x - z)] \qquad x = 0, \ldots, 8$$

$$d_i(x) = \text{value of } z \text{ that yields } f_i(x) \qquad \text{for } i = 2, 1$$

where $f_i(x)$ is the optimal return from investing x units in programs $i, i + 1, \ldots, 3$ and $d_i(x)$ is the optimal amount to invest in program i when x units are available to invest in programs $i, i + 1, \ldots, 3$ for $i = 1, 2, 3$.

In this section, we have basically examined the dynamic programming approach to the solution of the problem of allocating resource to activities in order to optimize the total return from all activities. In general, the resource could be people, money, machines, gasoline, grocery products, etc., and activities could be jobs, investment programs, manufacturing plants, refineries, grocery stores, etc. The basic assumptions in each case are:

1 The returns from all activities are measured in a common unit.
2 The return from a specific activity is independent of the returns from the other activities.
3 The return functions are nondecreasing.
4 The total return from all activities is equal to the sum of the individual returns.

2.3 DYNAMIC PROGRAMMING SOLUTION OF THE GENERAL ALLOCATION PROBLEM

In order to develop the dynamic programming functional equations for the general allocation problem, suppose

$R(x_1, \ldots, x_n) =$ total return from allocating x_i units of resource to the ith activity $(i = 1, 2, \ldots, n)$

$g_i(x_i) =$ return from the ith activity when x_i units of resource are allocated to that activity

$x^* =$ maximum number of units of resource available to allocate to the n activities

The allocation problem we want to solve is

$$\max \left[R(x_1, \ldots, x_n) \right] = \max_{\{x_k\}} \left[\sum_{k=1}^{n} g_k(x_k) \right]$$

$$\text{subject to: } \sum_{k=1}^{n} x_k = x^* \qquad x_k \geqslant 0$$

Heuristically, a sequence of functional equations $\{f_i(x)\}$ is defined as

$$f_i(x) = \max_{\{x_k\}} \left[\sum_{k=i}^{n} g_k(x_k) \right] \qquad \begin{array}{l} \text{for } x = 0, \Delta, 2\Delta, \ldots, x^* \\ i = n, n-1, \ldots, 1 \\ \Delta > 0 \end{array}$$

$$\text{subject to: } \sum_{k=i}^{n} x_k = x \qquad x_k \geqslant 0 \tag{2.1}$$

This is the optimal return from activities i, $i+1,\ldots,n$, when x units of resource are available for allocation to these activities only. Note that for $i=1$ and $x=x^*$ this is identically the problem we set out to solve. However, we have embedded the original problem in a family of problems where the number of activities under consideration, say m, is any positive integer less than or equal to n and the amount of resource is any amount, say x, less than or equal to x^*. This family of problems is solved sequentially until the original problem eventually is solved. We start by assuming that the last activity, activity n, is the only activity available for allocation of resource. If $x=0,\Delta,2\Delta,\ldots,x^*$ units are available to allocate, we should allocate all x units to activity n since the return from that activity is nondecreasing. This is represented by the functional equation

$$f_n(x) = \max_{x_n} \, [g_n(x_n)] = g_n(x) \qquad x = 0, \Delta, 2\Delta, \ldots, x^*$$

subject to: $x_n = x$

This is the optimal return from activity n when x units of resource are available for allocation to that activity only. Let $d_n(x)=x$ be the optimal amount of resource to allocate to the nth activity when it is the only activity, and x units of resource are available.

The next step is to assume that activities n and $(n-1)$ are the only activities to which the resource can be allocated. If x units of the resource are available, how many units should be allocated to activity $(n-1)$ to optimize the total return from activities $(n-1)$ and n? If we allocate x_{n-1} units to activity $(n-1)$ and use the remaining $(x-x_{n-1})$ units of resource to get a maximum return from activity n, then the total return from the two activities would be

$$g_{n-1}(x_{n-1}) + f_n(x - x_{n-1}) \qquad (2.2)$$

Thus, the total optimal return from activities $(n-1)$ and n when x units of resource are available to allocate to these activities is obtained by choosing x_{n-1} such that the quantity in Equation (2.2) is a maximum. That is,

$$f_{n-1}(x) = \max_{\substack{x_{n-1} = 0, \Delta, \ldots, x \\ x = 0, \Delta, 2\Delta, \ldots, x^*}} [g_{n-1}(x_{n-1}) + f_n(x - x_{n-1})] \qquad (2.3)$$

is the total optimal return from activities $(n-1)$ and n when x units of resource are available for allocation to these two activities only. Let $d_{n-1}(x)$ be the optimal number of units to allocate to activity $(n-1)$ when x units are available to allocate to activities $(n-1)$ and n only. Thus,

$$d_{n-1}(x) = \text{value of } x_{n-1} \text{ that yields } f_{n-1}(x)$$

We now assume that activities $(n-2)$, $(n-1)$, and n are the only activities available, and we want to know how many units of the resource should be allocated to them to obtain an optimal return. We repeat the same type of thinking process as before with only two activities. When x units of resource are available, x_{n-2} units are allocated to activity $(n-2)$ and the remaining $(x - x_{n-2})$ units are used to obtain an optimal return from the remaining two activities. Thus,

$$g_{n-2}(x_{n-2}) + f_{n-1}(x - x_{n-2}) \qquad (2.4)$$

would be the total return. Note that $f_{n-1}(k)$ was just calculated in the previous step for $k = 0, \Delta, 2\Delta, \ldots, x^*$, so it is readily available. Hence, evaluate Equation (2.4) for $x_{n-2} = 0, \Delta, 2\Delta, \ldots, x$ and let $f_{n-2}(x)$ be the maximum value obtained. Then,

$$f_{n-2}(x) = \max_{\substack{x_{n-2} = 0, \Delta, \ldots, x \\ x = 0, \Delta, 2\Delta, \ldots, x^*}} [g_{n-2}(x_{n-2}) + f_{n-1}(x - x_{n-2})]$$

is the total optimal return from the last three activities when x units are available to allocate to these three activities only. Define $d_{n-2}(x)$ to be the decision variable that represents the optimal amount of resource to allocate to activity $(n-2)$. Thus,

$$d_{n-2}(x) = \text{value of } x_{n-2} \text{ that yields } f_{n-2}(x)$$

The process is repeated for $i = n - 3, n - 4, \ldots, 1$, each time defining

$$f_i(x) = \max_{\substack{x_i = 0, \Delta, \ldots, x \\ x = 0, \Delta, \ldots, x^*}} [g_i(x_i) + f_{i+1}(x - x_i)]$$

$$d_i(x) = \text{value of } x_i \text{ that yields } f_i(x)$$

Since the functional equations are recursive, f_{i+1} is readily available from previous calculations. When $i = 1$, we have

$$f_1(x) = \max_{\substack{x_1 = 0, \Delta, \ldots, x \\ x = 0, \Delta, \ldots, x^*}} [g_1(x_1) + f_2(x - x_1)]$$

$$d_1(x) = \text{value of } x_1 \text{ that yields } f_1(x)$$

In this subproblem, we assume that activities $1, 2, \ldots, n$ are available and that x units of resource are available for allocation. This is the original problem we set out to solve for $x = x^*$. The problem can now be solved easily since all values of f_2 are available from previous computations. Necessarily, $f_1(x^*)$ is the optimal return from the n activities when x^* units of resource are available. The optimal amount to allocate to the various activities is given by the decision variables $d_i(x)$. For example, when x^* units of resource are available,

$$y_1 = d_1(x^*) \qquad \text{units are allocated to activity 1}$$

$$y_2 = d_2(x^* - y_1) \qquad \text{units are allocated to activity 2}$$

$$y_3 = d_3\left(x^* - \sum_{k=1}^{2} y_k\right) \qquad \text{units are allocated to activity 3}$$

$$\cdots \cdots \cdots \cdots \cdots \cdots \cdots \cdots \cdots \cdots$$

$$y_i = d_i\left(x^* - \sum_{k=1}^{i-1} y_k\right) \qquad \text{units are allocated to activity } i$$

$$\cdots \cdots \cdots \cdots \cdots \cdots \cdots \cdots \cdots \cdots$$

$$y_n = d_n\left(x^* - \sum_{k=1}^{n-1} y_k\right) \qquad \text{units are allocated to activity } n$$

Mathematically, the general functional equations are obtained by defining

$$f_i(x) = \max_{\substack{\{x_k\} \\ \sum_{k=i}^{n} x_k = x}} \left[\sum_{k=i}^{n} g_k(x_k)\right] \qquad i = n-1, n-2, \ldots, 1$$

Then

$$f_i(x) = \max_{0 \leqslant x_i \leqslant x} \left\{ \max_{\substack{\{x_{i+1}, \ldots, x_n\} \\ \sum_{k=i+1}^{n} x_k = x - x_i}} \left[\sum_{k=i}^{n} g_k(x_k)\right] \right\}$$

$$= \max_{0 \leqslant x_i \leqslant x} \left\{ g_i(x_i) + \max_{\substack{\{x_{i+1}, \ldots, x_n\} \\ \sum_{k=i+1}^{n} x_k = x - x_i}} \left[\sum_{k=i+1}^{n} g_k(x_k)\right] \right\}$$

$$= \max_{0 \leqslant x_i \leqslant x} \left[g_i(x_i) + f_{i+1}(x - x_i)\right] \qquad \begin{array}{l} i = n-1, n-2, \ldots, 1 \\ x = 0, \Delta, \ldots, x^* \\ \text{for each } i \end{array}$$

Note that for $i = 1$ and $x = x^*$

$$f_1(x^*) = \max_{\substack{\{x_k\} \\ \sum_{k=1}^{n} x_i = x^*}} \left[\sum_{k=1}^{n} g_k(x_k)\right] = \max\left[R(x_1, \ldots, x_n)\right]$$

Algorithm 2.1 is a concise computer-oriented presentation of the backward dynamic programming approach to the solution of a general allocation problem with K units of resource available to invest in N investment programs, with the returns from each program given in tabular form. The notation has been modified so the algorithm can be programmed in FORTRAN immediately without modifications. Since zero subscripts are not permitted in FORTRAN, the necessary adjustments have been made. FORTRAN notation and logic will be used.

2.3.1 Algorithm 2.1–Dynamic Programming Solution of Investment Problem–Tabular Return Functions

Assume K units of resource are available to invest in N investment programs. How many units should be invested in each program to maximize the total return? Let

$G(I,X) =$ the return from investing $(X-1)$ units of resource in program I; $I = 1, 2, \ldots, N$

$F(I,X) =$ the optimal return from investing $(X-1)$ units of resource in programs I, I + 1, ..., N

$D(I,X) =$ the optimal number of units to invest in program I when only programs I, I + 1, ..., N are being considered and $(X-1)$ units are available to invest

$XSTAR(I) =$ optimal number of units to invest in program I when all programs are being considered and K units of resource are available $(I = 1, 2, \ldots, N)$

We assume that K, N, and G(I,X) for $I = 1, 2, \ldots, N$ and $X = 1, 2, \ldots, K + 1$ have been read into the computer.

Step 1
Assume the last program is the only program. Initialize the optimal return and the optimal amount to invest for 0, 1, ..., K units of resource.
For $X = 1, 2, \ldots, K + 1$, let

$$F(N, X) = G(N, X)$$
$$D(N, X) = X - 1$$

Step 2
Assume the last two programs are the only programs. Set $I = N - 1$.

Step 3
Set the amount of resource to zero. Set $X = 1$.

Step 4
Calculate the optimal return from investing $X - 1$ units of resource in programs I, I + 1, ..., N. Calculate the optimal amount to invest in program I when $X - 1$ units of resource are available to invest in programs I, I + 1, ..., N.
Calculate

$$F(I, X) = \max_{Z = 1, 2, \ldots, X} [G(I, Z) + F(I + 1, X - Z + 1)]$$

$$D(I, X) = \text{value of Z that yields } F(I, X)$$

Step 5
Check to see if current amount of resource is at the maximum amount.
If $X = K + 1$, go to step 6; otherwise, increase X by 1 and return to step 4.

Step 6
Check to see if original problem has been solved. If $I = 1$, go to step 7; otherwise, decrease I by 1 and return to step 3.

Steps 7-11 determine the optimal number of units to invest in each program and print the results.

Step 7
Set

$$XSTAR(1) = D(1, K + 1)$$

Step 8
Set $I = 2$.

Step 9
Calculate

$$SUM = \sum_{J=1}^{I-1} XSTAR(J)$$

Step 10
Set

$$XSTAR(I) = D(I, K + 1 - SUM)$$

Step 11
If $I = N$, print results and stop; otherwise, increase I by 1 and return to step 9.

2.3.2 Computer Program for Algorithm 2.1

The comment cards at the beginning of the computer program for Algorithm 2.1 explain what the program is designed to do and exactly how to use it. The program is set up to handle a maximum of five investment programs and a maximum of 100 units of resource. To modify the maximum number of investment programs to P programs (P is any integer) and the maximum resource to Q units (Q is any integer), change the DIMENSION and INTEGER statements from

DIMENSION G(5,101),F(5,101)

INTEGER X,Z,SUM,D(5,101),XSTAR(5)

to

$$\text{DIMENSION } G(P,Q + 1), F(P,Q + 1)$$

$$\text{INTEGER } X, Z, SUM, D(P,Q + 1), XSTAR(P)$$

For example, if you have a maximum of 10 programs and 500 units of resource, the statements would be changed to:

$$\text{DIMENSION } G(10,501), F(10,501)$$

$$\text{INTEGER } X, Z, SUM, D(10,501), XSTAR(10)$$

The program as printed utilizes 44K bytes of core storage. The three-program problem from Section 2.2 took approximately 0.09 s of IBM 370/168 time. Consider the returns for each program:

x	$g_1(x)$	$g_2(x)$	$g_3(x)$
0	0	0	0
1	5	5	4
2	15	15	26
3	40	40	40
4	80	60	45
5	90	70	50
6	95	73	51
7	98	74	52
8	100	75	53

Assume the maximum of 8 units of resource. The data for the computer are punched as:

Columns									
Cards	1 2-----8	1 1 0-----6 7------4	2 2 5------2 3------0	3 3	4 4 1------8	4 4 9------6	5 5 7------4	6 6 5------2	7
1	THIS IS THE PROBLEM FROM SECTION 2.2								
2	8	3							
3	0.0	5.0	15.0	40.0	80.0	90.0	95.0	98.0	100.0
4	0.0	5.0	15.0	40.0	60.0	70.0	73.0	74.0	75.0
5	0.0	4.0	26.0	40.0	45.0	50.0	51.0	52.0	53.0

Card 1 is a title card that can contain anything the user desires in columns 2–80. Column 1 must be left blank. The information in this card will be printed on the output.

Although the comment cards state that the program is set up for the dynamic programming solution of investment problems, it can be used to solve any problem that involves allocating resource to activities when the return from each activity is given in tabular form.

```
C     ***************************************************************************
C     *                                                                         *
C     *           **    ALGORITHM 2.1      DYNAMIC PROGRAMMING    **            *
C     *        **  INVESTMENT PROGRAMS     TABULAR RETURN FUNCTIONS  **         *
C     *                                                                         *
C     *  THIS PROGRAM IS DESIGNED                                               *
C     *     TO READ                                                             *
C     *        CARD 1    COLS  2-80    TITLE  DESCRIPTION OF THE PROBLEM USING   *
C     *                                       ANY CHARACTERS ON KEYPUNCH         *
C     *                                       ** COLUMN 1 MUST BE LEFT BLANK **  *
C     *        CARD 2    COLS  1- 5    K  NUMBER OF UNITS AVAILABLE   (I5)       *
C     *                        6-10    N  NUMBER OF INVESTMENT PROGRAMS  (I5)    *
C     *        CARDS 3 TO ?   G(I,X)  THE RETURN FROM INVESTING X-1 UNITS IN     *
C     *                                PROGRAM I (I=1,N AND X=1,K+1)             *
C     *                                FOR EACH INVESTMENT PROGRAM,VALUES ARE    *
C     *                                READ ROWWISE WITH A MAXIMUM OF 10         *
C     *                                VALUES PER CARD IN 10F8.0 FORMAT.         *
C     *                                IF THERE ARE MORE THAN 10 VALUES,VALUES   *
C     *                                11,12,ETC. FOLLOW ON A SECOND CARD,ETC.   *
C     *                                VALUES FOR EACH INVESTMENT PROGRAM        *
C     *                                START ON A NEW CARD.                      *
C     *            TO SOLVE MORE THAN ONE PROBLEM AT A TIME, REPEAT THE          *
C     *            READ SEQUENCE, AND STACK THE DATA ONE BEHIND THE OTHER        *
C     *                                                                         *
C     *     TO CALCULATE                                                        *
C     *        F(I,X)     THE OPTIMAL RETURN FROM INVESTING (X-1) UNITS OF      *
C     *                   RESOURCE IN PROGRAMS I,I+1,...,N (I=1,N AND X=1,K+1)  *
C     *        D(I,X)     THE OPTIMAL NUMBER OF UNITS TO INVEST IN PROGRAM I    *
C     *                   WHEN ONLY PROGRAMS I,I+1,...,N ARE BEING CONSIDERED   *
C     *                   AND X-1 UNITS ARE AVAILABLE                           *
C     *                                                                         *
C     *     TO PRINT                                                            *
C     *        F(I,K+1)   OPTIMAL RETURN FROM INVESTING K UNITS OF RESOURCE     *
C     *                   IN PROGRAMS 1,2,...,N                                 *
C     *        D(I,X)     VALUES THAT REPRESENT THE OPTIMAL AMOUNT TO INVEST    *
C     *                   IN EACH PROGRAM                                       *
C     *                                                                         *
C     *  THE PROGRAM IS SET UP TO HANDLE A MAXIMUM OF 5 INVESTMENT PROGRAMS     *
C     *  AND 100 UNITS OF RESOURCE.  TO MODIFY THE MAXIMUM NUMBER OF PROGRAMS   *
C     *  TO SAY P PROGRAMS AND THE MAXIMUM RESOURCES TO SAY Q UNITS, CHANGE     *
C     *  THE DIMENSION AND INTEGER STATEMENTS TO                                *
C     *        DIMENSION G(P,Q+1),F(P,Q+1)                                      *
C     *        INTEGER X,Z,SUM,D(P,Q+1),XSTAR(P)                               *
C     *                                                                         *
C     ***************************************************************************
      DIMENSION G(5,101),F(5,101)
      INTEGER X,Z,SUM,D(5,101),XSTAR(5)
      REAL*4 TITLE(20)
C READ AND WRITE INPUT DATA
   50 READ(5,55,END=2000)TITLE
   55 FORMAT(20A4)
      WRITE(6,60)TITLE
   60 FORMAT('1',20A4,//)
      READ(5,100) K,N
  100 FORMAT(2I5)
      KP1=K+1
      WRITE(6,104)
  104 FORMAT(//  1X,'THE RETURN FUNCTION VALUES FOLLOW',/)
      WRITE(6,105)
  105 FORMAT(2X,'I/K=',4X,'0',9X'1',9X,'2',9X,'3',9X,'4',9X,'ETC',/)
      DO 4 I=1,N
      READ(5,101) (G(I,X),X=1,KP1)
  101 FORMAT(10F8.0)
      WRITE(6,106)I
  106 FORMAT(/1X,I2)
    4 WRITE(6,107)(G(I,X),X=1,KP1)
  107 FORMAT ('+',3X,7F10.2/(4X,7F10.2/))
```

```
C     ***********************************************************************
C     *   STEP 1                                                          *
C     *         ASSUME THE LAST PROGRAM IS THE ONLY PROGRAM.  INITIALIZE THE *
C     *         OPTIMAL RETURN AND THE OPTIMAL AMOUNT TO INVEST FOR        *
C     *         0,1,...,K UNITS OF RESOURCE.                              *
C     ***********************************************************************
      DO 10 X=1,KP1
      F(N,X)=G(N,X)
   10 D(N,X)=(X-1)
C     ***********************************************************************
C     *   STEP 2                                                          *
C     *         ASSUME THE LAST 2 PROGRAMS ARE THE ONLY PROGRAMS. (I=N-1)  *
C     ***********************************************************************
      I=N-1
C     ***********************************************************************
C     *   STEP 3                                                          *
C     *         SET THE AMOUNT OF RESOURCE TO ZERO.  (X=1)                *
C     ***********************************************************************
    3 X=1
C     ***********************************************************************
C     *   STEPS 4,5                                                       *
C     *         CALCULATE THE OPTIMAL RETURN FROM INVESTING X-1 UNITS OF  *
C     *         RESOURCE IN PROGRAMS I,I+1,...,N .                        *
C     *         CALCULATE THE OPTIMAL AMOUNT TO INVEST IN PROGRAM I WHEN  *
C     *         X-1 UNITS OF RESOURCE ARE AVAILABLE TO INVEST IN PROGRAMS *
C     *         I,I+1,...,N.                                              *
C     *         CHECK TO SEE IF CURRENT AMOUNT OF RESOURCE IS AT THE      *
C     *         MAXIMUM AMOUNT.                                           *
C     ***********************************************************************
      F(I,X)=G(I,1)+F(I+1,1)
      D(I,X)=0
      DO 5 X=2,KP1
      F(I,X)=G(I,1)+F(I+1,X)
      D(I,X)=0
      DO 5 Z=2,X
      IF(G(I,Z)+F(I+1,X-Z+1).LE.F(I,X)) GO TO 5
      F(I,X)=G(I,Z)+F(I+1,X-Z+1)
      D(I,X)=(Z-1)
    5 CONTINUE
C     ***********************************************************************
C     *   STEP 6                                                          *
C     *         CHECK TO SEE IF ORIGINAL PROBLEM HAS BEEN SOLVED.         *
C     ***********************************************************************
      IF(I.EQ.1) GO TO 6
      I=I-1
      GO TO 3
C     ***********************************************************************
C     *   STEPS 7,8,9,10,11                                               *
C     *         DETERMINE THE OPTIMAL NUMBER OF UNITS TO INVEST IN EACH   *
C     *         PROGRAM AND PRINT THE RESULTS.                            *
C     ***********************************************************************
    6 XSTAR(1)=D(1,KP1)
      DO 8 I=2,N
      SUM=0
      IM1=I-1
      DO 7 J=1,IM1
    7 SUM=SUM+XSTAR(J)
    8 XSTAR(I)=D(I,KP1-SUM)
      WRITE(6,102) F(1,KP1)
  102 FORMAT(//  1X,'THE OPTIMAL RETURN IS ',F15.2)
      WRITE(6,103) (I,XSTAR(I),I=1,N)
  103 FORMAT(//,1X,' THE OPTIMAL AMOUNT TO INVEST IN PROGRAM',I3,1X,'  I
     *S',I6)
      GO TO 50
 2000 STOP
      END
```

```
THIS IS THE PROBLEM FROM SECTION 2.2
```

```
THE RETURN FUNCTION VALUES FOLLOW

I/K=     0         1         2         3         4         ETC

1       0.0       5.00     15.00     40.00     80.00     90.00     95.00
        98.00    100.00

2       0.0       5.00     15.00     40.00     60.00     70.00     73.00
        74.00     75.00

3       0.0       4.00     26.00     40.00     45.00     50.00     51.00
        52.00     53.00


THE OPTIMAL RETURN IS              140.00

THE OPTIMAL AMOUNT TO INVEST IN PROGRAM  1   IS      4

THE OPTIMAL AMOUNT TO INVEST IN PROGRAM  2   IS      4

THE OPTIMAL AMOUNT TO INVEST IN PROGRAM  3   IS      0
```

2.4 STAGECOACH PROBLEM

A somewhat different type of problem that can be solved using dynamic programming is the well-known stagecoach problem. In some ways it resembles an allocation problem, but is enough different to be worth presenting. In reality, it is the problem of finding an optimal route through a network.

In the early days, a salesman located in a state on the East Coast of the United States decided to travel to the West Coast by stagecoach. It became apparent to him that the cost of an insurance policy would dictate the safest route. That is, the cheaper the policy, the safer the route. Figure 2.1 illustrates the various routes and the policy cost of traveling from one state to another. The object is to travel along the safest route from state 1 in stage 1 to state 10 in stage 5. The numbers in the circles represent the possible states he can travel through. The number on the arrow from one state to another is the corresponding policy cost. If we let C_{ij} represent the policy cost from state i to state j, then

$$C_{12} = 4 \quad C_{25} = 10 \quad C_{35} = 6 \quad C_{46} = 3 \quad C_{58} = 4$$
$$C_{13} = 2 \quad C_{26} = 9 \quad C_{36} = 7 \quad C_{47} = 8 \quad C_{59} = 8$$
$$C_{14} = 3 \quad \qquad \qquad C_{37} = 10$$

$$C_{68} = 9 \quad C_{78} = 5 \quad C_{8,10} = 8 \quad C_{9,10} = 4$$
$$C_{69} = 6 \quad C_{79} = 4$$

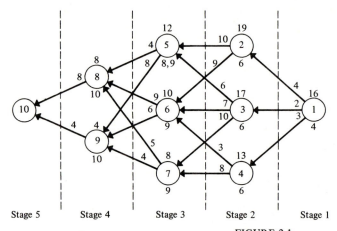

FIGURE 2.1
Stagecoach problem.

All other C_{ij} values are undefined.

The problem is to determine the safest route from state 1 to state 10. This is necessarily the route that minimizes the total insurance policy cost. The reasoning needed to obtain the dynamic programming solution is presented in the following steps.

Step 1

The stages in this example are analogous to the investment programs in Section 2.2. We start by assuming that the salesman has arrived at stage 4. Suppose for a moment that he finds himself in state 8. What is the least expensive policy to state 10? Since there is only one route possible, the minimum cost policy is from state 8 to state 10 at a cost of 8 units. Let $f_4(8) = 8$ represent this minimum cost, and let $d_4(8) = 10$ represent the next state he should go to from state 8.

But suppose he finds himself in state 9 in stage 4. Then the minimum policy cost from 9 to 10 would be $f_4(9) = 4$ and $d_4(9) = 10$. So if he arrives at state 8 or 9 in stage 4, the best policy is to go to state 10 since it is the *only* route. This is, of course, trivial, but necessary in order to establish the full dynamic programming algorithm for this example. Table 2.5 summarizes the results thus far.

Table 2.5 OPTIMAL POLICY—
STAGES 4–5

X	8	9
$f_4(X)$	8	4
$d_4(X)$	10	10

Step 2

We back up one stage and assume that the salesman has arrived at state 5, 6, or 7 and wants the minimum cost policy to state 10 by way of one of the states in stage 4. If he arrives at state 5, he would need to examine:

1 The sum of the cost of going from state 5 to 8 and the optimal policy cost from 8 to 10

2 The sum of the cost of going from state 5 to 9 and the optimal policy cost from 9 to 10

for the minimum value. The values are

1 $4 + f_4(8) = 12$ from 5 to 8 to 10
2 $8 + f_4(9) = 12$ from 5 to 9 to 10

The cost is the same, so the minimum policy cost from state 5 to state 10 by way of one of the states in stage 4 is 12 and is denoted by

$$f_3(5) = 12$$

The optimal route from 5 is either 8 or 9. Let

$$d_3(5) = 8 \text{ or } 9$$

denote this optimal route.

In a similar manner, if he arrives at state 6 in stage 3, the minimum policy cost from state 6 to state 10 by way of one of the states in stage 4 is

$$f_3(6) = \min \begin{bmatrix} 9 + f_4(8) \\ 6 + f_4(9) \end{bmatrix} = \min \begin{pmatrix} 9 + 8 \\ 6 + 4 \end{pmatrix} = 10$$

and the optimal route from state 6 is to state 9 in stage 4. That is,

$$d_3(6) = 9$$

Likewise,

$$f_3(7) = \min \begin{bmatrix} 5 + f_4(8) \\ 4 + f_4(9) \end{bmatrix} = 8$$

$$d_3(7) = 9$$

In each case, $f_3(X)$ represents the minimum policy cost to go from state X to state 10; $d_3(X)$ is the optimal state to go to from state X. The optimal policy from any state in stage 3 to state 10 is given in Table 2.6.

Table 2.6 OPTIMAL POLICY–STAGES 3–5

X	5	6	7	8	9
$f_4(X)$				8	4
$d_4(X)$				10	10
$f_3(X)$	12	10	8		
$d_3(X)$	8,9	9	9		

Step 3

We go to stage 2 where the salesman can theoretically find himself in state 2, 3, or 4. If he finds himself in state 2, he only needs to examine two sums to determine the minimum policy cost from state 2 to state 10 by way of stages 3 and 4, since he can only go to two states in stage 3, and the minimum policy cost from each of them has already been calculated in step 2. Thus, he can go to state 10 by way of state 5 at a minimum cost of

$$10 + f_3(5) = 10 + 12 = 22$$

or by way of state 6 at a minimum cost of

$$9 + f_3(6) = 9 + 10 = 19$$

Thus,

$$f_2(2) = \min \begin{bmatrix} 10 + f_3(5) \\ 9 + f_3(6) \end{bmatrix} = 19$$

$$d_2(2) = 6$$

Likewise,

$$f_2(3) = \min \begin{bmatrix} 6 + f_3(5) \\ 7 + f_3(6) \\ 10 + f_3(7) \end{bmatrix}$$

$$= \min \begin{pmatrix} 6 + 12 \\ 7 + 10 \\ 10 + 8 \end{pmatrix}$$

$$= 17$$

$$d_2(3) = 6$$

$$f_2(4) = \min \begin{bmatrix} 3 + f_3(6) \\ 8 + f_3(7) \end{bmatrix}$$

$$= \min \begin{pmatrix} 3 + 10 \\ 8 + 8 \end{pmatrix}$$

$$= 13$$

$$d_2(4) = 6$$

The optimal policy from any state in stage 2 to state 10 is illustrated in Table 2.7.

Step 4

Finally, we back up to stage 1, the starting point. In order to determine the minimum policy cost from state 1 to state 10, we only need to examine three sums for the minimum, namely,

1 The cost from state 1 to state 2 plus the minimum cost from 2 to 10
2 The cost from state 1 to state 3 plus the minimum cost from 3 to 10
3 The cost from state 1 to state 4 plus the minimum cost from 4 to 10

Of course, the minimum cost from any state in stage 2 to state 10 has already been calculated. Thus,

$$f_1(1) = \min \begin{bmatrix} C_{12} + f_2(2) \\ C_{13} + f_2(3) \\ C_{14} + f_2(4) \end{bmatrix}$$

$$= \min \begin{pmatrix} 4 + 19 \\ 2 + 17 \\ 3 + 13 \end{pmatrix}$$

$$= 16$$

$$d_1(1) = 4$$

Table 2.7 OPTIMAL POLICY–STAGES 2-5

X	2	3	4	5	6	7	8	9
$f_4(X)$							8	4
$d_4(X)$							10	10
$f_3(X)$				12	10	8		
$d_3(X)$				8,9	9	9		
$f_2(X)$	19	17	13					
$d_2(X)$	6	6	6					

The complete summary of the optimal policy from state 1 to state 10 is presented in Table 2.8.

From Table 2.8 we see that the minimum policy cost from state 1 to state 10 is 16 and the optimal route is $1 \rightarrow 4 \rightarrow 6 \rightarrow 9 \rightarrow 10$.

To recap, the optimal route is obtained as follows:

Stage 1—go from state 1 to state 4, $d_1(1) = 4$
Stage 2—go from state 4 to state 6, $d_2(4) = 6$
Stage 3—go from state 6 to state 9, $d_3(6) = 9$
Stage 4—go from state 9 to state 10, $d_4(9) = 10$

The number on top of each circle in Figure 2.1 is the minimum cost to go from the corresponding state to state 10. The number below each circle is the optimal state to go to in the next stage.

Algorithm 2.2 presents the dynamic programming approach to the generalized stagecoach problem.

2.4.1 Algorithm 2.2—Dynamic Programming Solution of Stagecoach Problem

Suppose there are N stages in a generalized stagecoach problem with M(I) states at stage I for I = 1, 2, . . . , N. Further, let

$S(I,J)$ = the Jth state in stage I for I = 1, 2, . . . , N and J = 1, 2, . . . , M(I)

$C(I,J,K)$ = the policy cost from state $S(I,J)$ to state $S(I+1,K)$ for I = 1, 2, . . . , N − 1; J = 1, 2, . . . , M(I); K = 1, 2, . . . , M(I + 1)

$F(I,J)$ = the minimum policy cost from state $S(I,J)$ to the final state in stage N for I = 1, 2, . . . , N − 1; and J = 1, 2, . . . , M(I)

$D(I,J)$ = the optimal state to go to in stage I + 1 from state $S(I,J)$ for I = 1, 2, . . . , N − 1; and J = 1, 2, . . . , M(I)

$XSTAR(I)$ = the optimal state to go to in stage I using the overall optimal policy, I = 1, 2, . . . , N

Table 2.8   OPTIMAL POLICY

X	1	2	3	4	5	6	7	8	9
$f_4(X)$								8	4
$d_4(X)$								10	10
$f_3(X)$					12	10	8		
$d_3(X)$					8,9	9	9		
$f_2(X)$		19	17	13					
$d_2(X)$		6	6	6					
$f_1(X)$	16								
$d_1(X)$	4								

Assume all values of S(I,J), C(I,J,K), and M(I) have been read into the computer. If a route does not exist for certain values of J and K, a very large positive number is read in for the corresponding C(I,J,K) value, say 10^{10}.

Steps 1–3 assume the process is in the next to last stage. These steps are used to initialize the minimum policy cost and the optimal state to go to in the last stage from every state in the next to last stage.

Step 1
Set J = 1.

Step 2
Set

$$F(N - 1, J) = C(N - 1, J, 1)$$
$$D(N - 1, J) = S(N, 1)$$

Note that S(N,1) is the final state and C(N− 1,J,1) is the policy cost from the *Jth* state in stage N − 1 to the first state in stage N, which is the final state.

Step 3
If J = M(N − 1), go to step 4; otherwise, increase J by 1 and return to step 2.

Steps 4–8 are used to calculate the minimum policy cost from every state to the final state and to calculate the optimal state to go to in the next stage from every state in the current stage.

Step 4
Set I = N − 2.

Step 5
Set J = 1.

Step 6
Calculate

$$F(I, J) = \min_{K = 1, 2, \ldots, M(I + 1)} [C(I, J, K) + F(I + 1, K)]$$

Suppose KSTAR is the value of K that yields F(I,J), then

$$D(I, J) = S(I + 1, KSTAR)$$

Step 7
If J = M(I), go to step 8; otherwise, increase J by 1 and return to step 6.

Step 8
If I = 1, go to step 9; otherwise, decrease I by 1 and return to step 5.

Steps 9–16 are used to calculate the minimum policy cost from state 1 to the final state and to calculate the optimal route through the network.

Step 9
Set

$$XSTAR(1) = S(1,1)$$
$$XSTAR(2) = D(1,1)$$

Step 10
Set KK = 1.

Step 11
Set I = 2.

Step 12
Set J = 1.

Step 13
If $S(I,J) \neq D(I-1,KK)$, go to step 16; otherwise, go to step 14.

Step 14
Set

$$XSTAR(I + 1) = D(I,J)$$
$$KK = J$$

Go to step 15.

Step 15
If $I = N - 1$, go to step 17; otherwise, increase I by 1 and return to step 12.

Step 16
Increase J by 1 and return to step 13.

Step 17 prints the minimum policy cost from state 1 to the final state and the optimal route through the network.

Step 17
Print F(1,1), the minimal policy cost from state 1 to the final state
Print XSTAR(I), the optimal state to go to in stage I using the overall optimal policy.
(I = 1, 2, . . . , N)
STOP

2.4.2 Computer Program for Algorithm 2.2

This computer program is designed to solve any stagecoach problem up to a maximum of eight stages and eight states per stage. To modify the program to solve larger problems with P stages and a maximum of Q states per stage, change the DIMENSION and INTEGER statements from

$$DIMENSION\ C(7,8,8), F(7,8), M(8)$$
$$INTEGER\ S(8,8), D(7,8), XSTAR(8)$$

Table 2.9 DATA FOR STAGECOACH PROBLEM

```
           1|1     1|1    2|2         3|3          4|4         5|5         6|6         7|7          8
2--5|6---0|1---5|6---0|1--------0|1--------0|1--------0|1--------0|1--------0|1--------0|1-----0
```

2–5	6–10	11–15	16–20	21–30	31–40	41–50	51–60	61–70	71–80
THIS	IS	THE	PROBLEM	FROM SECTION 2.4					
5									
1	3	3	2	1					
	4.	2.		3.					
	10.	9.	10.E10		6.	7.	10.	10.E10	3.
	8.								
	4.	8.	9.		6.	5.	4.		
	8.	4.							
1									
2	3	4							
5	6	7							
8	9								
10									

to

$$\text{DIMENSION } C(P - 1, Q, Q), F(P - 1, Q), M(P)$$

$$\text{INTEGER } S(P, Q), D(P - 1, Q), XSTAR(P)$$

The program as written occupies 40K bytes of core storage. The five-stage problem in Section 2.4 took 0.09 s of IBM 370/168 time to solve. The data for the problem are punched as in Table 2.9.

Card 1 is a title card that can contain anything the user desires in columns 2–80; column 1 must be left blank. The information in this card will be printed on the output. Card 2 contains the number of stages. Card 3 contains the number of states for each stage. Namely, there is one state in stage 1, three states in stage 2, three states in stage 3, two states in stage 4, and finally one state in stage 5. Cards 4–8 contain the policy costs, and cards 9–13 contain the state numbers in the various stages.

```
C     ********************************************************************
C     *                                                                *
C     *     **    ALGORITHM 2.2   DYNAMIC PROGRAMMING   STAGECOACH PROBLEM   **   *
C     *                                                                *
C     * THIS PROGRAM IS DESIGNED                                       *
C     *     TO READ                                                    *
C     *         CARD 1    COLS  2-80    TITLE  DESCRIPTION OF THE PROBLEM USING  *
C     *                                        ANY CHARACTERS ON KEYPUNCH       *
C     *                                        ** COLUMN 1 MUST BE LEFT BLANK ** *
C     *         CARD 2    COLS  1- 5    N  NUMBER OF STAGES   (I5)      *
C     *         CARDS 3 TO R            M(I)  NUMBER OF STATES IN STAGE I WHERE  *
C     *                                        I=1,2,...,N   (16I5)     *
C     *         CARDS R+1 TO T     C(I,J,K)  COST OF A POLICY FROM JTH STATE IN  *
C     *                                        STAGE I TO KTH STATE IN STAGE I+1 *
C     *                                        SUCH THAT FOR A FIXED VALUE OF I, *
C     *                                        VALUES ARE READ CONTINUOUSLY IN AN*
C     *                                        8F10.0 FORMAT FOR ALL J AND K     *
C     *                                          I:MAJOR SUBSCRIPT (I=1,2,...,N-1)*
C     *                                            EACH NEW VALUE OF I STARTS A NEW*
C     *                                            CARD                   *
C     *                                          J:INTERMEDIATE SUBSCRIPT  *
C     *                                            (J=1,2,...,M(I))        *
C     *                                          K:MINOR SUBSCRIPT (K=1,2,...,M(I+1))*
C     *         CARDS T+1 TO ?     S(I,J)  THE JTH STATE IN THE ITH STAGE WHERE *
C     *                                        I=1,2,...,N AND J=1,2,...,M(I)    *
C     *                                        PUNCH ROWWISE IN 16I5 FORMAT      *
C     *                                        EACH NEW ROW STARTS A NEW CARD    *
C     *                 TO SOLVE MORE THAN ONE PROBLEM AT A TIME, REPEAT THE     *
C     *                 READ SEQUENCE, AND STACK THE DATA ONE BEHIND THE OTHER   *
C     *                                                                *
C     *     TO CALCULATE                                               *
C     *         F(I,J)      MINIMUM POLICY COST TO TRAVEL FROM THE JTH STATE    *
C     *                     IN STAGE I TO THE FINAL STATE              *
C     *         D(I,J)      OPTIMAL STATE TO GO TO IN STAGE I+1 FROM THE JTH     *
C     *                     STATE IN STAGE I                          *
C     *         XSTAR(I)    OPTIMAL STATE TO GO TO IN STAGE I         *
C     *                                                                *
C     *     TO PRINT                                                   *
C     *         XSTAR(I), F(1,1)                                       *
C     *                                                                *
C     ********************************************************************
      DIMENSION C(7,8,8),F(7,8),M(8)
      INTEGER S(8,8),D(7,8),XSTAR(8)
C READ AND WRITE INPUT DATA.
      REAL*4 TITLE(20)
   50 READ(5,55,END=2000)TITLE
   55 FORMAT(20A4)
      WRITE(6,60)TITLE
   60 FORMAT('1',20A4,//)
      READ(5,100) N
  100 FORMAT(I5)
      READ(5,101) (M(I),I=1,N)
  101 FORMAT(16I5)
      NM1=N-1
      DO 2 I=1,NM1
      MI=M(I)
      MIP1=M(I+1)
    2 READ(5,102)((C(I,J,K),K=1,MIP1),J=1,MI)
  102 FORMAT(8F10.0)
      DO 3 I=1,N
      MI=M(I)
    3 READ(5,103)(S(I,J),J=1,MI)
  103 FORMAT(16I5)
C     ********************************************************************
C     *  STEPS 1,2,3                                                   *
C     *          ASSUME THE PROCESS IS IN THE NEXT TO THE LAST STAGE. INITIALIZE *
C     *          THE MINIMUM POLICY COST AND THE OPTIMAL STATE TO GO TO IN       *
C     *          THE LAST STAGE FROM EVERY STATE IN THE NEXT TO THE LAST STAGE.* *
C     ********************************************************************
```

```
      I=N-1
      MI=M(I)
      DO 4 J=1,MI
      F(I,J)=C(I,J,1)
    4 D(I,J)=S(N,1)
C     ********************************************************************
C     *  STEPS 4,5,6,7,8                                                *
C     *        CALCULATE THE MINIMUM POLICY COST FROM EVERY STATE TO THE FINAL *
C     *        STATE.  CALCULATE THE OPTIMAL STATE TO GO TO IN THE NEXT *
C     *        STAGE FROM EVERY STATE IN THE CURRENT STAGE.             *
C     ********************************************************************
      NM2=N-2
      DO 8 II=1,NM2
      I=N-II-1
      MI=M(I)
      MIP1=M(I+1)
      DO 8 J=1,MI
      F(I,J)=C(I,J,1)+F(I+1,1)
      D(I,J)=S(I+1,1)
      IF(MIP1.EQ.1) GO TO 8
      DO 5 K=2,MIP1
      IF(F(I,J).LE.C(I,J,K)+F(I+1,K)) GO TO 5
      F(I,J)=C(I,J,K)+F(I+1,K)
      D(I,J)=S(I+1,K)
    5 CONTINUE
    8 CONTINUE
C     ********************************************************************
C     *  STEPS 9,10,11,12,13,14,15,16                                   *
C     *        CALCULATE THE MINIMUM POLICY COST FROM STATE 1 TO THE FINAL *
C     *        STATE.  CALCULATE THE OPTIMAL ROUTE THROUGH THE NETWORK. *
C     ********************************************************************
      XSTAR(1)=S(1,1)
      XSTAR(2)=D(1,1)
      KK=1
      DO 7 I=2,NM1
      MI=M(I)
      DO 6 J=1,MI
      IF(S(I,J).NE.D(I-1,KK)) GO TO 6
      XSTAR(I+1)=D(I,J)
      KK=J
      GO TO 7
    6 CONTINUE
    7 CONTINUE
C     ********************************************************************
C     *  STEP 17                                                        *
C     *        PRINT THE MINIMUM POLICY COST FROM STATE 1 TO THE FINAL STATE, *
C     *        AND PRINT THE OPTIMAL ROUTE THROUGH THE NETWORK.         *
C     ********************************************************************
      WRITE(6,104) N
  104 FORMAT(    1X,'STAGECOACH PROBLEM WITH',I4,2X,'STAGES'//)
      WRITE(6,105)
  105 FORMAT(10X,'J=   1',4X,'2',4X,'3',4X,'4',4X,'5',4X,'6',4X,'7',4X,'8
     1',/)
      DO 10 I=1,N
      MI=M(I)
   10 WRITE(6,106) I,(S(I,J),J=1,MI)
  106 FORMAT(1X,'S(',I2,',J)=',1X,8I5)
      WRITE(6,107)
  107 FORMAT(//  12X,'K=   1',7X,'2',7X,'3',7X,'4',7X,'5',7X,'6',7X,'7',7
     1X,'8')
      DO 11 I=1,NM1
      MI=M(I)
      MIP1=M(I+1)
      DO 11 J=1,MI
   11 WRITE(6,108) I,J,(C(I,J,K),K=1,MIP1)
  108 FORMAT(1X,'C(',I2,',',I2,',K)=',8F8.2)
      WRITE(6,110) (XSTAR(I),I=1,N)
      WRITE(6,111) F(1,1)
```

```
 110 FORMAT(//  1X,'THE OPTIMAL ROUTE IS ',10I3)
 111 FORMAT(//,1X,'THE MINIMUM POLICY COST IS',F15.2)
     GO TO 50
2000 STOP
     END
```

```
THIS IS THE PROBLEM FROM SECTION 2.4

STAGECOACH PROBLEM WITH   5   STAGES

         J=  1    2    3    4    5    6    7    8

S( 1,J) =    1
S( 2,J) =    2    3    4
S( 3,J) =    5    6    7
S( 4,J) =    8    9
S( 5,J) =   10


          K=  1        2        3      4    5    6    7    8
C( 1, 1,K) =   4.00     2.00     3.00
C( 2, 1,K) =  10.00     9.00********
C( 2, 2,K) =   6.00     7.00    10.00
C( 2, 3,K) =********     3.00     8.00
C( 3, 1,K) =   4.00     8.00
C( 3, 2,K) =   9.00     6.00
C( 3, 3,K) =   5.00     4.00
C( 4, 1,K) =   8.00
C( 4, 2,K) =   4.00


THE OPTIMAL ROUTE IS   1  4  6  9 10

THE MINIMUM POLICY COST IS        16.00
```

2.5 PRODUCTION SCHEDULING

Consider the simple inventory problem of determining the production schedule for a certain item during the next N time periods, where there is a specific demand for the item during each period. For illustrative purposes, assume manufacturing time to be negligible; however, manufacturing costs go down as the production at the start of a given period goes up. Any excess produced at one time must be held in inventory, which, of course, costs money.

The object then is to determine a production schedule that will minimize the total production cost plus inventory holding cost subject to the constraints that all demands are met on time and the inventory level at the end of period N is zero. We assume that the amount in ending inventory at the end of period $I - 1$ plus the amount produced in period I is available for use anytime during the Ith period. Also assume that the inventory holding cost for the Ith period is based on the amount of ending inventory for period I.

We want to consider the following problem. Given:

$n =$ the number of periods $= 6$
$IO =$ inventory at the start of period $1 = 0$
$EI =$ inventory at the end of period $n = 0$
$PC_i(j) =$ cost to produce j units during period i:
$\qquad = 0 \qquad$ for $j = 0$ and $i = 1, 2, \ldots, n$
$\qquad = 20 + 5j \qquad$ for $j = 1, 2, \ldots$ and $i = 1, 2, \ldots, n$
$EIC_i(j) =$ cost of j units of ending inventory in period i
$\qquad = j \qquad$ for $j = 1, 2, \ldots$ and $i = 1, 2, \ldots, n$

The table of demands for the six periods is:

Period, i	1	2	3	4	5	6
Demand, d_i	8	4	6	2	10	4

Determine the amount to produce at the start of each period that will yield the minimum policy cost for n periods.

The dynamic programming approach is to assume that the process has reached the start of period n with a certain amount of inventory, and then, based on the demand for the last period, to determine the optimal number of units to produce to meet the demand for period n and end with 0 units of inventory. As in the previous examples, there is really no choice at the last stage (nth period). For example, if the ending inventory for period $(n-1)$ is 3, and the demand for period n is 4, there is no choice but to produce 1 unit. How many possible units of ending inventory can there be for period $(n-1)$? Certainly there can be no fewer than 0 units and there can be possibly as many as the demand for period n. Thus, let

$$
f_n(K) = \begin{cases} 0 & \text{for } K = d_n \\ 20 + 5(d_n - K) & \text{for } K = 0, 1, \ldots, d_n - 1 \end{cases}
$$

be the minimum policy cost for the nth period only, when the entering inventory for period n is K. Note that if the entering inventory for period n is d_n units, then the cost for the nth period will be zero, since there will be no production cost and no inventory cost. Recall that inventory cost for a period is based on the amount of inventory at the end of the period, which is zero in this case.

Let

$$
x_n(K) = \begin{cases} 0 & \text{for } K = d_n \\ d_n - K & \text{for } K = 0, 1, \ldots, d_n - 1 \end{cases}
$$

be the optimal number to produce at the start of period n when the entering inventory for the period is K. Since the ending inventory for period n must be zero, and since the demand for period n is 4 units, the entering inventory for period n can only be 0, 1, 2, 3, or 4 units. It should be clear that if the entering inventory for period n is K,

Table 2.10 $f_6(K)$ AND $x_6(K)$ VALUES

Entering inventory, K	$f_6(K)$	$x_6(K)$
0	40	4
1	35	3
2	30	2
3	25	1
4	0	0

then $4 - K$ units must be produced for use during the nth period. This is illustrated in Table 2.10.

The next step is to back up to the start of period 5, and assume that periods 5 and 6 are the only periods under consideration. The problem then is to determine the number of units to produce at the start of period 5 to minimize the total production and inventory cost over periods 5 and 6. If the fifth period is entered with an amount of inventory K which is less than the demand for period 5 ($d_5 = 10$), then at least $d_5 - K$ or $10 - K$ units must be produced; otherwise, the minimum amount that must be produced is 0 units. Likewise, if the fifth period is entered with an amount of inventory K, then the maximum amount that can be produced in order to have zero inventory at the end of the sixth period is the sum of the demands for periods 5 and 6 minus K. Consequently, the optimal amount to produce at the start of period 5, if the entering inventory is K units, is that amount z that yields $f_5(K)$, where

$$
f_5(K) = \min_{\max(0, d_5 - K) \leqslant z \leqslant d_5 + d_6 - K} [PC_5(z) + EIC_5(K + z - d_5)
$$
$$
+ f_6(K + z - d_5)] \qquad K = 0, 1, \ldots, d_5 + d_6
$$
$$
= \min_{\max(0, 10 - K) \leqslant z \leqslant 10 + 4 - K} [PC_5(z) + (K + z - 10)
$$
$$
+ f_6(K + z - 10)] \qquad K = 0, 1, \ldots, 14
$$

For $K = 0$

$$
f_5(0) = \min_{10 \leqslant z \leqslant 14} [20 + 5(z) + (z - 10) + f_6(z - 10)]
$$

$$
= \min \begin{pmatrix} z = 10: 20 + 50 + 0 + 40 = 110 \\ z = 11: 20 + 55 + 1 + 35 = 111 \\ z = 12: 20 + 60 + 2 + 30 = 112 \\ z = 13: 20 + 65 + 3 + 25 = 113 \\ z = 14: 20 + 70 + 4 + \ 0 = \ 94 \end{pmatrix}
$$

$$
= 94
$$
$$
x_5(0) = 14
$$

This says that if the fifth period is entered with 0 units of inventory, the minimum policy cost for periods 5 and 6 is $f_5(0) = 94$ and is obtained by producing $x_5(0) = 14$ units at the start of period 5. The cost to produce the 14 units is 90 units, and then it costs 4 units to carry the extra 4 units in inventory during the fifth period. For $K = 1$

$$f_5(1) = \min_{9 \leqslant z \leqslant 13} [20 + 5z + (z - 9) + f_6(z - 9)]$$

$$= \min \begin{pmatrix} z = 9: 20 + 45 + 0 + 40 = 105 \\ z = 10: 20 + 50 + 1 + 35 = 106 \\ z = 11: 20 + 55 + 2 + 30 = 107 \\ z = 12: 20 + 60 + 3 + 25 = 108 \\ z = 13: 20 + 65 + 4 + \quad 0 = \quad 89 \end{pmatrix}$$

$$= 89$$

$$x_5(1) = 13$$

Table 2.11 shows a summary of the results for $K = 0, 1, \ldots, 14$. Note that $14 - K$ units are produced for $K = 0, 1, \ldots, 9$, but 0 units are produced if the fifth period has a starting inventory of at least the amount of the demand for that period, namely 10 units. If the entering inventory is at least 10 units, it would be unwise to produce any of the product for period 6 before it is needed because of inventory costs.

Consider $f_5(K)$ and $x_5(K)$ for $K = 10$.

$$f_5(10) = \min_{0 \leqslant z \leqslant 4} [PC_5(z) + z + f_6(z)]$$

Table 2.11 OPTIMAL POLICY FOR PERIODS 5 AND 6 ONLY

Entering inventory, K	$f_6(K)$	$x_6(K)$	$f_5(K)$	$x_5(K)$
0	40	4	94	14
1	35	3	89	13
2	30	2	84	12
3	25	1	79	11
4	0	0	74	10
5	0	0	69	9
6	0	0	64	8
7	0	0	59	7
8	0	0	54	6
9	0	0	49	5
10	0	0	40	0
11	0	0	36	0
12	0	0	32	0
13	0	0	28	0
14	0	0	4	0

$$= \min \begin{pmatrix} z = 0: \ 0 + \ 0 + 0 + 40 = 40 \\ z = 1: \ 20 + \ 5 + 1 + 35 = 61 \\ z = 2: \ 20 + 10 + 2 + 30 = 62 \\ z = 3: \ 20 + 15 + 3 + 25 = 63 \\ z = 4: \ 20 + 20 + 4 + \ 0 = 44 \end{pmatrix}$$

$$= 40$$

$$x_5(10) = 0$$

The procedure at this point is to back off one additional period to the start of period 4 and repeat a similar process. The process is then repeated for periods 3 and 2 and finally for period 1. Of course, this will require defining $f_i(K)$ and $x_i(K)$ for $i = 4, 3, 2, 1$, where K is the amount of inventory at the start of period i. Thus, if the ith period ($i = 1, 2, \ldots, 5$) is entered with K units of inventory, the minimum cost for periods $i, i + 1, \ldots, 6$ is

$$f_i(K) = \min_{\max (0, d_i - K) \leqslant z \leqslant \sum_{j=i}^{6} d_j - K} [PC_i(z) + EIC_i(K + z - d_i)$$

$$+ f_{i+1}(K + z - d_i)]$$

and the optimal amount to produce at the start of period i is

$$x_i(K) = \text{value of } z \text{ that yields } f_i(K)$$

Consider the calculations for period 1 to further illustrate the dynamic programming process.

$$f_1(0) = \min_{\max (0, d_1) \leqslant z \leqslant \sum_{j=1}^{6} d_j} [PC_1(z) + (z - d_1) + f_2(z - d_1)]$$

$$= \min_{8 \leqslant z \leqslant 34} [20 + 5(z) + (z - 8) + f_2(z - 8)]$$

$$= \min \begin{pmatrix} z = \ 8: 20 + 40 \ + \ 0 + 184 = 244 \\ z = \ 9: 20 + 45 \ + \ 1 + 179 = 245 \\ \cdots\cdots\cdots\cdots\cdots\cdots\cdots\cdots\cdots \\ z = 12: 20 + 60 \ + \ 4 + 156 = 240 \\ z = 13: 20 + 65 \ + \ 5 + 152 = 242 \\ \cdots\cdots\cdots\cdots\cdots\cdots\cdots\cdots\cdots \\ z = 20 \ \ 20 + 100 + 12 + 104 = 236 \\ z = 21: 20 + 105 + 13 + 102 = 240 \\ \cdots\cdots\cdots\cdots\cdots\cdots\cdots\cdots\cdots \\ z = 34: 20 + 170 + 26 + \ 56 = 272 \end{pmatrix}$$

$$= 236$$

$$x_1(0) = 20$$

Of course, the values of $f_2(K)$ were calculated previously. A complete summary of all values of $f_i(K)$ and $x_i(K)$ is presented in Table 2.12. Note that $f_1(0) = 236$ is the minimum cost for the six periods under the assumptions of 0 units of initial inventory and 0 units of inventory at the end of period 6. Also, $x_1(0) = 20$ is the optimal number of units to produce at the start of period 1. The demand for period 1 is 8 units, so 12 units are available to start period 2. From Table 2.12, we see that $x_2(12) = 0$ is the optimal number to produce at the start of period 2. In a similar fashion, 4 units are used during period 2, so 8 units are available to start period 3. But $x_3(8) = 0$, so a demand of 6 during the third period leaves 2 units to start period 4. Then $x_4(2) = 0$, and 2 units are used during the fourth period, so period 5 is started with 0 units. Again from Table 2.12, we see that $x_5(0) = 14$ is the optimal number to produce at the start of period 5. These 14 units will supply the demands for the last two periods. In summary

$x_1(0) = 20$	$d_1 = 8$
$x_2(20 - d_1) = x_2(20 - 8) = x_2(12) = 0$	$d_2 = 4$
$x_3(20 - d_1 - d_2) = x_3(20 - 8 - 4) = x_3(8) = 0$	$d_3 = 6$
$x_4(20 - d_1 - d_2 - d_3) = x_4(20 - 8 - 4 - 6) = x_4(2) = 0$	$d_4 = 2$
$x_5(20 - d_1 - d_2 - d_3 - d_4) = x_5(20 - 8 - 4 - 6 - 2)$	
$\quad = x_5(0) = 14$	$d_5 = 10$
$x_6(14 - d_5) = x_6(14 - 10) = x_6(4) = 0$	

A complete step-by-step computer-oriented procedure for determining the optimal schedule over N periods is set forth in Algorithm 2.3. The algorithm has been generalized to handle a maximum ending inventory level for each period and a maximum production level for each period.

2.5.1 Algorithm 2.3—Dynamic Programming Solution of Production Scheduling Problems

The following notation will be used throughout the algorithm:

$\quad$ N = number of periods
$\quad$ MAXIL = maximum ending inventory level for each period
$\quad$ MAXP = maximum production during any period
$\quad$ D(I) = demand for Ith period, I = 1, 2, . . . , N
$\quad$ PC(I,J) = cost to produce J units during period I for I = 1, 2, . . . , N and J = 1, 2, . . . , MAXP
$\quad$ EIC(I,J) = cost of J units of ending inventory in period I for I = 1, 2, . . . , N and J = 1, 2, . . . , MAXIL

Table 2.12 OPTIMAL POLICY FOR PERIODS 1-6

Entering inventory, K	$f_6(K)$	$x_6(K)$	$f_5(K)$	$x_5(K)$	$f_4(K)$	$x_4(K)$	$f_3(K)$	$x_3(K)$	$f_2(K)$	$x_2(K)$	$f_1(K)$	$x_1(K)$
0	40	4	94	14	118	16	156	8	184	12	236	20
1	35	3	89	13	113	15	151	7	179	11		
2	30	2	84	12	94	0	146	6	174	10		
3	25	1	79	11	90	0	141	5	169	9		
4	0	0	74	10	86	0	136	4	156	0		
5	0	0	69	9	82	0	131	3	152	0		
6	0	0	64	8	78	0	118	0	148	0		
7	0	0	59	7	74	0	114	0	144	0		
8	0	0	54	6	70	0	96	0	140	0		
9	0	0	49	5	66	0	93	0	136	0		
10	0	0	40	0	62	0	90	0	124	0		
11	0	0	36	0	58	0	87	0	121	0		
12	0	0	32	0	50	0	84	0	104	0		
13	0	0	28	0	47	0	81	0	102	0		
14	0	0	4	0	44	0	78	0	100	0		
15	0	0	0	0	41	0	75	0	98	0		
16	0	0	0	0	18	0	72	0	96	0		
17	0	0	0	0	0	0	69	0	94	0		
18	0	0	0	0	0	0	62	0	92	0		
19	0	0	0	0	0	0	60	0	90	0		
20	0	0	0	0	0	0	58	0	88	0		
21	0	0	0	0	0	0	56	0	86	0		
22	0	0	0	0	0	0	34	0	80	0		
23	0	0	0	0	0	0	0	0	79	0		
24	0	0	0	0	0	0	0	0	78	0		
25	0	0	0	0	0	0	0	0	77	0		
26	0	0	0	0	0	0	0	0	56	0		
27	0	0	0	0	0	0	0	0	0	0		

$F(I,K)$ = minimum cost for the Ith through the Nth period when the ending inventory for period $(I - 1)$ is $(K - 1)$, where $I = 1, 2, \ldots, N$ and $K = 1, 2, \ldots, \min [\Sigma_{J=1}^{N} D(J) + 1, MAXIL + 1]$

$X(I,K)$ = optimal amount to produce at the start of period I when the ending inventory for period $(I - 1)$ is $(K - 1)$, $I = 1, 2, \ldots, N$ and $K = 1, 2, \ldots, \min [\Sigma_{J=1}^{N} D(J) + 1, MAXIL + 1]$

$XSTAR(I)$ = optimal amount to produce in the Ith period using the overall optimal policy, $I = 1, 2, \ldots, N$

IO = inventory level at the start of period 1

$$(IO + M \cdot MAXP) > \sum_{J=1}^{M} D(J) \text{ for } M = 1, 2, \ldots, N$$

Assume N, MAXIL, MAXP, IO, and D(I) have been read into the computer.

Steps 1–3 initialize the minimum cost for the last period and calculate the optimal amount to produce at the start of the last period.

Step 1

Set $KLIM = \max \{1, D(N) - MAXP + 1\}$

$K = KLIM$

$KPM1 = K - 1$

Step 2

Let

$$F(N,K) = PC(N, D(N) - K + 1)$$

$$X(N,K) = D(N) - K + 1$$

Step 3

If $K = D(N) + 1$, go to step 4; otherwise, increase K by 1 and return to step 2.

Steps 4–8 calculate the minimum cost to operate from any given period through the last period. These steps calculate the optimal amount to produce at the start of each period for every possible amount of entering inventory.

Step 4

Set $I = N - 1$.

Step 5

Set $KLIM = \max \{1, \sum_{J=1}^{N} D(J) - (N - I + 1) \cdot MAXP + 1, D(I) + KPM1 - MAXP + 1\}$

$K = KLIM$

Step 6

Calculate

$$F(I,K) = \min_{Z} \{PC(I,Z) + EIC[I,K + Z - D(I) - 1] + F[I + 1, K + Z - D(I)]\}$$

where

$$Z \geqslant \max \{0, D(I) + KPM1 - K + 1\}$$

$$Z \leqslant \min [MAXP, \sum_{J=I}^{N} D(J) - K + 1, D(I) + MAXIL - K + 1]$$

$X(I,K)$ = value of Z that yields $F(I,K)$

Step 7
If $K = \min [\sum_{J=I}^{N} D(J) + 1, \text{MAXIL} + 1]$, go to step 8; otherwise, increase K by 1 and return to step 6.

Step 8
If $I = 1$, go to step 9; otherwise, decrease I by 1, set $\text{KPM1} = \text{KLIM} - 1$, and return to step 5.

Steps 9-13 calculate the optimal amount to produce at the start of periods $1, 2, \ldots, N$, if the first period is started with IO units of inventory and 0 units are in inventory at the end of period N.

Step 9
Set

$$\text{XSTAR}(1) = X(1, \text{IO} + 1)$$

Step 10
Set

$$\text{NEI} = \text{IO} + 1$$
$$I = 2$$

Step 11
Calculate
$$\text{NNEI} = \text{XSTAR}(I - 1) - D(I - 1) + \text{NEI}$$
$$\text{XSTAR}(I) = X(I, \text{NNEI})$$

Step 12
Set $\text{NEI} = \text{NNEI}$.

Step 13
If $I = N$, go to step 14; otherwise, increase I by 1 and return to step 11.

Step 14 prints the total minimum cost to operate during periods $1, 2, \ldots, N$ and the optimal amount to produce at the start of each period.

Step 14
Print $F(1, \text{IO} + 1)$
Print $\text{XSTAR}(I), I = 1, 2, \ldots, N$
STOP

2.5.2 Computer Program for Algorithm 2.3

This program is set up to handle a maximum of 10 periods and a maximum ending inventory of 100 units for any given period. The maximum ending inventory level and the maximum production for any period are controlled by the input data. The comment cards explain what the program is designed to do and exactly how to use it.

To modify the program to handle a maximum of P periods and a maximum of Q units of ending inventory for each period, change the DIMENSION and INTEGER statements to

DIMENSION F(P,Q + 1)

INTEGER D(P),X(P,Q + 1),XSTAR(P),Z,SUM,DN,DNP1

where, of course, P and Q are replaced by their actual values.

The program as printed uses 48K bytes of core storage. The example problem in Section 2.5 was solved in 0.13 s of IBM 370/168 time. A 10-period inventory problem with a maximum of 100 units of ending inventory for each period would take approximately 0.25 s.

The data in Section 2.5 are entered as:

Columns Cards	1---5	6---0	1---5	6---0	1---5	6---0	1---5	6---0
1	T	HIS I	S THE	PROBL	EM FR	OM SE	CTION	2.5
2	6	100	100	0				
3	8	4	6	2	10	4		

```
C     ***********************************************************************
C     *                                                                     *
C     *    ** ALGORITHM 2.3   DYNAMIC PROGRAMMING   INVENTORY PROBLEM  **   *
C     *                                                                     *
C     * THIS PROGRAM IS DESIGNED                                            *
C     *    TO READ                                                          *
C     *        CARD 1    COLS  2-80   TITLE  DESCRIPTION OF THE PROBLEM USING*
C     *                                      ANY CHARACTERS ON KEYPUNCH      *
C     *                                      ** COLUMN 1 MUST BE LEFT BLANK **
C     *        CARD 2    COLS  1- 5   N NUMBER OF PERIODS  (I5)             *
C     *                        6-10   MAXIL  MAXIMUM ENDING INVENTORY LEVEL  (I5)*
C     *                       11-15   MAXP  MAXIMUM PRODUCTION FOR ANY GIVEN *
C     *                                      PERIOD (I5)                     *
C     *                       16-20   IO  INVENTORY AT START OF PERIOD 1  (I5)*
C     *        CARDS 3 TO ?      D(I)  DEMAND FOR ITH PERIOD (I=1,2,...,N)   *
C     *                                PUNCH ROWWISE IN 16I5 FORMAT         *
C     *              TO SOLVE MORE THAN ONE PROBLEM AT A TIME, REPEAT THE    *
C     *              READ SEQUENCE, AND STACK THE DATA ONE BEHIND THE OTHER  *
C     *                                                                     *
C     *     TO CALCULATE                                                     *
C     *        F(I,K)    MINIMUM COST FOR ITH THROUGH NTH PERIOD WHEN THE    *
C     *                  ENDING INVENTORY FOR PERIOD I-1 IS K-1 ,WHERE       *
C     *                  I=1,2,...,N AND K=1,2,...,MIN SUCH THAT MIN IS THE  *
C     *                  MINIMUM OF A. THE SUM OF D(J)+1 (J=1,2,...,N)       *
C     *                                B. MAXIL+1                            *
C     *        X(I,K)    OPTIMAL AMOUNT TO PRODUCE AT THE START OF PERIOD I  *
C     *                  WHEN THE ENDING INVENTORY FOR PERIOD I-1 IS K-1,    *
C     *                  WHERE I AND K ARE THE SAME AS ABOVE                 *
C     *                                                                     *
C     *     TO PRINT                                                         *
C     *        F(1,IO+1)  MINIMUM POLICY COST FOR N PERIODS STARTING WITH    *
C     *                   IO UNITS OF INVENTORY AND ENDING WITH ZERO UNITS   *
C     *                   OF INVENTORY                                       *
C     *        X(I,K)     THE VALUES THAT REPRESENT THE OPTIMAL AMOUNT TO    *
C     *                   PRODUCE EACH PERIOD                                *
C     *                                                                     *
C     * TO MODIFY THE PROGRAM TO HANDLE A MAXIMUM OF P PERIODS AND A MAXIMUM *
C     *   OF Q UNITS OF ENDING INVENTORY, CHANGE THE DIMENSION AND INTEGER   *
C     *   STATEMENTS TO:                                                     *
C     *              DIMENSION F(P,Q+1)                                      *
C     *              INTEGER D(P),X(P,Q+1),XSTAR(P),Z,SUM,DN,DNP1            *
C     *                                                                     *
C     * TO CHANGE PRODUCTION COST AND ENDING INVENTORY COST, CHANGE THE      *
C     *   STATEMENT FUNCTION CARDS, PC(I,J) AND EIC(I,J), ACCORDINGLY.       *
C     *                                                                     *
C     ***********************************************************************
      DIMENSION F(10,101)
      INTEGER D(10),X(10,101),XSTAR(10),Z,SUM,DN,DNP1
      REAL*4 TITLE(20)
C     ***********************************************************************
C     *    STATEMENT FUNCTIONS                                              *
C     *        PC(I,J)  COST TO PRODUCE J UNITS DURING PERIOD I,(J>0)       *
C     *                 PROGRAM ASSUMES PC(I,0)=0                           *
C     *        EIC(I,J) COST OF J UNITS OF ENDING INVENTORY IN PERIOD I     *
C     ***********************************************************************
      PC(I,J)=20+5*J
      EIC(I,J)=J
C     READ INPUT DATA
   50 READ(5,55,END=2000)TITLE
   55 FORMAT(20A4)
      WRITE(6,60)TITLE
   60 FORMAT('1',20A4,//)
      READ(5,100) N,MAXIL,MAXP,IO
  100 FORMAT(4I5)
      READ(5,101) (D(I),I=1,N)
  101 FORMAT(16I5)
      MAXP1=MAXP+1
      NM1=N-1
      MAXIL1=MAXIL+1
      DNP1=D(N)+1
```

```
      DN=D(N)
C     *****************************************************************************
C     *    STEPS 1,2,3                                                           *
C     *         INITIALIZE THE MINIMUM COST FOR THE LAST PERIOD.                 *
C     *         CALCULATE THE OPTIMAL AMOUNT TO PRODUCE AT THE START             *
C     *         OF THE LAST PERIOD.                                              *
C     *****************************************************************************
      KLIM=1
      IF(DNP1-MAXP.GT.KLIM) KLIM=DNP1-MAXP
      IF(KLIM.GT.MAXIL1) GO TO 25
      KPM1=KLIM-1
      IF(D(N).EQ.0) GO TO 5
      DO 4 K=KLIM,DN
      F(N,K)=PC(N,D(N)-K+1)
    4 X(N,K)=D(N)-K+1
C     *****************************************************************************
C     *    STEPS 4,5,6,7,8                                                       *
C     *         CALCULATE THE MINIMUM COST TO OPERATE FROM ANY GIVEN PERIOD      *
C     *         THROUGH THE LAST PERIOD.  CALCULATE THE OPTIMAL AMOUNT TO        *
C     *         PRODUCE AT THE START OF EACH PERIOD FOR EVERY POSSIBLE           *
C     *         AMOUNT OF ENTERING INVENTORY.                                    *
C     *****************************************************************************
    5 F(N,DNP1)=0
      X(N,DNP1)=0
      DO 20 II=1,NM1
      I=N-II
      SUM=0
      DO 6 J=I,N
    6 SUM=SUM+D(J)
      SUM=SUM+1
      IF(SUM.LT.MAXIL1) GO TO 7
      MINLIM=MAXIL1
      GO TO 8
    7 MINLIM=SUM
    8 KLIM=1
      IF(SUM-(N-I+1)*MAXP.GT.KLIM) KLIM=SUM-(N-I+1)*MAXP
      IF(D(I)+KPM1-MAXP+1.GT.KLIM) KLIM=D(I)+KPM1-MAXP+1
      IF(KLIM.GT.MAXIL1) GO TO 25
      DO 16 K=KLIM,MINLIM
      IF(D(I)+KPM1-K+1.LE.0) GO TO 10
      LLIM=D(I)+KPM1-K+1
      F(I,K)=PC(I,LLIM)+EIC(I,KPM1)+F(I+1,KPM1+1)
      X(I,K)=LLIM
      LLIM=LLIM+1
      GO TO 11
   10 LLIM=0
      F(I,K)=EIC(I,K-D(I)-1)+F(I+1,K-D(I))
      X(I,K)=0
      LLIM=LLIM+1
   11 IF(MAXP.GT.SUM-K) GO TO 12
      IF(MAXP.GT.D(I)+MAXIL1-K) GO TO 13
      MAXLIM=MAXP
      GO TO 14
   12 IF(SUM-K.GT.D(I)+MAXIL1-K) GO TO 13
      MAXLIM=SUM-K
      GO TO 14
   13 MAXLIM=D(I)+MAXIL1-K
      GO TO 14
   14 IF(LLIM-1.EQ.MAXLIM) GO TO 16
      DO 15 Z=LLIM,MAXLIM
      HOLD=PC(I,Z)+EIC(I,K+Z-D(I)-1)+F(I+1,K+Z-D(I))
      IF(F(I,K).LE.HOLD) GO TO 15
      F(I,K)=HOLD
      X(I,K)=Z
   15 CONTINUE
   16 CONTINUE
      KPM1=KLIM-1
   20 CONTINUE
C     *****************************************************************************
C     *    STEPS 9,10,11,12,13                                                   *
C     *         CALCULATE THE OPTIMAL AMOUNT TO PRODUCE AT THE START OF          *
C     *         PERIODS 1,2,...,N , IF THE FIRST PERIOD IS STARTED WITH          *
C     *         IO UNITS OF INVENTORY AND ZERO UNITS ARE IN INVENTORY AT         *
C     *         THE END OF PERIOD N.                                             *
C     *****************************************************************************
```

```
      XSTAR(1)=X(1,IO+1)
      NEI=IO+1
      DO 18 I=2,N
      NEI2=XSTAR(I-1)-D(I-1)+NEI
      XSTAR(I)=X(I,NEI2)
   18 NEI=NEI2
C     ****************************************************************************
C     *  STEP 14                                                                *
C     *        PRINT THE TOTAL MINIMUM COST TO OPERATE DURING PERIODS           *
C     *        1,2,....,N , AND THE OPTIMAL AMOUNT TO PRODUCE AT THE            *
C     *        START OF EACH PERIOD                                             *
C     ****************************************************************************
      WRITE(6,102) N,MAXIL,MAXP
  102 FORMAT(//  1X,'INVENTORY PROBLEM WITH',I4,1X,'PERIODS,',5X,'A MAXI
     1MUM INVENTORY LEVEL OF',I6,/,5X,'AND A MAXIMUM PRODUCTION OF',I6)
      WRITE(6,103) (I,D(I),I=1,N)
  103 FORMAT(/  ,(1X,'DEMAND FOR PERIOD',I4,4X,'IS',I6))
      WRITE(6,104) N,F(1,IO+1),IO
  104 FORMAT(//  1X,'THE MINIMUM POLICY COST FOR THE',I4,4X,'PERIODS IS'
     1 ,F12.2,2X,/,1X,'WITH',I4,2X,'UNITS OF INITIAL INVENTORY',/)
      WRITE(6,105) (I,XSTAR(I),I=1,N)
  105 FORMAT(1X,'THE OPTIMAL AMOUNT TO PRODUCE IN PERIOD',I4,4X,'IS',I6)
      GO TO 50
   25 WRITE(6,106)
  106 FORMAT(1X,'MINIMUM ENTERING INVENTORY LEVEL IS GREATER THAN THE MA
     1XIMUM INVENTORY LEVEL')
      GO TO 50
 2000 STOP
      END
```

```
THIS IS THE PROBLEM FROM SECTION 2.5

INVENTORY PROBLEM WITH   6 PERIODS,      A MAXIMUM INVENTORY LEVEL OF    100
      AND A MAXIMUM PRODUCTION OF    100

DEMAND FOR PERIOD    1    IS      8
DEMAND FOR PERIOD    2    IS      4
DEMAND FOR PERIOD    3    IS      6
DEMAND FOR PERIOD    4    IS      2
CEMAND FOR PERIOD    5    IS     10
DEMAND FOR PERIOD    6    IS      4


THE MINIMUM POLICY COST FOR THE   6    PERIODS IS      236.00
WITH   0   UNITS OF INITIAL INVENTORY

THE OPTIMAL AMOUNT TO PRODUCE IN PERIOD    1    IS    20
THE OPTIMAL AMOUNT TO PRODUCE IN PERIOD    2    IS     0
THE OPTIMAL AMOUNT TO PRODUCE IN PERIOD    3    IS     0
THE OPTIMAL AMOUNT TO PRODUCE IN PERIOD    4    IS     0
THE OPTIMAL AMOUNT TO PRODUCE IN PERIOD    5    IS    14
THE OPTIMAL AMOUNT TO PRODUCE IN PERIOD    6    IS     0
```

2.6 EQUIPMENT REPLACEMENT

Everyone has faced the problem of when to replace a piece of equipment, such as a car, that deteriorates with age. If reliable estimates of revenue, upkeep, and replacement costs can be obtained, dynamic programming can be used to determine a realistic optimal replacement policy. If the equipment is a car, revenue could be some measure of pleasure or the negative of the amount that would be spent on other modes of transportation or rentals. Equipment might be a combine, a dirt mover, a tractor, a chain saw, or a truck. In this example, it is a large-capacity truck.

Suppose the current truck is 2 years old at the start of 1975 (year 1), and the following estimates are available:

Truck made in 1973 (year minus 1)

Age	2	3	4	5	6
Revenue	10	8	8	6	4
Upkeep	3	3	4	4	5
Replacement	25	26	27	28	29

Truck made in 1975 (year 1)

Age	0	1	2	3	4
Revenue	14	16	16	14	12
Upkeep	1	1	2	2	3
Replacement	20	22	24	25	26

Truck made in 1976 (year 2)

Age	0	1	2	3
Revenue	16	14	14	12
Upkeep	1	1	2	2
Replacement	20	22	24	25

Truck made in 1977 (year 3)

Age	0	1	2
Revenue	18	16	16
Upkeep	1	1	2
Replacement	20	22	24

Truck made in 1978 (year 4)

Age	0	1
Revenue	18	16
Upkeep	1	1
Replacement	21	22

Truck made in 1979 (year 5)

Age	0
Revenue	20
Upkeep	1
Replacement	21

If the year 1975 (year 1) is started with a 2-year-old truck, what decision should be made at the start of this year and at the start of the next 4 years in order to maximize the total return.

In order to develop the dynamic programming functional equations for this example, consider the following notation:

$r_i(t) =$ revenue in period i from a truck that was made in year $(i-t)$ and is t years old at the start of period i

$u_i(t) =$ upkeep in period i on a truck that was made in year $(i-t)$ and is t years old at the start of period i

$c_i(t) =$ cost to replace a truck that was made in year $(i-t)$ and is t years old at the start of period i

$a =$ discount factor. For simplicity assume $a = 1$ for this example

$IT =$ age of the incumbent truck. $IT = 2$ in this example

$f_i(t) =$ optimal return for periods $i, i+1, \ldots, 5$ when the ith period is started with a truck that is t years old

$x_i(t) =$ decision to make at the start of period i that will yield $f_i(t)$. The only two possible decisions are to keep the old truck or to purchase a new one

If a new truck is purchased at the start of period i, the total profit from periods $i, i+1, \ldots, 5$ would be the revenue from a new truck in period i, minus the upkeep on the new truck in period i, minus the cost of replacing a truck that is t years old at the start of period i, plus the optimal return from periods $i+1, i+2, \ldots, 5$ starting with a 1-year-old truck discounted to the start of period i. Likewise, if a t-year-old truck is kept during the ith period, the total profit from periods $i, i+1, \ldots, 5$ would be the revenue from a t-year-old truck in period i, minus the upkeep on the t-year-old truck in period i, plus the optimal return from periods $i+1, \ldots, 5$ starting with a $(t+1)$-year-old truck discounted to the start of period i. This is expressed in the general dynamic programming functional equation for period i.

$$f_i(t) = \max \left[\begin{array}{c} \text{Purchase: } r_i(0) - u_i(0) - c_i(t) + a \cdot f_{i+1}(1) \\ \\ \text{Keep: } r_i(t) - u_i(t) + af_{i+1}(t+1) \end{array} \right]$$

for $i = 1, 2, \ldots, 5$ and $t = 1, 2, \ldots, (i-1), (i+IT-1)$. In order to use this equation, we assume $f_6(j) = 0$ for all j. Also, for $i = 1$, we assume $t = IT$ only.

The dynamic programming backward approach is to assume the fifth period is reached with a truck that is 1, 2, 3, 4, or 6 years old and to apply the general functional equation above. Thus, for $i = 5$ and

$$t = 1 \quad f_5(1) = \max \left[\begin{array}{c} \text{Purchase: } r_5(0) - u_5(0) - c_5(1) + f_6(1) \\ \\ \text{Keep: } r_5(1) - u_5(1) + f_6(2) \end{array} \right]$$

$$= \max \left(\begin{array}{c} \text{Purchase: } 20 - 1 - 22 + 0 \\ \\ \text{Keep: } 16 - 1 + 0 \end{array} \right) = 15$$

$x_5(1)$: Keep

$$t = 2 \quad f_5(2) = \max \begin{pmatrix} \text{Purchase: } 20 - 1 - 24 \\ \\ \text{Keep: } 16 - 2 \end{pmatrix} = 14$$

$$x_5(2) \; : \; \text{Keep}$$

$$t = 3 \quad f_5(3) = \max \begin{pmatrix} \text{Purchase: } 20 - 1 - 25 \\ \\ \text{Keep: } 12 - 2 \end{pmatrix} = 10$$

$$x_5(3) \; : \; \text{Keep}$$

$$t = 4 \quad f_5(4) = \max \begin{pmatrix} \text{Purchase: } 20 - 1 - 26 \\ \\ \text{Keep: } 12 - 3 \end{pmatrix} = 9$$

$$x_5(4) \; : \; \text{Keep}$$

$$t = 6 \quad f_5(6) = \max \begin{pmatrix} \text{Purchase: } 20 - 1 - 29 \\ \\ \text{Keep: } 4 - 5 \end{pmatrix} = -1$$

$$x_5(6) \; : \; \text{Keep}$$

We now assume that the start of the fourth period is reached with a 1-, 2-, 3-, or 5-year-old truck. What is the optimal decision to make in order to maximize the return from the last two periods? The functional equation for this period is

$$f_4(t) = \max \begin{bmatrix} \text{P: } r_4(0) - u_4(0) + c_4(t) + 1 \cdot f_5(1) \\ \\ \text{K: } r_4(t) - u_4(t) + 1 \cdot f_5(t + 1) \end{bmatrix} \quad t = 1, 2, 3, 5$$

Therefore,

$$f_4(1) = \max \begin{pmatrix} \text{P: } 18 - 1 - 22 + 15 \\ \\ \text{K: } 16 - 1 + 14 \end{pmatrix} = 29$$

$$x_4(1) \; : \; \text{Keep}$$

$$f_4(2) = \max \begin{pmatrix} \text{P: } 18 - 1 - 24 + 15 \\ \\ \text{K: } 14 - 2 + 10 \end{pmatrix} = 22$$

$$x_4(2) \; : \; \text{Keep}$$

$$f_4(3) = \max \begin{pmatrix} \text{P: } 18 - 1 - 25 + 15 \\ \\ \text{K: } 14 - 2 + 9 \end{pmatrix} = 21$$

$$x_4(3) \; : \; \text{Keep}$$

$$f_4(5) = \max \begin{pmatrix} \text{P: } 18 - 1 - 28 + 15 \\ \\ \text{K: } 6 - 4 - 1 \end{pmatrix} = 4$$

$x_4(5)$: Purchase

We now move back to the start of the third period and consider the optimal policy over the last three periods when the third period is started with a 1-, 2-, or 4-year-old truck.

$$f_3(1) = \max \begin{pmatrix} \text{P: } 18 - 1 - 22 + 29 \\ \\ \text{K: } 14 - 1 + 22 \end{pmatrix} = 35$$

$x_3(1)$: Keep

$$f_3(2) = \max \begin{pmatrix} \text{P: } 18 - 1 - 24 + 29 \\ \\ \text{K: } 16 - 2 + 21 \end{pmatrix} = 35$$

$x_3(2)$: Keep

$$f_3(4) = \max \begin{pmatrix} \text{P: } 18 - 1 - 27 + 29 \\ \\ \text{K: } 8 - 4 + 4 \end{pmatrix} = 19$$

$x_3(4)$: Purchase

Likewise, for period 2, $t = 1, 3$

$$f_2(1) = \max \begin{pmatrix} \text{P: } 16 - 1 - 22 + 35 \\ \\ \text{K: } 16 - 1 + 35 \end{pmatrix} = 50$$

$x_2(1)$: Keep

$$f_2(3) = \max \begin{pmatrix} \text{P: } 16 - 1 - 26 + 35 \\ \\ \text{K: } 8 - 3 + 19 \end{pmatrix} = 24$$

$x_2(3)$: Purchase or keep

Finally, we reach period 1 where we have a 2-year-old truck. Should we keep it or replace it in order to maximize the total return over the next five periods?

$$f_1(2) = \max \begin{pmatrix} \text{P: } 14 - 1 - 25 + 50 \\ \\ \text{K: } 10 - 3 + 24 \end{pmatrix} = 38$$

$x_1(2)$: Purchase

Table 2.13 OPTIMAL POLICY FOR PERIODS 1-5

Age of entering truck, t	$f_5(t)$	$x_5(t)$	$f_4(t)$	$x_4(t)$	$f_3(t)$	$x_3(t)$	$f_2(t)$	$x_2(t)$	$f_1(t)$	$x_1(t)$
1	15	K	29	K	35	K	50	K		
2	14	K	22	K	35	K			38	P
3	10	K	21	K			24	P,K		
4	9	K			19	P				
5			4	P						
6	−1	K								

Table 2.13 illustrates the complete set of $f_i(t)$ and $x_i(t)$ values for all applicable values of i and t.

The first period is entered with an incumbent truck of age 2, so the optimal policy is to purchase a new truck. Period 2 will then be entered with a 1-year-old truck, and the optimal policy is to keep the truck for at least one additional period $(x_2(1):K)$. Likewise, period 3 is entered with a 2-year-old truck which is kept $(x_3(2):K)$; period 4 is entered with a 3-year-old truck which is kept $(x_4(3):K)$; finally, period 5 is entered with a 4-year-old truck which is also kept $(x_5(4):K)$. The result of this overall 5-year policy is a maximum return of 38 units $[f_1(2) = 38]$. A summary of the optimal policy for the 5-year period is found in Table 2.14.

The general equipment replacement problem is treated in Algorithm 2.4. The notation has been modified to eliminate the problem of zero subscripts in programming. The notation and presentation of Algorithm 2.4 is designed for immediate programming without notational change. The notation that will be used in the algorithm is:

$$N = \text{number of periods under consideration}$$
$$XSTAR(I) = \text{optimal policy for period I, I} = 1, 2, \ldots, N$$
$$R(I,T) = \text{revenue in period I from a truck that was made in year}$$
$$(I - T + 1) \text{ and is } (T - 1) \text{ years old at the start of period I}$$

Table 2.14 OPTIMAL POLICY–5-YEAR PERIOD

Period	Age of entering truck	Policy
1	2	$x_1(2)$: Purchase
2	1	$x_2(1)$: Keep
3	2	$x_3(2)$: Keep
4	3	$x_4(3)$: Keep
5	4	$x_5(4)$: Keep

$U(I,T)$ = upkeep in period I on a truck that was made in year $(I - T + 1)$ and is $(T - 1)$ years old at the start of period I

$C(I,T)$ = cost to replace a truck that was made in year $(I - T + 1)$ and is $(T - 1)$ years old at the start of period I

$F(I,T)$ = optimal return for periods I, I + 1, . . . , N when the I*th* period is started with a $(T - 1)$-year-old truck

A = factor that discounts all returns during the 5-year process to the start of period 1

IT = age of incumbent truck

$POLICY(I,T)$ = the optimal decision for period I when the I*th* period is started with a $(T - 1)$-year-old truck

The general dynamic programming functional equation that represents the maximum return for periods I, I + 1, . . . , N when the I*th* period is entered with a $(T - 1)$-year-old truck is:

$$F(I,T) = \max \left[\begin{array}{l} \text{Purchase: } R(I,1) - U(I,1) - C(I,T) + A^*F(I + 1, 2) \\ \\ \text{Keep: } R(I,T) - U(I,T) + A^*F(I + 1, T + 1) \end{array} \right]$$

for I = 1, 2, . . . , N and T = 2, 3, . . . , I, I + IT. Assume T = I + IT only, for I = 1.

2.6.1 Algorithm 2.4—Dynamic Programming Solution of Equipment Replacement Problem

Assume the values for N, IT, $R(I,T)$, $U(I,T)$, and $C(I,T)$ have been read into the computer. Also assume $F(N + 1,T) = 0$ for all T = 2, 3, . . . , N + 1 and $(IT + N + 1)$.

Steps 1–2 set "period" to N and "age" to 1 year old.

Step 1
Set I = N.

Step 2
Set T = 2.

Steps 3–8 calculate the maximum return for periods I, I + 1, . . . , N, when the I*th* period is entered with a $(T - 1)$-year-old truck. These steps also calculate the optimal policy (keep or purchase) in each case.

Step 3
Calculate

$$F(I,T) = \max \left[\begin{array}{l} \text{PURCH: } R(I,1) - U(I,1) - C(I,T) + A^*F(I + 1, 2) \\ \\ \text{KEEP: } R(I,T) - U(I,T) + A^*F(I + 1, T + 1) \end{array} \right]$$

POLICY(I,T) = PURCH or KEEP, decision that yields F(I,T)

Step 4
If T = I, go to step 5; otherwise, increase T by 1 and return to step 3.

Step 5
Set T = I + IT, do step 3 only, and then go to step 6.

Step 6
If I = 2, go to step 7; otherwise, decrease I by 1 and return to step 2.

Step 7
Set I = 1 and T = IT + 1.

Step 8
Do step 3 only and then go to step 9.

Steps 9–13 calculate the optimal policy for each period starting with a truck of age IT.

Step 9
If POLICY(I,T) = KEEP, go to step 12; otherwise, go to step 10.

Step 10
Set XSTAR(I) = PURCH and T = 2.

Step 11
If I = N, go to step 14; otherwise, increase I by 1 and go to step 9.

Step 12
Set XSTAR(I) = KEEP.

Step 13
Increase T by 1 and go to step 11.

Step 14 prints the maximum return for N periods when the first period is entered with a truck of age IT. It also prints the optimal policy for each period.

Step 14
Print F(1, IT + 1) and XSTAR(I), I = 1,N
STOP

2.6.2 Computer Program for Algorithm 2.4

This program will solve a fairly general equipment replacement problem. It can handle a problem with a maximum of 10 periods and an incumbent machine that is no older than 10 units old at the start of the first period. It is assumed that a period represents a unit of age. To modify the program to handle a maximum of P periods and an incumbent machine that has a maximum age of Q units, change the COMMON and INTEGER statements to

COMMON F(P+1,P+Q+1),R(P,P+Q+1),U(P,P+Q+1),C(P,P+Q+1),
POLICY(P,P+Q+1),A

INTEGER XSTAR(P),POLICY,T

After the mainline program, there are two subroutines called DECIS and OUT. Change the first card in the subroutine DECIS from

COMMON F(11,21),R(10,21),U(10,21),C(10,21),POLICY(10,21),A

to

COMMON F(P+1,P+Q+1),R(P,P+Q+1),U(P,P+Q+1),C(P,P+Q+1),
POLICY(P,P+Q+1),A

also change the DIMENSION statement in the subroutine OUT to

DIMENSION X(P,P+Q+1)

The computer program as printed uses 44K bytes of core storage. The program solved the five-period problem from Section 2.6 in 0.12 s of IBM 370/168 time. The data were punched as:

```
          1|1            2|2            3|3            4|4            5
 2----7|8--------7|8--------7|8--------7|8--------7|8--------7
THIS IS THE PROBLEM FROM SECTION 2.6
 5    2    1.
    14.   10.
    16.   16.    8.
    18.   14.   16.    8.
    18.   16.   14.   14.    6.
    20.   16.   16.   12.   12.    4.
     1.    3.
     1.    1.    3.
     1.    1.    2.    4.
     1.    1.    2.    2.    4.
     1.    1.    2.    2.    3.    5.
    20.   25.
    20.   22.   26.
    20.   22.   24.   27.
    21.   22.   24.   25.   28.
    21.   22.   24.   25.   26.   29.
```

```
C     ***************************************************************************
C     *                                                                       *
C     *  **   ALGORITHM 2.4   DYNAMIC PROGRAMMING    EQUIPMENT REPLACEMENT  ** *
C     *                                                                       *
C     * THIS PROGRAM IS DESIGNED                                              *
C     *    TO READ                                                            *
C     *        CARD 1    COLS  2-80   TITLE  DESCRIPTION OF THE PROBLEM USING *
C     *                                      ANY CHARACTERS ON KEYPUNCH       *
C     *                                      ** COLUMN 1 MUST BE LEFT BLANK ** *
C     *        CARD 2    COLS  1- 5   N    # OF PERIODS UNDER CONSIDERATION (I5) *
C     *                        6-10   IT   AGE OF INCUMBENT MACHINE  (I5)      *
C     *                       11-20   A    DISCOUNT FACTOR  (F10.0)            *
C     *        CARDS 3 TO F    R(I,T)  REVENUE FROM A MACHINE MADE IN YEAR     *
C     *                               (I-T+1) AND IS (T-1) YEARS OLD AT THE    *
C     *                               START OF YEAR I (I=1,2,...,N)            *
C     *                               (T=1,2,...,I, AND I+IT)                  *
C     *                               PUNCH ROWWISE IN 8F10.0 FORMAT           *
C     *                               EACH NEW ROW STARTS A NEW CARD           *
C     *        CARDS F+1 TO G  U(I,T)  UPKEEP ON A MACHINE MADE IN YEAR        *
C     *                               (I-T+1) AND IS (T-1) YEARS OLD AT THE    *
C     *                               START OF YEAR I (I=1,2,...,N)            *
C     *                               (T=1,2,...,I, AND I+IT)                  *
C     *                               PUNCH ROWWISE IN 8F10.0 FORMAT           *
C     *                               EACH NEW ROW STARTS A NEW CARD           *
C     *        CARDS G+1 TO H  C(I,T)  COST TO REPLACE A MACHINE MADE IN YEAR  *
C     *                               (I-T+1) AND IS (T-1) YEARS OLD AT THE    *
C     *                               START OF YEAR I (I=1,2,...,N)            *
C     *                               (T=1,2,...,I, AND I+IT)                  *
C     *                               PUNCH ROWWISE IN 8F10.0 FORMAT           *
C     *                               EACH NEW ROW STARTS A NEW CARD           *
C     *            TO SOLVE MORE THAN ONE PROBLEM AT A TIME, REPEAT THE        *
C     *            READ SEQUENCE, AND STACK THE DATA ONE BEHIND THE OTHER      *
C     *                                                                       *
C     *     TO CALCULATE                                                       *
C     *        F(I,T)         OPTIMAL RETURN FOR A PROCESS STARTING YEAR I WITH *
C     *                       A (T-1) YEAR OLD MACHINE AND GOING THROUGH YEAR N *
C     *        POLICY(I,T)    OPTIMAL DECISION AT START OF YEAR I WITH A (T-1)  *
C     *                       YEAR OLD MACHINE                                 *
C     *        XSTAR(I)       OPTIMAL DECISION AT START OF YEAR I              *
C     *                                                                       *
C     *     TO PRINT                                                          *
C     *        F(1,IT+1)      OPTIMAL RETURN FROM AN N YEAR PROCESS STARTING WITH *
C     *                       AN IT YEAR OLD INCUMBENT MACHINE                 *
C     *        XSTAR(I)                                                       *
C     *                                                                       *
C     ***************************************************************************
      COMMON F(11,21), R(10,21),U(10,21),C(10,21), POLICY(10,21),A
      INTEGER XSTAR(10), POLICY,T
      REAL*4 TITLE(20)
C READ AND WRITE INPUT DATA
   50 READ(5,55,END=2000)TITLE
   55 FORMAT(20A4)
      WRITE(6,60)TITLE
   60 FORMAT('1',20A4,//)
      READ(5,100) N,IT,A
  100 FORMAT(2I5,F10.0)
      WRITE(6,110) N,IT
  110 FORMAT(     1X,I4,2X,'YEAR PROCESS STARTING WITH A',I3,2X,'YEAR OLD
     * MACHINE',/)
      WRITE(6,111) A
  111 FORMAT(1X,'THE DISCOUNT FACTOR IS',F10.3,/)
      NP1=N+1
      NM1=N-1
      ITPN1=IT+N+1
      WRITE(6,112)
  112 FORMAT(1X,'THE REVENUE VALUES FOLLOW ROWWISE',/)
      WRITE(6,115)
  115 FORMAT('  I/ T=    1',9X,'2',9X,'3',9X,'4',9X,'5',9X,'6',9X,'7')
      DO 20 I=1,N
   20 READ(5,101) (R(I,T),T=1,I),R(I,I+IT)
```

```
      CALL OUT(R,N,IT)
      WRITE(6,113)
  113 FORMAT(//  1X,'THE UPKEEP VALUES FOLLOW ROWWISE',/)
      WRITE(6,115)
      DO 21 I=1,N
   21 READ(5,101) (U(I,T),T=1,I),U(I,I+IT)
      CALL OUT(U,N,IT)
      WRITE(6,114)
  114 FORMAT(//  1X'THE COST TO REPLACE VALUES FOLLOW ROWWISE',/)
      WRITE(6,115)
      DO 22 I=1,N
   22 READ(5,101) (C(I,T),T=1,I),C(I,I+IT)
      CALL OUT(C,N,IT)
  101 FORMAT(8F10.0)
      DO 2 T=2,14
    2 F(NP1,T)=0.0
C     ****************************************************************************
C     *   STEPS 1,2                                                            *
C     *        SET 'PERIOD' TO N AND 'AGE' TO ONE YEAR OLD.                    *
C     ****************************************************************************
      DO 4 II=1,NM1
      I=N-II+1
C     ****************************************************************************
C     *   STEPS 2,3,4,5,6,7,8                                                  *
C     *        CALCULATE THE MAXIMUM RETURN FOR PERIODS I,I+1,...,N , WHEN     *
C     *        THE ITH PERIOD IS ENTERED WITH A  T-1  YEAR OLD TRUCK.         *
C     *        CALCULATE THE OPTIMAL POLICY (KEEP OR PURCHASE) IN EACH CASE.   *
C     ****************************************************************************
      DO 3 T=2,I
    3 CALL DECIS(I,T)
      T=I+IT
    4 CALL DECIS(I,T)
      I=1
      T=IT+1
      CALL DECIS(I,T)
C     ****************************************************************************
C     *   STEPS 9,10,11,12,13                                                  *
C     *        CALCULATE THE OPTIMAL POLICY FOR EACH PERIOD STARTING WITH      *
C     *        A TRUCK OF AGE IT.                                             *
C     ****************************************************************************
    9 IF(POLICY(I,T).EQ.2) GO TO 12
      XSTAR(I)=1
      T=2
   11 IF(I.EQ.N) GO TO 14
      I=I+1
      GO TO 9
   12 XSTAR(I)=2
      T=T+1
      GO TO 11
C     ****************************************************************************
C     *   STEP 14                                                              *
C     *        PRINT THE MAXIMUM RETURN FOR N PERIODS WHEN THE FIRST PERIOD    *
C     *        IS ENTERED WITH A TRUCK OF AGE IT.                             *
C     *        PRINT THE OPTIMAL POLICY FOR EACH PERIOD.                       *
C     ****************************************************************************
   14 WRITE(6,102)N,IT,F(1,IT+1)
  102 FORMAT(///5X,'OPTIMAL RETURN FROM A',I4,'  YEAR PROCESS'/7X,'START
     *ING WITH A',I4,'  YEAR OLD MACHINE IS',F10.2/)
      DO 15 I=1,N
      IF(XSTAR(I).EQ.1) GO TO 16
      WRITE(6,103) I
  103 FORMAT(1X,'AT THE START OF YEAR',I3,2X,'KEEP THE OLD MACHINE')
      GO TO 15
   16 WRITE(6,104) I
  104 FORMAT(1X,'AT THE START OF YEAR',I3,2X,'PURCHASE A NEW MACHINE')
   15 CONTINUE
      GO TO 50
 2000 STOP
      END
```

```
      SUBROUTINE DECIS(I,T)
      COMMON F(11,21), R(10,21),U(10,21),C(10,21), POLICY(10,21),A
      INTEGER T, POLICY
      REAL KEEP
      PURCH=R(I,1)-U(I,1)-C(I,T)+A*F(I+1,2)
      KEEP=R(I,T)-U(I,T)+A*F(I+1,T+1)
      IF(PURCH.GT.KEEP) GO TO 3
      F(I,T)=KEEP
      POLICY(I,T)=2
      GO TO 4
    3 F(I,T)=PURCH
      POLICY(I,T)=1
    4 RETURN
      END

      SUBROUTINE OUT(X,N,IT)
      DIMENSION X(10,21)
      INTEGER*2 ZX/'0X'/,FX/'4X'/
      INTEGER*2 NUMO/'  '/
      INTEGER*2 NUM(10)/' 1',' 2',' 3',' 4',' 5',' 6',' 7',' 8',' 9','10
     *'/
      INTEGER*2 FORM(9)/'(''','+''',', ',' ',' ',' ',F','10','.0',') '/
  200 FORMAT(I4)
  230 FORMAT(' ')
  235 FORMAT(F10.0)
      JT=IT-1
  201 DO 20 I=1,N
      FORM(5)=FX
      WRITE(6,230)
      WRITE(6,200)I
      CHECK=0
      DO 210 K=1,I
      IF(MOD(K,7).EQ.1) GO TO 245
      INC=MOD(K-1,7)
      FORM(4)=NUM(INC)
      GO TO 250
  245 FORM(4)=NUMO
  250 WRITE(6,FORM)X(I,K)
      CHECK=CHECK+1
      ITEST=I/7+1
      IJTEST=(I+JT)/7
      IF(ITEST-1.EQ.IJTEST)GO TO 247
      IF(I.LT.7*ITEST.AND.I+JT.GT.7*IJTEST.AND.I.EQ.K) GO TO 220
  247 IF(I+JT.EQ.7*IJTEST.AND.K.EQ.I) GO TO 225
      IF(AMOD(CHECK,7.).NE.0)GO TO 210
      WRITE(6,230)
      FORM(5)=ZX
      GO TO 210
  220 KJT=JT-7*IJTEST+I
      FORM(4)=NUM(KJT)
      FORM(5)=ZX
      WRITE(6,230)
      WRITE(6,FORM)X(I,I+IT)
      GO TO 20
  225 WRITE(6,235)X(I,I+IT)
      GO TO 20
  210 CONTINUE
      INK=MOD(I+JT,7)
      FORM(4)=NUM(INK)
      WRITE(6,FORM)X(I,I+IT)
   20 CONTINUE
      RETURN
      END
```

THIS IS THE PROBLEM FROM SECTION 2.6

5 YEAR PROCESS STARTING WITH A 2 YEAR OLD MACHINE

THE DISCOUNT FACTOR IS   1.000

THE REVENUE VALUES FOLLOW ROWWISE

I/ T=	1	2	3	4	5	6	7
1	14.		10.				
2	16.	16.		8.			
3	18.	14.	16.		8.		
4	18.	16.	14.	14.		6.	
5	20.	16.	16.	12.	12.		4.

THE UPKEEP VALUES FOLLOW ROWWISE

I/ T=	1	2	3	4	5	6	7
1	1.		3.				
2	1.	1.		3.			
3	1.	1.	2.		4.		
4	1.	1.	2.	2.		4.	
5	1.	1.	2.	2.	3.		5.

THE COST TO REPLACE VALUES FOLLOW ROWWISE

I/ T=	1	2	3	4	5	6	7
1	20.		25.				
2	20.	22.		26.			
3	20.	22.	24.		27.		
4	21.	22.	24.	25.		28.	
5	21.	22.	24.	25.	26.		29.

OPTIMAL RETURN FROM A   5   YEAR PROCESS
STARTING WITH A   2   YEAR OLD MACHINE IS   38.00

AT THE START OF YEAR 1 PURCHASE A NEW MACHINE
AT THE START OF YEAR 2 KEEP THE OLD MACHINE
AT THE START OF YEAR 3 KEEP THE OLD MACHINE
AT THE START OF YEAR 4 KEEP THE OLD MACHINE
AT THE START OF YEAR 5 KEEP THE OLD MACHINE

2.7 SUMMARY

Each example problem presented in this chapter conveyed the same idea. The original problem in each case was divided into N stages, and each stage was treated as a separate subproblem. The optimal solution of the subproblem at stage I was the optimal solution for stages I, $I + 1, \ldots, N$. Thus, the optimal solution of the subproblem at stage 1 was the optimal solution of the original problem.

The dynamic programming procedure used was the backward approach. That is, we started at stage N and backed through the various stages until finally stage 1 was reached. As we backed through the stages, a number of possible decisions were examined at each stage. Each possible decision resulted in

1 A certain return from the given stage
2 A corresponding optimal return from the remaining stages

The decision that optimized the sum of 1 and 2 was taken as the optimal decision at that point. Of course, 2 had already been calculated at the previous stage and was readily available.

In the process of solving the original problem, the optimal solutions to many subproblems were obtained; namely, all subproblems involving only the last K stages and all possible decisions at stage K ($K = 1, 2, \ldots, N$).

It should be clear that the time to solve a problem with dynamic programming is linear with respect to the number of stages, since the amount of time to solve the subproblem at each stage is relatively constant for all stages. If it takes 0.5 s of computer time to do the calculations at stage I and if there are 10 stages, then the total computation time will be approximately 5 s. On the other hand, 30 stages would take approximately 15 s. Thus, the computation time using dynamic programming is linear with respect to the number of stages, while the computation time for enumeration increases exponentially with the number of stages.

Many other types of problems in areas such as integer programming, nonlinear optimization, cargo loading, and reliability have been solved using dynamic programming. Readers who are interested in the dynamic programming approach to these and other problems should see Refs. [2], [3], or [9].

SELECTED BIBLIOGRAPHY

1 Aris, R.: "Discrete Dynamic Programming," Blaisdell, New York, 1964.
2 Bellman, R., and S. E. Dreyfus: "Applied Dynamic Programming," Princeton University Press, Princeton, N.J., 1962.
3 Denardo, E. V.: "Dynamic Programming: Theory and Application," Prentice-Hall, Inc., Englewood Cliffs, N.J., 1975.
4 Gluss, Brian: "An Elementary Introduction to Dynamic Programming," Allyn and Bacon, Inc., Boston, Mass., 1972.
5 Howard, R. A.: *Dynamic Programming, Manage. Sci.,* vol. 12, no. 5, pp. 317–345, January 1966.
6 Jacobs, C. L. R.: "An Introduction to Dynamic Programming," Chapman and Hall, London, England, 1967.
7 Kaufmann, A., and R. Cruon: "Dynamic Programming: Sequential Scientific Management," Academic Press, New York, N.Y., 1967.
8 Loomba, Narenda P., and Efraim Turban: "Applied Programming for Management," Holt, Rinehart and Winston, Inc., New York, N.Y., 1974.
9 Nemhauser, G. L.: "Introduction to Dynamic Programming," John Wiley & Sons, Inc., New York, N.Y., 1966.
10 Roberts, S. M.: "Dynamic Programming in Chemical Engineering and Process Control," Academic Press, Inc., New York, N.Y., 1964.
11 White, D. J.: "Dynamic Programming," Holden-Day, Inc., San Francisco, Calif., 1969.

EXERCISES

2.1 A total of 20 units of resource are available to allocate to 3 activities. The returns from these activities are given by

$$G(1,x) = 5\sqrt{x} \qquad 0 \leqslant x \leqslant 20$$
$$G(2,x) = x \qquad 0 \leqslant x \leqslant 20$$
$$G(3,x) = 0.07x^2 \qquad 0 \leqslant x \leqslant 20$$

Assume the resource is allocated in unit amounts.
(*a*) How many units should be allocated to each activity to maximize the total return from the 3 activities?
(*b*) What is the maximum return from the 3 activities?

2.2 Modify the computer program for Algorithm 2.1 to handle analytic return functions. Work Exercise 2.1 using the modified program.

2.3 In Section 2.4, suppose state 8 represents Las Vegas. The salesman is still interested in his own personal safety; however, he has a strong desire to visit Las Vegas, so he is willing to gamble somewhat to visit there. What is the minimum policy cost to travel from state 1 to state 10 by way of state 8?

2.4 In the early days the Easy-Ride Stagecoach Line was operating on a marginal budget, so they were interested in finding a route between city 1 and city 12 that would maximize their profit. The profit from operating between cities is given below. Note that only certain cities can be reached directly from a given city. For example, only cities 5, 6, 7, and 8 can be reached directly from city 2.

	To city										
From city	2	3	4	5	6	7	8	9	10	11	12
1	5	4	2								
2				8	10	5	7				
3				6	3	8	10				
4				8	9	6	4				
5								8	4	3	
6								5	2	7	
7								4	10	6	
8								12	5	2	
9											7
10											3
11											6

What route should be taken from city 1 to city 12 in order to maximize the total profit? (Note that the program for Algorithm 2.2 can be modified slightly to handle this problem.)

2.5 A new product has just been developed and the manufacturer is anxious to determine the optimal amount of resource that should be invested in the various advertising media in order to maximize the profit from the product. There are four types of advertising currently under consideration: newspaper, magazine, television, and radio. The table below shows the expected profit from investing in each type of advertising.

Investment, in thousands	Profit, in thousands			
	Newspaper	Magazine	Television	Radio
0	10.00	10.00	10.00	10.00
1	10.20	10.25	10.30	10.15
2	10.70	10.80	10.90	10.50
3	11.20	11.65	11.95	11.20
4	12.00	12.60	13.00	12.00
5	12.65	13.75	14.50	13.10
6	13.30	14.80	16.30	14.50
7	14.06	15.95	18.05	15.60
8	14.80	17.20	20.00	17.20
9	15.40	18.10	21.70	18.64
10	16.00	19.00	24.00	20.00

Note that a $10,000 investment in newspaper advertising will increase the profit from $10,000 to $16,000, a 60 percent return on investment. If $10,000 is available for advertising, how much should be invested in each media in order to maximize the total profit? If only $5000 is available, how should it be allocated to maximize profit?

2.6 A small lumber company has invested in 200 acres of trees. All trees can be harvested immediately, but of course they will yield more lumber if permitted to mature. To keep the problem manageable, suppose the company is interested in determining a harvesting policy over the next 5 years that will maximize the profit from the 200 acres of trees. For simplicity assume that all trees standing at the start of year 5 are harvested during that year. Reforestation is assumed but is ignored in this problem. All units are in millions of board feet. Assume the following notation:

A = number of units of lumber in the tract when it was purchased

$P(I)$ = profit per unit of lumber sold during the I*th* year; $I = 1, 2, \ldots, 5$

$X(I)$ = the maximum number of units available at the start of year I; $I = 1, 2, \ldots, 5$

$Y(I,K)$ = the optimal number of units to harvest during the I*th* year if K units are available; $I = 1, 2, \ldots, 5$; $K = 0, 1, \ldots, CX(I)$

C = unit return factor (i.e., each unit of lumber in trees at the start of any given year will result in C units of lumber at the end of the year)

Assume $A = 3$, $C = 1.1$, and

I	1	2	3	4	5
P(I)	10	11	9	8	8

(*a*) Formulate the dynamic programming functional equations for this problem.

(*b*) Construct a computer-oriented algorithm using dynamic programming to maximize the total profit.

(*c*) What is the optimal harvesting policy?

2.7 Formulate the dynamic programming functional equations to solve the problem:

$$\text{maximize:} \quad z = \prod_{i=1}^{n} x_i \quad 0 \leqslant x_i \leqslant 1$$

$$\text{subject to:} \quad \sum_{i=1}^{n} x_i = 1$$

Use the functional equations to solve the problem for $n = 4$ and each $x_i = 0.0, 0.1, 0.2, \ldots, 1.0$.

2.8 Use the concept of dynamic programming to find the maximum path through this network.

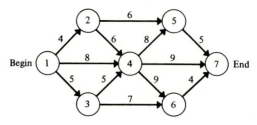

2.9 Use Algorithm 2.3 in Section 2.5.1 to solve the problem in Section 2.5 with a beginning inventory of 9 units and a maximum ending inventory of 10 units at the end of each period.

2.10 Consider an inventory problem with 10 periods, 15 units of beginning inventory, a maximum of 20 units of ending inventory at the end of each period, a cost of $(25 + 6j)$ to produce j units during each period, a cost of $(j/2)$ units for j units of ending inventory in each period, and the following demand table:

Period	1	2	3	4	5	6	7	8	9	10
Demand	15	12	30	15	24	6	18	25	12	40

Use the computer program in Section 2.5.2 to determine

(a) The optimal production schedule to minimize the total cost to operate for 10 periods

(b) The minimum policy cost for 10 periods

2.11 Consider an inventory problem with the following demands:

Month	Demand
January	5
February	3
March	2

The setup cost is $5, the production cost is $1 per unit produced, and the inventory holding cost is $1 per month based on ending inventory for the given month. Suppose the beginning inventory on January 1 is 1 unit and the inventory at the end of March is 0. Set up the dynamic programming functional equations to determine the optimal production schedule. Define all quantities. State exactly what $f_i(k)$ and $X_i(k)$ are for $i = 1, 2, 3$.

2.12 Use Algorithm 2.4 to solve the example problem in Section 2.6 with each revenue value increased by 2 units, each upkeep value increased by 3 units, and each replacement value increased by 1 unit.

3

LINEAR PROGRAMMING

3.1 INTRODUCTION

Linear programming (LP) is without a doubt one of the most used methods of operations research today. Problems from almost every phase of industry have been formulated successfully as linear programming models. Applications from the oil and gas industry include the initial extraction of the crude oil and gas from the earth, the determination of the refinery operating schedules, the determination of the optimal product mix when blending gasolines, and the final phase where the refined product is delivered to the consumer. Other applications include the use of linear programming to optimize the mixing of livestock feed, the transporting of goods from a number of plants to a number of warehouses, the utilization of timber in a forest, the production schedule in many manufacturing industries, the hiring of stewardesses, the flight schedule of airlines, the allocation of dollars for advertising, the selection of a portfolio, the assignment of jobs to people, etc. The list goes on and on. In each case the linear programming model involves a linear function of several variables to be optimized (maximized or minimized) subject to a set of linear constraints and nonnegativity restrictions on the variables.

In Chapter 2 we saw that a different formulation of dynamic programming functional equations was necessary from one problem to the next. Consequently, different computer programs were needed. This is not the case with linear programming. The form of each linear programming model is the same. Therefore, once a problem has been put into this unique form, the same procedure (usually the simplex method) can be used to obtain an optimal solution. The only real problem is to formulate the given problem as a linear programming model.

3.2   FORMULATION OF LINEAR PROGRAMMING MODELS

Each example problem in this section will be formulated as an LP model, but no attempt will be made to solve the model at this time. The objective is to illustrate the formulation of LP models.

The general form of each model will be

$$\text{maximize (or minimize): } z = c_1 x_1 + c_2 x_2 + \cdots + c_K x_K$$

$$\text{subject to: } a_{11} x_1 + a_{12} x_2 + \cdots + a_{1K} x_K (^*) b_1$$

$$a_{21} x_1 + a_{22} x_2 + \cdots + a_{2K} x_K (^*) b_2$$

$$\cdots\cdots\cdots\cdots\cdots\cdots\cdots\cdots\cdots\cdots\cdots\cdots$$

$$a_{m1} x_1 + a_{m2} x_2 + \cdots + a_{mK} x_K (^*) b_m$$

$$\text{all } x_i \geqslant 0$$

where c_j is a known "cost" coefficient of x_j, x_j is an unknown variable, a_{ij} is a known constant, b_i is a known constant, and $(^*)$ means $\geqslant, =,$ or $\leqslant$ for each constraint. The notation will become clear as we examine a number of examples.

EXAMPLE 3.2.1   *Diet Problem*   In this time of soaring food prices, every homemaker is faced with the difficult task of providing the family with a well-balanced diet while staying within a realistic budget. Of course, nutrition is only one factor to consider in planning a weekly menu. Suppose for a moment that the homemaker is contemplating the number of servings of each of the following six vegetables to put on this week's menu to minimize the cost while meeting all nutrient requirements. We assume that vegetables will provide only a fraction of the established minimum daily requirements of each nutrient. Table 3.1 summarizes the factors involved.

In addition, cabbage cannot be served more than twice during the week, and the other vegetables cannot be served more than four times each during the week. A total of 14 servings of vegetables are required during the week. How many times should each vegetable be served during the next week in order to minimize cost while satisfying the nutrient and taste requirements?

Let x_1 = number of times to serve green beans

x_2 = number of times to serve carrots

x_3 = number of times to serve broccoli

Table 3.1 DIET PROBLEM DATA

			Units per serving			Cost per serving, cents
			Vitamin			
Vegetable	Iron	Phosphorus	A	C	Niacin	
Green beans	0.45	10	415	8	0.3	5
Carrots	0.45	28	9065	3	0.35	5
Broccoli	1.05	50	2550	53	0.6	8
Cabbage	0.4	25	75	27	0.15	2
Beets	0.5	22	15	5	0.25	6
Potatoes	0.5	75	235	8	0.8	3
Minimum weekly requirements from vegetables	6.0 mg	325 mg	17,500 USP	245 mg	5.0 mg	

$$x_4 = \text{number of times to serve cabbage}$$
$$x_5 = \text{number of times to serve beets}$$
$$x_6 = \text{number of times to serve potatoes}$$

To solve the problem, the function

$$z = 5x_1 + 5x_2 + 8x_3 + 2x_4 + 6x_5 + 3x_6$$

must be minimized subject to the constraints

Iron: $\quad 0.45x_1 + 0.45x_2 + 1.05x_3 + 0.40x_4 + 0.50x_5 + 0.50x_6 \geqslant 6.0$

Phosphorus: $\quad 10x_1 + 28x_2 + 50x_3 + 25x_4 + 22x_5 + 75x_6 \geqslant 325$

Vitamin A: $\quad 415x_1 + 9065x_2 + 2550x_3 + 75x_4 + 25x_5 + 235x_6 \geqslant 17{,}500$

Vitamin C: $\quad 8x_1 + 3x_2 + 53x_3 + 27x_4 + 5x_5 + 8x_6 \geqslant 245$

Niacin: $\quad 0.3x_1 + 0.35x_2 + 0.6x_3 + 0.15x_4 + 0.25x_5 + 0.8x_6 \geqslant 5$

$$x_4 \leqslant 2$$
$$x_1 \leqslant 4$$
$$x_2 \leqslant 4$$
$$x_3 \leqslant 4$$
$$x_5 \leqslant 4$$
$$x_6 \leqslant 4$$
$$x_1 + x_2 + x_3 + x_4 + x_5 + x_6 = 14$$

and the nonnegativity restriction all $x_i \geqslant 0$.

The program in Section 3.9 provides the following optimal solution for this problem:

Vegetable	Number of times per week
Green beans	4.00
Carrots	0.99
Broccoli	2.27
Cabbage	2.00
Beets	0.74
Potatoes	4.00

at a total cost of $.6355 per person per week. Since the values are not all integers, the variables must be restricted to integer values and the problem resolved. We will do this in Chapter 4.

EXAMPLE 3.2.2 *Television Problem* A television manufacturer is concerned about how many units of three types of portable television sets should be produced during the next time period to maximize profit. Based on past demands, a minimum of 200, 250, and 100 units of types I, II, and III, respectively, are required. In addition, the manufacturer has available a maximum of 1000 units of time and 2000 units of raw materials during the next time period. Table 3.2 gives the essential data. Note that 1.5 units of raw materials and 1.2 units of time are required to produce one television set of type II.

Let x_i be the number of units of type i produced ($i = 1, 2, 3$). The objective function for the LP model is

$$\text{maximize:}\quad z = 10x_1 + 14x_2 + 12x_3$$

The constraints are

$$x_1 + 1.5x_2 + 4x_3 \leqslant 2000 \quad \text{raw materials}$$
$$2x_1 + 1.2x_2 + x_3 \leqslant 1000 \quad \text{time}$$
$$x_1 \geqslant 200$$
$$x_2 \geqslant 250$$
$$x_3 \geqslant 100$$

The nonnegativity restriction is all $x_i \geqslant 0$.

Table 3.2 REQUIREMENTS FOR TELEVISION PROBLEM

Type	Raw materials	Time	Minimum required	Profit
I	1.0	2.0	200	10
II	1.5	1.2	250	14
III	4.0	1.0	100	12
Available	2000	1000		

The computer solution using the simplex algorithm is

Produce 200 televisions of type I
Produce 250 televisions of type II
Produce 300 televisions of type III

for a maximum profit of 9100 units.

EXAMPLE 3.2.3 *Truck Production Problem* A truck manufacturer is capable of producing five types of trucks during a given month. The number of trucks of each type produced is restricted by the capacity of the various departments as follows:

1 The metal stamping department cannot handle more than the equivalent of 10,000 trucks of type I. The relationship between the types of trucks for metal stamping is given in Table 3.3.

2 The engine assembly department cannot handle more than the equivalent of 15,000 trucks of type I. The relationship between the types of trucks for engine assembly is given in Table 3.3.

3 The restrictions on the number of trucks of each type that can be handled by the final assembly department is given in Table 3.3.

If we let x_i be the number of trucks of type i ($i = 1, 2, \ldots, 5$) produced during the next month, the LP model can be written as

maximize: $z = 350x_1 + 450x_2 + 500x_3 + 300x_4 + 400x_5$

subject to: $x_1 + 1.4x_2 + 2.0x_3 + 0.8x_4 + 2.2x_5 \leqslant 10,000$ stamping

$x_1 + 1.6x_2 + 3.0x_3 + x_4 + 2.6x_5 \leqslant 15,000$ engine assembly

$x_1 \leqslant 7500$

$x_2 \leqslant 5000$

$x_3 \leqslant 1000$

$x_4 \leqslant 9000$

$x_5 \leqslant 3000$

all $x_i \geqslant 0$

Table 3.3   DATA FOR TRUCK PRODUCTION PROBLEM

Type	Final assembly constraint	Ratio to type I (stamping)	Ratio to type I (engine assembly)	Profit
I	7500	1.0	1.0	$350
II	5000	1.4	1.6	450
III	1000	2.0	3.0	500
IV	9000	0.8	1.0	300
V	3000	2.2	2.6	400

The computer solution using the simplex algorithm is

Type	Optimal number to produce
I	2800
II	0
III	0
IV	9000
V	0

for a maximum profit of $3,680,000.

EXAMPLE 3.2.4 *Machine Scheduling Problem* A plant has four machines, each capable of producing three variations of a single product. The profits per hour when producing the three variations on the respective machines are given in Table 3.4.

The production rates per hour of the four machines when producing the three variations of the product are given in Table 3.5. The demand for the three variations during the next month is expected to be 700, 500, and 400 units of variations 1, 2, and 3, respectively. The maximum available hours to produce the three variations during the next production period on the four machines are 90, 75, 90, and 85 hours, respectively.

If we let x_{ij} be the number of hours machine j should be scheduled to produce variation i for all i and j, the LP model can be written as

Table 3.4 PROFIT (DOLLARS PER HOUR) FOR EACH VARIATION BY MACHINE

Variation	Machine			
	1	2	3	4
1	5	6	4	3
2	5	4	5	4
3	6	7	2	8

Table 3.5 PRODUCTION RATE PER HOUR FOR EACH MACHINE BY VARIATION

Variation	Machine			
	1	2	3	4
1	8	2	4	9
2	7	6	6	3
3	4	8	5	2

Table 3.6 OPTIMAL SCHEDULE OF MACHINES (HOURS)

	Machine			
Variation	1	2	3	4
1	70.12	56.19	6.67	0
2	0	0	83.33	0
3	19.88	18.81	0	85.00

$$\text{maximize:} \quad z = 5x_{11} + 6x_{12} + 4x_{13} + 3x_{14}$$
$$+ 5x_{21} + 4x_{22} + 5x_{23} + 4x_{24}$$
$$+ 6x_{31} + 7x_{32} + 2x_{33} + 8x_{34}$$

$$\text{subject to:} \left. \begin{array}{l} 8x_{11} + 2x_{12} + 4x_{13} + 9x_{14} = 700 \\ 7x_{21} + 6x_{22} + 6x_{23} + 3x_{24} = 500 \\ 4x_{31} + 8x_{32} + 5x_{33} + 2x_{34} = 400 \end{array} \right\} \text{demand constraints}$$

$$\left. \begin{array}{l} x_{11} + x_{21} + x_{31} \leqslant 90 \\ x_{12} + x_{22} + x_{32} \leqslant 75 \\ x_{13} + x_{23} + x_{33} \leqslant 90 \\ x_{14} + x_{24} + x_{34} \leqslant 85 \end{array} \right\} \text{hour constraints}$$

$$\text{all } x_{ij} \geqslant 0$$

The optimal schedule for the four machines is given in Table 3.6. The maximum profit for the schedule in Table 3.6 is $2062.

3.3 GRAPHIC SOLUTION OF LINEAR PROGRAMMING MODELS

Although the graphic solution of LP models is limited to problems involving only two variables, it does provide valuable insight into the simplex method for solving larger problems. After the maximization problem is solved graphically in Section 3.3.1, the graphic procedure for solving minimization problems with two variables should be clear.

3.3.1 Television Problem Solved Graphically

Consider a simplified version of the television problem presented in Example 3.2.2.

Suppose only two types of television sets are produced with a profit of 6 units from each television of type I and 4 units from each television of type II. In addition,

2 and 3 units of raw materials are needed to produce one television of type I and II, respectively, and 4 and 2 units of time are required to produce one television of type I and II, respectively. If 100 units of raw materials and 120 units of time are available, how many units of each type of television should be produced to maximize profit and still meet all constraints on the problem?

We start by identifying the variables. Let x_1 be the number of units of type I produced and x_2 be the number of units of type II produced. Since each unit of type I and II yields a profit of 6 and 4 units, respectively, the function to be maximized is $z = 6x_1 + 4x_2$. The constraints on the problem are

$$2x_1 + 3x_3 \leqslant 100 \quad \text{raw materials}$$
$$4x_1 + 2x_2 \leqslant 120 \quad \text{time}$$
$$x_1, x_2 \geqslant 0 \quad \text{nonnegativity restriction}$$

Since type I yields a larger profit per unit, we would obviously want to produce as many units of type I as possible if there were no constraints.

The function to be optimized (maximized, in this case) is called the *objective function*. Since the objective function and all of the constraints are linear in the variables x_1 and x_2, the formulation is called a *linear programming (LP) model*. In general, the coefficients of the variables in the objective function are called *cost coefficients*. In this example, however, they could more appropriately be called *profit coefficients*.

Since only two variables are involved in this example, the problem can be solved graphically. Figure 3.1 (see p. 77) illustrates the details. The steps required to solve the problem are:

Step 1
Graph the first constraint as if it were an equality. That is, graph $2x_1 + 3x_2 = 100$.

Step 2
Determine the set of points that satisfy the first constraint, $2x_1 + 3x_2 \leqslant 100$. This can be done easily by checking to see if the origin (0,0) satisfies the constraint. In this case,

$$2 \cdot 0 + 3 \cdot 0 = 0 \leqslant 100$$

so all points below the line $2x_1 + 3x_2 = 100$ satisfy the first constraint. Note that the origin satisfies all less-than-or-equal-to constraints if the right side of the constraint is nonnegative.

Step 3
Graph the second and final constraint as if it were an equality. Let $4x_1 + 2x_2 = 120$.

Step 4
Determine the set of points that satisfy the second constraint $4x_1 + 2x_2 \leqslant 120$. Again, the origin satisfies the constraint so all points below the line $4x_1 + 2x_2 = 120$ must also satisfy the constraint.

Step 5

Determine the region where $x_1 \geqslant 0$ and $x_2 \geqslant 0$.

Step 6

Take the intersection of the regions determined in steps 2, 4, and 5. This gives the region of *feasible solutions*. That is, each point in this region satisfies all of the constraints and is a candidate for providing the maximum profit. But the region contains an infinity of feasible solutions. How can this number be reduced to a manageable finite number?

Step 7

With a little thought, it can be observed that the objective function $z = 6x_1 + 4x_2$ will take on its maximum value at one of the corners denoted by A, B, C, and D. Thus, by plotting

$$z = 6x_1 + 4x_2 = C_1$$
$$z = 6x_1 + 4x_2 = C_2$$

where C_1 and C_2 are two different constants, the slope of the objective function as well as the direction it moves with increasing values of z can be observed. The optimal solution is represented by the last corner of the region of feasible solutions that the objective function passes through as z is increased. This solution maximizes the value of z in the region of feasible solutions.

In the present example, we note that

$$z = 6x_1 + 4x_2 = 60$$

passes through the region of feasible solutions close to the point A. As z is increased to 120 and then to 192, the slope of the line representing the objective function remains the same but the line moves in the direction of point C. Each value of z will yield a straight line parallel to the line

$$z = 6x_1 + 4x_2 = d$$

for any constant d. If d is less than 120, the resulting line will be parallel but below and to the left of

$$z = 6x_1 + 4x_2 = 120$$

Likewise, for d greater than 120, the resulting line will be parallel but above and to the right of

$$z = 6x_1 + 4x_2 = 120$$

If d is increased too much, the resulting line will be completely out of the region of feasible solutions. Thus we can plot

$$z = 6x_1 + 4x_2 = d$$

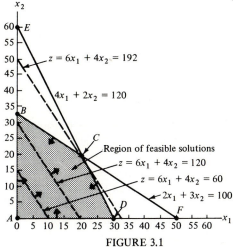

FIGURE 3.1
Graph of television problem.

for two values of d and observe the slope and direction the line moves as d is increased to determine the corner where the maximum (or minimum) value of the objective function occurs. Point C yields the maximum value in this case. This is the point where

$$2x_1 + 3x_2 = 100$$

and

$$4x_1 + 2x_2 = 120$$

intersect. Thus the solution of these two linear equations is the value of x_1 and x_2 that yields the maximum value of the objective function.

Step 8
To solve the equations

$$2x_1 + 3x_2 = 100$$
$$4x_1 + 2x_2 = 120$$

multiply the first equation by -2 and add the resulting equation to the second equation. The result is

$$-4x_1 - 6x_2 = -200$$
$$4x_1 + 2x_2 = 120$$
$$\overline{ - 4x_2 = -80}$$
$$x_2 = 20$$

If x_2 is substituted in the first original equation, then

$$2x_1 + 3(20) = 100$$

$$x_1 = 20$$

Hence, 20 units of type I and 20 units of type II should be produced to yield a maximum profit of

$$z = 6(20) + 4(20) = 200 \text{ units}$$

In preview, the simplex method is a procedure that starts at one corner of the region of feasible solutions and moves from one adjacent corner to the next as long as the objective function does not decrease. When it cannot move to an adjacent corner without *decreasing* the value of the objective function, the optimal solution is reached (maximization problem). The only exception is when there are multiple optimal solutions. In this case, the simplex method stops after finding the first optimal solution. For the minimization problem, the simplex method moves from one adjacent corner to the next until it can go no farther without *increasing* the value of the objective function.

3.3.2 Multiple Optimal Solutions

Suppose the problem in Section 3.3.1 were changed to

$$\text{maximize:} \quad z = 4x_1 + 6x_2$$

$$\text{subject to:} \quad 2x_1 + 3x_2 \leqslant 100$$

$$4x_1 + 2x_2 \leqslant 120$$

$$x_1, x_2 \geqslant 0$$

Since the cost coefficients in the objective function are both positive, it should be clear that the objective function should be pushed up and to the right as far as possible to maximize z. If the first constraint is written as an equality, we see that it would be parallel to the objective function. Hence, when z is increased to 200, we see in Figure 3.1 that every point from B to C on the line $2x_1 + 3x_2 = 100$ or, equivalently, $z = 4x_1 + 6x_2 = 200$ is an optimal solution.

3.4 MAXIMIZATION WITH LESS-THAN-OR-EQUAL-TO CONSTRAINTS

When an LP model has more than two variables, it is clear that the graphic procedure loses its appeal. Consequently, another procedure must be used to solve larger problems. The simplex method has proven to be an efficient procedure for solving LP models with any number of variables and constraints. In actual practice, however, the number of variables and constraints must be limited to the storage capacity of the computer available. Problems involving several hundred variables and constraints are not uncommon in industry.

In this section, a certain class of LP models will be examined to establish the rationale behind the simplex method, and then Sections 3.5 and 3.6 will extend the development to any LP model. Our discussion here will be limited to models where the objective function is to be maximized and all of the constraints are less-than-or-equal-to constraints. In particular, consider the problem from Section 3.3.1. We want to

$$\text{maximize:} \quad z^* = 6x_1 + 4x_2$$
$$\text{subject to:} \quad 2x_1 + 3x_2 \leqslant 100 \left.\vphantom{\begin{matrix}1\\1\end{matrix}}\right\} \text{constraints}$$
$$4x_1 + 2x_2 \leqslant 120$$
$$x_1, x_2 \geqslant 0 \quad \text{nonnegativity restriction}$$

To apply the simplex method, the original LP model must be converted to an equivalent model that expresses all of the constraints as equations. The two problems will be equivalent in the sense that an optimal solution of the new problem will also be an optimal solution of the original problem, if such a solution exists.

3.4.1 Slack Variables

To convert the LP model

$$\text{maximize:} \quad z^* = 6x_1 + 4x_2$$
$$\text{subject to:} \quad 2x_1 + 3x_2 \leqslant 100$$
$$4x_1 + 2x_2 \leqslant 120$$
$$x_1, x_2 \geqslant 0$$

to an equivalent problem, nonnegative variables x_3 and x_4, called *slack variables*, are added to the left side of the first and second constraints, respectively, to take up any possible slack. Also, a zero cost coefficient is assigned to each of these variables in the objective function. Thus, the new equivalent problem is to

$$\text{maximize:} \quad z = 6x_1 + 4x_2 + 0 \cdot x_3 + 0 \cdot x_4$$
$$\text{subject to:} \quad 2x_1 + 3x_2 + x_3 \qquad = 100$$
$$4x_1 + 2x_2 \qquad + x_4 = 120$$
$$x_1, x_2, x_3, x_4 \geqslant 0$$

Note that for any positive values of the slack variables, x_3 and x_4, the constraints are still satisfied in the original problem. Also, x_1 and x_2 should still be made as large as possible while satisfying the equations since positive values of x_3 and x_4 would not add anything to z.

The purpose of adding a slack variable to each less-than-or-equal-to constraint is to convert the constraints to equations that can be solved. Of course, there is still an infinity of solutions that satisfy the equations; however, only the solutions that correspond to the points A, B, C, and D in Figure 3.1 need to be examined.

3.4.2 Basic Solutions and Basic Feasible Solutions

Each solution that corresponds to one of the points A-F in Figure 3.1 is obtained by setting two of the four variables in the equivalent problem equal to zero and solving for the other two variables. Each solution obtained in this manner is called a *basic solution*, and the variables not set equal to zero are called *basic variables*. All of the basic solutions will not satisfy the original constraints and nonnegativity restrictions; however, those that do are called *basic feasible solutions*. The basic feasible solutions correspond to the points A, B, C, and D in Figure 3.1. In each LP problem, the optimal solution is selected from the manageable finite set of basic feasible solutions.

    In general, if the equivalent LP model contains m equations in n variables $(n > m)$, the following definitions hold.

> *1 Basic solution* Suppose $(n - m)$ variables are set equal to zero. If the resulting system of m linear equations in m unknowns has a unique solution (the columns of the corresponding coefficient matrix are linearly independent), then this unique solution is called a basic solution. The number of basic solutions must necessarily be less than or equal to the number of ways to choose m variables from the given n variables. This number is
>
> $$\binom{n}{m} = \frac{n!}{m!(n - m)!} = \frac{n(n - 1) \cdots 1}{[m(m - 1) \cdots 1][(n - m)(n - m - 1) \cdots 1]}$$
>
> *2 Basic feasible solution* A basic solution that satisfies all of the original constraints and nonnegativity restrictions is called a basic feasible solution.
> *3 Optimal basic feasible solution* A basic feasible solution that optimizes the objective function is called an optimal basic feasible solution.

The simplex method for maximizing the objective function starts at an extreme point or corner of the region of feasible solutions. This point corresponds to a basic feasible solution for the equivalent problem. The method then moves to an adjacent extreme point, which corresponds to a basic feasible solution that does not decrease the value of the objective function. This process continues until an optimal solution for the equivalent problem has been reached, if one exists. When the constraints are all less-than-or-equal-to constraints, the optimal solution for the equivalent problem is also optimal for the original problem. This is not necessarily true when there are greater-than-or-equal-to constraints or equalities in the original problem. This aspect of linear programming will be discussed in Section 3.5.

    To better illustrate the concept of basic solutions and basic feasible solutions, consider the example in Section 3.4.1. The equivalent problem is:

Table 3.7 BASIC SOLUTIONS

Nonbasic variables	Basic variables	z	Basic feasible solution	Point in Figure 3.1
$x_1 = x_2 = 0$	$x_3 = 100, x_4 = 120$	0	Yes	A
$x_1 = x_3 = 0$	$x_2 = 33.33, x_4 = 53.33$	133.32	Yes	B
$x_1 = x_4 = 0$	$x_2 = 60, x_3 = -80$	240	No	E
$x_2 = x_3 = 0$	$x_1 = 50, x_4 = -80$	300	No	F
$x_2 = x_4 = 0$	$x_1 = 30, x_3 = 40$	180	Yes	D
$x_3 = x_4 = 0$	$x_1 = 20, x_2 = 20$	200	Yes	C

$$\text{maximize:} \quad z = 6x_1 + 4x_2 + 0 \cdot x_3 + 0 \cdot x_4$$
$$\text{subject to:} \quad 2x_1 + 3x_2 + x_3 \qquad\quad = 100$$
$$4x_1 + 2x_2 \qquad\quad + x_4 = 120$$
$$\text{all } x_i \geqslant 0$$

Since there are two equations in four unknowns, the maximum number of basic solutions is

$$\binom{4}{2} = \frac{4!}{2!2!} = \frac{4 \cdot 3 \cdot 2 \cdot 1}{2 \cdot 1 \cdot 2 \cdot 1} = 6$$

In this example, if we set any two variables equal to zero, the solution of the remaining system of two equations in two unknowns is unique. Therefore, there will be six basic solutions. The data in Table 3.7 illustrate that not every basic solution is a basic feasible solution.

Thus, we see that the optimal basic feasible solution is attained at $x_1 = x_2 = 20$ with a maximum value of 200. Clearly the optimal solution is at point C in Figure 3.1.

In this example problem, the slack variables were both zero in the optimal solution. This means that the two constraints in the original problem are strict "equalities" for the values of x_1 and x_2 that maximize z^*. Many times one or more slack variables will be in the optimal solution at a positive level. This means that the corresponding constraint(s) in the original problem are strictly "less than" constraints for the optimal solution.

Before writing down the general simplex algorithm, we will illustrate its use by solving the problem we have been considering. As mentioned earlier, the simplex method will examine only a subset of all basic feasible solutions.

3.4.3 Simplex Method Illustrated

The simplex method is an iterative procedure that consists of moving from one basic feasible solution to another in such a way that the value of the objective function does not decrease (in the maximization problem). This process continues until an optimal solution is reached, if one exists. The simplex method will be illustrated with the example from Section 3.3.1.

Step 1
The original LP model

$$\text{maximize: } z^* = 6x_1 + 4x_2$$
$$\text{subject to: } 2x_1 + 3x_2 \leqslant 100$$
$$4x_1 + 2x_2 \leqslant 120$$
$$x_1, x_2 \geqslant 0$$

is converted to an equivalent model by adding slack variables to each constraint and assigning a zero cost coefficient to each slack variable in the objective function. Thus, the equivalent model is

$$\text{maximize: } z = 6x_1 + 4x_2 + 0 \cdot x_3 + 0 \cdot x_4$$
$$\text{subject to: } 2x_1 + 3x_2 + x_3 \quad\quad = 100$$
$$4x_1 + 2x_2 \quad\quad + x_4 = 120$$
$$\text{all } x_i \geqslant 0 \quad i = 1, 2, 3, 4$$

Step 2
Since each constant on the right side of each equation is greater than zero, go to step 3. The simplex method requires that all constants on the right side of the equals sign be greater than or equal to zero.

Step 3
Rewrite the equivalent problem as:

$$\text{maximize: } z$$
$$\text{subject to: } z - 6x_1 - 4x_2 \quad\quad\quad = 0 \quad\quad\quad (3.1)$$
$$2x_1 + 3x_2 + x_3 \quad\quad = 100 \quad\quad (3.2)$$
$$4x_1 + 2x_2 \quad\quad + x_4 = 120 \quad\quad (3.3)$$
$$\text{all } x_i \geqslant 0 \quad i = 1, 2, 3, 4$$

Step 4
Select an initial basic feasible solution. That is, set two variables equal to zero and solve for the other two variables. Let $x_1 = x_2 = 0$; then immediately by observation

$$x_3 = 100$$
$$x_4 = 120$$

from which we get $z = 0$. The variables x_3 and x_4 that were not set equal to zero are called *basic variables* and form a basis. The variables x_1 and x_2 that were set equal to zero are called *nonbasic variables*. This solution corresponds to point A in Figure 3.1.

The process now involves changing one of the basic variables to a nonbasic variable and changing one of the nonbasic variables to a basic variable. That is, either x_3 or x_4 is set equal to zero, and either x_1 or x_2 is allowed to take on a value greater than zero. The variable set equal to zero is said to "leave" the basis in the next basic feasible solution, whereas the nonbasic variable that is allowed to be greater than zero is said to "enter" the basis in the next basic feasible solution. But how is the selection done?

Step 5
To determine the variable to enter the basis in the next basic feasible solution, the coefficients of the nonbasic variables in Equation (3.1) are examined for the most negative coefficient. If all coefficients are greater than or equal to zero, an optimal solution has been reached. Each negative coefficient represents how much z will increase for each unit increase in the value of the corresponding nonbasic variable. In this case, the coefficient of x_1 is the most negative (-6), so variable x_1 will enter the next basic feasible solution.

Step 6
Examine the positive ratios of the constant on the right side of each equation to the corresponding coefficient of x_1 for the minimum value.

$$100/2 = 50 \quad \text{from Equation (3.2)}$$
$$120/4 = 30 \quad \text{from Equation (3.3)}$$

The minimum value occurs for Equation (3.3). Consequently, the current basic variable in Equation (3.3), variable 4, will leave the basis in the next basic feasible solution. If a positive ratio does not exist, then the objective function is not bounded above by the constraints. Thus, a finite optimal solution does not exist.

Step 7
Perform elementary transformations on each equation in step 3 until the coefficient of x_1 is 1 in the last equation and is 0 in the first two equations. This process is called *a change of basis*. By elementary transformation we mean

Multiply or divide an equation by a constant
Add a multiple of one equation to another

Neither of these operations will change the equations with respect to the possible solutions.

To get the coefficient of x_1 to be 1 in the third equation, merely divide Equation (3.3) by 4, the coefficient of x_1 in Equation (3.3),

$$z - 6x_1 - 4x_2 \qquad\qquad\qquad = 0 \qquad\qquad (3.4)$$
$$2x_1 + 3x_2 + x_3 \qquad\qquad = 100 \qquad (3.5)$$
$$x_1 + \frac{2}{4}x_2 \qquad + \frac{1}{4}x_4 = 30 \qquad (3.6)$$

Likewise, multiply Equation (3.6) by 6 and add the resulting equation to Equation (3.4) to get

$$z + 0 - x_2 \quad\quad + \frac{6}{4}x_4 = 180 \quad\quad (3.7)$$

$$2x_1 + 3x_2 + x_3 \quad\quad = 100 \quad\quad (3.8)$$

$$x_1 + \frac{2}{4}x_2 \quad\quad + \frac{1}{4}x_4 = 30 \quad\quad (3.9)$$

Then finally, multiply Equation (3.6) by -2 and add the resulting equation to Equation (3.5) to get

$$z \quad\quad -x_2 \quad\quad + \frac{6}{4}x_4 = 180 \quad\quad (3.10)$$

$$2x_2 + x_3 - \frac{2}{4}x_4 = 40 \quad\quad (3.11)$$

$$x_1 + \frac{2}{4}x_2 \quad\quad + \frac{1}{4}x_4 = 30 \quad\quad (3.12)$$

We determined in steps 5 and 6 that x_4 should leave the basis in the next basic feasible solution. Consequently, when x_2 and x_4 are set equal to 0, Equations (3.10)–(3.12) immediately yield

$$x_1 = 30$$
$$x_3 = 40$$
$$z = 180$$

This corresponds to the point D in Figure 3.1. Note that moving from point A to point D increases the value of the objective function from 0 to 180.

Once it was determined in steps 5 and 6 that x_4 would leave and x_1 would enter the next basis, we could have set $x_2 = x_4 = 0$, and solved Equations (3.2) and (3.3) for x_1 and x_3, as we did earlier in determining all of the basic solutions. However, the mathematical manipulations in step 7 (to be generalized later) allow us to write down the solution values of x_1 and x_3 immediately by observation, and also changes the equations to a form where the variable to enter and the variable to leave the next basis can easily be determined.

Step 8
The coefficients of the nonbasic variables in Equation (3.10) are examined for the most negative value. Obviously, since the coefficient of x_2 is the only negative coefficient, x_2 is chosen as the variable to enter the next basis.

Step 9
Examine the positive ratios of the constant on the right side of Equations (3.11) and (3.12) to the corresponding coefficient of x_2 for the minimum value.

$$40/2 = 20 \quad \text{from Equation (3.11)}$$

$$30/\frac{2}{4} = 60 \quad \text{from Equation (3.12)}$$

The minimum value occurs for Equation (3.11), so the current basic variable in Equation (3.11), variable 3, will leave the basis in the next basic feasible solution.

Step 10
Divide Equation (3.11) by 2, the coefficient of x_2 in that equation, to give

$$z \quad -x_2 \quad\quad +\frac{6}{4}x_4 = 180 \quad\quad (3.13)$$

$$x_2 + \frac{1}{2}x_3 - \frac{1}{4}x_4 = 20 \quad\quad (3.14)$$

$$x_1 + \frac{2}{4}x_2 \quad\quad +\frac{1}{4}x_4 = 30 \quad\quad (3.15)$$

Step 11
Add Equation (3.14) to Equation (3.13) to give

$$z \quad\quad +\frac{1}{2}x_3 + \frac{5}{4}x_4 = 200 \quad\quad (3.16)$$

$$x_2 + \frac{1}{2}x_3 - \frac{1}{4}x_4 = 20 \quad\quad (3.17)$$

$$x_1 + \frac{2}{4}x_2 \quad\quad +\frac{1}{4}x_4 = 30 \quad\quad (3.18)$$

Step 12
Multiply Equation (3.14) by $-\frac{2}{4}$ and add the resulting equation to Equation (3.15) to give

$$z \quad\quad +\frac{1}{2}x_3 + \frac{5}{4}x_4 = 200 \quad\quad (3.19)$$

$$x_2 + \frac{1}{2}x_3 - \frac{1}{4}x_4 = 20 \quad\quad (3.20)$$

$$x_1 \quad -\frac{1}{4}x_3 + \frac{6}{16}x_4 = 20 \quad\quad (3.21)$$

Thus, since x_3 and x_4 will be nonbasic variables in the next basic feasible solution ($x_3 = x_4 = 0$), and x_1 and x_2 will be basic variables, we see from Equations (3.19)–(3.21) that

$$x_1 = 20$$

$$x_2 = 20$$

$$z = 200$$

Since the coefficients of x_3 and x_4 are both positive in Equation (3.19), an optimal solution has been reached. The solution

$$x_1 = 20$$
$$x_2 = 20$$
$$x_3 = 0$$
$$x_4 = 0$$

is optimal for the equivalent problem, and the solution

$$x_1 = 20$$
$$x_2 = 20$$

is optimal for the original problem. Thus,

$$z^* = 6 \cdot 20 + 4 \cdot 20 = 200$$

is the maximum value of the objective function in the original problem.

Before presenting the general simplex algorithm, we will examine the remaining types of constraints as well as a minimization problem.

3.5 EQUALITIES AND GREATER-THAN-OR-EQUAL-TO CONSTRAINTS

If the problem in Section 3.3.1 is further restricted to the situation where exactly 14 televisions of type I and at least 22 televisions of type II must be produced, the corresponding LP model is

$$\text{maximize:} \quad z^* = 6x_1 + 4x_2$$

$$\begin{aligned}
\text{subject to:} \quad 2x_1 + 3x_2 &\leqslant 100 & (3.22)\\
4x_1 + 2x_2 &\leqslant 120 & (3.23)\\
x_1 &= 14 & (3.24)\\
x_2 &\geqslant 22 & (3.25)\\
x_1 &\geqslant 0
\end{aligned}$$

Here an equality and a greater-than-or-equal-to constraint have been added. The first objective with any LP model is to convert it to an equivalent model where the constraints are changed to equalities. Slack variables x_3 and x_4 can be added to the left side of constraints (3.22) and (3.23), respectively, to convert them to equalities. However, a positive amount must be subtracted from the left side of constraint (3.25) to force an equality. Thus, a positive variable x_5, called a *surplus variable*, is subtracted from the left side of constraint (3.25). A corresponding zero cost coefficient is assigned to each slack and surplus variable in the objective function. The resulting equivalent problem to this point is

$$\text{maximize:} \quad z = 6x_1 + 4x_2 + 0 \cdot x_3 + 0 \cdot x_4 + 0 \cdot x_5$$

$$\text{subject to:} \quad 2x_1 + 3x_2 + x_3 \qquad\qquad = 100 \qquad\qquad (3.26)$$

$$4x_1 + 2x_2 \qquad + x_4 \qquad = 120 \qquad\qquad (3.27)$$

$$x_1 \qquad\qquad\qquad\qquad = 14 \qquad\qquad (3.28)$$

$$x_2 \qquad\qquad -x_5 = 22 \qquad\qquad (3.29)$$

$$\text{all } x_i \geqslant 0 \qquad i = 1, 2, \ldots, 5$$

The simplex method requires that

1 All constants on the right side of the equations be greater than or equal to zero

2 Each equation have a variable whose coefficient is 1 in that equation and 0 in all of the remaining equations.

These conditions provide a set of variables that can be used as basic variables in the initial solution, and also assure that the resulting solution using these variables as basic variables will be a basic feasible solution for the equivalent LP model.

Condition 1 is satisfied in this example problem and variables 3 and 4 satisfy condition 2 in Equations (3.26) and (3.27), respectively. However, no variable in Equations (3.28) and (3.29) satisfies condition 2. Hence, additional variables must be added.

3.5.1 Artificial Variables

Even though equalities already exist in Equations (3.28) and (3.29), *artificial variables* x_6 and x_7 are added to the left side of these equations so they will have available variables that satisfy condition 2; namely, variables 6 and 7. Each of these artificial variables is assigned an arbitrarily small negative cost coefficient (algebraically), say $-T$, in the objective function.

Artificial variables merely provide a way of getting the simplex method started and give an artificial solution to the original problem as long as an artificial variable is in the basis at a positive nonzero level. As soon as an artificial variable leaves the basis, it can be ignored since it will never enter the basis again. However, if an artificial variable cannot be "driven" to zero and thus is in the basis at a positive nonzero level when an optimal solution for the equivalent problem is reached, then the original problem does not have a basic feasible solution.

The result of adding artificial variables x_6 and x_7 to Equations (3.28) and (3.29) is

$$\text{maximize:} \quad z = 6x_1 + 4x_2 + 0x_3 + 0x_4 + 0x_5 - Tx_6 - Tx_7 \qquad (3.30)$$

$$\text{subject to:} \quad 2x_1 + 3x_2 + x_3 \qquad\qquad = 100 \qquad (3.31)$$

$$4x_1 + 2x_2 \qquad + x_4 \qquad = 120 \qquad (3.32)$$

$$x_1 \qquad\qquad\qquad + x_6 \qquad\quad = 14 \qquad\qquad (3.33)$$

$$x_2 \qquad\qquad -x_5 \quad + x_7 = 22 \qquad\qquad (3.34)$$

$$\text{all } x_i \geqslant 0 \quad i = 1, 2, \ldots, 7$$

Variables x_3, x_4, x_6, and x_7 can now be used as basic variables for the initial solution, while variables x_1, x_2, and x_5 will be nonbasic variables. The solution of the equivalent problem is then

$$x_1 = 0 \qquad x_5 = 0$$
$$x_2 = 0 \qquad x_6 = 14$$
$$x_3 = 100 \qquad x_7 = 22$$
$$x_4 = 120$$

Note that this is a basic feasible solution of Equations (3.31)–(3.34); but, since the artificial variables are at a positive level, it is not a basic feasible solution for the original LP model. For example, $x_1 = 14$ and $x_2 \geqslant 22$ in the original model, but obviously this is not true in the above solution.

The purpose of assigning arbitrarily small negative cost coefficients (algebraically) to the artificial variables is to force them out of the basis, or at least to a zero level, since any positive value of an artificial variable makes the value of the objective function arbitrarily small.

One final step is necessary to prepare Equations (3.30)–(3.34) for the simplex method. Rewrite Equation (3.30) as

$$z - 6x_1 - 4x_2 + Tx_6 + Tx_7 = 0 \qquad (3.35)$$

and eliminate variables x_6 and x_7 from Equation (3.35). Hence, Equations (3.33) and (3.34) are each multiplied by $-T$ and added to Equation (3.35) to give the new equivalent LP model

maximize: z

subject to:
$$2x_1 + 3x_2 + x_3 \qquad\qquad\qquad\qquad = 100 \qquad (3.36)$$
$$4x_1 + 2x_2 \qquad + x_4 \qquad\qquad\qquad = 120 \qquad (3.37)$$
$$x_1 \qquad\qquad\qquad\qquad + x_6 \qquad\quad = 14 \qquad (3.38)$$
$$x_2 \qquad\qquad - x_5 \quad + x_7 = 22 \qquad (3.39)$$
$$z - (T + 6)x_1 - (T + 4)x_2 \qquad + Tx_5 \qquad\qquad = -36T \qquad (3.40)$$

Equations (3.36)–(3.40) are in a form suitable for solution using the simplex method.

3.6   MINIMIZATION OF THE OBJECTIVE FUNCTION

If the objective function in an LP model is to be minimized rather than maximized, it is a simple matter to convert the model to one where the objective function is to be maximized. The converted model can then be solved using the simplex method for maximization.

Given the LP model

$$\text{minimize: } z^* = \sum_{j=1}^{k} c_j x_j$$

$$\text{subject to: } \sum_{j=1}^{k} a_{ij} x_j (\leqslant, =, \geqslant) b_i \qquad i = 1, 2, \ldots, m$$

$$\text{all } x_j \geqslant 0 \qquad j = 1, 2, \ldots, k$$

the procedure is to multiply the objective function by -1 and then to

$$\text{maximize: } \hat{z} = -z^* = -\sum_{j=1}^{k} c_j x_j$$

$$\text{subject to: } \sum_{j=1}^{k} a_{ij} x_j (\leqslant, =, \geqslant) b_i \qquad i = 1, 2, \ldots, m$$

$$\text{all } x_j \geqslant 0 \qquad j = 1, 2, \ldots, k$$

The simplex maximization method can be used to solve this new problem, and then the value of the objective function for the original problem is just $z^* = -\hat{z}$. The value of the variables that maximize $\hat{z}$ also minimize z^*.

Consider the problem

$$\text{minimize: } z^* = x_1 + 2x_2$$
$$\text{subject to: } x_1 \geqslant 4$$
$$2x_1 - x_2 \leqslant 6$$
$$x_2 \geqslant 0$$

the new maximization problem is

$$\text{maximize: } \hat{z} = -x_1 - 2x_2$$
$$\text{subject to: } x_1 \geqslant 4$$
$$2x_1 - x_2 \leqslant 6$$
$$x_2 \geqslant 0$$

Figure 3.2 illustrates the graphic solution for this problem. The maximum value of $\hat{z}$ occurs at $x_1 = 4$ and $x_2 = 2$ and is equal to -8. Thus, $x_1 = 4$ and $x_2 = 2$ also minimize z^* in the original problem, and the minimum value of z^* is

$$\min (z^*) = - \max (\hat{z}) = - (-8) = 8$$

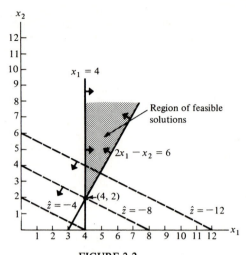

FIGURE 3.2
Solution of example in Section 3.6.

3.7 THE SIMPLEX METHOD

Basically the simplex method is an iterative procedure that can be used to solve any LP model if the needed computer time and storage are available. It is assumed that the original linear programming model

$$\text{maximize:} \quad \hat{z} = \sum_{j=1}^{r} \hat{c}_j x_j$$

$$\text{subject to:} \quad \sum_{j=1}^{r} a_{ij} x_j (\geqslant, =, \leqslant) b_i \quad b_i \geqslant 0 \quad i = 1, 2, \ldots, m$$

$$\text{all } x_j \geqslant 0$$

has been converted to the equivalent LP model

$$\text{maximize:} \quad z = \sum_{j=1}^{n} \hat{\hat{c}}_j x_j$$

$$\text{subject to:} \quad \sum_{j=1}^{n} a_{ij} x_j = b_i \quad i = 1, 2, \ldots, m$$

$$\text{all } x_j \geqslant 0$$

which includes slack variables that have been added to the left side of each less-than-or-equal-to constraint, surplus variables that have been subtracted from the left side of each greater-than-or-equal-to constraint, and artificial variables that have been added to the left side of each greater-than-or-equal-to constraint and each equality. It is also assumed that the cost coefficients for the slack and surplus variables are zero while the cost coefficients for the artificial variables are arbitrarily small negative numbers (algebraically), say $-T$. The equivalent model necessarily assures us that each equation contains a variable with a coefficient of 1 in that equation and a coefficient of zero in each of the other equations. If an original constraint was a less-than-or-equal-to constraint, the slack variable in the corresponding equation will satisfy the condition just stated. Likewise, the artificial variables added to the greater-than-or-equal-to constraints and equalities satisfy the condition for each of the remaining equations in the equivalent model. These slack and artificial variables are the basic variables in the initial basic feasible solution of the equivalent problem.

The equivalent model is now rewritten as

maximize: z

$$\text{subject to:}\quad z - \sum_{j=1}^{n} \hat{\hat{c}}_j x_j = 0 \tag{3.41}$$

$$\sum_{j=1}^{n} a_{ij} x_j = b_i \qquad i = 1, 2, \ldots, m \tag{3.42}$$

all $x_j \geqslant 0$

Since $\hat{\hat{c}}_j = -T$ for each artificial variable, we must multiply by $-T$ each equation represented by (3.42) that contains an artificial variable and add the resulting equations to Equation (3.41) to give

maximize: z

$$\text{subject to:}\quad z - \sum_{j=1}^{n} c_j x_j = b_0 \tag{3.43}$$

$$\sum_{j=1}^{n} a_{ij} x_j = b_i \qquad i = 1, 2, \ldots, m \tag{3.44}$$

all $x_j \geqslant 0$

where $b_0 = -T \sum_{*} b_k$ and * represents the equations containing artificial variables. This assures us that each equation in (3.44) contains a slack or artificial variable that has a coefficient of 1 in that equation and a coefficient of zero in each of the other equations in (3.44) as well as in Equation (3.43). Equation (3.43) will be referred to as the *objective function equation.*

We will now present the general simplex method. It will be followed by a computer-oriented algorithm to carry out the method.

(*a*) Obtain an initial basic feasible solution of the equivalent model; that is, let

$$x_{B_i} \qquad i = 1, 2, \ldots, m$$

be the initial basic feasible solution where x_{B_i} denotes the ith basic variable and corresponds to the slack or artificial variable in the ith equation.

(*b*) Select the nonbasic variable with the most negative coefficient in Equation (3.43) as the variable to enter as a basic variable in the new basic feasible solution. If all coefficients in Equation (3.43) are nonnegative, an optimal solution of the equivalent model has been obtained. However, the solution is optimal for the original model only if the basic variables are void of any artificial variables with a positive value. That is to say, if at least one basic variable is an artificial variable with a positive value in the optimal solution of the equivalent model, then there are no feasible solutions of the original model.

(*c*) Select a basic variable to leave the set of variables that are present in the current basic feasible solution. The basic variable in the equation corresponding to the minimum ratio of the b_i's to the corresponding positive coefficients of the entering variable in each equation represented by (3.44) will leave and not be a part of the next basic feasible solution. Let equation r contain the leaving variable. If there are no nonnegative ratios, then the objective function is unbounded above (i.e., no finite optimal solution exists).

(*d*) Perform elementary transformations on Equations (3.43) and (3.44) until the coefficient of the entering variable from step (*b*) is one in equation r and zero in every other equation including Equation (3.43). This can be accomplished by the Gauss-Jordan elimination method for solving a system of linear equations. The new basic feasible solution is

$$x_{B_i} = b_i^* \quad i = 1, 2, \ldots, m$$

where x_{B_i} $(i \neq r)$ corresponds to the same basic variables in the previous basic feasible solution and x_{B_r} corresponds to the new basic variable that just entered the basic solution.

(*e*) Let Equations (3.43) and (3.44) now represent the transformed system of linear equations from step (*d*) above. Return to step (*b*).

The simplex method will now be presented in algorithm form.

3.7.1 Algorithm 3.1—Simplex Algorithm

Step 1

Obtain an initial basic feasible solution of the equivalent model; that is, let

$$x_{B_i} = b_i \quad i = 1, 2, \ldots, m$$

be the initial basic feasible solution where x_{B_i} corresponds to the slack or artificial variable in the ith equation.

Step 2

If at least one of the coefficients of the nonbasic variables in the objective function Equation (3.43) is negative, then z can possibly be increased, so go to step 3. Otherwise, an optimal solution has been obtained, so go to step 9.

Step 3

The nonbasic variable with the most negative coefficient in Equation (3.43) is chosen to enter as a basic variable in the next basic feasible solution. Suppose x_k enters. Any nonbasic variable with a negative coefficient in Equation (3.43) could have been chosen and the value of the objective function would not have decreased; however, a good general rule is to choose the variable with the most negative coefficient. Further information about this will be found in Section 3.10.

Step 4

Examine the ratio of the b_i's to the corresponding positive coefficients of the entering variable x_k in each equation represented by (3.44). If at least one positive ratio exists, go to step 5; otherwise, the objective function is unbounded, so go to step 11.

Step 5

The current basic variable in the equation corresponding to the smallest nonnegative ratio from step 4 is chosen as the variable to leave the set of basic variables in the current basic feasible solution. Suppose

$$\frac{b_r}{a_{rk}} = \min\left(\frac{b_i}{a_{ik}}, a_{ik} > 0\right)$$

then the rth basic variable, the variable corresponding to x_{B_r}, will leave the set of basic variables. Since x_k is entering as a basic variable in the next solution, we will have

$$x_{B_r} \equiv x_k$$

in the new basic feasible solution.

The element a_{rk} is called the *pivotal element* and will play an important role in the transformations in steps 6–8. If the leaving variable is an artificial variable, it will never enter as a basic variable again because of its arbitrarily small, negative cost coefficient, so all calculations for that variable can be ignored in future steps.

Step 6

Perform elementary transformations on Equations (3.43) and (3.44) until the coefficient of the entering variable x_k is *1* in the rth equation and 0 in every other equation including Equation (3.43). This can be accomplished by the Gauss-Jordan method for solving a system of linear equations. The detailed procedure is:

(*a*) Divide the rth equation by the pivotal element, a_{rk}, to get

$$\frac{a_{r1}}{a_{rk}} x_1 + \frac{a_{r2}}{a_{rk}} x_2 + \cdots + \frac{a_{r,k-1}}{a_{rk}} x_{k-1} + x_k + \frac{a_{r,k+1}}{a_{rk}} x_{k+1} + \cdots + \frac{a_{rn}}{a_{rk}} x_n = \frac{b_r}{a_{rk}}$$

This new rth equation will be referred to as the pivotal equation.

(*b*) To force the coefficient of x_k to be zero in Equation (3.43), multiply the pivotal equation by c_k and add the resulting equation to Equation (3.43). As a result of this transformation, the new equation will have the form

$$z - c_1^* x_1 - c_2^* x_2 - \cdots - c_{k-1}^* x_{k-1} - c_{k+1}^* x_{k+1} - \cdots - c_n^* x_n = b_0^*$$

where $c_j^* = c_j + \dfrac{c_k a_{rj}}{a_{rk}}$ for $j = 1, 2, \ldots, k-1, k+1, \ldots, n$

$$b_0^* = b_0 + \frac{c_k b_r}{a_{rk}}$$

(c) To force the coefficient of x_k to be zero in each of the equations in (3.44) except the rth equation, multiply the pivotal equation by a_{ik} and subtract the resulting equation from equation i for $i = 1, 2, \ldots, r-1, r+1, \ldots, m$. The new coefficient of x_j in the ith equation will be

$$a_{ij}^* = a_{ij} - \frac{a_{rj} a_{ik}}{a_{rk}} \qquad \text{for } i \neq r \text{ and } j = 1, 2, \ldots, n$$

$$= \frac{a_{rj}}{a_{rk}} \qquad \text{for } i = r \text{ and } j = 1, 2, \ldots, n$$

Likewise, the new right-side constant for equation i is

$$b_i^* = b_i - \frac{a_{ik} b_r}{a_{rk}} \qquad \text{for } i \neq r$$

$$= \frac{b_r}{a_{rk}} \qquad \text{for } i = r$$

Step 7
The value of the rth basic variable in the new basic feasible solution is

$$x_{B_r} \equiv x_k = \frac{b_r}{a_{rk}} = b_r^*$$

and the value for each of the other basic variables is

$$x_{B_i} = b_i - \frac{a_{ik} b_r}{a_{rk}} = b_i^* \qquad i = 1, 2, \ldots, m$$

$$i \neq r$$

Note that x_{B_i} ($i \neq r$) corresponds to the same basic variables in the previous basic feasible solution.

Step 8
Let the constants c_j, b_0, a_{ij}, and b_i in Equations (3.43) and (3.44) represent the new transformed values obtained in step 6. Return to step 2.

Step 9
An optimal solution of the equivalent LP model has been obtained. Check to see if any of the artificial variables are in the solution at a positive level. If there is an artificial variable at a positive level (e.g., some artifical variable $x_{10} = 6$), go to step 10;

otherwise, the last solution obtained in step 8 is an optimal solution for the original model. (We assume the initial basic feasible solution consisting of all slack and artificial variables is not optimal.) If any of the coefficients of nonbasic variables in Equation (3.43) are zero, then there are multiple optimal solutions for the original model. When an optimal solution is found, if one exists, the simplex method does not continue to look for additional optimal solutions.

Print the results and stop.

Step 10
No feasible solution exists for the original model, so stop.

Step 11
The objective function is unbounded, so stop.

To further illustrate the simplex method, an example problem will be solved step by step using Algorithm 3.1.

3.8 EXAMPLE TO ILLUSTRATE SIMPLEX ALGORITHM

Suppose we want to solve the LP model

$$\text{minimize:} \quad z^* = -6x_1 - 4x_2$$
$$\text{subject to:} \quad 2x_1 + 3x_2 \leq 30$$
$$3x_1 + 2x_2 \leq 24$$
$$x_1 + x_2 \geq 3$$
$$x_1, x_2 \geq 0$$

Step 1
Convert the model to a maximization model.

$$\text{maximize:} \quad z = -z^* = 6x_1 + 4x_2$$
$$\text{subject to:} \quad 2x_1 + 3x_2 \leq 30$$
$$3x_1 + 2x_2 \leq 24$$
$$x_1 + x_2 \geq 3$$
$$x_1, x_2 \geq 0$$

Step 2
Introduce slack, surplus, and artificial variables. A slack variable is added to the left side of the first two constraints in step 1, and a surplus variable is subtracted from the left side of the third constraint to give

$$\text{maximize:} \quad z = 6x_1 + 4x_2$$

$$\text{subject to: } 2x_1 + 3x_2 + x_4 \qquad\qquad = 30 \tag{3.45}$$
$$3x_1 + 2x_2 \qquad\quad + x_5 = 24$$
$$x_1 + x_2 - x_3 \qquad\qquad = 3 \tag{3.46}$$
$$\text{all } x_i \geqslant 0 \qquad i = 1, 2, \ldots, 5$$

Step 3

To get a variable with a coefficient of 1 in Equation (3.46) and a coefficient of 0 in Equations (3.45), an artificial variable x_6 is added to the left side of Equation (3.46). An algebraically small, negative constant, say -100, is assigned to x_6 in the objective function. The result is

$$\text{maximize: } z = 6x_1 + 4x_2 - 100x_6$$
$$\text{subject to: } 2x_1 + 3x_2 \qquad + x_4 \qquad\qquad = 30$$
$$3x_1 + 2x_2 \qquad\qquad + x_5 \qquad = 24$$
$$x_1 + x_2 - x_3 \qquad\qquad + x_6 = 3$$

Step 4

Rewrite the equations in step 3 as

$$\text{maximize: } z$$
$$\text{subject to: } \quad 2x_1 + 3x_2 \qquad + x_4 \qquad\qquad = 30 \tag{3.47}$$
$$3x_1 + 2x_2 \qquad\qquad + x_5 \qquad = 24 \tag{3.48}$$
$$x_1 + x_2 - x_3 \qquad\qquad + x_6 = 3 \tag{3.49}$$
$$z - 6x_1 - 4x_2 \qquad\qquad + 100x_6 = 0 \tag{3.50}$$

Step 5

Multiply Equation (3.49) by -100 and add the resulting equation to Equation (3.50) to give

$$2x_1 + 3x_2 \qquad\qquad + x_4 \qquad\qquad = 30 \tag{3.51}$$
$$3x_1 + 2x_2 \qquad\qquad\qquad + x_5 \qquad = 24 \tag{3.52}$$
$$x_1 + x_2 - x_3 \qquad\qquad + x_6 = 3 \tag{3.53}$$
$$z - 106x_1 - 104x_2 + 100x_3 \qquad\qquad = -300 \tag{3.54}$$

Step 6

Let $x_1 = x_2 = x_3 = 0$; then from Equations (3.51)-(3.54)

$$x_{B_1} = x_4 = 30$$
$$x_{B_2} = x_5 = 24$$
$$x_{B_3} = x_6 = 3$$
$$z = -300$$

Of course, this solution is not feasible for the original LP model since the last constraint in step 1 is not satisfied. Note that x_4, x_5, and x_6 are the basic variables and form a basis. The value of the objective function for the equivalent problem is $z = -300$. x_{B_i} ($i = 1, 2, 3$) is the ith variable in the basis.

Step 7
The coefficient of x_1 is the most negative coefficient in Equation (3.54), so x_1 is chosen to enter as a basic variable in the next basic feasible solution.

Step 8
Examine the ratios:

$$30/2 = 15 \quad \text{from Equation (3.51)}$$
$$24/3 = 8 \quad \text{from Equation (3.52)}$$
$$3/1 = 3 \quad \text{from Equation (3.53)}$$

The smallest ratio is 3 and is obtained from Equation (3.53). Thus, the current basic variable in Equation (3.53), variable x_6, will leave the basis in the next basic solution. Replace variable x_6 with x_1 as the third variable in the basis. That is, let $x_{B_3} = x_1$. The coefficient of x_1 in Equation (3.53), namely 1, is called the *pivotal element.*

Step 9
Since the pivotal element is already 1, Equation (3.53) is called the *pivotal equation.*

Step 10
To force the coefficient of x_1 to be zero in Equations (3.51), (3.52), and (3.54),

(a) Multiply the pivotal equation by 106 and add the resulting equation to Equation (3.54).
(b) Multiply the pivotal equation by -2 and add the resulting equation to Equation (3.51).
(c) Multiply the pivotal equation by -3 and add the resulting equation to Equation (3.52).

The result of (a)–(c) is

$$
\begin{array}{llll}
x_2 + 2x_3 + x_4 & - & 2x_6 = 24 & (3.55) \\
- x_2 + 3x_3 & + x_5 - & 3x_6 = 15 & (3.56) \\
x_1 + x_2 - x_3 & + & x_6 = 3 & (3.57) \\
z + 2x_2 - 6x_3 & & + 106x_6 = 18 & (3.58)
\end{array}
$$

Step 11
The new basic feasible solution is

$$x_2 = x_3 = x_6 = 0$$
$$x_{B_1} = x_4 = 24$$

$$x_{B_2} = x_5 = 15$$
$$x_{B_3} = x_1 = 3$$

Since the artificial variable is not in the basis at a positive level, this is a basic feasible solution for the original model also. The value of the objective function, $z = 18$, is also the value of the objective function for the original maximization model.

Step 12

Since the coefficient of x_3 is the only negative coefficient in Equation (3.58), x_3 is chosen as the next variable to enter the basis.

Step 13

Examine the ratios:

$$24/2 = 12 \quad \text{from Equation (3.55)}$$
$$15/3 = 5 \quad \text{from Equation (3.56)}$$

Of course, the ratio from Equation (3.57) is not considered since it is negative. The smallest ratio comes from Equation (3.56), so the current basic variable in this equation, variable x_5, is chosen to leave the basis. Thus x_3 replaces x_5 as the second variable in the basis; that is, $x_{B_2} = x_3$. The coefficient of x_3 in Equation (3.56) is the pivotal element.

Step 14

Divide Equation (3.56) by the pivotal element to get the new pivotal equation

$$-\frac{1}{3}x_2 + x_3 \quad + \frac{1}{3}x_5 - x_6 = 5$$

Step 15

To force the coefficient of x_3 to be zero in Equations (3.55), (3.57), and (3.58),

(a) Multiply the pivotal equation by 6 and add the resulting equation to Equation (3.58).

(b) Multiply the pivotal equation by -2 and add the resulting equation to Equation (3.55).

(c) Add the pivotal equation to Equation (3.57).

The result is

$$\frac{5}{3}x_2 \quad + x_4 - \frac{2}{3}x_5 \quad = 14 \qquad (3.59)$$

$$-\frac{1}{3}x_2 + x_3 \quad + \frac{1}{3}x_5 - \quad x_6 = 5 \qquad (3.60)$$

$$x_1 + \frac{2}{3}x_2 \quad + \frac{1}{3}x_5 \quad = 8 \qquad (3.61)$$

$$z \qquad + 2x_5 + 100x_6 = 48 \qquad (3.62)$$

Step 16

The nonbasic variables are set equal to zero and the basic variables take on the values

$$x_{B_1} = x_4 = 14$$
$$x_{B_2} = x_3 = 5$$
$$x_{B_3} = x_1 = 8$$

This corresponds to point C in Figure 3.3. The value of the objective function is $z = 48$. Since an artificial variable is not in the basis at a positive level and all of the coefficients in Equation (3.62) are greater than or equal to zero, the current solution is an optimal solution for the original maximization problem. Also,

$$x_1 = 8$$
$$x_2 = 0$$

is an optimal solution of the original minimization problem and

$$z^* = -z = -48$$

is the minimum value of the objective function.

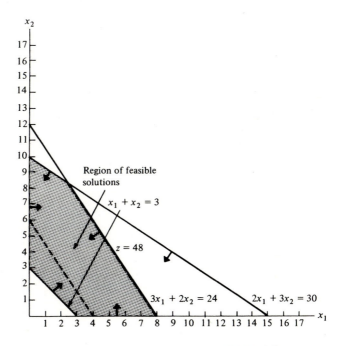

FIGURE 3.3
Example in Section 3.8.

It should be noted that since the nonbasic variable x_2 had a zero coefficient in Equation (3.62) when an optimal solution was reached, there is an infinity of optimal solutions. That is, every point on the line $3x_1 + 2x_2 = 24$ in the region of feasible solutions is an optimal solution for the original problem. Figure 3.3 illustrates the graphic solution.

3.9 COMPUTER PROGRAM FOR ALGORITHM 3.1

Most practical problems that can be solved with the simplex method involve a large number of variables and constraints. Cases involving several hundred variables and constraints are not uncommon. Computer programs have been written for the simplex algorithm that take advantage of special forms of the model such as in the transportation model presented in Section 3.11. Programs that use methods other than the ordinary simplex method to solve linear programming models are also available. The program presented in this section accepts the coefficients of the variables in the objective function and the constraints and converts the problem to the equivalent problem internally. The comment cards at the front of the program describe exactly how to use the program.

In particular, the simplex program consists of three parts. Part 1 is the mainline program that reads in the data; part 2 converts the constraints to equalities by adding slack, surplus, and artificial variables; and part 3 performs the actual work of the simplex method. Part 2 is handled with the subroutine SSARTV, while part 3 is handled with the subroutine SIMPLX.

The program is set up to handle a maximum of 25 constraints and 75 unknowns including slack, surplus, and artificial variables. To expand or contract the program to handle a maximum of M equations in N unknowns including slack, surplus, and artificial variables, change B(26), C(76), and CODE(26) in COMMON to B(M+1), C(N+1), and CODE(M+1). Also change the DIMENSION statement in the mainline to

$$\text{DIMENSION A(M+1,N+1),XB(N+1)}$$

The corresponding variables are dimensioned accordingly in the two subroutines SSARTV and SIMPLX.

The program as written occupies approximately 52K bytes of core storage. This includes both subroutines. It solved the problem in Section 3.8 in 0.09 s of IBM 370/168 time.

The computer program for the simplex algorithm is followed by the data and results for the problem in Section 3.8.

```
C     *********************************************************************
C     *                                                                  *
C     *       **    ALGORITHM 3.1   LINEAR PROGRAMMING   SIMPLEX    **    *
C     *                                                                  *
C     * THIS PROGRAM IS DESIGNED TO SOLVE ANY LINEAR PROGRAMMING MODEL UP TO *
C     * 25 CONSTRAINTS AND 75 VARIABLES INCLUDING SLACK, SURPLUS, AND ARTIFI- *
C     * CIAL VARIABLES.  LARGER PROBLEMS CAN BE SOLVED BY CHANGING THE COR- *
C     * RESPONDING NUMBERS IN THE DIMENSION AND COMMON STATEMENTS IN THE  *
C     * MAINLINE AS WELL AS IN THE SUBROUTINES SSARTV AND SIMPLX.         *
C     *     THE PROGRAM SUPPLIES THE NECESSARY SLACK, SURPLUS, AND ARTIFICIAL *
C     * VARIABLES.  IT WILL TREAT MINIMIZATION AS WELL AS MAXIMIZATION    *
C     * PROBLEMS.  EACH COST COEFFICIENT MUST BE LESS THAN 100 IN         *
C     * ABSOLUTE VALUE.                                                   *
C     * SUBROUTINE SSARTV SUPPLIES SLACK,SURPLUS,AND ARTIFICIAL VARIABLES. *
C     * SUBROUTINE SIMPLX DOES THE WORK OF THE SIMPLEX ALGORITHM.         *
C     *                                                                  *
C     * IT IS DESIGNED                                                    *
C     *     TO READ                                                       *
C     *         CARD 1   COLS  2-80   TITLE  DESCRIPTION OF THE PROBLEM USING *
C     *                                      ANY CHARACTERS ON KEYPUNCH   *
C     *                                      ** COLUMN 1 MUST BE LEFT BLANK ** *
C     *         CARD 2   COLS  1- 5   M  NUMBER OF CONSTRAINTS  (I5)       *
C     *                         6-10   K  NUMBER OF VARIABLES  (I5)        *
C     *                        11-15   NLET  NUMBER OF <OR= CONSTRAINTS  (I5) *
C     *                        16-20   NGET  NUMBER OF >OR= CONSTRAINTS  (I5) *
C     *                        21-25   NET   NUMBER OF = CONSTRAINTS  (I5) *
C     *                        26-30   NTYPE  0 MINIMIZATION PROBLEM       *
C     *                                       1 MAXIMIZATION PROBLEM  (I5) *
C     *         CARDS 3 TO T     M SETS OF CARDS, ONE SET FOR EACH CONSTRAINT *
C     *             CARD I   COLS  1-10   CODE(I)  0 IF <OR= CONSTRAINT    *
C     *                                            1 IF >OR= CONSTRAINT    *
C     *                                            2 IF = CONSTRAINT  (I10) *
C     *                        11-20   B(I)   CONSTANT IN CONSTRAINT I (F10.0)* 
C     *             CARD I+1    A(I,J)  J COEFFICIENTS OF CONSTRAINT I     *
C     *                                 PUNCH ROWWISE IN 8F10.0 FORMAT     *
C     *                                 IF K>8, CONTINUE ON NEXT CARD.     *
C     *         CARD T+1    C(J)  COST COEFFICIENTS OF OBJECTIVE FUNCTION  *
C     *                                 PUNCH ROWWISE IN 8F10.0 FORMAT     *
C     *                                 IF K>8, CONTINUE ON NEXT CARD.     *
C     *         CARD Z   COLS  1- 5   NOPT  0 PRINT ONLY OPTIMAL SOLUTION  *
C     *                                     1 PRINT ALL SOLUTIONS    (I5)  *
C     *             TO SOLVE MORE THAN ONE PROBLEM AT A TIME, REPEAT THE   *
C     *             READ SEQUENCE, AND STACK THE DATA ONE BEHIND THE OTHER *
C     *                                                                  *
C     *     TO CALCULATE AND PRINT                                        *
C     *         Z   OPTIMAL VALUE OF THE OBJECTIVE FUNCTION               *
C     *       XB(I)  THE SUBSCRIPT OF THE BASIC VARIABLES IN THE          *
C     *              OPTIMAL BASIC FEASIBLE SOLUTION                      *
C     *     A(I,NP1)  THE VALUE OF THE BASIC VARIABLES                    *
C     *********************************************************************
      COMMON B(26),C(76),CODE(26),KP1,MP1,N,K,M,NGET,NLET,NET,NTYPE,NP1,
     *NC,NC1,INDEXG,INDEXL,INDEXE,NFLAG,BASICS,OPTSOL,SUM,NOPT,IFLAG
      INTEGER CODE,XB,BASICS,OPTSOL
      DIMENSION A(26,76),XB(76)
      REAL*4 TITLE(20)
   50 READ(5,10,END=2000)TITLE
   10 FORMAT(20A4)
      WRITE(6,15)TITLE
   15 FORMAT('1',20A4,//)
      READ(5,20)M,K,NLET,NGET,NET,NTYPE
   20 FORMAT(6I5)
      DO 25 I=1,M
      READ(5,30)CODE(I),B(I)
   30 FORMAT(I10,F10.0)
      READ(5,29)(A(I,J),J=1,K)
   29 FORMAT(8F10.0)
   25 CONTINUE
      READ(5,29)(C(J),J=1,K)
      WRITE(6,40)
```

```
   40 FORMAT(5X,'THE ORIGINAL COEFFICIENTS OF THE CONSTRAINTS',//15X,'CO
     *DE 0 ==> <OR= CONSTRAINT',/15X,'CODE 1 ==> >OR= CONSTRAINT',/15X
     *,'CODE 2 ==> = CONSTRAINT',//)
      WRITE(6,55)
   55 FORMAT(' I CODE CONSTANT A(I,1) A(I,2) A(I,3) A(I,4) A(I,5)
     * A(I,6) A(I,7) A(I,8)',/)
      DO 45 I=1,M
      WRITE(6,51)I,CODE(I),B(I)
   51 FORMAT(I3,I4,F9.2)
      WRITE(6,52)(A(I,J),J=1,K)
   52 FORMAT('+',15X,8F8.2/(16X,8F8.2))
   45 CONTINUE
      IF(NTYPE.NE.0) GO TO 35
      WRITE(6,36)
   36 FORMAT(// 5X,'THE COEFFICIENTS IN THE ORIGINAL OBJECTIVE FUNCTION
     * TO BE MINIMIZED ARE:',/)
      GO TO 37
   35 WRITE(6,38)
   38 FORMAT(// 5X,'THE COEFFICIENTS IN THE ORIGINAL OBJECTIVE FUNCTION
     * TO BE MAXIMIZED ARE:',/)
   37 WRITE(6,39)(C(J),J=1,K)
   39 FORMAT(16X,8F8.2/16X,8F8.2)
      READ(5,20)NOPT
C     ***************************************************************************
  150 CALL SSARTV(A,XB)
      IF(IFLAG.EQ.1) GO TO 50
      BASICS=0
      OPTSOL=0
      WRITE(6,160)
  160 FORMAT(//)
      CALL SIMPLX(A,XB)
      IF(NFLAG.EQ.1.OR.NFLAG.EQ.2) GO TO 50
      IF(NTYPE.EQ.1) GO TO 220
      SUM=-SUM
  220 WRITE(6,230)SUM
  230 FORMAT(10X,'OPTIMAL VALUE OF THE ORIGINAL OBJECTIVE FUNCTION IS',
     *F12.2)
      GO TO 50
 2000 STOP
      END

      SUBROUTINE SSARTV(A,XB)
C     ***************************************************************************
C     *  SSARTV                                                               *
C     *          A SUBROUTINE THAT SUPPLIES THE SLACK, SURPLUS, AND ARTIFICIAL*
C     *          VARIABLES NEEDED TO PERFORM SIMPLEX METHOD.                  *
C     ***************************************************************************
      COMMON B(26),C(76),CODE(26),KP1,MP1,N,K,M,NGET,NLET,NET,NTYPE,NP1,
     *NC,NC1,INDEXG,INDEXL,INDEXE,NFLAG,BASICS,OPTSOL,SUM,NOPT,IFLAG
      INTEGER CODE,XB,BASICS,OPTSOL
      DIMENSION A(26,76),XB(76),ARTV(52)
C INITIALIZE VARIABLES
      IFLAG=0
      IA=1
      KP1=K+1
      MP1=M+1
      N=K+2*NGET+NLET+NET
      NP1=N+1
      NC=K+NGET+1
      NC1=NC+NLET
      INDEXG=K+1
      INDEXL=K+NGET+1
      INDEXE=K+NGET+NLET+1
      DO 69 I=1,MP1
      DO 69 J=KP1,NP1
   69 A(I,J)=0.
  150 DO 5 I=1,M
    5 A(I,NP1)=B(I)
      DO 4 I=1,M
      IF(CODE(I).EQ.0) GO TO 6
```

```
      IF(CODE(I).EQ.1) GO TO 8
      ARTV(IA)=I
      IA=IA+1
      XB(I)=INDEXE
      A(I,INDEXE)=1
      INDEXE=INDEXE+1
      GO TO 4
    8 XB(I)=INDEXE
      ARTV(IA)=I
      IA=IA+1
      INDEXE=INDEXE+1
      A(I,INDEXG)=-1.
      INDEXG=INDEXG+1
      GO TO 4
    6 XB(I)=INDEXL
      A(I,INDEXL)=1.
      INDEXL=INDEXL+1
    4 CONTINUE
C CHECK FOR CORRECT DATA
      IF(INDEXG.NE.NC) GO TO 100
      IF(INDEXL.NE.NC1) GO TO 110
      IF(INDEXE.NE.NP1) GO TO 120
      GO TO 151
  100 WRITE(6,101)
  101 FORMAT(///' NUMBER OF >OR= CONSTRAINTS DOES NOT MATCH VALUE READ I
     *N')
      IFLAG=1
      RETURN
  110 WRITE(6,111)
  111 FORMAT(///' NUMBER OF <OR= CONSTRAINTS DOES NOT MATCH VALUE READ I
     *N')
      IFLAG=1
      RETURN
  120 WRITE(6,121)
  121 FORMAT(//' NUMBER OF = CONSTRAINTS DOES NOT MATCH VALUE READ IN')
      IFLAG=1
      RETURN
C CHECK FOR MAXIMIZATION
  151 CONTINUE
      IF(NTYPE.EQ.0) GO TO 12
      DO 60 J=1,K
   60 A(MP1,J)=-C(J)
      GO TO 50
   12 DO 55 J=1,K
   55 A(MP1,J)=C(J)
   50 DO 61 J=KP1,NP1
      A(MP1,J)=0.
   61 C(J)=0.
      DO 62 J=1,K
   62 C(J)=-A(MP1,J)
      DO 63 J=NC1,N
   63 C(J)=-10.E2
      IF(NGET+NET.EQ.0) RETURN
      IA=IA-1
      KPGTE=K+NGET
      DO 64 J=1,KPGTE
      SUM=0
      DO 65 I=1,IA
   65 SUM=SUM+A(ARTV(I),J)
   64 A(MP1,J)=A(MP1,J)-10.E2*SUM
      SUM=0.
      DO 66 I=1,IA
   66 SUM=SUM+A(ARTV(I),NP1)
      A(MP1,NP1)=A(MP1,NP1)-10.E2*SUM
      RETURN
      END
```

```
      SUBROUTINE SIMPLX(A,XB)
C     ********************************************************************
C     *    SIMPLX                                                       *
C     *         SUBROUTINE TO PERFORM THE WORK OF THE SIMPLEX METHOD.   *
C     ********************************************************************
      COMMON B(26),C(76),CODE(26),KP1,MP1,N,K,M,NGET,NLET,NET,NTYPE,NP1,
     *NC,NC1,INDEXG,INDEXL,INDEXE,NFLAG,BASICS,OPTSOL,SUM,NOPT,IFLAG
      INTEGER CODE,XB,BASICS,OPTSOL
      DIMENSION A(26,76),XB(76)
      NFLAG=0
C     ********************************************************************
C     *    STEP 1                                                       *
C     *         OBTAIN BASIC FEASIBLE SOLUTION OF EQUIVALENT MODEL.     *
C     ********************************************************************
  100 BASICS=BASICS+1
      IF(NOPT.EQ.0) GO TO 200
  105 WRITE(6,104)BASICS
  104 FORMAT(5X,'BASIC SOLUTION',I4,/)
      DO 110 I=1,M
  110 WRITE(6,106)I,XB(I),A(I,NP1)
  106 FORMAT(7X,'XB(',I2,') = X(',I2,')=',F12.2)
      SUM=0.
      DO 111 I=1,M
  111 SUM=SUM+C(XB(I))*A(I,NP1)
      WRITE(6,130)SUM
  130 FORMAT( /7X,'CURRENT VALUE OF THE OBJECTIVE FUNCTION IS',E18.8//)
      IF(OPTSOL.EQ.1) GO TO 920
C     ********************************************************************
C     *    STEPS 2,3                                                    *
C     *         CHOOSE THE NONBASIC VARIABLE WITH THE MOST NEGATIVE COEFFICIENT *
C     *         TO ENTER AS A BASIS VARIABLE FOR THE NEXT FEASIBLE      *
C     *         SOLUTION.  IF NONE ARE NEGATIVE, AN OPTIMAL SOLUTION HAS *
C     *         BEEN REACHED, SO GO TO STEP 9.                          *
C     ********************************************************************
  200 NEG=0
      GNEG=0.
      DO 21 J=1,N
      IF(A(MP1,J).GE.GNEG) GO TO 21
      GNEG=A(MP1,J)
      NEG=J
   21 CONTINUE
      IF(NEG.EQ.0) GO TO 900
C     ********************************************************************
C     *    STEPS 4,11                                                   *
C     *         CHECK FOR UNBOUNDED OBJECTIVE FUNCTION.                 *
C     ********************************************************************
  400 SPR=10.E10
      DO 410 I=1,M
      IF(A(I,NEG).LE..00001) GO TO 410
      IF(A(I,NP1)/A(I,NEG).GE.SPR) GO TO 410
      SPR=A(I,NP1)/A(I,NEG)
      NSPR=I
  410 CONTINUE
      IF(SPR.LE.10.E8) GO TO 510
      WRITE(6,420)
  420 FORMAT(///' OBJECTIVE FUNCTION IS NOT BOUNDED BY CONSTRAINTS')
      NFLAG=1
      RETURN
C     ********************************************************************
C     *    STEP 5                                                       *
C     *         FIND PIVOTAL ELEMENT AND DIVIDE BY IT.                  *
C     ********************************************************************
  510 PELE =A(NSPR,NEG)
      DO 500 J=1,NP1
  500 A(NSPR,J)=A(NSPR,J)/PELE
      XB(NSPR)=NEG
C     ********************************************************************
C     *    STEPS 6,7,8                                                  *
C     *         PERFORM ELEMENTARY TRANSFORMATIONS, AND GO BACK TO STEP 1 TO *
C     *         PRINT OUT NEW BASIC FEASIBLE SOLUTION.                  *
C     ********************************************************************
```

```
  600 DO 610 I=1,MP1
      IF(I.EQ.NSPR) GO TO 610
      HOLD=A(I,NEG)
      DO 620 J=1,NP1
  620 A(I,J)=A(I,J)-HOLD*A(NSPR,J)
  610 CONTINUE
      GO TO 100
C     ************************************************************************
C     *     STEPS 9,10                                                      *
C     *          IF THERE IS AN ARTIFICIAL VARIABLE AT A POSITIVE LEVEL, A  *
C     *          FEASIBLE SOLUTION DOES NOT EXIST; OTHERWISE,AN OPTIMAL      *
C     *          SOLUTION OF THE EQUIVALENT LINEAR PROGRAMMING MODEL HAS     *
C     *          BEEN OBTAINED.                                             *
C     ************************************************************************
  900 OPTSOL=1
      IF(NOPT.EQ.1) GO TO 920
      GO TO 105
  920 DO 930 I=1,M
      IF(XB(I).LT.NC1) GO TO 930
      IF(A(I,NP1).LE.0) GO TO 930
      WRITE(6, 940)
  940 FORMAT(///' A FEASIBLE SOLUTION DOES NOT EXIST')
      NFLAG=2
      RETURN
  930 CONTINUE
      WRITE(6, 950)
  950 FORMAT(10X,'THE LAST BASIC FEASIBLE SOLUTION IS OPTIMAL')
      RETURN
      END


/DATA

EXAMPLE FROM SECTION 3.8
      3    2    2    1    0    0
           0         30.
          2.          3.
           0         24.
          3.          2.
          1           3.
          1.          1.
         -6.         -4.
      1
```

```
EXAMPLE FROM SECTION 3.8

    THE ORIGINAL COEFFICIENTS OF THE CONSTRAINTS

              CODE 0 ==>   <OR= CONSTRAINT
              CODE 1 ==>   >OR= CONSTRAINT
              CODE 2 ==>    = CONSTRAINT

I CODE CONSTANT  A(I,1)  A(I,2)  A(I,3)  A(I,4)  A(I,5)  A(I,6)  A(I,7)  A(I,8)

1   0    30.00    2.00    3.00
2   0    24.00    3.00    2.00
3   1     3.00    1.00    1.00


    THE COEFFICIENTS IN THE ORIGINAL OBJECTIVE FUNCTION TO BE MINIMIZED ARE:

                  -6.00    -4.00



    BASIC SOLUTION    1

       XB( 1)= X( 4)=       30.00
       XB( 2)= X( 5)=       24.00
       XB( 3)= X( 6)=        3.00

       CURRENT VALUE OF THE OBJECTIVE FUNCTION IS   -0.30000000E+04


    BASIC SOLUTION    2

       XB( 1)= X( 4)=       24.00
       XB( 2)= X( 5)=       15.00
       XB( 3)= X( 1)=        3.00

       CURRENT VALUE OF THE OBJECTIVE FUNCTION IS    0.18000000E+02


    BASIC SOLUTION    3

       XB( 1)= X( 4)=       14.00
       XB( 2)= X( 3)=        5.00
       XB( 3)= X( 1)=        8.00

       CURRENT VALUE OF THE OBJECTIVE FUNCTION IS    0.48000000E+02


          THE LAST BASIC FEASIBLE SOLUTION IS OPTIMAL
          OPTIMAL VALUE OF THE ORIGINAL OBJECTIVE FUNCTION IS     -48.00
```

3.10 PROPERTIES OF THE SIMPLEX METHOD

The important properties of the simplex method are summarized here for convenient ready reference.

1 The simplex method for maximizing the objective function starts at a basic feasible solution for the equivalent model and moves to an adjacent basic feasible solution that does not decrease the value of the objective function. If such a solution does not exist, an optimal solution for the equivalent model has been reached. That is, if all of the coefficients of the nonbasic variables in the objective function equation are greater-than-or-equal-to zero at some point, then an optimal solution for the equivalent model has been reached.

2 If an artificial variable is in an optimal solution of the equivalent model at a nonzero level, then no feasible solution for the original model exists. On the contrary, if the optimal solution of the equivalent model does not contain an artificial variable at a nonzero level, the solution is also optimal for the original model.

3 If all of the slack, surplus, and artificial variables are zero when an optimal solution of the equivalent model is reached, then all of the constraints in the original model are strict "equalities" for the values of the variables that optimize the objective function.

4 If a nonbasic variable has a zero coefficient in the objective function equation when an optimal solution is reached, there are multiple optimal solutions. In fact, there is an infinity of optimal solutions. The simplex method finds only one optimal solution and stops.

5 Once an artificial variable leaves the set of basic variables (the basis), it will never enter the basis again, so all calculations for that variable can be ignored in future steps.

6 When selecting the variable to leave the current basis:

(a) If two or more ratios are smallest, choose one arbitrarily.

(b) If a nonnegative ratio does not exist, the objective function in the original model is not bounded by the constraints. Thus, a *finite* optimal solution for the original model does not exist.

7 If a basis has a variable at the zero level, it is called a *degenerate basis*.

8 Although cycling is possible, there have never been any practical problems for which the simplex method failed to converge.

3.11 TRANSPORTATION PROBLEM

Quite often a manufacturer produces a certain commodity at a number of different plants and ships the commodity to holding points or warehouses for later distribution to stores and finally to the consumer. Suppose the commodity is produced at m plants for shipment to n warehouses. If it costs a certain amount to ship 1 unit from a given plant to a given warehouse, if each plant has a certain capacity for producing the commodity, and if each warehouse requires a certain amount of the commodity, the transportation problem is to determine the number of units to ship from each plant to each warehouse to minimize the overall shipping cost while satisfying the given constraints. Consider:

x_{ij} = amount shipped from plant i to warehouse j; $i = 1, 2, \ldots, m$; $j = 1, 2, \ldots, n$

c_{ij} = cost to ship 1 unit from plant i to warehouse j; $i = 1, 2, \ldots, m$; $j = 1, 2, \ldots, n$

d_j = required number of units at warehouse j; $j = 1, 2, \ldots, n$

s_i = capacity of plant i; $i = 1, 2, \ldots, m$

This problem can be easily formulated as an LP model, namely,

$$\text{minimize:} \quad z = \sum_{i=1}^{m} \sum_{j=1}^{n} c_{ij} x_{ij}$$

$$\text{subject to:} \quad \sum_{j=1}^{n} x_{ij} \leq s_i \quad i = 1, 2, \ldots, m \qquad (3.63)$$

$$\sum_{i=1}^{m} x_{ij} \geq d_j \quad j = 1, 2, \ldots, n \qquad (3.64)$$

$$\text{all } x_{ij} \geq 0$$

This model has the desirable property that if at least one feasible solution exists, then there exists an optimal solution where all of the x_{ij} values are integers or zero. The simplex method will produce this integer optimal solution.

If constraint (3.63) is summed over all i, then

$$\sum_{i=1}^{m} \sum_{j=1}^{n} x_{ij} \leq \sum_{i=1}^{m} s_i$$

Likewise, if contraint (3.64) is summed over all j, then

$$\sum_{j=1}^{n} \sum_{i=1}^{m} x_{ij} \geq \sum_{j=1}^{n} d_j$$

thus from these two relationships,

$$\sum_{i=1}^{m} s_i \geq \sum_{j=1}^{n} d_j$$

Suppose

$$\sum_{i=1}^{m} s_i = \sum_{j=1}^{n} d_j$$

Thus, constraints (3.63) and (3.64) can be rewritten as equalities so that the model becomes

$$\text{minimize:} \quad z = \sum_{i=1}^{m} \sum_{j=1}^{n} c_{ij} x_{ij}$$

$$\text{subject to: } \sum_{j=1}^{n} x_{ij} = s_i \quad i = 1, 2, \ldots, m$$

$$\sum_{i=1}^{m} x_{ij} = d_j \quad j = 1, 2, \ldots, n$$

$$\text{all } x_{ij} \geq 0$$

where $\sum_{i=1}^{m} s_i = \sum_{j=1}^{n} d_j$

3.11.1 Transportation of Automobiles

Suppose an automobile manufacturer is faced with the problem of determining the minimum cost policy for supplying dealers with the desired number of automobiles. The relevant data are given in Table 3.8. The value 2.2 represents the cost of shipping one car from plant 2 to dealer (warehouse) 3. Likewise, 2.4 represents the cost of shipping one car from plant 1 to dealer 5.

The corresponding LP model is

$$\text{minimize: } z = 1.2x_{11} + 1.7x_{12} + \cdots + 2.4x_{15}$$
$$+ 1.8x_{21} + 1.5x_{22} + \cdots + 1.6x_{25}$$
$$+ 1.5x_{31} + 1.4x_{32} + \cdots + 1.0x_{35}$$

$$\text{subject to: } \sum_{j=1}^{5} x_{1j} = 300$$

$$\sum_{j=1}^{5} x_{2j} = 400$$

$$\sum_{j=1}^{5} x_{3j} = 100$$

Table 3.8 TRANSPORATION DATA FOR AUTOMOBILE EXAMPLE

Plant	Dealer					Plant capacity
	1	2	3	4	5	
1	1.2	1.7	1.6	1.8	2.4	300
2	1.8	1.5	2.2	1.2	1.6	400
3	1.5	1.4	1.2	1.5	1.0	100
Dealer requirements	100	50	300	150	200	

$$\sum_{i=1}^{3} x_{i1} = 100$$

$$\sum_{i=1}^{3} x_{i2} = 50$$

$$\sum_{i=1}^{3} x_{i3} = 300$$

$$\sum_{i=1}^{3} x_{i4} = 150$$

$$\sum_{i=1}^{3} x_{i5} = 200$$

$$\text{all } x_{ij} \geqslant 0$$

where x_{ij} is the cost of shipping a car from plant i to dealer j.

The simplex program in Section 3.9 was used to obtain the optimal solution:

$x_{11} = 100$	$x_{24} = 150$
$x_{22} = 50$	$x_{25} = 200$
$x_{13} = 200$	all other $x_{ij} = 0$
$x_{33} = 100$	

The minimum cost is 1135 units.

3.12 ASSIGNMENT PROBLEM

Suppose a company has m tasks that must be completed and it has at least m employees who can perform any of the m tasks but possibly in a different amount of time. Which employee should be assigned to each task to minimize the overall time to complete all m tasks, if each employee is assigned to one and only one task? This is but one example of the classical assignment problem where tasks could be any type of activity, employees could be any type of resource, and time for an employee to complete a task could be considered the effectiveness associated with using a given type of resource on a given activity. If effectiveness represents a loss such as cost, then the overall effectiveness associated with assigning one and only one type of resource to each activity is a minimization problem; otherwise, it is a maximization problem. The effectiveness for the various assignments of resource to activities is generally put in tabular form, and it is called the *effectiveness matrix*. Table 3.9 represents the

Table 3.9   EFFECTIVENESS MATRIX FOR
FOUR–TASK, FOUR–EMPLOYEE
ASSIGNMENT PROBLEM

| | Task | | | |
Employee	1	2	3	4
1	5	8	8	6
2	4	6	5	8
3	6	10	7	4
4	9	9	7	3

effectiveness matrix for a four-task, four-employee assignment problem. The effectiveness of assigning employee 1 to task 1 is 5, of assigning employee 2 to task 1 is 4, etc.

3.12.1   Linear Programming Formulation

If we let

$$x_{ij} = \begin{cases} 0 \text{ if resource } i \text{ is not assigned to activity } j \\ 1 \text{ if resource } i \text{ is assigned to activity } j \end{cases}$$

c_{ij} = effectiveness associated with assigning resource i to activity j

where $i = 1, 2, \ldots, m$ and $j = 1, 2, \ldots, m$, then mathematically the assignment problem can be stated as:

$$\text{minimize(maximize): } z = \sum_{i=1}^{m} \sum_{j=1}^{m} c_{ij} x_{ij}$$

$$\text{subject to: } \sum_{j=1}^{m} x_{ij} = 1 \qquad \text{for } i = 1, 2, \ldots, m$$

$$\sum_{i=1}^{m} x_{ij} = 1 \qquad \text{for } j = 1, 2, \ldots, m$$

$$x_{ij} = 0 \text{ or } 1 \qquad \text{for all } i \text{ and } j$$

This is just a special case of the more general transportation problem where

$$s_i = 1 \qquad i = 1, 2, \ldots, m$$
$$d_j = 1 \qquad j = 1, 2, \ldots, m$$

Note that the above linear programming formulation assumes that there are m units of resource and m activities. Every assignment problem can be reformulated to satisfy this assumption by adding dummy resources or activities with corresponding rows or columns of zero effectiveness to force the effectiveness matrix to be square.

If we wish to minimize the total effectiveness in the assignment problem in Table 3.9, the LP model would be

$$
\begin{aligned}
\text{minimize:} \quad z = {} & 5x_{11} + 8x_{12} + 8x_{13} + 6x_{14} \\
& + 4x_{21} + 6x_{22} + 5x_{23} + 8x_{24} \\
& + 6x_{31} + 10x_{32} + 7x_{33} + 4x_{34} \\
& + 9x_{41} + 9x_{42} + 7x_{43} + 3x_{44}
\end{aligned}
$$

$$
\text{subject to:} \quad \sum_{j=1}^{4} x_{ij} = 1 \qquad i = 1, 2, 3, 4
$$

$$
\sum_{i=1}^{4} x_{ij} = 1 \qquad j = 1, 2, 3, 4
$$

$$
\text{all } x_{ij} = 0 \text{ or } 1
$$

The regular simplex method or special methods that take advantage of the form of the transportation problem could be used to solve the assignment problem since the solution would necessarily satisfy the integer restriction on all x_{ij}. However, a special method called the *Hungarian method* has been developed which takes advantage of the further restriction on the transportation problem.

3.12.2 Hungarian Method

The Hungarian method is credited to the Hungarian mathematician D. König who proved an essential theorem for the development of the method. Basically, the method successively modifies the rows and columns of the effectiveness matrix until there is at least one zero component in each row and column such that a complete assignment corresponding to these zeros can be made. This complete assignment will be an optimal assignment in that when it is applied to the original effectiveness matrix, the resulting total effectiveness will be a *minimum*. The method will always converge to an optimal assignment in a finite number of steps. The basis of the method is the fact that a constant can be added to or subtracted from any row or column without changing the set of optimal assignments. For example, if 3 units are subtracted from the ith row and 2 units are added to the jth column, then the objective function in the LP model would be

$$
\begin{aligned}
\text{minimize:} \quad z &= \sum_{i=1}^{m} \sum_{j=1}^{m} c_{ij} x_{ij} - 3 \sum_{j=1}^{m} x_{ij} + 2 \sum_{i=1}^{m} x_{ij} \\
&= \sum_{i=1}^{m} \sum_{j=1}^{m} c_{ij} x_{ij} - 3 + 2
\end{aligned}
$$

since $\Sigma_{j=1}^{m} x_{ij} = 1$ and $\Sigma_{i=1}^{m} x_{ij} = 1$ (from the constraints). Adding a constant to or subtracting a constant from the objective function does not change the optimal solution, since every basic feasible solution would have the same amount added to or subtracted from the objective function.

This concept can be generalized to the case in which a_i is subtracted from each element in the ith row of the effectiveness matrix and b_j is subtracted from each element in the jth column for $i = 1, 2, \ldots, m$ and $j = 1, 2, \ldots, m$. The new objective function would then be

$$\text{minimize:} \quad z = \sum_{i=1}^{m} \sum_{j=1}^{m} c_{ij} x_{ij} - \sum_{i=1}^{m} a_i \sum_{j=1}^{m} x_{ij} - \sum_{j=1}^{m} b_j \sum_{i=1}^{m} x_{ij}$$

$$= \sum_{i=1}^{m} \sum_{j=1}^{m} c_{ij} x_{ij} - \sum_{i=1}^{m} a_i - \sum_{j=1}^{m} b_j$$

where again subtracting the constants $\Sigma_{i=1}^{m} a_i$ and $\Sigma_{j=1}^{m} b_j$ from the original objective function does not change the set of basic feasible solutions.

The Hungarian method will now be illustrated and will be presented in algorithmic form in Section 3.12.3.

Suppose four professors are each capable of teaching any one of four different courses. However, because of their background and experience, the average weekly amount of class preparation necessary to get each professor equally prepared to teach a given course is not constant. Since the professors' department is highly research-oriented, the chairperson would like to assign each professor to one and only one course to minimize the total course preparation time for all four courses. Table 3.10 gives the preparation time needed by each professor for each course.

The first step of the Hungarian method is to modify the effectiveness matrix to get at least one zero in each row and each column of the effectiveness matrix with the hope of being able to make a complete assignment that corresponds to zeros in the reduced matrix. This would necessarily minimize the total effectiveness. To accomplish this first step, subtract the smallest element (algebraically) in each row of the

Table 3.10   CLASS PREPARATION TIME, FOUR–PROFESSOR, FOUR–COURSE ASSIGNMENT PROBLEM

	Course			
Professor	Linear programming	Queueing theory	Dynamic programming	Regression analysis
Blazer	2	10	9	7
Toumi	15	4	14	8
Hillendorf	13	14	16	11
Smith	4	15	13	9

Table 3.11 EFFECTIVENESS MATRIX AFTER ROW REDUCTION

Professor	Course			
	Linear programming	Queueing theory	Dynamic programming	Regression analysis
Blazer	0	8	7	5
Toumi	11	0	10	4
Hillendorf	2	3	5	0
Smith	0	11	9	5

effectiveness matrix from each element in the row. Table 3.11 is the reduced matrix after 2, 4, 11, and 4 have been subtracted from each element in rows 1, 2, 3, and 4 of Table 3.10, respectively. The sum of these numbers

$$s_1 = 2 + 4 + 11 + 4 = 21$$

must be added to the total effectiveness for any complete assignment using Table 3.11 since 2 additional units of preparation time would be required by Professor Blazer regardless of her assignment, 4 additional units of preparation time would be required by Professor Toumi regardless of his assignment, etc.

Since column 3 in Table 3.11 does not contain a zero, subtract the smallest element (algebraically), namely 5, from each element in column 3 to give the resulting effectiveness matrix in Table 3.12.

The second step in the method is to try to make a complete assignment involving only zero elements in Table 3.12. To do this, examine rows successively, beginning with row 1, until a row with exactly one unmarked zero is found. A zero is marked if it has one of the symbols △ or ✕ over it. Mark the unmarked zero with the symbol △ to represent an assignment of the professor in that row to the course in that column. Cross out (✕) the other zeros in the same column. Repeat this process until each row has no unmarked zeros or at least two zeros. Since row 1 has a single zero,

Table 3.12 EFFECTIVENESS MATRIX AFTER ROW
AND COLUMN REDUCTIONS

Professor	Course			
	Linear programming	Queueing theory	Dynamic programming	Regression analysis
Blazer	0	8	2	5
Toumi	11	0	5	4
Hillendorf	2	3	0	0
Smith	0	11	4	5

mark it ($\triangle$) and cross out ($\times$) the zero in row 4, column 1. Mark ($\triangle$) the zero in row 2, column 2. Row 3 has two zeros, so the results so far are

$$\begin{bmatrix} \boxed{0} & 8 & 2 & 5 \\ 11 & \boxed{0} & 5 & 4 \\ 2 & 3 & 0 & 0 \\ \cancel{0} & 11 & 4 & 5 \end{bmatrix}$$

We now examine columns successively for single unmarked zeros and mark them with the symbol $\triangle$. Cross out ($\times$) the other zeros in the same row, if there are any. Repeat the process until each column has no unmarked zeros or has at least two zeros. For this case, column 3 has a single zero, so mark it ($\triangle$) and cross out ($\times$) the zero in row 3, column 4 to give

$$\begin{bmatrix} \boxed{0} & 8 & 2 & 5 \\ 11 & \boxed{0} & 5 & 4 \\ 2 & 3 & \boxed{0} & \cancel{0} \\ \cancel{0} & 11 & 4 & 5 \end{bmatrix}$$

Since a complete assignment cannot be made that involves zero elements only, draw the minimum number of vertical and horizontal lines that are needed to cover each zero element at least once. This is accomplished by:

(*a*) Check ($\checkmark$) all rows for which assignments ($\triangle$) have not been made
(*b*) Check ($\checkmark$) columns not already checked which have zeros in checked rows

$$\begin{bmatrix} \boxed{0} & 8 & 2 & 5 \\ 11 & \boxed{0} & 5 & 4 \\ 2 & 3 & \boxed{0} & \cancel{0} \\ \cancel{0} & 11 & 4 & 5 \end{bmatrix} \checkmark$$

(*c*) Check ($\checkmark$) rows not already checked which have assignments in checked columns.

$$\begin{bmatrix} \boxed{0} & 8 & 2 & 5 \\ 11 & \boxed{0} & 5 & 4 \\ 2 & 3 & \boxed{0} & \cancel{0} \\ \cancel{0} & 11 & 4 & 5 \end{bmatrix} \begin{matrix} \checkmark \\ \\ \\ \checkmark \end{matrix}$$

(*d*) Repeat steps (*b*) and (*c*) until no further checks can be made. In this case, the checkings stop after the first time through.

(*e*) Draw lines through all unchecked rows and through all checked columns.

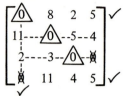

If the effectiveness matrix has *m* rows and *m* columns, then the minimum number of lines needed to cover each zero in the current reduced effectiveness matrix at least once is necessarily *m*, if a complete assignment can be made that has a total effectiveness of zero. In this example, only three lines are needed to cover each zero at least once, so a complete feasible assignment cannot be made at this time. In other words, a complete assignment with a total of 21 or fewer units of preparation time is impossible.

A procedure that will eventually obtain a complete solution with a minimum total effectiveness, starting with the reduced matrix in step (*e*), is:

(*f*) Examine the elements in the latest reduced matrix that do not have at least one line through them. Let *k* be the smallest element. *Subtract k from every element in each row containing uncovered elements.* In the present example $k = 2$, so subtract 2 from rows 1 and 4 to give

$$\begin{bmatrix} -2 & 6 & 0 & 3 \\ 11 & 0 & 5 & 4 \\ 2 & 3 & 0 & 0 \\ -2 & 9 & 2 & 3 \end{bmatrix}$$

(*g*) Step (*f*) will cause certain elements in columns with vertical lines through them in step (*e*) to go negative, so add *k* to every element in each column that has a vertical line through it in step (*e*). Thus, add 2 to each element in column 1 of the present example to give

$$\begin{bmatrix} 0 & 6 & 0 & 3 \\ 13 & 0 & 5 & 4 \\ 4 & 3 & 0 & 0 \\ 0 & 9 & 2 & 3 \end{bmatrix}$$

It can be shown that if a complete assignment involving zero elements only can be made with the reduced matrix in step (*g*), the total effectiveness using the same assignment with the original matrix will necessarily be minimum.

To determine a complete assignment, the general procedure for making assignments is now repeated using the new effectiveness matrix in step (*g*) above. Specifically,

(*i*) Make an assignment in row 2.
(*ii*) Make an assignment in row 4 and mark out (✕) the zero in row 1, column 1.
(*iii*) Make an assignment in row 1 and mark out (✕) the zero in row 3, column 3.
(*iv*) Make an assignment in row 3.

The result is

$$\begin{bmatrix} \cancel{0} & 6 & \boxed{0} & 3 \\ 13 & \boxed{0} & 5 & 4 \\ 4 & 3 & \cancel{0} & \boxed{0} \\ \boxed{0} & 9 & 2 & 3 \end{bmatrix}$$

A complete optimal assignment has been made. Thus, assign

Blazer to dynamic programming
Toumi to queueing theory
Dillendorf to regression analysis
Smith to linear programming

with a minimum total preparation time of

$$9 + 4 + 11 + 4 = 28 \text{ units}$$

This total could be obtained either from the original effectiveness matrix or by summing the constants that were subtracted and added to the various rows and columns throughout the procedure.

3.12.3 Algorithm 3.2—Hungarian Method to Solve the Assignment Problem

Suppose each of m units of resource such as drivers, salespeople, employees, equipment, etc., can be assigned to any one of m different activities such as routes, territories, jobs, space, etc., with a given effectiveness. The assignment problem is to determine which unit of resource should be assigned to each activity to optimize the overall effectiveness if each unit of resource must be assigned to one and only one activity. If there are more units of resource to assign than there are activities available, add dummy activities to make the effectiveness matrix square. Each column for dummy activities will be all zeros in the effectiveness matrix. If there are more activities than units of resource, add on rows of zeros to the effectiveness matrix for each dummy resource added. When the complete optimal assignment is obtained, ignore all assignments involving dummy resources or dummy activities, whichever the case may be.

The following is a step-by-step algorithm that uses the Hungarian method to solve the general m-resource, m-activity assignment problem for the *minimum* total effectiveness.

Step 1
If the total effectiveness is to be maximized, change the sign of each element in the effectiveness matrix and go to step 2; otherwise, go directly to step 2.

Step 2
If the minimum element in row i is not zero, then subtract this minimum element from each element in row i $(i = 1, 2, \ldots, m)$.

Step 3
If the minimum element in column j is not zero, then subtract this minimum element from each element in column j $(j = 1, 2, \ldots, m)$.

Step 4
Examine rows successively, beginning with row 1, for a row with exactly one unmarked zero. If at least one exists, mark this zero with the symbol ($\triangle$) to denote an assignment. Cross out ($\times$) the other zeros in the same column so additional assignments will not be made to that column (activity). Repeat the process until each row has no unmarked zeros or at least two unmarked zeros.

Step 5
Examine the columns successively for single, unmarked zeros and mark them with the symbol ($\triangle$) to denote an assignment. Cross out ($\times$) the other zeros in the same row so the corresponding resource will not be assigned to other activities. Repeat the process until each column has no unmarked zeros or has at least two unmarked zeros.

Step 6
Repeat steps 4 and 5 successively (if necessary) until one of three things occurs:

(a) Every row has an assignment ($\triangle$).
(b) There are at least two unmarked zeros in each row and each column.
(c) There are no zeros left unmarked and a complete assignment has not been made.

Step 7
If (a) occurs, the assignment is complete and it is an optimal assignment. If (b) occurs, arbitrarily make an assignment ($\triangle$) to one of the zeros and cross out ($\times$) all of the zeros in the same row *and* column, and then go to step 4. If (c) occurs, go to step 8.

Step 8
Check ($\checkmark$) all rows for which assignments ($\triangle$) have not been made.

Step 9
Check columns not already checked which have a zero in checked rows.

Step 10
Check rows not already checked which have assignments in checked columns.

Step 11
Repeat steps 9 and 10 until the chain of checkings ends.

Step 12
Draw lines through all *unchecked* rows and through all *checked* columns. This will necessarily give the minimum number of lines needed to cover each zero at least one time.

Step 13
Examine the elements that do not have at least one line through them. Select the smallest of these and subtract it from every element in each row that contains at least one uncovered element. Add the same element to every element in each column that has a vertical line through it. Return to step 4.

Another example will illustrate how to solve an assignment problem where there are more items to assign than there are objects to assign. The reverse of this is taken care of in a manner similar to that which follows.

Suppose a manager must order five trucks out of a fleet of eight to be present at five specific locations for loading goods that are awaiting shipment. The eight trucks are at eight different locations. The problem is to select the five for which the total transportation cost to get to the five locations is minimized. The costs are given in Table 3.13.

Since there are more trucks than loading locations, three dummy locations are added to the table and the corresponding costs are zero for each truck. Table 3.14 shows the new transportation costs. The idea is that each truck has an equal opportunity to be assigned to F, G, and H so the five trucks that can service locations A-E most cheaply will be assigned to them.

The Hungarian algorithm applied to this problem yielded this optimal assignment:

Truck	Loading location
1	Unassigned
2	Unassigned
3	A
4	B
5	C
6	E
7	D
8	Unassigned

with a minimum cost of 870.

3.12.4 Computer Program for Algorithm 3.2

This program solves the M-resource, M-activity assignment problem for the assignment that will optimize the total effectiveness. The problem can be either maximization or minimization, but the elements in the effectiveness matrix must be integers.

Table 3.13 TRANSPORATION COSTS

| | | Loading location | | | |
Truck	A	B	C	D	E
1	300	290	280	290	210
2	250	310	290	300	200
3	180	190	300	190	180
4	320	180	190	240	170
5	270	210	190	250	160
6	190	200	220	190	140
7	220	300	230	180	160
8	260	190	260	210	180

The program is written in two parts. Part I inputs and outputs the data. Part II is a subroutine called HUNGRY that actually carries out the Hungarian algorithm. It was written as a subroutine so it could be used intact in the Eastman algorithm for the traveling salesman problem in Section 5.3.1.

Problems with a maximum of 15 resources and 15 activities can be solved with the program as listed. To increase the maximum size of the effectiveness matrix to M resources and M activities, change the DIMENSION statement in the mainline program to

$$\text{DIMENSION MATRIX(M,M),IASMAT(M)}$$

and change the components of the variables in the DIMENSION statement in the subroutine HUNGRY to M.

If the original matrix is not square (either more resources than activities or vice versa), the user must supply the necessary rows or columns of zeros before using the program.

The problem in Table 3.14 was solved in 0.09 s of IBM 370/168 time.

Table 3.14 TRANSPORATION COSTS–NEW PROBLEM

| | | Loading location | | | | | | |
Truck	A	B	C	D	E	F	G	H
1	300	290	280	290	210	0	0	0
2	250	310	290	300	200	0	0	0
3	180	190	300	190	180	0	0	0
4	320	180	190	240	170	0	0	0
5	270	210	190	250	160	0	0	0
6	190	200	220	190	140	0	0	0
7	220	300	230	180	160	0	0	0
8	260	190	260	210	180	0	0	0

```
C     ********************************************************************
C     *                                                                  *
C     *       **    ALGORITHM 3.2    HUNGARIAN ALGORITHM    **            *
C     *                                                                  *
C     * THIS PROGRAM IS A METHOD FOR SOLVING THE GENERAL M-RESOURCE,     *
C     * M-ACTIVITY ASSIGNMENT PROBLEM FOR TOTAL EFFECTIVENESS.  THE      *
C     * PROBLEM MAY BE EITHER MINIMIZATION OR MAXIMIZATION.  THE PROGRAM *
C     * USES A SUBROUTINE CALLED HUNGRY TO CARRY OUT THE STEPS OF THE    *
C     * ALGORITHM.                                                        *
C     * ** ALL ELEMENTS OF THE EFFECTIVENESS MATRIX MUST BE INTEGER **   *
C     *                                                                  *
C     * THIS PROGRAM IS DESIGNED                                         *
C     *    TO READ                                                       *
C     *       CARD 1    COLS  2-80    TITLE  DESCRIPTION OF THE PROBLEM USING *
C     *                                      ANY CHARACTERS ON KEYPUNCH  *
C     *                                      ** COLUMN 1 MUST BE LEFT BLANK ** *
C     *       CARD 2    COLS  1- 5    M  # OF RESOURCES AND ACTIVITIES  (I5) *
C     *                       6-10    KODE  0 FOR MINIMIZATION PROBLEM   *
C     *                                     1 FOR MAXIMIZATION PROBLEM  (I5) *
C     *       CARDS 3 TO ?    MATRIX(I,J)    ORIGINAL EFFECTIVENESS MATRIX *
C     *                                      DATA IS PUNCHED ROWWISE IN 10I8 *
C     *                                      FORMAT.  EACH NEW ROW BEGINS A *
C     *                                      NEW CARD.                   *
C     *          TO SOLVE MORE THAN ONE PROBLEM AT A TIME, REPEAT THE    *
C     *          READ SEQUENCE, AND STACK THE DATA ONE BEHIND THE OTHER  *
C     *                                                                  *
C     *    TO CALCULATE AND PRINT                                        *
C     *    IASMAT      ASSIGNMENT MATRIX                                 *
C     *    NCOST       OPTIMAL COST OF ASSIGNMENTS                       *
C     *                                                                  *
C     ********************************************************************
      DIMENSION MATRIX(15,15),IASMAT(15)
      REAL*4 TITLE(20)
   50 READ(5,55,END=2000)TITLE
   55 FORMAT(20A4)
      WRITE(6,60)TITLE
   60 FORMAT('1',20A4,//)
      READ(5,1)N,KODE
    1 FORMAT(2I5)
      WRITE(6,4)
    4 FORMAT('  THE ORIGINAL MATRIX',/)
      DO 2 I=1,N
      READ(5,3)(MATRIX(I,J),J=1,N)
    3 FORMAT(10I8)
      WRITE(6,5)(MATRIX(I,J),J=1,N)
    5 FORMAT(/10I8/10I8)
    2 CONTINUE
      CALL HUNGRY(N,MATRIX,IASMAT,NCOST,KODE)
      WRITE(6,120)NCOST
  120 FORMAT(//  5X,'THE OPTIMAL SOLUTION OF THE ASSIGNMENT PROBLEM HAS
     *TOTAL COST OF',I8,/)
      DO 130 I=1,N
      WRITE(6,135)I,IASMAT(I)
  135 FORMAT(10X,'THE ASSIGNMENT FOR ',I3,'  IS ==>',I8)
  130 CONTINUE
      GO TO 50
 2000 STOP
      END


      SUBROUTINE HUNGRY(N,IIF,IROW,TOTAL,KODE)
      DIMENSION IIF(15,15),IEFF(15,15),IROW(15),ICOL(15),ICHECK(15),
     *          JCHECK(15)
      INTEGER TOTAL
C     ********************************************************************
C     * STEP 1                                                           *
C     *       CONSTRUCT THE EFFECTIVENESS MATRIX.  IF TOTAL EFFECTIVENESS *
C     *       IS TO BE MAXIMIZED, LET THE EFFECTIVENESS MATRIX BE THE    *
C     *       NEGATIVE OF THE ORIGINAL MATRIX; OTHERWISE, THE EFFECTIVE- *
C     *       NESS MATRIX EQUALS THE ORIGINAL MATRIX.                    *
C     ********************************************************************
```

```
      IF(KODE.EQ.1) GO TO 100
      DO 110 I=1,N
      DO 110 J=1,N
  110 IEFF(I,J)=IIF(I,J)
      GO TO 200
  100 DO 120 I=1,N
      DO 120 J=1,N
  120 IEFF(I,J)=-IIF(I,J)
C     **************************************************************************
C     *   STEP 2                                                            *
C     *        FIND THE SMALLEST ELEMENT OF EACH ROW AND SUBTRACT IT FROM   *
C     *             THE OTHER ELEMENTS OF THE SAME ROW.                     *
C     **************************************************************************
  200 DO 210 I=1,N
      MINROW=IEFF(I,1)
      DO 220 J=1,N
      IF(IEFF(I,J).LE.MINROW)MINROW=IEFF(I,J)
  220 CONTINUE
      DO 210 J1=1,N
      IEFF(I,J1)=IEFF(I,J1)-MINROW
  210 CONTINUE
C     **************************************************************************
C     *   STEP 3                                                            *
C     *        FIND THE SMALLEST ELEMENT OF EACH COLUMN AND SUBTRACT IT     *
C     *             FROM THE OTHER ELEMENTS IN THE SAME COLUMN.             *
C     **************************************************************************
      DO 300 J=1,N
      MINCOL=IEFF(1,J)
      DO 310 I=1,N
      IF(IEFF(I,J).LE.MINCOL)MINCOL=IEFF(I,J)
  310 CONTINUE
      DO 300 I1=1,N
      IEFF(I1,J)=IEFF(I1,J)-MINCOL
  300 CONTINUE
C     **************************************************************************
C     *   STEP 4                                                            *
C     *        ROW ASSIGNMENTS                                              *
C     **************************************************************************
  400 DO 410 I=1,N
      IROW(I)=0
  410 ICOL(I)=0
      NOMADE=0
  420 LOOP=0
      NZEROS=0
      DO 430 I=1,N
      NOZR=0
      IF(IROW(I).NE.0) GO TO 430
      DO 440 J=1,N
      IF(ICOL(J).NE.0) GO TO 440
      IF(IEFF(I,J).NE.0) GO TO 440
      NOZR=NOZR+1
      NZEROS=NZEROS+1
      NRPT=J
      NREFF=I
  440 CONTINUE
      IF(NOZR.NE.1) GO TO 430
      IROW(I)=NRPT
      ICOL(NRPT)=1
      NOMADE=NOMADE+1
      LOOP=LOOP+1
  430 CONTINUE
C     **************************************************************************
C     *   STEP 5                                                            *
C     *        COLUMN ASSIGNMENTS                                           *
C     **************************************************************************
      DO 500 I=1,N
      NOZC=0
      IF(ICOL(I).NE.0) GO TO 500
      DO 510 J=1,N
      IF(IROW(J).NE.0) GO TO 510
```

```
      IF(IEFF(J,I).NE.0) GO TO 510
      NOZC=NOZC+1
      NZEROS=NZEROS+1
      IRPT=J
  510 CONTINUE
      IF(NOZC.NE.1) GO TO 500
      ICOL(I)=1
      IROW(IRPT)=I
      NOMADE=NOMADE+1
      LOOP=LOOP+1
  500 CONTINUE
C     *********************************************************************
C     *  STEP 6                                                          *
C     *        CHECK RESULTS SO FAR.                                     *
C     *            IF COMPLETE ASSIGNMENT HAS BEEN MADE, GO TO STEP 15.  C
C     *            IF AT LEAST ONE ASSIGNMENT HAS BEEN MADE, RETURN TO   C
C     *            STEP 4 TO MAKE ADDITIONAL ASSIGNMENTS.                *
C     *********************************************************************
      IF(NOMADE.EQ.N) GO TO 1500
      IF(LOOP.NE.0) GO TO 420
      IF(NZEROS.EQ.0) GO TO 800
C     *********************************************************************
C     *  STEP 7                                                          *
C     *        PICK AN ARBITRARY ZERO AND RETURN TO STEP 4.             *
C     *********************************************************************
  700 IROW(NREFF)=NRPT
      NOMADE=NOMADE+1
      ICOL(NRPT)=1
      GO TO 420
C     *********************************************************************
C     *  STEP 8                                                          *
C     *        CHECK FOR UNASSIGNED ROW.                                 *
C     *********************************************************************
  800 DO 810 I=1,N
      ICHECK(I)=0
      JCHECK(I)=0
      IF(IROW(I).NE.0) GO TO 810
      ICHECK(I)=I
  810 CONTINUE
C     *********************************************************************
C     *  STEP 9                                                          *
C     *        CHECK COLUMNS THAT HAVE ZEROS IN CHECKED ROWS.            *
C     *********************************************************************
  900 NCHECK=0
      DO 910 I=1,N
      IF(ICHECK(I).EQ.0) GO TO 910
      DO 920 J=1,N
      IF(JCHECK(J).NE.0) GO TO 920
      IF(IEFF(I,J).NE.0) GO TO 920
      JCHECK(J)=J
      NCHECK=NCHECK+1
  920 CONTINUE
  910 CONTINUE
C     *********************************************************************
C     *  STEPS 10,11,12                                                  *
C     *        CHECK ROWS THAT HAVE ASSIGNMENTS IN CHECKED COLUMNS.      *
C     *            REPEAT UNTIL CHAIN OF CHECKING IS COMPLETED.          *
C     *            ELIMINATE ALL UNCHECKED ROWS AND ALL CHECKED COLUMNS. *
C     *********************************************************************
      IF(NCHECK.EQ.0) GO TO 1300
      DO 1010 I=1,N
      IF(JCHECK(I).LE.0) GO TO 1010
      DO 1020 J=1,N
      IF(JCHECK(I).NE.IROW(J)) GO TO 1020
      ICHECK(J)=J
      NCHECK=NCHECK+1
 1020 CONTINUE
 1010 CONTINUE
      IF(NCHECK.NE.0) GO TO 900
```

```
C     ****************************************************************************
C     *   STEP 13                                                             *
C     *        FIND THE MINIMUM UNMARKED ELEMENT.                             *
C     ****************************************************************************
 1300 MINELM=99999999
      DO 1310 I=1,N
      IF(ICHECK(I).EQ.0) GO TO 1310
      DO 1320 J=1,N
      IF(JCHECK(J).NE.0) GO TO 1320
      IF(IEFF(I,J).GE.MINELM) GO TO 1320
      MINELM=IEFF(I,J)
 1320 CONTINUE
 1310 CONTINUE
C     ****************************************************************************
C     *   STEP 14                                                             *
C     *        REDUCE MATRIX AND GO TO STEP 4.                                *
C     ****************************************************************************
      DO 1400 I=1,N
      DO 1400 J=1,N
      IF(ICHECK(I).LT.0) GO TO 1400
      IF(ICHECK(I).EQ.0) GO TO 1410
      IF(JCHECK(J).NE.0) GO TO 1400
      IEFF(I,J)=IEFF(I,J)-MINELM
      GO TO 1400
 1410 IF(JCHECK(J).LE.0) GO TO 1400
      IEFF(I,J)=IEFF(I,J)+MINELM
 1400 CONTINUE
      GO TO 400
C     ****************************************************************************
C     *   STEP 15                                                             *
C     *        CALCULATE TOTAL AND RETURN TO MAIN PROGRAM.                    *
C     ****************************************************************************
 1500 TOTAL=0
      DO 1510 I=1,N
      K=IROW(I)
 1510 TOTAL=TOTAL+IIF(I,K)
      RETURN
      END


/DATA

EXAMPLE USING TABLE 3.14
    8    0
     300      290      280      290      210       0        0        0
     250      310      290      300      200       0        0        0
     180      190      300      190      180       0        0        0
     320      180      190      240      170       0        0        0
     270      210      190      250      160       0        0        0
     190      200      220      190      140       0        0        0
     220      300      230      180      160       0        0        0
     260      190      260      210      180       0        0        0
```

EXAMPLE USING TABLE 3.14

THE ORIGINAL MATRIX

300	290	280	290	210	0	0	0
250	310	290	300	200	0	0	0
180	190	300	190	180	0	0	0
320	180	190	240	170	0	0	0
270	210	190	250	160	0	0	0
190	200	220	190	140	0	0	0
220	300	230	180	160	0	0	0
260	190	260	210	180	0	0	0

THE OPTIMAL SOLUTION OF THE ASSIGNMENT PROBLEM HAS TOTAL COST OF   870

```
THE ASSIGNMENT FOR   1  IS ==>      6
THE ASSIGNMENT FOR   2  IS ==>      7
THE ASSIGNMENT FOR   3  IS ==>      1
THE ASSIGNMENT FOR   4  IS ==>      2
THE ASSIGNMENT FOR   5  IS ==>      3
THE ASSIGNMENT FOR   6  IS ==>      5
THE ASSIGNMENT FOR   7  IS ==>      4
THE ASSIGNMENT FOR   8  IS ==>      8
```

SELECTED BIBLIOGRAPHY

1 Garvin, W. W.: "Introduction to Linear Programming," McGraw-Hill Book Company, New York, N.Y., 1960.
2 Gass, S. I.: "Linear Programming," 3d ed. McGraw-Hill Book Company, New York, N.Y., 1970.
3 Glickman, A. M.: "An Introduction to Linear Programming and the Theory of Games," John Wiley & Sons, Inc., New York, N.Y., 1963.
4 Hadley, G.: "Linear Programming," Addison-Wesley Publishing Co., Inc., Reading, Mass., 1962.
5 Kim, C.: "Introduction to Linear Programming," Holt, Rinehart and Winston, Inc., New York, N.Y., 1971.
6 Kwak, N. K.: "Mathematical Programming with Business Applications," McGraw-Hill Book Company, New York, N.Y., 1973.
7 Loomba, Narenda P., and Efraim Turban: "Applied Programming for Management," Holt, Rinehart and Winston, Inc., New York, N.Y., 1974.
8 Orchard-Hays, W.: "Advanced Linear Programming Computing Techniques," McGraw-Hill Book Company, New York, N.Y., 1968.
9 Singleton, R. R., and W. F. Tyndall: "Games and Programs," W. H. Freeman and Company, San Francisco, Calif., 1974.
10 Zionts, S.: "Linear and Integer Programming," Prentice-Hall, Inc., Englewood Cliffs, N.J., 1974.

EXERCISES

3.1 Solve the following linear programming problems graphically:

(a)

$$\text{minimize:} \quad Z = 5x_1 + 2x_2$$
$$\text{subject to:} \quad 4x_1 + x_2 \geqslant 8$$
$$x_1 + x_2 \leqslant 5$$
$$x_2 \geqslant 2$$
$$x_1 \geqslant 0$$

(b)

$$\text{maximize:} \quad Z = x_1 + 2x_2$$
$$\text{subject to:} \quad -3x_1 + 3x_2 \leqslant 9$$
$$x_1 - x_2 \leqslant 2$$
$$x_1 + x_2 \leqslant 6$$
$$x_1 + 3x_2 \leqslant 6$$
$$x_1, x_2 \geqslant 0$$

(c)

$$\text{maximize:} \quad Z = x_1 + x_2$$
$$\text{subject to:} \quad x_1 + x_2 \leqslant 3$$
$$x_1 \leqslant 2$$
$$x_1, x_2 \geqslant 0$$

(d)

$$\text{minimize:} \quad Z = 3x_1 - x_2$$
$$\text{subject to:} \quad x_1 - 2x_2 \geqslant 4$$
$$x_1 + x_2 \leqslant 8$$
$$-4x_1 + 2x_2 \leqslant 20$$
$$x_2 \leqslant 4$$
$$x_1 \geqslant 4$$
$$x_1 \leqslant 8$$
$$x_1, x_2 \geqslant 0$$

3.2 A company wants to purchase at most 1800 units of a product. There are two types of the product, M_1 and M_2, available. M_1 occupies 2 ft^3, costs $12, and the company makes a profit of $3. M_2 occupies 3 ft^3, costs $15, and the company makes a profit of $4. If the budget is $15,000 and the warehouse has 3000 ft^3 for the product,
(a) Set up the problem as a linear programming problem.
(b) Solve the problem graphically.

3.3 The BW Dog-Food manufacturer has four plants which ship to 10 warehouses for distribution. The shipping cost per case, the number of cases desired by each warehouse, and the capacity of each plant in cases are given by:

| | Warehouse | | | | | | | | | | Plant |
Plant	1	2	3	4	5	6	7	8	9	10	capacity
1	5	4	8	4	9	2	9	4	8	6	10
2	6	8	3	3	1	6	8	5	4	3	14
3	8	3	7	5	4	4	2	3	4	5	16
4	7	9	6	9	3	8	8	3	1	6	12
Number of cases desired	2	4	3	3	4	5	2	2	1	6	

    (*a*) Formulate the linear programming model to minimize the shipping costs while meeting all demands.

    (*b*) Solve the model in (*a*) using the simplex program in Section 3.9.

    (*c*) What is the minimum cost production-shipping schedule if the variable production costs per case at plants 1, 2, 3, and 4 are 12, 15, 10, and 16, respectively?

3.4   Solve the diet problem (Example 3.2.1) using the simplex program in Section 3.9.

3.5   Rework Exercise 3.4 with the cost per serving of each vegetable changed to: green beens ($.08), carrots ($.07), broccoli ($.10), cabbage ($.03), beets ($.09), potatoes ($.05).

3.6   Solve the television problem (Example 3.2.2) using the simplex method.

3.7   Solve the truck production problem (Example 3.2.3) using the simplex method.

3.8   Solve the machine scheduling problem (Example 3.2.4) using the simplex method.

3.9   Given the following LP model, introduce slack, surplus, and artificial variables to form an equivalent problem that can be presented to the simplex method to obtain an optimal solution.

$$\text{maximize:} \quad Z = 3X_1 + 2X_2 + 8X_3$$
$$\text{subject to:} \quad 4X_1 - 3X_2 + 12X_3 \geqslant 12$$
$$X_1 \qquad\quad + 4X_3 \leqslant 6$$
$$X_2 - X_3 = 2 \qquad \text{all } X_i \geqslant 0$$

    (*a*) Write out the new equivalent model.

    (*b*) Solve the model in (*a*) using the simplex algorithm.

3.10 Solve the following linear programming problem using the simplex method:

$$\text{maximize:} \quad Z = -X_1 + 2X_2$$
$$\text{subject to:} \quad X_1 + 2X_2 \leqslant 4$$
$$2X_1 + 5X_2 \leqslant 10$$
$$X_1, X_2 \geqslant 0$$

3.11 Three secretaries are being considered for three open positions. Each secretary has been given a rating for each position as shown in the table below.

	Positions		
Secretaries	1	2	3
1	7	5	6
2	8	4	7
3	9	6	4

Assign each secretary to one and only one position in such a way that the sum of the ratings for all three secretaries is a maximum.

(*a*) Set up this problem as an LP model.

(*b*) Solve this problem using the Hungarian algorithm discussed in Section 3.12.3.

3.12 Solve the following assignment problems using the Hungarian algorithm.

(*a*)

Person	Job		
	1	2	3
1	7	3	5
2	2	2	1
3	6	5	3
4	3	4	7

(*b*)

Person	Job			
	1	2	3	4
1	∞	2	2	5
2	2	∞	4	4
3	1	2	∞	2
4	2	4	3	∞

State who should perform each job to minimize the overall effectiveness. What is the overall minimum effectiveness?

3.13 Use the computer program for the Hungarian algorithm to solve the following assignment problem for the total maximum effectiveness.

Employee	Job														
	1	2	3	4	5	6	7	8	9	10	11	12	13	14	15
1	48	91	31	15	64	29	16	97	9	38	63	10	34	1	71
2	73	9	57	70	30	4	32	73	26	91	57	19	84	89	70
3	79	3	43	34	71	89	51	93	58	74	9	51	13	45	56
4	21	19	31	61	50	6	16	19	16	60	99	42	7	40	75
5	79	66	80	13	26	40	94	63	37	40	53	92	62	98	92
6	4	1	63	50	69	54	27	5	99	97	41	54	92	93	18
7	91	96	97	79	48	59	96	32	82	42	29	78	47	45	28
8	29	10	66	38	85	61	35	35	31	50	76	72	21	19	76
9	1	35	73	3	59	39	93	96	64	4	18	96	75	61	68
10	46	30	26	22	99	87	7	45	17	49	26	82	44	52	2
11	89	79	74	19	58	73	57	57	38	26	10	77	46	2	12
12	74	30	46	39	91	31	47	36	93	20	30	65	86	10	68
13	92	48	60	22	95	76	40	4	27	40	65	84	7	37	45
14	26	86	48	74	82	43	11	8	13	22	89	93	96	77	32
15	26	93	65	20	28	49	41	18	1	95	37	49	56	92	15

4

INTEGER PROGRAMMING

4.1 INTRODUCTION

The simplex method is the basis for the solution of any LP model for which the variables must only be nonnegative. However, if at least one of the variables is further restricted to be a nonnegative *integer*, the model becomes an all-integer or mixed-integer linear programming model. Unfortunately, there is no single method, such as the simplex method, that has been accepted as "the" method for solving all types of integer linear programming models. However, all of the known methods are primarily based on one of these four approaches:

1 Cutting plane [4]
2 Some type of enumeration [11]
3 Bender's decomposition [6]
4 Group theory [6]

We will center our attention in this book on the first two approaches only.

The problem to be solved in this chapter is the all-integer linear programming model:

$$\text{minimize:} \quad z = \sum_{j=1}^{n} c_j x_j$$

$$\text{subject to:} \quad \sum_{j=1}^{n} a_{ij}x_j \, (\geqslant, =, \leqslant) b_i \quad i = 1, 2, \ldots, m$$

$$x_j \text{ is a nonnegative integer} \quad j = 1, 2, \ldots, n$$

where the c_j's, a_{ij}'s, and b_i's are known constants and the x_j's are the variables we wish to determine.

In this chapter we will discuss an implicit enumeration algorithm and a cutting-plane algorithm for the solution of all-integer linear programming (LP) models. The implicit enumeration algorithm is only applicable to the special case where each variable takes on the value *0* or *1*. Consequently, any integer LP model which allows one or more of the variables to take on any integer value must be converted to an all-integer model where the variables can take on only the value 0 or 1. The necessary transformation procedure for this case is discussed in Section 4.2.6. The cutting-plane algorithm, on the other hand, is applicable to the general all-integer LP model in which the variables can take on any integer values. In Chapter 5, we will present a branch-and-bound algorithm derived by Dakin that is equally applicable for the solution of mixed-integer as well as all-integer LP models.

4.2 IMPLICIT ENUMERATION

One procedure to solve the 0-1 integer programming model is to examine every possible combination of the variables set equal to 0 and 1. This is total or explicit enumeration. The combination that satisfies all of the constraints and minimizes z is declared the optimal solution. However, this requires examining 2^n combinations of the variables which is out of the question for $n > 15$. Hence, it would be desirable to have a procedure that would systematically examine only a small subset of all possible combinations of the variables before reaching an optimal solution. This is what the implicit enumeration algorithm does.

In order to use the implicit enumeration algorithm, the integer programming model must have the form

$$\text{minimize:} \quad z = \sum_{j=1}^{n} c_j x_j$$

$$\text{subject to:} \quad Q_i = -b_i + \sum_{j=1}^{n} a_{ij}x_j \geqslant 0 \quad \text{for } i = 1, 2, \ldots, m$$

$$\text{all } x_j = 0, 1$$

where $c_j \geqslant 0$ for $j = 1, 2, \ldots, n$. The procedure to transform any integer linear programming model into this form is discussed in Sections 4.2.4 and 4.2.6.

Basically, the implicit enumeration algorithm starts out with all variables set equal to 0, and then systematically specifies certain variables to take on the value *1* until a feasible solution is obtained. This first feasible solution is then considered to be the best feasible solution to date. Since the variables are chosen heuristically, it is quite possible that the first feasible solution will not be optimal. Consequently, the algorithm systematically looks at various combinations of the variables set equal to 0 and 1 that can possibly improve on the best feasible solution to date, until an optimal solution is obtained. Many combinations that cannot possibly lead to a better feasible solution are not examined and are thus said to be *implicitly enumerated.*

The details of how variables are chosen to be 0 or 1 and how blocks of possible solutions can be eliminated without *explicitly* enumerating them are quite lengthy, so we will first illustrate how the algorithm works and then follow with a complete description of the algorithm.

4.2.1 Implicit Enumeration Illustrated

Consider the 0-1 integer programming model

$$\text{minimize:} \quad z = 4x_1 + 3x_2 + 2x_3$$
$$\text{subject to:} \quad 2x_1 - 5x_2 + 3x_3 \leqslant 4$$
$$4x_1 + x_2 + 3x_3 \geqslant 3$$
$$x_2 + x_3 \geqslant 1$$
$$\text{all } x_j = 0,1$$

A step-by-step analysis is presented to illustrate how implicit enumeration can be used to solve the given model.

Step 1

If any of the cost coefficients in the objective function are negative, make a transformation that will make them all positive. (This transformation will be discussed in Section 4.2.4.) In this example all of the cost coefficients are positive, so go to step 2.

Step 2

Convert each equality constraint to a greater-than-or-equal-to-zero constraint (to be discussed in Section 4.2.4.). None of the constraints are equalities in this example, so go to step 3.

Step 3

Convert each nonequality constraint to a greater-than-or-equal-to-zero constraint. Write the first constraint as

$$Q_1 = 4 - 2x_1 + 5x_2 - 3x_3 \geqslant 0$$

and the next two constraints as

$$Q_2 = -3 + 4x_1 + x_2 + 3x_3 \geqslant 0$$
$$Q_3 = -1 \qquad + x_2 + x_3 \geqslant 0$$

Step 4

Steps 1–3 have prepared the problem for implicit enumeration. We start the enumeration by setting all of the variables equal to 0 since clearly this solution would minimize z. However, all of the constraints may not be satisfied. In fact, at $x_1 = x_2 = x_3 = 0$

$$Q_1 = \quad 4 \geqslant 0$$
$$Q_2 = -3 \ngeqslant 0$$
$$Q_3 = -1 \ngeqslant 0$$

so constraints 2 and 3 are violated. Consequently, the solution $x_1 = x_2 = x_3 = 0$, which corresponds to node 1 in Figure 4.1 (see p. 134), is not a feasible solution. The variables x_1, x_2, and x_3 are called *free variables* since they have not been specified as being 0 or 1. To determine if further branching can be done from node 1, go to step 5.

Step 5

Check to see if the violated constraints (constraints 2 and 3) can be made feasible ($\geqslant 0$) by setting to *1* each of the variables with positive coefficients in the violated constraints. (Note that if variables with negative coefficients in violated constraints are set equal to 1, they would only make the constraints "more" infeasible.) If all of the violated constraints cannot be made feasible, no solution emanating from node 1 can be feasible.

Variables x_1, x_2, and x_3 each have positive coefficients in constraint 2, so when they are set equal to *1*, we have

$$Q_2 = -3 + 4 + 1 + 3 = 5 > 0$$

Thus, constraint 2 can be made feasible. Likewise, variables x_2 and x_3 each have positive coefficients in constraint 3, so when they are set equal to *1* we have

$$Q_3 = -1 + 1 + 1 = 1 > 0$$

Constraint 3 is also satisfied. Since both of the violated constraints can be made feasible by setting certain variables equal to 1, we know there is possibly a feasible solution emanating from node 1 in Figure 4.1. Go to step 6.

Step 6

We will add one variable at a time to the set of variables that have specified values at a given node. (*Note:* No variables have specified values at node 1.) Basically we would like to choose a free variable from the variables with positive coefficients in violated constraints in step 4 that would move us closest to feasibility (all of the constraints satisfied). Variables with positive coefficients in violated constraints (step 4) are the only possible variables that have a chance to make a violated constraint feasible. Let

$$T = \{1, 2, 3\}$$

represent the set of subscripts of these variables.

A number of heuristic procedures for selecting the variable from T have been proposed. One procedure is to choose the variable in T that would minimize the total distance from feasibility over all constraints. The distance from feasibility for a nonnegative constraint is 0, whereas for a negative constraint it is the amount that must be added to the constraint to make it 0.

For variable 1 ($x_1 = 1$):

	Distance from feasibility
$Q_1 = 4 - 2 = 2$	0
$Q_2 = -3 + 4 = 1$	0
$Q_3 = -1$	$\underline{1}$
	Total = 1

For variable 2 ($x_2 = 1$):

	Distance from feasibility
$Q_1 = 4 + 5 = 9$	0
$Q_2 = -3 + 1 = -2$	2
$Q_3 = -1 + 1 = 0$	$\underline{0}$
	Total = 2

For variable 3 ($x_3 = 1$):

	Distance from feasibility
$Q_1 = 4 - 3 = 1$	0
$Q_2 = -3 + 3 = 0$	0
$Q_3 = -1 + 1 = 0$	$\underline{0}$
	Total = 0

The variable that would move us closest to feasibility is taken to be the one with the smallest total distance from feasibility, namely, variable 3. Keep in mind that this is an arbitrary heuristic procedure for choosing a variable to add to the specified variables. In this case x_3 is specified to be 1 and x_1 and x_2 are still free to take on either 0 or 1. (See Figure 4.1.) Note that the variable FREE represents the variables that are unspecified or free at a given node.

Step 7
The partial solution at node 2 is $x_3 = 1$. The complete solution at node 2 is obtained by setting the free variables equal to 0. Thus, the complete solution at node 2 is

$$x_1 = x_2 = 0 \quad \text{and} \quad x_3 = 1$$

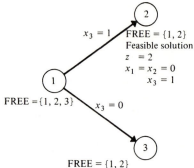

FIGURE 4.1
Partial solution tree.

Check to see if the complete solution at node 2 is feasible. That is, evaluate all of the constraints using $x_1 = x_2 = 0$ and $x_3 = 1$.

$$Q_1 = 4 - 3 = 1 \geqslant 0$$
$$Q_2 = -3 + 3 = 0 \geqslant 0$$
$$Q_3 = -1 + 1 = 0 \geqslant 0$$

so all three constraints are feasible (satisfied). Thus

$$x_1 = x_2 = 0 \quad \text{and} \quad x_3 = 1$$

is a feasible solution with

$$z = 4(0) + 3(0) + 2(1) = 2$$

Let ZMIN $= z = 2$. This is the best solution value to date.

Since any solution with $x_3 = 1$ and some other variable set equal to 1 would increase the value of z, there is no need to examine any solution emanating from node 2. Thus, all solutions emanating from node 2 have been implicitly enumerated.

Step 8
Backtrack. Go back to node 1 and specify $x_3 = 0$. The variables x_1 and x_2 are still free.

Step 9
At node 3 check to see if completing the partial solution $x_3 = 0$ with the free variables set equal to 0 is a feasible solution. For $x_1 = x_2 = x_3 = 0$,

$$Q_1 = 4 \geqslant 0$$
$$Q_2 = -3 \ngeqslant 0$$
$$Q_3 = -1 \ngeqslant 0$$

so constraints 2 and 3 are violated. Thus, the solution $x_1 = x_2 = x_3 = 0$ is not a feasible solution. To determine if further branching can be done from node 3, go to step 10.

Step 10
Let T be the set of free variables which have

1 An objective function coefficient less than ZMIN $- 0 = 2 - 0 = 2$ (to be explained later)
2 A positive coefficient in some violated constraint

Each variable has a cost coefficient larger than 2 so

$$T = \emptyset$$

where $\emptyset$ represents the empty set.

Step 11
Since both of the free variables that could possibly make Q_2 and Q_3 feasible have cost coefficients greater than or equal to 2 (the best feasible solution value to date), no feasible solution with $x_3 = 0$ can have a solution value less than 2. Hence, no solution emanating from node 3 is better than the current best feasible solution,

$$x_1 = x_2 = 0 \quad \text{and} \quad x_3 = 1$$

Thus,

$$x_1 = x_2 = 0 \quad \text{and} \quad x_3 = 1$$

is an optimal solution. Stop.

4.2.2 Algorithm 4.1—Implicit Enumeration Solution of the 0-1 Integer Programming Problem

Assume the 0-1 integer program to be solved has the form:

$$\text{minimize:} \quad Z = \sum_{j=1}^{N} C(J) * X(J)$$

$$\text{subject to:} \quad Q(I) = -B(I) + \sum_{j=1}^{N} A(I,J) * X(J) \geqslant 0 \quad I = 1, 2, \ldots, M$$

$$X(J) = 0 \text{ or } 1 \quad J = 1, 2, \ldots, N$$

where $C(J) \geqslant 0$; $J = 1, 2, \ldots, N$. The procedure for transforming any integer LP model to this form is presented in Section 4.2.4.

The notation used is:

FREE = the set of subscripts of the variables that have not been specified to be 0 or 1

NFREE = the set of subscripts of the variables that have been specified to be 0 or 1. If an element of NFREE is negative, the corresponding variable has been specified to be 0, otherwise, it has been specified to be 1. The first element (leftmost) in NFREE corresponds to the first variable specified to be 0 or 1. Likewise, the second element in NFREE corresponds to the second variable specified to be 0 or 1, etc.

ZMIN = the value of the objective function corresponding to the best feasible solution to date

VC = the set of violated constraints

T = the variables in FREE that have

(*a*) An objective function coefficient less than BOUND, where

$$\text{BOUND} = \text{ZMIN} - \sum_{I \,\epsilon\, \text{NFREE}} C(I) * X(I)$$

(*b*) A positive coefficient in some constraint in VC

$\sum_{I \,\epsilon\, \text{FREE}}$ = sum over all subscripts in NFREE

Step 1

Set

$$\text{FREE} = \{1, 2, \ldots, N\}$$
$$\text{NFREE} = \emptyset, \text{ the empty set}$$
$$\text{ZMIN} = 10^{10}$$

Step 2

Calculate

$$Z = \sum_{I \,\epsilon\, \text{NFREE}} C(I) * X(I)$$

Note that some of the X(I)'s in the above sum may be specified to have the value 0.

Step 3

Evaluate each constraint Q(I), (I = 1, 2, ..., M) using the NFREE variables with their specified values plus the FREE variables each set equal to 0. If each of the constraints are feasible (satisfied), then the values of the variables used to evaluate the constraints constitute a feasible solution.

Let VC denote the set of violated constraints.

Step 4

If VC is empty, go to step 12; otherwise, go to step 5.

Step 5

Set BOUND = ZMIN − Z.

Step 6

Select the FREE variables that have a chance to make all of the constraints feasible. That is, let T be the set of variables in FREE that have

1 A positive coefficient in some constraint in VC
2 An objective function coefficient < BOUND

A violated constraint can only be made "more" infeasible by setting to *1* a variable with a negative coefficient in the constraint, so only variables with a positive coefficient in a given constraint have a chance to make the constraint feasible ($\geqslant 0$). Likewise, a variable X(K) in FREE such that

$$\sum_{I \,\epsilon\, \text{NFREE}} C(I) * X(I) + C(K) \geqslant \text{ZMIN}$$

should not be considered for inclusion in NFREE since the feasible solution corresponding to ZMIN is already at least as good.

Step 7

If T empty, go to step 11; otherwise, go to step 8.

Step 8

For each constraint in VC

Set to 1 the FREE variables in T that have positive coefficients in the given constraint

Set the NFREE variables equal to their specified values

Step 9

If any of the constraints are still violated, go to step 11; otherwise, go to step 10.

Step 10

Remove from FREE and add to NFREE the variable in T that would minimize the total distance from feasibility over all constraints. This process is covered in detail in steps 10A-10C.

Step 10A

For each variable, say X(K), in T, evaluate each constraint Q(I), (I = 1, 2, . . . , M), using the NFREE variables with their specified values, X(K) = 1, and the remaining FREE variables each set equal to 0.

Step 10B

Sum the negative results from step 10A and let ASUM be the absolute value of the sum. The absolute value of each negative result is the amount the corresponding constraint must be increased to be feasible. Hence, ASUM represents in some sense the total distance from feasibility using X(K) = 1.

Step 10C

Remove from FREE and add to NFREE the variable in T that has the smallest total distance from feasibility (the smallest ASUM). Go to step 2.

Step 11
If NFREE is empty, go to step 21; otherwise, no feasible completion of the partial solution represented by NFREE has a smaller value than the current ZMIN, so go to step 16.

Step 12
The variables in NFREE with their specified values, along with the variables in FREE set equal to 0, form a complete solution. Go to step 13.

Step 13
If Z < ZMIN, go to step 14; otherwise, go to step 15.

Step 14
Set ZMIN = Z. Save the complete solution and go to step 15.

Step 15
Backtrack. If NFREE is empty, the feasible solution $X(I) = 0$ $(I = 1, 2, \ldots, N)$ is optimal, so go to step 20; otherwise, go to step 16.

Step 16
If the last element in NFREE is negative, go to step 18; otherwise, go to step 17. The rightmost element in NFREE is considered to be the last element in NFREE.

Step 17
Make the last (rightmost) element in NFREE negative and go to step 2. The variable corresponding to the last element has been specified to be *1* (corresponding subscript in NFREE has been positive). We now specify the variable to be 0 (change the sign of the last element in NFREE to minus).

Step 18
If all elements in NFREE are negative, an optimal solution has been reached, so go to step 20; otherwise, go to step 19.

Step 19
Make the rightmost *positive* element in NFREE negative and remove the remaining elements to the right from NFREE. Add the dropped elements to FREE. Go to step 2.

Step 20
The complete solution corresponding to ZMIN is optimal. If ZMIN = 10^{10}, no feasible solution. Print results. Stop.

Step 21
No feasible solution to the problem. Stop.

4.2.3 Backpack-Loading Problem—Implicit Enumeration Solution

A wilderness wanderer is preparing for a 2-week backpacking trip to the Lizard Creek lakes in the Selway Crags area of Idaho. Since she is an experienced backpacker, she is able to do an exceptionally good job of minimizing the total weight of her cargo. In fact, after all of the essential items are loaded into the backpack, she realizes that she can carry an additional 5 lb without undue hardship. She ponders over the long list of items that she could take along to make the trip more enjoyable, but to her dismay, all of the additional items would add 15 lb to her pack. What then should she take? She decides to assign a value to each item and to maximize the total value of her extra cargo within the 5-lb limitation.

Suppose we constrain the problem to the case where no more than one of each item can be taken. Thus, given the weight of each item w_j and the value of each item v_j, the problem is to determine which items should be loaded to maximize the value of the extra cargo within the weight limitation. It is assumed that each item is indivisible. If there are n possible items to load and a maximum load limit of w units, we want to determine the values of x_j $(j = 1, 2, \ldots, n)$ that will

$$\text{maximize:} \quad z = \sum_{j=1}^{n} v_j x_j$$

$$\text{subject to:} \quad \sum_{j=1}^{n} w_j x_j \leqslant w$$

$$x_j = 0 \text{ or } 1 \quad \text{for } j = 1, 2, \ldots, n$$

where $x_j = 1$ if item j is included and 0 otherwise. This is an all-integer (0-1) linear programming problem.

To illustrate the use of implicit enumeration to solve the problem, the number of different items has been set at 4, and the maximum additional load has been reduced to 5 oz. The complete problem is treated in an exercise at the end of the chapter. Table 4.1 gives the abbreviated list of items that will be considered in this example, along with their corresponding weights and values.

The integer programming formulation of this problem is:

$$\text{maximize:} \quad z^* = 6x_1 + 3x_2 + x_3 + 5x_4$$
$$\text{subject to:} \quad 5x_1 + 2x_2 + x_3 + 3x_4 \leqslant 5$$
$$\text{all } x_j = 0 \text{ or } 1$$

Table 4.1 BACKPACK DATA

Item number, i	Item	Weight, w_i	Value v_i
1	Book	5	6
2	Lure	2	3
3	Flashlight, 1 battery	1	1
4	Food	3	5

Since this is a maximization problem we must convert it to an equivalent minimization problem to use Algorithm 4.1. The new objective function is:

$$\text{minimize:} \quad -z^* = -6x_1 - 3x_2 - x_3 - 5x_4$$

However, all of the cost coefficients must be positive, so let

$$y_j = 1 - x_j \quad j = 1, 2, 3, 4$$

or

$$x_j = 1 - y_j$$

The new problem to be solved, then, is

$$\text{minimize:} \quad z = -z^* = -6(1 - y_1) - 3(1 - y_2) - (1 - y_3) - 5(1 - y_4)$$
$$\text{subject to:} \quad 5(1 - y_1) + 2(1 - y_2) + (1 - y_3) + 3(1 - y_4) \leqslant 5$$
$$\text{all } y_j = 0 \text{ or } 1$$

or

$$\text{minimize:} \quad z = 6y_1 + 3y_2 + y_3 + 5y_4 - 15$$
$$\text{subject to:} \quad -5y_1 - 2y_2 - y_3 - 3y_4 \leqslant -6$$

Note that if $y_j = 0$, then $x_j = 1$. Likewise, if $y_j = 1$, then $x_j = 0$. The number -15 in the objective function can be dropped since it would be subtracted from each solution, and thus would have no effect on which variables should be 0 and which variables should be 1 in the optimal solution.

The step-by-step solution of the problem using implicit enumeration is:

Step 1
Write the constraint as

$$Q_1 = -6 + 5y_1 + 2y_2 + y_3 + 3y_4 \geqslant 0$$

Set

$$\text{FREE} = \{1, 2, 3, 4\}$$
$$\text{NFREE} = \emptyset$$
$$\text{ZMIN} = 10^{10}$$

Step 2
Calculate

$$z = \sum_{i \,\epsilon\, \text{NFREE}} c_i y_i = 0$$

since NFREE is empty.

Step 3
Evaluate Q_1 using the FREE variable each set equal to 0.

$$Q_1 = -6 \ngeqslant 0$$

Set VC = $\{Q_1\}$. Recall that VC is the set of violated constraints when $y_i = 0$ for $i = 1, 2, 3,$ and 4.

Step 4
VC is not empty, so go to step 5.

Step 5
Calculate

$$\text{BOUND} = \text{ZMIN} - z = 10^{10} - 0 = 10^{10}$$

Step 6
Every FREE variable has a positive coefficient in Q_1 and the corresponding cost coefficients are all less than BOUND, so all four variables are candidates to make Q_1 feasible.

$$T = \{1, 2, 3, 4\}$$

represents these variables.

Step 7
T is not empty, so go to step 8.

Step 8
Evaluate Q_1 with the variables in T set equal to 1. This is to determine if there is any possibility at all of making Q_1 feasible.

$$Q_1 = -6 + 5 + 2 + 1 + 3 = 5 > 0$$

The constraint is not violated, so go to step 9.

Step 9
Remove from FREE and add to NFREE the variable in T that would minimize the total distance from feasibility over all constraints. The variable subscript is put in NFREE as a positive number.

	Total distance from feasibility
For variable 1: $Q_1 = -6 + 5 = -1$	1
For variable 2: $Q_1 = -6 + 2 = -4$	4
For variable 3: $Q_1 = -6 + 1 = -5$	5
For variable 4: $Q_1 = -6 + 3 = -3$	3

The smallest total distance from feasibility is obtained by letting variable 1 take on the value 1, so remove variable 1 from FREE and put it in NFREE.

$$\text{NFREE} = \{1\}$$
$$\text{FREE} = \{2, 3, 4\}$$

This is represented by a branch on variable 1 to node 2 in Figure 4.2.

Go to step 2A.

Note: Step 2A indicates the first return to step 2 in the general algorithm, step 2B indicates the second return to step 2, etc.

Step 2A
Evaluate

$$z = \sum_{i \in \text{NFREE}} c_i y_i = c_1 y_1 = 6 y_1 = 6$$

Step 3A

$$Q_1 = -6 + 5 = -1 \not\geq 0$$
$$\text{VC} = \{Q_1\}$$

Step 4A
VC is not empty, so go to step 5A.

Step 5A

$$\text{BOUND} = \text{ZMIN} - z = 10^{10} - 6$$

Step 6A

$$T = \{2, 3, 4\}$$

Step 7A
T is not empty, so go to step 8A.

Step 8A

$$Q_1 = -6 + 5 + 2 + 1 + 3 = 5 > 0$$

Q is not violated, so go to step 9A.

Step 9A

	Total distance from feasibility
For variable 2: $Q_1 = -6 + 5 + 2 = 1$	0
For variable 3: $Q_1 = -6 + 5 + 1 = 0$	0
For variable 4: $Q_1 = -6 + 5 + 3 = 2$	0

any one of the variables 2, 3, or 4 set equal to 1 will cause Q_1 to be feasible, so we can choose any one of them to be removed from FREE and to be put in NFREE. A choice that tends to speed up the search for the optimal solution is to choose the variable with the smallest cost coefficient. Thus, select variable 3.

$$\text{NFREE} = \{1, 3\}$$
$$\text{FREE} = \{2, 4\}$$

This is represented by the branch on variable 3 to node 3 in Figure 4.2.
    Go to step 2B.

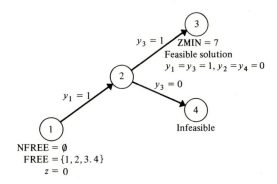

FIGURE 4.2
Partial solution tree for backpack-loading problem.

Step 2B
Evaluate

$$z = c_1y_1 + c_3y_3 = 6(1) + 1(1) = 7$$

Step 3B

$$Q_1 = -6 + 5 + 1 = 0$$
$$VC = \emptyset$$

Step 4B
VC is empty, so go to step 10.

Step 10
$y_1 = y_3 = 1$ and $y_2 = y_4 = 0$ is a complete feasible solution.
Go to step 11.

Step 11
$z = 7 < ZMIN = 10^{10}$, so go to step 12.

Step 12
Set $ZMIN = z = 7$. Save the current complete feasible solution.

Step 13
Backtrack. NFREE = $\{1, 3\}$ is not empty, so go to step 14.

Step 14
The last element in NFREE, namely 3, is positive, so go to step 15.

Step 15
Make the last (rightmost) element in NFREE negative and go to step 2. This makes variable 3 specified to be 0. NFREE = $\{1, -3\}$. This is represented by a branch on variable 3 to node 4 in Figure 4.2.

Step 2C
Evaluate

$$z = \sum_{i \,\epsilon\, \text{NFREE}} c_i y_i = 6y_1 + 1y_3 = 6(1) + 1(0) = 6$$

Step 3C

$$Q_1 = -6 + 5 = -1 \not> 0$$
$$\text{VC} = \{Q_1\}$$

Step 4C
VC is not empty, so go to step 5C.

Step 5C
Set

$$\text{BOUND} = \text{ZMIN} - z = 7 - 6 = 1$$

Step 6C
The only two variables in FREE, namely variables 2 and 4, have cost coefficients of 3 and 5, respectively, which are both greater than BOUND = 1. Therefore, $T = \emptyset$.

Step 7C
T is empty, so no feasible completion of the partial solution represented by NFREE $(y_1 = 1, y_3 = 0)$ has a smaller ZMIN value. Go to step 14.

Step 14
The last element in NFREE = $\{1, -3\}$ is negative, so go to step 16.

Step 16
All elements in NFREE are not negative, so go to step 17.

Step 17
Make the rightmost positive element in NFREE negative and remove the remaining elements to the right from NFREE. Add the dropped elements to FREE. Go to step 2D.

$$\text{NFREE} = \{-1\}$$
$$\text{FREE} = \{2, 3, 4\}$$

This is represented by the branch on variable 1 to node 5 in Figure 4.3 on p. 148.

Step 2D
Calculate

$$z = \sum_{i \,\epsilon\, \text{NFREE}} c_i y_i = 6y_1 = 6(0) = 0$$

Step 3D

$$Q_1 = -6 + 0 = -6 < 0$$
$$\text{VC} = \{Q_1\}$$

Step 4D
VC is not empty, so go to step 5D.

Step 5D
Set

$$\text{BOUND} = \text{ZMIN} - z = 7 - 0 = 7$$

Step 6D
$T = \{2, 3, 4\}$ since each cost coefficient is less than BOUND $= 7$.

Step 7D
T is not empty, so go to step 8D.

Step 8D

$$Q_1 = -6 + 0 + 3 + 1 + 5 = 3 > 0$$

Go to step 9D.

Step 9D

	Total distance from feasibility
For variable 2: $Q_1 = -6 + 0 + 2 = -4$	4
For variable 3: $Q_1 = -6 + 0 + 1 = -5$	5
For variable 4: $Q_1 = -6 + 0 + 3 = -3$	3

Variable 4 has the smallest total distance from feasibility, so remove it from FREE and place in NFREE.

$$\text{NFREE} = \{-1, 4\}$$
$$\text{FREE} = \{2, 3\}$$

This is represented by a branch on variable 4 to node 6 in Figure 4.3. Go to step 2E.

Step 2E
Calculate

$$z = \sum_{i \in \text{NFREE}} c_i y_i = 6y_1 + 5y_4 = 6(0) + 5(1) = 5$$

Step 3E

$$Q_1 = -6 + 0 + 3 = -3 < 0$$
$$\text{VC} = \{Q_1\}$$

Step 4E
VC is not empty, so go to step 5E.

Step 5E
Set

$$\text{BOUND} = \text{ZMIN} - z = 7 - 5 = 2$$

Step 6E
$T = \{3\}$.
Note that variable 3 is the only FREE variable with a cost coefficient less than $\text{BOUND} = 2$.

Step 7E
T is not empty, so go to step 8E.

Step 8E

$$Q_1 = -6 + 0 + 1 + 3 = -2$$

Since Q_1 is negative no feasible completion of the partial solution represented by NFREE has a smaller ZMIN value. Go to step 14A.

Step 14A
The last element in NFREE is positive, so go to step 15A.

Step 15A
Make the rightmost element in NFREE negative and go to step 2F.

$$\text{NFREE} = \{-1, -4\}$$
$$\text{FREE} = \{2, 3\}.$$

This is represented by a branch on variable 4 to node 7 in Figure 4.3 on p. 148.

Step 2F
Calculate

$$z = \sum_{i \,\epsilon\, \text{NFREE}} c_i y_i = 6y_1 + 5y_4 = 6(0) + 5(0) = 0$$

Step 3F
$$Q_1 = -6 + 0 + 0 + 0 + 0 = -6$$
$$\text{VC} = \{Q_1\}$$

Step 4F
VC is not empty, so go to step 5F.

Step 5F
Set

$$\text{BOUND} = \text{ZMIN} - z = 7 - 0 = 7$$

Step 6F
$$T = \{2, 3\}$$

Step 7F
T is not empty, so go to step 8F.

Step 8F

$$Q_1 = -6 + 0 + 2 + 1 + 0 = -3 < 0$$

Therefore, no feasible completion of the partial solution represented by NFREE ($y_1 = 0, y_4 = 0$) has a smaller ZMIN value, so go to step 14B.

Step 14B

The last element in NFREE is negative, so go to step 16A.

Step 16A

All elements of NFREE are negative, so an optimal solution has been reached. Go to step 18.

Step 18

The complete solution corresponding to ZMIN = 7 is optimal; namely,

$$y_1 = 1 \quad y_3 = 1$$
$$y_2 = 0 \quad y_4 = 0$$

Add −15 to ZMIN to give

$$\min (z) = +7 - 15 = -8$$

In terms of the x_j's,

$$x_1 = 1 - y_1 = 0$$
$$x_2 = 1 - y_2 = 1$$
$$x_3 = 1 - y_3 = 0$$
$$x_4 = 1 - y_4 = 1$$

Hence,

$$\min (-z^*) = -6(0) - 3(1) - (0) - 5(1)$$
$$= -8$$

The value of the objective function for the original problem is then

$$\max (z^*) = \min (-z^*) = 8$$

Thus, the maximum value of the cargo, 8 units, is obtained by taking a lure and extra food. This corresponds to node 3 in Figure 4.3.

Obviously, this is a long-drawn-out process to solve such a simple problem; nevertheless, it does illustrate the implicit enumeration method for solving integer (0-1) linear programming problems. The backpack-loading problem can be solved more efficiently using a branch-and-bound algorithm derived by Kolesar [9]. Dynamic programming would also be generally more efficient than implicit enumeration for this type of problem, but it too would be less efficient than Kolesar's algorithm.

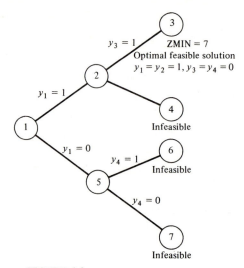

FIGURE 4.3
Complete solution tree for backpack problem.

In Figure 4.3 the word "infeasible" means that there is no solution emanating from the given node that is better than the current best feasible solution.

4.2.4 Preparation of any 0-1 Integer Program for Algorithm 4.1

In order to use Algorithm 4.1 the 0-1 integer linear program to be solved must have the form

$$\text{minimize:} \quad Z = \sum_{J=1}^{N} C(J) * X(J)$$

$$\text{subject to:} \quad Q(I) = -B(I) + \sum_{J=1}^{N} A(I,J) * X(J) \geqslant 0 \quad I = 1, 2, \ldots, M$$

$$X(J) = 0 \text{ or } 1 \quad J = 1, 2, \ldots, N$$

where $C(J) \geqslant 0; J = 1, 2, \ldots, N$.

The purpose for having all $C(J) \geqslant 0$ is so we can determine quickly whether a feasible solution emanating from a given node would be a more attractive solution than the current best feasible solution. If a variable in the objective function has a negative cost coefficient $[C(J) < 0]$, simply replace the variable with another variable that is the one's complement of the first variable. That is, if $C(2) = -4$, let

$$X(2) = 1 - Y(2)$$

then

$$Y(2) = 1 - X(2)$$

Thus, if $X(2) = 0$, then $Y(2) = 1$. Likewise, if $X(2) = 1$, then $Y(2) = 0$. Consider the example

$$\text{minimize: } z = 2X_1 - 4X_2 + 6X_3$$
$$\text{subject to: } 3X_1 + 2X_2 + X_3 \leqslant 4$$
$$X_1 - 3X_2 + 4X_3 \geqslant 2$$
$$\text{all } X_i = 0 \text{ or } 1$$

Since X_2 has the only negative cost coefficient in the objective function, let

$$Y_2 = 1 - X_2$$

or

$$X_2 = 1 - Y_2$$

The new problem then is

$$\text{minimize: } z = 2X_1 - 4(1 - Y_2) + 6X_3$$
$$\text{subject to: } 3X_1 + 2(1 - Y_2) + X_3 \leqslant 4$$
$$X_1 - 3(1 - Y_2) + 4X_3 \geqslant 2$$
$$X_1, Y_2, X_3 = 0 \text{ or } 1$$

or

$$\text{minimize: } z = 2X_1 + 4Y_2 + 6X_3 - 4$$
$$\text{subject to: } 3X_1 - 2Y_2 + X_3 \leqslant 2$$
$$X_1 + 3Y_2 + 4X_3 \geqslant 5$$
$$X_1, Y_2, X_3 = 0 \text{ or } 1$$

When each constraint is written as a greater-than-or-equal-to constraint, we are able to recognize where variables with positive coefficients in a violated constraint can help bring about feasibility by raising them to 1. Each constraint can be written as a greater-than-or-equal-to constraint as follows:

1 Write $\displaystyle\sum_{j=1}^{N} a_{ij}X_j \leqslant b_i$ as $Q(i) = b_i - \displaystyle\sum_{j=1}^{N} a_{ij}X_j \geqslant 0$

2 Write $\displaystyle\sum_{j=1}^{N} a_{ij}X_j \geqslant b_i$ as $Q(i) = -b_i + \displaystyle\sum_{j=1}^{N} a_{ij}X_j \geqslant 0$

3 Write $\sum_{j=1}^{N} a_{ij} X_j = b_i$ as two constraints, namely,

$$-b_i + \sum_{j=1}^{N} a_{ij} X_j \geqslant 0$$

$$-b_i + \sum_{j=1}^{N} a_{ij} X_j \leqslant 0$$

or

$$Q(i) = -b_i + \sum_{j=1}^{N} a_{ij} X_j \geqslant 0$$

$$Q(i + 1) = b_i - \sum_{j=1}^{N} a_{ij} X_j \geqslant 0$$

To write each equality as two greater-than-or-equal-to constraints may not be too appealing if there are a number of equalities. Hence, if there are K equalities

$$Q(i) = -b_i + \sum_{j=1}^{N} a_{ij} X_j = 0 \qquad i = 1, 2, \ldots, K$$

replace them with the $(K + 1)$ greater-than-or-equal-to constraints

$$Q(i) = -b_i + \sum_{j=1}^{N} a_{ij} X_j \geqslant 0 \qquad i = 1, 2, \ldots, K$$

$$Q(K + 1) = \sum_{i=1}^{K} b_i - \sum_{i=1}^{K} \sum_{j=1}^{N} a_{ij} X_j \geqslant 0$$

For example, suppose we have the two equalities

$$2X_1 + 4X_2 + 4X_3 - X_4 = 5$$
$$-4X_1 + X_2 + 5X_3 + X_4 = 2$$

They can be replaced by the three greater-than-or-equal-to constraints

$$-5 + 2X_1 + 4X_2 + 4X_3 - X_4 \geqslant 0$$
$$-2 - 4X_1 + X_2 + 5X_3 + X_4 \geqslant 0$$
$$7 + 2X_1 - 5X_2 - 9X_3 \qquad \geqslant 0$$

The only solution that satisfies the two equalities is the solution that satisfies the three greater-than-or-equal-to-zero constraints; namely,

$$X_1 = X_3 = X_4 = 1 \qquad \text{and} \qquad X_2 = 0$$

4.2.5   Computer Program for Algorithm 4.1

This program is designed to solve (0-1) integer linear programming problems with a maximum of 15 constraints and 10 variables. To modify the program to handle P constraints in R variables, change the three INTEGER statements at the beginning of the program to

INTEGER CCS(R), X$(R + 1)$, Y$(R + 1)$, FLAG(R), CODE(P), FREE(R), VC$(P + 1)$

INTEGER C(R), B$(P + 1)$, A(P, R), Q$(P + 1, R + 1)$, ASUM(R), NFREE(R)

INTEGER T(R), LAST(R), ZMIN, Z, BOUND, SUM, ZFLAG

The program will solve both maximization and minimization problems with positive or negative cost coefficients. The problem is presented to the program in its original form and the program takes care of the necessary bookwork to get it in the standard form for the implicit enumeration algorithm. The comment cards at the beginning of the program explain exactly how to input the data. The only restriction is that the user must multiply the objective function and/or constraints by the proper constants to force all of the input data to be in integer form. For example, the constraint

$$3.1x_1 - 4.5x_2 + 6.8x_3 \geqslant 4$$

must be multiplied by 10 to give

$$31x_1 - 45x_2 + 68x_3 \geqslant 40$$

This is the constraint that would be entered into the computer.

The program as written occupies 44K bytes of core storage. The three problems following the program listing took a total of 0.13 s of IBM 370/168 time.

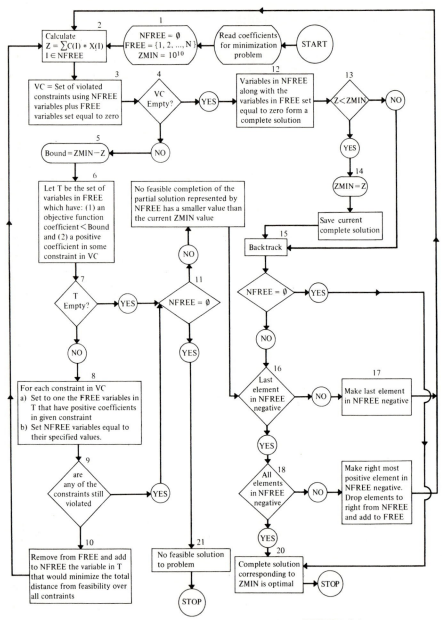

FIGURE 4.4
Flowchart for Algorithm 4.1.

```
C     ****************************************************************************
C     *                                                                        *
C     *  **    ALGORITHM 4.1    INTEGER PROGRAMMING    IMPLICIT ENUMERATION  ** *
C     *                                                                        *
C     * THIS PROGRAM WILL SOLVE 0-1 INTEGER LINEAR PROGRAMMING PROBLEMS        *
C     * WITH A MAXIMUM SIZE OF 10 VARIABLES AND 15 CONSTRAINTS.                *
C     *  **   ALL COEFFICIENTS AND CONSTANTS MUST BE INTEGERS. **             *
C     *                                                                        *
C     * IT IS DESIGNED                                                         *
C     *    TO READ                                                             *
C     *         CARD 1    COLS  2-80    TITLE  DESCRIPTION OF THE PROBLEM USING *
C     *                                        ANY CHARACTERS ON KEYPUNCH      *
C     *                                        ** COLUMN 1 MUST BE LEFT BLANK ***
C     *         CARD 2    COLS  1- 5    M  NUMBER OF CONSTRAINTS  (I5)          *
C     *                         6-10    K  NUMBER OF VARIABLES  (I5)           *
C     *                        11-15    NLET  NUMBER OF <OR= CONSTRAINTS  (I5)  *
C     *                        16-20    NGET  NUMBER OF >OR= CONSTRAINTS  (I5)  *
C     *                        21-25    NET   NUMBER OF = CONSTRAINTS  (I5)     *
C     *                        26-30    NTYPE 0 MINIMIZATION PROBLEM           *
C     *                                       1 MAXIMIZATION PROBLEM  (I5)     *
C     *         CARDS 3 TO T    M SETS OF CARDS, ONE SET FOR EACH CONSTRAINT   *
C     *             CARD I    COLS  1-10    CODE(I) 0 IF <OR= CONSTRAINT       *
C     *                                             1 IF >OR= CONSTRAINT       *
C     *                                             2 IF = CONSTRAINT  (I10)   *
C     *                            11-20    B(I)  CONSTANT IN CONSTRAINT (I10) *
C     *             CARD I+1    A(I,J)  J COEFFICIENTS OF CONSTRAINT I         *
C     *                                 PUNCH ROWWISE IN 8I10 FORMAT          *
C     *                                 IF K>8, CONTINUE ON NEXT CARD.         *
C     *         CARD T+1    C(J)  COST COEFFICIENTS OF OBJECTIVE FUNCTION      *
C     *                           PUNCH ROWWISE IN 8I10 FORMAT                *
C     *                           IF K>8, CONTINUE ON NEXT CARD.               *
C     *         TO SOLVE MORE THAN ONE PROBLEM AT A TIME, REPEAT THE          *
C     *         READ SEQUENCE, AND STACK THE DATA ONE BEHIND THE OTHER        *
C     *                                                                        *
C     *    TO CALCULATE AND PRINT                                             *
C     *         ZMIN       OPTIMAL VALUE OF OBJECTIVE FUNCTION                *
C     *         LAST(I)    VALUES OF VARIABLES YIELDING ZMIN                  *
C     *                                                                        *
C     ****************************************************************************
      INTEGER CCS(10),X(11),Y(11),FLAG(10),CODE(15),FREE(10),VC(16)
      INTEGER   C(10),B(16),A(15,10),Q(16,11),ASUM(10),NFREE(10)
      INTEGER T(10),LAST(10),ZMIN,Z,BOUND,SUM,ZFLAG
      REAL*4 TITLE(20)
    5 READ(5,10,END=2000)TITLE
   10 FORMAT(20A4)
      WRITE(6,15)TITLE
   15 FORMAT('1',20A4,//)
      READ(5,20)M,K,NLET,NGET,NET,NTYPE
   20 FORMAT(6I5)
      DO 25 I=1,M
      READ(5,30)CODE(I),B(I)
   30 FORMAT(8I10)
      READ(5,30)(A(I,J),J=1,K)
   25 CONTINUE
      READ(5,30)(C(J),J=1,K)
      WRITE(6,40)
   40 FORMAT(5X,'THE ORIGINAL COEFFICIENTS OF THE CONSTRAINTS',//15X,'CO
     *DE 0 ==>  <OR= CONSTRAINT',/15X,'CODE 1 ==>  >OR= CONSTRAINT',/15X
     *,'CODE 2 ==>  = CONSTRAINT',//)
      WRITE(6,55)
   55 FORMAT('  I CODE CONSTANT  A(I,1)  A(I,2)  A(I,3)  A(I,4)  A(I,5)
     * A(I,6)  A(I,7)  A(I,8)',/)
      DO 45 I=1,M
      WRITE(6,51)I,CODE(I),B(I)
   51 FORMAT(I3,I4,I9)
      WRITE(6,52)(A(I,J),J=1,K)
   52 FORMAT('+',15X,8I8/(16X,8I8))
   45 CONTINUE
      IF(NTYPE.NE.0) GO TO 35
      WRITE(6,36)
```

```
   36 FORMAT(//  5X,'THE COEFFICIENTS IN THE ORIGINAL OBJECTIVE FUNCTION
      * TO BE MINIMIZED ARE:',/)
      GO TO 37
   35 WRITE(6,38)
   38 FORMAT(//  5X,'THE COEFFICIENTS IN THE ORIGINAL OBJECTIVE FUNCTION
      * TO BE MAXIMIZED ARE:',/)
   37 WRITE(6,39)(C(J),J=1,K)
   39 FORMAT(16X,8I8/16X,8I8)
C     *********************************************************************
C     *  STEP A                                                          *
C     *          IF THE PROBLEM IS MAXIMIZATION, CHANGE TO MINIMIZATION; *
C     *          OTHERWISE, GO TO STEP B.                                *
C     *********************************************************************
      IF(NTYPE.EQ.0) GO TO 99
      DO 60 J=1,K
   60 C(J)=-C(J)
C     *********************************************************************
C     *  STEP B                                                          *
C     *          IF ANY OF THE COST COEFFICIENTS IN THE OBJECTIVE FUNCTION ARE *
C     *          NEGATIVE, MAKE A TRANSFORMATION THAT WILL MAKE THEM POSITIVE. *
C     *********************************************************************
   99 CSUM=0
      DO 100 J=1,K
      IF(C(J).GE.0  ) GO TO 105
      CSUM=CSUM+C(J)
      C(J)=-C(J)
      FLAG(J)=1
      DO 110 I=1,M
      B(I)=B(I)-A(I,J)
      A(I,J)=-A(I,J)
  110 CONTINUE
      GO TO 100
  105 FLAG(J)=0
  100 CONTINUE
C     *********************************************************************
C     *  STEP C                                                          *
C     *          CONVERT EQUALITY CONSTRAINTS TO >= 0 CONSTRAINTS.       *
C     *********************************************************************
      K1=K+1
      M1=0
      IF(NET.EQ.0) GO TO 300
      M1=M+1
      CODE(M1)=1
      B(M1)=0
      DO 205 J=1,K
      A(M1,J)=0
  205 CONTINUE
      DO 200 I=1,M
      IF(CODE(I).NE.2) GO TO 200
      B(M1)=B(M1)-B(I)
      CODE(I)=1
      DO 210 J=1,K
  210 A(M1,J)=A(M1,J)-A(I,J)
  200 CONTINUE
C     *********************************************************************
C     *  STEP D                                                          *
C     *          CONVERT ALL CONSTRAINTS TO >OR= CONSTRAINTS.            *
C     *********************************************************************
  300 IF(M1.EQ.0)M1=M
      DO 310 I=1,M1
      IF(CODE(I).EQ.2) GO TO 310
      IF(CODE(I).EQ.1) GO TO 320
      Q(I,K1)=B(I)
      DO 315 J=1,K
  315 Q(I,J)=-A(I,J)
      GO TO 310
  320 Q(I,K1)=-B(I)
      DO 325 J=1,K
  325 Q(I,J)=A(I,J)
  310 CONTINUE
```

```
      WRITE(6,321)
  321 FORMAT(//  5X,'CONVERTED CONSTRAINTS',/)
      DO 322 I=1,M1
      WRITE(6,323)I,Q(I,K1)
  323 FORMAT(I3,I13)
      WRITE(6,52)(Q(I,J),J=1,K)
  322 CONTINUE
      WRITE( 6,235)
  235 FORMAT(//  ' STEP #     PARTIAL SOLUTIONS   (NFREE)',36X,'ZMIN',/)
C     ********************************************************************
C     *  STEP 1                                                         *
C     *          SET INITIAL VALUES OF FREE, NFREE, ZMIN,ZFLAG,NSTEP    *
C     ********************************************************************
      DO 120 I=1,K
      FREE(I)=I
      NFREE(I)=0
  120 CONTINUE
      ZMIN=10000000
      ZFLAG=0
      NSTEP=-1
C     ********************************************************************
C     *  STEP 2                                                         *
C     *          CALCULATE VALUE OF THE OBJECTIVE FUNCTION USING X(I) SUCH THAT *
C     *              I IS IN NFREE.                                     *
C     ********************************************************************
  201 CONTINUE
      NSTEP=NSTEP+1
      SUM=0
      DO 220 I=1,K
      IF(NFREE(I).EQ.0) GO TO 230
      IF(NFREE(I).LE.0) GO TO 220
      IN=NFREE(I)
      SUM=SUM+C(IN)
  220 CONTINUE
  230 Z=SUM
C     ********************************************************************
C     *  STEP 3                                                         *
C     *          EVALUATE EACH CONSTRAINT USING THE NFREE VARIABLES PLUS THE *
C     *              FREE VARIABLES SET TO 0. LET VC DENOTE THE VIOLATED *
C     *              CONSTRAINTS.                                       *
C     ********************************************************************
  350 CONTINUE
      DO 360 I=1,K
      Y(I)=0
  360 CONTINUE
      Y(K1)=1
      DO 370 I=1,K
      IF(NFREE(I).LE.0) GO TO 370
      IN=NFREE(I)
      Y(IN)=1
  370 CONTINUE
      DO 375 I=1,M1
      SUM=0
      DO 380 J=1,K1
      SUM=SUM+Q(I,J)*Y(J)
  380 CONTINUE
      IF(SUM.GE.0  ) GO TO 385
      VC(I)=1
      GO TO 375
  385 VC(I)=0
  375 CONTINUE
C     ********************************************************************
C     *  STEP 4                                                         *
C     *          IF VC IS EMPTY GO TO STEP 12, OTHERWISE, GO TO STEP 5. *
C     ********************************************************************
      DO 400 I=1,M1
      IF(VC(I).EQ.1) GO TO 500
  400 CONTINUE
      GO TO 1200
```

```
C     *******************************************************************************
C     *   STEP 5                                                                   *
C     *           SET BOUND=ZMIN-Z.                                                *
C     *******************************************************************************
  500 BOUND=ZMIN-Z
      WRITE( 6,206)NSTEP,(NFREE(I),I=1,K)
  206 FORMAT(I6,4X,10I6,/(10X,10I6/))
      WRITE( 6,207)ZMIN
  207 FORMAT('+',70X,I8)
C     *******************************************************************************
C     *   STEP 6                                                                   *
C     *           SELECT THE FREE VARIABLES THAT HAVE A CHANCE TO MAKE ALL OF THE  *
C     *           CONSTRAINTS FEASIBLE.  LET T BE THE SET OF VARIABLES IN FREE     *
C     *           THAT HAVE 1) A POSITIVE COEFFICIENT IN SOME CONSTRAINT IN VC     *
C     *           AND 2) AN OBJECTIVE FUNCTION COEFFICIENT < BOUND                 *
C     *******************************************************************************
      DO 600 J=1,K
      T(J)=0
      IF(FREE(J).EQ.0) GO TO 600
      IF(C(J).GE.BOUND) GO TO 600
      DO 610 I=1,M1
      IF(VC(I).EQ.0) GO TO 610
      IF(Q(I,J).GT.0  ) GO TO 630
  610 CONTINUE
      GO TO 600
  630 T(J)=1
  600 CONTINUE
C     *******************************************************************************
C     *   STEP 7                                                                   *
C     *           IF T IS EMPTY, GO TO STEP 11; OTHERWISE,GO TO STEP 8.            *
C     *******************************************************************************
      DO 700 J=1,K
      IF(T(J).EQ.1) GO TO 800
  700 CONTINUE
      GO TO 1100
C     *******************************************************************************
C     *   STEPS 8,9                                                                *
C     *           FOR EACH CONSTRAINT IN VC                                        *
C     *             A) SET TO ONE THE FREE VARIABLES IN T THAT HAVE POSITIVE       *
C     *                COEFFICIENTS IN THE GIVEN CONSTRAINT                        *
C     *             B) SET THE NFREE VARIABLES EQUAL TO THEIR SPECIFIED VALUES.    *
C     *           IF ANY OF THE CONSTRAINTS ARE STILL VIOLATED, GO TO STEP 11;     *
C     *           OTHERWISE, GO TO STEP 10.                                        *
C     *******************************************************************************
  800 DO 810 J=1,K
  810 Y(J)=0
      DO 830 J=1,K
      IF(NFREE(J).LE.0) GO TO 830
      IN=NFREE(J)
      Y(IN)=1
  830 CONTINUE
      T(K1)=0
      Y(K1)=1
      DO 840 I=1,M1
      IF(VC(I).EQ.0) GO TO 840
      SUM=0
      DO 850 J=1,K1
      IF(T(J).EQ.1.AND.Q(I,J).GT.0.AND.J.NE.K1) Y(J)=1
      SUM=SUM+Q(I,J)*Y(J)
      IF(T(J).EQ.1.AND.Q(I,J).GT.0.AND.J.NE.K1) Y(J)=0
  850 CONTINUE



      IF(SUM.LT.0  ) GO TO 1100
  840 CONTINUE
C     *******************************************************************************
C     *   STEP 10                                                                  *
C     *           REMOVE FROM FREE AND ADD TO NFREE THE VARIABLE IN T THAT WOULD   *
C     *             MINIMIZE THE TOTAL DISTANCE FROM FEASIBILITY OVER ALL OF THE   *
C     *             CONSTRAINTS.                                                    *
C     *******************************************************************************
```

```
      MIN=1000000
      DO 910 J=1,K
      IF(T(J).NE.1) GO TO 910
      KOUNT=J
      DO 920 JJ=1,K
      IF(JJ.NE.KOUNT) Y(JJ)=0
  920 CONTINUE
      Y(KOUNT)=1
      DO 930 JJ=1,K
      IF(NFREE(JJ).LE.0) GO TO 930
      IN=NFREE(JJ)
      Y(IN)=1
  930 CONTINUE
      Y(K1)=1
      ASUM(KOUNT)=0
      DO 940 I=1,M1
      SUM=0
      DO 950 IJ=1,K1
  950 SUM=SUM+Q(I,IJ)*Y(IJ)
      IF(SUM.GE.0  ) GO TO 940
      ASUM(KOUNT)=ASUM(KOUNT)-SUM
  940 CONTINUE
      MIN=MINO(MIN,ASUM(KOUNT))
      IF( MIN.EQ.ASUM(KOUNT))KTOT=KOUNT
  910 CONTINUE
      FREE(KTOT)=0
      DO 960 I=1,K
      IF(NFREE(I).EQ.0) GO TO 970
  960 CONTINUE
  970 NFREE(I)=KTOT
      GO TO 201
C     ***************************************************************************
C     *    STEP 11                                                           *
C     *          IF NFREE IS EMPTY, GO TO STEP 21; OTHERWISE, NO FEASIBLE    *
C     *          COMPLETION OF THE PARTIAL SOLUTION REPRESENTED BY NFREE HAS *
C     *          A SMALLER VALUE THAN THE CURRENT ZMIN, SO GO TO STEP 16.    *
C     ***************************************************************************
 1100 DO 1110 I=1,K
      IF(NFREE(I).NE.0) GO TO 1600
 1110 CONTINUE
      GO TO 2100
C     ***************************************************************************
C     *    STEP 12                                                           *
C     *          VARIABLES IN NFREE WITH SPECIFIED VALUES, ALONG WITH VARIABLES *
C     *          IN FREE SET EQUAL TO ZERO, FORM A COMPLETE SOLUTION.        *
C     *          GO TO STEP 13.                                              *
C     ***************************************************************************
 1200 CONTINUE
      DO 1210 I=1,K
 1210 CCS(I)=0
      DO 1220 I=1,K
      IF(NFREE(I).LE.0) GO TO 1220
      IN=NFREE(I)
      CCS(IN)=1
 1220 CONTINUE
C     ***************************************************************************
C     *    STEP 13                                                           *
C     *          IF  Z < ZMIN  GO TO STEP 14; OTHERWISE, GO TO STEP 15.      *
C     ***************************************************************************
      IF(Z.LT.ZMIN) GO TO 1400
      GO TO 1500
C     ***************************************************************************
C     *    STEP 14                                                           *
C     *          SET ZMIN=Z AND SAVE CURRENT COMPLETE SOLUTION.              *
C     ***************************************************************************
 1400 ZMIN=Z
      ZFLAG=1
      DO 1410 I=1,K
      LAST(I)=CCS(I)
```

```
 1410 CONTINUE
C     *********************************************************************
C     *   STEP 15                                                        *
C     *          BACKTRACK.  IF NFREE IS EMPTY, THE FEASIBLE SOLUTION IS OPTIMAL *
C     *          SO GO TO STEP 20; OTHERWISE, GO TO STEP 16.             *
C     *********************************************************************
 1500 CONTINUE
      WRITE( 6,206)NSTEP,(NFREE(I),I=1,K)
      WRITE( 6,207)ZMIN
      DO 1510 I=1,K
      IF(NFREE(I).NE.0) GO TO 1600
 1510 CONTINUE
      GO TO 2010
C     *********************************************************************
C     *   STEP 16                                                        *
C     *          IF THE LAST ELEMENT IN NFREE IS NEGATIVE, GO TO STEP 18; *
C     *          OTHERWISE, GO TO STEP 17.                               *
C     *********************************************************************
 1600 CONTINUE
      KK=K-1
      DO 1610 I=1,KK
      II=I+1
      IF(NFREE(II).EQ.0) GO TO 1620
      GO TO 1610
 1620 KOUNTR=I
      IF(NFREE(I).LT.0) GO TO 1800
      GO TO 1700
 1610 CONTINUE
      KOUNTR=K
      IF(NFREE(K).LT.0) GO TO 1800
      GO TO 1700
C     *********************************************************************
C     *   STEP 17                                                        *
C     *          MAKE THE LAST ELEMENT IN NFREE NEGATIVE, AND GO TO STEP 2. *
C     *********************************************************************
 1700 NFREE(KOUNTR)=-NFREE(KOUNTR)
      GO TO 201
C     *********************************************************************
C     *   STEP 18                                                        *
C     *          IF ALL ELEMENTS IN NFREE ARE NEGATIVE, AN OPTIMAL SOLUTION HAS *
C     *          BEEN REACHED, SO GO TO STEP 20; OTHERWISE, GO TO STEP 19. *
C     *********************************************************************
 1800 CONTINUE
      KOUNTR=KOUNTR+1
      DO 1810 I=1,K
      N=KOUNTR-I
      IF(N.LE.0) GO TO 2010
      IF(NFRFE(N).GE.0) GO TO 1900
 1810 CONTINUE
C     *********************************************************************
C     *   STEP 19                                                        *
C     *          MAKE THE RIGHTMOST POSITIVE ELEMENT IN NFREE NEGATIVE, AND *
C     *          AND REMOVE THE REMAINING ELEMENTS TO THE RIGHT FROM NFREE. *
C     *          ADD THE DROPPED ELEMENTS TO FREE.  GO TO STEP 2.        *
C     *********************************************************************
 1900 NFREE(N)=-NFREE(N)
      N1=N+1
      DO 1910 I=N1,K
      IF(NFREE(I).EQ.0) GO TO 201
      IN=IABS(NFREE(I))
      NFREE(I)=0
      FREE(IN)=IN
      IF(I.EQ.K) GO TO 201
 1910 CONTINUE
C     *********************************************************************
C     *   STEP 20                                                        *
C     *          IF NO FEASIBLE SOLUTION HAS BEEN REACHED, GO TO STEP 21; *
C     *          OTHERWISE, THE COMPLETE SOLUTION CORRESPONDING TO ZMIN  *
C     *          IS OPTIMAL, SO PRINT THE RESULTS AND STOP.             *
C     *********************************************************************
```

```
 2010 CONTINUE
      IF(ZFLAG.EQ.0) GO TO 2100
      DO 2020 I=1,K
      IF(FLAG(I).EQ.0) GO TO 2020
      LAST(I)=1-LAST(I)
 2020 CONTINUE
      WRITE(6,2025)
 2025 FORMAT(//' OPTIMAL SOLUTION',/)
      DO 2030 I=1,K
      WRITE( 6,2040)I,LAST(I)
 2040 FORMAT( 5X,'VARIABLE ',I3,'  HAS VALUE OF ',I2)
 2030 CONTINUE
      NEWMIN=ZMIN+CSUM
      IF(NTYPE.EQ.0) GO TO 2035
      NEWMIN=-NEWMIN
 2035 WRITE( 6,2050)NEWMIN
 2050 FORMAT(// 5X,'THE OPTIMAL VALUE OF THE OBJECTIVE FUNCTION IS',I10)
      GO TO 5
C     ***********************************************************************
C     *  STEP 21                                                          *
C     *        THERE IS NO FEASIBLE SOLUTION TO THE PROBLEM, SO STOP.     *
C     ***********************************************************************
 2100 WRITE( 6,2110)
 2110 FORMAT(//  5X,'NO FEASIBLE SOLUTION TO PROBLEM')
      GO TO 5
 2000 STOP
      END


/DATA

SAMPLE 0-1 INTEGER PROGRAMMING PROBLEM FROM SECTION 4.2.1
    3    3    1    2    0    0
         0         4
         2        -5         3
         1         3
         4         1         3
         1         1
         0         1         1
         4         3         2
BACKPACK PROBLEM FROM SECTION 4.2.3
    1    4    1    0    0    1
         0         5
         5         2         1         3
         6         3         1         5
   SAMPLE OF 0-1 INTEGER PROGRAMMING    SECTION 4.2.4
    2    3    1    1    0    0
         0         4
         3         ?         1
         1         2
         1        -3         4
         2        -4         6
```

```
SAMPLE 0-1 INTEGER PROGRAMMING PROBLEM FROM SECTION 4.2.1

    THE ORIGINAL COEFFICIENTS OF THE CONSTRAINTS

              CODE 0 ==>   <OR= CONSTRAINT
              CODE 1 ==>   >OR= CONSTRAINT
              CODE 2 ==>   = CONSTRAINT


I CODE CONSTANT  A(I,1)   A(I,2)   A(I,3)   A(I,4)   A(I,5)   A(I,6)   A(I,7)   A(I,8)

1  0      4        2        -5        3
2  1      3        4         1        3
3  1      1        0         1        1


    THE COEFFICIENTS IN THE ORIGINAL OBJECTIVE FUNCTION TO BE MINIMIZED ARE:

                    4         3        2


    CONVERTED CONSTRAINTS

1            4       -2        5       -3
2           -3        4        1        3
3           -1        0        1        1


STEP #      PARTIAL SOLUTIONS   (NFREE)                                        ZMIN

   0          0    0    0                                                   10000000
   1          3    0    0                                                          2
   2         -3    0    0                                                          2


OPTIMAL SOLUTION

      VARIABLE    1   HAS VALUE OF   0
      VARIABLE    2   HAS VALUE OF   0
      VARIABLE    3   HAS VALUE OF   1


    THE OPTIMAL VALUE OF THE OBJECTIVE FUNCTION IS              2
```

BACKPACK PROBLEM FROM SECTION 4.2.3

THE ORIGINAL COEFFICIENTS OF THE CONSTRAINTS

        CODE 0 ==>   <OR= CONSTRAINT
        CODE 1 ==>   >OR= CONSTRAINT
        CODE 2 ==>   = CONSTRAINT

I CODE CONSTANT A(I,1) A(I,2) A(I,3) A(I,4) A(I,5) A(I,6) A(I,7) A(I,8)

1   0   5   5   2   1   3

THE COEFFICIENTS IN THE ORIGINAL OBJECTIVE FUNCTION TO BE MAXIMIZED ARE:

            6   3   1   5

CONVERTED CONSTRAINTS

1   -6   5   2   1   3

STEP #	PARTIAL SOLUTIONS			(NFREE)	ZMIN
0	0	0	0	0	10000000
1	1	0	0	0	10000000
2	1	4	0	0	11
3	1	-4	0	0	11
4	1	-4	3	0	7
5	1	-4	-3	0	7
6	-1	0	0	0	7
7	-1	4	0	0	7
8	-1	-4	0	0	7

OPTIMAL SOLUTION

    VARIABLE   1 HAS VALUE OF 0
    VARIABLE   2 HAS VALUE OF 1
    VARIABLE   3 HAS VALUE OF 0
    VARIABLE   4 HAS VALUE OF 1

THE OPTIMAL VALUE OF THE OBJECTIVE FUNCTION IS   8

```
SAMPLE OF 0-1 INTEGER PROGRAMMING    SECTION 4.2.4

THE ORIGINAL COEFFICIENTS OF THE CONSTRAINTS

            CODE 0 ==>   <OR= CONSTRAINT
            CODE 1 ==>   >OR= CONSTRAINT
            CODE 2 ==>   = CONSTRAINT

I CODE CONSTANT  A(I,1)  A(I,2)  A(I,3)  A(I,4)  A(I,5)  A(I,6)  A(I,7)  A(I,8)

1   0      4       3       2       1
2   1      2       1      -3       4

    THE COEFFICIENTS IN THE ORIGINAL OBJECTIVE FUNCTION TO BE MINIMIZED ARE:

              2      -4       6

    CONVERTED CONSTRAINTS

1          2       -3       2      -1
2         -5        1       3       4

STEP #     PARTIAL SOLUTIONS   (NFREE)                                ZMIN

   0       0    0    0                                              10000000
   1       3    0    0                                              10000000
   2       3    2    0                                                    10
   3       3   -2    0                                                    10
   4       3   -2    1                                                    10
   5       3   -2   -1                                                    10
   6      -3    0    0                                                    10

OPTIMAL SOLUTION

    VARIABLE   1   HAS VALUE OF   0
    VARIABLE   2   HAS VALUE OF   0
    VARIABLE   3   HAS VALUE OF   1

    THE OPTIMAL VALUE OF THE OBJECTIVE FUNCTION IS          6
```

4.2.6 Summary of Implicit Enumeration

Implicit enumeration has a number of important advantages that make it attractive as a method for solving integer LP problems. However, like most methods for solving problems it has some disadvantages. Some of the positive attributes for implicit enumeration are:

1 Addition and subtraction are the only arithmetic operations used to carry out the algorithm in the computer. These operations are extremely fast compared to multiplication and division.

2 The algorithm is very fast because of attribute 1.

3 Attribute 1 makes it possible to use integer arithmetic in the computer thus eliminating the accumulation of round-off errors.

4 The number of constraints in the original problem does not grow as it does with other methods.

5 Attribute 4 cuts down on memory requirements so the algorithm may use less storage than other methods.

6 The algorithm usually reaches a feasible solution very quickly. Hence, branches of the solution tree can be pruned early, which ultimately should lead to the optimal solution in a reasonable amount of time.

Some of the negative attributes of implicit enumeration are:

1 The implicit enumeration procedure described in Algorithm 4.1 is only capable of solving 0-1 integer LP problems. Consequently it is not too practical for a very large general problem where each of the variables must be represented by many binary (0-1) variables before it can be solved using implicit enumeration. For example, if the variable X in a given problem can take on any integer value between 0 and 10 inclusively, then it could be replaced by four variables as follows:

$$X = 2^0 X_0 + 2^1 X_1 + 2^2 X_2 + 3X_3$$

where $X_0, X_1, X_2, X_3 = 0$ or 1.

The general transformation for a variable X that can take on any integer value between 0 and T inclusively is:

$$X = 2^0 X_0 + 2^1 X_1 + 2^2 X_2 + \cdots + 2^{k-2} X_{k-2} + \left(T - \sum_{j=0}^{k-2} 2^j \right) X_{k-1}$$

where k is the smallest integer such that $2^k - 1 \geqslant T$ and $X_i = 0$ or 1; $i = 0, 1, \ldots, k - 1$. In a very large general integer programming problem where the variables can take on large integer values, the number of binary (0-1) variables needed could very easily prohibit the use of implicit enumeration.

2 The number of nodes of the solution tree to check before reaching the optimal solution may be extremely large, thus prohibiting the use of implicit enumeration.

The cutting plane algorithm described in Section 4.3 tends to converge rapidly in many cases, so in general, a good rule of thumb for solving integer LP problems is to use a cutting-plane algorithm first. If it does not converge to the optimal solution in a reasonable amount of time, switch to an implicit enumeration or branch-and-bound algorithm.

4.3 CUTTING-PLANE TECHNIQUE

The cutting-plane technique for solving integer LP problems is simply a technique that squeezes down on the set of all feasible solutions of the corresponding noninteger LP problem by sequentially introducing additional constraints (cuts) until an optimal solution of the integer programming problem is reached. The main problem associated with the cutting-plane technique is how to construct new constraints.

Basically the cutting-plane technique involves three steps:

Step 1
Ignore the integrality constraints and solve the corresponding linear programming problem using the simplex algorithm.

Step 2
If the solution from step 1 is an all-integer solution, the integer programming problem is solved; otherwise, go to step 3.

Step 3
Add a new constraint (cut) to the problem and return to step 1.

4.3.1 Gomory's Cutting-Plane Algorithm Illustrated

Consider the integer LP problem

$$\text{maximize:} \quad z = x_1 + x_2$$
$$\text{subject to:} \quad 2x_1 + x_2 \leqslant 6$$
$$4x_1 + 5x_2 \leqslant 20$$
$$x_1, x_2 \text{ are nonnegative integers}$$

The solution of this problem using Gomory's cutting-plane algorithm is obtained as follows:

Step 1
Add a slack variable to each constraint to give the equivalent problem

$$\text{maximize:} \quad z = x_1 + x_2$$
$$\text{subject to:} \quad 2x_1 + x_2 + x_3 \quad\quad = 6$$
$$4x_1 + 5x_2 \quad\quad + x_4 = 20$$
$$x_1, x_2 \text{ are nonnegative integers}$$
$$x_3, x_4 \geqslant 0$$

We will see later that the coefficients and constants in the constraint equations must be integer-valued to use this algorithm, which necessarily makes x_3 and x_4 integer values in the optimal solution.

Step 2

Drop the integrality restriction and rewrite the equivalent problem as

$$\text{maximize: } z$$

$$
\begin{aligned}
\text{subject to: } z - x_1 - x_2 \qquad\qquad &= 0 && (4.1)\\
2x_1 + x_2 + x_3 \qquad &= 6 && (4.2)\\
4x_1 + 5x_2 \qquad\quad + x_4 &= 20 && (4.3)\\
x_1, x_2, x_3, x_4 &\geqslant 0
\end{aligned}
$$

Step 3

Solve the equivalent problem using the simplex method.

(*a*) The first basic feasible solution is

$$x_3 = 6$$
$$x_4 = 20$$
$$z = 0$$

(*b*) Variable x_1 is selected to enter the basis and variable x_3 is selected to leave the basis.

(*c*) The transformed equations are

$$z \quad -\frac{1}{2}x_2 + \frac{1}{2}x_3 \qquad = 3$$

$$x_1 + \frac{1}{2}x_2 + \frac{1}{2}x_3 \qquad = 3$$

$$3x_2 - 2x_3 + x_4 = 8$$

and the new basic feasible solution is

$$x_1 = 3$$
$$x_4 = 8$$
$$z = 3$$

(*d*) Variable x_2 is selected to enter the basis and variable x_4 is chosen to leave the basis.

(*e*) The transformed equations are

$$z \qquad +\frac{1}{6}x_3 + \frac{1}{6}x_4 = \frac{13}{3} \qquad (4.4)$$

$$x_1 \qquad +\frac{5}{6}x_3 - \frac{1}{6}x_4 = \frac{5}{3} \qquad (4.5)$$

$$x_2 - \frac{2}{3}x_3 + \frac{1}{3}x_4 = \frac{8}{3} \qquad (4.6)$$

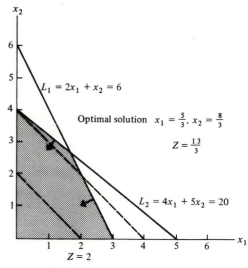

FIGURE 4.5
Graphic solution of noninteger LP problem.

and the new basic solution is

$$x_1 = \frac{5}{3}$$

$$x_2 = \frac{8}{3}$$

$$z = \frac{13}{3}$$

This is an optimal LP solution. Figure 4.5 illustrates this solution graphically.

Since we have merely performed elementary transformations on the original system of equations, Equations (4.5) and (4.6) must be satisfied by every feasible solution of the LP problem when the variables are not restricted to integer values. Consequently, to get a finer cut or constraint on the set of feasible solutions of the noninteger LP problem, we select an equation that contains a variable with a noninteger value in the solution just obtained. Since $x_1 = \frac{5}{3}$ and $x_2 = \frac{8}{3}$ in the above solution, arbitrarily select the equation that contains x_2, namely, Equation (4.6) for further restriction.

Step 4
Rewrite Equation (4.6) as

$$0 \cdot x_1 + (1 + 0)x_2 + \left(-1 + \frac{1}{3}\right)x_3 + \left(0 + \frac{1}{3}\right)x_4 = \left(2 + \frac{2}{3}\right)$$

or

$$0 \cdot x_1 + 0 \cdot x_2 + \frac{1}{3}x_3 + \frac{1}{3}x_4 = \frac{2}{3} + (2 - x_2 + x_3)$$

Step 5

Assume all of the variables in the equation

$$\frac{1}{3}x_3 + \frac{1}{3}x_4 = \frac{2}{3} + (2 - x_2 + x_3) \qquad (4.7)$$

have their optimal integer solution values (including the slack variables x_3 and x_4). We assume the original problem was formulated such that when the original variables take on their optimal integer values, the slack variables will also have integer values. This can always be done by multiplying each constraint in the original problem by the appropriate value to remove the fractional coefficients.

From Equation (4.7), we have

$$\frac{1}{3}x_3 + \frac{1}{3}x_4 \geqslant 0$$

since x_3 and x_4 are positive integers (possibly 0). Thus,

$$\frac{2}{3} + (2 - x_2 + x_3) \geqslant 0 \qquad (4.8)$$

and $2 - x_2 + x_3 = 0$ or a positive integer value, which implies that $\frac{2}{3}$ is a lower bound on the quantity on the right side of Equation (4.7) and thus, is a lower bound on the quantity on the left side. Hence,

$$\frac{1}{3}x_3 + \frac{1}{3}x_4 \geqslant \frac{2}{3}$$

or

$$x_3 + x_4 \geqslant 2 \qquad (4.9)$$

Step 6

Subtract a surplus variable *from* and add an artificial variable *to* the left side of constraint (4.9) to give

$$x_3 + x_4 - x_5 + x_6 = 2 \qquad (4.10)$$

Assign an arbitrarily small negative cost coefficient, $-T$, to the artificial variable x_6. Use Equation (4.10) and Equations (4.4)-(4.6) as the new constraint equations and find the new LP solution. That is,

maximize: z

subject to: $z \quad + \frac{1}{6}x_3 + \frac{1}{6}x_4 \quad + Tx_6 = \frac{13}{3}$

$\qquad x_1 \quad + \frac{5}{6}x_3 - \frac{1}{6}x_4 \qquad = \frac{5}{3}$

$$x_2 - \frac{2}{3}x_3 + \frac{1}{3}x_4 \qquad\qquad = \frac{8}{3}$$

$$x_3 + \quad x_4 - x_5 + \quad x_6 = 2$$

The last equation is multiplied by $-T$ and added to the first equation to give

$$z \qquad + \left(-T + \frac{1}{6}\right)x_3 + \left(-T + \frac{1}{6}\right)x_4 + Tx_5 \qquad = \frac{13}{3} - 2T$$

$$x_1 \quad + \qquad \frac{5}{6}x_3 - \qquad \frac{1}{6}x_4 \qquad\qquad = \frac{5}{3}$$

$$x_2 - \qquad \frac{2}{3}x_3 + \qquad \frac{1}{3}x_4 \qquad\qquad = \frac{8}{3}$$

$$x_3 + \qquad\qquad x_4 - \quad x_5 + x_6 = 2$$

(a) Select x_4 to enter and then x_6 will leave.

(b) The transformed equations are

$$z \qquad\qquad\qquad + \frac{1}{6}x_5 + \left(T - \frac{1}{6}\right)x_6 = 4$$

$$x_1 \quad + x_3 \qquad -\frac{1}{6}x_5 + \qquad \frac{1}{6}x_6 = 2$$

$$x_2 - x_3 \qquad + \frac{1}{3}x_5 - \qquad \frac{1}{3}x_6 = 2$$

$$x_3 + x_4 - \quad x_5 + \qquad x_6 = 2$$

and the basic feasible solution is

$$x_1 = 2$$
$$x_2 = 2$$
$$z = 4$$

This is an optimal integer solution, so stop.

Each time an optimal LP solution is obtained, we check to see if it is an integer solution. If it is not, all artificial variables (basic and nonbasic) are eliminated from the final LP solution equations before a new cut is constructed. In this example, no artificial variables were added to the original problem, so none had to be eliminated before constructing the cut [constraint (4.9)]. Also, the second LP solution was an optimal integer solution, so no further constraining was necessary. Had we chosen to use Equation (4.5) (the equation containing x_1) to construct the initial cut, more than one cut would have been required to get an optimal integer solution. This is illustrated by the computer solution of this problem which is printed after the program in Section 4.3.3.

Note: To illustrate graphically the cut [constraint (4.9)] that was developed in steps 4 and 5, we observe that the slack variable in Equation (4.2) can be expressed as a function of x_1 and x_2. This is,

$$2x_1 + x_2 + x_3 = 6$$

can be expressed as

$$x_3 = 6 - 2x_1 - x_2$$

Likewise, x_4 in Equation (4.3) can be expressed as

$$x_4 = 20 - 4x_1 - 5x_2$$

If we substitute into constraint (4.9), we get

$$(6 - 2x_1 - x_2) + (20 \; - 4x_1 - 5x_2) \geqslant 2$$
$$- \; 6x_1 - 6x_2 + 26 \quad \geqslant 2$$
$$x_1 + x_2 \quad \leqslant 4 \qquad (4.11)$$

Figure 4.6 illustrates this cut. Constraint (4.11) "cuts" away the feasible region of the noninteger problem that is above the line $x_1 + x_2 = 4$. Thus, constraint (4.11) acts as a cutting plane to reduce the size of the feasible region for the noninteger problem. It is important to note that this procedure of adding constraints (cuts) to the noninteger problem will never cut away feasible integer solutions.

Since the equation $x_1 + x_2 = 4$ is parallel to the objective function $z = x_1 + x_2$, it should be clear from Figure 4.6 that the optimal solutions are

$$x_1 = 0, x_2 = 4$$
$$x_1 = 1, x_2 = 3$$
$$x_1 = 2, x_2 = 2$$

with $z = 4$.

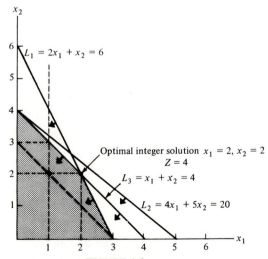

FIGURE 4.6
Graphic solution of integer LP problem.

4.3.2   Algorithm 4.2—Gomory's Cutting-Plane Solution for Integer Programming

Assume the integer LP problem to be solved has the form

$$\text{maximize:} \quad z = \sum_{j=1}^{n} c_j x_j$$

$$\text{subject to:} \quad \sum_{j=1}^{n} a_{ij} x_j = b_i \quad i = 1, 2, \ldots, m \qquad (4.12)$$

where b_i is a nonnegative integer for $i = 1, 2, \ldots, m$, and the a_{ij}'s have integer values for all i and j. If any of the coefficients or constants in the original constraints were not integers, it is assumed that the corresponding constraints were multiplied by an appropriate constant to remove the fractional values before slack, surplus, and/or artificial variables were introduced to give Equation (4.12). For example, if one of the original constraints had been

$$0.92x_1 + 0.2x_2 + 6.43x_3 \geqslant 16.25$$

it should have been multiplied by 100 to give

$$92x_1 + 20x_2 + 643x_3 \geqslant 1625$$

A surplus variable x_4 and an artificial variable x_5 should then have been subtracted and added, respectively, to the left side of the constraint to give

$$92x_1 + 20x_2 + 643x_3 - x_4 + x_5 = 1625$$

Step 1
Solve the associated LP problem without the integer restriction on the variables using the simplex algorithm.

Step 2
If the solution from the previous simplex solution (from step 1 the first time through) is an all-integer solution, the original integer LP problem is solved, so print the results and stop; otherwise, go to step 3.

Steps 3–6 select an additional constraint (cut) to add to the problem.

Step 3
Eliminate all artificial variables (basic and nonbasic) from the final LP solution equations before selecting a variable, say x_k, that does not have an integer value in the simplex solution of the last LP model solved.

Step 4
The variable x_k has a coefficient of *1* in one of the equations, say equation Q_t, in the final solution of the simplex algorithm, and a coefficient of *0* in each of the other equations. Replace each coefficient in Q_t and the constant on the right side of Q_t with

their fractional parts. For example, replace -2 with 0, $2\frac{4}{7}$ with $\frac{4}{7}$, $-\frac{2}{3}$ with $-\frac{2}{3}$, $-3\frac{1}{7}$ with $-\frac{1}{7}$, etc.

Step 5

Add 1 to each negative fractional result from step 4. Write the resulting equation as a greater-than-or-equal-to constraint.

Step 6

Subtract a surplus *from* and add an artificial variable *to* the left side of the *new* Q_t constraint from steps 4 and 5 to give an equality. Place the resulting equation after the last equation in the final solution of the last LP model solved. Assign an arbitrarily small negative cost coefficient $-T$ to the artificial variable. Multiply the new equation by $-T$ and add the resulting equation to the objective function constraint equation in the final solution of the last LP model solved. (See step 6 of the example in Section 4.3.1.)

Step 7

Carry out additional iterations of the simplex algorithm starting with the newly formed equations from step 6. Continue the process until an optimal LP solution is obtained. Return to step 2.

Algorithm 4.2 makes use of the regular simplex method that was presented in Chapter 4. However, to make the cutting-plane algorithm more efficient, a method called the *dual simplex method* is generally used to solve the linear programming problem after each cut.

Readers interested in the dual simplex method and its use in cutting-plane algorithms should see Garfinkel and Nemhauser [4], Salkin [11], or Hadley [8].

4.3.3   Computer Program for Algorithm 4.2

This program for Gomory's cutting-plane algorithm is set up to solve small all-integer LP problems (maximum of 15 constraints and 15 variables in the original problem). It will solve minimization as well as maximization problems. The comments at the beginning of the program explain how to enter the data. In particular, all coefficients and constants in the constraints must be entered as integers. The user can supply an upper limit on the number of cuts that will be tolerated, or if an upper limit is not supplied, the program will stop if an optimal integer solution has not been obtained after 15 cuts.

The diet problem in Section 4.3.4 took 2.1 s of IBM 370/168 time to solve. The data for the problem follow the program listing.

The program as listed occupies 52K bytes of core storage. This includes the space needed for the two subroutines—SSARTV and SIMPLX—which are called in the mainline Gomory program. The subroutines are listed after the mainline of the simplex program and can be lifted intact and placed after the mainline Gomory program.

The last row of the final tableau (table) in the printout is the transformed objective function constraint equation of the *maximization* problem without the z variable. For example, in the printout of the first "final tableau" for the example from Section 4.3.1, row 3 is printed as

$$0.0 \quad 0.0 \quad 0.167 \quad 0.167 \quad 4.333$$

when in reality, we mean

$$z + 0x_1 + 0x_2 + 0.167x_3 + 0.167x_4 = 4.333$$

Thus, when $x_3 = x_4 = 0$, the optimal LP basic feasible solution is

$$x_1 = 1.67$$
$$x_2 = 2.67$$

and $z = 4.333$.

The data and results for the problems in Sections 4.3.1 and 4.3.4 follow the program. For the diet problem in Section 4.3.4, basic feasible solutions 1–12 for the original LP problem are omitted. The diet problem was solved with only two cuts when the *first* fractional variable in the basic solution of the final LP solution was used to build the next cut. If a cut is built using the equation corresponding to the basic variable with the *maximum* fractional part, the algorithm will not converge in 15 cuts. This illustrates the sensitivity of cutting-plane algorithms.

In the printout for this example, note that the optimal LP solution values of the objective function are

$$z = 63.55 \quad \text{first solution}$$
$$z = 62.90 \quad \text{after first cut}$$
$$z = 65.00 \quad \text{after second cut}$$

Of course, z should not have decreased after the first cut was introduced; however, the decrease was due to round-off error that was introduced by the large difference between the values of the original coefficients. Likewise, the value -77.74 in the last column of the last row of the final tableau before an optimal integer solution is reached should be -65.00. Here again, round-off error took its toll. In any case, the program converged in two cuts.

```
C     *****************************************************************
C     *                                                               *
C     *     **   ALGORITHM 4.2 INTEGER PROGRAMMING  GOMORY'S CUTTING PLANE  **  *
C     *                                                               *
C     * THIS PROGRAM IS DESIGNED TO SOLVE INTEGER LINEAR PROGRAMMING MODELS  *
C     *   USING GOMORY'S CUTTING PLANE ALGORITHM.  IT WILL NORMALLY SOLVE    *
C     *   MODELS WITH UP TO 15 CONSTRAINTS AND 15 VARIABLES IN THE ORIGINAL  *
C     *   MODEL.  LARGER PROBLEMS CAN BE SOLVED BY CHANGING THE NUMBERS IN THE *
C     *   DIMENSION AND COMMON STATEMENTS IN THE MAINLINE AS WELL AS IN THE   *
C     *   SUBROUTINES SSARTV AND SIMPLX.  ALL COEFFICIENTS AND CONSTANTS IN   *
C     *   THE CONSTRAINTS MUST BE ENTERED AS WHOLE NUMBERS (REAL FORM).       *
C     *   THE USER CAN SUPPLY AN UPPER LIMIT ON THE NUMBER OF CUTS HE WILL    *
C     *   TOLERATE, OR IF AN UPPER LIMIT IS NOT SUPPLIED, THE PROGRAM WILL    *
C     *   TERMINATE IF AN OPTIMAL INTEGER SOLUTION HAS NOT BEEN OBTAINED AFTER *
C     *   15 CUTS.  THE PROGRAM SUPPLIES THE NECESSARY SLACK, SURPLUS, AND    *
C     *   ARTIFICIAL VARIABLES.  IT WILL TREAT MINIMIZATION AS WELL AS MAX-   *
C     *   IMIZATION PROBLEMS.  EACH COST COEFFICIENT MUST BE LESS THAN 100    *
C     *   IN ABSOLUTE VALUE.                                                  *
C     *   SUBROUTINE SSARTV SUPPLIES SLACK,SURPLUS,AND ARTIFICIAL VARIABLES.  *
C     *   SUBROUTINE SIMPLX DOES THE WORK OF THE SIMPLEX ALGORITHM.           *
C     *                                                               *
C     * IT IS DESIGNED                                                *
C     *   TO READ                                                     *
C     *       CARD 1    COLS 2-80   TITLE  DESCRIPTION OF THE PROBLEM USING *
C     *                                    ANY CHARACTERS ON KEYPUNCH       *
C     *                                    ** COLUMN 1 MUST BE LEFT BLANK ** *
C     *       CARD 2    COLS 1- 5   M NUMBER OF CONSTRAINTS (I5)       *
C     *                      6-10   K NUMBER OF VARIABLES (I5)         *
C     *                     11-15   NLET NUMBER OF <OR= CONSTRAINTS (I5) *
C     *                     16-20   NGET NUMBER OF >OR= CONSTRAINTS (I5) *
C     *                     21-25   NET  NUMBER OF = CONSTRAINTS (I5)  *
C     *                     26-30   NTYPE 0 MINIMIZATION PROBLEM       *
C     *                                   1 MAXIMIZATION PROBLEM (I5)  *
C     *       CARDS 3 TO T    M SETS OF CARDS, ONE SET FOR EACH CONSTRAINT *
C     *           CARD I    COLS 1-10   CODE(I)  0 IF <OR= CONSTRAINT  *
C     *                                          1 IF >OR= CONSTRAINT  *
C     *                                          2 IF = CONSTRAINT (I10) *
C     *                          11-20   B(I)  CONSTANT IN CONSTRAINT I (F10.0)*
C     *           CARD I+1   A(I,J) J COEFFICIENTS OF CONSTRAINT I     *
C     *                             PUNCH ROWWISE IN 8F10.0 FORMAT     *
C     *                             IF K>8, CONTINUE ON NEXT CARD.     *
C     *       CARD T+1      C(J)  COST COEFFICIENTS OF OBJECTIVE FUNCTION *
C     *                          PUNCH ROWWISE IN 8F10.0 FORMAT        *
C     *                          IF K>8, CONTINUE ON NEXT CARD.        *
C     *       CARD Z    COLS 1- 5   NOPT 0 PRINT ONLY OPTIMAL SOLUTION *
C     *                                  1 PRINT ALL SOLUTIONS (I5)    *
C     *                      6-10   MAXCT MAXIMUM NUMBER OF ITERATIONS (CUTS) *
C     *                             USER WILL TOLERATE.  IF LEFT BLANK *
C     *                             PROGRAM WILL STOP AFTER 15 CUTS IF *
C     *                             AN OPTIMAL INTEGER SOLUTION HAS NOT *
C     *                             BEEN OBTAINED. (I5)               *
C     *           TO SOLVE MORE THAN ONE PROBLEM AT A TIME, REPEAT THE *
C     *           READ SEQUENCE, AND STACK THE DATA ONE BEHIND THE OTHER *
C     *                                                               *
C     *   TO CALCULATE AND PRINT                                      *
C     *           Z  OPTIMAL VALUE OF THE OBJECTIVE FUNCTION          *
C     *       XB(I)  THE SUBSCRIPT OF THE BASIC VARIABLES IN THE      *
C     *              OPTIMAL BASIC FEASIBLE SOLUTION                   *
C     *   A(I,NP1)  THE VALUE OF THE BASIC VARIABLES                  *
C     *                                                               *
C     *****************************************************************
```

```
      COMMON B(26),C(76),CODE(26),KP1,MP1,N,K,M,NGET,NLET,NET,NTYPE,NP1,
     *NC,NC1,INDEXG,INDEXL,INDEXE,NFLAG,BASICS,OPTSOL,SUM,NOPT,IFLAG
      INTEGER CODE, XB(76),BASICS,OPTSOL
      DIMENSION A(26,76)
      REAL*4 TITLE(20)
   50 READ(5,10,END=2000)TITLE
   10 FORMAT(20A4)
      WRITE(6,15)TITLE
   15 FORMAT('1',20A4,//)
      READ(5,20)M,K,NLET,NGET,NET,NTYPE
   20 FORMAT(6I5)
      DO 25 I=1,M
      READ(5,30)CODE(I),B(I)
   30 FORMAT(I10,F10.0)
      READ(5,29)(A(I,J),J=1,K)
   29 FORMAT(8F10.0)
   25 CONTINUE
      READ(5,29)(C(J),J=1,K)
      WRITE(6,40)
   40 FORMAT(5X,'THE ORIGINAL COEFFICIENTS OF THE CONSTRAINTS',//15X,'CO
     *DE 0 ==>  <OR= CONSTRAINT',/15X,'CODE 1 ==>  >OR= CONSTRAINT',/15X
     *,'CODE 2 ==>  = CONSTRAINT',//)
      WRITE(6,55)
   55 FORMAT(' I CODE CONSTANT  A(I,1)  A(I,2)  A(I,3)  A(I,4)  A(I,5)
     * A(I,6)  A(I,7)  A(I,8)',/)
      DO 45 I=1,M
      WRITE(6,51)I,CODE(I),B(I)
   51 FORMAT(I3,I4,F9.2)
      WRITE(6,52)(A(I,J),J=1,K)
   52 FORMAT('+',15X,8F8.2,/(16X,8F8.2))
   45 CONTINUE
      IF(NTYPE.NE.0) GO TO 35
      WRITE(6,36)
   36 FORMAT(//  5X,'THE COEFFICIENTS IN THE ORIGINAL OBJECTIVE FUNCTION
     * TO BE MINIMIZED ARE:',/)
      GO TO 37
   35 WRITE(6,38)
   38 FORMAT(//  5X,'THE COEFFICIENTS IN THE ORIGINAL OBJECTIVE FUNCTION
     * TO BE MAXIMIZED ARE:',/)
   37 WRITE(6,39)(C(J),J=1,K)
   39 FORMAT(16X,8F8.2/16X,8F8.2)
      READ(5,20) NOPT,MAXCT
      KOUNT=K
      NCUT=0
      NVS=0
C     ***********************************************************************
  150 CALL SSARTV(A,XB)
      IF(IFLAG.EQ.1) GO TO 50
      ICOUNT=1
  300 BASICS=0
      OPTSOL=0
      WRITE(6,160)
  160 FORMAT(// )
      CALL SIMPLX(A,XB)
      IF(NFLAG.EQ.1.OR.NFLAG.EQ.2) GO TO 50
      WRITE(6,121)
  121 FORMAT(//' FINAL TABLEAU  (LAST ELEMENT OF ITH ROW IS VALUE OF XB(
     *I))',/)
      DO 119  I=1,MP1
  119 WRITE(6,120)I,(A(I,J),J=1,NP1)
  120 FORMAT(/I4,7F10.3,/,(4X,7F10.3))




      IF(NTYPE.NE.1) SUM=-SUM
  220 WRITE(6,230) SUM
  230 FORMAT(//5X,'** THE OPTIMAL VALUE OF THE OBJECTIVE FUNCTION IS **
     *',F12.2)
C     ***********************************************************************
C     *            ELIMINATE ARTIFICIAL VARIABLES IN BASIS                 *
C     ***********************************************************************
      ID=1
```

```
   63 DO 60 KK=ID,M
      IF(XB(KK).GE.NC1) GO TO 61
   60 CONTINUE
      GO TO 70
   61 IF(KK.EQ.M) GO TO 64
      M=M-1
      DO 62 II=KK,M
      XB(II)=XB(II+1)
      DO 62 JJ=1,NP1
   62 A(II,JJ)=A(II+1,JJ)
      ID=KK
      GO TO 63
   64 M=M-1
C     *****************************************************************
C     *        IF MP1=M+1, THEN NO EQUATIONS IN FINAL L.P. SOLUTION  *
C     *         WERE ELIMINATED, SO GO TO STATEMENT 67, OTHERWISE, MOVE *
C     *          OBJECTIVE FUNCTION COEFFICIENTS TO THE M+1 ROW      *
C     *****************************************************************
   70 IF(MP1.EQ.M+1) GO TO 67
      DO 66 JJ=1,NP1
   66 A(M+1,JJ)=A(MP1,JJ)
   67 IF(NP1.EQ.NC1) GO TO 71
      N=NC1-1
C     *****************************************************************
C     *        ELIMINATE COLUMNS IN FINAL L.P. SOLUTION CORRESPONDING TO *
C     *             ARTIFICIAL VARIABLES.                           *
C     *****************************************************************
      DO 72 II=1,MP1
   72 A(II,N+1)=A(II,NP1)
      NP1=N+1
      MP1=M+1
   71 MP2=M+2
      NP2=N+2
      NP3=N+3
C     *****************************************************************
C     *        CHECK TO SEE IF CURRENT BASIC FEASIBLE SOLUTION IS ALL-INTEGER *
C     *****************************************************************
      NSW=0
      DO 4 I=1,M
      NA=A(I,NP1)
      DIFF=A(I,NP1)-NA
      N1=A(I,NP1)
      N2=A(I,NP1)+.0001
      IF(N1.NE.N2)GO TO 4
      IF(DIFF.LT..001)  GO TO 4
      IF(XB(I).GT.KOUNT) GO TO 4
      IF(XB(I).NE.NVS) GO TO 517
      NSW=XB(I)
    4 CONTINUE
      IF(NSW.EQ.0) GO TO 519
  517 NCUT=NCUT+1
      NVS=XB(I)
      WRITE(6,127)NCUT,I,XB(I)
  127 FORMAT(//' COEFFICIENTS OF CUT',I4,'  INVOLVING'/5X,'BASIC VARIABL
     *E',I4,'  (ORIGINAL VARIABLE',I4,'  ) FOLLOW:'/)
      GO TO 11
C     *****************************************************************
C     *        OPTIMAL LP SOLUTION IS ALSO AN OPTIMAL INTEGER SOLUTION *
C     *             PRINT MESSAGE AND STOP                          *
C     *****************************************************************
  519 WRITE(6,520)
  520 FORMAT(//' ** LAST BASIC FEASIBLE SOLUTION IS AN OPTIMAL INTEGER S
     *OLUTION **',/)
      WRITE(6,548)SUM
  548 FORMAT(' OPTIMAL VALUE OF OBJECTIVE FUNCTION IS',F12.2)
      WRITE(6,549)
  549 FORMAT(' VARIABLE     VALUE')
      DO 550 I=1,M
  550 WRITE(6,551)XB(I),A(I,NP1)
```

```
  551 FORMAT(I6,F12.2)
      GO TO 50
C     ***********************************************************************
C     *    STEPS 4,5,6                                                     *
C     *           CURRENT BFS IS NOT ALL-INTEGER SO BUILD A NEW GOMORY CUT *
C     ***********************************************************************
   11 DO 5 J=1,NP1
      A(MP2,J)=A(MP1,J)
      N1=ABS(A(I,J))
      N2=ABS(A(I,J))+.0001
      IF(N1.EQ.N2) GO TO 73
      A(MP1,J)=0.0
      GO TO 5
   73 NA=A(I,J)
      A(MP1,J)=A(I,J)-NA
      IF(A(MP1,J).LT.-10.E-5) A(MP1,J)=A(MP1,J)+1
      A(MP2,J)=A(MP2,J)-10.E2*A(MP1,J)
    5 CONTINUE
      DO 6 K=1,MP2
      A(K,NP3)=A(K,NP1)
      A(K,NP2)=0.0
    6 A(K,NP1)=0.0
      A(MP1,NP1)=-1
      A(MP1,NP2)=1
      A(MP2,NP1)=10.E2
      DO 7 J=1,NP2
    7 WRITE(6,522) J,A(MP1,J)
  522 FORMAT(1X,'A(M,',I2,')=',F12.3)
      WRITE(6,523) A(MP1,NP3)
  523 FORMAT(1X,'B(M)=',F12.3//)
      N=NP2
      NP1=N+1
      M=MP1
      MP1=M+1
C     ***********************************************************************
C     *           IF GOMORY'S CUTTING PLANE ALGORITHM HAS NOT CONVERGED IN MAXCT  *
C     *           ITERATIONS ** STOP ** OTHERWISE, CONTINUE TO BUILD CUTS. *
C     ***********************************************************************
      IF(MAXCT.EQ.0) GO TO 16
      IF(ICOUNT.GT.MAXCT) GO TO 18
C     ***********************************************************************
C     *    STEP 7                                                          *
C     *           CARRY OUT ADDITIONAL ITERATIONS OF SIMPLEX ALGORITHM STARTING  *
C     *           WITH THE NEWLY FORMED EQUATIONS.                         *
C     ***********************************************************************
   17 ICCUNT=ICCUNT+1
      XB(M)=N
      NC1=N
      C(N-1)=0
      C(N)=-10.E2
      GO TO 300
   16 IF(ICOUNT.GT.15) GO TO 19
      GO TO 17
   18 WRITE(6,524)
  524 FORMAT(1X,'GOMORY''S CUTTING PLANE ALGORITHM DID NOT CONVERGE TO T
     *HE')
      WRITE(6,525) MAXCT
  525 FORMAT(10X,'OPTIMAL INTEGER SOLUTION IN',I4,' CUTS',////)
      GO TO 50
   19 WRITE(6,524)
      WRITE(6,526)
  526 FORMAT(10X,'OPTIMAL INTEGER SOLUTION IN 15 CUTS'////)
      GO TO 50
 2000 STOP
      END
```

/DATA

```
-EXAMPLE FROM SECTION 4.3.1-
  2     2     2     0     0     1
        0           6.
        2.          1.
        0          20.
        4.          5.
        1.          1.
  1     5
  - DIET PROBLEM FROM SECTION 4.3.4
12    6     6     5     1     0
        1         600.
       45.        45.       105.       40.       50.       50.
        1         325.
       10.        28.        50.       25.       22.       75.
        1       17500.
      415.      9065.      2550.       75.       15.      235.
        1         245.
        8.         3.        53.       27.        5.        8.
        1         500.
       30.        35.        60.       15.       25.       80.
        0          2.
        0          0          0        1.         0         0
        0          4.
        1.         0          0         0         0         0
        0          4.
        0          1.         0         0         0         0
        0          4.
        0          0          1.        0         0         0
        0          4.
        0          0          0         0        1.         0
        0          4.
        0          0          0         0         0        1.
        2         14.
        1.         1.         1.        1.        1.        1.
        5.         5.         8.        2.        6.        3.
  0    10
```

```
-EXAMPLE FROM SECTION 4.3.1-

    THE ORIGINAL COEFFICIENTS OF THE CONSTRAINTS

                CODE 0 ==>  <OR= CONSTRAINT
                CODE 1 ==>  >OR= CONSTRAINT
                CODE 2 ==>  = CONSTRAINT

I CODE CONSTANT  A(I,1)  A(I,2)  A(I,3)  A(I,4)  A(I,5)  A(I,6)  A(I,7)  A(I,8)

1   0    6.00    2.00    1.00
2   0   20.00    4.00    5.00


    THE COEFFICIENTS IN THE ORIGINAL OBJECTIVE FUNCTION TO BE MAXIMIZED ARE:

                1.00    1.00


    BASIC SOLUTION   1

       XB( 1)= X( 3)=        6.00
       XB( 2)= X( 4)=       20.00

    CURRENT VALUE OF THE OBJECTIVE FUNCTION IS    0.0


    BASIC SOLUTION   2

       XB( 1)= X( 1)=        3.00
       XB( 2)= X( 4)=        8.00

    CURRENT VALUE OF THE OBJECTIVE FUNCTION IS    0.30000000E+01


    BASIC SOLUTION   3

       XB( 1)= X( 1)=        1.67
       XB( 2)= X( 2)=        2.67

    CURRENT VALUE OF THE OBJECTIVE FUNCTION IS    0.43333330E+01


        THE LAST BASIC FEASIBLE SOLUTION IS OPTIMAL

FINAL TABLEAU  (LAST ELEMENT OF ITH ROW IS VALUE OF XB(I))

   1    1.000     0.0      0.833    -0.167     1.667

   2    0.0       1.000   -0.667     0.333     2.667

   3    0.0       0.0      0.167     0.167     4.333

    ** THE OPTIMAL VALUE OF THE OBJECTIVE FUNCTION IS **        4.33
```

COEFFICIENTS OF CUT   1   INVOLVING
   BASIC VARIABLE   1   (ORIGINAL VARIABLE   1   ) FOLLOW:

```
A(M, 1)=        0.0
A(M, 2)=        0.0
A(M, 3)=        0.833
A(M, 4)=        0.833
A(M, 5)=       -1.000
A(M, 6)=        1.000
B(M)=           0.667
```

   BASIC SOLUTION   1

```
      XB( 1)= X( 1)=        1.67
      XB( 2)= X( 2)=        2.67
      XB( 3)= X( 6)=        0.67
```

      CURRENT VALUE OF THE OBJECTIVE FUNCTION IS   -0.66233325E+03

   BASIC SOLUTION   2

```
      XB( 1)= X( 1)=        1.00
      XB( 2)= X( 2)=        3.20
      XB( 3)= X( 3)=        0.80
```

      CURRENT VALUE OF THE OBJECTIVE FUNCTION IS   0.41999989E+01

         THE LAST BASIC FEASIBLE SOLUTION IS OPTIMAL

FINAL TABLEAU   (LAST ELEMENT OF ITH ROW IS VALUE OF XB(I))

1	1.000	0.0	0.0	-1.000	1.000	-1.000	1.000
2	0.0	1.000	0.0	1.000	-0.800	0.800	3.200
3	0.0	0.0	1.000	1.000	-1.200	1.200	0.800
4	0.0	0.0	0.0	0.0	0.200	999.800	4.200

      ** THE OPTIMAL VALUE OF THE OBJECTIVE FUNCTION IS **   4.20

COEFFICIENTS OF CUT   2   INVOLVING
   BASIC VARIABLE   2   (ORIGINAL VARIABLE   2   ) FOLLOW:

```
A(M, 1)=        0.0
A(M, 2)=        0.0
A(M, 3)=        0.0
A(M, 4)=        0.0
A(M, 5)=        0.200
A(M, 6)=       -1.000
A(M, 7)=        1.000
B(M)=           0.200
```

```
BASIC SOLUTION   1

   XB( 1)= X( 1)=        1.00
   XB( 2)= X( 2)=        3.20
   XB( 3)= X( 3)=        0.80
   XB( 4)= X( 7)=        0.20

CURRENT VALUE OF THE OBJECTIVE FUNCTION IS   -0.19579884E+03


BASIC SOLUTION   2

   XB( 1)= X( 1)=        0.00
   XB( 2)= X( 2)=        4.00
   XB( 3)= X( 3)=        2.00
   XB( 4)= X( 5)=        1.00

CURRENT VALUE OF THE OBJECTIVE FUNCTION IS    0.39999990E+01


      THE LAST BASIC FEASIBLE SOLUTION IS OPTIMAL


FINAL TABLEAU   (LAST ELEMENT OF ITH ROW IS VALUE OF XB(I))


   1     1.000      0.0       0.0      -1.000      0.0       5.000     -5.000
         0.000

   2     0.0        1.000     0.0       1.000      0.0      -4.000      4.000
         4.000

   3     0.0        0.0       1.000     1.000      0.0      -6.000      6.000
         2.000

   4     0.0        0.0       0.0       0.0        1.000     -5.000      5.000
         1.000

   5     0.0        0.0       0.0       0.0        0.0        1.002    998.998
         4.000


   ** THE OPTIMAL VALUE OF THE OBJECTIVE FUNCTION IS **          4.00


** LAST BASIC FEASIBLE SOLUTION IS AN OPTIMAL INTEGER SOLUTION **

OPTIMAL VALUE OF OBJECTIVE FUNCTION IS          4.00
VARIABLE     VALUE
   1         0.00
   2         4.00
   3         2.00
   5         1.00
```

- DIET PROBLEM FROM SECTION 4.3.4

THE ORIGINAL COEFFICIENTS OF THE CONSTRAINTS

CODE 0 ==>   <OR= CONSTRAINT
CODE 1 ==>   >OR= CONSTRAINT
CODE 2 ==>   = CONSTRAINT

I	CODE	CONSTANT	A(I,1)	A(I,2)	A(I,3)	A(I,4)	A(I,5)	A(I,6)	A(I,7)	A(I,8)
1	1	600.00	45.00	45.00	105.00	40.00	50.00	50.00		
2	1	325.00	10.00	28.00	50.00	25.00	22.00	75.00		
3	1	17500.00	415.00	9065.00	2550.00	75.00	15.00	235.00		
4	1	245.00	8.00	3.00	53.00	27.00	5.00	8.00		
5	1	500.00	30.00	35.00	60.00	15.00	25.00	80.00		
6	0	2.00	0.0	0.0	0.0	1.00	0.0	0.0		
7	0	4.00	1.00	0.0	0.0	0.0	0.0	0.0		
8	0	4.00	0.0	1.00	0.0	0.0	0.0	0.0		
9	0	4.00	0.0	0.0	1.00	0.0	0.0	0.0		
10	0	4.00	0.0	0.0	0.0	0.0	1.00	0.0		
11	0	4.00	0.0	0.0	0.0	0.0	0.0	1.00		
12	2	14.00	1.00	1.00	1.00	1.00	1.00	1.00		

THE COEFFICIENTS IN THE ORIGINAL OBJECTIVE FUNCTION TO BE MINIMIZED ARE:

5.00   5.00   8.00   2.00   6.00   3.00

BASIC SOLUTION 13

```
XB( 1)= X( 1)=       4.00
XB( 2)= X( 5)=       0.74
XB( 3)= X( 2)=       0.99
XB( 4)= X( 7)=     179.93
XB( 5)= X( 6)=       4.00
XB( 6)= X(16)=       3.26
XB( 7)= X(15)=       1.73
XB( 8)= X(14)=       3.01
XB( 9)= X( 3)=       2.27
XB(10)= X( 8)=     222.49
XB(11)= X(11)=     159.33
XB(12)= X( 4)=       2.00
```

CURRENT VALUE OF THE OBJECTIVE FUNCTION IS $-0.63553268E+02$

THE LAST BASIC FEASIBLE SOLUTION IS OPTIMAL

FINAL TABLEAU   (LAST ELEMENT OF ITH ROW IS VALUE OF XB(I))

```
1    1.000      0.0        0.0        0.0        0.0        0.0        0.0
     0.0       -0.000     -0.000      0.0       -0.000      1.000      0.0
     0.0        0.0       -0.000      0.0        0.0        0.0        0.0
     0.0       -0.000      4.000

2    0.0        0.0        0.0        0.0        1.000      0.0        0.0
     0.0        0.000      0.015      0.0       -0.667     -0.910      0.0
     0.0        0.0       -0.930      0.0        0.0        0.0        0.0
     0.0        1.076      0.742

3    0.0        1.000      0.0        0.0        0.0        0.0        0.0
     0.0       -0.000      0.006      0.0        0.120     -0.026      0.0
     0.0        0.0       -0.007      0.0        0.0        0.0        0.0
     0.0        0.027      0.987
```

4	0.0	0.0	0.0	0.0	0.0	0.0	1.000
	0.0	0.000	−1.161	0.0	−35.534	−8.366	0.0
	0.0	0.0	−3.419	0.0	0.0	0.0	0.0
	0.0	44.157	179.930				
5	0.0	0.0	0.0	0.0	0.0	1.000	0.0
	0.0	−0.000	0.0	0.0	0.000	0.000	0.0
	0.0	0.0	1.000	0.0	0.0	0.0	0.0
	0.0	−0.000	4.000				
6	0.0	0.0	0.0	0.0	0.0	0.0	0.0
	0.0	−0.000	−0.015	0.0	0.667	0.910	0.0
	0.0	1.000	0.930	0.0	0.0	0.0	0.0
	0.0	−1.076	3.258				
7	0.0	0.0	0.0	0.0	0.0	0.0	0.0
	0.0	0.000	0.021	0.0	0.453	0.064	0.0
	1.000	0.0	0.063	0.0	0.0	0.0	0.0
	0.0	0.103	1.730				
8	0.0	0.0	0.0	0.0	0.0	0.0	0.0
	0.0	0.000	−0.006	0.0	−0.120	0.026	1.000
	0.0	0.0	0.007	0.0	0.0	0.0	0.0
	0.0	−0.027	3.013				
9	0.0	0.0	1.000	0.0	0.0	0.0	0.0
	0.0	−0.000	−0.021	0.0	−0.453	−0.064	0.0
	0.0	0.0	−0.063	0.0	0.0	0.0	0.0
	0.0	−0.103	2.270				
10	0.0	0.0	0.0	0.0	0.0	0.0	0.0
	1.000	−0.001	−0.542	0.0	−8.971	−13.939	0.0
	0.0	0.0	51.202	0.0	0.0	0.0	0.0
	0.0	19.278	222.492				
11	0.0	0.0	0.0	0.0	0.0	0.0	0.0
	0.0	−0.001	−0.663	1.000	−24.663	2.510	0.0
	0.0	0.0	52.735	0.0	0.0	0.0	0.0
	0.0	21.666	159.333				
12	0.0	0.0	0.0	1.000	0.0	0.0	0.0
	0.0	0.000	0.000	0.0	1.000	−0.000	0.0
	0.0	0.0	−0.000	0.0	0.0	0.0	0.0
	0.0	0.000	2.000				
13	0.0	0.0	0.0	0.0	0.0	0.0	0.0
	0.0	0.000	0.037	0.0	4.940	1.209	0.0
	0.0	0.0	3.233	0.0	0.0	0.0	0.0
	0.0	994.152	−76.345				

** THE OPTIMAL VALUE CF THE OBJECTIVE FUNCTION IS **   63.55

```
COEFFICIENTS OF CUT   1   INVOLVING
    BASIC VARIABLE   2   (ORIGINAL VARIABLE   5  ) FOLLOW:

A(M, 1)=        0.0
A(M, 2)=        0.0
A(M, 3)=        0.0
A(M, 4)=        0.0
A(M, 5)=        0.0
A(M, 6)=        0.0
A(M, 7)=        0.0
A(M, 8)=        0.0
A(M, 9)=        0.000
A(M,10)=        0.015
A(M,11)=        0.0
A(M,12)=        0.333
A(M,13)=        0.090
A(M,14)=        0.0
A(M,15)=        0.0
A(M,16)=        0.0
A(M,17)=        0.070
A(M,18)=       -1.000
A(M,19)=        1.000
B(M)=      0.742
```

```
    BASIC SOLUTION   7

        XB( 1)= X( 1)=        4.00
        XB( 2)= X(16)=        4.00
        XB( 3)= X( 2)=        1.70
        XB( 4)= X( 7)=      178.00
        XB( 5)= X( 6)=        4.00
        XB( 6)= X( 4)=        2.00
        XB( 7)= X(15)=        1.70
        XB( 8)= X(14)=        2.30
        XB( 9)= X( 3)=        2.30
        XB(10)= X( 8)=      227.60
        XB(11)= X(11)=      167.50
        XB(12)= X( 9)=     6525.55
        XB(13)= X(13)=        0.00
```

CURRENT VALUE OF THE OBJECTIVE FUNCTION IS $-0.62899872E+02$

THE LAST BASIC FEASIBLE SOLUTION IS OPTIMAL

FINAL TABLEAU   (LAST ELEMENT OF ITH ROW IS VALUE OF XB(I))

```
1    1.000    0.0      0.0      0.0      1.000    0.0      0.0
     0.0      0.0     -0.000    0.0     -1.000    0.0      0.0
     0.0      0.0     -1.000    1.000   -1.000    4.000

2    0.0      0.0      0.0      0.0      1.000    0.0      0.0
     0.0      0.0      0.000    0.0     -0.000    0.0      0.0
     0.0      1.000   -0.000    0.000   -0.000    4.000

3    0.0      1.000    0.0      0.0      0.060    0.0      0.0
     0.0      0.0      0.020    0.0      0.380    0.0      0.0
     0.0      0.0      0.000   -0.900    0.900    1.700

4    0.0      0.0      0.0      0.0     -8.600    0.0      1.000
     0.0      0.0     -1.200    0.0    -27.800    0.0      0.0
     0.0      0.0      5.000   -6.000    6.000  178.000
```

5	0.0	0.0	0.0	0.0	0.000	1.000	0.0
	0.0	0.0	0.000	0.0	0.000	0.0	0.0
	0.0	0.0	1.000	−0.000	0.000	4.000	
6	0.0	0.0	0.0	1.000	0.000	0.0	0.0
	0.0	0.0	0.000	0.0	1.000	0.0	0.0
	0.0	0.0	−0.000	−0.000	0.000	2.000	
7	0.0	0.0	0.0	0.0	0.060	0.0	0.0
	0.0	0.0	0.020	0.0	0.380	0.0	0.0
	1.000	0.0	0.000	0.100	−0.100	1.700	
8	0.0	0.0	0.0	0.0	−0.060	0.0	0.0
	0.0	0.0	−0.020	0.0	−0.380	0.0	1.000
	0.0	0.0	−0.000	0.900	−0.900	2.300	
9	0.0	0.0	1.000	0.0	−0.060	0.0	0.0
	0.0	0.0	−0.020	0.0	−0.380	0.0	0.0
	0.0	0.0	−0.000	−0.100	0.100	2.300	
10	0.0	0.0	0.0	0.0	−13.320	0.0	0.0
	1.000	0.0	−0.440	0.0	6.640	0.0	0.0
	0.0	0.0	65.000	−20.200	20.200	227.600	
11	0.0	0.0	0.0	0.0	3.500	0.0	0.0
	0.0	0.0	−0.500	1.000	−24.500	0.0	0.0
	0.0	0.0	50.000	−7.500	7.500	167.500	
12	0.0	0.0	0.0	0.0	790.902	0.0	0.0
	0.0	1.000	130.300	0.0	2135.710	0.0	0.0
	0.0	0.0	−179.997	−7998.504	7998.504	6525.555	
13	0.0	0.0	0.0	0.0	−1.000	0.0	0.0
	0.0	0.0	0.000	0.0	1.000	1.000	0.0
	0.0	0.0	1.000	−1.000	1.000	0.000	
14	0.0	0.0	0.0	0.0	1.163	0.0	0.0
	0.0	0.0	0.029	0.0	3.608	0.0	0.0
	0.0	0.0	2.035	1.669	998.331	−76.720	

** THE OPTIMAL VALUE OF THE OBJECTIVE FUNCTION IS **   62.90

COEFFICIENTS OF CUT   2   INVOLVING
   BASIC VARIABLE   3 (ORIGINAL VARIABLE   2) FOLLOW:

```
A(M,  1)=      C.C
A(M,  2)=      0.0
A(M,  3)=      0.0
A(M,  4)=      C.0
A(M,  5)=      0.060
A(M,  6)=      0.0
A(M,  7)=      0.0
A(M,  8)=      0.0
A(M,  9)=      0.0
A(M,10)=       C.020
A(M,11)=       0.0
A(M,12)=       0.380
A(M,13)=       0.0
A(M,14)=       0.0
A(M,15)=       0.0
A(M,16)=       0.0
A(M,17)=       0.000
A(M,18)=       C.100
A(M,19)=      −1.000
A(M,20)=       1.000
B(M)=        0.700
```

```
BASIC SOLUTION   5

    XB(  1)= X(  1)=       4.00
    XB(  2)= X(16)=       4.00
    XB(  3)= X(  2)=       1.00
    XB(  4)= X(  7)=     220.00
    XB(  5)= X(  6)=       4.00
    XB(  6)= X(  4)=       2.00
    XB(  7)= X(15)=       1.00
    XB(  8)= X(14)=       3.00
    XB(  9)= X(  3)=       3.00
    XB(10)= X(  8)=     243.00
    XB(11)= X(11)=     185.00
    XB(12)= X(  9)=    1965.03
    XB(13)= X(13)=       0.00
    XB(14)= X(10)=      35.00
```

CURRENT VALUE OF THE OBJECTIVE FUNCTION IS   -0.64999863E+02

THE LAST BASIC FEASIBLE SOLUTION IS OPTIMAL

FINAL TABLEAU   (LAST ELEMENT OF ITH ROW IS VALUE OF XB(I))

```
 1    1.000     C.0      0.0       0.0       1.000     0.0       0.0
      0.0       0.0      0.0       0.0      -1.000     0.0       0.0
      0.0       0.0     -1.000     1.000     0.000    -0.000     4.000

 2    0.0       0.0      0.0       0.0       1.000     0.0       0.0
      0.0       0.0      0.0       0.0      -0.000     0.0       0.0
      0.0       1.000   -0.000     0.000     0.000    -0.000     4.000

 3    0.0       1.000    0.0       0.0      -0.000     0.0       0.0
      0.0       0.0      0.0       0.0       0.000     0.0       0.0
      0.0       0.0     -0.000    -1.000     1.000    -1.000     1.000

 4    0.0       0.0      C.0       0.0      -5.000     0.0       1.000
      0.0       0.0      0.0       0.0      -5.000     0.0       0.0
      0.0       0.0      5.000    -0.000    -60.000    60.000    220.000

 5    0.0       0.0      0.0       0.0       0.000     1.000     0.0
      0.0       0.0      0.0       0.0       0.000     0.0       0.0
      0.0       0.0      1.000    -0.000     0.000    -0.000     4.000

 6    0.0       0.0      0.0       1.000    -0.000     0.0       0.0
      0.0       0.0      0.0       0.0       1.000     0.0       0.0
      0.0       0.0      0.000    -0.000     0.000    -0.000     2.000

 7    0.0       0.0      C.0       0.0      -0.000     0.0       0.0
      0.0       0.0      0.0       0.0      -0.000     0.0       0.0
      1.000     0.0     -C.000    -0.000     1.000    -1.000     1.000

 8    0.0       0.0      0.0       0.0       0.000     0.0       0.0
      0.0       0.0      0.0       0.0      -0.000     0.0       1.000
      0.0       0.0      0.000     1.000    -1.000     1.000     3.000

 9    0.0       0.0      1.000     0.0       0.000     0.0       0.0
      0.0       0.0      0.0       0.0       0.000     0.0       0.0
      0.0       0.0      0.000     0.000    -1.000     1.000     3.000

10    0.0       0.0      0.0       0.0      -12.000    0.0       0.0
      1.000     0.0      0.0       0.0       15.000    0.0       0.0
      0.0       0.0      65.000   -18.000   -22.000    22.000    243.000

11    0.0       0.0      0.0       0.0       5.000     0.0       0.0
      0.0       0.0      0.0       1.000    -15.000    0.0       0.0
      0.0       0.0      50.000   -5.000    -25.000    25.000    185.000
```

12	0.0	0.0	0.0	0.0	400.000	0.0	0.0
	0.0	1.000	0.0	0.0	-339.996	0.0	0.0
	0.0	0.0	-130.004	-8650.004	6515.000	-6515.000	1965.030
13	0.0	0.0	0.0	0.0	-1.000	0.0	0.0
	0.0	0.0	0.0	0.0	1.000	1.000	0.0
	0.0	0.0	1.000	-1.000	0.000	-0.000	0.000
14	0.0	0.0	0.0	0.0	3.000	0.0	0.0
	0.0	0.0	1.000	0.0	19.000	0.0	0.0
	0.0	0.0	0.000	5.000	-50.000	50.000	35.000
15	0.0	0.0	0.0	0.0	1.076	0.0	0.0
	0.0	0.0	0.0	0.0	3.054	0.0	0.0
	0.0	0.0	2.035	1.523	1.458	998.542	-77.741

```
    ** THE OPTIMAL VALUE OF THE OBJECTIVE FUNCTION IS **        65.00

** LAST BASIC FEASIBLE SOLUTION IS AN OPTIMAL INTEGER SOLUTION **

OPTIMAL VALUE OF OBJECTIVE FUNCTION IS        65.00
VARIABLE        VALUE
    1           4.00
   16           4.00
    2           1.00
    7         220.00
    6           4.00
    4           2.00
   15           1.00
   14           3.00
    3           3.00
    8         243.00
   11         185.00
    9        1965.03
   13           0.00
   10          35.00
```

4.3.4 Diet Problem

Consider the diet problem from Section 3.2.1. A homemaker is contemplating the number of servings of each of the following six vegetables to put on this week's menu to minimize the cost while meeting all nutrient and taste requirements. We assume that vegetables will provide only a fraction of the established minimum daily requirements of each nutrient. Table 4.2 summarizes the factors involved.

Cabbage cannot be served more than twice during the week, and the other vegetables cannot be served more than four times each during the week. A total of 14 servings of vegetables are required each week. How many times should each vegetable be served during the next week in order to minimize cost while satisfying the nutrient and taste requirements? The computer program in Section 4.3.3 yielded the optimal at a total cost of $.65 per person per week.

Table 4.2 DIET PROBLEM DATA

			Units per serving			
				Vitamin		Cost per serving, cents
Vegetable	Iron	Phosphorus	A	C	Niacin	
Green beans	0.45	10	415	8	0.30	5
Carrots	0.45	28	9065	3	0.35	5
Broccoli	1.05	50	2550	53	0.60	8
Cabbage	0.40	25	75	27	0.15	2
Beets	0.50	22	15	5	0.25	6
Potatoes	0.50	75	235	8	0.80	3
Minimum weekly requirements from vegetables	6.00 mg	325 mg	17,500 USP	245 mg	5.00 mg	

The optimal solution at a total cost of $.65 per person per week:

Vegetable	Number of times per week
Green beans	4
Carrots	1
Broccoli	3
Cabbage	2
Beets	0
Potatoes	4

4.3.5 Summary of the Cutting-Plane Technique

The cutting-plane technique for integer LP involves cycling through two steps repeatedly until an optimal solution for the *integer* LP problem is obtained. The two steps are:

1 Solve the associated noninteger LP problem.
2 Trim the region of feasible solutions for the noninteger problem and return to step 1.

The cutting-plane technique has a number of good points with the strongest possibly being the fact that algorithms using the technique usually converge with relatively few cuts if they are going to converge to the optimal solution in a reasonable amount of time. On the other hand, if they do not converge to the optimal solution rather quickly, they very likely will take an extremely large number of cuts to converge. Theoretically, Algorithm 4.2 will converge in a finite number of cuts; however, the number may push the computer time needed to solve the problem beyond reason.

Another negative aspect of cutting-plane algorithms is the fact that the value of the objective function may reach a plateau and remain there for an extremely large number of cuts. This aspect coupled with the fact that algorithms for this technique must necessarily use noninteger arithmetic makes it quite possible for the round-off error to build up to the extent that when an optimal solution is reached, it is completely unreliable.

Quite often these negative aspects can be removed or at least improved upon by

1 Using double-precision arithmetic in the computer
2 Changing the order of the constraints in the computer
3 Reducing the coefficients and constants in each constraint to the least common integer denominator

As stated in Section 4.2.6, it is generally a good policy to use a cutting-plane algorithm for several cuts and if it does not converge to the optimal solution of the integer problem, switch to an implicit enumeration or branch-and-bound algorithm.

Dakin's branch-and-bound algorithm to solve integer LP problems will be presented in Chapter 5 as a method to illustrate the branch-and-bound technique.

Salkin [11] lists general algorithms that can usually solve integer LP problems with 50 to 100 variables and as many constraints.

SELECTED BIBLIOGRAPHY

1 Abadie, J. (ed.): "Integer and Nonlinear Programming," American Elsevier Publishing Co., Inc., New York, N.Y., 1970.
2 Balas, E.: An Additive Algorithm for Solving Linear Programs with Zero-One Variables, *Oper. Res.,* vol. 13, pp. 517–546, 1965.
3 Beale, E. M. L.: Survey of Integer Programming, *Oper. Res. Q.,* vol. 16, pp. 219–228, 1965.
4 Garfinkel, Robert S., and George L. Nemhauser: "Integer Programming," John Wiley & Sons, Inc., New York, N.Y., 1972.
5 Geoffrion, A. M.: Integer Programming by Implicit Enumeration and Balas' Method, *SIAM Rev.,* vol. 7, pp. 178–190, 1967.
6 Geoffrion, A. M., and R. E. Marsten: Integer Programming: A Framework and State-of-the-Art Survey, *Manage. Sci.,* vol. 18, pp. 465–491, 1972.
7 Gorry, G. A., J. F. Shapiro, and L. A. Wolsey: Relaxation Methods for Pure and Mixed Integer Programming Problems, *Manage. Sci.,* vol. 18, pp. 229–239, 1972.
8 Hadley, G.: "Linear Programming," Addison-Wesley Publishing Co., Inc., Reading, Mass., 1962.
9 Kolesar, P. J.: A Branch and Bound Algorithm for the Knapsack Problem, *Manage. Sci.,* vol. 13, pp. 723–735, 1967.

*Reference list for integer programming is very complete.

10 Plane, D. R., and C. McMillan, Jr.: "Discrete Optimization," Prentice-Hall, Inc., Englewood Cliffs, N.J., 1971.

*11 Salkin, Harvey M.: "Integer Programming," Addison-Wesley Publishing Co., Inc., Reading, Mass., 1975.

12 Zionts, S.: "Linear and Integer Programming," Prentice-Hall, Inc., Englewood Cliffs, N.J., 1974.

EXERCISES

Exercises 4.1–4.5 can be worked without the aid of a computer, whereas a computer should be available to aid in the solution of Exercises 4.6–4.9.

4.1 Solve the following 0-1 integer LP problem using implicit enumeration

$$\text{maximize:} \quad z = -3x_1 - 5x_2 - 3x_3$$
$$\text{subject to:} \quad x_1 + x_2 + x_3 \geqslant 1$$
$$-x_2 + x_3 \geqslant 1$$
$$x_1 - x_2 + 4x_3 \geqslant 5$$
$$\text{all } x_i = 0 \text{ or } 1$$

4.2 Prepare the following problem for solution via implicit enumeration:

$$\text{minimize:} \quad z = 3x_1 + 3x_2 - 3x_3 + 5x_4 - x_5$$
$$\text{subject to:} \quad x_1 + 2x_2 - 3x_3 + x_4 + 6x_5 \geqslant 4$$
$$2x_1 - x_2 + 4x_3 - x_4 + 4x_5 \leqslant 10$$
$$x_2 - x_4 + x_5 \leqslant 0$$
$$6x_1 - 4x_2 + 2x_3 + 4x_4 + x_5 \geqslant 8$$
$$x_1 - x_2 + x_3 - x_4 + x_5 = 2$$
$$\text{all } x_i = 0 \text{ or } 1$$

4.3 Use implicit enumeration to solve the following 0-1 integer programming problem.

$$\text{minimize:} \quad z = x_1 + 2x_2 + x_3$$
$$\text{subject to:} \quad x_1 - 2x_2 - x_3 \leqslant -2$$
$$-2x_1 + x_2 + x_3 \leqslant 0$$
$$2x_1 - x_2 + x_3 \geqslant 2$$
$$\text{all } x_i = 0 \text{ or } 1$$

4.4 Consider the backpack-loading problem with the following data:

Item	Weight	Value
1	25	20
2	40	50
3	30	25
4	20	30
5	50	60

Assume a maximum of 80 units of weight can be loaded. Use implicit enumeration to determine which items to load in order to maximize the value of the cargo.

4.5 Solve the following integer programming problems by the cutting-plane method. As cuts are added, plot them in order to show what portion of the feasible region has been removed from consideration.

(a)

$$\text{maximize:} \quad z = x_1 + 2x_2$$

$$\text{subject to:} \quad x_1 + 2x_2 \leqslant 12$$

$$4x_1 + 3x_2 \leqslant 14$$

all x_i are nonnegative integers

(b)

$$\text{maximize:} \quad z = 6x_1 + 4x_2$$

$$\text{subject to:} \quad 3x_1 + 2x_2 \leqslant 20$$

$$6x_1 + 5x_2 \leqslant 25$$

$$x_1 + 3x_2 \leqslant 10$$

x_1, x_2 are nonnegative integers

(c)

$$\text{maximize:} \quad z = x_1 + 2x_2$$

$$\text{subject to:} \quad x_1 + x_2 \leqslant 100$$

$$5x_1 \qquad \leqslant 100$$

$$x_2 \leqslant 150$$

x_1, x_2 are nonnegative integers

(d)

$$\text{maximize:} \quad z = x_1 - x_2$$

$$\text{subject to:} \quad x_1 + 2x_2 \leqslant 4$$

$$6x_1 + 2x_2 \leqslant 9$$

x_1, x_2 are nonnegative integers

Computer-Oriented Exercises

4.6 Use the computer program for implicit enumeration in Section 4.2.5 to solve the following 0-1 integer programming problem.

$$\text{minimize:} \quad z = 3x_1 + x_2 + 3x_3 + x_4 + 3x_5 + x_6 + x_7 + x_8$$

$$\text{subject to:} \quad x_1 + x_2 + 2x_3 - x_4 + x_5 - x_6 \qquad + x_8 \geqslant 3$$

$$-x_1 + 3x_2 + 3x_3 \qquad + x_5 \qquad + x_7 + 2x_8 \geqslant 4$$
$$- 3x_3 - x_4 \qquad + 7x_6 \qquad \leqslant 1$$
$$2x_1 + x_2 \qquad + 5x_4 \qquad + 2x_7 + x_8 \geqslant 5$$
$$2x_2 + 8x_3 \qquad + 2x_5 + 6x_6 - 3x_7 - 3x_8 \geqslant 3$$
$$-x_1 \qquad - 3x_3 + x_4 - x_5 + 2x_6 + 3x_7 + 8x_8 \geqslant 6$$
$$\text{all } x_i = 0 \text{ or } 1$$

4.7 A mining company would like to schedule its mining operation to control the grade of lead going to the mill. Specifically, suppose the company has 15 different faces that can be mined on a given shift. The percent of lead in each face and the tons of ore that can be mined per shift from each face are given by these tables.

Face	1	2	3	4	5	6	7	8
Percent lead	2	5	8	20	25	4	8	10
Tons of ore	540	520	480	600	580	575	555	540

Face	9	10	11	12	13	14	15
Percent lead	12	18	12	4	2	1	3
Tons of ore	530	535	585	530	510	500	620

Five faces are to be mined on each shift. The combined ore going to the mill must contain at least 8 percent lead.
(a) Model the problem as a 0-1 integer LP problem.
(b) Solve the model using the computer program in Section 4.2.5.

4.8 Solve the following integer LP problems using the computer program in Section 4.3.3.

(a)

$$\text{maximize: } z = 6x_1 + 4x_2 + x_3$$
$$\text{subject to: } 3x_1 + 2x_2 + x_3 \leqslant 20$$
$$6x_1 + 5x_2 + x_3 \leqslant 25$$
$$x_1 + 3x_2 + 3x_3 \leqslant 10$$
$$\text{all } x_i \text{ are nonnegative integers}$$

(b)

$$\text{minimize: } z = -2x_1 - x_2$$
$$\text{subject to: } x_1 - x_2 \leqslant 3$$
$$2x_1 - x_2 \leqslant 8$$

$$x_1 + 4x_2 \leqslant 24$$
$$x_1 + 2x_2 \leqslant 14$$

x_1, x_2 are nonnegative integers

(c) maximize: $z = 2x_1 - 8x_2 + x_3$

subject to: $-2.4x_1 + 6.4x_2 + x_3 \geqslant 10.2$

$$x_1 - 2.8x_2 + 6x_3 \leqslant 4.4$$

$$3.7x_1 + 4.2x_2 - x_3 \geqslant 6.8$$

all x_i are nonnegative integers

(d) maximize: $z = 3x_1 + 2x_2 + x_3 + x_4 + x_5 + 2x_6 + 3x_7 + 4x_8$

$$x_1 \qquad + x_3 \qquad + x_5 \qquad + x_7 \qquad \geqslant 10$$

$$x_2 \qquad - x_4 \qquad + x_6 \qquad - x_8 \geqslant 6$$

$$-x_1 - x_2 - x_3 \qquad - x_7 - x_8 \geqslant -2$$

$$x_1 - x_2 - x_3 + x_4 - x_5 - x_6 + x_7 + x_8 \geqslant 0$$

all x_i are nonnegative integers

4.9 How is the solution of the example problem in Section 4.3.4 changed if
   (a) Cabbage can be served no more than four times during the week?
   (b) Potatoes can be served no more than two times during the week?

5

BRANCH–AND–BOUND TECHNIQUE

5.1 INTRODUCTION

The branch-and-bound technique involves a well-structured systematic search of the space of all feasible solutions of constrained optimization problems that have a finite number of feasible solutions.

Usually the space of all feasible solutions is repeatedly partitioned into smaller and smaller subsets (*branching*) and a lower bound (for a minimization problem) is calculated for the cost of solutions within each subset (*bounding*). After each partitioning, those subsets with a bound that exceeds the cost of a known feasible solution are excluded from all further partitionings. Thus, large subsets of solutions may be excluded from consideration without examining each solution in these subsets. The partitioning continues until a feasible solution is found such that its cost is no greater than the bound for any subset. Of course, the success of the technique depends upon the number of solutions examined before an optimal solution is reached.

Branch-and-bound algorithms have been used with some degree of success to solve integer programming problems, the scheduling problem, the traveling salesman problem, the plant location problem, the knapsack problem, the assignment problem, and a variety of other problems with a finite number (usually very large) of feasible solutions. Until recently, the branch-and-bound algorithm developed by Little, Murty,

Sweeney, and Karel [10] was the best-known algorithm for solving fairly large traveling salesman problems exactly. The paper by Little et al. and a branch-and-bound algorithm by Land and Doig [7] for general integer LP problems are generally given credit for demonstrating the usefulness of the branch-and-bound technique and for generating research interest in the technique.

The general principle of the branch-and-bound technique remains constant from one algorithm to the next; however, the procedure for branching, bounding, and pruning may vary considerably.

At any point in a branch-and-bound algorithm where a branching decision must be made, any subset with a bound that is less than the least upper bound for all feasible solutions discovered to date is a possible candidate for branching (minimization problem). To this end, there are basically two branching decision rules used in all branch-and-bound algorithms; namely,

Branch from lowest bound

Branch from newest active bound

The "branch from lowest bound" decision rule says that the next branching should be from the subset of possible solutions that has the lowest bound on the optimal solution. In general, this policy has the advantage that it examines fewer subproblems than the other rule, but has the disadvantage of requiring more computer storage because more intermediate data must be stored. The "branch from newest active bound" rule chooses from the subsets most recently generated the subset with the lowest bound to branch from next. This rule generally requires many more branching operations than the other decision rule but requires much less storage.

It should be noted that the *branch-and-bound technique* involves branching from one problem to a set of subproblems and establishing bounds on the new subproblems. A procedure for branching to a set of subproblems and bounding them is a *branch-and-bound algorithm*. Thus, there are as many branch-and-bound algorithms as there are decision rules to do the branching and bounding, but only one branch-and-bound technique.

The branch-and-bound technique will become more meaningful as we examine a number of algorithms that use the technique to solve a variety of problems.

5.2 BRANCH-AND-BOUND ALGORITHM FOR ASSIGNMENT PROBLEM

Although the Hungarian algorithm for solving the assignment problem is much more efficient than branch-and-bound algorithms, a branch-and-bound algorithm to solve the problem is presented in order to provide insight into the basic branch-and-bound technique.

EXAMPLE 5.2.1 Suppose four people can each perform any one of four different jobs but possibly in different amounts of time. If one and only one person is to

Table 5.1 TIME TO PERFORM JOBS

Person	Job			
	1	2	3	4
A	2	10	9	7
B	15	4	14	8
C	13	14	16	11
D	4	15	13	9

perform each job, which person should be assigned to each job to minimize the total time to perform all four jobs? Table 5.1 gives the corresponding times to perform the various jobs.

One approach to the solution of this problem is the branch-and-bound technique. We might observe that there are only $4! = 4 \cdot 3 \cdot 2 \cdot 1 = 24$ feasible solutions for this problem. However, for 20 people and 20 jobs, there are well over 10^{18} feasible solutions. Hopefully, the branch-and-bound algorithm used will examine only a small subset of these solutions.

A feasible solution for the assignment problem is defined to be an assignment of people to jobs such that

$$\text{one and only one person is assigned to each job} \qquad (5.1)$$

Step 1

Ignore constraint (5.1) and solve for the minimum total time (*relaxation*). This solution is obtained by observing the minimum time in each column of Table 5.1.

SOLUTION

	Assignment	
Person	Job	Time
A	1	2
B	2	4
A	3	9
A	4	7
	Total time =	22

This represents the minimum total time for all solutions; however, this is not a feasible solution since person A is assigned to more than one job. The number 22 represents a lower bound on all solutions. That is, no assignment—feasible or not—will yield a smaller total time than 22.

Step 2

Partition the 24 feasible solutions into four subsets of six feasible solutions each. One way to get each of the subsets is to assign a certain person to job 1, then there will be

$3! = 6$ ways the remaining three people can be assigned to jobs 2, 3, and 4. Of course, each of the resulting solutions would be feasible. In reality, however, the branch-and-bound algorithm assigns a certain person to job 1 and assigns the remaining people to the remaining jobs to minimize the total time, ignoring constraint (5.1). The process is then repeated with a different person assigned to job 1 until all four people have been assigned to job 1. In each case, the total time from the resulting assignment is a lower bound on all solutions with the given person assigned to job 1. The exact procedure is given by steps 2A–2D.

Step 2A

Assign person A to job 1 and assign persons B, C, and D to jobs 2, 3, and 4 to minimize the total time, ignoring constraint (5.1). Thus from Table 5.1, we observe that after row 1 is marked out (person A is assigned to job 1), the minimum elements in columns 2, 3, and 4 are 4, 13, and 8, respectively. The resulting assignment is:

Assignment		
Person	Job	Time
A	1	2
B	2	4
D	3	13
B	4	8
	Total time	= 27

This is not a feasible solution since person B is assigned to more than one job. However, the lower bound on all solutions with person A assigned to job 1 is 27.

Step 2B

Assign person B to job 1 and assign persons A, C, and D to jobs 2, 3, and 4 to minimize the total time, ignoring constraint (5.1).

Assignment		
Person	Job	Time
B	1	15
A	2	10
A	3	9
A	4	7
	Total time	= 41

Again, this is not a feasible solution. The lower bound on all solutions with person B assigned to job 1 is 41.

Step 2C

Assign person C to job 1, and assign persons A, B, and D to jobs 2, 3, and 4, ignoring constraint (5.1), to minimize the total time.

Assignment		
Person	**Job**	**Time**
C	*1*	*13*
B	2	4
A	3	9
A	4	7
	Total time = 33	

The lower bound is 33, a nonfeasible solution.

Step 2D
Assign person D to job 1 and assign persons A, B, and C to jobs 2, 3, and 4 to minimize the total time, ignoring constraint (5.1).

Assignment		
Person	**Job**	**Time**
D	*1*	*4*
B	2	4
A	3	9
A	4	7
	Total time = 24	
	Lower bound = 24	
	Nonfeasible solution.	

Step 3
The results of steps 1 and 2 are given in Figure 5.1. The circles in Figure 5.1 are called *nodes* and represent the set of all possible feasible solutions that can be reached from that node. For example, all feasible solutions of the original problem

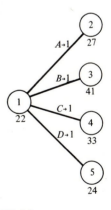

FIGURE 5.1
First branch of solution tree.

can be reached from node 1. Only those feasible solutions with person A assigned to job 1 can be reached from node 2. Likewise, only those feasible solutions with person B assigned to job 1 can be reached from node 3, etc.

The number in each circle is the node number and sequentially represents the order in which the branch-and-bound algorithm is carried out. The number below each node is the lower bound on all feasible solutions emanating from that node. The lines connecting the nodes are called *branches*. Nodes 2-5 are called *terminal nodes* at this point because branches do not emanate from them. By the same reasoning, node 1 is not a terminal node.

In step 2 of the algorithm, person A is assigned to job 1 first and the resulting subproblem, ignoring constraint (5.1), has the solution value listed under node 2, namely 27. Thus, 27 is a lower bound on all feasible solutions of the original problem with the added constraint that person A is assigned to job 1. To say it another way, any feasible solution with person A assigned to job 1 cannot have a smaller total time than 27. Similar statements hold when person B is assigned to job 1 (node 3), when person C is assigned to job 1 (node 4), and when person D is assigned to job 1 (node 5).

Step 4

Since node 5 has the smallest lower bound, it is chosen first for further branching. With the constraint that person D is assigned to job 1, either person A, B, or C is assigned to job 2, and the remaining people are assigned to jobs 3 and 4 to minimize the total time, ignoring constraint (5.1). The results corresponding to nodes 6, 7, and 8 in Figure 5.2 are:

Assignment				Assignment				Assignment		
Person	Job	Time		Person	Job	Time		Person	Job	Time
D	1	4		D	1	4		D	1	4
A	2	10		B	2	4		C	2	14
B	3	14		A	3	9		A	3	9
B	4	8		A	4	7		A	4	7
Total time = 36 Nonfeasible				Total time = 24 Nonfeasible				Total time = 34 Nonfeasible		

Step 5

The results of steps 1-4 are given in Figure 5.2. None of the solutions are feasible, so all terminal nodes (2, 3, 4, 6, 7, 8) are still candidates to lead to the optimal solution. The number below each node is a lower bound on all solutions emanating from that node. Also, the minimum value at all terminal nodes provides a lower bound for the problem, 24 at node 7 at this point.

Step 6

Branch from node 7 since it has a smaller lower bound than any other terminal node. With the constraint that person D is assigned to job 1 and person B is assigned to job 2, perform steps 6A and 6B.

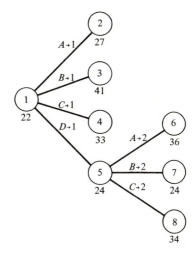

FIGURE 5.2
Second branch of solution tree.

Step 6A

Assign person A to job 3 and person C to job 4 for a total time of 28. This is a feasible solution (one and only one assigned to each job). Thus, 28 is an *upper bound* on the set of feasible solutions. This says that any node with a total time greater than or equal to 28 can be ignored. Further constraints on a node with a larger total time would keep the total time the same or increase it. Hence, all nodes that have a larger total time can be trimmed from the tree. In this case, all solutions emanating from nodes 3, 4, 6, and 8 can be ignored in searching for the optimal solution.

Step 6B

Assign person C to job 3 and person A to job 4 for a total time of 31. This is a feasible solution, but it yields a larger total time than the current upper bound of 28. Thus, it can be ignored.

Step 7

Examine all terminal nodes that have a total time that is less than the best upper bound on all feasible solutions (node 9 with value 28 at this point). Since node 2 is the only remaining terminal node (only node with a value less than 28), further branching from it is done.

  With the constraints that person A is assigned to job 1, either person B, C, or D is assigned to job 2 and the remaining people are assigned to jobs 3 and 4 to minimize the total time, ignoring constraint (5.1). The results corresponding to nodes 11, 12, and 13 in Figure 5.3 are:

Assignment		
Person	Job	Time
A	1	2
B	2	4
D	3	13
D	4	9

Total time = 28
Nonfeasible

Assignment		
Person	Job	Time
A	1	2
C	2	14
D	3	13
B	4	8

Total time = 37
Feasible

Assignment		
Person	Job	Time
A	1	2
D	2	15
B	3	14
B	4	8

Total time = 39
Nonfeasible

Step 8

The results of steps 1–7 are given in Figure 5.3. Note that node 9 yields a feasible solution with a value of 28 and that no other terminal node has a smaller value. Thus, the solution corresponding to node 9 must be optimal; namely,

Assignment		
Person	Job	Time
D	1	4
B	2	4
A	3	9
C	4	11

Total time = 28

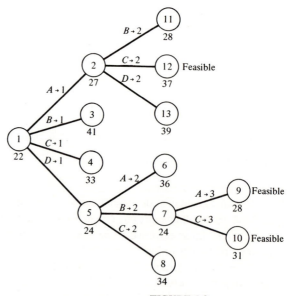

FIGURE 5.3
Third branch of solution tree.

Node 12 yields a feasible solution, but its value is larger than 28, so it can be ignored.

5.3 BRANCH–AND–BOUND ALGORITHMS FOR TRAVELING SALESMAN PROBLEM

A salesman located in a given city wishes to visit each of $N - 1$ cities once and only once and then return to the city he started from. In what order should he visit the cities to minimize the total distance traveled? The purpose of this section is to explore a branch-and-bound algorithm that solves this problem.

One industrial example of this type of problem is production scheduling. Suppose that during some production cycle an assembly line must produce each of N different models. The cost to switch from model i to model j is c_{ij}. In what order should the models be produced to minimize total switching cost?

Although a great deal of research effort has been put forth in the past 10 years to solve the general traveling salesman problem, algorithms that find the exact optimal solution are still limited to fewer than 100 cities. Lin and Kernighan [9] have an algorithm that will obtain a "good" solution for problems with fewer than 250 cities in a reasonable amount of time on the fastest computers. However, algorithms that will find the exact solution for "large" problems are still very much in demand.

A number of branch-and-bound algorithms that find the exact solution for small-to-moderate-size traveling salesman problems (fewer than 50 cities) have appeared in the literature during the past 10 years; however, most, if not all, are based on the algorithm by Eastman [4]. Little et al. [10] modified both the branching and bounding procedures used by Eastman, and Shapiro [13] modified Eastman's algorithm to eliminate two-city subtours. Since the Eastman and Little et al. algorithms form the basis for all traveling salesman branch-and-bound algorithms, one of them, namely, Eastman's algorithm, will be presented at this time.

5.3.1 Algorithm 5.1—Eastman Algorithm

Let $D(I,J)$ be the distance from city I to city J for $I = 1, 2, \ldots, N$ and $J = 1, 2, \ldots, N$, where N is the number of cities. Let $D(I,I) = \infty$ for $I = 1, 2, \ldots, N$. A *tour* is a complete route or cycle through the N cities where no city is visited more than once. If the salesman visits a certain city and returns to that city later, the cities involved form a *subtour*. Of course, this cannot occur if a route is feasible (each city is visited once and only once). Eastman's algorithm solves the easier assignment problem that allows subtours and then systematically forbids subtours until finally a tour is obtained that is optimal.

An illustrative example follows the algorithm.

Step 1
Let CLUB represent the current least upper bound on the optimal solution of the traveling salesman problem. Set

$$CLUB = 10^{10}$$

Step 2
Solve the associated assignment problem, where the distances $D(I,J)$ are the elements of the effectiveness matrix. The solution provides a lower bound on the optimal solution of the traveling salesman problem. If at least one subtour exists in the solution, go to step 3, otherwise the optimal solution of the assignment problem is also an optimal solution of the traveling salesman problem, so stop.

Step 3
Select a subtour and let k be the number of arcs (links) in the selected subtour. Eastman [4] selects the subtour with the smallest number of arcs. (An *arc* is just the line connecting two cities.) All other subtours at this node can be ignored.

Step 4
Branch into k subproblems. If the subtour is

$$I_1 \rightarrow I_2 \rightarrow \cdot \cdot \cdot I_k \rightarrow I_1$$

then for subproblem 1 let $D(I_1,I_2) = \infty$, for subproblem 2 let $D(I_2,I_3) = \infty$, etc., and for subproblem k let $D(I_k,I_1) = \infty$.

Step 5
Solve the k new assignment problems. Each solution distance is a lower bound for the corresponding subproblem.

Step 6
If there are one or more feasible solutions from step 5 and if the smallest total distance for these feasible solutions, say STD, is smaller than CLUB, set CLUB = STD and save the corresponding feasible solution. Otherwise CLUB remains unchanged.

Step 7
If CLUB is less than the lower bounds on all other unexplored subproblems, then the solution corresponding to CLUB is an optimal solution of the traveling salesman problem, so stop; otherwise, go to step 8. By unexplored subproblems, we mean subproblems that have not been divided into further subproblems.

Step 8
From the set of *all* unexplored nonfeasible (subtours present) subproblems with a bound less than CLUB, select the subproblem with the smallest lower bound for further branching. Go to step 3.

EXAMPLE 5.3.1 Consider the traveling salesman problem with the following table of distances:

	To city				
From city	1	2	3	4	5
1	∞	1	7	4	3
2	2	∞	6	3	4
3	1	6	∞	2	1
4	1	5	4	∞	6
5	7	5	4	5	∞

The Eastman solution is:

Step 1
Solve the problem as if it were an assignment problem. Two methods are available: branch-and-bound and the Hungarian method. We will use the Hungarian method from Chapter 3.

$$\begin{bmatrix} \infty & 1 & 7 & 4 & 3 \\ 2 & \infty & 6 & 3 & 4 \\ 1 & 6 & \infty & 2 & 1 \\ 1 & 5 & 4 & \infty & 6 \\ 7 & 5 & 4 & 5 & \infty \end{bmatrix} \sim \begin{bmatrix} \infty & 0 & 6 & 3 & 2 \\ 0 & \infty & 4 & 1 & 2 \\ 0 & 5 & \infty & 1 & 0 \\ 0 & 4 & 3 & \infty & 5 \\ 3 & 1 & 0 & 1 & \infty \end{bmatrix} \sim \begin{bmatrix} \infty & \boxed{0} & 6 & 2 & 2 \\ \cancel{0} & \infty & 4 & \boxed{0} & 2 \\ \cancel{0} & 5 & \infty & \cancel{0} & \boxed{0} \\ \boxed{0} & 4 & 3 & \infty & 5 \\ 3 & 1 & \boxed{0} & \cancel{0} & \infty \end{bmatrix}$$

$\sim$ denotes *is equivalent with respect to the optimal solution*. The optimal assignment is

$$1 \to 2$$
$$2 \to 4$$
$$3 \to 5$$
$$4 \to 1$$
$$5 \to 3$$

with a total distance of 10. In this assignment there are two subtours, namely

$$1 \to 2 \to 4 \to 1$$
$$3 \to 5 \to 3$$

Step 2
Since the solution of the assignment problem in step 1 did not yield a tour, 10 is a lower bound on all feasible solutions of the traveling salesman problem.

Step 3
The subtour with the smallest number of arcs (links) is clearly $3 \to 5 \to 3$ since it has two arcs, while $1 \to 2 \to 4 \to 1$ has three arcs. Thus $k = 2$.

Step 4
Branch into two subproblems, one with $D(3,5) = \infty$ and one with $D(5,3) = \infty$.

Step 5

Let $D(3,5) = \infty$ and solve the resulting assignment problem.

$$\begin{bmatrix} \infty & 1 & 7 & 4 & 3 \\ 2 & \infty & 6 & 3 & 4 \\ 1 & 6 & \infty & 2 & \infty \\ 1 & 5 & 4 & \infty & 6 \\ 7 & 5 & 4 & 5 & \infty \end{bmatrix} \sim \begin{bmatrix} \infty & \boxed{0} & 6 & 2 & \boxtimes \\ \boxtimes & \infty & 4 & \boxtimes & \boxed{0} \\ \boxtimes & 5 & \infty & \boxed{0} & \infty \\ \boxed{0} & 4 & 3 & \infty & 3 \\ 3 & 1 & \boxed{0} & \boxtimes & \infty \end{bmatrix}$$

The optimal assignment is a tour with a total distance of 12. The assignment is

$$1 \to 2 \to 5 \to 3 \to 4 \to 1$$

Since this is a feasible solution of the traveling salesman problem, it is a least upper bound on the optimal solution at this point. This solution is represented by node 2 in Figure 5.4. No further branching from this node will be done because the solution is feasible.

Let $D(5,3) = \infty$:

$$\begin{bmatrix} \infty & 1 & 7 & 4 & 3 \\ 2 & \infty & 6 & 3 & 4 \\ 1 & 6 & \infty & 2 & 1 \\ 1 & 5 & 4 & \infty & 6 \\ 7 & 5 & \infty & 5 & \infty \end{bmatrix} \sim \begin{bmatrix} \infty & \boxed{0} & 3 & 3 & 2 \\ \boxed{0} & \infty & 1 & 1 & 2 \\ \boxtimes & 5 & \infty & 1 & \boxed{0} \\ \boxtimes & 4 & \boxed{0} & \infty & 5 \\ 2 & \boxtimes & \infty & \boxed{0} & \infty \end{bmatrix}$$

This optimal assignment has two subtours

$$1 \to 2 \to 1$$
$$3 \to 5 \to 4 \to 3$$

with a total distance of 13.

Step 6

Since the solution of the first subproblem $D(3,5) = \infty$ is feasible with a value (12) that is less than the lower bound (13) on the other subproblem, it is the optimal solution of the traveling salesman problem. Figure 5.4 illustrates the solution process.

Note that there is no need to check out the subproblems arising from the other subtour at node 1 $(1 \to 2 \to 4 \to 1)$. It would also lead to the optimal solution, but possibly in more steps. Branching must be done for *only one* subtour at each node.

If the value at node 3 were *less than 12* and the solution nonfeasible, only the branches resulting either from setting $D(1,2) = \infty$ and $D(2,1) = \infty$ or from setting $D(3,5) = \infty$, $D(5,4) = \infty$, and $D(4,3) = \infty$ would need to be examined, but not both. Eastman used the rule that selects the subtour with the fewest arcs. Thus, in this example, two new subproblems would need to be solved, one with $D(1,2) = \infty$ and one with $D(2,1) = \infty$.

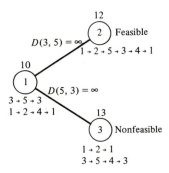

FIGURE 5.4
Complete solution tree for traveling
salesman problem.

Shapiro [13] modified Eastman's algorithm to eliminate subtours of length 2 for symmetric problems and Little et al. [10] modified both the branching and bounding procedures. Currently, the most efficient methods for solving large-scale traveling salesman problems are heuristic methods derived by Christofides and Eilon [1] and Lin and Kernighan [9]. One of the most efficient *exact* methods was developed by Held and Karp [5]. However, it is limited in the size of problems it can solve.

5.3.2 Computer Program for Algorithm 5.1

This program as listed will solve traveling salesman problems with 15 or fewer cities. It occupies 88K bytes of core storage. It solved the 10-city problem listed after the program in 1.79 s of IBM 370/168 time. However, computation times grow exponentially as the number of cities increases. Generally, a 30-city problem can be solved in a reasonable amount of time, but larger problems get out of hand quickly.

The program uses the subroutine HUNGRY that was developed for the Hungarian algorithm. The subroutine HUNGRY is listed after the mainline program for Algorithm 3.2 in Section 3.12.4. It can be placed intact after the mainline program for Eastman's algorithm. To increase the maximum number of cities to M, change the 15 component of the variables in the DIMENSION statements (mainline and subroutine) to M. Change the 500 component of the variables in the DIMENSION statement in the mainline program to 30M.

The input data and results for a 10-city problem follow the computer program.

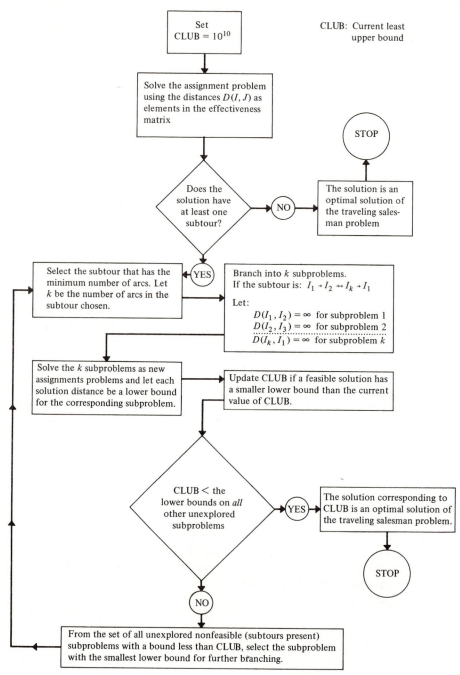

FIGURE 5.5
Flowchart for Eastman algorithm.

```
C     ******************************************************************
C     *                                                                *
C     *         **    ALGORITHM 5.1    EASTMAN'S ALGORITHM    **        *
C     *               FOR TRAVELING SALESMAN PROBLEM                    *
C     *                                                                *
C     *  THIS PROGRAM WILL SOLVE THE TRAVELING SALESMAN PROBLEM WHEN 15 OR *
C     *  FEWER CITIES ARE INVOLVED, BY USING THE HUNGARIAN ALGORITHM TO SOLVE *
C     *  THE ASSOCIATED ASSIGNMENT PROBLEM. SUBROUTINE HUNGRY MUST BE SUPPLIED.*
C     *  THIS SUBROUTINE IS LISTED WITH THE PROGRAM FOR THE HUNGARIAN ALGORITHM*
C     *  IN SECTION 3.12.4 .                                            *
C     *                                                                *
C     *  THIS PROGRAM IS DESIGNED                                       *
C     *     TO READ                                                     *
C     *          CARD 1    COLS  2-80    TITLE  DESCRIPTION OF THE PROBLEM USING *
C     *                                         ANY CHARACTERS ON KEYPUNCH *
C     *                                         ** COLUMN 1 MUST BE LEFT BLANK ** *
C     *          CARD 2    COLS  1- 5    N  NUMBER OF CITIES INVOLVED   (I5)  *
C     *          CARDS 3 TO ?   IDIST(I,J)  DISTANCE MATRIX             *
C     *                                DATA ENTERED ROWWISE IN 10I8 FORMAT *
C     *                                EACH NEW ROW MUST START ON A NEW CARD *
C     *                                ALL ENTRIES ARE INTEGER, WITH THE *
C     *                                DIAGONAL ELEMENTS SET TO 1000000 *
C     *                     TO SOLVE MORE THAN ONE PROBLEM AT A TIME, REPEAT THE *
C     *                     READ SEQUENCE, AND STACK THE DATA ONE BEHIND THE OTHER *
C     *                                                                *
C     *     TO CALCULATE                                                *
C     *        IAS    THE ASSIGNMENT MATRIX                             *
C     *        MD     MINIMUM DISTANCE OF THE ASSOCIATED ASSIGNMENT PROBLEM *
C     *                                                                *
C     *     TO PRINT                                                    *
C     *        CLUB   DISTANCE OF OPTIMAL FEASIBLE SOLUTION             *
C     *        IAS                                                      *
C     *                                                                *
C     ******************************************************************
      DIMENSION IAS(15),IDIST(15,15),ISDIST(15,15),JCOMP(15),
     *          BFSD(15),IIAS(500,15),BRANCH(500),R(500),C(500),
     *          P(500),TD(500),NARCS(500),SUBT(500)
      REAL*4 TITLE(20)
   50 READ(5,55,END=2000)TITLE
   55 FORMAT(20A4)
      WRITE(6,60)TITLE
   60 FORMAT('1',20A4,//)
      READ(5,1)N
    1 FORMAT(I5)
      DO 2 I =1,N,1
      READ(5,3)(IDIST(I,J),J=1,N)
    3 FORMAT(10I8)
    2 CONTINUE
      KODE=0
      WRITE(6,710)
  710 FORMAT(' THE DISTANCE MATRIX:',/)
      DO 707 I = 1,N,1
      WRITE(6,702) (IDIST(I,J),J = 1,N)
  702 FORMAT(10I8)
  707 CONTINUE
C     ******************************************************************
C     *  STEP 1                                                        *
C     *        SET MINIMUM TOTAL DISTANCE (CLUB) TO LARGE POSITIVE NUMBER *
C     ******************************************************************
      CLUB = .1E11
C     ******************************************************************
C     *  STEP 2                                                        *
C     *        CALL SUBROUTINE HUNGRY TO SOLVE THE ASSOCIATED ASSIGNMENT *
C     *        PROBLEM BY THE HUNGARIAN METHOD.                         *
C     *        IF AT LEAST ONE SUBTOUR EXISTS, GO TO STEP 3.  OTHERWISE, AN *
C     *        OPTIMAL SOLUTION OF THE ASSIGNMENT PROBLEM IS THE OPTIMAL *
C     *        SOLUTION OF THE TRAVELING SALESMAN PROBLEM, SO STOP.     *
C     ******************************************************************
      CALL HUNGRY(N,IDIST,IAS,MD,KODE)
      NN = N -2
```

```
      DO 71 I = 1,N,1
      JCOMP(I) = IAS(I)
   71 CONTINUE
      DO 70 II = 2,NN,1
      DO 72 I=1,N,1
      J = JCOMP(I)
      JCOMP(I) = IAS(J)
      IF(JCOMP(I).EQ.I) GO TO 80
   72 CONTINUE
   70 CONTINUE
      GO TO 200
C     ********************************************************************
C     *    STEP 3                                                       *
C     *         A SUBTOUR EXISTS OF WHICH WE HAVE THE SHORTEST.  DETERMINE *
C     *         THE PARAMETERS OF THE SHORTEST SUBTOUR                  *
C     ********************************************************************
   80 IARS = II
      INT = I
      DO 701  KK = 1,N,1
      IIAS(1,KK) =IAS(KK)
  701 CONTINUE
      K = 1
C     ********************************************************************
C     *    STEPS 4,5                                                    *
C     *         BRANCH INTO  K  SUBPROBLEMS                             *
C     *         SOLVE THE K SUBPROBLEMS AS NEW ASSIGNMENT PROBLEMS, AND LET *
C     *         EACH SOLUTION DISTANCE BE A LOWER BOUND FOR THE CORRESPONDING *
C     *         SUBPROBLEM                                              *
C     ********************************************************************
      P(1) = 1
      IPRED=1
      GO TO 110
  700 LL1 = IPRED
  111 IF(P(LL1).EQ.1) GO TO 112
      LL2 = R(LL1)
      LL3 = C (LL1)
      ISDIST(LL2,LL3)=IDIST(LL2,LL3)
      IDIST(LL2,LL3) = 9999999
      LL1 = P(LL1)
      GO TO 111
  112 LL2=R(LL1)
      LL3=C(LL1)
      ISDIST(LL2,LL3) =IDIST(LL2,LL3)
      IDIST(LL2,LL3) = 9999999
      IARS = NARCS(IPRED)
      INT = SUBT(IPRED)
  110 ITERM = INT
      DO 90 IJ = 1,IARS
      IBEGIN = ITERM
      ITERM=  IIAS(IPRED,IBEGIN)
      K=K+1
      R(K)=IBEGIN
      C(K)=ITERM
      ITEMP = IDIST(IBEGIN,ITERM)
      IDIST(IBEGIN,ITERM) = 9999999
      CALL HUNGRY(N,IDIST,IAS,MD,KODE)
      TD(K) = MD
      P(K) = IPRED
      IDIST(IBEGIN,ITERM) = ITEMP
      DO 125 MM = 1,N,1
      IIAS(K,MM) = IAS(MM)
  125 CONTINUE
      DO 73 I=1,N
      JCOMP(I)=IAS(I)
   73 CONTINUE
      DO 75 II=2,NN
      DO 74 I=1,N
      J=JCOMP(I)
      JCOMP(I)=IAS(J)
      IF(JCOMP(I).EQ.I) GO TO 131
```

```
   74 CONTINUE
   75 CONTINUE
C     ***********************************************************************
C     *     STEP 6                                                         *
C     *        IF THERE EXISTS ONE OR MORE FEASIBLE SOLUTIONS FROM STEP 5, AND *
C     *        IF THE SMALLEST TOTAL DISTANCE FOR THAT FEASIBLE SOLUTION IS *
C     *        SMALLER THAN CLUB, SET CLUB = STD AND SAVE THE CORRESPONDING *
C     *        FEASIBLE SOLUTION                                           *
C     ***********************************************************************
      IF( CLUB.LT.TD(K)) GO TO 130
      CLUB = TD(K)
      DO 129 JJ = 1,N,1
      BFSD(JJ) = IAS(JJ)
  129 CONTINUE
  130 BRANCH(K) = 0
      GO TO 90
  131 BRANCH(K) = 1
      SUBT(K) = I
      NARCS(K) = II
   90 CONTINUE
      IF(IPRED.EQ.1) GO TO 160
      LL1 =IPRED
  150 IF(P(LL1).EQ.1) GO TO 152
      LL2 = R(LL1)
      LL3 = C(LL1)
      LL1 = P(LL1)
      IDIST(LL2,LL3) = ISDIST(LL2,LL3)
      GO TO 150
  152 LL2 = R(LL1)
      LL3 = C(LL1)
      IDIST(LL2,LL3) = ISDIST(LL2,LL3)
C     ***********************************************************************
C     *     STEP 7                                                         *
C     *        IF CLUB IS LESS THAN THE LOWER BOUNDS ON ALL OF THE UNEXPLORED *
C     *        SUBPROBLEMS,THE SOLUTION CORRESPONDING TO CLUB IS AN OPTIMAL *
C     *        SOLUTION, SO STOP.  OTHERWISE, GO TO STEP 8.               *
C     ***********************************************************************
  160 DO 132  I = 2,K,1
      IF(BRANCH(I).EQ.0) GO TO 132
      IF( CLUB .GT.TD(I)) GO TO 134
  132 CONTINUE
      GO TO 135
C     ***********************************************************************
C     *     STEP 8                                                         *
C     *        SELECT THE UNEXPLORED SUBPROBLEM WITH THE SMALLEST VALUE.   *
C     *        FIND THE MINIMUM DISTANCE FOR THE UNFEASIBLE NODES.         *
C     *        SET THE INITIAL MINIMAL NODE TO THE VALUE OF THE COUNTER IN THE *
C     *        PREVIOUS LOOP, AND RETURN FOR FURTHER BRANCHING.            *
C     ***********************************************************************
  134 MINND = I
      DO 142  J = I,K,1
      IF(BRANCH(J).EQ. 0) GO TO 142
      IF(TD(J).LT.TD(MINND)) MINND=J
  142 CONTINUE
      BRANCH(MINND) = 0
      IPRED = MINND
      GO TO 700
C     ***********************************************************************
C     *     OUTPUT THE FINAL MINIMAL DISTANCE.                             *
C     *     OUTPUT THE ASSIGNMENT FOR THE OPTIMAL SOLUTION.                *
C     ***********************************************************************
  135 WRITE(6,222)CLUB
  222 FORMAT(//,' THE OPTIMAL FEASIBLE SOLUTION DISTANCE IS', F12.0)
      DO 136 I = 1,N,1
      WRITE(6,220) I, BFSD(I)
  220 FORMAT(' THE ASSIGNMENT FOR',I3,'  IS ==>',F12.0)
  136 CONTINUE
      GO TO 50
```

```
C     ************************************************************************
C     *   THE SOLUTION TO THE ASSIGNMENT PROBLEM IS THE OPTIMAL SOLUTION    *
C     *   TO THE TRAVELING SALESMAN PROBLEM.                                *
C     ************************************************************************
  200 WRITE(6,201)
  201 FORMAT(////5X,'THE SOLUTION HAS NO SUBTOURS,HENCE THE OPTIMAL SOLU
     *TION OF THE ASSIGNMENT',/5X,'PROBLEM IS ALSO AN OPTIMAL SOLUTION O
     *F THE TRAVELING SALESMAN PROBLEM',//)
      WRITE(6,202) MD
  202 FORMAT(5X,'THE TOTAL MINIMAL DISTANCE IS',I8,//)
      DO 203 I = 1,N,1
      WRITE(6,204) I,IAS(I)
  203 CONTINUE
  204 FORMAT(5X,'THE ASSIGNMENT FOR ',I3,'  IS ==>',I8)
      GO TO 50
 2000 STOP
      END
```

/DATA

```
TEN CITY PROBLEM
   10
1000000      184      292      449      670      516      598      618      881      909
     184 1000000      195      310      540      357      514      434      697      964
     292      195 1000000      215      380      232      434      493      719      955
     449      310      215 1000000      288      200      566      787      790     1020
     670      540      380      288 1000000      211      436      814      632      974
     516      357      232      200      211 1000000      381      642      697      952
     598      514      434      566      436      381 1000000      295      224      541
     618      434      493      787      814      642      295 1000000      320      341
     881      697      719      790      632      697      224      320 1000000      318
     909      964      955     1020      974      952      541      341      318 1000000
```

```
TEN CITY PROBLEM


THE DISTANCE MATRIX:

1000000      184      292      449      670      516      598      618      881      909
     184 1000000      195      310      540      357      514      434      697      964
     292      195 1000000      215      380      232      434      493      719      955
     449      310      215 1000000      288      200      566      787      790     1020
     670      540      380      288 1000000      211      436      814      632      974
     516      357      232      200      211 1000000      381      642      697      952
     598      514      434      566      436      381 1000000      295      224      541
     618      434      493      787      814      642      295 1000000      320      341
     881      697      719      790      632      697      224      320 1000000      318
     909      964      955     1020      974      952      541      341      318 1000000


THE OPTIMAL FEASIBLE SOLUTION DISTANCE IS        2855.
THE ASSIGNMENT FOR  1  IS ==>        2.
THE ASSIGNMENT FOR  2  IS ==>        8.
THE ASSIGNMENT FOR  3  IS ==>        1.
THE ASSIGNMENT FOR  4  IS ==>        3.
THE ASSIGNMENT FOR  5  IS ==>        6.
THE ASSIGNMENT FOR  6  IS ==>        4.
THE ASSIGNMENT FOR  7  IS ==>        5.
THE ASSIGNMENT FOR  8  IS ==>       10.
THE ASSIGNMENT FOR  9  IS ==>        7.
THE ASSIGNMENT FOR 10  IS ==>        9.
```

5.4 BRANCH–AND–BOUND ALGORITHM FOR INTEGER PROGRAMMING

Consider the general mixed-integer linear programming problem in canonical form (constraints have been converted to less-than-or-equal-to constraints).

$$\text{minimize:} \quad z = \sum_{j=1}^{r} c_j x_j + \sum_{j=r+1}^{n} c_j y_j$$

$$\text{subject to:} \quad \sum_{j=1}^{r} a_{ij} x_j + \sum_{j=r+1}^{n} a_{ij} y_j \leqslant b_i \quad i = 1, 2, \ldots, m$$

$$x_j \geqslant 0, y_j \geqslant 0 \quad \text{for all } j$$

$$x_j \text{ is an integer}$$

where the c_j elements are the cost coefficients and the a_{ij} and b_i elements are known constants.

5.4.1 Dakin's Modification of the Land and Doig Algorithm Illustrated

Consider the constrained optimization problem:

$$\text{minimize:} \quad Z = x_1 + 4x_2$$
$$\text{subject to:} \quad 2x_1 + x_2 \leqslant 8$$
$$x_1 + 2x_2 \geqslant 6$$
$$x_1, x_2 \quad \geqslant 0$$
$$x_1, x_2 \text{ are integers}$$

Dakin's algorithm to solve this problem is:

Step 1
Ignore the integrality constraints and solve the problem as a regular LP problem. The graphic solution is given in Figure 5.6.
The optimal solution is: $x_1 = \frac{10}{3}$, $x_2 = \frac{4}{3}$, $Z = \frac{26}{3}$. $Z = \frac{26}{3} = 8\frac{2}{3}$ is a lower bound on the set of all feasible solutions (node 1 in Figure 5.9).

Step 2
Since x_1 and x_2 both have fractional values in step 1, arbitrarily select one to branch on next. Suppose we select x_1 to branch on. The set of feasible solutions is partitioned into two subsets. One set contains all feasible solutions with the constraint

$$x_1 \leqslant \left[\frac{10}{3}\right] = 3$$

and the other contains the set of all feasible solutions with the constraint

$$x_1 \geqslant \left[\frac{10}{3}\right] + 1 = 4$$

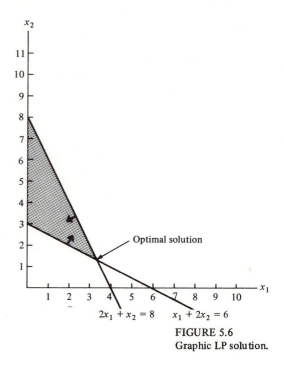

FIGURE 5.6
Graphic LP solution.

This reduces the region of feasible solutions of the LP problem, but leaves the region of feasible solutions of the integer LP problem unchanged since there are no integers between $[\frac{10}{3}]$ and $[\frac{10}{3}] + 1$.

The problem corresponding to node 2 in Figure 5.9 is

$$\text{minimize:} \quad Z = x_1 + 4x_2$$
$$\text{subject to:} \quad 2x_1 + \ x_2 \leqslant 8$$
$$x_1 + 2x_2 \geqslant 6$$
$$x_1 \qquad \leqslant 3$$
$$x_1, x_2 \qquad \geqslant 0$$
$$x_1, x_2 \text{ are integers}$$

Ignore the integer constraint on x_2 and solve the corresponding LP problem. The graphic solution is given in Figure 5.7.

The optimal solution is: $x_1 = 3$, $x_2 = \frac{3}{2}$, $Z = 9$. The solution is still nonfeasible for the original problem, but $Z = 9$ is a lower bound on the set of all feasible solutions with $x_1 \leqslant 3$ (node 2 in Figure 5.9).

Likewise, the problem corresponding to node 3 in Figure 5.9 is

$$\text{minimize:} \quad Z = x_1 + 4x_2$$

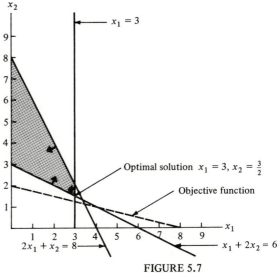

FIGURE 5.7
Graphic solution with $x_1 \leq 3$.

$$\text{subject to:} \quad 2x_1 + x_2 \leq 8$$
$$x_1 + 2x_2 \geq 6$$
$$x_1 \qquad \geq 4$$
$$x_2 \qquad \geq 0$$
$$x_1, x_2 \text{ are integers}$$

Ignore the integer restriction and solve the corresponding LP problem. The graphic solution is given in Figure 5.8. There is no feasible solution, by observation.

Step 3
Since node 2 is the only candidate for branching, a fractional-valued variable is selected (of course, x_2 is the *only* fractional-valued variable in this case) for further branching. The set of feasible solutions with $x_1 \leq 3$ (node 2) is partitioned into two subsets, one with $x_2 \leq [\frac{3}{2}] = 1$ and one with $x_2 \geq [\frac{3}{2}] + 1 = 2$. These subsets correspond to nodes 4 and 5, respectively (Figure 5.11).

The subproblem to solve at

node 4 is

minimize: $Z = x_1 + 4x_2$
subject to: $2x_1 + x_2 \leq 8$
$\qquad\qquad x_1 + 2x_2 \geq 6$
$\qquad\qquad x_1 \qquad \leq 3$

node 5 is

minimize: $Z = x_1 + 4x_2$
subject to: $2x_1 + x_2 \leq 8$
$\qquad\qquad x_1 + 2x_2 \geq 6$
$\qquad\qquad x_1 \qquad \leq 3$

$$x_2 \leqslant 1 \qquad\qquad\qquad x_2 \geqslant 2$$

$$x_1, x_2 \geqslant 0 \qquad\qquad\qquad x_1 \geqslant 0$$

By observation, the subproblem at node 4 is infeasible. The graphic solution of the subproblem at node 5 is given in Figure 5.10.

The optimal solution is: $x_1 = 2, x_2 = 2, Z = 10$. This is a feasible solution of the original problem and, since nodes 3 and 4 yielded nonfeasible solutions, the above feasible solution is optimal. That is, $x_1 = 2, x_2 = 2$ is an optimal solution of the original problem with an optimal value of the objective function equal to 10.

5.4.2 Algorithm 5.2—Dakin's Modification of the Land and Doig Algorithm

The notation and framework presented in Section 5.4 will be used throughout this section. Specifically,

IOP = initial optimization problem (minimization)
Z_0 = current least upper bound on optimal solution
$(CP)_I$ = current candidate problem being explored
$(CP_R)_I$ = same as $(CP)_I$ except with the integrality restriction relaxed
Candidate list = active subproblems (subproblems that are still candidates to be explored)

Step 1
Set

$$Z_0 = 10^{10}$$

$$K = 1$$

$$(CP)_1 = IOP$$

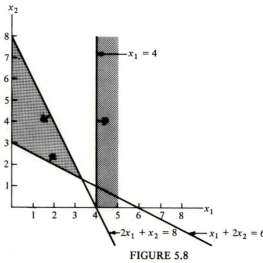

FIGURE 5.8
Graphic solution with $x_1 \geqslant 4$.

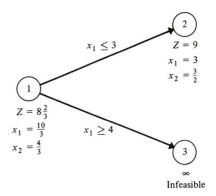

FIGURE 5.9
Partial solution tree.

Thus, $(CP)_1$ is the initial mixed-integer LP problem we wish to solve.

Step 2
Set $I = 1$.

Step 3
Relax all integrality restrictions in $(CP)_I$. $(CP_R)_I$ is the new problem with the integrality restrictions ignored.

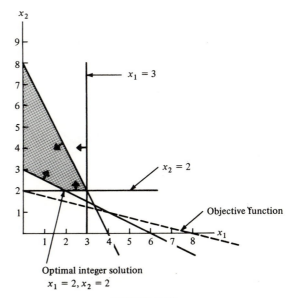

FIGURE 5.10
Graphic solution with $x_1 \leq 3$, $x_2 \geq 2$.

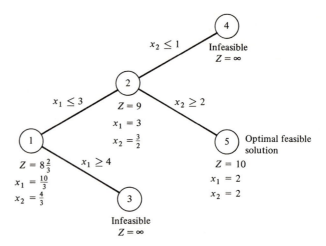

FIGURE 5.11
Complete solution tree—Dakin's algorithm.

Step 4
Solve $(CP_R)_I$ with an LP algorithm, say with the simplex algorithm. The value of the objective function is a bound for $(CP)_I$. If $(CP_R)_I$ does not have a feasible solution, set the corresponding bound equal to 10^{10}.

Step 5
If the solution of $(CP_R)_I$ yields a feasible solution for IOP, go to step 6; otherwise, go to step 8.

Step 6
If the value of the objective function using the feasible solution from step 5 is less than Z_0, go to step 7; otherwise, go to step 10.

Step 7
Set Z_0 equal to the value of the objective function using the feasible solution in step 5 and go to step 10.

Step 8
If the bound calculated in step 4 is less than Z_0, go to step 9; otherwise, go to step 10.

Step 9
Add $(CP)_I$ to candidate list and go to step 10.

Step 10
If $I = K$, go to step 12; otherwise, go to step 11.

Step 11
Set $I = I + 1$ and go to step 3.

Step 12
If the candidate list is empty, go to step 15; otherwise, go to step 13.

Step 13
Remove a problem from the candidate list for branching using the LIFO (last-in-first-out) rule. That is, the last subproblem added to the candidate list is removed and labeled CP. K = 2.

Step 14
Select a fractional-valued x variable, say x_j, from the solution of CP_R and partition CP into two new subproblems, $(CP)_1$ and $(CP)_2$. $(CP)_1$ is the same as problem CP with the added constraint that

$$x_j \leqslant [x_j^*]$$

where x_j^* is the value of x_j in the solution of (CP_R). $(CP)_2$ is the same as problem CP with the added constraint that

$$x_j \geqslant [x_j^*] + 1$$

Recall that $[x_j^*]$ means the integer part of x_j^*. This reduces the feasible region of the LP problem, but leaves the feasible region of the corresponding integer LP problem unchanged since there are no integers between $[x_j^*]$ and $[x_j^*] + 1$. Go to step 2.

Step 15
If a feasible solution has not been reached, go to step 17; otherwise go to step 16.

Step 16
The best feasible solution to date is an optimal solution for IOP. Go to step 18.

Step 17
No feasible solution for IOP exists. Go to step 18.

Step 18
Stop.
     A flowchart for Algorithm 5.2 is shown in Figure 5.12.

5.5 BRANCH-AND-BOUND ALGORITHM FOR BACKPACK-LOADING PROBLEM

Suppose we now constrain the backpack-loading problem to the case where no more than one of each item can be loaded. Thus, given the weight of each item W(I) and the value of each item V(I), which items should be loaded to maximize the value of the load when the maximum weight is W? It is assumed that each item is indivisible. Mathematically, the problem is to determine the values of X(I), I = 1, 2, . . . , N that will

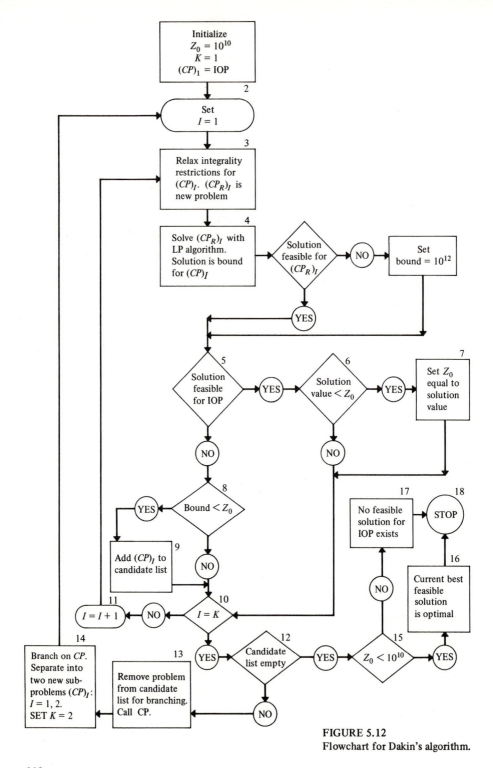

FIGURE 5.12
Flowchart for Dakin's algorithm.

218

$$\text{maximize:}\quad Z = \sum_{I=1}^{N} X(I) * V(I)$$

$$\text{subject to:}\quad \sum_{I=1}^{N} X(I) * W(I) \leqslant W$$

$$X(I) = \begin{cases} 0 \\ 1 \end{cases} \quad \text{for } I = 1, 2, \ldots, N$$

This is an all-integer (0-1) linear programming problem that can be solved by a number of algorithms (see [2], [8], and [12]); however, the special nature of the problem can be taken advantage of to solve the problem with an algorithm that is faster than general integer programming algorithms. One such algorithm to solve the problem at hand was derived by Kolesar [6].

5.5.1   Algorithm 5.3—Kolesar Algorithm for the Backpack-loading Problem

Consider the following notation:

N = number of items
$W(I)$ = weight of item I; $I = 1, 2, \ldots, N$
$V(I)$ = value of item I; $I = 1, 2, \ldots, N$
$B(K)$ = bound at node K
$SETI(K)$ = set of items included at node K
$SETE(K)$ = set of items excluded at node K
$SETF(K)$ = set of items that are "free" at node K
Z_0 = current greatest lower bound on the set of all feasible solutions
WL = maximum weight limit

Step 1
If $\min_{I} [W(I)] > WL$ no feasible solution exists, so stop; otherwise, go to step 2.

Step 2
If $\sum_{I=1}^{N} W(I) \leqslant WL$, then all items may be loaded and the problem is trivial, so stop; otherwise, go to step 3.

Step 3
Order the items by decreasing magnitude of $V(I)/W(I)$ and go to step 4.

Step 4
Set

$$B(1) = 10^{10}$$

$$SETI(1) = \emptyset$$

$$SETE(1) = \emptyset$$

$$SETF(1) = \{1, 2, \ldots, N\}$$

Go to step 5.

Step 5
Let K represent the terminal node with the largest bound. A node is terminal if it does not have branches emanating from it. The next branching will take place from node K. Initially node 1 is the only terminal node. Go to step 6.

Step 6
If SETF(K) = $\emptyset$ (all items included or excluded), an optimal solution is given by the indices contained in SETI(K). The maximum value of the cargo is

$$\max (Z) = \sum_{I \in SETI(K)} V(I)$$

Stop. If SETF(K) $\neq \emptyset$, go to step 7.

Step 7
Branch on the item with max [V(I)/W(I)] over all I ϵ SETF(K). Let ISTAR be the item. One branch includes item ISTAR and the other excludes item ISTAR. Go to step 8.

Step 8
Consider the node where ISTAR is excluded first. Set

$$K = K + 1$$
$$SETI(K) = SETI(K - 1)$$
$$SETE(K) = SETE(K - 1) \cup ISTAR$$
$$COUNT = 1$$

Go to step 9.

Step 9
Compute the upper bound B(K) by first loading all items in the set SETI(K) and then proceed in sequence (by maximum value) loading as much as possible of each item belonging to SETF(K) until the total weight loaded is exactly WL. The total value of the loaded items is denoted by B(K). Go to step 10.

Step 10
If COUNT = 1, go to step 11; otherwise, go to step 13.

Step 11
Consider the node where ISTAR is included. Set

$$K = K + 1$$
$$SETI(K) = SETI(K - 2) \cup ISTAR$$
$$SETE(K) = SETE(K - 2)$$
$$COUNT = 0$$

Go to step 12.

Step 12

Test the feasibility of the solution corresponding to node K by verifying if

$$\sum_{I \in SETI(K)} W(I) \leqslant WL$$

If the test fails, set $B(K) = -10^{10}$ and go to step 13; otherwise, go to step 9.

Step 13

Set

$$SETF(K-1) = SETF(K-2) - ISTAR$$
$$SETF(K) = SETF(K-2) - ISTAR$$

Go to step 5.

EXAMPLE 5.5.1 Consider a backpack-loading problem with the data given in Table 5.2. If no more than one of each item can be loaded, which items should be loaded to maximize the total value subject to the constraint that the total weight is less than or equal to 100? The solution using Kolesar's algorithm follows.

Step 1

$$\min_{I} [W(I)] = 10 < 100 = WL \quad \text{at least one item can be loaded}$$

Go to step 2.

Step 2

$$\sum_{I=1}^{7} W(I) = 210 > 100 = WL \quad \text{all items cannot be loaded}$$

Go to step 3.

Table 5.2 BACKPACK-LOADING DATA

Item number	Weight	Value
1	40	40
2	50	60
3	20	10
4	10	9
5	20	3
6	40	20
7	30	60

Table 5.3

New order	Item number	Weight	Value	Ratio: V(I)/W(I)
1	7	30	60	2
2	2	50	60	6/5
3	1	40	40	1
4	4	10	9	9/10
5	6	40	20	1/2
6	3	20	10	1/2
7	5	20	3	3/20

Step 3
Order the items by decreasing magnitude of V(I)/W(I). (See Table 5.3.) The new order will be used in the future when reference is made to the item numbers.

Step 4
Set

$$Z_0 = -10^{10}$$
$$B(1) = 10^{10}$$
$$SETI(1) = \emptyset$$
$$SETE(1) = \emptyset$$
$$SETF(1) = \{1, 2, \ldots, 7\}$$

Go to step 5.

Step 5
The original node is the only terminal node; go to step 6.

Step 6
$SETF(1) \neq \emptyset$, go to step 7.

Step 7

$$ISTAR = 1, \text{ since } V(1)/W(1) = 2 = \max_{I \in SETF(1)} [V(I)/W(I)]$$

Step 8
Set

$$K = K + 1 = 1 + 1 = 2$$
$$SETI(2) = SETI(1) = \emptyset$$
$$SETE(2) = SETE(1) \cup ISTAR = \{1\} \quad \text{exclude ISTAR}$$
$$COUNT = 1$$

Let node 2 be the node where ISTAR $= 1$ is excluded.

Step 9

SETI(2) is empty and item 1 is excluded, so load as much as possible of each item beginning with the most valuable item (item 2) until the total weight loaded is exactly WL $= 100$.

$$
\begin{array}{llllll}
\text{Load item 2,} & \text{weight} & 50, & \text{value} & 60 \\
\text{Load item 3,} & \text{weight} & 40, & \text{value} & 40 \\
\text{Load item 4,} & \text{weight} & 10, & \text{value} & 9 \\
\hline
& & \text{Total} = 100 & \text{Total} = 109
\end{array}
$$

Thus, $B(2) = 109$.

Step 10

Count $= 1$, so go to step 11.

Step 11

Consider the node where ISTAR $= 1$ is included (node 3). Set

$$K = K + 1 = 3$$
$$\text{SETI}(3) = \text{SETI}(1) \cup \text{ISTAR} = \{1\}$$
$$\text{SETE}(3) = \text{SETE}(1) = \emptyset$$
$$\text{COUNT} = 0$$

Go to step 12.

Step 12

$$\sum_{I \in \text{SETI}(3)} W(I) = \sum_{I \in \{1\}} W(I) = W(1) = 30 \leqslant 100 = WL$$

so go to step 9A.

Step 9A

Compute $B(3)$ at node 3.

$$
\begin{array}{lll}
\text{Load item 1, weight 30, value} & 60 \\
\text{Load item 2, weight 50, value} & 60 \\
\text{Load one-half of item 3, weight 20, value} & 20 \\
\hline
& \text{Total} = 140
\end{array}
$$

Thus, $B(3) = 140$.

Step 10A

Count is equal to 0, so go to step 13.

Step 13

Set

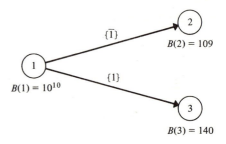

FIGURE 5.13
Partial solution tree—step 9A. ($\overline{1}$ denotes that
item 1 is excluded.)

$$SETF(2) = SETF(1) - \{1\} = \{2,3,4,5,6,7\}$$
$$SETF(3) = SETF(1) - \{1\} = \{2,3,4,5,6,7\}$$

Go to step 5A.

Step 5A
Since node 3 has the largest bound, set K = 3.

Step 6A
Since SETF(3) = {2,3,4,5,6,7}, go to step 7A.

Step 7A
ISTAR = 2, since $V(2)/W(2) = \frac{6}{5} = \max_{I \in SETF(3)} [V(I)/W(I)]$.

Step 8A
Set

$$K = K + 1 = 3 + 1 = 4$$
$$SETI(4) = SETI(3) = \{1\}$$
$$SETE(4) = SETE(3) \cup ISTAR = \{2\}$$
$$COUNT = 1$$

Node 4 is the node where item 1 is included and item 2 excluded.

Step 9B
Load items in SETI(4) (item 1), and as much as possible of each item beginning with
the most valuable item after item 2, namely, item 3, until the total weight is exactly
WL = 100.

Load item 1, weight 30, value		60
Load item 3, weight 40, value		40
Load item 4, weight 10, value		9
Load one-half of item 5, weight 20, value		10
	Total =	119

Thus, B(4) = 119.

Step 10B
COUNT = 1, so go to step 11B.

Step 11B
Consider the node where ISTAR = 2 is included (node 5). Set

$$K = K + 1 = 5$$
$$\text{SETI}(5) = \text{SETI}(3) \cup \text{ISTAR} = \{1,2\}$$
$$\text{SETE}(5) = \text{SETE}(3) = \emptyset$$
$$\text{COUNT} = 0$$

Go to step 12B.

Step 12B

$$\sum_{I \in \text{SETI}(5)} W(I) = \sum_{I \in \{1,2\}} W(I) = W(1) + W(2) = 30 + 50 = 80 < 100$$

so go to step 9C.

Step 9C
Compute B(5) at node 5.

$$\begin{array}{lr}
\text{Load item 1, weight 30, value} & 60 \\
\text{Load item 2, weight 50, value} & 60 \\
\text{Load one-half of item 3, weight 20, value} & \underline{20} \\
\text{Total} = & 140
\end{array}$$

Thus, B(5) = 140.

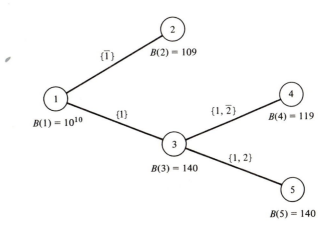

FIGURE 5.14
Partial solution tree—step 9C.

Step 10C

COUNT = 0, so go to step 13C.

Step 13C

Set

$$\text{SETF}(4) = \text{SETF}(3) - \{1,2\} = \{3,4,5,6,7\}$$
$$\text{SETF}(5) = \text{SETF}(3) - \{1,2\} = \{3,4,5,6,7\}$$

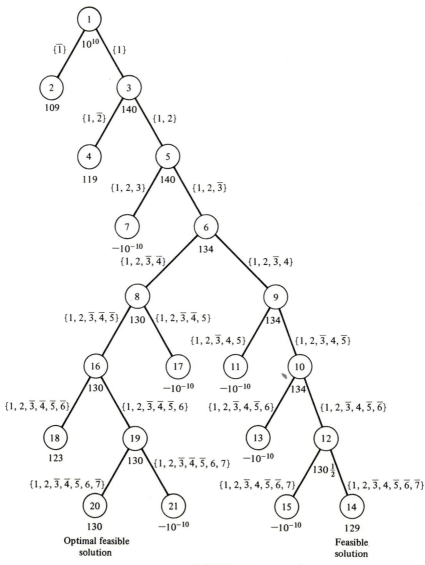

FIGURE 5.15
Complete solution tree—backpack-loading problem.

Go to step 5C.

The process eventually yields the tree in Figure 5.15.

Thus, the optimal feasible solution is to load items 1, 2, and 6 with a total value of 130. This corresponds to original items 2, 3, and 7.

EXAMPLE 5.5.2 Consider another example. A backpacking enthusiast has planned a 7-day backpacking trip into the Selway-Bitterroot wilderness area in Idaho. After all of the essential items were loaded, she discovered she could comfortably carry an additional 60 oz. She is now faced with the difficult problem of deciding which optional items should be loaded to maximize the comfort and enjoyability of her trip. Table 5.4 lists the possible items to be loaded with their corresponding weight and relative value to the backpacker.

Which items should be loaded to maximize the total value of the cargo if a maximum of an additional 60 oz are allowed and if no more than one of each item is loaded? The computer program in Section 5.5.2 was used to determine the optimal solution.

5.5.2 Computer Program for Algorithm 5.3

This program will solve backpack (knapsack) problems with a maximum of 25 items. Larger problems can be solved by changing the components of the variables in the INTEGER and DIMENSION statements. The program as listed is set up to handle a maximum of 500 nodes or a maximum number of nodes as specified by the variable

Table 5.4 BACKPACK ITEMS, WEIGHTS, AND VALUES

Item	Item number	Weight, oz	Value
Sleeping bag liner	1	12	2
Book	2	5	3
Camera and film	3	20	9
Extra rope	4	1	2
Plastic wash basin	5	5	4
Playing cards	6	3	4
Extra fishing equipment	7	10	2
Extra socks	8	6	7
Vest	9	8	8
Popcorn	10	7	10
Extra candy bars	11	4	3
Pancake mix and syrup	12	12	6
Grill	13	3	5
Extra flashlight batteries	14	3	5
Reflector oven	15	20	7
Saw	16	1	8
Wire	17	2	6

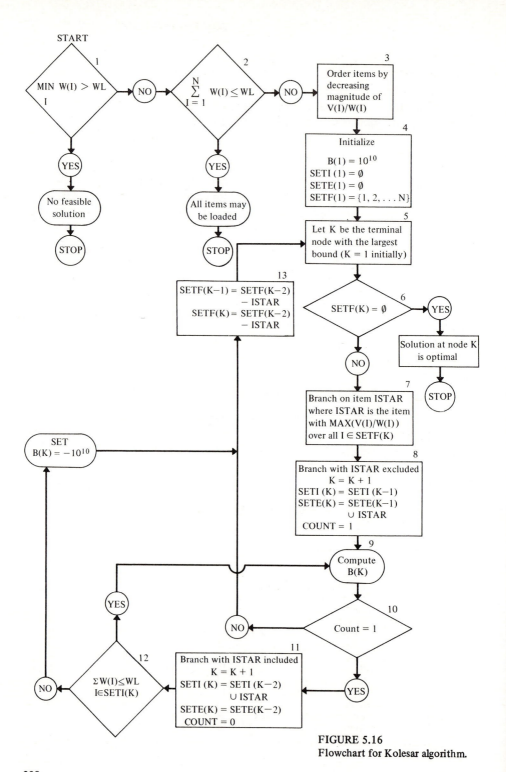

FIGURE 5.16
Flowchart for Kolesar algorithm.

228

MAXNOD. Generally, a value of MAXNOD should be read-in that is one less than the number in the first component of the variable STATUS in the INTEGER statement.

The program follows Algorithm 5.3 closely with the exception that the variable STATUS takes the place of the three variables SETI, SETE, and SETF. In the algorithm SETI(K), SETE(K), and SETF(K) represent the set of items that are included, excluded, and free at node K, respectively. In the program

$$STATUS(K,J) = \begin{cases} -1 & \text{if item J is included at node K} \\ 0 & \text{if item J is excluded at node K} \\ 1 & \text{if item J is free at node K} \end{cases}$$

The program occupies 92K bytes of core storage and required 0.13 s of IBM 370/168 time to solve the problem in Table 5.4.

```
C     ********************************************************************
C     *                                                                *
C     *    ** ALGORITHM 5.3  KOLESAR'S ALGORITHM **                    *
C     *        FOR BACKPACK LOADING PROBLEM                            *
C     *    THIS PROGRAM IS CURRENTLY SET UP TO HANDLE A MAXIMUM OF 25 ITEMS *
C     *    AND 500 NODES. IF AN OPTIMAL SOLUTION IS NOT OBTAINED BEFORE *
C     *    THE MAXIMUM NUMBER OF NODES IS REACHED, A MESSAGE WILL PRINT *
C     *    STATING SUCH.  TO INCREASE THE NUMBER OF ITEMS AND/OR THE MAXIMUM *
C     *    NUMBER OF NODES THE PROGRAM WILL HANDLE, CHANGE THE CORRESPONDING *
C     *    NUMBERS IN THE INTEGER AND DIMENSION STATEMENT.  IF THE MAXIMUM *
C     *    NUMBER OF NODES IS CHANGED, THE NUMBER READ IN FOR -MAXNOD- *
C     *    (THE MAXIMUM NUMBER OF NODES THE USER WILL TOLERATE) MUST ALSO *
C     *    BE CHANGED TO REFLECT THIS CHANGE.                          *
C     *                                                                *
C     * THIS PROGRAM IS DESIGNED                                       *
C     *    TO READ                                                     *
C     *        CARD 1   COLS  2-80   TITLE  DESCRIPTION OF THE PROBLEM USING *
C     *                                     ANY CHARACTERS ON KEYPUNCH *
C     *                                     ** COLUMN 1 MUST BE LEFT BLANK ** *
C     *        CARD 2   COLS  1- 5   N  NUMBER OF ITEMS  (I5)          *
C     *                       6-10   MAXNOD  MAXIMUM NUMBER OF NODES   *
C     *                                      USER WILL TOLERATE  (I5)  *
C     *                      11-20   WL  WEIGHT LIMIT  (F10.0)         *
C     *        CARDS 3 TO N+2   N CARDS SUCH THAT THE ITH CARD OF EACH *
C     *                          (I=1,2,...,N) PUNCHED AS:            *
C     *                 COLS  1- 5   ITEM(I)  ITEM NUMBER  (I5)        *
C     *                       6-15   W(I)  WEIGHT OF ITEM I  (F10.0)   *
C     *                      16-25   V(I)  VALUE OF ITEM I  (F10.0)    *
C     *                 TO SOLVE MORE THAN ONE PROBLEM AT A TIME, REPEAT THE *
C     *                 READ SEQUENCE, AND STACK THE DATA ONE BEHIND THE OTHER *
C     *                                                                *
C     *    TO CALCULATE                                                *
C     *        STATUS(I,J)  -1  ITEM J IS INCLUDED AT NODE I          *
C     *                      0  ITEM J IS EXCLUDED AT NODE I          *
C     *                      1  ITEM J IS FREE AT NODE I              *
C     *        B(K)         VALUE OF THE CARGO AT NODE K              *
C     *        WT(K)        WEIGHT OF THE CARGO AT NODE K             *
C     *                                                                *
C     *    TO PRINT                                                    *
C     *                                                                *
C     *        INPUT DATA                                              *
C     *        THE MAXIMUM VALUE OF THE CARGO                          *
C     *        THE WEIGHT OF THE CARGO THAT PRODUCES THE MAXIMUM VALUE *
C     *        THE LIST OF ITEMS TO INCLUDE IN THE BACKPACK            *
C     ********************************************************************
```

```
      INTEGER *4 STATUS(500,25),COUNT
      DIMENSION ITEM(25),W(25),V(25),WT(500),B(500),RATIO(25)
      REAL*4 TITLE(20)
    1 READ(5,110,END=9999) TITLE
  110 FORMAT(20A4)
      WRITE(6,111) TITLE
  111 FORMAT('1',20A4,//)
      READ(5,100) N,MAXNOD,WL
  100 FORMAT(2I5,F10.0)
      WRITE(6,117)
  117 FORMAT(' ITEM #      WEIGHT      VALUE')
      DO 4 I=1,N
      READ(5,101) ITEM(I),W(I),V(I)
  101 FORMAT(I5,2F10.0)
      WRITE(6,118)ITEM(I),W(I),V(I)
  118 FORMAT(I5,F14.2,F10.2)
    4 CONTINUE
      AMINWT=W(1)
      DO 5 I=2,N
      IF(W(I).LT.AMINWT)AMINWT=W(I)
    5 CONTINUE
C     ****************************************************************************
C     *    STEP 1                                                             *
C     *           IF MIN W(I)>MAXIMUM WEIGHT LIMIT, NO SOLUTION, OTHERWISE,   *
C     *              GO TO STEP 2                                             *
C     ****************************************************************************
      IF(AMINWT.LE.WL) GO TO 8
      WRITE(6,102)
  102 FORMAT(/' NO FEASIBLE SOLUTION')
      GO TO 1
C     ****************************************************************************
C     *    STEP 2                                                             *
C     *           IF SUM W(I)< OR = MAXIMUM WEIGHT LIMIT, ALL ITEMS CAN BE    *
C     *              LOADED, OTHERWISE GO TO STEP 3.                          *
C     ****************************************************************************
    8 TOT=W(1)
      DO 10 I=2,N
   10 TOT=TOT+W(I)
      IF(TOT.GT.WL) GO TO 12
      WRITE(6,103)
  103 FORMAT(/' ALL ITEMS CAN BE LOADED')
      GO TO 1
C     ****************************************************************************
C     *    STEP 3                                                             *
C     *           ORDER THE ITEMS BY DECREASING MAGNITUDE OF V(I)/W(I)        *
C     ****************************************************************************
   12 DO 14 I=1,N
   14 RATIO(I)=V(I)/W(I)
      M=N-1
   15 IFLAG=0
      DO 18 I=1,M
      IF(RATIO(I).GE.RATIO(I+1)) GO TO 18
      SAVE=RATIO(I+1)
      RATIO(I+1)=RATIO(I)
      RATIO(I)=SAVE
      ISAVE=ITEM(I+1)
      ITEM(I+1)=ITEM(I)
      ITEM(I)=ISAVE
      IFLAG=10
   18 CONTINUE
      IF(IFLAG.GT.0) GO TO 15
C     ****************************************************************************
C     *    STEP 4                                                             *
C     *           INITIALIZE THE UPPER BOUND AT NODE 1 AND THE INCLUDED,      *
C     *              EXCLUDED AND FREE VECTORS AT NODE 1.                     *
C     ****************************************************************************
      B(1)=10.E10
C     ****************************************************************************
C     *           SET ALL ITEMS FREE AT ALL NODES                            *
C     ****************************************************************************
```

```
      DO 20 I=1,MAXNOD
      DO 20 J=1,N
   20 STATUS(I,J)=1
C     ********************************************************************
C     *          SET K=1 AND BRANCH FROM NODE K.  L IS THE CURRENT NODE NO.  *
C     ********************************************************************
      L=1
      K=1
      GO TO 21
C     ********************************************************************
C     *  STEP 5                                                          *
C     *          FIND THE NODE WITH THE LARGEST BOUND AND CALL IT NODE K. *
C     ********************************************************************
   34 K=1
      BIG=B(1)
      DO 35 KK=2,L
      IF(B(KK).LE.BIG) GO TO 35
      BIG=B(KK)
      K=KK
   35 CONTINUE
C     ********************************************************************
C     *  STEPS 6 AND 7                                                   *
C     *          IF ALL ITEMS ARE INCLUDED OR EXCLUDED (NOT FREE) AT THE  *
C     *          CURRENT NODE, AN OPTIMAL SOLUTION HAS BEEN OBTAINED,     *
C.    *          OTHERWISE, BRANCH ON ITEM WITH MAX V(I)/W(I).            *
C     ********************************************************************
   21 DO 23 II=1,N
      IF(STATUS(K,ITEM(II)).EQ.1) GO TO 22
   23 CONTINUE
C               AN OPTIMAL SOLUTION HAS BEEN REACHED, PRINT RESULTS.      *
      WRITE(6,105) B(K)
  105 FORMAT(1X,'THE MAXIMUM VALUE OF THE CARGO IS',F10.2)
      WRITE(6,106) WT(K)
  106 FORMAT(1X,'THE WEIGHT OF THE CARGO IS',F10.2)
      WRITE(6,107)
  107 FORMAT(1X,'THE MAXIMUM VALUE OF THE CARGO IS OBTAINED BY')
      WRITE(6,109)
  109 FORMAT(6X,'INCLUDING THE FOLLOWING ITEMS:')
      DO 50 J=1,N
      IF(STATUS(K,J).NE.-1) GO TO 50
      WRITE(6,108) J
  108 FORMAT(5X,I5)
   50 CONTINUE
      GO TO 1
   22 ISTAR=ITEM(II)
      L=L+1
      IF(L.GT.MAXNOD) GO TO 40
      B(K)=-10.E10
      DO 24 J=1,N
      STATUS(L,J)=STATUS(K,J)
   24 STATUS(L+1,J)=STATUS(K,J)
      STATUS(L,ISTAR)=0
      STATUS(L+1,ISTAR)=-1
      COUNT=1
C     ********************************************************************
C     *  STEP 9                                                          *
C     *          COMPUTE UPPER BOUND AT CURRENT NODE BY FIRST LOADING ALL *
C     *          INCLUDED ITEMS AT CURRENT NODE AND THEN PROCEED IN SEQ.  *
C     *          (BY MAX VALUE), LOADING AS MUCH AS POSSIBLE OF EACH FREE *
C     *          ITEM UNTIL THE TOTAL WEIGHT LOADED IS EXACTLY EQUAL TO   *
C     *          THE MAXIMUM LOAD LIMIT.                                  *
C     ********************************************************************
      B(L)=0.0
      WT(L)=0.0
      DO 26 J=1,N
      IF(STATUS(L,J).NE.-1) GO TO 26
      B(L)=B(L)+V(J)
      WT(L)=WT(L)+W(J)
   26 CONTINUE
   29 DO 27 J=1,N
```

```
          IF(STATUS(L,ITEM(J)).NE.1) GO TO 27
          IF(WT(L)+W(ITEM(J)).GT.WL) GO TO 28
          WT(L)=WT(L)+W(ITEM(J))
          B(L)=B(L)+V(ITEM(J))
          GO TO 27
       28 DIFF=WT(L)+W(ITEM(J))-WL
          B(L)=B(L)+(1.-DIFF/W(ITEM(J)))*V(ITEM(J))
          WT(L)=WT(L)+(1.-DIFF/W(ITEM(J)))*W(ITEM(J))
          GO TO 30
       27 CONTINUE
C
C     ****************************************************************
C     *   STEP 10                                                   *
C     *         IF BOTH BRANCHES FROM NODE K HAVE BEEN EXPLORED, GO TO *
C     *             STEP 5, OTHERWISE, GO TO STEPS 11-12.           *
C     ****************************************************************
       30 CONTINUE
          IF(COUNT.NE.1) GO TO 34
          COUNT=0
C
C     ****************************************************************
C     *   STEPS 11-12                                               *
C     *         CALCULATE THE VALUE OF THE INCLUDED ITEMS AT THE CURRENT NODE *
C     ****************************************************************
          L=L+1
          IF(L.GT.MAXNOD) GO TO 40
          B(L)=0.0
          WT(L)=0.0
          DO 31 J=1,N
          IF(STATUS(L,J).NE.-1) GO TO 31
          B(L)=B(L)+V(J)
          WT(L)=WT(L)+W(J)
       31 CONTINUE
C
C     ****************************************************************
C     *         IF ALL INCLUDED ITEMS AT THE CURRENT NODE CAN BE INCLUDED, *
C     *             RETURN TO STEP 9, OTHERWISE GO TO STEP 5.       *
C     ****************************************************************
          IF(WT(L).LE.WL) GO TO 29
          B(L)=-10.E10
          GO TO 34
       40 WRITE(6,115)
      115 FORMAT(/' MAXIMUM NUMBER OF NODES EXCEEDED')
          GO TO 1
     9999 STOP
          END
```

```
/DATA

    -- BACKPACK LOADING PROBLEM FROM TABLE 5.3 --
   17    499        60.
    1         12.          2.
    2          5.          3.
    3         20.          9.
    4          1.          2.
    5          5.          4.
    6          3.          4.
    7         10.          2.
    8          6.          7.
    9          8.          8.
   10          7.         10.
   11          4.          3.
   12         12.          6.
   13          3.          5.
   14          3.          5.
   15         20.          7.
   16          1.          8.
   17          2.          6.
```

```
        -- BACKPACK LOADING PROBLEM FROM TABLE 5.3 --


ITEM #      WEIGHT       VALUE
   1         12.00        2.00
   2          5.00        3.00
   3         20.00        9.00
   4          1.00        2.00
   5          5.00        4.00
   6          3.00        4.00
   7         10.00        2.00
   8          6.00        7.00
   9          8.00        8.00
  10          7.00       10.00
  11          4.00        3.00
  12         12.00        6.00
  13          3.00        5.00
  14          3.00        5.00
  15         20.00        7.00
  16          1.00        8.00
  17          2.00        6.00
THE MAXIMUM VALUE OF THE CARGO IS       71.00
THE WEIGHT OF THE CARGO IS        60.00
THE MAXIMUM VALUE OF THE CARGO IS OBTAINED BY
      INCLUDING THE FOLLOWING ITEMS:
          2
          4
          5
          6
          8
          9
         10
         11
         12
         13
         14
         16
         17
```

5.6 ALGORITHM 5.4–GENERAL ALGORITHM FOR THE BRANCH–AND–BOUND TECHNIQUE

Now that we have presented three branch-and-bound algorithms, the general branch-and-bound principle embedded in each algorithm should be clear. However, to provide additional insight, a general algorithm for the technique will now be presented. It is applicable to all branch-and-bound algorithms. The following notation will be used throughout the presentation.

IOP = initial optimization problem (minimization assumed)

Z_0 = current least upper bound on the optimal solution

$F(A)$ = set of all feasible solutions for problem A

$(A_1, \ldots, A_k)$ = subproblems of A such that

(a) Every feasible solution of A is a feasible solution for exactly one A_I

(b) A feasible solution of any A_I is a feasible solution for A

Thus, $F(A_1), \ldots, F(A_k)$ is a partition of $F(A)$

$(CP)_I$ = current candidate problem being explored

Candidate list = active subproblems (subproblems that are still candidates to be explored)

Step 1

Initialize Z_0 to be an arbitrarily large positive constant. Set $K = 1$. Consider IOP as $(CP)_1$.

Step 2

Set $I = 1$.

Step 3

Choose a relaxation criterion $(CP_R)_I$ for $(CP)_I$. Generally, $(CP)_I$ is impossible or very difficult to solve, so constraints are relaxed to give a new problem $(CP_R)_I$ that is easy to solve. Clearly,

If $(CP_R)_I$ has no feasible solutions, neither does $(CP)_I$.

The minimum value of $(CP)_I$ is no less than the minimum value of $(CP_R)_I$.

The relaxation in Algorithm 5.1 is to ignore the constraint that one and only one person is assigned to each job.

Step 4

Bound $(CP)_I$. Apply an appropriate algorithm to $(CP_R)_I$ to bound all solutions emanating from $(CP)_I$. For example, in solving the traveling salesman problem, Eastman's algorithm solves the appropriate assignment problem to obtain this bound.

Step 5

If the solution of $(CP_R)_I$ revealed a feasible solution of IOP, go to step 6; otherwise, go to step 8.

Step 6

If the solution value of $(CP)_I$ is less than Z_0, the current least upper bound on the optimal solution of IOP, go to step 7; otherwise, go to step 10.

Step 7

Set Z_0 equal to the solution value of $(CP)_I$ and go to step 10.

Step 8

If the bound calculated in step 4 is less than Z_0, go to step 9; otherwise, go to step 10.

Step 9

Add $(CP)_I$ to candidate list and go to step 10.

Step 10

If all of the subproblems created by the last branch have been explored (bounded and analyzed), go to step 12; otherwise, go to step 11. That is, if $I = K$, go to step 12; otherwise, go to step 11.

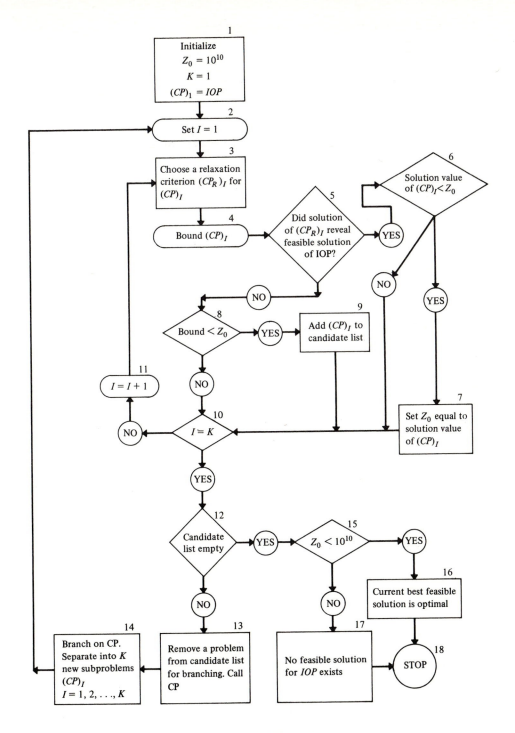

FIGURE 5.17
Flowchart for general branch-and-bound technique.

235

Step 11

Explore next subproblem among those created by the last branch. That is, let $I = I + 1$ and go to step 3.

Step 12

If the candidate list is empty, go to step 15; otherwise, go to step 13.

Step 13

Remove a problem from the candidate list for branching. Label the problem CP. Decision rules to "branch from lowest bound" or "branch from newest active bound" or a combination of the two are generally used. The decision rule to branch from newest active bound, sometimes referred to as *last-in-first-out* (*LIFO*), selects the last subproblem added to the candidate list.

Step 14

Branch on CP. Partition CP into K new subproblems $(CP)_I$, $I = 1, 2, \ldots, K$ and go to step 2.

Step 15

If a feasible solution has not been reached, go to step 17; otherwise, go to step 16.

Step 16

The best feasible solution to date is an optimal solution for IOP. Go to step 18.

Step 17

No feasible solution for IOP exists. Go to step 18.

Step 18

Stop.

SELECTED BIBLIOGRAPHY

1   Christofides, N., and S. Eilon: Algorithms for Large-Scale Travelling Salesman Problems, *Oper. Res. Q.*, vol. 23, pp. 511–518, 1972.

2   Cooper, Leon, and David Steinberg: "Introduction to Methods of Optimization," W. B. Saunders Company, Philadelphia, Pa., 1970.

3   Dakin, R. J.: A Tree-Search Algorithm for Mixed Integer Programming Problems, *Comput. J.*, vol. 8, pp. 250–255, 1965.

4   Eastman, W. L.: "Linear Programming with Pattern Constraints," Ph.D. dissertation, Harvard University, Cambridge, 1968.

5   Held, M., and R. M. Karp: The Traveling-Salesman Problem and Minimum Spanning Trees: Part II, *Math. Programming*, vol. 1, pp. 6–25, 1971.

6   Kolesar, P. J.: A Branch and Bound Algorithm for the Knapsack Problem, *Manage. Sci.*, vol. 13, pp. 723–735, 1967.

7   Land, A. H., and A. Doig: An Automatic Method of Solving Discrete Programming Problems, *Econometrica*, vol. 28, pp. 497–520, 1960.

8   Lawler, E. L., and D. E. Wood: Branch and Bound Methods: A Survey, *Oper. Res.*, vol. 14, pp. 699–719, 1966.

9 Lin, S., and B. W. Kernighan: A Heuristic Algorithm for the Traveling Salesman Problem, *Comput. Sci. Tech. Rept.* 1, Bell Laboratories, 1972.

10 Little, J. D., K. G. Murty, D. W. Sweeney, and C. Karel: An Algorithm for the Traveling Salesman Problem, *Oper. Res.,* vol. 11, pp. 979–989, 1963.

11 Mitten, L. G.: Branch and Bound Methods: General Formulation and Properties, *Oper. Res.,* vol. 18, pp. 24–34, 1970.

12 Plane, Donald R., and C. McMillan, Jr.: "Discrete Optimization," Prentice-Hall, Inc., Englewood Cliffs, N.J., 1971.

13 Shapiro, D.: "Algorithms for the Solution of the Optimal Cost Traveling Salesman Problem," Sc.D. thesis, Washington University, St. Louis, 1966.

14 Tomlin, J. A.: An Improved Branch and Bound Method for Integer Programming, *Oper. Res.,* vol. 19, pp. 1070–1074, 1971.

EXERCISES

Exercises 5.1–5.5 can be worked without the aid of a computer, whereas a computer should be available to aid in the solution of Exercises 5.6–5.12.

5.1 Solve the following assignment problems using the branch-and-bound algorithm in Section 5.2.

(a)

	Job			
Person	1	2	3	4
A	6	5	8	3
B	10	5	4	15
C	13	7	2	11
D	13	9	7	10

(b)

	Job			
Truck	1	2	3	4
A	10	6	8	12
B	13	5	6	15
C	12	7	5	14
D	8	9	7	13

5.2 Use Eastman's algorithm in Section 5.3.1 to solve the traveling salesman problems with following distance matrices:

(a)

	To city				
From city	1	2	3	4	5
1	∞	8	5	8	6
2	1	∞	3	1	8
3	1	7	∞	6	7
4	3	4	6	∞	9
5	6	5	3	7	∞

(b)

	To city				
From city	1	2	3	4	5
1	∞	11	16	21	31
2	18	∞	21	21	19
3	22	25	∞	29	24
4	24	34	31	∞	18
5	17	18	31	23	∞

(c)

	To city				
From city	1	2	3	4	5
1	∞	14	10	24	41
2	6	∞	10	12	10
3	7	13	∞	8	15
4	11	14	30	∞	17
5	6	8	12	16	∞

5.3 In Exercise 5.2(c), suppose it is impossible to travel from city 2 to city 1 and from city 1 to city 3. How does this affect the solution?

5.4 Use Dakin's algorithm to solve the constrained optimization problems

(a)

minimize: $z = 2x_1 + 5x_2$

subject to: $3x_1 + x_2 \leqslant 10$

$x_1 + 2x_2 \geqslant 8$

x_1, x_2 are nonnegative integers

(b)

maximize: $z = x_1 + x_2$

subject to: $x_1 + 2x_2 \leqslant 8$

$4x_1 - 3x_2 \leqslant 8$

x_1, x_2 are nonnegative integers

(c)

maximize: $z = x_1 + 3x_2$

subject to: $x_1 + x_2 \geqslant 2$

$3x_1 + 4x_2 \leqslant 12$

$x_1 - x_2 \geqslant 0$

x_1, x_2 are nonnegative integers

5.5 Use Kolesar's algorithm given in Section 5.5.1 to solve the following backpack-loading problem. Assume a maximum of 90 units of weight.

Item number	Weight	Value
1	30	10
2	40	40
3	25	25
4	10	50
5	60	30

Which items should be loaded to maximize the total value of the cargo?

Computer-oriented Exercises

5.6 Use the computer program for Eastman's algorithm given in Section 5.3.2 to verify your solution for Exercises 5.2(a)–(c).

5.7 Use the computer program for Eastman's algorithm given in Section 5.3.2 to solve the following traveling salesman problem.

	To city							
From city	1	2	3	4	5	6	7	8
1	∞	5	17	1	18	2	4	7
2	5	∞	13	15	4	5	11	10
3	17	13	∞	20	15	5	6	12
4	1	15	20	∞	12	3	15	4
5	18	4	15	12	∞	7	6	13
6	2	5	5	3	7	∞	3	8
7	4	11	6	15	6	3	∞	12
8	7	10	12	4	13	8	12	∞

5.8 Write a computer program for Dakin's algorithm (Algorithm 5.2) given in Section 5.4.2.

5.9 Use the computer program developed in Exercise 5.8 to solve the following integer programming problems:

(a)
$$\text{minimize: } z = 2x_1 + 3x_2$$
$$\text{subject to: } 3x_1 + x_2 \leqslant 10$$
$$x_1 + 2x_2 \geqslant 8$$
$$x_1, x_2 \text{ are nonnegative integers}$$

(b)
$$\text{maximize: } z = x_1 + x_2$$
$$\text{subject to: } 2x_1 + x_2 \leqslant 8$$
$$x_1 + 2x_2 \leqslant 8$$
$$x_1, x_2 \text{ are nonnegative integers}$$

(c)

$$\text{minimize:} \quad z = 4x_1 + 5x_2 + 6x_3 + 7x_4$$

$$\text{subject to:} \quad 25x_1 + 4x_2 + 9x_3 + 2x_4 + 4x_5 \geqslant 0$$

$$30x_1 + 3x_2 + x_3 + 4x_4 + 2x_5 \geqslant 0$$

$$35x_1 + 8x_2 + 7x_3 + 6x_4 + 5x_5 \geqslant 0$$

$$0 \leqslant x_i \leqslant 50$$

x_i is a nonnegative integer

(d)

$$\text{minimize:} \quad z = 6x_1 + 5x_2 + 8x_3 + 3x_4$$

$$+ 10x_5 + 5x_6 + 4x_7 + 15x_8$$

$$+ 13x_9 + 7x_{10} + 2x_{11} + 11x_{12}$$

$$+ 13x_{13} + 9x_{14} + 7x_{15} + 10x_{16}$$

$$\text{subject to:} \quad x_1 + x_2 + x_3 + x_4 = 1$$

$$x_5 + x_6 + x_7 + x_8 = 1$$

$$x_9 + x_{10} + x_{11} + x_{12} = 1$$

$$x_{13} + x_{14} + x_{15} + x_{16} = 1$$

$$x_1 + x_5 + x_9 + x_{13} = 1$$

$$x_2 + x_6 + x_{10} + x_{14} = 1$$

$$x_3 + x_7 + x_{11} + x_{15} = 1$$

$$x_4 + x_8 + x_{12} + x_{16} = 1$$

all x_i = 0 or 1

Your solution should agree with the solution of Exercise 5.1(a) if you let $x_i = 0$ if an assignment is not made and $x_i = 1$ if an assignment is made, where x_1 is the variable associated with assigning person A to job 1, x_2 is person A to job 2, ..., x_4 is person A to job 4, x_5 is person B to job 1, ..., x_9 is person C to job 1, ..., x_{16} is person D to job 4.

5.10 Consider the backpack data in Table 5.2. Verify the given solution by using the computer program for Kolesar's algorithm given in Section 5.5.2.

5.11 If the saw (item 16) and the wire (item 17) are deleted from the possible items to choose from in Table 5.4, which items should be loaded to maximize the value of the cargo? Assume the maximum additional ounces remain at 60.

5.12 Suppose you and a friend are preparing for a week of backpacking. Listed below are potential items that can be taken. Assign your own value to each item and then use the computer program for Kolesar's algorithm (Algorithm 5.3) to maximize the value of your cargo if the total contents is limited to 25 percent of your combined weights. You will need to change the INTEGER and DIMENSION statements to handle 60 items.

Item	Item number	Weight, oz	Item	Item number	Weight, oz
Two-man tent	1	56	Can opener-turner, etc.	31	10
Sleeping bags (2)	2	104	Detergent-scratcher	32	5
Ground cloth	3	21	Compass-matches-whistle	33	3
Ensolite pads (2)	4	32	Stove	34	27
Flashlight	5	3	Wire	35	2
Canteens (2), filled	6	74	Canned heat	36	3
Rope (30 ft)	7	1	Handcream-chapstick	37	3
Toilet articles	8	10	Insect repellant	38	4
Knife	9	2	Petroleum jelly	39	3
Packframes and bags (2)	10	109	Aluminum foil	40	2
First-aid kit	11	8	Jackets (2)	41	40
Bar soap	12	4	Snakebite kit	42	2
Toilet tissue	13	4	Notebook and pencil	43	1
Tape	14	3	Chewing gum	44	4
Pliers	15	4	Gloves	45	10
Maps	16	3	Plastic bags-pack cover	46	4
Fishing equipment	17	32	Sewing kit	47	1
Sleeping bag liners (2)	18	24	Popcorn	48	7
Book	19	5	Extra candy bars	49	4
Saw	20	4	Grill	50	3
Nail file	21	1	Extra batteries	51	3
Camera and film	22	40	Reflector oven	52	20
Playing cards	23	2	Long johns	53	18
Extra socks	24	16	Binoculars	54	14
Raincoat	25	4	Signal flare	55	3
Food	26	378	Canvas shoes	56	48
Aluminum pans (2)	27	11	Extra photographic equipment	57	42
Aluminum skillet	28	11	Extra shirts (2)	58	18
Food soaking jar	29	4	Sweaters (2)	59	56
Plates and cups	30	5	Extra cooking gear	60	23

6

DETERMINISTIC INVENTORY MODELS

6.1 INTRODUCTION

One of the most pressing problems in the manufacturing and sale of goods is the control of inventory. Many companies fail each year due to the lack of adequate control of their inventory. Whether it be raw materials used to manufacture a product or products waiting to be sold, problems arise when too few or too many items are held in inventory. For our purposes, we consider items to be in inventory if they are waiting to be used or sold. The greatest number of problems arise because too many items are held in inventory. Measures are usually taken to increase the inventory level of items that are frequently out of stock (items that have a lot of activity); however, items with a slow use or sale rate (items with minimal activity) tend to be ignored, and quite often too many of them are carried in inventory, in which case,

> Money is tied up in unnecessary inventory.
> Valuable space is used unnecessarily.
> Items may depreciate, deteriorate, or become obsolete.

On the other hand, if too few items are held in inventory,

> There may be a loss of profit because of the loss of sales and because of the loss of goodwill due to unfilled demands.

Additional manpower and/or costs may be associated with stockouts (items out of stock).

The annual cost to replenish inventory stock may be excessive because stock must be ordered frequently.

The manufacturing plant may have to be shut down because of the lack of raw materials.

Suppose we concentrate on the control of a single type of product that is being held in inventory with other types of products. When the inventory level of one type of product is low or the product is out of stock, we assume the space is available for use by other products. When the inventory level of a given product reaches a certain value, two alternatives are available.

1 A replacement order can be placed with an outside source for future delivery.

2 A production run can be started to produce enough of the product to raise the inventory to a certain level.

In each case, the complete order of stock can be received into inventory at one time or can be received in partial orders. If an order is placed with an outside source, an ordering cost c_0 is incurred each time an order is placed. On the other hand, if the product is produced internally, c_0 is a setup or changeover cost incurred in preparation for a production run. This assumes, of course, that the production of the given product takes only a fraction of the available production time. Inherent in this statement is the fact that the production rate exceeds the use or sale rate. Unfilled orders that can be filled at a later date are known as *backorders*. In this case, orders which are received after the inventory level reaches zero are backordered for delivery when a new order of stock is received. When backordering is allowed, it is necessary to determine

The number of backorders to allow before starting a production run *or* before receiving an order placed earlier with an outside source.

The number of units to produce once a production run has started *or* the number of units to order from an outside source.

Figure 6.1 is a general diagram of the inventory use and replacement process to be analyzed in this chapter.

Basically, the problem in inventory control is to minimize the sum of the costs associated with maintaining an inventory. These costs include

Costs associated with placing an order *or* setting up for a production run, c_0 (ordering costs)

Costs associated with holding stock in inventory, c_1 (inventory holding cost)

Costs associated with backordering stock, c_2 (backorder cost), if applicable

The key to minimizing inventory costs is deciding *when to order, how much to order,* and *how much backordering to allow* (if applicable). If the demand is known and the time to receive an order (lead time) is constant, then *when to order* is not a problem.

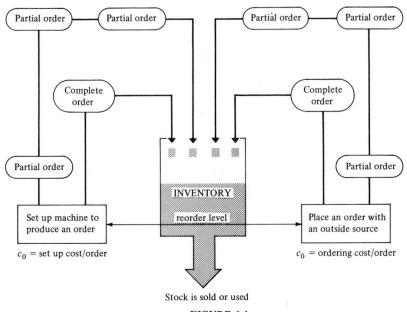

FIGURE 6.1
General inventory use and replacement process.

We will assume this is the case throughout this chapter, as we analyze the following inventory models:

1 Infinite delivery rate with no backordering (Section 6.2)
2 Finite delivery rate with no backordering (Section 6.3)
3 Infinite delivery rate with backordering (Section 6.4)
4 Finite delivery rate with backordering (Section 6.5)

In this chapter, we assume

A single type of product is analyzed even though many types are held in inventory for use or sale.
The planning period is 1 year.
The demand for the product is known and is constant throughout the year.
The lead time is known and is constant (time between the requisition and receipt of an order).

6.2 INFINITE DELIVERY RATE WITH NO BACKORDERING

In this section we assume

1 Complete orders are delivered at one time (infinite delivery rate).

2 Unfilled orders are lost sales (no backordering allowed).

3 All assumptions from Section 6.1 hold.

Thus, there are only two costs associated with this inventory model: ordering cost and inventory holding cost.

An analysis of a single-type product in inventory is valid in some rare cases, but generally is not valid because the space and costs associated with one type of product are interrelated to other types of products. However, the study of the control of one type of product will form the basis for the inventory control of many products. Likewise, the assumption that the demand for the product is known and is constant is probably only valid when the product is raw materials needed in a manufacturing process. For example, the constant production of fan-blade assemblies throughout the year requires a constant supply of steel. Thus, the demand for steel is known and is constant from week to week. In contrast, the demand for most items held in inventory to be sold is not constant throughout the year.

Basically, there are two broad classes of inventory items: those that will be used in manufacturing and those that will be sold. Items that are held in inventory for use in manufacturing will be referred to as raw materials. If management allows the stock of raw materials to be depleted, several conditions may result; namely,

Substitute or borrowed raw materials may be used.

Emergency measures may be taken to get a new supply of raw materials.

The company may switch to the production of a different product.

The manufacturing process may shut down completely.

In any case, loss of profit usually results when the stock of raw materials is allowed to be depleted.

For salable items, we assume unfilled demands are lost sales. No backordering of the product is allowed. Consequently, profit will suffer because of lost sales and, possibly, lost customers due to ill will.

In some inventory systems, the item carried in inventory is produced by the company that is holding it in inventory. In other systems, the product held in inventory is ordered and delivered from an outside source in a fixed length of time. In either case, the lead time, which is the time between the requisition and receipt of an order, is known and is constant.

Let $Q = $ order quantity (the amount to order each time

an order is placed) (6.1)

$D = $ annual demand for the product (6.2)

$c_0 = $ ordering cost/order (cost to place an order) (6.3)

$c_1 = $ annual inventory holding cost/unit (this is the cost

to hold one unit of stock in inventory for 1 year) (6.4)

$Q/2 = $ average inventory level (6.5)

$N = \frac{D}{Q} = $ number of orders/year (6.6)

$\mathrm{AOC}(Q) = c_0(D/Q) = $ annual ordering cost (6.7)

$$AIHC(Q) = c_1(Q/2) = \text{annual inventory holding cost} \qquad (6.8)$$

$$
\begin{aligned}
TAIC(Q) &= \text{total annual inventory cost} \\
&= AOC(Q) + AIHC(Q) \\
&= c_0(D/Q) + c_1(Q/2) \qquad (6.9)
\end{aligned}
$$

$$
\begin{aligned}
EOQ &= \text{economic order quantity [value of } Q \text{ that minimizes} \\
&\quad TAIC(Q)] \qquad (6.10)
\end{aligned}
$$

Figure 6.2 illustrates the relationship between Equations (6.7)–(6.10).

Note that the annual ordering cost decreases as Q increases and the annual inventory holding cost increases as Q increases. The EOQ is the value of Q that minimizes the sum of these two cost quantities.

EXAMPLE 6.2.1   A small manufacturing company specializes in the production of a certain type of goose-down sleeping bag. Based on the past records, it is estimated that the company will be able to produce 1500 bags during the next year if raw materials are available when needed $(D = 1500)$. The raw materials for each bag cost $48. Assume the bags are produced at a constant rate during the 300 working days that are available. It is estimated that the annual inventory holding cost for the raw materials for each bag is 22 percent of the cost of the raw materials for each bag

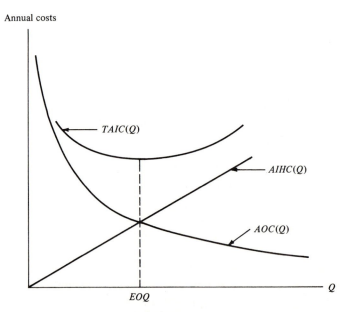

FIGURE 6.2
Relationship between Equations (6.7)–(6.10).

Table 6.1 EVALUATION OF TAIC(Q)

Q	TAIC(Q)
80	$891.15
81	890.64
82	890.28
83	890.05
EOQ → 84	889.95
85	889.98
86	890.13
87	890.39
88	890.78
89	891.27
90	891.87

$[c_1 = 0.22(48) = \$10.56]$. In addition, a \$25 cost is incurred each time an order for raw materials is placed ($c_0 = \$25$). Lead time is 7 days. Thus,

$$\text{TAIC}(Q) = \$25\,\frac{1500}{Q} + \$10.56\,\frac{Q}{2} \qquad (6.11)$$

One approach to finding the EOQ for this problem is enumeration. For example, we could enumerate TAIC(Q) for $Q = 7, 8, \ldots, K$, until $\text{TAIC}(K) > \text{TAIC}(K-1)$, then $Q = K - 1$ would be the EOQ. This is illustrated in Table 6.1. Of course, the disadvantage of this approach is that TAIC(Q) must be evaluated many times. We see from Table 6.1 that the EOQ is 84, which means that enough raw materials for 84 bags should be ordered each time an order is placed. In addition, the total cost of this policy is

$$\text{TC} = \text{cost of materials for 1500 bags} + \text{TAIC}(84)$$

$$= 1500(\$48) + \$889.95$$

$$= \$72,889.95$$

This is a long-run average total cost since

$$N = \frac{D}{Q} = \frac{1500}{84} = 17.85 \text{ orders/year}$$

is not an integer value. Hence, in some years 17 orders will be placed, while in others 18 orders will be placed. Figure 6.3 illustrates the reordering process.

Note that a reorder occurs 7 days prior to the time when there will be material for fewer than 5 bags. The daily use rate is material for 5 bags (1500 bags/300 working days = 5 bags/day). We assume the year is started with material for 84 bags. After 16 working days the inventory level will be down to 4, so an order for material to make 84 more bags is placed on day 9 for receipt on day 16. On day 16, the inventory level is replenished to 88 (4 on hand + 84 received). On day 33 (17 days later) the

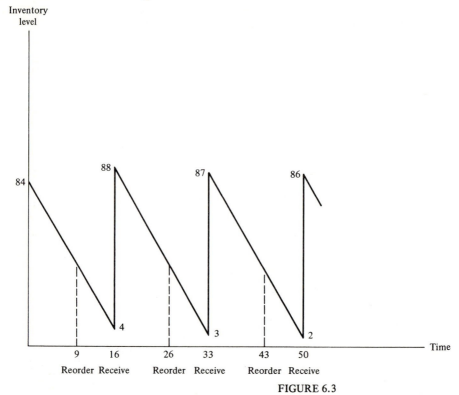

FIGURE 6.3
Reordering process for Example 6.2.1.

inventory level will reach 3 units, so a reorder for 84 units is placed on day 26 for delivery on day 33. The process continues in this manner throughout the year.

The simplest approach to finding the EOQ is to differentiate the $\text{TAIC}(Q)$ with respect to Q, and set the result equal to zero. That is,

$$\frac{d[\text{TAIC}(Q)]}{dQ} = \frac{d[25(1500/Q) + 10.56(Q/2)]}{dQ}$$

$$= -\frac{37{,}500}{Q^2} + \frac{10.56}{2} = 0$$

Then,

$$Q^2 = 7102.27$$

$$Q = 84.27$$

To determine the optimal integer value of Q, it would be necessary to evaluate Equation (6.11) for $Q = 84$ and $Q = 85$, and then choose the value of Q with the smallest TAIC value. Table 6.1 indicates that the EOQ is $Q = 84$.

This same result could have been obtained by equating the annual ordering cost and the annual inventory holding cost, since the value of Q that yields the EOQ occurs where these two cost equations intersect. Thus, from Equations (6.7) and (6.8), set

$$\text{AOC}(Q) = \text{AIHC}(Q)$$

$$c_0 \left(\frac{D}{Q}\right) = c_1 \left(\frac{Q}{2}\right)$$

$$25 \, \frac{1500}{Q} = 10.56 \, \frac{Q}{2}$$

$$Q^2 = \frac{25(1500)(2)}{10.56}$$

$$Q = 84.27$$

6.2.1 Derivation of the EOQ Formula

To derive the EOQ formula using differentiation, take the derivative of $\text{TAIC}(Q)$ with respect to Q, set the result equal to zero, and solve for Q.

$$\frac{d[\text{TAIC}(Q)]}{dQ} = \frac{d[c_0(D/Q) + c_1(Q/2)]}{dQ}$$

$$= -\frac{c_0 D}{Q^2} + \frac{c_1}{2} = 0$$

Then

$$Q^2 = \frac{2c_0 D}{c_1}$$

$$Q = \sqrt{\frac{2c_0 D}{c_1}} \qquad (6.12)$$

Equation (6.12) yields the EOQ.

We could have just as easily equated the annual ordering cost and the annual inventory holding cost, and then solved for Q. The result would have been exactly the same. That is,

$$\text{AOC}(Q) = \text{AIHC}(Q)$$

$$c_0 \, \frac{D}{Q} = c_1 \, \frac{Q}{2}$$

$$Q^2 = \frac{2c_0 D}{c_1}$$

$$Q = \sqrt{\frac{2c_0 D}{c_1}} \qquad (6.13)$$

EXAMPLE 6.2.2 *Quantity Discount* Suppose the supplier of the raw materials for the goose-down sleeping bags in Example 6.2.1 will give the manufacturer a 5 percent discount if he buys a 6 months' supply of raw materials each time an order is placed. Should the manufacturer accept the offer?

Although a general formula could be developed to determine the break-even point with respect to the maximum amount of raw materials that could be ordered each time an order is placed, the easiest procedure is to compare the total annual cost of operation for the two alternatives. It was determined earlier that the total annual cost using the EOQ ordering policy was

$$\text{TC} = \text{cost of materials for 1500 bags} + \text{TAIC}(84)$$
$$= 1500(\$48) + \$889.95$$
$$= \$72,889.95$$

Under the proposed offer of a 5 percent discount for large orders, the new cost of raw material for one bag is

$$\text{cost/bag} = \$48 - (0.05)(\$48) = \$45.60$$

Likewise,

$$c_0 = \$25$$
$$c_1 = 0.22(\$45.60) = \$10.03$$
$$Q = 750$$
$$D = 1500$$

Hence, the total cost under the proposed offer is

$$\text{TC} = \left(\begin{matrix}\text{cost of materials}\\\text{for 1500 bags}\end{matrix}\right) + \left(\begin{matrix}\text{annual}\\\text{order cost}\end{matrix}\right) + \left(\begin{matrix}\text{annual inventory}\\\text{holding cost}\end{matrix}\right)$$

$$= 1500(\$45.60) + \frac{25(1500)}{750} + \frac{(\$10.03)(750)}{2}$$

$$= \$68,400 + \$50 + \$3,761.25$$

$$= \$72,211.25$$

The proposed offer should be accepted since it would result in a savings of \$678.70.

6.3 FINITE DELIVERY RATE WITH NO BACKORDERING

Quite often a complete order of stock does not arrive at one time, as we assumed in Section 6.2. This may be because the complete order is not available for delivery, so it must be shipped in partial orders as it is produced or obtained from another source.

Another reason for partial shipments might be because the order is too bulky for shipment at one time. In any case, for simplicity, we assume that, after a fixed lead time, stock arrives at a certain fixed rate (finite delivery rate) until the complete order is received. We also assume that the arrival rate is greater than the use or sale rate, thus avoiding unfilled demands.

Let A = arrival rate of an order in units/day

U = use or sale rate in units/day

Q = order quantity

D = annual demand for the product

c_0 = ordering cost/order

c_1 = annual inventory holding cost/unit

$\frac{Q}{A}$ = time to receive complete order of Q units (in days)

$A > U$

Since units are used or sold while others are arriving to be put in inventory, the inventory level will never reach the EOQ value. To determine the average inventory level, let

$$U \frac{Q}{A} = \text{number of units used or sold while the new stock is arriving} \tag{6.14}$$

$$Q - U \frac{Q}{A} = \text{maximum inventory level} \tag{6.15}$$

$$\frac{1}{2} \left[Q - U \frac{Q}{A} \right] = \text{average inventory level} \tag{6.16}$$

We can now obtain

$$\frac{c_1}{2} \left[Q - U \frac{Q}{A} \right] = \text{annual inventory holding cost} \tag{6.17}$$

$$c_0 \frac{D}{Q} = \text{annual ordering cost} \tag{6.18}$$

As with the model in Section 6.1, the EOQ can be determined by equating Equations (6.17) and (6.18), and then solving for Q.

$$\frac{c_1}{2} \left[Q - U \frac{Q}{A} \right] = \frac{c_0 D}{Q}$$

$$c_1 Q^2 \left(1 - \frac{U}{A} \right) = 2 c_0 D$$

$$Q^2 = \frac{2 c_0 D}{c_1 (1 - U/A)}$$

$$Q = \sqrt{\frac{2 c_0 D}{c_1 (1 - U/A)}} \tag{6.19}$$

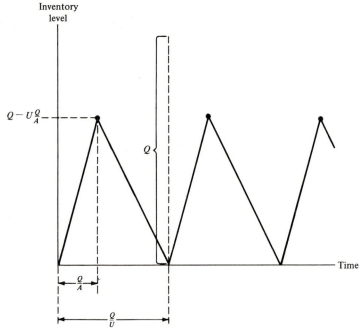

FIGURE 6.4
Finite delivery rate inventory model.

Figure 6.4 shows the partial order delivery model.

To illustrate, assume the conditions in Example 6.2.1 with an arrival (delivery) rate of 30/day.

$$D = 1500$$
$$A = 30/\text{day}$$
$$U = 5/\text{day}$$
$$c_0 = \$25 \text{ per order}$$
$$c_1 = \$10.56$$

Thus, the corresponding EOQ is

$$Q = \sqrt{\frac{2(25)(1500)}{(10.56)[1 - (5/30)]}}$$
$$= 92.3$$

Suppose we accept the policy of ordering materials for 92 bags each time an order is placed. The total annual cost is then

$$TC = 1500(\$48) + \frac{c_0 D}{Q} + \frac{c_1 Q}{2}\left(1 - \frac{U}{A}\right)$$

$$= 1500(\$48) + \frac{\$25(1500)}{92} + \frac{\$10.56(92)}{2}\left(1 - \frac{5}{30}\right)$$

$$= \$72,000 + \$407.61 + \$404.80$$

$$= \$72,812.41$$

This amounts to a considerable savings over the total annual cost ($72,889.95) when the complete order is delivered at once. Under the original policy of one delivery per order (EOQ = 84),

$$AOC(84) = \$446.42$$
$$AIHC(84) = \$443.52$$

and under the new policy of multiple deliveries per order (EOQ = 92),

$$AOC(92) = \$407.61$$
$$AIHC(92) = \$404.80$$

The savings attributed to annual ordering cost (fewer orders) is

$$\$446.42 - \$407.61 = \$38.81$$

while the savings attributed to annual inventory holding cost (smaller average inventory level) is

$$\$443.52 - \$404.80 = 38.72$$

Hence, approximately one-half of the savings is attributed to fewer orders and one-half to a smaller average inventory level. This will always be true, since under either policy AOC and AIHC will be equal when the corresponding EOQ is used. Thus, the difference between the AOC values using the new policy as opposed to the original policy will be equal to the difference between the AIHC values using the new policy as opposed to the original policy.

It should be clear that a policy that offers a partial order delivery will always be superior to a policy with a single delivery of the complete order.

6.4 INFINITE DELIVERY RATE WITH BACKORDERING

In the previous sections, we assumed that unfilled demands were lost. However, unfilled demands for salable items do not always result in lost sales. Quite often customers will wait for an ordered item to arrive, or they will permit the merchant to place an order for the item of interest. An unfilled demand that can be filled at a later date is known as a *backorder*. As might be expected, there is generally a cost associated with backorders. Clearly, if all demands could be backordered, and if there were no cost for backorders, there would be no need for inventory. The merchant could take orders and then wait until the most economical time for him to place an order for future delivery. But this is rarely the case. If an item is backordered, there are generally costs associated with

Loss of goodwill
Repeated delays in delivery
Additional bookkeeping
Loss of cash that would have been available for immediate use

The basic problem, then, is to decide how much to order each time an order is placed and how many backorders to allow before receiving a new shipment. We assume

1 Backorders are allowed.
2 Complete orders are delivered at one time.
3 All assumptions from Section 6.1 hold.

Let Q = order quantity
D = annual demand for the product
B = number of backorders allowed before replenishing inventory
c_0 = ordering cost/order
c_1 = annual inventory holding cost/unit
c_2 = annual backorder cost/unit (this is the cost of one backorder for 1 year)
t_1 = time from the receipt of an order until the inventory level is again zero
t_2 = time from a zero inventory level until a new order is received
t_3 = time between consecutive orders
LT = lead time
$N = \frac{D}{Q}$ = number of orders/year

Figure 6.5 illustrates the model under consideration. Note in Figure 6.5 that the following relationships hold:

$$\frac{t_1}{t_3} = \frac{Q - B}{Q} \qquad (6.20)$$

$$\frac{t_2}{t_3} = \frac{B}{Q} \qquad (6.21)$$

Also note that the average inventory level during time t_1 is $(Q - B)/2$ units. Since the inventory level is zero during time t_2, the annual inventory holding cost is given by

$$\text{AIHC}(Q, B) = c_1 \begin{pmatrix} \text{average inventory} \\ \text{level during time} \\ t_1 \end{pmatrix} \begin{pmatrix} \text{fraction of} \\ \text{time inventory} \\ \text{level is positive} \end{pmatrix}$$

$$= c_1 \frac{Q - B}{2} \frac{t_1}{t_3}$$

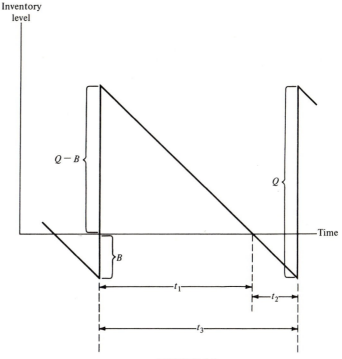

Inventory
level

$Q - B$

Q

Time

t_1

t_2

t_3

B

FIGURE 6.5
Infinite delivery rate with backordering.

From Equation (6.20), we see that

$$\text{AIHC}(Q, B) = c_1 \frac{Q - B}{2} \frac{Q - B}{Q}$$

$$= \frac{c_1(Q - B)^2}{2Q} \qquad (6.22)$$

Likewise, backorders occur only during time t_2, so the annual backorder cost is

$$\text{ABC}(Q, B) = c_2 \begin{pmatrix} \text{average number of} \\ \text{backorders during} \\ \text{time } t_2 \end{pmatrix} \begin{pmatrix} \text{fraction of the} \\ \text{time backorders} \\ \text{occur} \end{pmatrix}$$

$$= c_2 \frac{B}{2} \frac{t_2}{t_3}$$

$$= \frac{c_2 B}{2} \frac{B}{Q} \qquad \text{from Equation (6.21)}$$

$$= \frac{c_2 B^2}{2Q} \qquad (6.23)$$

The annual ordering cost is the same as in Section 6.2, namely,

$$\text{AOC}(Q) = \frac{c_0 D}{Q} \qquad (6.24)$$

Finally, the total annual inventory cost is

$$\text{TAIC}(Q,B) = \text{AOC}(Q) + \text{AIHC}(Q,B) + \text{ABC}(Q,B)$$
$$= \frac{c_0 D}{Q} + \frac{c_1 (Q - B)^2}{2Q} + \frac{c_2 B^2}{2Q} \qquad (6.25)$$

To minimize TAIC(Q,B), we take the partial derivative of TAIC(Q,B) with respect to Q and with respect to B, set the results equal to zero, and solve for Q and B. When this is done, the results are

$$Q = \sqrt{\frac{2c_0 D}{c_1} \frac{c_1 + c_2}{c_2}} \qquad (6.26)$$

$$B = \frac{c_1}{c_1 + c_2} Q \qquad (6.27)$$

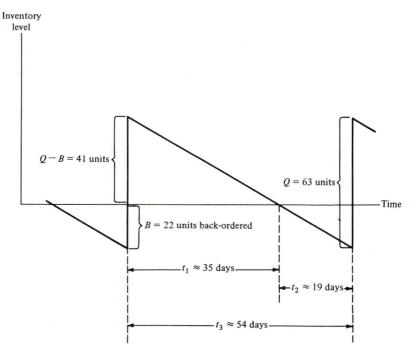

FIGURE 6.6
Results from Example 6.4.1.

EXAMPLE 6.4.1   Suppose a retailer has the following information available:

$D = 350$ units/year
$c_0 = \$50$ per order
$c_1 = \$13.75$ per unit
$c_2 = \$25$ per unit
$LT = 5$ days

To minimize the total annual inventory cost when backordering is allowed, how many units should be ordered each time an order is placed, and how many backorders should be allowed? The solution is

$$Q = \sqrt{\frac{2(50)(350)}{13.75} \frac{13.75 + 25}{25}}$$

$$\approx 63 \text{ units}$$

$$B = \frac{13.75}{13.75 + 25} 63$$

$$\approx 22 \text{ units}$$

Thus, the optimal policy is to allow approximately 22 backorders before replenishing the inventory with approximately 63 units. The results are illustrated in Figure 6.6.

6.5   FINITE DELIVERY RATE WITH BACKORDERING

This section is the same as Section 6.4 except we assume that each order for more stock arrives in partial orders at a constant rate each day until the complete order is received. Thus, all assumptions from Section 6.4 hold with the exception of the one just stated. Let

A = arrival (delivery) rate/day
U = use or sale rate/day
Q = order quantity
B = number of backorders allowed before replenishing inventory
c_0 = ordering cost/order
c_1 = annual inventory holding cost/unit
c_2 = annual backorder cost/unit
t_1 = time from zero inventory until the complete order is received
t_2 = time from receipt of complete order until the inventory level reaches zero again
t_3 = time from when backordering starts until a new order starts coming in
t_4 = time from when a new order starts coming in until all backorders are filled (inventory level comes back to zero again)

$$t_5 = \Sigma_{i=1}^{4} \, t_i$$
$$N = \frac{D}{Q} = \text{number of orders/year}$$
$$LT = \text{lead time}$$

Figure 6.7 illustrates the model under consideration.
Based on the above notation,

$$\text{AOC}(Q) = \frac{c_0 D}{Q} \tag{6.28}$$

$$\text{AIHC}(Q,B) = c_1 \, \frac{t_1 + t_2}{t_5} \, \frac{Q - t_1 U - B}{2} \tag{6.29}$$

$$\text{ABC}(Q,B) = c_2 \, \frac{t_3 + t_4}{t_5} \, \frac{B}{2} \tag{6.30}$$

$$\text{TAIC}(Q,B) = \frac{c_0 D}{Q} + \frac{c_1 A}{2Q(A - U)} \left(Q \, \frac{A - U}{A} - B \right)^2 + \frac{c_2 A B^2}{2Q(A - U)} \tag{6.31}$$

To find the value of Q and B that will minimize $\text{TAIC}(Q,B)$, take the partial derivative of $\text{TAIC}(Q,B)$ with respect to Q and with respect to B, set the results equal to zero, and solve for Q and B. When this is done,

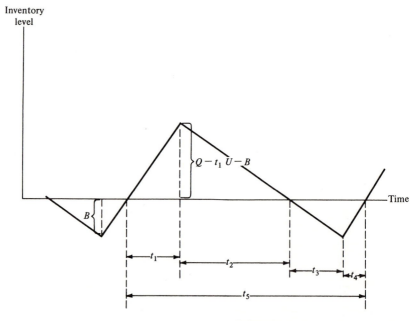

FIGURE 6.7
Finite delivery rate with backordering.

$$Q = \sqrt{\frac{2c_0 D}{c_1(1 - U/A)} \frac{c_1 + c_2}{c_2}} \qquad (6.32)$$

$$B = \frac{c_1}{c_1 + c_2}\left(1 - \frac{U}{A}\right)Q \qquad (6.33)$$

EXAMPLE 6.5.1 Suppose we have the same data as in Example 6.4.1, except each order arrives in partial shipments at the rate of 10/day. What should the value of Q and B be in order to minimize the total annual inventory cost? For example,

$$A = 10/\text{day}$$

$$U = \frac{350 \text{ units/year}}{300 \text{ days/year}}$$

$$= 1.1667 \text{ units/day}$$

Thus, from Equations (6.32) and (6.33), we have

$$Q = \sqrt{\frac{2(50)(350)}{13.75\left(1 - \frac{1.1667}{10}\right)} \frac{13.75 + 25}{25}}$$

$$\simeq 67 \text{ units}$$

$$B = \frac{13.75}{13.75 + 25}\left(1 - \frac{1.1667}{10}\right)(67)$$

$$\simeq 21 \text{ units}$$

The total annual inventory cost using these values is

$$\text{TAIC}(67,21) = \frac{50(350)}{67} + \left[\frac{13.75(10)}{2(67)(10 - 1.1667)}\right]\left[(67)\left(\frac{10 - 1.1667}{10}\right)\right.$$

$$\left. - 21\right]^2 + \frac{25(10)(21)^2}{2(67)(10 - 1.1667)}$$

$$= \$261.19 + \$169.36 + \$93.14$$

$$= \$523.69$$

6.6 SUMMARY

In this chapter, the annual cost of the product was ignored in the minimization of the total annual inventory cost, since the annual cost of the product is strictly a function of the annual demand and is completely independent of Q and B.

As mentioned earlier, a constant demand for a salable item is rarely realized. Likewise, lead time is generally not a constant. Instead, the demand and lead time are usually considered to be random variables with some distribution function. These cases will be discussed in Chapter 15.

Basically, this chapter serves as a general introduction to the subject of inventory control. Analytical solutions are readily available for the deterministic inventory models that were studied, so no computer programs were developed. However, two programs will be presented in Chapter 15 to solve probabilistic inventory models.

SELECTED BIBLIOGRAPHY

1 Buffa, E. S., and W. H. Taubert: "Production Inventory Systems: Planning and Control," rev. ed., Richard D. Irwin, Inc., Homewood, Ill., 1972.
2 Hadley, G., and T. M. Whitin: "Analysis of Inventory Systems," Prentice-Hall, Inc., Englewood Cliffs, N.J., 1963.
3 Magee, John F., and D. M. Boodman: "Production Planning and Inventory Control," 2d ed., McGraw-Hill Book Company, New York, 1967.
4 Naddor, Eliezer: "Inventory Systems," John Wiley & Sons, Inc., New York, 1966.
5 Plossl, G. W., and O. W. Wright: "Production and Inventory Control," Prentice-Hall, Inc., Englewood Cliffs, N.J., 1967.
6 Prichard, J. W., and R. H. Eagle: "Modern Inventory Management," John Wiley & Sons, Inc., New York, 1965.
7 Starr, M. K., and D. W. Miller: "Inventory Control: Theory and Practice," Prentice-Hall, Inc., Englewood Cliffs, N.J., 1962.

EXERCISES

6.1 The demand for a given product is exactly 10/day. The inventory holding cost/year is $20 per unit. Each time an order for a quantity of the product is placed, it costs $10. Each item costs $5 and sells for $7.50. How many units of the product should be ordered each time an order is placed to minimize the total annual cost of ordering and holding in inventory? Assume 360 demand days/year. Lead time is 1 day. No backordering is allowed.

6.2 In Example 6.2.1, suppose the company can produce 2000 sleeping bags per year, the raw materials cost $52 per bag, the ordering cost is $20, and the annual inventory holding cost per bag is 20 percent of the cost of the raw materials per bag. The lead time remains at 7 days and the number of working days remains at 300 days/year. What is the EOQ?

6.3 The supplier of the raw materials for the sleeping bags in Exercise 6.2 will give the manufacturer a 4 percent discount if he buys a 6-month supply of raw materials each time an order is placed. Should the manufacturer accept the offer? Why?

6.4 Assume the conditions in Exercise 6.2 with the exception that the delivery of raw materials comes in partial orders at the rate of 30/day. What is the EOQ?

6.5 If the cost of raw materials in Example 6.2.1 is reduced to $38 per bag, how are the answers to Exercises 6.2–6.4 affected?

6.6 In Example 6.4.1 where backordering is allowed and a complete order is delivered at one time, what is the optimal number of backorders to allow and what is the EOQ if the annual backordering cost is increased to $50 per unit?

6.7 What should be the values of Q and B in order to minimize the total annual inventory cost in Exercise 6.6 if orders arrive at an average rate of 5/day?

6.8 Suppose the CDPCA uses 25 boxes of data-processing cards per month. It costs $20 to place a replenishment order. The inventory holding cost per box per year is $5. What is the EOQ if backordering is not allowed and a complete order is received at one time?

7

SEQUENCING PROBLEMS

7.1 INTRODUCTION

The well-known sequencing problem is to determine the sequence in which two or more jobs should be processed on one or more machines in order to optimize some measure of effectiveness. The problem may have some constraints placed on it, such as due date for each job, processing order of each job on each machine, or variable processing times. The measure of effectiveness could be the total elapsed time between the start of the first job on machine 1 and the completion of the last job on the last machine or it could be maximum tardiness or total tardiness. Of course, other constraints or measures of effectiveness may be appropriate for a given problem.

Consider a simple sequencing problem where n jobs waiting to be done must each be processed on two machines in such a way that the total elapsed time between the start of the first job on the first machine and the completion of the last job on the last machine is minimum. We assume that the processing times are known and the no passing rule is in effect. That is, when a job is finished on machine 1, it goes directly on machine 2 if it is empty; otherwise, it starts a waiting line or joins the end of the waiting line if one already exists. Jobs which form a waiting line are processed on machine 2 in the same order that they joined the waiting line. Thus, if job k is processed seventh on machine 1, it will be the seventh job processed on machine 2 regardless of whether it joined a waiting line or not.

7.2 TWO-MACHINE SEQUENCING PROBLEM

We will now focus our attention on a simple example.

EXAMPLE 7.2.1 Ten jobs must be processed through two machines each day with no passing allowed between machines. That is, a job is placed on machine 1 first and as soon as it is processed it is placed on machine 2 if it is empty; otherwise, it is placed in a waiting line from which jobs are taken and placed on machine 2 on a first-come first-served basis.

Each job requires the amount of time given in Table 7.1 on the two machines.

The problem is to determine the sequence in which the jobs should be processed through the two machines in order to minimize the time between the start of the first job on machine 1 and the finish of the last job on machine 2. Table 7.2 illustrates the actual flow of jobs through the machines using the current sequence:

$$1\text{-}2\text{-}3\text{-}4\text{-}5\text{-}6\text{-}7\text{-}8\text{-}9\text{-}10$$

From Table 7.2 we see that the idle time on machine 1 is just the time between the finish of job 10 on machine 2 and the finish of job 10 on machine 1, namely, $94 - 72 = 22$.

The idle time on machine 2 is given by:

Idle time on machine 2 = time first job starts on machine 2

$$+ \sum_{k=2}^{10} (\text{time } k\text{th job starts on machine 2}$$

$$- \text{time } (k-1)\text{st job finished on machine 2})$$

$$= 20 + 6 + 0 + \cdots + 0$$

$$= 26$$

Table 7.1 10 JOBS, TWO MACHINES–
PROCESSING TIMES, minutes

Job number	Machine 1	Machine 2
1	20	4
2	10	12
3	3	5
4	10	8
5	5	6
6	2	12
7	8	4
8	7	10
9	3	6
10	4	1

Table 7.2   FLOW OF JOBS THROUGH MACHINES USING
THE SEQUENCE 1-2-3-4-5-6-7-8-9-10

Job	Machine 1		Machine 2		Idle time machine 2
	Time in	Time out	Time in	Time out	
1	0	20	20	24	20
2	20	30	30	42	6
3	30	33	42	47	0
4	33	43	47	55	0
5	43	48	55	61	0
6	48	50	61	73	0
7	50	58	73	77	0
8	58	65	77	87	0
9	65	68	87	93	0
10	68	72	93	94	0

We might ask the question, "Is there a sequence which would reduce the total processing time through the two machines?" It can be shown that the procedure of successively placing the job with the smallest processing time as close to the beginning of the sequence as possible if the processing time is on machine 1 and as close to the end of the sequence as possible if it is on machine 2 will yield an optimal sequence if jobs are deleted from consideration after they are assigned a position in the sequence. We will formalize this statement in Algorithm 7.1.

When all processing times are considered for both machines in the present example, we see that job 10 has the smallest processing time and it is on machine 2, so job 10 is placed last in the sequence. After job 10 is deleted from consideration, job 6 has the smallest processing time, namely, 2 units of time on machine 1. Thus job 6 is placed at the beginning of the sequence. When job 6 is deleted from consideration we see that jobs 3 and 9 both have the smallest processing time, 3 units on machine 1. Either of the two jobs can be processed second behind job 6; the other should be processed third. This process of assigning each job a position in the sequence continues until all jobs are assigned. The final sequences using the above procedure would be

$$6\text{-}3\text{-}9\text{-}5\text{-}8\text{-}2\text{-}4\text{-}1\text{-}7\text{-}10$$

or

$$6\text{-}9\text{-}3\text{-}5\text{-}8\text{-}2\text{-}4\text{-}1\text{-}7\text{-}10$$

or

$$6\text{-}3\text{-}9\text{-}5\text{-}8\text{-}2\text{-}4\text{-}7\text{-}1\text{-}10$$

or

$$6\text{-}9\text{-}3\text{-}5\text{-}8\text{-}2\text{-}4\text{-}7\text{-}1\text{-}10$$

All four sequences are optimal in the sense that the total time to process all jobs on the two machines is minimum among all possible sequences.

Table 7.3 illustrates the flow of the jobs through the machines using the first optimal sequence

$$6\text{-}3\text{-}9\text{-}5\text{-}8\text{-}2\text{-}4\text{-}1\text{-}7\text{-}10$$

Table 7.3 FLOW OF JOBS THROUGH MACHINES USING
THE SEQUENCE 6-3-9-5-8-2-4-1-7-10

Job	Machine 1		Machine 2		Idle time machine 2
	Time in	Time out	Time in	Time out	
6	0	2	2	14	2
3	2	5	14	19	0
9	5	8	19	25	0
5	8	13	25	31	0
8	13	20	31	41	0
2	20	30	41	53	0
4	30	40	53	61	0
1	40	60	61	65	0
7	60	68	68	72	3
10	68	72	72	73	0

With this sequence the total elapsed time to process all 10 jobs through the two machines is reduced from 94 to 73 units, a reduction of 22 percent. Likewise, the idle time on machines 1 and 2 has been reduced from 22 to 1 and from 26 to 5, respectively.

EXAMPLE 7.2.2 Each morning a general Fix-It Shop receives a supply of small household appliances (jobs) which are in need of repair. The appliances come from large discount stores that demand 1-day service. Past experience indicates that the shop has been able to meet its demand 99 percent of the time, even though the employees have had to work a great deal of overtime on occasions.

The owner, being progressive in her thinking, decides to investigate the use of OR methods in her shop to determine if she can increase her profit. The shop currently has two employees, a fault-detection analyst who receives $5 per hour and a general repairman who repairs or replaces defective parts at a rate of $2.50 per hour. In the past 6 months the owner has had to pay out $2514.38 in overtime pay.

$$(189 \text{ hr} \times 1.5 \times \$5.00) + (292.5 \text{ hr} \times 1.5 \times \$2.50) = \$2514.38$$
$$\text{Analyst} \qquad\qquad\qquad \text{Repair}$$

Since the owner had to pay time and a half for all hours over 8, she felt she was losing a great deal of profit, so she decided to determine if the amount of overtime could be reduced by optimizing the sequence in which the items are processed through the shop. Currently, the appliances are examined for defects in the order they are listed in Table 7.4. After the defect is detected, the appliance is given directly to the repairman for repair. If the analyst finishes one or more appliances before the repairman finishes a given appliance, the appliances waiting for repair are repaired in the order they were completed by the analyst (no passing rule). Table 7.4 gives the

Table 7.4   AVERAGE TIME MINUTES TO DETECT AND REPAIR DEFECTIVE ITEMS

Item number	Item	Number of each item	Detect fault	Repair fault
1	Iron	8	17	15
2	Toaster (type A)	5	12	20
3	Radio	4	20	25
4	Mixer	6	16	12
5	Waffle iron	3	10	8
6	Toaster (type B)	4	14	12
7	Electric skillet	6	15	10
8	Electric knife	3	6	11

number of each type of appliance received on a given day along with the average times to detect and repair a fault.

If the items are processed through the shop in the order given in Table 7.4, that is, the eight irons, then the five toasters (type A), then the four radios, and so forth, the analyst will work 566 min or 9.433 hr while the repairman will be on the job 591 min or 9.85 hr. This is shown in Table 7.5. If an 8-hour day is used as a base, the analyst will work 1.433 hr overtime at a cost of $1.433 \times 1.5 \times \$5 = \$10.73$ and the repairman will work 1.85 hr overtime at a cost of $1.85 \times 1.5 \times \$2.50 = \$6.94$.

Intuitively, it seems that it would be good to get the repairman working as soon as possible and that an appliance that takes the smallest time to repair should be put last so the repairman can finish for the day as soon as possible after the analyst detects the last fault.

In order to determine an optimal sequence to process the appliances through the repair shop, we can ignore for a moment the fact that there are eight irons, five toasters (type A), etc.

Based on the data in Table 7.4, we see that the electric knife has the smallest time when all fault detection and repair times are considered, namely, 6 min to detect the fault. Thus, the three electric knives are placed first in the sequence. The next smallest time is 8 min and this is the time to repair a waffle iron. Since this time is in the repair column, the three waffle irons are placed last in the sequence of items to be serviced. If this process is continued, an optimal sequence that will result is:

First—three electric knives
Second—five toasters (type A)
Third—four radios
Fourth—eight irons
Fifth—six mixers
Sixth—four toasters (type B)
Seventh—six electric skillets
Eighth—three waffle irons

Table 7.5 FLOW OF APPLIANCES THROUGH REPAIR
SHOP USING THE SEQUENCE 1-2-3-4-5-6-7-8

	Detect fault		Repair fault		Idle time machine 2
Item	In	Out	In	Out	
1	0	17	17	32	17
1	17	34	34	49	2
1	34	51	51	66	2
1	51	68	68	83	2
1	68	85	85	100	2
1	85	102	102	117	2
1	102	119	119	134	2
1	119	136	136	151	2
2	136	148	151	171	0
2	148	160	171	191	0
2	160	172	191	211	0
2	172	184	211	231	0
2	184	196	231	251	0
3	196	216	251	276	0
3	216	236	276	301	0
3	236	256	301	326	0
3	256	276	326	351	0
4	276	292	351	363	0
4	292	308	363	375	0
4	308	324	375	387	0
4	324	340	387	399	0
4	340	356	399	411	0
4	356	372	411	423	0
5	372	382	423	431	0
5	382	392	431	439	0
5	392	402	439	447	0
6	402	416	447	459	0
6	416	430	459	471	0
6	430	444	471	483	0
6	444	458	483	495	0
7	458	473	495	505	0
7	473	488	505	515	0
7	488	503	515	525	0
7	503	518	525	535	0
7	518	533	535	545	0
7	533	548	548	558	3
8	548	554	558	569	0
8	554	560	569	580	0
8	560	566	580	591	0

Total = 34

Table 7.6   FLOW OF APPLIANCES THROUGH REPAIR
SHOP USING THE SEQUENCE 8-2-3-1-4-6-7-5

Item	Detect fault In	Detect fault Out	Repair fault In	Repair fault Out	Idle time of repairman
8	0	6	6	17	6
8	6	12	17	28	0
8	12	18	28	39	0
2	18	30	39	59	0
2	30	42	59	79	0
2	42	54	79	99	0
2	54	66	99	119	0
2	66	78	119	139	0
3	78	98	139	164	0
3	98	118	164	189	0
3	118	138	189	214	0
3	138	158	214	239	0
1	158	175	239	254	0
1	175	192	254	269	0
1	192	209	269	284	0
1	209	226	284	299	0
1	226	243	299	314	0
1	243	260	314	329	0
1	260	277	329	344	0
1	277	294	344	359	0
4	294	310	359	371	0
4	310	326	371	383	0
4	326	342	383	395	0
4	342	358	395	407	0
4	358	374	407	419	0
4	374	390	419	431	0
6	390	404	431	443	0
6	404	418	443	455	0
6	418	432	455	467	0
6	432	446	467	479	0
7	446	461	479	489	0
7	461	476	489	499	0
7	476	491	499	509	0
7	491	506	509	519	0
7	506	521	521	531	2
7	521	536	536	546	5
5	536	546	546	554	0
5	546	556	556	564	2
5	556	566	566	574	2

Total = 17

If this sequence is used, the analyst still works 566 min or 9.433 hr because once the work is started, it can continue straight through until all of the applicances have been examined. However, Table 7.6 illustrates how the repairman's idle time will be reduced from 34 to 17 min/day so that he only works 574 min or 9.566 hr, a reduction of 17 min/day. This appears to be a small savings with respect to the amount of time lost in small talk, etc.; however, with respect to production time, this would amount to a savings of $368 per year.

Although we have concentrated on a sequence which would minimize the overtime for the repairman, the same optimum sequence will minimize the elapsed time from the start of the analysis of the first appliance until the final repair of the last appliance. Generally, the emphasis in sequencing problems is on the total time to process all jobs through all machines.

Example 7.2.2 has been a realistic look at an actual problem in sequencing and, like many other cases which have been studied, OR methods did not help a great deal in increasing the owner's profit; however, this should in no way discourage the OR analyst in his investigation of sequencing problems.

One might be tempted to just multiply the detection and repair time for each type of item by the corresponding number of items of the given type and to use the resulting table of processing times to obtain an optimal sequence. Inherent in this procedure is the assumption that the analyst must detect the fault of every item of a given type before the repairman can start repairing any of the items of the given type. For example, the fault of all three electric knives must be detected by the analyst before the repairman can start on any of the knives. A similar statement holds for each of the other types of items. This is quite a different problem from the one we just solved. To solve this problem we first must cumulate the detect and repair times for each type of appliance. This is done in Table 7.7.

The optimal sequence for this problem would be

$$8\text{-}2\text{-}3\text{-}1\text{-}4\text{-}7\text{-}6\text{-}5$$

Table 7.7 CUMULATIVE DETECTION AND REPAIR TIMES FOR EXAMPLE 7.2.2

Item number	Items	Cumulative fault detection time	Cumulative repair time
1	Irons	8(17) = 136	8(15) = 90
2	Toasters (type A)	5(12) = 60	5(20) = 100
3	Radios	80	100
4	Mixers	96	72
5	Waffle irons	30	24
6	Toasters (type B)	56	48
7	Electric skillets	90	60
8	Electric knives	18	33

Table 7.8 FLOW OF APPLIANCES THROUGH SHOP
USING CUMULATIVE TIMES AND THE
SEQUENCE 8-2-3-1-4-7-6-5

Item	Detect fault		Repair fault		Idle time of repairman
	In	Out	In	Out	
8	0	18	18	51	18
2	18	78	78	178	27
3	78	158	178	278	0
1	158	294	294	384	16
4	294	390	390	462	6
7	390	480	480	540	18
6	480	536	540	588	0
5	536	566	588	612	0
					85

Table 7.8 illustrates that the idle time for the repairman is 85 min and that he will be on the job 612 min or 10.2 hr. This means the repairer will work 2.2 hr of overtime at a cost of

$$2.2 \times 1.5 \times \$2.50 = \$8.25 \text{ per day}$$

7.2.1 Algorithm 7.1—Sequencing N Jobs through Two Machines

Suppose N jobs are to be processed through two machines M_1 and M_2 in the same order with no passing between machines.

Let $T(I,J)$ = time to process job I on machine M_J; $I = 1, 2, \ldots, N$; $J = 1, 2$

$TIM1(K)$ = time the Kth job in a sequence starts on machine M_1; $K = 1, 2, \ldots, N$

$TOM1(K)$ = time the Kth job in a sequence finishes on machine M_1; $K = 1, 2, \ldots, N$

$TIM2(K)$ = time the Kth job in a sequence starts on machine M_2; $K = 1, 2, \ldots, N$

$TOM2(K)$ = time the Kth job in a sequence finishes on machine M_2; $K = 1, 2, \ldots, N$

TET = total elapsed time from the start of the first job on machine M_1 to the finish of the last job on machine M_2

$ITM1$ = idle time on machine M_1

$ITM2$ = idle time on machine M_2

Step 1

Select the smallest $T(I,J)$ element, say $T(I_0,J_0)$, for those jobs that have not been assigned. If there are two or more smallest elements, arbitrarily select one of them.

Step 2
If J_0 is equal to 1, this means the selected smallest processing time is on machine M_1, so assign job I_0 as close to the beginning of the sequence as possible; otherwise, the selected smallest processing time is on machine M_2, so assign job I_0 as close to the end of the sequence as possible.

Step 3
Eliminate job I_0 from further consideration.

Step 4
If all jobs have been assigned a position in the sequence, go to step 5; otherwise, go to step 1.

Step 5
Calculate the time each job in the sequence will be out of machine M_1.

$$TOM1(K) = TOM1(K-1) + \text{processing time of } Kth \text{ job}$$
$$\text{on machine } M_1 \quad K = 1, 2, \ldots, N$$

where $TOM1(0) \equiv 0$

Step 6
Calculate the time each job in the sequence will start on machine M_1.

$$TIM1(1) = 0$$
$$TIM1(K) = TOM1(K-1) \quad K = 2, 3, \ldots, N$$

Step 7
Iteratively calculate the time each job in the sequence will start and finish on machine M_2.

$$TIM2(1) = TOM1(1)$$
$$TOM2(K) = TIM2(K) + \text{processing time of } Kth \text{ job on machine } M_2$$
$$TIM2(K+1) = \max [TOM1(K+1), TOM2(K)] \quad K = 1, 2, \ldots, N$$

except define $TIM2(N+1) = 0$.

Step 8
Calculate the total elapsed time to process all jobs through the two machines.

$$TET = TOM2(N)$$

Step 9
Calculate the idle time for machines M_1 and M_2.

$$ITM1 = TOM2(N) - TOM1(N)$$

$$ITM2 = TOM1(1) + \sum_{K=2}^{N} [TIM2(K) - TOM2(K-1)]$$

Table 7.9 EIGHT JOBS, TWO MACHINES— PROCESSING TIME

Job	Machine	
	1	2
1	4	6
2	8	3
3	7	6
4	8	4
5	2	6
6	1	5
7	3	7
8	9	2

Step 10

Print results and stop.

Johnson [2] gives a proof that this algorithm will produce an optimal sequence.

EXAMPLE 7.2.3 Suppose eight jobs are to be processed on two machines. The processing times are given in Table 7.9.

1 The smallest t_{ij} element is $t_{61} = 1 = t_{i_0 j_0}$.
2 Job 6 is assigned to machine 1 first since the smallest t_{ij} element is in column 1; $j_0 = 1$.
3 Eliminate job 6 from further consideration.
4 The current partial assignment is

6							

5 The smallest remaining processing time is $t_{51} = t_{82} = 2$.
6 Job 5 is assigned to machine 1 as close to the front as possible since $j_0 = 1$.
7 Eliminate job 5 from further consideration.
8 The current partial assignment is

6	5						

9 The smallest remaining processing time is $t_{82} = 2$.

$$t_{i_0 j_0} = t_{82} = 2$$

10 Job 8 is assigned to machine 1 as close to the end as possible since $j_0 = 2$.
11 Eliminate job 8 from further consideration.

12 The current partial assignment becomes

| 6 | 5 | | | | | 8 |

13 Further applications of Algorithm 7.1 lead to the following list of partial assignments

| 6 | 5 | 7 | | | | 8 |

| 6 | 5 | 7 | | | 2 | 8 |

| 6 | 5 | 7 | | 4 | 2 | 8 |

| 6 | 5 | 7 | 1 | 4 | 2 | 8 |

with an optimal sequence being:

| 6 | 5 | 7 | 1 | 3 | 4 | 2 | 8 |

The total elapsed time from the time job 6 is placed on machine 1 until job 8 is finished on machine 2 is 44 units of time and is calculated in Table 7.10.

The idle time for machine 1 is equal to the time when job 8 finishes on machine 2 minus the time job 8 finishes on machine 1. That is, $44 - 42 = 2$ units of time. The idle time for machine 2 is equal to the time job 6 starts on machine 2 plus the time job 8 starts on machine 2 minus the time job 2 finishes on machine 2; namely, $1 + 42 - 38 = 5$ units of time. In general, the idle time for machine 1 is just the time the last job finishes on machine 2 minus the time the last job finishes on machine 1, while the idle time for machine 2 is given by:

Table 7.10 ELAPSED TIME—EXAMPLE 7.2.3

	Machine 1		Machine 2		
Job	Time in	Time out	Time in	Time out	Idle time machine 2
6	0	1	1	6	1
5	1	3	6	12	0
7	3	6	12	19	0
1	6	10	19	25	0
3	10	17	25	31	0
4	17	25	31	35	0
2	25	33	35	38	0
8	33	42	42	44	4

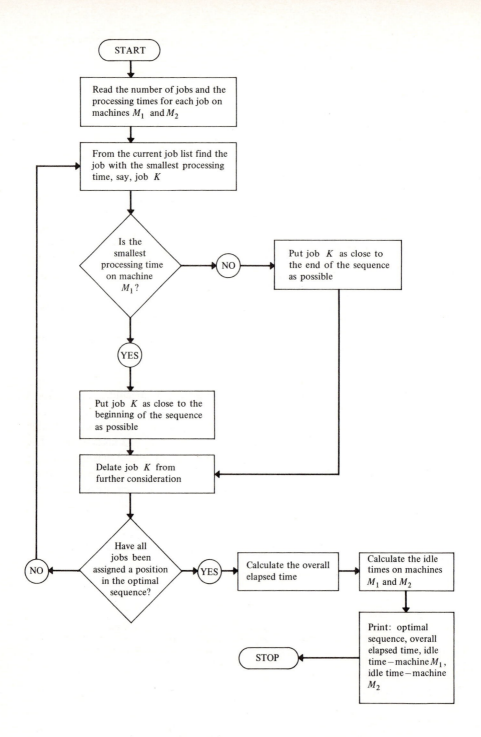

FIGURE 7.1
Flowchart for Algorithm 7.1.

274

Idle time machine $2 =$ time first job starts on machine 2

$$+ \sum_{k=2}^{n} [\text{time } k\text{th job starts on machine } 2 - \text{time } (k-1)\text{st job finishes on machine } 2]$$

7.2.2 Computer Program for Algorithm 7.1

The comment cards at the beginning of the computer program explain exactly what the program is designed to do and how to use it. The data for Example 7.2.3 follow the computer program. In this sample problem, there are eight jobs to be performed on two machines, so an 8 is punched in column 5 of the second data card (the first data card is the title card—Example 7.2.3—in this case). The first job takes 4 units of time on machine A and 6 units of time on machine B, so *4.* is punched in columns 9 and 10, and *6.* is punched in columns 19 and 20 of the third data card. Likewise, *8.* and *3.* are punched in columns 9 and 10 and in columns 19 and 20 of the fourth card, respectively. The data for the remaining jobs follow in cards 5-10.

The computer program as printed occupies 48K bytes of core storage. Example 7.2.3 took 0.13 s of IBM 370/168 time.

```
C
C     *********************************************************************
C     *                                                                 *
C     *     **   ALGORITHM 7.1     SEQUENCING  N-JOBS THROUGH 2 MACHINES  **  *
C     *                                                                 *
C     * THIS PROGRAM WILL HANDLE A MAXIMUM OF 250 JOBS BEING SEQUENCED   *
C     * THROUGH 2 MACHINES.  TO CHANGE THIS BOUND, CHANGE THE DIMENSION  *
C     * AND INTEGER STATEMENTS THAT CORRESPOND.                          *
C     *                                                                 *
C     * THIS PROGRAM IS DESIGNED                                         *
C     *     TO READ                                                      *
C     *         CARD 1    COLS   2-80    TITLE   DESCRIPTION OF THE PROBLEM USING  *
C     *                                          ANY CHARACTERS ON KEYPUNCH       *
C     *                                          ** COLUMN 1 MUST BE LEFT BLANK ** *
C     *         CARD 2    COLS   1- 5    N   NUMBER OF JOBS  (I5)         *
C     *         CARDS 3 TO N+2   COLS   1-10    T(I,1)   TIME TO PROCESS JOB I ON  *
C     *                                                  MACHINE 1  (F10.0)       *
C     *                                 11-20   T(I,2)   TIME TO PROCESS JOB I ON  *
C     *                                                  MACHINE 2  (F10.0)       *
C     *             TO SOLVE MORE THAN ONE PROBLEM AT A TIME, REPEAT THE  *
C     *             READ SEQUENCE AND STACK THE DATA ONE BEHIND THE OTHER. *
C     *                                                                 *
C     *     TO CALCULATE                                                 *
C     *         OSVECT        OPTIMAL SEQUENCE FOR PROCESSING N JOBS THROUGH  *
C     *                       TWO MACHINES                               *
C     *         TIM1,TOM1     TIME IN AND TIME OUT FOR MACHINE 1 FOR EACH JOB  *
C     *         TIM2,TOM2     TIME IN AND TIME OUT FOR MACHINE 2 FOR EACH JOB  *
C     *         TET           TOTAL ELAPSED TIME FOR THE OPTIMAL SEQUENCE *
C     *         ITM1          IDLE TIME ON MACHINE 1                      *
C     *         ITM2          IDLE TIME ON MACHINE 2                      *
C     *                                                                 *
C     *     TO PRINT                                                     *
C     *         T(I,J), OSVECT(N), TET, ITM1, ITM2                       *
C     *                                                                 *
C     *********************************************************************
      DIMENSION T(250,2), S(250,2)
      DIMENSION TIM1(250), TIM2(250), TOM1(250), TOM2(250)
      REAL*4 ITM1,ITM2,TITLE(20)
      INTEGER OSVECT(250)
```

```
    50 READ(5,55,END=2000)TITLE
    55 FORMAT(20A4)
       WRITE(6,60)TITLE
    60 FORMAT('1',20A4,//)
C  READ N, READ T(I,J)
       READ(5,100) N
   100 FORMAT(I5)
       DO 11 I=1,N
    11 READ(5,104)(T(I,J),J=1,2)
   104 FORMAT(2F10.0)
       WRITE(6,101) N
   101 FORMAT(    1X,'SEQUENCING',I5,1X,'JOBS THROUGH 2 MACHINES',///)
       WRITE(6,102)
   102 FORMAT(1X,'JOB',5X,'PROCESSING TIME PROCESSING TIME')
       WRITE(6,103)
   103 FORMAT(12X,'MACHINE 1',7X,'MACHINE 2',/)
       DO 1 I=1,N
     1 WRITE(6,105) I,(T(I,J),J=1,2)
   105 FORMAT(I3,2F16.2)
C  SAVE ORIGINAL VALUES FOR LATER USE
       DO 2 I=1,N
       DO 2 J=1,2
     2 S(I,J)=T(I,J)
       K=1
       L=1
C   **********************************************************************
C   *   STEP 1                                                          *
C   *           SELECT THE SMALLEST T(I,J) OF THOSE JOBS NOT YET ASSIGNED *
C   *           CALL IT T(IZERO,JZERO)                                  *
C   *           CALCULATE THE OPTIMAL SEQUENCE AND PLACE IN OSVECT      *
C   **********************************************************************
     8 IF(T(1,1).GT.T(1,2)) GO TO 3
       SMALL=T(1,1)
       IZERO=1
       JZERO=1
       GO TO 4
     3 SMALL=T(1,2)
       IZERO=1
       JZERO=2
     4 DO 5 I=2,N
       DO 5 J=1,2
       IF(T(I,J).GE.SMALL) GO TO 5
       SMALL=T(I,J)
       IZERO=I
       JZERO=J
     5 CONTINUE
C   **********************************************************************
C   *   STEP 2                                                          *
C   *           IF JZERO = 1, ASSIGN JOB IZERO AS CLOSE TO FRONT AS POSSIBLE *
C   *           IF JZERO ¬= 1, ASSIGN JOB IZERO AS CLOSE TO END AS POSSIBLE *
C   **********************************************************************
       IF(JZERO.EQ.1) GO TO 6
       OSVECT(N-L+1)=IZERO
       L=L+1
       GO TO 7
     6 OSVECT(K)=IZERO
       K=K+1
C   **********************************************************************
C   *   STEP 3                                                          *
C   *           ELIMINATE JOB IZERO FROM FURTHER CONSIDERATION          *
C   **********************************************************************



     7 T(IZERO,1)=10.E10
       T(IZERO,2)=10.E10
C   **********************************************************************
C   *   STEP 4                                                          *
C   *           IF ALL JOBS HAVE BEEN ASSIGNED, GO TO STEP 5; OTHERWISE, *
C   *           GO TO STEP 1.                                           *
C   **********************************************************************
       IF(L+K.NE.N+2) GO TO 8
```

```
C     ****************************************************************
C     *    STEPS 5,6,7,8,9                                          *
C     *         CALCULATE TIME IN AND TIME OUT OF EACH MACHINE, AND *
C     *         CALCULATE IDLE TIME FOR EACH MACHINE.               *
C     ****************************************************************
      TIM1(1)=0
      TOM1(1)=S(OSVECT(1),1)
      TIM2(1)=TOM1(1)
      TOM2(1)=TIM2(1)+S(OSVECT(1),2)
      ITM2=TIM2(1)
      DO 10 K=2,N
      TIM1(K)=TOM1(K-1)
      TOM1(K)=TIM1(K)+S(OSVECT(K),1)
      IF(TOM2(K-1).GE.TOM1(K)) GO TO 9
      TIM2(K)=TOM1(K)
      ITM2 =ITM2 +TOM1(K)-TOM2(K-1)
      GO TO 10
    9 TIM2(K)=TOM2(K-1)
   10 TOM2(K)=TIM2(K)+S(OSVECT(K),2)
      ITM1 =TOM2(N)-TOM1(N)
C     ****************************************************************
C     *    STEP 10                                                  *
C     *         PRINT RESULTS AND STOP.                             *
C     ****************************************************************
      WRITE(6,106)
  106 FORMAT(////,1X,'OPTIMAL SEQUENCE FOLLOWS',/)
      WRITE(6,107) (OSVECT(I),I=1,N)
  107 FORMAT(1X,25I4)
      TET=TOM2(N)
      WRITE(6,108)TET
  108 FORMAT(//,1X,'TOTAL ELAPSED TIME =',F10.2)
      WRITE(6,109) ITM1,ITM2
  109 FORMAT(/,1X,'IDLE TIME ON MACHINE 1 =',F10.2,// 1X,'IDLE TIME ON M
     *ACHINE 2 =',F10.2)
      GO TO 50
 2000 STOP
      END


/DATA

EXAMPLE 7.2.3
      8
          4.          6.
          8.          3.
          7.          6.
          8.          4.
          2.          6.
          1.          5.
          3.          7.
          9.          2.
```

EXAMPLE 7.2.3

SEQUENCING   8 JOBS THROUGH 2 MACHINES

JOB	PROCESSING TIME MACHINE 1	PROCESSING TIME MACHINE 2
1	4.00	6.00
2	8.00	3.00
3	7.00	6.00
4	8.00	4.00
5	2.00	6.00
6	1.00	5.00
7	3.00	7.00
8	9.00	2.00

OPTIMAL SEQUENCE FOLLOWS

  6   5   7   1   3   4   2   8

TOTAL ELAPSED TIME =   44.00

IDLE TIME ON MACHINE 1 =   2.00

IDLE TIME ON MACHINE 2 =   5.00

7.3 N–JOB, THREE–MACHINE SEQUENCING PROBLEM

An optimal solution to the general N-job, M-machine sequencing problem was not found until 1967. The solution for the general case is quite complicated; however, for $M = 3$, if either or both of the following conditions hold, the solution is straightforward. (See Johnson [2] for a proof.)

1 The smallest processing time for the first machine is at least as great as the largest processing time for the second machine.

2 The smallest processing time for the third machine is at least as great as the largest processing time for the second machine.

If either or both of the above conditions hold, then a procedure that can be used to solve the N-job, three-machine sequencing problem is:

1 Sum the processing times on machines 1 and 2 for each job.

2 Sum the processing times on machines 2 and 3, for each job.

3 Use the sums calculated in steps 1 and 2 for each job as the processing times on the two machines in an N-job, two-machine sequencing problem and solve this new problem using Algorithm 7.1.

4 The optimal sequence for the two-machine sequencing problem in step 3 is also optimal for the original three-machine sequencing problem.

Table 7.11 FIVE JOBS,
THREE MACHINES–
PROCESSING TIME

Job	Machine		
	1	2	3
1	4	5	5
2	2	2	6
3	8	3	8
4	10	3	9
5	5	4	7

Table 7.12 FIVE JOBS,
TWO MACHINES–
PROCESSING TIME

Job	Machine	
	1	2
1	9	10
2	4	8
3	11	11
4	13	12
5	9	11

EXAMPLE 7.3.1 Suppose five jobs must be processed through three machines. The processing times on each machine are given in Table 7.11. Since the minimum processing time on machine 3 is equal to the largest processing time on machine 2, Algorithm 7.2 can be used. The processing times for the new problem are given in Table 7.12.

The processing time for job i on machine j in the new problem is calculated as follows:

$$s_{11} = t_{11} + t_{12} = 4 + 5 = 9$$
$$s_{12} = t_{12} + t_{23} = 5 + 5 = 10$$
$$s_{21} = t_{21} + t_{22} = 2 + 2 = 4$$
$$s_{22} = t_{22} + t_{23} = 2 + 6 = 8$$
. . . .

When Algorithm 7.1 is applied to the new problem, an optimal sequence is

2	5	1	3	4

The total elapsed time of 41 units is calculated in Table 7.13.

Table 7.13 ELAPSED TIME FOR AN OPTIMAL SEQUENCE–
EXAMPLE 7.3.1

Job	Machine 1		Machine 2		Machine 3	
	Time in	Time out	Time in	Time out	Time in	Time out
2	0	2	2	4	4	10
5	2	7	7	11	11	18
1	7	11	11	16	18	23
3	11	19	19	22	23	31
4	19	29	29	32	32	41

The idle time on machine 1 is just the time the last job, job 4, is finished on machine 3 minus the time job 4 is finished on machine 1; namely,

$$\text{Idle time for machine } 1 = 41 - 29 = 12 \text{ units}$$

The idle time on machine 2 is calculated as follows:

$$
\begin{aligned}
\text{Idle time for machine 2} = {} & \text{time first job finishes on machine 1} \\
& + \Sigma_{k=2}^{5} \, [\text{time in machine 2 for } k\text{th job} - \\
& \qquad \text{time out machine 2 for } (k-1)\text{st job}] \\
& + \text{time last job finishes on machine 3} - \\
& \quad \text{time last job finishes on machine 2} \\
= {} & 2 + (7-4) + (11-11) + (19-16) \\
& + (29-22) + (41-32) \\
= {} & 24 \text{ units}
\end{aligned}
$$

Similarly,

$$
\begin{aligned}
\text{Idle time for machine 3} = {} & \text{time first job is finished on machine 2} \\
& + \Sigma_{k=2}^{5} \, [\text{time in machine 3 for } k\text{th job} - \\
& \qquad \text{time out machine 3 for } (k-1)\text{st job}] \\
= {} & 4 + (11-10) + (18-18) + (23-23) \\
& + (32-31) \\
= {} & 6 \text{ units}
\end{aligned}
$$

7.3.1 Algorithm 7.2—Sequencing N Jobs through Three Machines

Suppose the smallest processing time on the first or third machine is at least as great as the largest processing time on the second machine. This algorithm will then provide an optimal sequence for the three-machine problem.

Step 1
Let

$$S(I, 1) = T(I, 1) + T(I, 2)$$
$$S(I, 2) = T(I, 2) + T(I, 3) \qquad I = 1, 2, \ldots, N$$

where $T(I,J)$ is the processing time for job I on machine J. $S(I,J)$ represents the processing time for job I on machine J in the new N-job, two-machine sequencing problem.

Step 2
Solve the new N-job, two-machine sequencing problem using Algorithm 7.1. An optimal sequence for this problem is an optimal sequence for the original N-job, three-machine sequencing problem. Use the sequence determined at this step in the steps to follow. Also, the notation from Algorithm 7.1 will be used.

Step 3
Calculate the time each job will be out of machine 1.

$$TOM1(K) = TOM1(K - 1) + \text{processing time of } K\textit{th} \text{ job on machine 1}$$
$$K = 1, 2, \ldots, N$$

where $TOM1(0) = 0$.

Step 4
Calculate the time each job will start on machine 1.

$$TIM1(1) = 0$$
$$TIM1(K) = TOM1(k - 1) \quad K = 2, 3, \ldots, N$$

Step 5
Iteratively calculate the time each job will start and finish on machine 2.

$$TIM2(1) = TOM1(1)$$
$$TOM2(K) = TIM2(K) + \text{processing time of } K\textit{th} \text{ job on machine 2}$$
$$TIM2(K + 1) = \max [TOM1(K + 1), TOM2(K)] \quad K = 1, 2, \ldots, N$$

except define $TIM2(N + 1) = 0$.

Step 6
Iteratively calculate the time each job will start and finish on machine 3.

$$TIM3(1) = TOM2(1)$$
$$TOM3(K) = TIM3(K) + \text{processing time of } K\textit{th} \text{ job on machine 3}$$
$$TIM3(K + 1) = \max [TOM2(K + 1), TOM3(K)] \quad K = 1, 2, \ldots, N$$

except define $TIM3(N + 1) = 0$.

Step 7
Calculate the total elapsed time to process all jobs through the three machines

$$TET = TOM3(N)$$

Step 8
Calculate the idle times for machines 1, 2, and 3.

$$ITM1 = TOM3(N) - TOM1(N)$$

$$ITM2 = TOM1(1) + \sum_{K=2}^{N} [(TIM2(K) - TOM2(K - 1)]$$

$$+ [TOM3(N) - TOM2(N)]$$

$$ITM3 = TOM2(1) + \sum_{K=2}^{N} [TIM3(K) - TOM3(K - 1)]$$

Step 9
Print results and stop.

7.3.2 Computer Program for Algorithm 7.2

This program will determine the optimal sequence of N jobs through three machines when the smallest processing time on machine 1 and/or machine 3 is at least as great as the largest processing time on machine 2. In its present form, it will handle a maximum of 100 jobs. To increase the maximum size to N jobs, change the 100 component of the variables in the DIMENSION and INTEGER statements.

The program currently occupies 44K bytes of core storage. It took 0.09 s of IBM 370/168 time to solve the problem in Section 7.3.1.

```
C      ****************************************************************
C      *                                                            *
C      *       **   ALGORITHM 7.2    SEQUENCING    N-JOBS THROUGH 3 MACHINES **   *
C      *                                                            *
C      * THE MAXIMUM NUMBER OF JOBS THAT MAY BE SOLVED BY THIS PROGRAM IS 100. *
C      * TO CHANGE THIS BOUND, CHANGE THE CORRESPONDING DIMENSION AND *
C      * INTEGER STATEMENTS.                                        *
C      *                                                            *
C      * THIS PROGRAM IS DESIGNED                                   *
C      *     TO READ                                                *
C      *        CARD 1    COLS  2-80   TITLE  DESCRIPTION OF THE PROBLEM USING *
C      *                                      ANY CHARACTERS ON KEYPUNCH *
C      *                                      ** COLUMN 1 MUST BE LEFT BLANK ** *
C      *        CARD 2    COLS  1- 5   N  NUMBER OF JOBS   (I5)      *
C      *        CARDS 3 TO N+2   COLS  1-10   T(I,1)  PROCESSING TIME FOR JOB I *
C      *                                      ON MACHINE 1   (F10.0) *
C      *                              11-20   T(I,2)  PROCESSING TIME FOR JOB I *
C      *                                      ON MACHINE 2   (F10.0) *
C      *                              21-30   T(I,3)  PROCESSING TIME FOR JOB I *
C      *                                      ON MACHINE 3   (F10.0) *
C      *           TO SOLVE MORE THAN ONE PROBLEM AT A TIME, REPEAT THE *
C      *           READ SEQUENCE, AND STACK THE DATA ONE BEHIND THE OTHER *
C      *                                                            *
C      *     TO CALCULATE                                           *
C      *        OSVECT        THE OPTIMAL SEQUENCE OF N JOBS THROUGH 3 MACHINES *
C      *                      WHEN THE SMALLEST PROCESSING TIME FOR MACHINE 1 *
C      *                      AND/OR 3 IS AT LEAST AS GREAT AS THE LARGEST *
C      *                      PROCESSING TIME FOR MACHINE 2         *
C      *        TIM1,TOM1     TIME IN AND TIME OUT FOR MACHINE 1 FOR EACH JOB *
C      *        TIM2,TOM2     TIME IN AND TIME OUT FOR MACHINE 2 FOR EACH JOB *
C      *        TIM3,TOM3     TIME IN AND TIME OUT FOR MACHINE 3 FOR EACH JOB *
C      *        TET           THE TOTAL ELAPSED TIME FROM THE TIME THE FIRST *
C      *                      JOB OF THE OPTIMAL SEQUENCE WAS PUT ON MACHINE 1 *
C      *                      UNTIL THE LAST JOB FINISHED ON MACHINE 3. *
C      *        ITM1          IDLE TIME FOR MACHINE 1               *
C      *        ITM2          IDLE TIME FOR MACHINE 2               *
C      *        ITM3          IDLE TIME FOR MACHINE 3               *
C      *                                                            *
C      *     TO PRINT                                               *
C      *        T(I,J)                                              *
C      *        OSVECT(N)                                           *
C      *        TIM1, TOM1, TIM2, TOM2, TIM3, TOM3                  *
C      *        TET                                                 *
C      *        ITM1, ITM2, ITM3                                    *
C      *                                                            *
C      ****************************************************************
       DIMENSION T(100,3), S(100,3), TIM1(100), TOM1(100)
       DIMENSION TIM2(100), TOM2(100), TIM3(100), TOM3(100)
       REAL*4 ITM1,ITM2,ITM3,TITLE(20)
       INTEGER OSVECT(100)
    50 READ(5,55,END=2000)TITLE
    55 FORMAT(20A4)
       WRITE(6,60)TITLE
    60 FORMAT('1',20A4,//)
       READ(5,100) N
   100 FORMAT(I5)
       DO 21 I=1,N
    21 READ(5,104)(T(I,J),J=1,3)
   104 FORMAT(3F10.0)
       WRITE(6,101) N
   101 FORMAT(    1X,'SEQUENCING',I5,1X,'JOBS THROUGH 3 MACHINES',//)



       WRITE(6,102)
   102 FORMAT(1X,'JOB',5X,'PROCESSING TIME PROCESSING TIME PROCESSING TIM
      1E')
       WRITE(6,103)
   103 FORMAT(11X,'MACHINE 1',7X,'MACHINE 2',7X,'MACHINE 3',/)
       DO 1 I=1,N
     1 WRITE(6,105) I,(T(I,J),J=1,3)
   105 FORMAT(I3,3F16.2)
C  SAVE ORIGINAL TIMES
```

```
      DO 2 I=1,N
      DO 2 J=1,3
    2 S(I,J)=T(I,J)
C     ****************************************************************************
C     *    STEP 1                                                             *
C     *           CONVERT TO A 2-MACHINE PROBLEM                              *
C     ****************************************************************************
      DO 13 I=1,N
      T(I,1)=T(I,1)+T(I,2)
   13 T(I,2)=T(I,2)+T(I,3)
      K=1
      L=1
C     ****************************************************************************
C     *    STEP 2                                                             *
C     *           USE STEPS 1 TO 4 OF ALGORITHM 7.1 TO FIND THE OPTIMAL       *
C     *               SEQUENCE OF THE NEW N-JOB,2-MACHINE PROBLEM.            *
C     ****************************************************************************
    8 IF(T(1,1).GT.T(1,2)) GO TO 3
      SMALL=T(1,1)
      IZERO=1
      JZERO=1
      GO TO 4
    3 SMALL=T(1,2)
      IZERO=1
      JZERO=2
    4 DO 5 I=2,N
      DO 5 J=1,2
      IF(T(I,J).GE.SMALL) GO TO 5
      SMALL=T(I,J)
      IZERO=I
      JZERO=J
    5 CONTINUE
      IF(JZERO.EQ.1) GO TO 6
      OSVECT(N-L+1)=IZERO
      L=L+1
      GO TO 7
    6 OSVECT(K)=IZERO
      K=K+1
    7 T(IZERO,1)=10.E10
      T(IZERO,2)=10.E10
      IF(L+K.NE.N+2) GO TO 8
C     ****************************************************************************
C     *    STEPS 3,4,5,6,7,8                                                  *
C     *           CALCULATE TIME IN AND TIME OUT FOR EACH MACHINE, AND        *
C     *               CALCULATE THE IDLE TIME FOR EACH MACHINE.               *
C     ****************************************************************************
      TIM1(1)=0
      TOM1(1)=S(OSVECT(1),1)
      TIM2(1)=TOM1(1)
      TOM2(1)=TIM2(1)+S(OSVECT(1),2)
      TIM3(1)=TOM2(1)
      TOM3(1)=TIM3(1)+S(OSVECT(1),3)
      ITM2 =TIM2(1)
      ITM3 =TIM3(1)
      DO 12 K=2,N
      TIM1(K)=TOM1(K-1)
      TOM1(K)=TIM1(K)+S(OSVECT(K),1)
      IF(TOM2(K-1).GE.TOM1(K)) GO TO 9
      TIM2(K)=TOM1(K)
      ITM2 =ITM2 +TOM1(K)-TOM2(K-1)
      GO TO 10
    9 TIM2(K)=TCM2(K-1)
   10 TOM2(K)=TIM2(K)+S(OSVECT(K),2)
      IF(TOM3(K-1).GE.TOM2(K)) GO TO 11
      TIM3(K)=TOM2(K)
      ITM3 =ITM3 +TOM2(K)-TOM3(K-1)
      GO TO 12
   11 TIM3(K)=TOM3(K-1)
   12 TOM3(K)=TIM3(K)+S(OSVECT(K),3)
      ITM1 =TOM3(N)-TOM1(N)
```

```
      ITM2 =ITM2 +TOM3(N)-TOM2(N)
      TET=TOM3(N)
C     ******************************************************************
C     *    STEP 9                                                      *
C     *          PRINT RESULTS AND STOP.                               *
C     ******************************************************************
      WRITE(6,106)
  106 FORMAT(//  ,1X,'OPTIMAL SEQUENCE FOLLOWS',/)
      WRITE(6,107) (OSVECT(I),I=1,N)
  107 FORMAT(1X,25I4,//)
      WRITE(6,108) TET
  108 FORMAT(// 1X,'TOTAL ELAPSED TIME =',F10.2,/)
      WRITE(6,109) ITM1,ITM2,ITM3
  109 FORMAT(1X,'IDLE TIME ON MACHINE 1 =',F10.2,/ 11X,'ON MACHINE 2 =',
     *F10.2,/ 11X,'ON MACHINE 3 =',F10.2)
      WRITE(6,110)
  110 FORMAT(//  13X,'MACHINE 1',13X,'MACHINE 2',13X,'MACHINE 3')
      WRITE(6,111)
  111 FORMAT(11X,'TIME',7X,'TIME',7X,'TIME',7X,'TIME',7X,'TIME',7X,'TIME
     1')
      WRITE(6,112)
  112 FORMAT(2X,'JOB',7X,'IN',9X,'OUT',8X,'IN',9X,'OUT',8X,'IN',9X,'OUT'
     1,/)
      DO 16 I=1,N
   16 WRITE(6,113) OSVECT(I),TIM1(I),TOM1(I),TIM2(I),TOM2(I),TIM3(I),TOM
     13(I)
  113 FORMAT(I4,6F11.2)
      GO TO 50
 2000 STOP
      END


/DATA

EXAMPLE FROM SECTION 7.3.1
    5
      4.          5.          5.
      2.          2.          6.
      8.          3.          8.
     10.          3.          9.
      5.          4.          7.
```

```
EXAMPLE FROM SECTION 7.3.1

SEQUENCING    5 JOBS THROUGH 3 MACHINES

JOB     PROCESSING TIME PROCESSING TIME PROCESSING TIME
            MACHINE 1       MACHINE 2       MACHINE 3

1           4.00            5.00            5.00
2           2.00            2.00            6.00
3           8.00            3.00            8.00
4          10.00            3.00            9.00
5           5.00            4.00            7.00

OPTIMAL SEQUENCE FOLLOWS

    2    1    5    3    4

TOTAL ELAPSED TIME =       41.00

IDLE TIME ON MACHINE 1 =       12.00
            ON MACHINE 2 =       24.00
            ON MACHINE 3 =        6.00

            MACHINE 1               MACHINE 2               MACHINE 3
         TIME      TIME         TIME       TIME         TIME       TIME
JOB       IN       OUT          IN         OUT          IN         OUT

2        0.0       2.00         2.00       4.00         4.00      10.00
1        2.00      6.00         6.00      11.00        11.00      16.00
5        6.00     11.00        11.00      15.00        16.00      23.00
3       11.00     19.00        19.00      22.00        23.00      31.00
4       19.00     29.00        29.00      32.00        32.00      41.00
```

SELECTED BIBLIOGRAPHY

1 Ackoff, Russell L., and Maurice W. Sasieni: "Fundamentals of Operations Research," John Wiley & Sons, Inc., New York, 1968.
2 Johnson, S. M.: Optimal Two- and Three-Stage Production Schedules with Setup Times Included, *Nav. Res. Logistics Q.,* vol. 1, no. 1, 1954.

EXERCISES

7.1 In a manufacturing process several types of fan blades must be processed on the same two machines just before final assembly. Each type requires a certain processing time on each machine. Assume each type must be processed on machine 1, then on machine 2 with no passing. The processing times are:

Type	Machine 1	Machine 2
1	2	4
2	6	3
3	7	8
4	10	11
5	4	5
6	9	1

(a) Use Algorithm 7.1 to determine an optimal sequence to process the various types of fan blades each day if the object is to minimize total time through both machines.

(b) What is the total elapsed time for an optimal sequence?

(c) What is the total idle time on machine 1? On machine 2?

7.2 In Exercise 7.1 suppose the number of fan blades of the various types are:

Type	Number
1	4
2	6
3	10
4	2
5	6
6	5

(a) Determine an optimal sequence to process the various fan blades each day. Assume each type must be processed on machine 1, then on machine 2 with no passing.

(b) What is the total elapsed time for an optimal sequence?

(c) What is the total idle time on machines 1 and 2?

7.3 Suppose several types of furniture must pass through three prefinishing stages in the same order. Because of the size and complexity of each type of furniture, the processing time at each stage varies considerably.

Type	Stage 1	Stage 2	Stage 3
Chair	7	2	5
Desk	10	3	8
Lamp	6	4	4
End table	7	3	2
Coffee table	8	5	2

(a) Determine an optimal sequence for processing the five types of furniture through the three stages in order to minimize the total elapsed time.

(b) What is the total elapsed time for an optimal sequence?

(c) What is the total idle time at stages 1, 2, and 3?

7.4 The data processing supervisor for CDPCA, a small consulting firm, has a number of jobs that must be prepared and processed on the computer each day. On a given day the supervisor is faced with the problem of how to sequence 10 jobs through the preparation and processing stages. Once a job is prepared it must go on the computer for processing as soon as possible. The preparation and processing times are:

Type of job	Preparation	Processing
1	10	2
2	30	5
3	15	1
4	60	3
5	5	10
6	10	12
7	20	4
8	25	10
9	10	20
10	6	2

(a) Determine the sequence in which the jobs should be prepared and processed in order to minimize the total preparation and processing time for all jobs. (Assume the computer can be interrupted immediately to process any of the 10 jobs.)

(b) How much time will elapse before all 10 jobs are ready for distribution?

7.5 In the N-job, two-machine sequencing problem, show that minimizing the idle time on machine 2 will minimize the total elapsed time.

7.6 Use the computer program for Algorithm 7.2 to answer parts (a), (b), and (c) of Exercise 7.3 using the data below.

Type	Stage 1	Stage 2	Stage 3
End table	12	4	8
Coffee table	4	6	9
Chair (type A)	8	3	7
Chair (type B)	13	6	8
Chair (type C)	12	5	10
Stool	7	5	6
Table (type A)	4	4	9
Table (type B)	6	2	10
Bench	10	3	8

7.7 Suppose the number of jobs in Exercise 7.4 is increased to 30 jobs. Use the computer program for Algorithm 7.1 to determine the optimal sequence to process the jobs. The preparation and processing times follow.

Type of job	Preparation	Processing
1	61	97
2	11	68
3	50	48
4	86	51
5	25	24
6	6	97
7	60	54
8	80	44
9	19	90
10	88	49
11	25	6
12	24	60
13	68	92
14	37	77
15	78	38
16	37	39
17	4	84
18	32	47
19	75	43
20	21	44
21	47	91
22	40	1
23	71	85
24	85	60
25	88	94
26	15	64
27	24	12
28	61	22
29	19	94
30	90	86

PART TWO

Probabilistic Operations Research Models

8

BASIC PROBABILITY AND
STATISTICAL CONCEPTS

8.1 INTRODUCTION

To this point we have dealt with mathematical models and techniques that were completely deterministic in nature. There was no randomness or variation due to chance in the assumed models or in the methods that were used to solve the models. The models were exact representations of the real systems under study and, in the absence of round-off errors, the methods would find the optimal solution of the models in a finite number of steps.

Since there is random variation or some degree of uncertainty in the components of many realistic systems, it is important that we study some basic probability and statistical concepts that can be incorporated into mathematical models of such systems. These same concepts can be further extended to the techniques needed to solve probabilistic models. The elements of probability and statistics that have direct application to the probabilistic models and techniques in this book will be presented in an intuitive manner for ease of understanding.

8.2 BASIC PROBABILITY

An experiment is generally thought of as one or more acts that result in some outcome or response. If the experiment is repeated many times under identical conditions, we

Table 8.1 BACKPACK SALES FOR 20-WEEK PERIOD

Week	1	2	3	4	5	6	7	8	9	10	11	12	13	14	15	16	17	18	19	20
Sales	4	8	2	6	12	5	8	2	5	9	4	7	6	8	3	1	4	5	9	14

might get the same outcome each time, or there may be variation in the outcomes. In the latter case, we might be interested in predicting the possibility of each outcome if the experiment is repeated again under the same conditions. The possibility of each outcome from an experiment could be called the *probability of an outcome* and is defined as the relative frequency of the outcome in past experiments. For example, a merchant might be interested in the probability of selling $0, 1, 2, \ldots, 9, 10$ or more backpacks during the next week. To determine these probabilities, a series of experiments could be conducted under the same conditions (ignore seasonal variations) and, based on the outcomes from each experiment, have some basis for approximating the desired probabilities. The experiment would be the observance of the sales for a given week in the past. The actual number of sales would be the outcome for that particular experiment. Suppose the experiment is repeated for each of the past 20 weeks. Table 8.1 illustrates the various outcomes.

Based on the possible outcomes of $0, 1, 2, \ldots, 9, 10$ or more sales per week for 20 weeks, the relative frequency or probability of selling k backpacks next week is determined by dividing the number of weeks k backpacks were sold during the 20-week period by the total number of weeks under consideration, namely 20. Thus, the probability of selling 12 backpacks next week is

$$\Pr(12) = \frac{1}{20}$$

Likewise the probability of selling 8 backpacks is

$$\Pr(8) = \frac{3}{20}$$

The complete set of probabilities is given in Table 8.2. Note that the set of probabilities sum to 1. This is reasonable since one of the possible outcomes must occur.

Suppose we formalize the concept by presenting some definitions and properties of probability.

Table 8.2 RELATIVE FREQUENCY OR PROBABILITY OF EACH OUTCOME

Sales	0	1	2	3	4	5	6	7	8	9	10 or more
Relative frequency or probability	0	1/20	2/20	1/20	3/20	3/20	2/20	1/20	3/20	2/20	2/20

Definition 8.2.1 Sample Point Each possible outcome of an experiment is called a sample point.

For the present example, each of the sales $0, 1, \ldots, 9, 10$ or more is a sample point. A sample point could be a point in time between two limits, say t_0 and t_n.   ////

Definition 8.2.2 Sample Space The sample space is the set of all sample points of an experiment.

The set of all possible sales for a given week is the sample space in the backpack example. The sample space could be the infinity of points in time between two limits t_0 and t_n.   ////

Definition 8.2.3   Event Defined on the Sample Space An event is defined to be a set of sample points of an experiment.

The set may be empty, it may contain only one sample point, or it may contain any number of sample points up to and including the entire sample space.

Some examples of events are:

A = event that the sales will be 0, 1, 2, or 3 during a given week
B = event that the sales will be 2, 3, or 8 during a given week
C = event that the sales will be 1 during a given week

Note that different events can have one or more sample points in common.   ////

Definition 8.2.4 Occurrence of an Event An event A is said to occur in an experiment if one of the outcomes (sample points) in A occurs.   ////

Definition 8.2.5 Mutually Exclusive Events Two events A and B are mutually exclusive if they both cannot occur in the same experiment.

Let A = event of 0, 1, 2, or 3 sales/week
B = event of 7, 8, or 9 sales/week

then the occurrence of event A precludes the occurrence of event B and vice versa. Thus, events A and B are mutually exclusive.   ////

8.2.1 Probability of an Event

Since each possible outcome and/or set of possible outcomes of an experiment can be defined as an event, probability is usually defined in terms of "the probability of an event." The probability of an event could be thought of as the relative frequency of the event based on an infinite number of repeated experimentations under identical conditions. For example, if

A = event of 0, 1, 2, or 3 sales/week
n = number of weeks that sales were observed
m = number of times event A occurred

then the probability of the event A is

$$\Pr(A) = \lim_{n \to \infty} \frac{m}{n}$$

Of course, this is a classical definition that cannot be used to actually determine the probability of event A. However, it will suffice to allow us to develop further concepts that are needed for probabilistic OR models.

The probability of an event, in a practical sense, could be thought of as the relative frequency of the event based on the outcomes from a finite number of experiments under identical conditions. This interpretation of probability was used in the backpack sales example to determine the values in Table 8.2.

Although several approaches could be used to define probability, it is essential that every definition be such that the following properties hold.

1 $0 \leqslant \Pr(A) \leqslant 1$, where $\Pr(A)$ is the probability event A will occur.
2 $\Pr(A_0) = 0$, where A_0 is an event that cannot occur.
3 $\Pr(A) = 1$, where A is the event that one of the outcomes will occur. That is, A consists of all of the sample points in the sample space.
4 $\Pr(A \text{ or } B) = \Pr(A) + \Pr(B)$ if A and B are mutually exclusive events.

Other properties of probability are based on conditional probability, joint probability, and the independence of two or more events.

Definition 8.2.6 Conditional Probability The conditional probability that event A will occur, given that some other event has already occurred, is defined to be

$$\Pr(A|B) = \frac{\Pr(A \text{ and } B)}{\Pr(B)}$$

where $\Pr(B) > 0$.

If $\Pr(B) = 0$, then event B cannot occur, so it does not make sense to talk about the occurrence of A given that B has occurred.   ////

Conditional probabilities are usually associated with experiments where there are two or more attributes associated with each outcome, or with experiments that require the observation of outcomes at two or more points in time. In the first case, suppose backpacks are available in two colors, orange and blue, in the backpack sales example. The two attributes are number sold and color. The new sample space is illustrated in Figure 8.1.

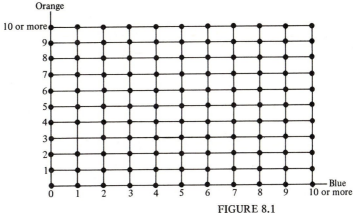

FIGURE 8.1
Sample space—backpack sales.

Note that there are 121 sample points in the experiment with each sample point being represented by a two-dimensional coordinate (x,y), where x is the number of blue backpacks sold and y is the number of orange backpacks sold. For example, the point $(2,5)$ represents the sale of 2 blue and 5 orange backpacks, $(4,7)$ represents the sale of 4 blue and 7 orange backpacks, etc. Now let

A = event that four backpacks were sold
B = event that one blue backpack was sold

Event A consists of the sample points $\{(0,4),(1,3),(2,2),(3,1),(4,0)\}$; event B consists of the sample points $\{(1,0),(1,1),(1,2),(1,3),(1,4),(1,5),\ldots,(1,10)\}$. If it is known that one blue backpack was sold (event B occurred), then the conditional probability that four backpacks were sold (event A occurs) is

$$\Pr(A|B) = \frac{\Pr(A \text{ and } B)}{\Pr(B)}$$

$$= \frac{\Pr[\text{outcome is sample point }(1,3)]}{\Pr[\text{outcome is }(1,0),(1,1),\ldots,\text{or }(1,10)]} \quad (8.1)$$

Sample point $(1,3)$ is the only sample point common to both events, so the probability that events A and B both occur is just the probability that sample point $(1,3)$ occurs. The probability associated with each sample point is generally approximated from past experimentation, intuition, or simulation. Once these probabilities are determined, the probability of any event A is just the probability that the sample points or outcomes in A occur. For example, if each sample point represented in Figure 8.1 is equally likely, i.e.,

$$\Pr[\text{sample point }(x,y)\text{ occurs}] = \frac{1}{121} \quad \begin{array}{l} \text{for } x = 0, 1, \ldots, 10 \\ y = 0, 1, \ldots, 10 \end{array}$$

and if

> A = event that four backpacks were sold
> B = event that one blue backpack was sold

then

$$\Pr(A) = \Pr \{\text{sample points } (0,4), (1,3), (2,2), (3,1), \text{ or } (4,0) \text{ occurs}\}$$

$$= \frac{1}{121} + \frac{1}{121} + \frac{1}{121} + \frac{1}{121} + \frac{1}{121} \qquad \text{all outcomes mutually exclusive}$$

$$= \frac{5}{121}$$

$$\Pr(B) = \Pr \{\text{sample point } (1,0), (1,1), \ldots, (1,10) \text{ occurs}\}$$

$$= \frac{11}{121}$$

$$\Pr(A|B) = \frac{\Pr(A \text{ and } B)}{\Pr(B)}$$

$$\Pr(A|B) = \frac{\Pr[\text{sample point } (1,3) \text{ occurs})]}{\Pr(B)}$$

$$= \frac{1/121}{11/121}$$

$$= \frac{1}{11}$$

In Figure 8.1, we see that knowledge of the fact that only one blue pack was sold reduces the *effective* sample space to the 11 points

$$\{(1,0),(1,1),(1,2), \ldots, (1,10)\}$$

each occurring with equal probability, so the probability of four sales using this sample space is just the probability the sample point $(1,3)$ occurs, namely $\frac{1}{11}$.

Consider the definition of the term $\Pr(A \text{ and } B)$, which is called the *joint probability of A and B*.

Definition 8.2.7 Joint Probability The joint probability of events A and B is the probability that events A and B both occur.

It is defined in terms of the conditional probabilities as

$$\Pr(AB) = \Pr(A \text{ and } B) \qquad (8.2)$$

$$= \Pr(A) \cdot \Pr(B|A)$$

$$= \Pr(B) \cdot \Pr(A|B) \qquad (8.3)$$

////

Definition 8.2.8 Independent Events Two or more events are independent if it is possible for all of the events to occur in the same experiment, and the occurrence of any one event does not affect the occurrence of the others.

Thus, two events A and B are independent if

$$\Pr(AB) = \Pr(A) \cdot \Pr(B) \qquad (8.4)$$

That is,

$$\Pr(A|B) = \Pr(A)$$
$$\Pr(B|A) = \Pr(B) \qquad ////$$

In the revised backpack sales example (two colors of backpacks available), if the fact that four packs were sold per week was not affected by the fact that one of the packs was blue, and if the fact that one of the packs was blue was not affected by the fact that four packs were sold, then the two events were independent. Ordinarily we would not expect this to be the case since the number of blue packs would probably be dependent on the total number of packs sold.

8.2.2 Additional Properties of Probability

We can now state two additional properties of probability.

5 $\Pr(A$ or B or both$) = \Pr(A) + \Pr(B) - \Pr(AB)$

$\qquad\qquad\qquad\qquad = \Pr(A) + \Pr(B) - \Pr(A)\Pr(B|A)$

$\qquad\qquad\qquad\qquad = \Pr(A) + \Pr(B) - \Pr(B)\Pr(A|B) \qquad (8.5)$

if A and B are two dependent events.

6 $\Pr(A$ or B or both$) = \Pr(A) + \Pr(B) - \Pr(A)\Pr(B) \qquad (8.6)$

if events A and B are independent.

8.3 RANDOM VARIABLES

A number of numerically valued variables can be defined on the sample space of a given experiment. These variables are given the name *random variables* because they take on each of their values with a certain probability in the discrete sample space case, and a value between two limits with a certain probability in the continuous or infinite sample space case. For example, we might let X be the number of backpack sales per week. If a probability can be associated with each value X can take on, then X is a discrete random variable. Likewise, we could let T be the time between consecutive arrivals at the outdoor equipment store. If we could determine the probability that an arrival would occur between time 0 and time t for $t > 0$, then T

would be a continuous random variable. We will treat the discrete random variable and its properties first and then extend the concept of a random variable to the continuous case.

8.4 DISCRETE RANDOM VARIABLES

A discrete random variable is a numerically valued variable which can assume only a finite or denumerable number of values, each with a certain probability. (By denumerable we mean that the values can be put into a one-to-one correspondence with the positive integers.) Random variables will be denoted by capital letters while the values of the random variable will be denoted by small letters. For example, if X is the number of blue backpacks sold per week, then X is the random variable, and

$$x = 0, 1, 2, \ldots$$

denotes the possible values X can take on. Generally, it is of interest to know the various probabilities with which X takes on its values. If the probability of each sample point can be determined, it is a simple matter to calculate the probabilities associated with each value of the variables defined on the sample space.

Suppose we let

X = number of blue backpacks sold per week
Y = number of backpacks sold per week

be two discrete random variables associated with a given experiment. For simplicity, assume there are only two colors of packs, orange and blue, and the maximum allowable sales for any week is two packs. Figure 8.2 illustrates the sample space for this problem.

Assume the probabilities in Table 8.3 for the various sample points. Let Pr $(X = x)$ denote the probability that the random variable X takes on the value x.

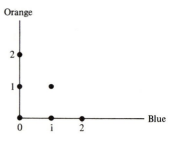

FIGURE 8.2
Sample space.

Table 8.3   **PROBABILITIES FOR EACH SAMPLE POINT IN FIGURE 8.2**

Sample point	(0,0)	(0,1)	(0,2)	(1,0)	(1,1)	(2,0)
Probability	1/8	1/8	1/4	1/8	1/4	1/8

In the current example, X takes on the values 0, 1, and 2 with probabilities

$$\text{Pr}\,(X = 0) = \text{Pr}\,[(0,0)\text{ occurs}] + \text{Pr}\,[(0,1)\text{ occurs}] + \text{Pr}\,[(0,2)\text{ occurs}]$$

$$= \frac{1}{8} + \frac{1}{8} + \frac{1}{4}$$

$$= \frac{1}{2}$$

$$\text{Pr}\,(X = 1) = \text{Pr}\,[(1,0)\text{ occurs}] + \text{Pr}\,[(1,1)\text{ occurs}]$$

$$= \frac{1}{8} + \frac{1}{4}$$

$$= \frac{3}{8}$$

$$\text{Pr}\,(X = 2) = \text{Pr}\,[(2,0)\text{ occurs}]$$

$$= \frac{1}{8}$$

The random variable Y takes on the values 0, 1, and 2 with probabilities

$$\text{Pr}\,(Y = 0) = \text{Pr}\,[(0,0)\text{ occurs}]$$

$$= \frac{1}{8}$$

$$\text{Pr}\,(Y = 1) = \text{Pr}\,[(0,1)\text{ occurs}] + \text{Pr}\,[(1,0)\text{ occurs}]$$

$$= \frac{1}{8} + \frac{1}{8}$$

$$= \frac{1}{4}$$

$$\text{Pr}\,(Y = 2) = \text{Pr}\,[(0,2)\text{ occurs}] + \text{Pr}\,(1,1)\text{ occurs}] + \text{Pr}\,[(2,0)\text{ occurs}]$$

$$= \frac{1}{4} + \frac{1}{4} + \frac{1}{8}$$

$$= \frac{5}{8}$$

Table 8.4 SUMMARY OF RANDOM VARIABLES X AND Y

X	0	1	2	Y	0	1	2
$\Pr(X = x)$	1/2	3/8	1/8	$\Pr(Y = y)$	1/8	1/4	5/8

A summary of the random variables X and Y with their corresponding probabilities is presented in Table 8.4.

The relationship between the values of a random variable X and their corresponding probabilities can be expressed as a function called the *frequency function,* the *probability density function* or, sometimes, the *probability distribution function* of X. We will use the latter name and denote it by PDF.

8.4.1 Probability Distribution Function of a Discrete Random Variable

A function $f(x)$ that yields the probability that the random variable X will assume any particular value in its range is called the *probability distribution function* of the random variable X. Thus,

$$f(x) = \Pr(X = x)$$

Table 8.4 gives the random variables X and Y with their corresponding PDFs. That is, for the random variable X,

$$f(0) = \Pr(X = 0) = \frac{1}{2}$$

$$f(1) = \Pr(X = 1) = \frac{3}{8}$$

$$f(2) = \Pr(X = 2) = \frac{1}{8}$$

Many times the PDF is a table of probabilities associated with the values of the corresponding random variable as in Table 8.4. At other times it might be expressed in closed form, such as

$$f(x) = \Pr(X = x) = p^x(1 - p)^{1-x} \qquad \begin{matrix} x = 0, 1 \\ 0 < p < 1 \end{matrix} \qquad (8.7)$$

The PDF for a random variable X has the properties

$$f(x) \geqslant 0 \qquad \text{for every } x \text{ in } R(x) \qquad (8.8)$$

$$\underset{R(X)}{\Sigma}\ f(x) = 1 \qquad (8.9)$$

where $R(X)$ denotes the range of the random variable X. For the random variable X with the PDF in Table 8.4

$$f(x) \geqslant 0 \qquad \text{for } x = 0, 1, 2$$

$$f(0) + f(1) + f(2) = \frac{1}{2} + \frac{3}{8} + \frac{1}{8} = 1$$

8.4.2 Cumulative Distribution Function of a Discrete Random Variable

Closely related to the PDF is a function called the *cumulative distribution function* of a random variable X. It is defined as

$$F(x) = \Pr(X \leqslant x) = \sum_{z \leqslant x} f(z) = \sum_{z \leqslant x} \Pr(X = z) \qquad (8.10)$$

$F(x)$ represents the probability that the random variable X takes on a value less than or equal to x. For the example represented by Table 8.4

$$F(1) = \Pr(X \leqslant 1) = f(0) + f(1)$$

$$= \frac{1}{2} + \frac{3}{8}$$

$$= \frac{7}{8}$$

$$F(2) = \Pr(X \leqslant 2) = f(0) + f(1) + f(2)$$

$$= \frac{1}{2} + \frac{3}{8} + \frac{1}{8}$$

$$= 1$$

8.4.3 Expected Value of a Discrete Random Variable

Every random variable has associated with it a quantity called the *expected value* of the random variable. Intuitively, it is a linear combination of all the values the random variable takes on, where the coefficient of each value is the probability the random variable takes on that value. Specifically the expected value of a discrete random variable X is defined to be

$$E(X) = \sum_{R(X)} \Pr(X = x) \cdot x$$

$$= \sum_{R(X)} f(x) \cdot x \qquad (8.11)$$

where $R(x)$ denotes the range of X.

For the random variable X in Table 8.4, we have

$$E(X) = \left(\frac{1}{2}\right)(0) + \left(\frac{3}{8}\right)(1) + \left(\frac{1}{8}\right)(2)$$

$$= \frac{5}{8} \qquad (8.12)$$

and for the random variable Y, we have

$$E(Y) = \left(\frac{1}{8}\right)(0) + \left(\frac{1}{4}\right)(1) + \left(\frac{5}{8}\right)(2)$$

$$= \frac{3}{2} \tag{8.13}$$

Note that it is not required that the expected value be one of the values the random variable can take on.

8.4.4 Variance of a Discrete Random Variable

Another quantity closely associated with every random variable is its variance. Basically, the variance is a measure of the relative spread in the values the random variable takes on. In particular, the variance of a discrete random variable is defined as

$$\text{var}(X) = E\{[X - E(X)]^2\}$$
$$= \sum_{R(X)} \text{Pr}(X = x)[x - E(X)]^2$$
$$= \sum_{R(X)} f(x)[x - E(X)]^2 \tag{8.14}$$

The variance of the random variable X in Table 8.4 is

$$\text{var}(X) = \frac{1}{2}\left(0 - \frac{5}{8}\right)^2 + \frac{3}{8}\left(1 - \frac{5}{8}\right)^2 + \frac{1}{8}\left(2 - \frac{5}{8}\right)^2$$

$$= \frac{1}{2}\left(\frac{25}{64}\right) + \frac{3}{8}\left(\frac{9}{64}\right) + \frac{1}{8}\left(\frac{121}{64}\right)$$

$$= 0.484375$$

Quite often a problem can be formulated such that one or more of the random variables involved will have a PDF which is well known. In fact, many of the recurring PDFs have been given special names such as binomial, Poisson, geometric, hypergeometric, etc. We will now examine a few of these special distributions.

8.4.5 Binomial Distribution Function

Suppose an experiment can yield only two possible outcomes, say 0 or 1, where 0 represents a failure and 1 represents a success. Let p be the probability of a success (an outcome of 1) in each experiment. Now repeat the experiment n times under identical conditions. If we let X represent the number of successes in the n experiments, then X is said to have a binomial distribution which is given by

$$f(x) = \text{Pr}(X = x) = \binom{n}{x} p^x (1-p)^{n-x} \quad \begin{array}{l} x = 0, 1, \ldots, n \\ 0 < p < 1 \end{array} \tag{8.15}$$

where $\binom{n}{x}$ denotes the number of ways x successes can occur in n-independent experiments or trials and is given by

$$\binom{n}{x} = \frac{n!}{x!\,(n-x)!} = \frac{n \cdot (n-1) \cdot (n-2) \cdot (n-3) \cdots 1}{x \cdot (x-1) \cdots 1 \cdot (n-x) \cdot (n-x-1) \cdots 1} \qquad (8.16)$$

The symbol also denotes the number of ways to choose x things from n different things. Note that

$$\sum_{x=0}^{n} \binom{n}{x} p^x (1-p)^{n-x} = 1$$

The binomial distribution arises quite naturally. Since p is the probability of success in each experiment, and since the experiments are completely independent (the outcome of one does not affect any others), the probability of getting x successes in a specific way is

$$p^x (1-p)^{n-x}$$

For example, the probability of getting x successes on the first x trials and failures on the remaining $n - x$ trials is

$$\underbrace{p \cdot p \cdots p}_{x \text{ of these}} \ \underbrace{(1-p) \cdot (1-p) \cdots (1-p)}_{n-x \text{ of these}} = p^x (1-p)^{n-x}$$

But there are $\binom{n}{x}$ different ways to get x successes in n-independent trials. Thus,

$$f(x) = \binom{n}{x} p^x (1-p)^{n-x} \qquad \begin{matrix} x = 0, 1, \ldots, n \\ 0 < p < 1 \end{matrix} \qquad (8.17)$$

Suppose 20 computer programs are submitted to the computer and $p = 0.1$ is the probability each program will execute correctly. What is the probability none of them will be executed correctly? Let X be the random variable that represents the number of programs that executed correctly. Each program is considered an independent experiment where the probability of success is $p = 0.1$. Therefore,

$$f(x) = \Pr(X = x) = \binom{20}{x} (0.1)^x (0.9)^{20-x} \qquad x = 0, 1, \ldots, 20$$

Thus,

$$f(0) = \binom{20}{0} (0.1)^0 (0.9)^{20}$$

$$= 0.121577$$

The quantity $\binom{20}{0} = 20!/(0!20!) = 1$, since 0! is defined to be 1. Likewise, the probability that two programs will be executed correctly is

$$f(2) = \Pr(X = 2) = \binom{20}{2} (0.1)^2 (0.9)^{18}$$

$$= \frac{20 \cdot 19 \cdot 18!}{2 \cdot 1 \cdot 18!} (0.01)(0.15)$$

$$= 0.258$$

The expected value of a binomial random variable X is

$$E(X) = \sum_{x=0}^{n} x \binom{n}{x} p^x (1-p)^{n-x}$$

$$= \sum_{x=1}^{n} \frac{x \cdot n \cdot (n-1)!}{x(x-1)!(n-x)!} p^x (1-p)^{n-x}$$

$$= np \sum_{x=1}^{n} \frac{(n-1)!}{(x-1)!(n-x)!} p^{x-1} (1-p)^{n-x}$$

Let $y = x - 1$, then

$$E(X) = np \sum_{y=0}^{n-1} \frac{(n-1)!}{y!(n-1-y)!} p^y (1-p)^{(n-1)-y}$$

$$= np \underbrace{\sum_{y=0}^{n-1} \binom{n-1}{y} p^y (1-p)^{(n-1)-y}}_{1}$$

$$= np \tag{8.18}$$

In a similar manner, it can be shown that the variance of a binomial random variable is

$$\text{var}(X) = np(1-p) \tag{8.19}$$

8.4.6 Poisson Distribution

Another distribution that occurs quite frequently in queueing problems is the Poisson. If customers arrive at a service facility completely at random, then the random variable representing the number of arrivals per unit of time will have a Poisson distribution. Arrivals could be shoppers arriving to check out at a grocery store, planes arriving to land, ships arriving to unload, etc.

The PDF for a Poisson random variable is

$$f(x) = \Pr(X = x)$$

$$= \frac{e^{-\lambda} \lambda^x}{x!} \quad \begin{array}{l} x = 0, 1, 2, \ldots \\ \lambda > 0 \end{array} \tag{8.20}$$

The expected value and variance of a Poisson random variable are

$$E(X) = \lambda \tag{8.21}$$

$$\text{var}(X) = \lambda \tag{8.22}$$

8.4.7 Geometric Distribution

The geometric distribution is closely related to the binomial in the sense that both are based on the same type of experimentation. That is, independent trials are conducted where the probability of success is p and the probability of failure is $1-p$. With the geometric distribution, we are interested in the time until the first failure occurs.

Let X be the random variable that represents the time until the first failure. The PDF of X is

$$f(x) = \Pr(X = x)$$
$$= p^{x-1}(1-p) \qquad \begin{matrix} x = 1, 2, \ldots \\ 0 < p < 1 \end{matrix} \qquad (8.23)$$

Thus, $f(x)$ represents the probability that the first $x-1$ trials were successes and the xth trial was a failure. This is known as the *geometric distribution*.

The expected value of X is

$$E(X) = \sum_{x=1}^{\infty} x p^{x-1}(1-p)$$

$$= \frac{1}{1-p} \qquad (8.24)$$

8.4.8 Hypergeometric Distribution

Suppose we take a random sample of size n from a population of N items without replacement. If N_A of the items in the population have an attribute A, and if we let X be a random variable describing the number of items drawn that have attribute A, then

$$f(x) = \Pr(X = x)$$
$$= \frac{\binom{N_A}{x}\binom{N-N_A}{n-x}}{\binom{N}{n}} \qquad x = 0, 1, 2, \ldots, N_A \qquad (8.25)$$

is the *hypergeometric distribution*.

Consider the example where 10 students are chosen from a class of 30 to work on a certain project. If the class consists of 25 undergraduates and 5 graduate students, what is the PDF for the number of graduate students chosen? If X is the number of graduate students chosen, then from the PDF in Equation (8.25), we have

$$f(x) = \frac{\binom{5}{x}\binom{25}{10-x}}{\binom{30}{10}} \qquad x = 0, 1, \ldots, 5 \qquad (8.26)$$

From (8.26), we see that the probability of two graduate students being chosen is

$$f(2) = \frac{\binom{5}{2}\binom{25}{8}}{\binom{30}{10}}$$

$$= \frac{[5!/(2!3!)]\ [25!/(8!17!)]}{30!/(10!20!)}$$

$$= 0.359985$$

There are other discrete distributions that are used occasionally; however, we will now turn our attention to continuous random variables and their corresponding distributions.

8.5 CONTINUOUS RANDOM VARIABLES

A variable X that can take on a nondenumerable number of values is said to be a continuous random variable if there exists a function $f(x)$, called the *distribution or density function of X*, such that

$$\Pr(A \leqslant X \leqslant B) = \int_A^B f(x)\, dx \qquad (8.27)$$

In the discrete case, $f(x)$ is the probability that the random variable X takes on the value x, whereas in the continuous case, $f(x)$ is just the height of the curve $f(x)$ at $X = x$. Thus, in the continuous case we only talk about the probability that the random variable X takes on a value between two limits, say A and B, which is just the area under the curve $f(x)$ over $[A,B]$. That is,

$$\Pr(A \leqslant X \leqslant B) = \int_A^B f(x)\, dx$$

This is illustrated in Figure 8.3.

8.5.1 Properties of Continuous Random Variables and Their Density Functions

A density function also satisfies two essential properties, namely

$$f(x) \geqslant 0 \quad \text{for all } x \text{ in } R(X) \qquad (8.28)$$

$$\int_{R(X)} f(x)\, dx = 1 \qquad (8.29)$$

where $R(X)$ denotes the range of the continuous random variable X.

Each continuous random variable X also has an expected value, a variance, and a cumulative distribution function defined as follows:

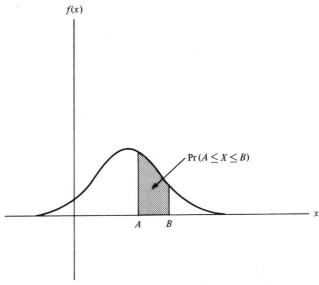

FIGURE 8.3
Continuous density function.

The expected value of X is

$$E(X) = \int_{R(X)} xf(x)\,dx \qquad (8.30)$$

The variance of X is

$$\text{var}\,(X) = \int_{R(X)} [x - E(X)]^2 f(x)\,dx \qquad (8.31)$$

The cumulative distribution of X is

$$F(x) = \text{Pr}\,(X \leq x) = \int_{-\infty}^{x} f(t)\,dt \qquad (8.32)$$

where $f(t)$ is the density of X with the dummy variable of integration t substituted. We will illustrate these properties with a few of the more useful continuous distribution functions.

8.5.2 Normal Distribution Function

Many practical situations arise where the distribution of the random variable involved can be approximated with the normal distribution. It is probably the best known and possibly the most used continuous distribution, primarily because many statistical models assume the errors are normal and independently distributed. This assumption is generally valid because of the extremely important central limit theorem which essentially states that the sum of many independent effects tends to be normally distributed as the number of effects becomes large.

8.5.2.1 Central limit theorem If the random variables X_1, X_2, ..., X_n are independently distributed according to some common distribution function with mean (expected value) μ and finite variance σ^2, then as the number of random variables increases without bound, the random variable

$$Y = \frac{\sum_{i=1}^{n} X_i - n\mu}{\sqrt{n\sigma^2}}$$

converges to a normal random variable with mean 0 and variance 1.

The *normal distribution* of a continuous random variable X is given by

$$f(x) = \frac{1}{\sigma\sqrt{2\pi}}\, e^{-1/2[(x-\mu)/\sigma]^2} \qquad -\infty \leqslant x \leqslant \infty \qquad (8.33)$$

where μ and σ are two parameters such that $\sigma > 0$. It turns out that the mean or expected value of X is μ and the variance is σ^2. The parameter μ shifts the distribution to the right or left as it is increased or decreased, respectively. The parameter σ squeezes the distribution in around μ as it is decreased and expands the distribution as it is increased. It should be noted that the normal distribution is symmetric about the mean μ regardless of the values of μ and σ. This is illustrated in Figure 8.4.

The cumulative distribution of a normally distributed random variable X is

$$F(x) = \Pr\,(X \leqslant x) = \int_{-\infty}^{x} \frac{1}{\sigma\sqrt{2\pi}}\, e^{-1/2[(t-\mu)/\sigma]^2}\, dt \qquad (8.34)$$

However, it is not possible to integrate the normal distribution analytically. Consequently, we can make a transformation on any normal distribution with mean μ and variance σ^2 to reduce it to the so-called *unit normal distribution*, namely a normal distribution with mean 0 and variance 1. The cumulative distribution of the normal random variable with mean 0 and variance 1 can then be put in table form for easy reference. Such a table appears in Table A.1. The transformation needed to convert any normal random variable X to a unit normal random variable is

$$Y = \frac{X - \mu}{\sigma} \qquad (8.35)$$

where X is normally distributed with mean μ and variance σ^2. If we use the symbol

$$X \sim N(\mu,\sigma^2) \qquad (8.36)$$

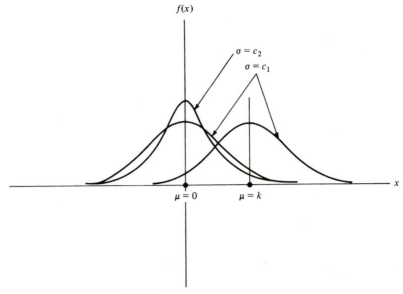

FIGURE 8.4
Normal distribution with constants c_1, c_2, $k > 0$ and $c_1 > c_2$.

to denote that X is distributed normally with mean μ and variance σ^2, then it can be shown that

$$Y = \frac{X - \mu}{\sigma} \sim N(0, 1) \qquad (8.37)$$

Hence,

$$F(x) = \Pr(X \leqslant x) = \int_{-\infty}^{x} N(\mu, \sigma^2)\, dt$$

$$= \int_{-\infty}^{(x-\mu)/\sigma} N(0,1)\, dt$$

$$= \int_{-\infty}^{y} N(0,1)\, dt$$

$$= \alpha \qquad (8.38)$$

Table A.1 gives the value of α, which is the area under the unit normal distribution from $-\infty$ to y for $y = 0.0, 0.01, 0.02, \ldots, 3.49$. The procedure to calculate $F(x)$ when X is distributed as a normal with mean μ and variance σ^2 is

(a) Let $y = \frac{x - \mu}{\sigma}$, x, μ, and σ are known.

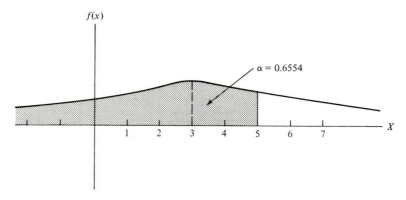

FIGURE 8.5
Normal distribution with mean 3 and variance 25.

(b) If y is negative, go to step (c); otherwise select the value of α from Table A.1 that corresponds to the value of y. The selected value of α will necessarily be the value of $F(x) = \Pr(X \leqslant x)$. Stop.

(c) Change the sign of y and select the value of α from Table A.1 that corresponds to the new value of y. Let $\beta = 1 - \alpha$, then $F(x) = \Pr(X \leqslant x) = \beta$. Stop.

Suppose we want $F(5)$ when X is distributed as a normal random variance with mean 3 and variance $\sigma^2 = 25$.

(a) Let $y = \frac{x - \mu}{\sigma} = \frac{5 - 3}{5} = 0.40$.

(b) $y > 0$, so read off the value of α for $y = 0.4$ from Table A.1, namely, $\alpha = 0.6554$. Therefore $F(5) = \Pr(X \leqslant 5) = 0.6554$.

Suppose we want $F(2)$ in the above example.

(a) Let $y = \frac{x - \mu}{\sigma} = \frac{2 - 3}{5} = -\frac{1}{5} = -0.2$.

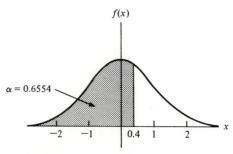

FIGURE 8.6
Normal distribution with mean 0 and variance 1.

(b) $y < 0$, so go to step (c).
(c) Let $y = -(-0.2) = 0.2$ and read off the value of α for $y = 0.2$ from Table A.1, namely, $\alpha = 0.5793$.

Let

$$\beta = 1 - \alpha$$
$$= 1 - 0.5793$$
$$= 0.4207$$

Then $F(2) = \Pr(X \leqslant 2) = 0.4207$.

One further example should clarify the procedure. To determine $\Pr(2 \leqslant X \leqslant 5)$, we merely need to observe that

$$\Pr(2 \leqslant X \leqslant 5) = \int_2^5 N(3,25)\, dt$$

$$= \int_{-\infty}^5 N(3,25)\, dt - \int_{-\infty}^2 N(3,25)\, dt$$

$$= F(5) - F(2)$$
$$= 0.6554 - 0.4207$$
$$= 0.2347$$

8.5.3 Gamma Distribution Function

Another much used distribution in OR is the gamma distribution which is given by

$$f(t) = \frac{t^{\alpha-1} e^{-t/\beta}}{\Gamma(\alpha)\beta^\alpha} \qquad \begin{matrix} t \geqslant 0 \\ \alpha,\, \beta > 0 \end{matrix} \qquad (8.39)$$

where α and β are positive parameters and

$$\Gamma(\alpha) = \int_0^\infty x^{\alpha-1} e^{-x}\, dx \qquad \text{for all } \alpha > 0 \qquad (8.40)$$

If α is an integer, then repeated integration by parts yields

$$\Gamma(\alpha) = (\alpha - 1)!$$

In this case, the gamma distribution is known as the *Erlang distribution* which will be discussed in Section 8.5.3.2.

It can be shown that the gamma-distributed random variable T has mean and variance

$$E(T) = \alpha\beta \qquad (8.41)$$
$$\text{var}(T) = \alpha\beta^2 \qquad (8.42)$$

Quite often the distribution of a given set of data can be approximated by the gamma distribution for certain values of α and β. In particular, if $\alpha = 1$ the distribution reduces to the so-called *exponential distribution.*

8.5.3.1 Exponential distribution function The exponential distribution is obtained by letting $\alpha = 1$ in the gamma distribution; however, it arises quite naturally in situations in which the time for something to occur is involved. For example, the distribution of a continuous random variable T that denotes the time between consecutive arrivals for service, the time to perform a service, or the life of a computer component might be approximated with an exponential distribution.

Suppose we let $\alpha = 1$ and $\beta = 1/\mu$ in the gamma distribution. The result is the exponential distribution

$$f(t) = \mu e^{-\mu t} \quad \begin{matrix} t \geqslant 0 \\ \mu > 0 \end{matrix} \qquad (8.43)$$

with mean and variance

$$E(T) = \frac{1}{\mu}$$

$$\text{var } (T) = \frac{1}{\mu^2}$$

Figure 8.7 gives the general form of the exponential distribution.

The cumulative distribution of an exponentially distributed random variable is useful in simulation. It is given by

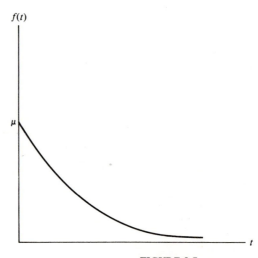

FIGURE 8.7
Exponential distribution.

$$F(t) = \Pr(T \leqslant t)$$

$$= \int_0^t \mu e^{-\mu x}\, dx$$

$$= 1 - e^{-\mu t} \qquad (8.44)$$

The important relationship that exists between the exponential and Poisson distributions is useful in waiting-line or queueing problems as well as in simulation. In particular, if the time between consecutive arrivals at a service facility has an exponential distribution with parameter λ, then it can be shown that the number of arrivals per unit of time has a Poisson distribution with parameter λ. That is, if

$T =$ time between consecutive arrivals
$X =$ number of arrivals per unit of time

with $f(t) = \lambda e^{-\lambda t} \quad \begin{array}{l} t \geqslant 0 \\ \lambda > 0 \end{array}$ \hfill (8.45)

then $f(x) = \dfrac{e^{-\lambda}\lambda^x}{x!} \quad \begin{array}{l} x = 0, 1, 2, \ldots \\ \lambda > 0 \end{array}$ \hfill (8.46)

8.5.3.2 Erlang distribution function We have noted that the gamma distribution is called the *Erlang distribution* when the parameter α is an integer. The distribution can arise as the result of summing a number of independent exponentially distributed random variables. That is, if $T_1, T_2, \ldots, T_k$ are k-independent exponentially distributed random variables with a common parameter $k\mu$, [that is, $f(t_i) = k\mu e^{-k\mu t_i}$], then the random variable

$$T = \sum_{i=1}^{k} T_i$$

has a gamma (Erlang) distribution with mean $1/\mu$ and variance $1/k\mu^2$. Note that with $\alpha = k$ and $\beta = 1/k\mu$ in the gamma, the resulting distribution, known as the Erlang, has the form

$$f(t) = \frac{(k\mu)^k t^{k-1} e^{-k\mu t}}{(k-1)!} \qquad \begin{array}{l} t \geqslant 0 \\ k > 0 \\ \mu > 0 \end{array} \qquad (8.47)$$

with mean

$$E(T) = \frac{1}{\mu}$$

$$\mathrm{var}\,(T) = \frac{1}{k\mu^2}$$

Figure 8.8 illustrates the Erlang distribution for $k = 1, 2,$ and 3.

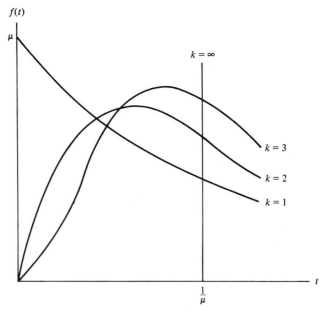

FIGURE 8.8
Erlang distribution with $k = 1, 2, 3$.

Suppose customers arrive at a service facility where k distinct phases of the service must be performed on each customer. If the time to perform each phase has an exponential distribution

$$f(t_i) = k\mu e^{-k\mu t_i} \quad \begin{array}{l} t_i \geq 0 \\ k > 0 \\ \mu > 0 \end{array}$$

and is independent of the time to perform each of the other phases, then the total time T to perform all k phases of service has the Erlang distribution

$$f(t) = \frac{(k\mu)^k t^{k-1} e^{-k\mu t}}{(k-1)!} \quad \begin{array}{l} t \geq 0 \\ k > 0 \\ \mu > 0 \end{array}$$

The Erlang distribution is useful in its own right to approximate the service time distribution in many waiting-line or queueing problems because of the wide diversity provided by the two positive parameters in the distribution.

8.5.3.3 Chi-Square distribution function An important distribution that is used to determine if a given set of observations came from a certain distribution or not is the chi-square distribution. It also has wide use in the area of regression analysis. In particular if we let $\alpha = \delta/2$, $\beta = 1$, and $t = y/2$ in the gamma distribution in Equation

(8.39), the resulting random variable will have a chi-square distribution with δ degrees of freedom (df). Primarily, we will be interested in selecting certain critical points from Table A.2.

The chi-square distribution is sometimes defined in terms of the sum of independent normal random variables that each have a mean 0 and variance 1. That is, if X_1, X_2, ..., X_δ are independent normal random variables each with mean 0 and variance 1, then the distribution of

$$Y = X_1{}^2 + X_2{}^2 + \cdots + X_\delta{}^2$$

is called the *chi-square or χ^2 distribution with δ degrees of freedom.* Figure 8.9 illustrates χ^2 distributions with 10 and 25 degrees of freedom.

To determine the critical point χ_0^2 for $\alpha = 0.05$ and $\delta = 10$, observe $\delta = 10$ in the left column of Table A.2, and move to the right until $1 - \alpha = 1 - 0.05 = 0.95$ is directly above. The correct value, $\chi_0^2 = 18.31$, is read off the table at this point of intersection. This aspect of the chi-square distribution will be discussed further in Section 8.6.

8.5.4 Uniform Distribution

If the distribution of a random variable X is constant on the interval of definition, say $[a,b]$, then X is said to have a uniform distribution which is defined as

$$f(x) = \frac{1}{b - a} \qquad a \leqslant x \leqslant b$$

The special case where $a = 0$ and $b = 1$ will be of interest in simulation. Figure 8.10 illustrates the uniform distribution on $[a,b]$.

8.6 SELECTING THE APPROPRIATE DISTRIBUTION

The first concern in any OR project should be the selection of appropriate models to represent the system and subsystems under study. If uncertainty is involved, this

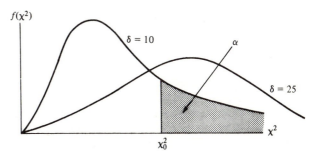

FIGURE 8.9
χ^2 distributions with 10 and 25 degrees of freedom.

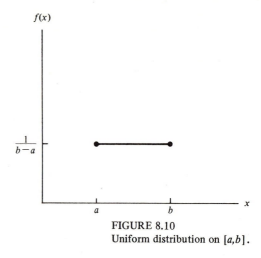

FIGURE 8.10
Uniform distribution on $[a,b]$.

necessitates the use of random variables whose distributions may or may not be known. When the distribution of certain sample data is unknown, it is usually appropriate to represent the distribution of the data with a distribution function whose properties are well known. For example, in regression analysis the underlying assumption throughout the analysis is that the random errors are normally distributed with mean 0 and variance σ^2. How valid is this assumption? Many times in simulation it is appropriate to represent the distribution of random variables in each phase of the project with well-known distributions that approximate the distribution of sample data which are obtained from prior experimentation. In this case, we might assume the number of arrivals per unit of time at a service facility has some form of the Poisson distribution and the time to service an arrival has an Erlang distribution. But how good are our assumptions, and what are the appropriate values of the parameters in each case?

From a practical standpoint, the first step to take in answering these questions is to plot the sample data to see if the resulting distribution "looks like" a known distribution function. If one or more known distributions look like they would do an adequate job of representing the distribution of the data, then statistical tests should be applied to the data to determine which distribution would be the most appropriate to use. One could also plot the sample cumulative distribution to see if it looks like a certain known cumulative distribution before making any statistical tests. Keep in mind that statistics is nothing more than an aid in the decision-making process. More than one distribution might do an adequate job of representing a given set of sample data, but statistics can be used to assist in finding the most appropriate distribution based on the given data. Of course, the results of any statistical test are based on the basic assumptions that the sample data used in the test are representative of the population from which they came and that the sample size is sufficiently large enough to indicate such.

Suppose a given set of sample data is represented by $y_1, y_2, \ldots, y_n$ where y_1 is the smallest value and y_n is the largest value. If we divide the closed interval $[y_1, y_n]$ into m equally spaced subintervals $I_1, I_2, \ldots, I_m$, each of width h, and let $f(I_j)$ be the number of data points in the jth subinterval, then the plot or histogram of the data would appear as in Figure 8.11.

Note that $f(I_1) = 2, f(I_2) = 2, f(I_3) = 3, f(I_4) = 5$, etc. Based on this histogram, we might want to test the hypothesis that the data came from a normal distribution with a specific mean and variance. A good rule of thumb is to consider several distributions as candidates to represent the given set of data, and then to apply one or more statistical tests to determine which is most appropriate.

Generally, the chi-square test and the Kolmogorov-Smirnov test are used to test the hypothesis that a given set of data came from a specific distribution. If either or both of the tests indicate that the hypothesis should be rejected, then the hypothesized distribution is not used. However, if neither of the tests indicate that the hypothesis should be rejected, then the hypothesized distribution is usually accepted as being an appropriate distribution for the data. In reality, if a hypothesis is not rejected, the correct statement is that there is insufficient information to reject the hypothesis at the specified level of significance. Consequently, there is potential danger in accepting a hypothesis. In fact, neither of the aforementioned tests should be used to determine if a hypothesized distribution *should be used* to represent the given set of data, but should only be used to determine if a hypothesized distribution is *not appropriate* for the data. A procedure for selecting an appropriate distribution will be discussed in Section 8.6.3. It is based on the test to be discussed in Section 8.6.1.

8.6.1 Chi-Square Goodness-of-Fit Test

This test is appropriate for testing the hypothesis that a given set of data came from a certain distribution with all parameters specified. It is primarily used to determine

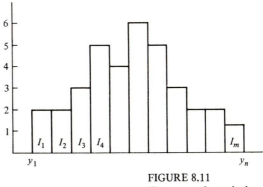

FIGURE 8.11
Histogram of sample data.

when a hypothesized distribution is not an adequate distribution to use; however, many authors recommend using the hypothesized distribution when it cannot be rejected. There is potential danger in this recommendation unless the hypothesized distribution *cannot* be rejected at the 50 or 60 percent level of significance. We will clarify this point after the discussion of the chi-square test.

If the parameters are not specified in the hypothesized distribution, they must be estimated from the data using the maximum likelihood or least-squares estimates. For example, if the hypothesis is that the data came from a normal distribution without specifying the mean or variance, the mean and variance are estimated with

$$\bar{y} = \sum_{i=1}^{n} y_i/n$$

$$s^2 = \sum_{i=1}^{n} \frac{(y_i - \bar{y})^2}{n-1}$$

and we test the hypothesis that

$$y \sim N(\bar{y}, s^2)$$

The general chi-square goodness-of-fit test procedure is:

(*a*) Hypothesize that the sample data came from a certain distribution with all parameters specified or estimated.

(*b*) Divide the range of the hypothesized distribution into m subintervals such that the expected number of values, say E_j, in each subinterval is at least five for $j = 1, 2, \ldots, m.$

(*c*) Let O_j be the number of sample data points in the jth subinterval for $j = 1, 2, \ldots, m.$

(*d*) The quantity

$$\text{Calculated } \chi^2 = \sum_{j=1}^{m} \frac{(O_j - E_j)^2}{E_j}$$

approaches the χ^2 distribution with $m - k - 1$ degrees of freedom as m becomes large, where k is the number of parameters that must be estimated from the sample data in order to calculate the expected number of values E_j for $j = 1, 2, \ldots, m.$ (Degrees of freedom will be discussed in Chapter 9.)

(*e*) If calculated χ^2 is greater than the critical χ^2 value in Table A.2, using $m - k - 1$ degrees of freedom and a $100 (1 - \alpha)$ percent significance level, reject the hypothesis that the sample data came from the hypothesized distribution; otherwise, consider some other distributions before accepting the hypothesized distribution as being adequate.

Suppose we have a sample of size $N = 100$, and we wish to determine whether we can reject the hypothesis that the random variable X which yielded the 100 values has a normal distribution with mean 0 and variance 1. To do this we:

(a) Hypothesize that X has a normal distribution with mean 0 and variance 1, which can be written as:

$$H_0 : X \sim N(0,1)$$

(b) Divide the range of X into m subintervals. In general $m = 10$ is appropriate for $N \geqslant 100$. The 10 subintervals, the corresponding probability that a normally distributed random variable with mean 0 and variance 1 will fall in each subinterval, the expected number of values in each subinterval, and the number of sample data points in each subinterval, O_j, are given in Table 8.5.

(c) The quantity

$$\text{Calculated } \chi^2 = \sum_{j=1}^{10} \frac{(O_j - E_j)^2}{E_j} = 17.798$$

is greater than

$$\text{Tabulated } \chi^2_{0.05}(9) = 16.919$$

which is the critical χ^2 value with $m - k - 1 = 10 - 0 - 1 = 9$ degrees of freedom at the $100(1 - 0.05)$ percent $= 95$ percent significance level. Hence we reject the hypothesis that the given data came from a normal distribution with mean 0 and variance 1 and look for another potential distribution.

If the calculated χ^2 were equal to say, 5.00, we could not reject the hypothesis even at the $100(1 - 0.75) = 25$ percent significance level since tabulated $\chi^2_{0.75}(9) = 5.899$. This means that we cannot be 25 percent confident that X is not a normal random variable with mean 0 and variance 1. Therefore, we would be rather safe in accepting a normal distribution with mean 0 and variance 1 as an appropriate representation for the data. Basically, the chi-square test should only be used when the

Table 8.5   EXPECTED NUMBER OF OBSERVATIONS IN EACH SUBINTERVAL OF AN $N(0,1)$ FOR $N = 100$ AND THE NUMBER OF SAMPLE DATA POINTS IN EACH SUBINTERVAL

Subinterval I_j	Pr $[X \epsilon I_j]$	$E_j = 100\text{Pr }[X \epsilon I_j]$	O_j
$I_1 = [-\infty, -1.6]$	0.0548	5.48	3
$I_2 = [-1.6, -1.2]$	0.0603	6.03	8
$I_3 = [-1.2, -0.8]$	0.0968	9.68	7
$I_4 = [-0.8, -0.4]$	0.1327	13.27	12
$I_5 = [-0.4, 0]$	0.1554	15.54	18
$I_6 = [0, 0.4]$	0.1554	15.54	25
$I_7 = [0.4, 0.8]$	0.1327	13.27	16
$I_8 = [0.8, 1.2]$	0.0968	9.68	2
$I_9 = [1.2, 1.6]$	0.0603	6.03	7
$I_{10} = [1.6, \infty]$	0.0548	5.48	2

sample size is large (say, $N \geqslant 20$) and the expected number of values in most of the subintervals is at least five.

The Kolmogorov-Smirnov test (discussed in Section 8.6.2) can be used with a small sample size and is generally accepted as being more powerful than the chi-square test when all of the parameters are specified in the hypothesized distribution.

8.6.2 Kolmogorov-Smirnov Goodness-of-Fit Test

In this test, the maximum absolute difference between the sample cumulative distribution and the cumulative distribution under the assumed hypothesis is calculated and compared with a critical value to determine if the hypothesized distribution can be rejected. Specifically, given a sample of size N,

(a) Hypothesize that the sample data came from a certain distribution with all parameters specified.

(b) Divide the range of the hypothesized distribution into m equally spaced subintervals.

(c) Let $F(y)$ be the hypothesized cumulative distribution and $F_0(y)$ be the sample cumulative distribution.

(d) Calculate

$$D_N = \max_{\text{over all subintervals}} [|F_0(y) - F(y)|]$$

(e) If

$$D_N > D_N^*(\alpha)$$

reject the hypothesis that the data came from the hypothesized distribution; otherwise, examine other potential distribution before making a final decision, where $D_N^*(\alpha)$ is the critical value obtained from Table A.3.

Consider the problem in which we hypothesize that a given sample of size $N = 100$ came from a uniform distribution on $[0,1]$. Suppose we use the 10 equally spaced subintervals, $[0,0.1]$, $[0.1,0.2]$, ..., $[0.9,1.0]$, then

$$F(y) = y \qquad 0 \leqslant y \leqslant 1$$

$$F_0(y) = \frac{k}{100}$$

where k is the number of sample values less than or equal to y. The sample cumulative distribution is shown in Table 8.6 along with the hypothesized cumulative distribution and the absolute difference between the two. From Table 8.6 we see that $D_{100} = 0.08$ and from Table A.3, $D_{100}^*(0.05) = 0.136$. Therefore, the hypothesis cannot be rejected at the $100(1 - \alpha)$ percent $= 95$ percent significance level, so many authors recommend that the hypothesized distribution be accepted at this point. An alternative procedure will be discussed in Section 8.6.3.

Table 8.6   CUMULATIVE DISTRIBUTIONS FOR KOLMOGOROV–SMIRNOV TEST

	Subinterval									
Distribution	[0,0.1]	[0.1,0.2]	[0.2,0.3]	[0.3,0.4]	[0.4,0.5]	[0.5,0.6]	[0.6,0.7]	[0.7,0.8]	[0.8,0.9]	[0.9,1.0]
$F(y)$	0.1	0.2	0.3	0.4	0.5	0.6	0.7	0.8	0.9	1.0
$F_0(y)$	0.12	0.18	0.24	0.45	0.5	0.63	0.78	0.85	0.92	1.0
$\lvert F_0(y) - F(y) \rvert$	0.02	0.02	0.06	0.05	0.0	0.03	0.08	0.05	0.02	0

8.6.3   Procedure to Select an Appropriate Distribution

An alternative to testing the hypothesis that a given set of data came from a specific distribution is to:

(*a*)   Select a number of potential distributions by examining a histogram of the data.

(*b*)   Calculate the quantity

$$\text{Calculated } \chi^2 = \sum_{j=1}^{m} \frac{(O_j - E_j)^2}{E_j}$$

for each potential distribution.

(*c*)   Select the distribution with the smallest calculated χ^2.

If the smallest calculated χ^2 is greater than the tabulated critical χ^2 value at the 75 percent level, it might be appropriate to add more distributions to the set of potential distributions and go back to step (*b*).

Another alternative is to apply the Kolmogorov-Smirnov test to each of the potential distributions, and to select the distribution with the smallest D_N value.

SELECTED BIBLIOGRAPHY

1   Afifi, A. A., and S. P. Azen: "Statistical Analysis, A Computer Oriented Approach," Academic Press, Inc., New York, 1972.

2   Birnbaum, Z. W.: Numerical Tabulation of the Distribution of Kolmogorov's Statistic for Finite Sample Size, *J. Am. Statistical Assoc.*, vol. 47, pp. 425–441, 1952.

3   Edwards, A. L.: "Probability and Statistics," Holt, Rinehart and Winston, Inc., New York, 1971.

4   Hodges, J. L., Jr., and E. L. Lehmann: "Basic Concepts of Probability and Statistics," Holden-Day, Inc., San Francisco, 1964.

5   Hoel, P. G.: "Introduction to Mathematical Statistics," 3d ed., John Wiley & Sons, Inc., New York, 1963.

6   Lass, H., and P. Gottlieb: "Probability and Statistics," Addison-Wesley Publishing Company, Inc., Reading, Mass., 1971.

7 Massey, F. J.: The Kolmogorov-Smirnov Test for Goodness-of-Fit, *J. Am. Statistical Assoc.*, vol. 46, pp. 68–78, 1951.

8 Mood, A. M., and F. A. Graybill: "Introduction to the Theory of Statistics," 2d ed., McGraw-Hill Book Company, New York, 1963.

9 Ross, S.: "Introduction to Probability Models," Academic Press, Inc., New York, 1972.

10 Schlaifer, R.: "Introduction to Statistics for Business Decisions," McGraw-Hill Book Company, New York, 1961.

11 Winkler, R. L.: "Statistics, Probability, Influence, and Decision," Holt, Rinehart and Winston, Inc., New York, 1970.

EXERCISES

8.1 The following data were obtained by a random number generator which was designed to generate values from a uniform distribution on the interval [0,1].

(0.2, 0.6, 0.8, 0.3, 0.9, 0.5, 0.8, 0.6, 0.2, 0.3, 0.7, 0.9, 0.6, 0.7,

0.4, 0.8, 0.7, 0.1, 0.6, 0.5, 0.8)

(a) Use the chi-square test to determine if the hypothesis that the data came from a uniform distribution on [0,1] can be rejected at the 95 percent confidence level ($\alpha = 0.05$).

(b) Test the data using the Kolmogorov-Smirnov test at the 95 percent confidence level to see if it can be concluded that the data did not come from the hypothesized distribution.

8.2 Let X be a random variable with the distribution function

$$f(x) = k(1 - x^2) \qquad -1 \leqslant x \leqslant 1$$
$$= 0 \qquad\qquad \text{otherwise}$$

What is the value of k?

8.3 Suppose the probability distribution function of demand for a product is given by:

Demand D	0	1	2	3
$f(d) = P(D = d)$	0.2	0.1	0.2	0.5

(a) What is the expected demand?

(b) What is the variance of demand?

(c) What is the probability the demand will be less than 2?

8.4 Let X be the number of radios sold per week. Assume X has a Poisson distribution with parameter $\lambda = 20$.

(a) Find $P(X \geqslant 20)$.

(b) If the number of radios in inventory is 25, what is the probability of a shortage occurring during the next week?

8.5 If the numbers 1, 2, ..., n are arranged in a random order, what is the probability that the digits 1 and 2 will appear next to each other?

8.6   Given the probability distribution function (PDF)

$$f(x) = \frac{e^{-1}}{x!} \qquad x = 0, 1, 2, \ldots$$

(a) Calculate $F(2) = P(X \leq 2)$
(b) Show that e^{-1} is the proper constant for this PDF.

8.7   From a group of 50 people, 3 are chosen. Find the probability that none of 10 certain people in the group will be chosen.

8.8   Calculate the expected value of a random variable which has the PDF

$$f(x) = \left(\frac{1}{2}\right)^x \qquad x = 1, 2, 3, 4$$

$$= \left(\frac{1}{2}\right)^{x-1} \qquad x = 5$$

8.9   In the binomial PDF with $n = 4$ and $p = 2/3$, what is the probability of one success?

8.10   Given a family with five children, what is the PDF for the number of girls in the family if the probability for having a girl is 0.6?

8.11   Suppose 5 cards are selected from a deck of 52 cards. What is the PDF for the number of aces?

8.12   Give an example of each of the following
(a) Independent events
(b) Mutually exclusive events
(c) Discrete random variable
(d) Continuous random variable

8.13   Suppose a computer component has a probability $q = 10^{-6}$ of failing during a given hour. What is the probability the component will last at least 10,000 hr?

8.14   Let $p = \frac{3}{4}$ be the probability of a success on independent trials of an experiment. What is the probability that the first failure will occur on the third trial?

8.15   If arrivals at a supermarket occur completely at random, the number of arrivals per minute has a Poisson distribution. Suppose the mean number of arrivals per minute is 5. What is the probability of more than 5 arrivals/min?

8.16   A random variable X has a normal distribution with mean 5 and variance 9. Find
(a) $P(X < 2)$
(b) $P(X > 5)$
(c) $P(X > 8)$
(d) $P(4 < X < 6)$

9
REGRESSION ANALYSIS

9.1 INTRODUCTION

The basic objective of any OR project is to study a given system, such as a university computer center or the U.S. Treasury Department, to gain useful information. In the study of most realistic systems, variation can be observed in many components of the system. For example, in a university computer center the turnaround time for computer programs is not constant but varies from time to time. Logical questions might be, "What factors affect turnaround time?," "Can a functional relationship be established between turnaround time and these factors?" The process of establishing answers for these questions is the essence of regression analysis.

In general, *regression analysis* is the process of constructing and analyzing functional relationships between a response, the dependent variable Y, and important factors, the independent variables X_1, X_2, $\ldots$, X_k, that affect the response. The relationship that "best," in some sense, represents the response as a function of the independent variables is selected for use in predicting future responses for fixed values of the independent variables. In the computer center example, turnaround time could be the response variable. Factors such as priority level of the program, core requirements for the program, time of day when the program was submitted, and special instructions to the operator could be the independent variables that might affect turnaround time.

The word "independent" means that the variables can be set or observed at specific values. It does not mean that the variables are statistically independent. In fact, if they are set at specific values, they are completely deterministic mathematical variables. If the independent variables take on values that can be observed, but not controlled (such as the salinity of ocean water, water temperature, etc.), they are random variables which may or may not be statistically independent. The dependent variable is considered to be a random variable that is dependent upon, or a function of, one or more independent variables. Although the independent variables may be mathematical variables, we will denote both the dependent and independent *variables* with *capital letters,* and the *values* they take on with *small letters.*

In order to construct a functional relationship between dependent and independent variables, data must be available or collected that consist of responses y_i with $i = 1, 2, \ldots, n$, and corresponding values of all independent variables that possibly have any relationship to the response. For example, if it is believed that factors represented by the independent variables X_1, X_2, and X_3 are related to a response Y in some way, a set of data similar to that in Table 9.1 must be available from past records, or must be collected, in order to establish a functional relationship between Y and X_1, X_2, and X_3.

Once the data are available, functional relationships such as

$$Y = \alpha_0 + \alpha_1 X_1$$
$$Y = \alpha_0 + \alpha_1 X_1 + \alpha_2 X_2$$
$$Y = \alpha_0 + \alpha_1 X_3$$
$$Y = \alpha_0 + \alpha_1 X_1 + \alpha_2 X_2 + \alpha_3 X_3 + \alpha_4 X_1 X_2{}^2$$
$$Y = \alpha_0 + \alpha_1 X_2$$

can be analyzed to determine a relationship that is "best," in some sense, based on the given data. The α_j's in each case are parameters to be determined. In fact, for each functional relationship, the given data are used to determine the corresponding values of the α_j's that will force the particular relationship to fit the data "best" in some sense. Generally, we will be interested in determining the α_j's that are "best" in the sense of *least squares*. This concept will be discussed in Section 9.2.

Although nonlinear relationships exist quite often, we will restrict our discussion to relationships that are linear in the parameters. That is, we will concentrate on fitting models of the form

Table 9.1 SAMPLE DATA

X_1	1	1	4	5	8	6	12	16	12
X_2	2	4	6	12	12	8	4	4	8
X_3	32	16	18	42	5	12	19	3	1
Y	32	16	48	69	92	74	42	50	85

$$Y = \alpha_0 + \alpha_1 X_1 + \alpha_2 X_2 + \cdots + \alpha_k X_k + \epsilon$$

to determine the least-squares estimates of the parameters $\alpha_0, \alpha_1, \ldots, \alpha_k$, where ϵ is an error term. Note that the model is linear in the α_j's. It need not be linear in the X_j's however. In fact, the X_j's can themselves be nonlinear functions of other independent variables, such as

$$X_1 = Z_1$$
$$X_2 = Z_1^2$$
$$X_3 = Z_2$$
$$X_4 = Z_2^2$$
$$X_5 = Z_1 Z_2$$

where Z_1 and Z_2 are independent variables. Also, the variable Z might be a single independent variable of interest, and X_i might be Z raised to the ith power, that is,

$$X_i = Z^i \qquad i = 1, 2, \ldots$$

The basics of any regression analysis can be stated simply as

1 Gather available data, or conduct experiments with the important independent variables set or observed at specific values, and observe the response each time. For example, we might set an independent variable X at a specific value x_1 and observe the response y_1. The experiment is repeated many times with X set at the same or different values and the response y_i observed each time. The resulting set of data is $\{x_i, y_i\}; i = 1, 2, \ldots, n$.

2 Fit the observed data to a number of different models of the form

$$Y = f(X_1, X_2, \ldots, X_k; \beta_0, \beta_1, \ldots, \beta_p) + \epsilon$$

using a method such as least squares to determine the "best" fit for a given model, where $f(\ )$ is a function of the X_j's and the parameters $\beta_0, \beta_1, \ldots, \beta_p$, and ϵ is an error term. Denote the least-squares fit by

$$\hat{Y} = f(X_1, X_2, \ldots, X_k; \hat{\beta}_0, \hat{\beta}_1, \ldots, \hat{\beta}_p)$$

3 Select the least-squares equation from step 2 above that will do the "best" job of predicting future responses.

In a general regression analysis, certain assumptions must be made about the error term in the model

$$Y = \beta_0 + \sum_{j=1}^{k} \beta_j X_j + \epsilon$$

before statistical tests can be applied to determine the best prediction equation. A regression analysis usually begins by estimating the parameters in a very simple model involving only one independent variable. Statistical tests are then made to determine if additional variables should be added to the model, etc. Polynomial regression can also be handled as a special case by letting $X_i = Z^i$ in the general model above, where Z is a single independent variable of interest. However, in Section 9.2 we will not make any assumptions needed for statistical tests, but rather will ignore statistics and proceed to fit linear, quadratic, cubic, and higher-order polynomials in one independent variable until a least-squares polynomial is found that satisfies a deterministic test.

9.2 POLYNOMIAL REGRESSION

Before looking at regression in general, consider the very simple problem of representing a given set of data $\{x_i, y_i\}$ with a polynomial relationship. Quite often a researcher sets or observes an independent factor or variable X at specified values, and observes the corresponding values of the response or dependent variable Y. Thus the researcher has a set of n data points $\{x_i, y_i\}$, and is interested in representing the response Y as a polynomial in X. The researcher is not interested in determining if other factors might have affected the responses, if there are random errors in the responses, or if the responses were measured correctly. The researcher simply wants to represent Y as a polynomial in X. The reason for wanting such a relationship is probably important to the researcher, but is immaterial to the development of an adequate polynomial relationship. The solution of this problem will be applicable to a similar subproblem in a general regression analysis.

Consider the problem in which the management of a store dealing exclusively in outdoor supplies has reason to believe that the total sales on each Monday is an excellent predictor of the total sales for that week. Table 9.2 presents data collected over 10 weeks. The data are plotted in Figure 9.1.

Based on the data from the 10-week period, management wants to determine a polynomial relationship between Monday sales and the total weekly sales. This relationship will then be used to predict future weekly sales as a function of Monday sales for any given week.

If the values for X were all distinct, then the data could be fit exactly with a unique ninth-degree polynomial. For example, a unique first-degree polynomial will pass through two distinct points, a unique second-degree polynomial will pass through

Table 9.2 SALES FOR OUTDOOR SUPPLIES
(IN THOUSANDS)

X: Sales on Monday	5.2	4.8	6.4	3.1	6.5	9.7	4.3	6.4	8.9	10.4
Y: Total sales for week	40	33	42	20	45	55	27	50	60	62

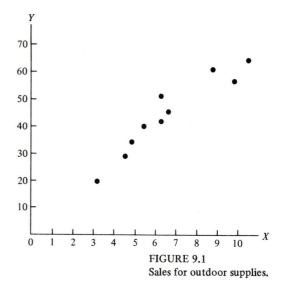

FIGURE 9.1
Sales for outdoor supplies.

three distinct points, etc. However, we generally want a polynomial of low degree that will "adequately" represent Y as a polynomial in X. "Adequately" in a practical sense usually means that the researcher is personally satisfied that a polynomial of higher degree would not do a significantly better job of representing the data.

The problem of representing Y as a polynomial in X poses two additional problems:

Which method, among several, should be used to determine polynomials of degree $1, 2, \ldots$?
What should the degree of the polynomial be?

Although several methods are available, the method of least squares is generally accepted as one of the best methods to use to fit a polynomial to a given set of data. The process of successively applying the method of least squares to determine polynomials of degree $1, 2, \ldots$ until a polynomial of adequate degree is found will be referred to as *least-squares polynomial regression*. We will now develop this procedure, concluding with recommendations on how to choose the degree of the polynomial that will adequately represent the data.

9.2.1 Least-squares Polynomial Regression

Based on a given set of data $\{x_i, y_i\}$ where $i = 1, 2, \ldots, n$, we want to determine a polynomial of low degree that will adequately represent the data. We start by assuming a linear relationship between the independent variable X and the dependent variable Y. That is, we assume each value of Y, y_i, can be represented by a constant amount

$\beta_0 + \beta_1 x_i$ plus some unknown amount ϵ_{i1}; $i = 1, 2, \ldots, n$, where β_0 and β_1 are constants. This representation

$$y_i = \beta_0 + \beta_1 x_i + \epsilon_{i1} \qquad (9.1)$$

is called the *observation model*. Although an infinity of straight lines can be drawn through the data as shown in Figure 9.2, we want to determine the values of β_0 and β_1 such that

$$\sum_{i=1}^{n} \epsilon_{i1}^{2} = \sum_{i=1}^{n} (y_i - \beta_0 - \beta_1 x_i)^2 \qquad (9.2)$$

is a minimum. The resulting polynomial is the least-squares polynomial of degree 1. Note that each straight line in Figure 9.2 is obtained by using specific values for β_0 and β_1 in the general form

$$Y = \beta_0 + \beta_1 X$$

If we let

$$\epsilon_{i1} = y_i - \beta_0^* - \beta_1^* x_i \qquad (9.3)$$

be the difference between the response y_i and the predicted value of the response at x_i using the specific values β_0^* and β_1^* as shown in Figure 9.3, then

$$\sum_{i=1}^{n} \epsilon_{i1}^{2} = \sum_{i=1}^{n} (y_i - \beta_0^* - \beta_1^* x_i)^2 \qquad (9.4)$$

is the sum of squares of the differences over all data points. This is a measure of how close the given straight line fits the data. Note that each specific pair of values for β_0

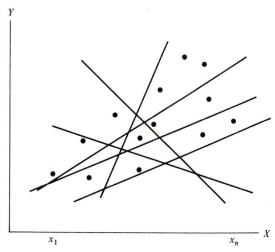

FIGURE 9.2
Linear equations for a given set of data.

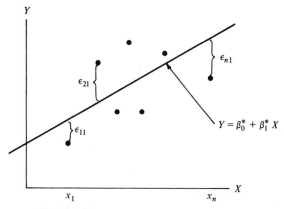

FIGURE 9.3
Difference between response and predicted response.

and β_1 will yield a different sum of squares. The method of least squares finds the unique values for β_0 and β_1 that will minimize $\Sigma_{i=1}^{n} \epsilon_{i1}{}^2$.

To do this, the first partial derivatives of $\Sigma_{i=1}^{n} \epsilon_{i1}{}^2$ are taken with respect to β_0 and β_1, and the results set equal to zero.

$$\frac{\partial \sum_{i=1}^{n} \epsilon_{i1}{}^2}{\partial \beta_0} = 2 \sum_{i=1}^{n} (y_i - \hat{\beta}_0 - \hat{\beta}_1 x_i)(-1) = 0 \qquad (9.5)$$

$$\frac{\partial \sum_{i=1}^{n} \epsilon_{i1}{}^2}{\partial \beta_1} = 2 \sum_{i=1}^{n} (y_i - \hat{\beta}_0 - \hat{\beta}_1 x_i)(-x_i) = 0 \qquad (9.6)$$

When the terms are rearranged in Equations (9.5) and (9.6) we get

$$\hat{\beta}_0 n + \hat{\beta}_1 \Sigma x_i = \Sigma y_i \qquad (9.7)$$

$$\hat{\beta}_0 \Sigma x_i + \hat{\beta}_1 \Sigma x_i{}^2 = \Sigma x_i y_i \qquad (9.8)$$

Equations (9.7) and (9.8) are called the *normal equations*, and $\hat{\beta}_0$ and $\hat{\beta}_1$ are called the *least-squares estimates* of β_0 and β_1 based on the given set of data. The solution of the normal equations is

$$\hat{\beta}_1 = \frac{\sum_{i=1}^{n} (x_i - \bar{x})(y_i - \bar{y})}{\sum_{i=1}^{n} (x_i - \bar{x})^2} \qquad (9.9)$$

$$\hat{\beta}_0 = \bar{y} - \hat{\beta}_1 \bar{x} \qquad (9.10)$$

where
$$\bar{x} = \frac{\sum\limits_{i=1}^{n} x_i}{n} \qquad (9.11)$$

$$\bar{y} = \frac{\sum\limits_{i=1}^{n} y_i}{n} \qquad (9.12)$$

Appendix C contains a discussion of the Gauss-Jordan method for the solution of a system of linear equations. The least-squares polynomial of degree 1 based on the given set of data $\{x_i, y_i\}$ is

$$
\begin{aligned}
\hat{Y}_1 &= \hat{\beta}_0 + \hat{\beta}_1 X \\
&= \bar{y} - \hat{\beta}_1 \bar{x} + \hat{\beta}_1 X \\
&= \bar{y} + \hat{\beta}_1 (X - \bar{x}) \qquad (9.13)
\end{aligned}
$$

There is no other linear equation in X that will yield a smaller sum of squares of the differences ϵ_{i1}; $i = 1, 2, \ldots, n$. That is,

$$
\sum_{i=1}^{n} \epsilon_{i1}^{2} = \sum_{i=1}^{n} (y_i - \hat{\beta}_0 - \hat{\beta}_1 x_i)^2
$$

$$
= \sum_{i=1}^{n} (y_i - \hat{y}_{i1})^2
$$

is a minimum, where y_i is the response at x_i and $\hat{y}_{i1}$ is the predicted value of the response at x_i using the least-squares polynomial of degree 1.

We see that $\hat{\beta}_0$ and $\hat{\beta}_1$ are functions of the given data, so it is imperative that the data be a good representation of the real population from which they came.

EXAMPLE 9.2.1.1 To illustrate the least-squares concept, consider an example where the data are given by

X	−1	0	1	2
Y	−4	0	4	2

From Equations (9.9) and (9.10) we see that we need

$$n = 4$$

$$\bar{x} = \frac{\sum x_i}{n} = \frac{2}{4} = \frac{1}{2}$$

$$\bar{y} = \frac{\sum y_i}{n} = \frac{2}{4} = \frac{1}{2}$$

$$\Sigma (x_i - \bar{x})(y_i - \bar{y}) = \left(-1 - \frac{1}{2}\right)\left(-4 - \frac{1}{2}\right) + \left(0 - \frac{1}{2}\right)\left(0 - \frac{1}{2}\right)$$

$$+ \left(1 - \frac{1}{2}\right)\left(4 - \frac{1}{2}\right) + \left(2 - \frac{1}{2}\right)\left(2 - \frac{1}{2}\right)$$

$$= 11$$

$$\Sigma (x_i - \bar{x})^2 = 5$$

Therefore,

$$\hat{\beta}_1 = \frac{\Sigma (x_i - \bar{x})(y_i - \bar{y})}{\Sigma (x_i - \bar{x})^2} = \frac{11}{5}$$

$$\hat{\beta}_0 = \bar{y} - \hat{\beta}_1 \bar{x} = \frac{1}{2} - \frac{11}{5}\left(\frac{1}{2}\right) = -\frac{3}{5}$$

Thus, the least-squares linear polynomial for the above data is

$$\hat{Y}_1 = -\frac{3}{5} + \frac{11}{5} X \qquad (9.14)$$

From Table 9.3 we see that

$$\sum_{i=1}^{4} \epsilon_{i1}^2 = \sum_{i=1}^{4} \left[y_i - \left(-\frac{3}{5}\right) - \frac{11}{5} x_i \right]^2$$

$$= \left(-4 + \frac{3}{5} + \frac{11}{5}\right)^2 + \left(0 + \frac{3}{5} + 0\right)^2 + \left(4 + \frac{3}{5} - \frac{11}{5}\right)^2$$

$$+ \left(2 + \frac{3}{5} - \frac{22}{5}\right)^2 = 10.8$$

The least-squares linear polynomial is shown in Figure 9.4.

Although it appears that a linear fit is adequate for this example, the next step in the general least-squares polynomial fitting procedure is to assume that a quadratic polynomial would fit the data better. Thus, we assume the quadratic observation model

$$y_i = \gamma_0 + \gamma_1 x_i + \gamma_2 x_i^2 + \epsilon_{i2} \qquad (9.15)$$

and determine the values of γ_0, γ_1, and γ_2 such that the quantity

Table 9.3 CALCULATIONS FOR EXAMPLE DATA

x_i	−1	0	1	2
y_i	−4	0	4	2
$\hat{y}_i$	−14/5	−3/5	8/5	19/5
$y_i - \hat{y}_i$	−6/5	3/5	12/5	−9/5
$(y_i - \hat{y}_i)^2$	36/25	9/25	144/25	81/25

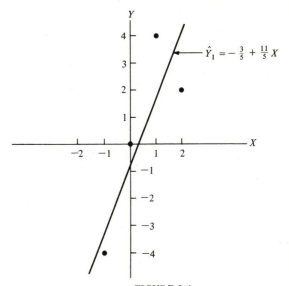

FIGURE 9.4
Least-squares linear polynomial.

$$\sum_{i=1}^{n} \epsilon_{i2}^{2} = \sum_{i=1}^{n} (y_i - \gamma_0 - \gamma_1 x_i - \gamma_2 x_i^2)^2$$

is a minimum. Since the parameters γ_0, γ_1, and γ_2 are the only quantities that can be changed, we take the first partial derivatives of $\sum_{i=1}^{n} \epsilon_{i2}^{2}$ with respect to γ_0, γ_1, and γ_2 and then set the results equal to zero.

$$\frac{\partial \Sigma \, \epsilon_{i2}^{2}}{\partial \gamma_0} = 2\Sigma \, (y_i - \hat{\gamma}_0 - \hat{\gamma}_1 x_i - \hat{\gamma}_2 x_i^2)(-1) = 0 \qquad (9.16)$$

$$\frac{\partial \Sigma \, \epsilon_{i2}^{2}}{\partial \gamma_1} = 2\Sigma \, (y_i - \hat{\gamma}_0 - \hat{\gamma}_1 x_i - \hat{\gamma}_2 x_i^2)(-x_i) = 0 \qquad (9.17)$$

$$\frac{\partial \Sigma \, \epsilon_{i2}^{2}}{\partial \gamma_2} = 2\Sigma \, (y_i - \hat{\gamma}_0 - \hat{\gamma}_1 x_i - \hat{\gamma}_2 x_i^2)(-x_i^2) = 0 \qquad (9.18)$$

This leads to the normal equations

$$\hat{\gamma}_0 n + \hat{\gamma}_1 \Sigma \, x_i + \hat{\gamma}_2 \Sigma \, x_i^2 = \Sigma \, y_i \qquad (9.19)$$

$$\hat{\gamma}_0 \Sigma \, x_i + \hat{\gamma}_1 \Sigma \, x_i^2 + \hat{\gamma}_2 \Sigma \, x_i^3 = \Sigma \, x_i y_i \qquad (9.20)$$

$$\hat{\gamma}_0 \Sigma \, x_i^2 + \hat{\gamma}_1 \Sigma \, x_i^3 + \hat{\gamma}_2 \Sigma \, x_i^4 = \Sigma \, x_i^2 y_i \qquad (9.21)$$

where $\hat{\gamma}_0$, $\hat{\gamma}_1$, and $\hat{\gamma}_2$ are the least-squares estimates of γ_0, γ_1 and γ_2. The solution of these three normal equations in the three unknowns $\hat{\gamma}_0$, $\hat{\gamma}_1$, and $\hat{\gamma}_2$ yields the least-squares polynomial of degree 2

$$\hat{Y}_2 = \hat{\gamma}_0 + \hat{\gamma}_1 X + \hat{\gamma}_2 X^2 \qquad (9.22)$$

from which we get

$$\sum_{i=1}^{n} \epsilon_{i_2}{}^2 = \sum_{i=1}^{n} (y_i - \hat{y}_{i2})^2 \qquad (9.23)$$

Theoretically, $\Sigma_{i=1}^{n} \epsilon_{i2}{}^2 \leqslant \Sigma_{i=1}^{n} \epsilon_{i1}{}^2$. Why? However, this will not necessarily be true in practice because more calculations are required to determine $\Sigma_{i=1}^{n} \epsilon_{i2}{}^2$, thus introducing a greater possibility of round-off error. Consequently, a good rule of thumb is to continue fitting higher-order polynomials using least squares until

$$\frac{\displaystyle\sum_{i=1}^{n} \epsilon_{ik}{}^2}{n-k-1} > \frac{\displaystyle\sum_{i=1}^{n} \epsilon_{i,k-1}^2}{n-k} \qquad (9.24)$$

or until a polynomial of degree $n-1$ is obtained. That is, continue to fit higher-order polynomials until the round-off errors in the computations override the contribution from the last term added. When the condition in Equation (9.24) occurs, the polynomial of degree $k-1$ is chosen to represent the data. Figure 9.5 illustrates this concept. Other stopping rules are used but this one will suffice for all practical purposes.

In Example 9.2.1.1, the normal equations to determine the least-squares quadratic polynomial are

$$4\hat{\gamma}_0 + 2\hat{\gamma}_1 + 6\hat{\gamma}_2 = 2$$
$$2\hat{\gamma}_0 + 6\hat{\gamma}_1 + 8\hat{\gamma}_2 = 12$$
$$6\hat{\gamma}_0 + 8\hat{\gamma}_1 + 18\hat{\gamma}_2 = 8$$

The Gauss-Jordan method in Appendix C yielded the solution

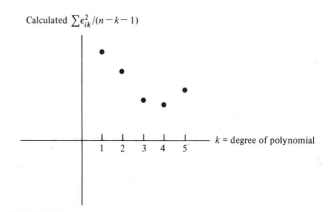

FIGURE 9.5
Relative sum of squares of differences against degree of polynomial.

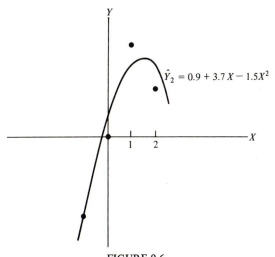

FIGURE 9.6
Least-squares quadratic polynomial.

$$\hat{\gamma}_0 = 0.9$$
$$\hat{\gamma}_1 = 3.7$$
$$\hat{\gamma}_2 = -1.5$$

and

$$\sum_{i=1}^{4} \epsilon_{i2}{}^2 = 1.8$$

which is a significant reduction from $\Sigma_{i=1}^{4} \epsilon_{i1}{}^2 = 10.8$. Figure 9.6 illustrates the plot of

$$\hat{Y}_2 = 0.9 + 3.7X - 1.5X^2$$

Since

$$\frac{\sum_{i=1}^{4} \epsilon_{i2}{}^2}{4-2-1} = 1.8 < \frac{\sum_{i=1}^{4} \epsilon_{i1}{}^2}{4-1-1} = \frac{10.8}{2} = 5.4$$

we would ordinarily fit a higher-order polynomial, however, in this case, a cubic polynomial would fit the data exactly, so we assume the least-squares quadratic polynomial is adequate.

To determine the kth-degree least-squares polynomial based on the given set of data, the observation model

$$y_i = \gamma_0 + \gamma_1 x_i + \gamma_2 x_i^2 + \cdots + \gamma_k x_i{}^k + \epsilon_{ik} \qquad (9.25)$$

is written in terms of the error ϵ_{ik}

$$\epsilon_{ik} = (y_i - \gamma_0 - \gamma_1 x_i - \cdots - \gamma_k x_i^k) \qquad (9.26)$$

The errors are squared and summed over all data points to give

$$\sum_{i=1}^{n} \epsilon_{ik}^2 = \sum_{i=1}^{n} (y_i - \gamma_0 - \gamma_1 x_i - \cdots - \gamma_k x_i^k)^2 \qquad (9.27)$$

The first partial derivatives of $\sum_{i=1}^{n} \epsilon_{ik}^2$ with respect to $\gamma_0, \gamma_1, \ldots, \gamma_k$ yield the normal equations

$$\hat{\gamma}_0 n + \hat{\gamma}_1 \Sigma x_i + \cdots + \hat{\gamma}_k \Sigma x_i^k = \Sigma y_i$$
$$\hat{\gamma}_0 \Sigma x_i + \hat{\gamma}_1 \Sigma x_i^2 + \cdots + \hat{\gamma}_k \Sigma x_i^{k+1} = \Sigma x_i y_i \qquad (9.28)$$
$$\cdots\cdots\cdots\cdots\cdots\cdots\cdots\cdots\cdots\cdots\cdots\cdots\cdots\cdots$$
$$\hat{\gamma}_0 \Sigma x_i^k + \hat{\gamma}_1 \Sigma x_i^{k+1} + \cdots + \hat{\gamma}_k \Sigma x_i^{2k} = \Sigma x_i^k y_i$$

These $k + 1$ normal equations in the $k + 1$ unknowns $\hat{\gamma}_0, \hat{\gamma}_1, \ldots, \hat{\gamma}_k$ can be solved using the Gauss-Jordan method in Appendix C.

Since the normal equations become quite ill-conditioned (are subject to large round-off errors) as k becomes large, it is recommended that all calculations be carried out in double precision, and that k should be no larger than about 8. The use of orthogonal polynomials will also reduce the number of calculations, and consequently the round-off errors in doing polynomial regression; however, their use will not be discussed at this time.

9.2.2 Algorithm 9.1—Least-squares Polynomial Regression

The basic notation used in this algorithm is

$n =$ number of data points
$x_i =$ ith observed or set value of the independent variable X
$y_i =$ ith response

We assume the data have been read into the computer.

Step 1
Obtain the least-squares linear polynomial based on the given set of data by solving the normal equations

$$\hat{\beta}_0 n + \hat{\beta}_1 \Sigma x_i = \Sigma y_i$$
$$\hat{\beta}_0 \Sigma x_i + \hat{\beta}_1 \Sigma x_i^2 = \Sigma x_i y_i$$

for $\hat{\beta}_0$ and $\hat{\beta}_1$ using the Gauss-Jordan subroutine (Appendix C). The least-squares linear polynomial is then

$$\hat{Y}_1 = \hat{\beta}_0 + \hat{\beta}_1 X$$

Step 2
Let $k = 1$ represent the degree of the current least-squares polynomial. Calculate the quantity

$$\frac{\sum\limits_{i=1}^{n} \epsilon_{i1}^{2}}{n - 2} = \frac{\sum\limits_{i=1}^{n} (y_i - \hat{y}_{i1})^2}{n - 2} = \frac{\sum\limits_{i=1}^{n} (y_i - \hat{\beta}_0 - \hat{\beta}_1 x_i)^2}{n - 2}$$

where $\hat{y}_{i1}$ denotes the predicted response at x_i.

Step 3
Increase the degree k of the polynomial being fitted by one (k will now be 2 the first time through this step), and obtain the least-squares polynomial of degree k by solving the normal equations

$$\hat{\gamma}_0 n + \hat{\gamma}_1 \Sigma x_i + \cdots + \hat{\gamma}_k \Sigma x_i^{k} = \Sigma y_i$$
$$\hat{\gamma}_0 \Sigma x_i + \hat{\gamma}_1 \Sigma x_i^2 + \cdots + \hat{\gamma}_k \Sigma x_i^{k+1} = \Sigma x_i y_i \qquad (9.29)$$
$$\cdots\cdots\cdots\cdots\cdots\cdots\cdots\cdots\cdots\cdots\cdots\cdots$$
$$\hat{\gamma}_0 \Sigma x_i^{k} + \hat{\gamma}_1 \Sigma x_i^{k+1} + \cdots + \hat{\gamma}_k \Sigma x_i^{2k} = \Sigma x_i^{k} y_i$$

for $\hat{\gamma}_0, \hat{\gamma}_1, \ldots, \hat{\gamma}_k$ using the Gauss-Jordan subroutine (Appendix C). The least-squares polynomial of degree k is then

$$\hat{Y}_k = \hat{\gamma}_0 + \hat{\gamma}_1 X + \hat{\gamma}_2 X^2 + \cdots + \hat{\gamma}_k X^k \qquad (9.30)$$

Step 4
Calculate the sum of squares

$$\sum_{i=1}^{n} \epsilon_{ik}^{2} = \sum_{i=1}^{n} (y_i - \hat{y}_{ik})^2 = \sum_{i=1}^{n} \left(y_i - \hat{\gamma}_0 - \sum_{j=1}^{k} \hat{\gamma}_j x_i^{j} \right)^2 \qquad (9.31)$$

Step 5
If $k = n - 1$, go to step 7. If $k \neq n - 1$ and

$$\frac{\sum\limits_{i=1}^{n} \epsilon_{ik}^{2}}{n - k - 1} \geq \frac{\sum\limits_{i=1}^{n} \epsilon_{i,\,k-1}^{2}}{n - k} \qquad (9.32)$$

go to step 6; otherwise, X^k reduces the sum of squares significantly, so check the next higher-order term by returning to step 3.

Step 6
The round-off errors and the unit decrease in the denominator has overshadowed the contribution X^k made to the reduction of the sum of squares, so accept the least-squares polynomial of degree $k - 1$ as an adequate representation of Y in terms of X and stop.

Step 7

If round-off errors are ignored, the current polynomial of degree $n-1$ would fit the n data points exactly. Accept the least-squares polynomial of degree $n-1$ as an adequate representation of Y in terms of X and stop.

9.2.3 Computer Program for Algorithm 9.1

This program is designed to find the least-squares polynomial that will adequately represent a given set of data. It will handle a maximum of 200 observations and will fit least-squares polynomials up to and including degree 10. The Gauss-Jordan subroutine, GSJOR, is used to solve the normal equations. It appears in Appendix C as well as after the least-squares program listing.

The program occupies 40K bytes of core storage. It took 0.10 s of IBM 370/168 time to find the first- and second-degree least-squares polynomials for the data in Table 9.2. The details of entering the data are explained by the comment cards at the beginning of the program. The data and results for the data in Table 9.2 are listed after the program.

```
C     ****************************************************************************
C     *                                                                          *
C     *     *** ALGORITHM 9.1 - LEAST SQUARES POLYNOMIAL REGRESSION  ***         *
C     *                                                                          *
C     * THIS PROGRAM IS DESIGNED TO FIND THE LEAST SQUARES POLYNOMIAL THAT       *
C     *   WILL ADEQUATELY REPRESENT A GIVEN SET OF DATA.  THE PROGRAM WILL       *
C     *   HANDLE UP TO 200 OBSERVATIONS,(X(I),Y(I)), AND WILL FIT LEAST          *
C     *   SQUARES POLYNOMIALS UP TO AND INCLUDING DEGREE 10.  THE GAUSS-         *
C     *   JORDAN SUBROUTINE (GSJOR) IS USED TO SOLVE THE NORMAL EQUATIONS.       *
C     *   THE PROGRAM CONTINUES TO FIT HIGHER ORDER POLYNOMIALS UNTIL            *
C     *          CMSSQ = SUM(Y(I)-YHAT(I))**2/(NUM-K-1)                          *
C     *   INCREASES OR UNTIL A 10TH DEGREE POLYNOMIAL IS OBTAINED, WHERE         *
C     *   K IS THE DEGREE OF THE POLYNOMIAL, YHAT(I) IS THE PREDICTED RE-        *
C     *   SPONSE AT X(I), AND NUM IS THE NUMBER OF OBSERVATIONS.                 *
C     *                                                                          *
C     * THE PROGRAM WILL                                                         *
C     *   READ                                                                   *
C     *     CARD 1    COLS  2-80    TITLE   DESCRIPTION OF THE PROBLEM USING      *
C     *                                     ANY CHARACTERS ON KEYPUNCH           *
C     *                                     ** COLUMN 1 MUST BE LEFT BLANK **     *
C     *     CARD 2    COLS  1- 5    NUM     NUMBER OF OBSERVATIONS  (I5)          *
C     *   CARDS 3 TO T COLS  1-10    X(I)    ITH X VALUE  (F10.0)                 *
C     *                     11-20   Y(I)    ITH Y VALUE  (F10.0)                  *
C     *                                     EACH OBSERVATION IS ON A SEPARATE CARD.*
C     *           TO SOLVE MORE THAN ONE PROBLEM AT A TIME, REPEAT THE           *
C     *           READ SEQUENCE, AND STACK THE DATA ONE BEHIND THE OTHER         *
C     *                                                                          *
C     *   CALCULATE                                                              *
C     *     XPX(I,J)   THE COEFFICIENTS OF THE UNKNOWNS IN THE NORMAL            *
C     *                EQUATIONS                                                 *
C     *     XPY(I)     THE CONSTANTS ON THE RIGHT SIDE OF THE NORMAL             *
C     *                EQUATIONS                                                 *
C     *     YHAT(I)    THE PREDICTED VALUE OF Y AT X(I) FOR A GIVEN              *
C     *                DEGREE POLYNOMIAL                                         *
C     *     SUMSQ      SUM OF SQUARES OF THE DIFFERENCE BETWEEN THE OBSERVED     *
C     *                RESPONSE, Y(I), AND THE PREDICTED RESPONSE,YHAT           *
C     *     CMSSQ      CURRENT MODIFIED SUM OF SQUARES,NAMELY,                   *
C     *                     CMSSQ = SUMSQ/(NUM-K-1)                             *
C     *     A(I,M)     LEAST SQUARES SOLUTION VALUES                            *
C     *                                                                          *
C     *   PRINT                                                                  *
C     *     K          THE CURRENT DEGREE OF THE LEAST SQUARES POLYNOMIAL        *
C     *     A(I,M)                                                               *
C     *     CMSSQ                                                                *
C     *                                                                          *
C     * TO MODIFY THE PROGRAM TO HANDLE MORE THAN 200 OBSERVATIONS, CHANGE       *
C     *   THE COMPONENTS OF X AND Y IN THE DIMENSION STATEMENT TO THE            *
C     *   DESIRED NUMBER OF OBSERVATIONS.                                        *
C     *                                                                          *
C     ****************************************************************************
      DIMENSION A(11,12),XPX(11,11),XPY(11),X(200),Y(200),TITLE(20)
      DIMENSION B(11)
C     ****************************************************************************
C     * READ THE TITLE CARD AND THE NUMBER OF OBSERVATIONS                       *
C     ****************************************************************************
    1 READ(5,100,END=2000) TITLE
  100 FORMAT(20A4)
      WRITE(6,101) TITLE
  101 FORMAT('1',20A4,//)
      READ(5,102) NUM
  102 FORMAT(I5)




C     ****************************************************************************
C     * READ THE OBSERVATIONS AND CALCULATE THE COEFFICIENTS FOR THE NORMAL     *
C     *   EQUATIONS TO FIT A FIRST DEGREE POLYNOMIAL                            *
C     ****************************************************************************
      SUMY=0.0
      SUMX=0.0
      SUMXY=0.0
      SUMXS=0.0
      DO 4 I=1,NUM
```

```
      READ(5,103) X(I),Y(I)
  103 FORMAT(2F10.0)
      SUMY=SUMY+Y(I)
      SUMX=SUMX+X(I)
      SUMXY=SUMXY+X(I)*Y(I)
    4 SUMXS=SUMXS+X(I)*X(I)
      PMSSQ=10.E8
      K=1
      N=K+1
      M=N+1
      XPX(1,1)=NUM
      XPX(1,2)=SUMX
      XPX(2,1)=SUMX
      XPX(2,2)=SUMXS
      XPY(1)=SUMY
      XPY(2)=SUMXY
C     ***************************************************************************
C     * TRANSFER THE XPX AND XPY QUANTITIES TO THE A MATRIX AND SAVE THE       *
C     *   XPX AND XPY QUANTITIES.  THE GAUSS-JORDAN METHOD WILL PERFORM        *
C     *   ELEMENTARY TRANSFORMATIONS UNTIL THE SOLUTION OF THE NORMAL          *
C     *   EQUATIONS IS IN A(I,M), I=1,N.                                       *
C     ***************************************************************************
   18 DO 12 I=1,N
      DO 10 J=1,N
   10 A(I,J)=XPX(I,J)
   12 A(I,M)=XPY(I)
C     ***************************************************************************
C     * SOLVE THE NORMAL EQUATIONS TO GET THE LEAST SQUARES ESTIMATES OF       *
C     *   THE PARAMETERS                                                       *
C     ***************************************************************************
      CALL GSJOR(N,M,A)
C     ***************************************************************************
C     * CALCULATE THE SUM OF SQUARES OF THE DIFFERENCE BETWEEN THE OBSERVED    *
C     *   RESPONSE AND THE PREDICTED RESPONSE                                  *
C     ***************************************************************************
      SUMSQ=0.0
      DO 16 I=1,NUM
      PROD=0.0
      DO 17 J=1,K
   17 PROD=PROD+A(J+1,M)*X(I)**J
      YHAT=A(1,M)+PROD
   16 SUMSQ=SUMSQ+(Y(I)-YHAT)**2
      IF(NUM-K-1.EQ.0) GO TO 42
C     ***************************************************************************
C     * CALCULATE THE CURRENT MODIFIED SUM OF SQUARES                          *
C     ***************************************************************************
      CMSSQ=SUMSQ/(NUM-K-1)
C     ***************************************************************************
C     * IF THE CURRENT MODIFIED SUM OF SQUARES IS GREATER THAN THE PREVIOUS    *
C     *   MODIFIED SUM OF SQUARES, AN ADEQUATE DEGREE POLYNOMIAL HAS BEEN      *
C     *   OBTAINED, SO GO TO STATEMENT 42; OTHERWISE, WRITE THE DEGREE OF THE  *
C     *   POLYNOMIAL JUST OBTAINED, THE CORRESPONDING LEAST SQUARES ESTIMATES  *
C     *   OF THE PARAMETERS, AND THE CURRENT MODIFIED SUM OF SQUARES.          *
C     ***************************************************************************
      IF(CMSSQ.GE.PMSSQ) GO TO 42
      WRITE(6,104) K
  104 FORMAT(1X,'THE COEFFICIENTS OF THE LEAST SQUARES POLYNOMIAL OF DEG
     1REE',I2,1X,'ARE',/)
      DO 15 I=1,N
      IM=I-1
   15 WRITE(6,105) IM,A(I,M)
  105 FORMAT(1X,'BETA(',I2,')=',F12.6)
      WRITE(6,106) CMSSQ
  106 FORMAT(/,1X,'CMSSQ=',F12.6,//)
      PMSSQ=CMSSQ
      IF(K.EQ.10) GO TO 1
C     ***************************************************************************
C     * INCREASE THE DEGREE OF THE POLYNOMIAL BEING FITTED, K, BUILD THE       *
C     *   NEW NORMAL EQUATIONS, AND THEN RETURN TO STATEMENT 18.               *
C     ***************************************************************************
```

```
      K=K+1
      N=K+1
      M=N+1
      KP1=K+1
      KM1=K-1
      DO 20 I=1,KM1
      XPX(KP1,I)=XPX(K,I+1)
   20 XPX(I,KP1)=XPX(KP1,I)
      SUM1=0.0
      SUM2=0.0
      SUM3=0.0
      DO 21 I=1,NUM
      XK=X(I)**K
      SUM1=SUM1+XK*X(I)**(K-1)
      SUM2=SUM2+XK*XK
   21 SUM3=SUM3+XK*Y(I)
      XPX(KP1,K)=SUM1
      XPX(KP1,KP1)=SUM2
      XPX(K,KP1)=SUM1
      XPY(KP1)=SUM3
      DO 27 J=1,K
   27 B(J)=A(J,N)
      GO TO 18
C     ***************************************************************************
C     * PRINT X, Y, YHAT, AND (Y-YHAT) FOR THE POLYNOMIAL THAT ADEQUATELY      *
C     *  REPRESENTS THE DATA.
C     ***************************************************************************
   42 KM1=K-1
      WRITE(6,107) KM1
  107 FORMAT(//,1X,'THE POLYNOMIAL OF DEGREE',I3,1X,'ADEQUATELY REPRESEN
     1TS THE DATA')
      WRITE(6,108)
  108 FORMAT(//,8X,'X',13X,'Y',11X,'YHAT',8X,'(Y-YHAT)',/)
      DO 25 I=1,NUM
      PROD=0.0
      DO 26 J=1,KM1
   26 PROD=PROD+B(J+1)*X(I)**J
      YHAT=B(1)+PROD
      DIFF=Y(I)-YHAT
   25 WRITE(6,109) X(I),Y(I),YHAT,DIFF
  109 FORMAT(4F14.6)
      GO TO 1
 2000 STOP
      END

      SUBROUTINE GSJOR (N,M,A)
      DIMENSION A(11,12)
      DO 16 K=1,N
      KP1=K+1
      DO 9 J=KP1,M
      A(K,J)=A(K,J)/A(K,K)
    9 CONTINUE
      DO 12 I=1,N
      IF(I.EQ.K) GO TO 12
      DO 14 J=KP1,M
      A(I,J)=A(I,J)-A(I,K)*A(K,J)
   14 CONTINUE
   12 CONTINUE
   16 CONTINUE
   13 RETURN
      END
```

```
/DATA

    SALES FOR OUTDOOR SUPPLIES - TABLE 9.2
   10
        5.2         40.
        4.8         33.
        6.4         42.
        3.1         20.
        6.5         45.
        9.7         55.
        4.3         27.
        6.4         50.
        8.9         60.
       10.4         62.
```

SALES FOR OUTDOOR SUPPLIES - TABLE 9.2

THE COEFFICIENTS OF THE LEAST SQUARES POLYNOMIAL OF DEGREE 1 ARE

BETA(0)=   7.286163
BETA(1)=   5.496784

CMSSQ=   20.543701

THE COEFFICIENTS OF THE LEAST SQUARES POLYNOMIAL OF DEGREE 2 ARE

BETA(0)=   -18.560730
BETA(1)=   13.886235
BETA(2)=   -0.605026

CMSSQ=   11.654689

THE POLYNOMIAL OF DEGREE 2 ADEQUATELY REPRESENTS THE DATA

X	Y	YHAT	(Y-YHAT)
5.200000	40.000000	37.287796	2.712204
4.800000	33.000000	34.153397	-1.153397
6.400000	42.000000	45.529312	-3.529312
3.100000	20.000000	18.672302	1.327698
6.500000	45.000000	46.137466	-1.137466
9.700000	55.000000	59.208878	-4.208878
4.300000	27.000000	29.963135	-2.963135
6.400000	50.000000	45.529312	4.470688
8.900000	60.000000	57.102661	2.897339
10.400000	62.000000	60.416519	1.583481

9.2.4 Fitting a kth-Degree Least-squares Polynomial through a Given Data Point

A question asked quite often is, "How can the least-squares polynomial be forced through an arbitrary y intercept, say $(0, y_p^*)$?" This question can be answered by noting that the constant $\hat{\gamma}_0$ in the general kth-degree least-squares polynomial

$$\hat{Y}_k = \hat{\gamma}_0 + \sum_{j=1}^{k} \hat{\gamma}_j X^j \qquad (9.33)$$

is the Y intercept, so we just replace γ_0 with y_p^* in the observation model

$$y_i = \gamma_0 + \sum_{j=1}^{k} \gamma_j x_i^j + \epsilon_{ik} \qquad (9.34)$$

to give

$$y_i = y_p^* + \sum_{j=1}^{k} \gamma_j x_i^j + \epsilon_{ik} \qquad (9.35)$$

The normal equations will be

$$\frac{\partial \Sigma \, \epsilon_{ik}^2}{\partial \gamma_1} = 2 \sum_{i=1}^{n} \left(y_i - y_p^* - \sum_{j=1}^{k} \hat{\gamma}_j x_i^j \right)(-x_i) = 0$$

$$\frac{\partial \Sigma \, \epsilon_{ik}^2}{\partial \gamma_2} = 2 \sum_{i=1}^{n} \left(y_i - y_p^* - \sum_{j=1}^{k} \hat{\gamma}_j x_i^j \right)(-x_i^2) = 0$$

$$\cdots \cdots \cdots \cdots \cdots \cdots \cdots \cdots \cdots \cdots \cdots \cdots \cdots$$

$$\frac{\partial \Sigma \, \epsilon_{ik}^2}{\partial \gamma_k} = 2 \sum_{i=1}^{n} \left(y_i - y_p^* - \sum_{j=1}^{k} \hat{\gamma}_j x_i^j \right)(-x_i^k) = 0$$

If the equations are rearranged, we get

$$\begin{aligned}
\hat{\gamma}_1 \Sigma \, x_i^2 + \hat{\gamma}_2 \Sigma \, x_i^3 + \cdots + \hat{\gamma}_k \Sigma \, x_i^{k+1} &= \Sigma \, x_i y_i - y_p^* \Sigma \, x_i \\
\hat{\gamma}_1 \Sigma \, x_i^3 + \hat{\gamma}_2 \Sigma \, x_i^4 + \cdots + \hat{\gamma}_k \Sigma \, x_i^{k+2} &= \Sigma \, x_i^2 y_i - y_p^* \Sigma \, x_i^2 \\
\cdots \cdots \cdots \cdots \cdots \cdots \cdots \cdots \cdots \cdots & \qquad\qquad (9.36) \\
\hat{\gamma}_1 \Sigma \, x_i^{k+1} + \hat{\gamma}_2 \Sigma \, x_i^{k+2} + \cdots + \hat{\gamma}_k \Sigma \, x_i^{2k} &= \Sigma \, x_i^k y_i - y_p^* \Sigma \, x_i^k
\end{aligned}$$

These k normal equations can now be solved for $\hat{\gamma}_1, \ldots, \hat{\gamma}_k$ using the Gauss-Jordan subroutine (Appendix C). The resulting kth-degree polynomial that passes through the point $(0, y_p^*)$ is

$$\hat{Y}_k = y_p^* + \sum_{j=1}^{k} \hat{\gamma}_j X^j \qquad (9.37)$$

For the linear case ($k = 1$), we have only one equation in one unknown:

$$\hat{\gamma}_1 \Sigma \, x_i^2 = \Sigma \, x_i y_i - y_p^* \Sigma \, x_i$$

Thus,

$$\hat{\gamma}_1 = \frac{\Sigma \, x_i y_i - y_p^* \Sigma \, x_i}{\Sigma \, x_i^2} \qquad (9.38)$$

Then,

$$\hat{Y}_1 = y_p^* + \hat{\gamma}_1 X$$

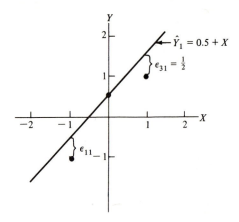

FIGURE 9.7
Modified least-squares linear polynomial.

EXAMPLE 9.2.4.1   Given the data

x	−1	0	1
y	−1	0.5	1

what is the least-squares linear polynomial that passes through the point (0,0.5)? From Equation (9.38) we have

$$\hat{\gamma}_1 = \frac{(-1)(-1) + (0)(0.5) + (1)(1) - (0.5)(-1 + 0 + 1)}{(-1)^2 + (0)^2 + (1)^2} = 1.0$$

Hence,

$$\hat{Y}_1 = 0.5 + \hat{\gamma}_1 X$$
$$= 0.5 + 1.0 \cdot X$$

Figure 9.7 illustrates these results. Note that

$$\sum_{i=1}^{3} \epsilon_{i1}^2 = \left(\frac{1}{2}\right)^2 + (0)^2 + \left(\frac{1}{2}\right)^2 = \frac{1}{2}$$

cannot be decreased by rotating the line $Y = 0.5 + \gamma_1 X$ about the point (0,0.5).

To force the kth-degree least-squares polynomial through any specific point (x_p^*, y_p^*), make the transformation

$$Z = X - x_p^* \qquad (9.39)$$

and fit the observation model

$$y_i = y_p^* + \sum_{j=1}^{k} \delta_j z_i{}^j + \epsilon_{ik} \qquad (9.40)$$

This model is in the form of Equation (9.35), so Equation (9.36) can be solved, where each x_i is replaced by z_i. Then

$$\hat{Y}_k = y_p^* + \sum_{j=1}^{k} \hat{\delta}_j Z^j$$

$$= y_p^* + \sum_{j=1}^{k} \hat{\delta}_j (X - x_p^*)^j \qquad (9.41)$$

is the least-squares polynomial of degree k that passes through the point (x_p^*, y_p^*).

For $k = 1$, we have

$$\hat{\delta}_1 = \frac{\sum z_i y_i - y_p^* \sum z_i}{\sum z_i{}^2} \qquad (9.42)$$

Then,

$$\hat{Y}_1 = y_p^* + \hat{\delta}_1 Z$$
$$= y_p^* + \hat{\delta}_1 (X - x_p^*)$$
$$= (y_p^* - \hat{\delta}_1 x_p^*) + \hat{\delta}_1 X \qquad (9.43)$$

EXAMPLE 9.2.4.2 Consider the data in Table 9.4. Suppose we want the first-degree least-squares polynomial that passes through the point (3,2), that is, $x_p^* = 3$, $y_p^* = 2$. By this we mean we want the first-degree polynomial that passes through the point (3,2) and minimizes the sum of squares of the differences between the observed and predicted responses over all the given data. It should be noted that (x_p^*, y_p^*) need not be one of the given data points although it is in this case.

Let $Z = X - x_p^*$
$\quad\quad = X - 3$

Then, from Equation (9.42) and the data in Table 9.4, we have

$$\hat{\delta}_1 = \frac{(-2) + (-1)(3) + (0)(2) + (1)(4) - 2(-2 - 1 + 0 + 1)}{(-2)^2 + (-1)^2 + (0)^2 + (1)^2} = 0.5$$

Table 9.4 SAMPLE DATA

x_i	1	2	3	4
y_i	1	3	2	4
z_i	-2	-1	0	1

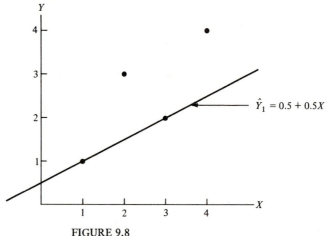

FIGURE 9.8
Least-squares linear polynomial through the point (3,2).

Therefore, from Equation (9.43),

$$\hat{Y}_1 = [2 - 0.5(3)] + 0.5X$$
$$= 0.5 + 0.5X$$

The results are displayed in Figure 9.8. There is no other straight line through the point (3,2) that would yield a smaller sum of squares than

$$\sum_{i=1}^{4} \epsilon_{i1}^2 = 0 + (1.5)^2 + 0 + (1.5)^2 = 4.5$$

9.3 SIMPLE LINEAR REGRESSION

Simple linear regression is the process of analyzing models of the form

$$Y = \beta_0 + \beta_1 X + \epsilon \qquad (9.44)$$

where X = an independent variable whose values can be set or observed but not controlled

Y = a dependent or response variable

β_0, β_1 = unknown parameters to be determined

ϵ = a random error that may be the sum of one or more other random errors. It is considered to be a random variable.

Note that since ϵ is a random variable so is Y since it is just a constant plus a random variable. Thus, we assume for a fixed value of X that Y can be written as the constant $\beta_0 + \beta_1 X$ plus an amount ϵ. Also note that for fixed values of β_0 and β_1 the error ϵ will change with different values of X. We will be interested in setting or observing X at n values $x_1, x_2, \ldots, x_n$, where some of the x_i's may be the same, and observing a corresponding value of each random variable Y_i with $i = 1, 2, \ldots, n$, namely $y_1, y_2, \ldots, y_n$. Based on the model in Equation (9.44), y_i is assumed to be a value of the random variable Y_i where

$$Y_i = \beta_0 + \beta_1 x_i + \epsilon_i \qquad i = 1, 2, \ldots, n$$

That is, we set $X = x_1$ and then observe a response y_1 which is assumed to be a value of the random variable

$$Y_1 = \beta_0 + \beta_1 x_1 + \epsilon_1$$

Thus,

$$y_1 = \beta_0 + \beta_1 x_1 + e_1$$

where e_1 is a value of the random variable ϵ_1. A similar process is repeated for $X = x_2$, $x_3, \ldots, x_n$.

If we assume that the mean of each random error ϵ_i with $i = 1, 2, \ldots, n$ is zero, then the expected value of Y_i is

$$E(Y_i) = E(\beta_0 + \beta_1 x_i + \epsilon_i)$$
$$= \beta_0 + \beta_1 x_i \qquad (9.45)$$

Figure 9.9 illustrates the concept of drawing a random sample from the distribution of Y_i with $i = 1, 2, \ldots, n$.

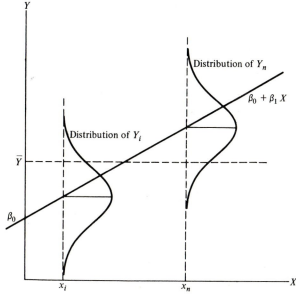

FIGURE 9.9
Distribution of $Y_i, i = 1, 2, \ldots, n$.

Keep in mind that x_i is the ith value of the mathematical variable X, ϵ_i is a random variable with mean zero, Y_i is a random variable with mean $\beta_0 + \beta_1 x_i$ and y_i is a value from Y_i for $i = 1, 2, \ldots, n$. The linear equation

$$Y = \beta_0 + \beta_1 X$$

is the *regression line* of Y on X, and β_1 is the *regression coefficient* of X.

9.3.1 Least-squares Estimates

Suppose we have obtained the set of data $\{x_i, y_i\}$ with $i = 1, 2, \ldots, n$, and wish to use it to determine the least-squares estimates of the parameters β_0 and β_1 in the model

$$Y = \beta_0 + \beta_1 X + \epsilon$$

Observe that the general form of each observation y_i is

$$y_i = \beta_0 + \beta_1 x_i + e_i \qquad (9.46)$$

where e_i is a value from the random variable ϵ_i with $i = 1, 2, \ldots, n$. Thus Equation (9.46) is called the *observation model*. Recall from Section 9.2 that the least-squares procedure is to write

$$e_i = y_i - \beta_0 - \beta_1 x_i$$

$$\sum_{i=1}^{n} e_i^2 = \sum_{i=1}^{n} (y_i - \beta_0 - \beta_1 x_i)^2$$

When the first partial derivations of Σe_i^2 with respect to β_0 and β_1 are set equal to zero, we obtain the normal equations

$$\hat{\beta}_0 n + \hat{\beta}_1 \Sigma x_i = \Sigma y_i$$
$$\hat{\beta}_0 \Sigma x_i + \hat{\beta}_1 \Sigma x_i^2 = \Sigma x_i y_i$$

The solution of this system of two linear equations in two unknowns is

$$\hat{\beta}_0 = \bar{y} - \hat{\beta}_1 \bar{x} \qquad (9.47)$$

$$\hat{\beta}_1 = \frac{\Sigma (x_i - \bar{x})(y_i - \bar{y})}{\Sigma (x_i - \bar{x})^2} \qquad (9.48)$$

where

$$\bar{x} = \frac{\displaystyle\sum_{i=1}^{n} x_i}{n}$$

$$\bar{y} = \frac{\displaystyle\sum_{i=1}^{n} y_i}{n}$$

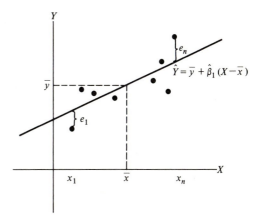

FIGURE 9.10
Least-squares linear prediction equation.

The least-squares regression line is then

$$\hat{Y} = \hat{\beta}_0 + \hat{\beta}_1 X$$
$$= \bar{y} - \hat{\beta}_1 \bar{x} + \hat{\beta}_1 X$$
$$= \bar{y} + \hat{\beta}_1(X - \bar{x}) \qquad (9.49)$$

This line can be used as a prediction equation to predict future responses. However, it may do a very poor job if additional independent variables and/or higher-order powers of X are needed to predict Y adequately. Note that the prediction equation passes through the point $(\bar{x}, \bar{y})$ as illustrated in Figure 9.10. That is, for $X = \bar{x}$

$$\hat{Y} = \bar{y} + \hat{\beta}_1(\bar{x} - \bar{x})$$
$$= \bar{y}$$

Also note that $\sum_{i=1}^{n}(y_i - \hat{y}_i) = 0$, where $\hat{y}_i$ is the predicted value at x_i using Equation (9.49). That is,

$$\sum_{i=1}^{n}(y_i - \hat{y}_i) = \sum_{i=1}^{n}[y_i - \bar{y} - \hat{\beta}_1(x_i - \bar{x})]$$

$$= \sum_{i=1}^{n}[(y_i - \bar{y}) - \hat{\beta}_1(x_i - \bar{x})]$$

$$= \sum_{i=1}^{n}(y_i - \bar{y}) - \hat{\beta}_1 \sum_{i=1}^{n}(x_i - \bar{x})$$

$$= \sum_{i=1}^{n} y_i - n\bar{y} - \hat{\beta}_1\left(\sum_{i=1}^{n} x_i - n\bar{x}\right)$$

$$= \sum_{i=1}^{n} y_i - \frac{n\Sigma\, y_i}{n} - \hat{\beta}_1 \left(\sum_{i=1}^{n} x_i - \frac{n\Sigma\, x_i}{n} \right)$$

$$= 0$$

Recall from Section 9.2 that the least-squares estimates of the parameters, namely $\hat{\beta}_0$ and $\hat{\beta}_1$, are such that

$$\sum_{i=1}^{n} \epsilon_i^2 = \sum_{i=1}^{n} (y_i - \hat{y}_i)^2$$

$$= \sum_{i=1}^{n} (y_i - \hat{\beta}_0 - \hat{\beta}_1 x_i)^2$$

$$= \sum_{i=1}^{n} [y_i - \bar{y} - \hat{\beta}_1 (x_i - \bar{x})]^2$$

is a minimum. No other straight line through the data will yield a smaller sum of squares.

9.3.2 Preliminaries to Test for Linear Effect

The next step in a regression analysis is to determine if the linear term in the model

$$Y = \beta_0 + \beta_1 X + \epsilon$$

is statistically significant based on the given set of data. This is accomplished by hypothesizing that β_1 is zero, that is,

$$H_0 : \beta_1 = 0$$

and making a statistical test, called the *F test*, to determine if the hypothesis can be rejected with a fair degree of confidence. If it can be rejected, β_1 is considered statistically significant and left in the model, otherwise it is removed.

Keep in mind that we are interested in accounting for the total variation of the responses about the mean response $\bar{y}$. Is it due to linear effect in the independent variable X, or is it due to random errors or to other important independent variables? Consider the data in Figure 9.11. It appears that there is no increasing or decreasing trend in the response as X is increased, so it is doubtful that Y is dependent on X in any way. The responses seem to vary about the mean response $\bar{y}$ completely at random with no noticeable pattern. It may be that other important variables that affect Y are changing, which in turn causes Y to vary. Also, it may be that we cannot find important factors that affect Y, so the variation will be attributed solely to random errors.

The data in Figure 9.12 indicate a definite downward trend in the responses as X increases, so we might expect linear effect to be significant ($\beta_1 \neq 0$). However, the

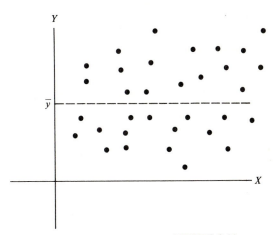

FIGURE 9.11
Observed data set A.

responses are scattered a great deal around the trend line, so the test that will be used may not be able to pick up the linear effect in X.

Basically, we will be interested in determining how much of the total variation of the responses about the mean $\bar{y}$ can be accounted for by the linear term in the model, and how much can be accounted for by random errors and the need for more independent variables. The various types of variations that will be needed to test the hypothesis

$$H_0 : \beta_1 = 0$$

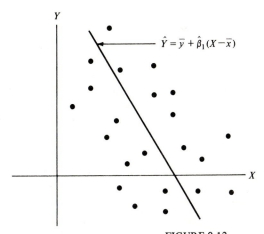

$$\hat{Y} = \bar{y} + \hat{\beta}_1 (X - \bar{x})$$

FIGURE 9.12
Observed data set B.

are measured in terms of sums of squares (SSQ). Specifically, we will initially need

$\sum_{i=1}^{n} (y_i - \bar{y})^2$ = total variation or sum of squares about the mean response $\bar{y}$ (SSQ about the mean)

$\sum_{i=1}^{n} (y_i - \hat{y}_i)^2$ = total variation or sum of squares of the given responses about the predicted responses (SSQ about the regression)

$\sum_{i=1}^{n} (\hat{y}_i - \bar{y})^2$ = total variation or sum of squares of the predicted responses about the mean response $\bar{y}$ (SSQ due to regression)

These sums of squares arise quite naturally when we observe

$$\hat{y}_i = \bar{y} + \hat{\beta}_1(x_i - \bar{x})$$

$$\hat{y}_i - \bar{y} = \hat{\beta}_1(x_i - \bar{x}) \tag{9.50}$$

$$\hat{\beta}_1 = \frac{\Sigma(x_i - \bar{x})(y_i - \bar{y})}{\Sigma(x_i - \bar{x})^2} \tag{9.51}$$

$$\hat{\beta}_1 \Sigma(x_i - \bar{x})^2 = \Sigma(x_i - \bar{x})(y_i - \bar{y})$$

$$y_i - \bar{y} = (y_i - \hat{y}_i) + (\hat{y}_i - \bar{y}) \tag{9.52}$$

then $\Sigma(y_i - \bar{y})^2 = \Sigma[(y_i - \hat{y}_i) + (\hat{y}_i - \bar{y})]^2$

$$= \Sigma(y_i - \hat{y}_i)^2 + \Sigma(\hat{y}_i - \bar{y})^2 + 2\Sigma(y_i - \hat{y}_i)(\hat{y}_i - \bar{y})$$

$$= \Sigma(y_i - \hat{y}_i)^2 + \Sigma(\hat{y}_i - \bar{y})^2 + 2\Sigma(y_i - \bar{y})(\hat{y}_i - \bar{y})$$

$$- 2\Sigma(\hat{y}_i - \bar{y})(\hat{y}_i - \bar{y})$$

$$= \Sigma(y_i - \hat{y}_i)^2 + \Sigma(\hat{y}_i - \bar{y})^2 + 2\hat{\beta}_1\Sigma(y_i - \bar{y})(x_i - \bar{x})$$

$$- 2\hat{\beta}_1^2\Sigma(x_i - \bar{x})^2 \quad \text{from (9.50)}$$

$$= \Sigma(y_i - \hat{y}_i)^2 + \Sigma(\hat{y}_i - \bar{y})^2 + 2\hat{\beta}_1^2\Sigma(x_i - \bar{x})^2$$

$$- 2\hat{\beta}_1^2\Sigma(x_i - \bar{x})^2 \quad \text{from (9.51)}$$

$$= \Sigma(y_i - \hat{y}_i)^2 + \Sigma(\hat{y}_i - \bar{y})^2$$

Therefore,

$$\sum_{i=1}^{n} (y_i - \bar{y})^2 = \sum_{i=1}^{n} (y_i - \hat{y}_i)^2 + \sum_{i=1}^{n} (\hat{y}_i - \bar{y})^2 \tag{9.53}$$

$$\underbrace{\phantom{\sum_{i=1}^{n}(y_i-\bar{y})^2}}_{\substack{\text{SSQ about the}\\\text{mean}}} \quad \underbrace{\phantom{\sum_{i=1}^{n}(y_i-\hat{y}_i)^2}}_{\substack{\text{SSQ about}\\\text{regression}}} \quad \underbrace{\phantom{\sum_{i=1}^{n}(\hat{y}_i-\bar{y})^2}}_{\substack{\text{SSQ due to}\\\text{regression}}}$$

This concept is illustrated in Figure 9.13.

Equation (9.52) results from noting that the distance of an observed response from the mean $\bar{y}$ can be expressed as the distance between the observed response and the corresponding predicted response, plus the distance of the corresponding predicted response from $\bar{y}$, that is,

$$y_i - \bar{y} = (y_i - \hat{y}_i) + (\hat{y}_i - \bar{y})$$

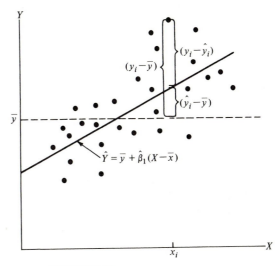

FIGURE 9.13
Observed and predicted response about the mean.

This is illustrated in Figure 9.13.

If the SSQ about regression is very close to zero, then all of the observed responses would be very close to the prediction equation, so we could, in a practical sense, conclude that linear effect is significant, and accounts for almost all of the total variation about the mean response. On the other hand, if the SSQ about regression is quite large, it may not be possible to detect linear effect in X even though it exists. These aspects of regression will be discussed thoroughly in Section 9.3.3.

9.3.3 Degrees of Freedom

Every sum of squares of random variables has associated with it a number called its *degrees of freedom*. Basically this is a number that indicates how many independent linear functions of the random variables are needed to compute the sum of squares. The importance of degrees of freedom should become apparent as we develop statistical tests to determine if certain terms in a given model are significant. Consider the sum of squares in Equation (9.53). Note that

$$\Sigma (y_i - \bar{y})^2 = \Sigma (y_i^2 - 2\bar{y}y_i + \bar{y}^2)$$
$$= \Sigma y_i^2 - 2\bar{y}\Sigma y_i + n\bar{y}^2$$
$$= \Sigma y_i^2 - 2n\bar{y}^2 + n\bar{y}^2$$
$$= \Sigma y_i^2 - n\bar{y}^2$$

Now $\Sigma_{i=1}^{n} y_i^2$ is the sum of squares of n independent linear functions of the y_i, namely,

$$y_1 = f_1(y_1, y_2, \ldots, y_n) = y_1$$
$$y_2 = f_2(y_1, y_2, \ldots, y_n) = y_2$$
$$\cdots\cdots\cdots\cdots\cdots\cdots\cdots$$
$$y_n = f_n(y_1, y_2, \ldots, y_n) = y_n$$

Therefore, $\sum_{i=1}^{n} y_i^2$ has n degrees of freedom. Likewise, if we have only one independent linear function

$$\bar{y} = f(y_1, \ldots, y_n) = \frac{y_1 + y_2 + \cdots + y_n}{n}$$

then $n\bar{y}^2$ can be calculated. Thus $n\bar{y}^2$ has 1 degree of freedom. Since the degrees of freedom associated with the sum or difference of two or more sum-of-squares quantities is just the sum or difference of the corresponding degrees of freedom associated with each sum of squares, we say that degrees of freedom are additive. In the above example, then,

$$\sum_{i=1}^{n} (y_i - \bar{y})^2 = \sum_{i=1}^{n} y_i^2 - n\bar{y}^2 \qquad (9.54)$$

has $n - 1$ degrees of freedom.

Consider the SSQ due to regression:

$$\sum_{i=1}^{n} (\hat{y}_i - \bar{y})^2 = \sum_{i=1}^{n} [\hat{\beta}_1 (x_i - \bar{x})]^2$$
$$= \hat{\beta}_1^2 \Sigma (x_i - \bar{x})^2$$

Since $\hat{\beta}_1$ is calculated from a single linear function of the y_i's, namely,

$$\hat{\beta}_1 = \frac{\Sigma (x_i - \bar{x})(y_i - \bar{y})}{\Sigma (x_i - \bar{x})^2}$$
$$= \frac{\Sigma (x_i - \bar{x}) y_i}{\Sigma (x_i - \bar{x})^2} - \frac{\bar{y} \Sigma (x_i - \bar{x})}{\Sigma (x_i - \bar{x})^2}$$
$$= \sum_{i=1}^{n} \left[\frac{(x_i - \bar{x})}{\Sigma (x_i - \bar{x})^2} \right] y_i$$

since $\sum_{i=1}^{n} (x_i - \bar{x}) = 0$, the SSQ due to regression has only 1 degree of freedom. It can also be shown that the SSQ about regression $\Sigma (y_i - \hat{y}_i)^2$ has $n - 2$ degrees of freedom. Since degrees of freedom are additive, we could have obtained this result by subtraction. That is, from Equation (9.53),

$$\sum_{i=1}^{n} (y_i - \bar{y})^2 = \sum_{i=1}^{n} (y_i - \hat{y}_i)^2 + \sum_{i=1}^{n} (\hat{y}_i - \bar{y})^2$$

or

$$\sum_{i=1}^{n} y_i^2 = n\bar{y}^2 + \sum_{i=1}^{n} (y_i - \hat{y}_i)^2 + \sum_{i=1}^{n} (\hat{y}_i - \bar{y})^2 \qquad (9.55)$$

$$n \text{ df} \qquad 1 \text{ df} \qquad\qquad\qquad 1 \text{ df}$$

Therefore, the sum of squares about regression must have $n - 2$ degrees of freedom.

9.3.4 Analysis of Variance

Equation (9.55) expresses the total variation in the responses (Total SSQ) as the SSQ due to the mean $\bar{y}$ *plus* the SSQ about regression *plus* the SSQ due to regression. This breakdown of the variation in the data is generally displayed in a table called the *analysis of variance (AOV) table* (see Table 9.5).

The symbols in Table 9.5 are defined as

$R(\beta_1|\beta_0) =$ reduction in the total SSQ due to regression after adjusting for the constant term β_0. It is a measure of just the effect of the linear term $\beta_1 X$ being in the model.

Residual = an error term; a measure of how far the predicted values miss the observed values. It is the variation in the responses that is not accounted for by the mean and the linear term (in this case). The SSQ for this quantity can be obtained by subtraction. See Equation (9.55).

rms = regression mean square.

s^2 = error mean square.

cal F = calculated F value to be compared with a corresponding critical tabulated value.

Under the assumption that

Table 9.5 AOV TABLE

Source of variation	df	SSQ	Mean square (MS)	F
Total	n	$\sum_{i=1}^{n} y_i^2$		
Mean	1	$n\bar{y}^2$		
Due to regression $R(\beta_1|\beta_0)$	1	$\sum_{i=1}^{n} (\hat{y}_i - \bar{y})^2 = R(\beta_1|\beta_0)\text{SSQ}$	$\text{rms} = R(\beta_1|\beta_0)\text{SSQ}/1$	$\text{cal } F = \dfrac{\text{rms}}{s^2}$
About regression (residual)	$n-2$	$\sum_{i=1}^{n} (y_i - \hat{y}_i)^2$ (subtraction)	$s^2 = \dfrac{(\text{residual SSQ})}{(n-2)}$	

$$\epsilon_i \sim \text{NID}(0,\sigma^2)$$

we can use the quantities in the AOV table to test the hypothesis

$$H_0 : \beta_1 = 0$$

at the $100(1 - \alpha)$ percent confidence level. Specifically, if

$$\text{cal } F > F^*(v_1, v_2, 1 - \alpha) = F^*(1, n - 2, 1 - \alpha)$$

we reject the hypothesis and conclude that the term $\beta_1 X$ should be in the model, otherwise we conclude that there is no evidence that $\beta_1 X$ should be in the model. The quantity $F^*(1, n - 2, 1 - \alpha)$ is the critical point of an F distribution, and is obtained from a table in Appendix A. Specifically, an F distribution has the form

$$f(w; v_1, v_2) = \frac{\left(\dfrac{v_1 + v_2 - 2}{2}\right)! \left(\dfrac{v_1}{v_2}\right)^{v_1/2} \left[w^{(v_1/2-1)}\right]}{\left(\dfrac{v_1 - 2}{2}\right)! \left(\dfrac{v_2 - 2}{2}\right)! \left(1 + \dfrac{v_1 w}{v_2}\right)^{(v_1+v_2)/2}} \qquad w > 0 \qquad (9.56)$$

where v_1 and v_2 are integer parameters called the *numerator and denominator degrees of freedom,* respectively. Figure 9.14 illustrates an F distribution with $v_1 = 1$ and $v_2 = 18$.

In general the critical point $F^*(v_1, v_2, 1 - \alpha)$ is the value of w such that

$$\int_0^{F^*(v_1, v_2, 1-\alpha)} f(w; v_1, v_2)\, dw = 1 - \alpha$$

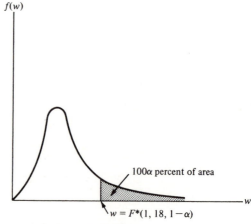

FIGURE 9.14
F distribution with $v_1 = 1$, $v_2 = 18$.

The value of $F^*(v_1, v_2, 1 - \alpha)$ has been calculated for numerous values of v_1 and v_2 with specific values of α (see Tables A.4 and A.5).

The question now is, "Why can we reject the hypothesis that $\beta_1 = 0$ in the model

$$Y = \beta_0 + \beta_1 X + \epsilon$$

at the $100(1 - \alpha)$ percent level just because

$$\text{cal } F > F^*(1, n - 2, 1 - \alpha)$$

where cal F is from the AOV in Table 9.6?"

The question can be resolved by noting that the SSQ, mean squares, and the calculated F quantities in the AOV table are sample values that are calculated from the given data $\{x_i, y_i\}$. The given Y_i's,

$$Y_i = \beta_0 + \beta_1 x_i + \epsilon_i$$

are random variables so every function of them is also a random variable with a certain distribution. Specifically, under the assumptions

$$\epsilon_i \sim \text{NID}(0, \sigma^2) \quad \text{for } i = 1, 2, \ldots, n \qquad (9.57)$$

$$\beta_1 = 0 \qquad (9.58)$$

in the model

$$Y_i = \beta_0 + \beta_1 x_i + \epsilon_i \quad \text{for } i = 1, 2, \ldots, n$$

it can be shown that

$$\frac{\text{RMS}}{\sigma^2} = \frac{\sum_{i=1}^{n} (\hat{Y}_i - \bar{Y})^2}{\sigma^2} \sim \chi^2(1) \qquad (9.59)$$

$$\frac{(n-2)S^2}{\sigma^2} = \frac{(n-2)\sum_{i=1}^{n}(Y_i - \hat{Y}_i)}{(n-2)\sigma^2} = \frac{\sum_{i=1}^{n}(Y_i - \hat{Y}_i)}{\sigma^2} \sim \chi^2(n-2) \qquad (9.60)$$

and the random variables RMS/σ^2 and $[(n-2)S^2]/\sigma^2$ are independent. In addition, the ratio

$$W = \frac{\left(\dfrac{\text{RMS}}{\sigma^2}\right)/1}{\left(\dfrac{(n-2)S^2}{\sigma^2}\right)/(n-2)} = \frac{\left(\dfrac{\text{RMS}}{\sigma^2}\right)}{\left(\dfrac{S^2}{\sigma^2}\right)} = \frac{\text{RMS}}{S^2} \qquad (9.61)$$

has an F distribution with 1 and $n - 2$ numerator and denominator degrees of freedom, respectively. That is,

$$W = \frac{\text{RMS}}{S^2} \sim F(1, n-2) \qquad (9.62)$$

Thus under assumptions (9.57) and (9.58), the calculated F value in Table 9.5 is just a value from W in Equation (9.62).

If we assume Equation (9.57) holds, and if cal F in Table 9.5 is greater than $F^*(1, n-2, 1-\alpha)$, we reject the hypothesis that cal F came from W, whose distribution is denoted as $f(w; 1, n-2)$, and run a 100α percent risk of rejecting a true hypothesis. For example, if cal $F = 5.62$, then

$$\text{cal } F = 5.62 > F^*(1, 18, 0.95) = 4.41$$

so we reject the hypothesis that cal F came from $f(w; 1, 18)$ and run a 5 percent risk of being wrong. In other words, cal F could be a value of the random variable W with density $f(w; 1, 18)$ and be greater than 4.41 5 percent of the time. Figure 9.15 illustrates this concept.

When we reject the hypothesis that cal F is a value of W whose density is $f(w; 1, n-2)$, we are actually saying that assumption (9.58) does not hold, that is, $\beta_1 \neq 0$. Thus, to test the hypothesis

$$H_0 : \beta_1 = 0$$

in the model

$$Y = \beta_0 + \beta_1 X + \epsilon$$

at the $100(1-\alpha)$ percent significance level we collect a set of data $\{x_i, y_i\}$ with $i = 1, 2, \ldots, n$, and calculate the AOV according to Table 9.5. If

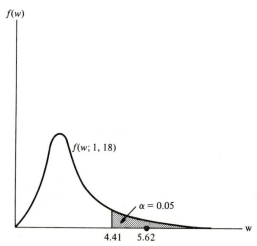

FIGURE 9.15

F distribution with $v_1 = 1$, $v_2 = 18$, $\alpha = 0.05$.

$$\text{cal } F > F^*(1, n-2, 1-\alpha)$$

we reject the hypothesis that $\beta_1 = 0$ and conclude that the term $\beta_1 X$ is significant and should be in the model. Otherwise, we assume $\beta_1 = 0$ and do not put the term $\beta_1 X$ in the model. We will see in Section 9.3.8 that if assumption (9.58) does not hold, then the above test is not valid and should not be used. The only problem that arises when we use the test under the false assumption is that we may leave out terms that should be in the model.

If the only errors in ϵ_i with $i = 1, 2, \ldots, n$ are truly random errors, then the assumption

$$\epsilon_i \sim \text{NID}(0, \sigma^2)$$

is usually valid by the central limit theorem (see Section 8.5.2.1). However, if ϵ_i contains variation caused by the need for more independent variables or higher-order powers of X in the model, the quantity

$$s^2 = \frac{\sum_{i=1}^{n} (y_i - \hat{y}_i)^2}{n-2}$$

contains more than just random errors and in fact also contains the variation due to not having enough independent variables and/or higher-order powers of X in the model. Consequently, there may be a need for the linear term $\beta_1 X$ in the model, but the extra variation picked up in s^2 will cause the quantity

$$\frac{\text{rms}}{s^2}$$

to be smaller than it would be if s^2 only contained variation due to random errors. In this case, we may possibly conclude that $\beta_1 = 0$ when in reality it is not. One way to determine if s^2 contains more than just random errors is to examine a quantity called the *square of the multiple correlation coefficient*.

9.3.5 R^2—Square of the Multiple Correlation Coefficient

One measure of the goodness of a model is the relative size of the square of the multiple correlation coefficient which is given by

$$R^2 = \frac{\text{SSQ due to regression}}{\text{SSQ about the mean}} \qquad (9.63)$$

This is the proportion of the total variation about the mean $\bar{y}$ that is explained or accounted for by regression. In the model

$$Y = \beta_0 + \beta_1 X + \epsilon$$

R^2 is the proportion of the variation about the mean explained by the $\beta_1 X$ term, and is given by

$$R^2 = \frac{\Sigma \, (\hat{y}_i - \bar{y})^2}{\Sigma \, (y_i - \bar{y})^2} \qquad (9.64)$$

If R^2 is close to zero, very little of the variation is explained by $\beta_1 X$. In fact, most of the variation is unaccounted for and can be found in the residual

$$\sum_{i=1}^{n} (y_i - \hat{y}_i)^2$$

Thus, if $R^2 = 0.05$, then necessarily from Equation (9.53)

$$\frac{\Sigma \, (y_i - \hat{y}_i)^2}{\Sigma \, (y_i - \bar{y})^2} = 0.95$$

since

$$\frac{\Sigma \, (y_i - \hat{y})^2}{\Sigma \, (y_i - \bar{y})^2} + \frac{\Sigma \, (\hat{y}_i - \bar{y})^2}{\Sigma \, (y_i - \bar{y})^2} = 1 \qquad (9.65)$$

Clearly, if R^2 is close to 1, almost all of the variation about the mean is accounted for by the current model, so the residual SSQ will be very small. The whole idea behind regression analysis is to find important independent variables, and keep putting them in an initial model until the only variation in s^2 is just random errors. At this point, R^2 will be very near 1, and regression will have accounted for almost all of the variation about the mean.

9.3.6 Track Meet Example

Suppose data are available from a number of track meets and are given in Table 9.6. Based on these data, we would like to use linear regression analysis to predict the average speed a runner should run if he expects to win a race of any distance between 440 yd and 5280 yd under similar conditions.

Let X be the distance of the race in yards, and Y be the average speed in yards per second. The first step is to fit the model

$$Y = \beta_0 + \beta_1 X + \epsilon$$

to the data. The least-squares estimates of β_0 and β_1 based on the data in Table 9.6 are

Table 9.6 TRACK MEET DATA

X: distance, yd	440	880	1760	5280	440	880	1760	440	1760	5280
Y: Winning average speed, yd/s	9.06	8.12	7.02	6.49	9.52	7.55	7.38	8.76	7.13	5.77

Table 9.7 AOV TABLE–TRACK MEET EXAMPLE

Source	df	SSQ	MS	F
Total	10	602.3832		
Mean	1	589.8240		
$R(\beta_1\|\beta_0)$	1	9.04976	9.04976/1	20.6295
Residual	8	3.50944	$3.50944/8 = 0.43868$	

$$\hat{\beta}_1 = \frac{\Sigma\,(x_i - \bar{x})(y_i - \bar{y})}{\Sigma\,(x_i - \bar{x})^2} = \frac{\Sigma\,(x_i - \bar{x})y_i}{\Sigma\,x_i^2 - n\bar{x}^2} = \frac{\Sigma\,x_i y_i - \bar{x}\Sigma\,y_i}{\Sigma\,x_i^2 - n\bar{x}^2}$$

$$= \frac{128,444.8 - (1892)(76.8)}{67,179,200 - 35,796,640}$$

$$= \frac{-16,860.8}{31,382,560}$$

$$\hat{\beta}_1 = -0.000537$$

$$\hat{\beta}_0 = \bar{y} - \hat{\beta}_1\bar{x}$$

$$= 7.68 - (-0.000537)(1892)$$

$$= 8.696004$$

Therefore, the least-squares linear prediction equation is

$$\hat{y} = 8.696004 - 0.000537X$$

The quantities needed for the AOV table are

$$\Sigma\,y_i^2 = 602.3832$$

$$n\bar{y}^2 = 589.8240$$

$$\Sigma\,(\hat{y}_i - \bar{y})^2 = \hat{\beta}_1^2\,\Sigma\,(x_i - \bar{x})^2$$

$$= (-0.000537)^2(31,382,560)$$

$$= 9.04976$$

$$\Sigma\,(y_i - \hat{y}_i)^2 = \Sigma\,e_i^2$$

$$= \Sigma\,y_i^2 - n\bar{y}^2 - \Sigma\,(\hat{y}_i - \bar{y})^2$$

$$= 602.3832 - 589.8240 - 9.04976$$

$$= 3.50944$$

The AOV for this data is given in Table 9.7.
From Table A.4,

$$F^*(1,8,0.95) = 5.32$$

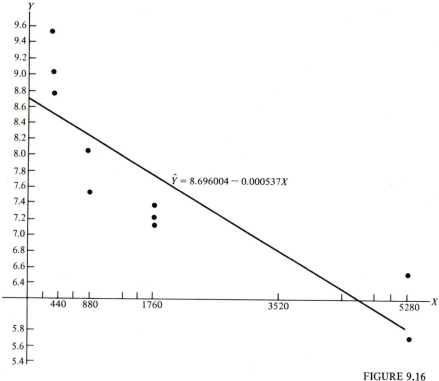

FIGURE 9.16
Track meet data.

Since cal $F = 20.6295 > F^*(1,8,0.95) = 5.32$, reject the hypothesis that $\beta_1 = 0$ and leave the $\beta_1 X$ term in the model. It appears from Figure 9.16 that a negative exponential model would be more appropriate. However, a quadratic term in X will give a good approximation. Also, it appears that some other factors, such as the altitude where the race was run and wind velocity, may have caused the variation in the speed for races of the same distance. This aspect of regression will be discussed in Section 9.4. In any event, an R^2 value of

$$R^2 = \frac{\Sigma (\hat{y}_i - \bar{y})^2}{\Sigma (y_i - \bar{y})^2} = \frac{9.04976}{12.55920} = 0.72$$

indicates that additional terms are needed in the model to adequately predict the average speed a runner should travel to win a race of fixed distance.

9.3.7 Tire Mileage Example

A certain tire manufacturer would like to develop a least-squares prediction equation to estimate tire life (in miles) for a specific size of a new type of tire that has been developed recently. It was determined that some of the more important factors that might affect tire life are

Average speed car is driven
Number of drivers under 20 years of age
Number of drivers between 20 and 25 years of age
Average weight of loaded car
Average number of miles between rotation of tires
Average number of miles between front end alignments on car
Percent of time on highway as opposed to city driving

To simplify matters, suppose we only have access to data that involves tire life (in miles), average speed car is driven, number of drivers under 20 years of age, and miles between rotation of tires. The data are given in Table 9.8.

The tire life is plotted against X_1, X_2, and X_3 in Figures 9.17, 9.18, and 9.19, respectively. Based on these plots, it appears that there is a definite linear relationship between tire life and average speed. Thus, suppose we start our analysis by assuming the model

$$Y = \beta_0 + \beta_1 X_1 + \epsilon$$

For the data in Table 9.8, we have

Table 9.8 TIRE MILEAGE DATA

X_1, average speed	X_2, number of drivers under 20	X_3, miles between rotation of tires, thousands	Y Tire life, thousands of miles
50	0	5.5	30
45	1	6.2	28
48	0	8.2	27
52	0	4.8	26
55	2	2.0	23
43	1	4.0	30
48	2	3.7	25
45	1	6.2	30
44	0	5.8	32
53	0	4.8	26
53	2	5.6	28
46	1	6.6	27
46	2	2.5	34
40	0	4.3	35
47	1	5.4	29
47	1	5.4	31
49	0	4.7	30
53	0	4.8	32
48	1	6.0	33
52	1	5.0	26

$$\sum_{i=1}^{20} y_i{}^2 = 17{,}128$$

$$\bar{y} = 29.1$$

$$n\bar{y}^2 = 16{,}936.2$$

$$\bar{x} = 48.2$$

$$\Sigma (x_i - \bar{x})^2 = 293.2$$

$$\Sigma (x_i - \bar{x})y_i = -141.4$$

therefore,

$$\hat{\beta}_1 = \frac{-141.4}{293.2}$$

$$= -0.482265$$

$$\hat{\beta}_0 = 29.1 - (-0.482265)(48.2)$$

$$= 52.345157$$

$$\hat{Y} = 52.345157 - 0.482265X_1$$

$$\Sigma (\hat{y}_i - \bar{y})^2 = \hat{\beta}_1{}^2 \Sigma(x_i - \bar{x})^2$$

$$= 68.192318$$

The AOV is given in Table 9.9.
From Table A.4, with $\alpha = 0.05$,

$$F^*(1,18,0.95) = 4.41$$

Since cal $F = 9.93 > F^*(1,18,0.95) = 4.41$, reject the hypothesis that $\beta_1 = 0$, and leave $\beta_1 X_1$ in the model. It appears from Figure 9.17 that most of the unaccounted-for variation is due to the need for more independent variables.

Note that

$$R^2 = \frac{\Sigma (\hat{y}_i - \bar{y})^2}{\Sigma (y_i - \bar{y})^2} = \frac{68.19}{17{,}128.0 - 16{,}936.2}$$

$$= 0.36$$

Hence, the linear term in the average speed accounts for only 36 percent of the total variation about the mean. Additional variables should be added to the model.

Table 9.9 AOV TABLE-TIRE MILEAGE EXAMPLE

Source	df	SSQ	MS	F
Total	20	17,128.0		
Mean	1	16,936.2		
$R(\beta_1|\beta_0)$	1	68.19	68.19	9.93
Residual	18	123.61	6.87	

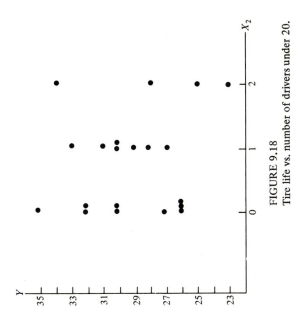

FIGURE 9.18
Tire life vs. number of drivers under 20.

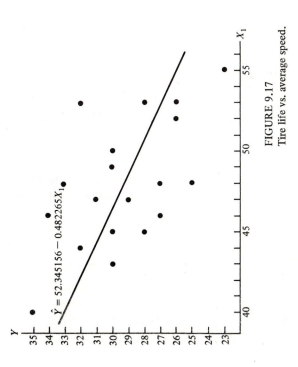

$\hat{Y} = 52.345156 - 0.482265X_1$

FIGURE 9.17
Tire life vs. average speed.

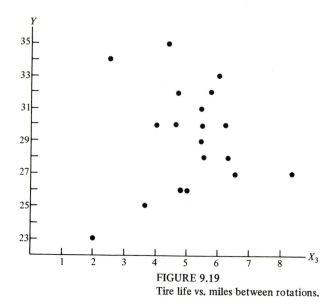

FIGURE 9.19
Tire life vs. miles between rotations.

9.3.8 Lack of Fit and Pure Errors

The SSQ about regression (residual SSQ) contains only random errors if the assumed model is correct. However, if higher-order terms, cross products, and/or additional independent variables are needed in the model, then the residual SSQ also contains the variation due to not having these terms in the model. If we have repeated responses or observations at some of the values of X, then we can break the residual SSQ into *pure error SSQ* and *lack of fit SSQ*. Suppose we set or observe X at k distinct values, $x_1, x_2,$ ..., x_k, and observe n_i responses at x_i with $i = 1, 2, \ldots, k$. Let y_{ij} denote the jth response at x_i for $i = 1, 2, \ldots, k; j = 1, 2, \ldots, n_i$. Also, let $n = \Sigma_{i=1}^{k} n_i$ be the total number of responses. For a fixed value of X, say x_i, the two things that could cause the y_{ij} to vary are

$$\text{Random errors} \tag{9.66}$$

$$\text{Other independent variables not in the model} \tag{9.67}$$

For example, if X is the time of day and Y is the outside temperature, we would not expect the temperature to be the same at 2:00 P.M. each day, since the temperature is a function of several variables.

Consider the observations in Figure 9.20. If time of day is the only variable needed to predict outside temperature accurately, then almost all of the temperatures for a given hour should be essentially the same. From Figure 9.20 we see that this is not true, which means either the measuring device is faulty, or other factors are causing the temperature to vary. Based on our knowledge of the problem, we would assume other factors cause most of the variation. Certainly putting higher-order terms in the model

$$Y = \beta_0 + \beta_1 X + \epsilon$$

would not decrease the variation in Y at a fixed value of X. Consequently, we can calculate the sum of squares

$$\sum_{j=1}^{n_i} (y_{ij} - \bar{y}_i)^2 \qquad (9.68)$$

where $\bar{y}_i = \sum_{j=1}^{n_i} y_{ij}/n_i$ for each x_i. This sum of squares is the variation in the responses due to conditions (9.66) and (9.67). This is called the *pure error SSQ at x_i.* If we repeat the process for all x_i, we have

$$\text{Total pure error SSQ} = \sum_{i=1}^{k} \sum_{j=1}^{n_i} (y_{ij} - \bar{y}_i)^2 \qquad (9.69)$$

The degrees of freedom for the quantity in Equation (9.68) is $n_i - 1$, therefore, the degrees of freedom for the total pure error SSQ in Equation (9.69) is

$$n_e = \sum_{i=1}^{k} (n_i - 1) = \sum_{i=1}^{k} n_i - k = n - k \qquad (9.70)$$

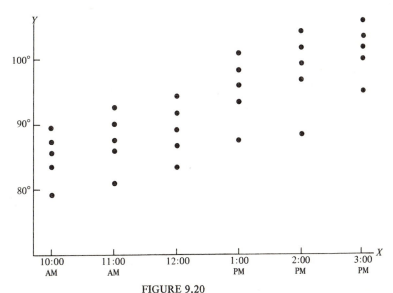

FIGURE 9.20
Outside temperature for five consecutive days in July.

The *lack of fit SSQ* (LF SSQ) is a quantity that represents the variation about the mean that is still unaccounted for after the *pure error* variation is removed from the *residual* variation. Thus,

$$\text{LF SSQ} = \text{residual SSQ} - \text{pure error SSQ}$$

and has $n - 2 - n_e = n - 2 - n + k = k - 2$ degrees of freedom.

Given the set of data $\{x_i, y_{ij}\}$, where $i = 1, 2, \ldots, k$ and $j = 1, 2, \ldots, n_i$, and the assumed observation model

$$y_{ij} = \beta_0 + \beta_1 x_i + \epsilon_{ij} \qquad \epsilon_{ij} \sim \text{NID}(0, \sigma^2) \qquad (9.71)$$

the least-squares estimates of β_0 and β_1 are

$$\hat{\beta}_0 = \bar{y} - \hat{\beta}_1 \bar{x} \qquad (9.72)$$

$$\hat{\beta}_1 = \frac{\displaystyle\sum_{i=1}^{k} \sum_{j=1}^{n_i} (x_i - \bar{x})(y_{ij} - \bar{y})}{\displaystyle\sum_{i=1}^{k} \sum_{j=1}^{n_i} (x_i - \bar{x})^2}$$

$$= \frac{\displaystyle\sum_{i=1}^{k} \sum_{j=1}^{n_i} (x_i - \bar{x}) y_{ij} - \bar{y} \sum_{i=1}^{k} \sum_{j=1}^{n_i} (x_i - \bar{x})}{\displaystyle\sum_{i=1}^{k} n_i (x_i - \bar{x})^2}$$

$$= \frac{\displaystyle\sum_{i=1}^{k} n_i (x_i - \bar{x}) \bar{y}_i}{\displaystyle\sum_{i=1}^{k} n_i (x_i - \bar{x})^2} \qquad (9.73)$$

where

$$\bar{y} = \frac{\displaystyle\sum_{i=1}^{k} \sum_{j=1}^{n_i} y_{ij}}{n}$$

$$\bar{x} = \frac{\displaystyle\sum_{i=1}^{k} \sum_{j=1}^{n_i} x_i}{n} = \frac{\displaystyle\sum_{i=1}^{k} n_i x_i}{n}$$

$$\bar{y}_i = \frac{\displaystyle\sum_{j=1}^{n_i} y_{ij}}{n_i}$$

The prediction equation is then

$$\hat{Y} = \hat{\beta}_0 + \hat{\beta}_1 X$$

and the predicted value at each x_i is

$$\hat{Y}_i = \hat{\beta}_0 + \hat{\beta}_1 x_i \qquad (9.74)$$

Table 9.10 illustrates the AOV when repeated observations are available. It should be noted that s^2 contains variation due to

Random errors	(9.75)
Not enough independent variables in model	(9.76)
Not enough higher-order powers and/or cross products of X with other independent variables	(9.77)

Likewise, s_e^2 contains variation due to conditions (9.75) and (9.76), while LFMS contains only variation due to condition (9.77). Thus, to test for lack of fit (i.e., need for higher-order terms in X and/or cross products), calculate $LFMS/s_e^2$. If

$$\text{cal } F_{LF} = \frac{LFMS}{s_e^2} > F^*(k-2, n_e, 1-\alpha)$$

reject the hypothesis of no lack of fit, and conclude that higher-order terms in X and/or cross products of X with other independent variables are needed in the model. Otherwise, conclude that there is no lack of fit. Of course, we could run into the same problem here as we did in using s^2 to test for linear effect. If s_e^2 contains variation due

Table 9.10   AOV TABLE WITH REPEATED OBSERVATIONS

Source of variation	df	SSQ	MS	F
Total	n	$\displaystyle\sum_{i=1}^{k}\sum_{j=1}^{n_i} y_{ij}^2$		
Mean	1	$n\bar{y}^2$		
$R(\beta_1\lvert\beta_0)$ Regression	1	$\displaystyle\sum_{i=1}^{k}\sum_{j=1}^{n_i}(\hat{y}_i-\bar{y})^2 = \hat{\beta}_1^{\,2}\sum_{i=1}^{k} n_i(x_i-\bar{x})^2$	$\dfrac{R(\beta_1\lvert\beta_0)SSQ}{(1)} = \text{rms}$	$\dfrac{\text{rms}}{s^2}$
Residual (about regression)	$n-2$	Total SSQ $-$ mean SSQ $-R(\beta_1\lvert\beta_0)SSQ$	$\dfrac{\text{Residual SSQ}}{n-2} = s^2$	
LF	$k-2$	Residual SSQ $-$ pure error SSQ	$\dfrac{\text{LF SSQ}}{k-2} = \text{LFMS}$	$\dfrac{\text{LFMS}}{s_e^2}$
Pure error	n_e	$\displaystyle\sum_{i=1}^{k}\sum_{j=1}^{n_i}(y_{ij}-\bar{y}_i)^2$	$\dfrac{\text{Pure error SSQ}}{n_e} = s_e^2$	

to the need for more independent variables, it will cause cal F_{LF} to be smaller than it would be if s_e^2 contained random errors only. Consequently, the above test may not be able to detect lack of fit even though it is present.

Since the track meet data appear to have lack of fit variation, we will test it to determine if higher-order terms in X should be used. The data can be considered as

$$
\begin{array}{lll}
x_1 = 440 & y_{11} = 9.06 & n_1 = 3 \\
& y_{12} = 9.52 & \\
& y_{13} = 8.76 & \\
x_2 = 880 & y_{21} = 8.12 & n_2 = 2 \\
& y_{22} = 7.55 & \\
x_3 = 1760 & y_{31} = 7.02 & n_3 = 3 \\
& y_{32} = 7.38 & \\
& y_{33} = 7.13 & \\
x_4 = 5280 & y_{41} = 6.49 & n_4 = 2 \\
& y_{42} = 5.77 &
\end{array}
$$

All of the results from Section 9.3.6 remain the same even though the labeling of the data and the formulas for calculating the results have changed. For example,

$$
\hat{\beta}_1 = \frac{\displaystyle\sum_{i=1}^{4} n_i(x_i - \bar{x})\bar{y}_i}{\displaystyle\sum_{i=1}^{4} n_i(x_i - \bar{x})^2}
$$

where

$$
\bar{y}_1 = \frac{9.06 + 9.52 + 8.76}{3} = 9.1133
$$

$$
\bar{y}_2 = \frac{8.12 + 7.55}{2} = 7.8350
$$

$$
\bar{y}_3 = \frac{7.02 + 7.38 + 7.13}{3} = 7.1767
$$

$$
\bar{y}_4 = \frac{6.49 + 5.77}{2} = 6.1300
$$

$$
\bar{x} = \frac{\displaystyle\sum_{i=1}^{4} n_i x_i}{10} = \frac{3(440) + 2(880) + 3(1760) + 2(5280)}{10}
$$

$$
= 1892
$$

Therefore,

$$\hat{\beta}_1 = \frac{3(440 - 1892)(9.1133) + \cdots + 2(5280 - 1892)(6.13)}{3(440 - 1892)^2 + \cdots + 2(5280 - 1892)^2}$$

$$= \frac{-16,860.67}{31,382,560}$$

$$= -0.000537$$

This is the same value of $\hat{\beta}_1$ that we calculated in Section 9.3.6. The only new quantity that must be calculated is the pure error SSQ, which is given by

$$\sum_{i=1}^{4} \sum_{j=1}^{n_i} (y_{ij} - \bar{y}_i)^2 = (9.06 - 9.1133)^2 + (9.52 - 9.1133)^2 + (8.76 - 9.1133)^2$$

$$+ (8.12 - 7.835)^2 + (7.55 - 7.835)^2 + \cdots + (5.77 - 6.13)^2$$

$$= 0.7828$$

The complete AOV is given in Table 9.11.

The corresponding critical value at the 95 percent level is

$$F^*(2,6,0.95) = 5.14$$

Since

$$\text{cal } F = 10.44 > F^*(2,6,0.95) = 5.14$$

reject the hypothesis that there is no lack of fit and conclude that higher-order powers in X and/or cross-product terms are needed.

The general procedure for simple linear regression is illustrated with a flowchart in Figure 9.21.

9.3.9 Computer Program for Simple Linear Regression

This program basically follows the general procedure for simple linear regression that is shown in Figure 9.21. It calculates

Table 9.11 AOV TABLE–TRACK MEET EXAMPLE
WITH LF AND PURE ERROR

Source	df	SSQ	MS	F
Total	20	602.3832		
Mean	1	589.8240		
$R(\beta_1|\beta_0)$	1	9.04976	9.04976	20.629525
Residual	8	3.50944	0.43868	
LF	2	2.72624	1.36312	10.442697
Pure error	6	0.78320	0.13053	

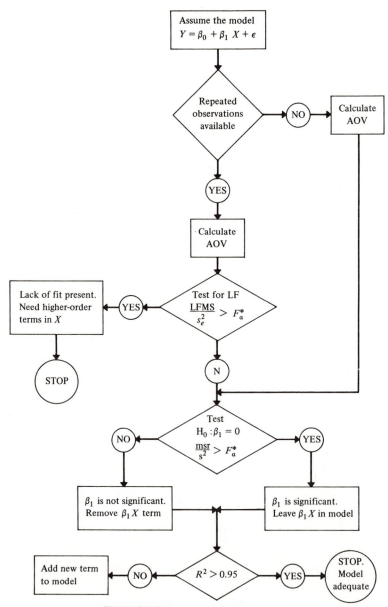

FIGURE 9.21
Flowchart for general procedure to do simple linear regression.

1 The least-squares estimates of the parameters in the model

$$Y = \beta_0 + \beta_1 X + \epsilon$$

2 The AOV for testing for lack of fit if repeated observations are available and for testing the hypothesis $H_0: \beta_1 = 0$.

```
C
C      *****************************************************************
C      *                                                             *
C      *          ***  SIMPLE LINEAR REGRESSION  ***                 *
C      *                                                             *
C      * THIS PROGRAM IS DESIGNED                                    *
C      *                                                             *
C      *    TO READ                                                  *
C      *      CARD 1   COLS  2-80   TITLE  DESCRIPTION OF THE PROBLEM USING *
C      *                                   ANY CHARACTERS ON KEYPUNCH *
C      *                            ** COLUMN 1 MUST BE LEFT BLANK ** *
C      *      CARD 2   COLS  1- 5   N   TOTAL # OF OBSERVATIONS    (I5) *
C      *                     6-10   K   # OF UNIQUE VALUES OF THE INDEPENDENT *
C      *                                VARIABLE  (I5)              *
C      *      CARDS 3 TO T   K SETS OF CARDS, ONE SET FOR EACH IND. VALUE *
C      *        CARD A   COLS  1-10   NI  # OF OBSERVATIONS AT X(I)  (I10) *
C      *                      11-20   X(I)  INDEPENDENT VALUE   (F10.0) *
C      *        CARD B   Y(I,J)  J=1,...,NI   OBSERVATIONS AT X(I)  *
C      *                                PUNCH 8 TO A CARD IN 8F10.0 *
C      *                                FORMAT.  IF NI>8, CONTINUE ON *
C      *                                NEXT CARD.                  *
C      *        TO SOLVE MORE THAN ONE PROBLEM AT A TIME, REPEAT THE *
C      *        READ SEQUENCE, AND STACK THE DATA ONE BEHIND THE OTHER *
C      *                                                             *
C      *    TO CALCULATE                                             *
C      *      SUMX       TOTAL SUM OF VALUES OF INDEPENDENT VARIABLE *
C      *      SUMY       TOTAL SUM OF VALUES OF DEPENDENT VARIABLE  *
C      *      SUMYI      SUM OF THE VALUES OF THE DEPENDENT VARIABLE AT EACH *
C      *                 VALUE OF THE INDEPENDENT VARIABLES          *
C      *      SUMX2      TOTAL SUM OF SQUARES OF THE INDEPENDENT VARIABLE *
C      *      SUMY2      TOTAL SUM OF THE SQUARES OF THE DEPENDENT VARIABLE *
C      *      SUMXY      TOTAL SUM OF THE PRODUCTS OF THE INDEPENDENT VARIABLE *
C      *                 WITH THE CORRESPONDING DEPENDENT VARIABLE   *
C      *      XBAR       MEAN OF THE INDEPENDENT VARIABLE            *
C      *      YBAR       MEAN OF THE DEPENDENT VARIABLE              *
C      *      YBARK(I)   PARTIAL MEANS OF THE DEPENDENT VARIABLE  WHEN MULTIPLE *
C      *                 OBSERVATIONS ARE INVOLVED                   *
C      *      BHAT0, BHAT1   LEAST SQUARES ESTIMATES OF THE PARAMETERS IN *
C      *                 THE MODEL   Y=BETA0 + BETA1*X + EPSILON     *
C      *      SSQM       SUM OF SQUARES FOR THE MEAN                 *
C      *      SSQDR      SUM OF SQUARES DUE TO REGRESSION            *
C      *      SSQAR      SUM OF SQUARES ABOUT REGRESSION             *
C      *      SSQLF      SUM OF SQUARES DUE TO LACK OF FIT           *
C      *      SSQPE      SUM OF SQUARES DUE TO PURE ERROR            *
C      *      RMS        REGRESSION MEAN SQUARE                      *
C      *      SQUARE     RESIDUAL MEAN SQUARE                        *
C      *      LFMS       LACK OF FIT MEAN SQUARE                     *
C      *      ERRMS      PURE ERROR MEAN SQUARE                      *
C      *      FVAL       REGRESSION MEAN SQUARE / RESIDUAL MEAN SQUARE *
C      *      FLOF       LACK OF FIT MEAN SQUARE / ERROR MEAN SQUARE *
C      *      RSQR       PART OF SUM OF SQUARES ABOUT THE MEAN ACCOUNTED FOR *
C      *                 BY THE PRESENCE OF B1 IN THE MODEL          *
C      *                                                             *
C      *    TO PRINT                                                 *
C      *      ANALYSIS OF VARIANCE TABLE                            *
C      *      XBAR, YBAR, BHAT0, BHAT1, RSQR                         *
C      *                                                             *
C      * THE PROGRAM, AS WRITTEN, DOES NOT ALLOW MORE THAN 100 VALUES, OR *
C      * MORE THAN 15 OBSERVATIONS AT A GIVEN X(K).  TO CHANGE THESE LIMITS, *
C      * CHANGE THE CORRESPONDING DIMENSION STATEMENTS.             *
C      *                                                             *
C      *****************************************************************
C
```

```
      DIMENSION X(100),Y(100,15),NYOBX(100),YBARK(100),TITLE(20)
      REAL LFMS
C  READ DATA
   95 READ(5,96,END=2000)TITLE
   96 FORMAT(20A4)
      WRITE(6,97) TITLE
   97 FORMAT('1',20A4,//)
      READ(5,100)N,K
  100 FORMAT(2I5)
      DO 110 I=1,K
      READ(5,115)NI,X(I)
  115 FORMAT (I10,F10.0)
      READ (5,116)(Y(I,J),J=1,NI)
  116 FORMAT(8F10.0)
      NYOBX(I)=NI
  110 CONTINUE
C  PRINT OUT THE DATA AS A CHECK
      WRITE(6,111)
  111 FORMAT(6X,'K    N(I)    X(K)',7X,'Y(K,1)',4X,'Y(K,2)',4X,'Y(K,3)',
     *4X,'Y(K,4)',4X,'Y(K,5)',/)
      DO 113 I=1,K
      NI=NYOBX(I)
      WRITE(6,112)I,NI,X(I),(Y(I,J),J=1,NI)
  112 FORMAT( 5X,I2,3X,I3,1X,6F10.4,(/24X,5F10.4))
  113 CONTINUE
      WRITE(6,144)
  144 FORMAT(///3X,75('_')/2X,'|',75X,'|')
C     ****************************************************************************
C     * CALCULATE SUMMATIONS NECESSARY FOR AN ANALYSIS OF VARIANCE            *
C     ****************************************************************************
C  INITIALIZE SUMMATIONS
      SUMX=0.0
      SUMY=0.0
      SUMX2=0.0
      SUMY2=0.0
      SUMXY=0.0
      SUMYI=0.0
      BNUM=0.0
      BDEN=0.0
C   CALCULATE SUMMATIONS AND AVERAGES
      DO 120 I=1,K
      SUMYI=0.0
      NI=NYOBX(I)
      SUMX2=SUMX2+NI*X(I)*X(I)
      SUMX=SUMX+NI*X(I)
      DO 125 J=1,NI
      SUMXY=SUMXY+X(I)*Y(I,J)
      SUMY2=SUMY2+Y(I,J)*Y(I,J)
      SUMY=SUMY+Y(I,J)
      SUMYI=SUMYI+Y(I,J)
  125 CONTINUE
      YBARK(I)=SUMYI/NI
  120 CONTINUE
      XBAR=SUMX/N
      YBAR=SUMY/N
C SET FLAG FOR REPEATED OBSERVATIONS
      DO 121 I=1,K
      IF(NYOBX(I).NE.1) GO TO 122
  121 CONTINUE
      IFLAG=0
      GO TO 123
  122 IFLAG=1
  123 CONTINUE
    C  CALCULATE VALUES FOR  AOV  TABLE
      DO 130 I=1,K
      DIFF=X(I)-XBAR
      BNUM=BNUM+NYOBX(I)*DIFF*YBARK(I)
      BDEN=BDEN+NYOBX(I)*DIFF*DIFF
  130 CONTINUE
      BHAT1=BNUM/BDEN
      BHATO=YBAR-BHAT1*XBAR
```

```
      SSQM=N*YBAR*YBAR
      SSQDR=BHAT1*BHAT1*BDEN
      SSQAR=SUMY2-SSQM-SSQDR
      RMS=SSQDR/1
      N2=N-2
      SQUARE=SSQAR/N2
      FVAL=RMS/SQUARE
      RSQR=SSQDR/(SUMY2-SSQM)
C   PRINT TABLE IF NO REPEATED OBSERVATIONS
      IF(IFLAG.EQ.0) GO TO 150
      SSQPE=0.0
      DO 135 I=1,K
      NI=NYOBX(I)
      DO 135 J=1,NI
      SDIF=Y(I,J)-YBARK(I)
      SSQPE=SSQPE+SDIF*SDIF
  135 CONTINUE
      SSQLF=SSQAR-SSQPE
      K2=K-2
      LFMS=SSQLF/K2
      NE=N-K
      ERRMS=SSQPE/NE
      FLOF=LFMS/ERRMS
      GO TO 160
C     ********************************************************************
C     * PRINT  ANALYSIS OF VARIANCE  TABLE                             *
C     ********************************************************************
  150 WRITE(6,155)
  155 FORMAT(13X,'ANALYSIS OF VARIANCE TABLE WITH NO REPEATED OBSERVATIO
     *NS'/'+',1X,'|',75X,'|'/2X,'|',75X,'|')
      WRITE(6,148)
  148 FORMAT(3X,75('_')/'+',1X,'|',75X,'|')
      GO TO 170
  160 WRITE(6,165)
  165 FORMAT(13X,'ANALYSIS OF VARIANCE TABLE WITH REPEATED OBSERVATIONS'
     */'+',1X,'|',75X,'|'/2X,'|',75X,'|')
      WRITE(6,148)
  170 WRITE(6,145)
      WRITE(6,145)
      WRITE(6,175)
  175 FORMAT(5X,'SOURCE OF VARIATION   D.F.   SUM OF SQUARES   MEAN SQUA
     *RES     CAL.F.'/
     *'+',1X,'|',22X,'|',6X,'|',16X,'|',15X,'|',12X,'|')
      WRITE(6,147)
  147 FORMAT(3X,75('_')/
     *'+',1X,'|',22X,'|',6X,'|',16X,'|',15X,'|',12X,'|')
      WRITE(6,145)
  145 FORMAT(2X,'|',22X,'|',6X,'|',16X,'|',15X,'|',12X,'|')
      WRITE(6,145)
      WRITE(6,180)N,SUMY2
  180 FORMAT(19X,'TOTAL',3X,I3,5X,F12.4/
     *'+',1X,'|',22X,'|',6X,'|',16X,'|',15X,'|',12X,'|')
      WRITE(6,147)
      WRITE(6,145)
      WRITE(6,185)SSQM
  185 FORMAT(20X,'MEAN       1     ',F12.4/
     *'+',1X,'|',22X,'|',6X,'|',16X,'|',15X,'|',12X,'|')
      WRITE(6,147)
      WRITE(6,190)SSQDR,RMS,FVAL
  190 FORMAT(16X,'R(B1|B0)'/
     *'+',1X,'|',22X,'|',6X,'|',16X,'|',15X,'|',12X,'|'/
     *7X,'DUE TO REGRESSION     1',5X,F12.4,4X,F12.4,3X,F10.5/
     *'+',1X,'|',22X,'|',6X,'|',16X,'|',15X,'|',12X,'|')
      WRITE(6,147)
      WRITE(6,195)N2,SSQAR,SQUARE
  195 FORMAT(16X,'RESIDUAL'/
     *'+',1X,'|',22X,'|',6X,'|',16X,'|',15X,'|',12X,'|'/
     *8X,'ABOUT REGRESSION',3X,I3,5X,F12.4,4X,F12.4/
     *'+',1X,'|',22X,'|',6X,'|',16X,'|',15X,'|',12X,'|')
      WRITE(6,147)
```

```
      IF (IFLAG.EQ.0) GO TO 210
      WRITE(6,145)
      WRITE(6,200)K2,SSQLF,LFMS,FLOF
  200 FORMAT(13X,'LACK OF FIT',3X,I3,5X,F12.4,4X,F12.4,3X,F10.5/
     *'+',1X,'|',22X,'|',6X,'|',1oX,'|',15X,'|',12X,'|')
      WRITE(6,147)
      WRITE(6,145)
      WRITE(6,205)NE,SSQPE,ERRMS
  205 FORMAT(14X,'PURE ERROR',3X,I3,5X,F12.4,4X,F12.4/
     *'+',1X,'|',22X,'|',6X,'|',16X,'|',15X,'|',12X,'|')
      WRITE(6,147)
  210 CONTINUE
      WRITE(6,215)XBAR,YBAR
  215 FORMAT(///10X,'XBAR =',F12.4,10X,'YBAR =',F12.4/)
      WRITE(6,225)BHAT0,BHAT1
  225 FORMAT(10X,'BETA(0) =',F12.4,10X,'BETA(1) =',F12.4,/)
      WRITE(6,230)RSQR
  230 FORMAT(10X,'R**2 =',F12.4/)
      GO TO 95
 2000 STOP
      END


/DATA

 TRACK MEET WITH REPEATED OBSERVATIONS
   10    4
          3         440.
        9.06        9.52        8.76
          2         880.
        8.12        7.55
          3        1760.
        7.02        7.38        7.13
          2        5280.
        6.49        5.77
```

TRACK MEET WITH REPEATED OBSERVATIONS

K	N(I)	X(K)	Y(K,1)	Y(K,2)	Y(K,3)	Y(K,4)	Y(K,5)
1	3	440.0000	9.0600	9.5200	8.7600		
2	2	880.0000	8.1200	7.5500			
3	3	1760.0000	7.0200	7.3800	7.1300		
4	2	5280.0000	6.4900	5.7700			

ANALYSIS OF VARIANCE TABLE WITH REPEATED OBSERVATIONS				
SOURCE OF VARIATION	D.F.	SUM OF SQUARES	MEAN SQUARES	CAL.F.
TOTAL	10	602.3823		
MEAN	1	589.8223		
R(B1|B0) DUE TO REGRESSION	1	9.0587	9.0587	20.69763
RESIDUAL ABOUT REGRESSION	8	3.5014	0.4377	
LACK OF FIT	2	2.7186	1.3593	10.41886
PURE ERROR	6	0.7828	0.1305	

XBAR =   1892.0000   YBAR =   7.6800

BETA(0) =   8.6965   BETA(1) =   -0.0005

R**2 =   0.7212

9.4 SUMMARY

In this chapter we have examined

1 A nonstatistical approach to polynomial regression with a single independent variable

2 A statistical approach to linear regression with one independent variable

The discussion of polynomial regression was rather complete; however, the statistical approach to linear regression was only a brief introduction. Most realistic regression situations involve a dependent variable which is a function of several independent variables. Consequently, regression analysis involves determining the important independent variables and adding them one at a time to the model until a "good" fit is obtained. This involves using somewhat more statistics than has been covered in this textbook.

Some general procedures for doing the basics of a regression analysis are forward regression, backward regression, and stepwise regression. The stepwise procedure is usually preferred. Hence, most computer systems have a stepwise procedure available.

The potential user of regression should be aware that regression procedures are not cut-and-dried OR tools to be used without a great deal of discretion. They are merely tools to aid in the decision-making process. Consequently, a much deeper study of regression analysis than we have made here should be undertaken before seriously using it.

SELECTED BIBLIOGRAPHY

1 Afifi, A. A., and S. P. Azen: "Statistical Analysis, A Computer Oriented Approach," Academic Press, Inc., New York, 1972.
2 Draper, N. R., and H. Smith: "Applied Regression Analysis," John Wiley & Sons, Inc., New York, 1968.
3 Graybill, F. A.: "An Introduction to Linear Statistical Models," McGraw-Hill Book Company, New York, 1961.
4 Williams, E. J.: "Regression Analysis," John Wiley & Sons, Inc., New York, 1959.

EXERCISES

Exercises 9.1–9.6 do not require the use of a computer while Exercises 9.7–9.11 can best be solved by utilizing the computer.

9.1　Given the following set of data:

x	−2	−1	0	1	2
y	2	3	6	9	10

　　(*a*)　Determine the least-squares linear prediction equation.
　　(*b*)　Calculate the sum of squares of the errors for the linear fit in (*a*).
　　(*c*)　Determine the least-squares quadratic prediction equation.
　　(*d*)　Calculate the sum of squares of the errors for the quadratic fit in (*c*).

9.2　Determine the least-squares linear prediction equation for the data

x	0	1	2	3	4
y	−5	−1	0	2	4

9.3　For the following data, determine the least-squares linear prediction equation which passes through the origin.

x	−1	3	5	6	9
y	−2	1	8	6	15

9.4   For the data in Exercise 9.3, determine the least-squares linear prediction equation which passes through the point (3,2).

9.5   Suppose the model $Y = \beta_0 + \beta_1 X + \epsilon$ is fit using least squares. Analyze the AOV in Table 9.12 and state your conclusions.

Table 9.12

AOV

Source	df	SSQ	MS	Cal F
Total	15	536		
$R(\beta_0)$	1	366		
$R(\beta_1\|\beta_0)$	1	50	50	5.4
Residual	13	120	9.2	
LF	4	70	17.5	3.18
Pure error	9	50	5.5	

9.6   Suppose the model $Y = \beta_0 + \beta_1 X + \epsilon$ is assumed and the partial AOV is given by Table 9.13.

Table 9.13

Source	df	SSQ	MS	Cal F
Total	32	5780		
$R(\beta_0)$		5000		
$R(\beta_1\|\beta_0)$				
Residual		600		
LF				
Pure error	10	100		

(a)   Complete the AOV table.

(b)   Does the model suffer from lack of fit at the 95 percent confidence level? Why?

(c)   What is the value of the square of the multiple correlation coefficient R^2?

(d)   Should the linear term $\beta_1 X$ remain in the model? Why?

(e)   Should more independent variables be added to the model? Why?

(f)   Should higher-order terms in X be added to the current model? Why?

9.7   Consider the track meet data in Table 9.6 in Section 9.3.6.

(a)   Determine the least-squares quadratic prediction equation.

(b)   Calculate the sum of squares of the errors.

(c)   Calculate R^2.

(d)   Would you consider the quadratic fit an adequate fit? Why?

9.8   Extend the AOV in Table 9.9 to include lack of fit and pure error. Does the model $Y = \beta_0 + \beta_1 X_1 + \epsilon$, where X_1 is average speed, suffer from lack of fit at the 95 percent confidence level?

9.9 Fit the model $Y = \beta_0 + \beta_3 X_3 + \epsilon$ to the tire mileage data in Table 9.8, where X_3 is the miles between the rotation of tires in thousands of miles. Set up the complete AOV including lack of fit and pure error.
(a) Does the model suffer from lack of fit?
(b) Can the hypothesis, $H_0: \beta_3 = 0$, be rejected at the 95 percent confidence level?
(c) What is R^2?
(d) Plot the residuals.
(e) What are the least-squares estimates of β_0 and β_3?
(f) Would you recommend using the prediction equation based on the estimates in (e)? Why?

9.10 Write a computer program to find the least-squares estimates of β_0, β_1, and β_3 in the model $Y = \beta_0 + \beta_1 X_1 + \beta_3 X_3 + \epsilon$ using the tire mileage data in Table 9.8. Also calculate R^2.

9.11 Consider the wind chill index data in Table 9.14.

Table 9.14

Wind speed, mi/h	Temperature, degrees								
	50	40	30	20	10	0	−10	−20	−30
0	50	40	30	20	10	0	−10	−20	−30
5	48	37	27	16	6	−5	−15	−26	−36
10	40	28	16	4	−9	−21	−33	−46	−58
15	36	22	9	−5	−18	−36	−45	−58	−72
20	32	18	4	−10	−25	−39	−53	−67	−82
25	30	16	0	−15	−29	−44	−59	−74	−88
30	28	13	−2	−18	−33	−48	−63	−79	−94
35	27	11	−4	−20	−35	−49	−67	−82	−98
40	26	10	−6	−21	−37	−53	−69	−85	−100

(a) Fit the model: $Y = \beta_0 + \beta_1 X_1 + \epsilon$ using least squares, where X_1 is temperature. Analyze the AOV and state your conclusions. Include
   (i) Test for lack of fit.
   (ii) Test for regression ($\beta_1 \neq 0$).
   (iii) R^2.
   (iv) Should more terms be added to the model?
   (v) Plot of residuals $y_i - \hat{y}_i$.
(b) Fit the model: $Y = \beta_0 + \beta_2 X_2 + \epsilon$ using least squares, where X_2 is wind speed. Analyze the AOV and state your conclusions.
(c) Fit the model: $Y = \beta_0 + \beta_1 X_1 + \beta_2 X_2 + \epsilon$ using least squares. (Use the computer program from Exercise 9.10 to obtain the least-squares estimates.) Calculate R^2 and plot the residuals $y_i - \hat{y}_i$. Do you consider this model adequate? Why?

10
DECISION THEORY

10.1 INTRODUCTION

Stochastic OR methods generally are classified as tools that can be used to assist management in making decisions under uncertainty. For example, predicting a future response or outcome may involve a great deal of uncertainty. Consequently, a statistical tool, such as *regression analysis*, can be used to determine the relationship between the important factors and the response to provide management with an equation that will adequately predict future responses. Likewise, *queueing theory* can be used to determine the number of service facilities to provide for customer service, the arrangement of queues to feed the service facilities, etc. In general, each stochastic OR method is used to solve problems that can be formulated as a certain type of model.

Decision theory is one such stochastic OR tool that can be used to assist management in making decisions under uncertainty. We will consider the situation that involves

1 A decision maker who has a finite number of courses of action available
2 A finite number of possible outcomes or states of nature for each action
3 A loss that is incurred for each action–state of nature combination

The decision maker would naturally like to choose an action that would minimize loss, regardless of the actual state of nature. However, this is rarely ever realized. For example, on any given morning we have the option of taking or not taking a raincoat to work. Thus, we have two courses of action available. Likewise, there can be two possible states of nature: it *will* rain, or it *will not* rain. If we take a raincoat and it rains, we could say that no loss is incurred. However, if we take a raincoat and it does not rain, we are inconvenienced unnecessarily, so we might say that a loss of 3 units is incurred. If we do not take a raincoat and it rains, a loss of 6 units is incurred. Finally, if we do not take a raincoat and it does not rain, there is no loss. Table 10.1 illustrates the courses of action, the states of nature, and the corresponding losses. In this example, no single action would minimize the loss for all states of nature.

Basically, the amount of uncertainty associated with a problem influences the approach used by the decision maker. For example, if the state of nature is known with certainty for each action, and if the corresponding loss is known or can be calculated, the problem is easily solved. The decision-making process in this case is called *decision making under certainty*. If only the probability of each state of nature for each action is *known*, then the process is called *decision making under risk*. On the other hand, if a course of action must be chosen without any knowledge of the state of nature, then this is *decision making under uncertainty*. The latter two cases will be examined in detail since they are the only two of real interest.

Consider the general framework of the decision problem we have been discussing. Suppose we let

$A = \{a_1, a_2, \ldots, a_m\}$ be the class of all possible actions available to the decision maker

$\theta = \{\theta_1, \theta_2, \ldots, \theta_n\}$ be the class of all states of nature

$l(a_i, \theta_j)$ = the loss from using action a_i when the true state of nature is θ_j

Specifically, consider the courses of action, the states of nature, and the corresponding losses illustrated in Table 10.2.

The decision maker is interested in minimizing loss, so the decision maker would like to choose an action a_i that would minimize the loss, regardless of the true state of nature. Usually this is not possible. Hence, the decision maker must resort to methods that will keep the loss at a minimum, based on the amount of available information about the state of nature.

Table 10.1 DECISION TABLE

Actions	States of nature	
	Rain	No rain
Take raincoat	0	3
Do not take raincoat	6	0

Table 10.2 GENERAL DECISION TABLE

Actions	States of nature					
	θ_1	θ_2	$\cdots$	θ_j	$\cdots$	θ_n
a_1	$l(a_1,\theta_1)$	$l(a_1,\theta_2)$	$\cdots$	$l(a_1,\theta_j)$	$\cdots$	$l(a_1,\theta_n)$
a_2	$l(a_2,\theta_1)$	$l(a_2,\theta_2)$	$\cdots$	$l(a_2,\theta_j)$	$\cdots$	$l(a_2,\theta_n)$
$\vdots$						
a_i	$l(a_i,\theta_1)$	$l(a_i,\theta_2)$	$\cdots$	$l(a_i,\theta_j)$	$\cdots$	$l(a_i,\theta_n)$
$\vdots$						
a_m	$l(a_m,\theta_1)$	$l(a_m,\theta_2)$	$\cdots$	$l(a_m,\theta_j)$	$\cdots$	$l(a_m,\theta_n)$

10.2 MINIMAX DECISION PROCEDURE

Generally, some type of information is known about the likelihood of the occurrence of each state of nature. However, in the absence of any information about the states of nature, a number of decision procedures are available to use. The most conservative of these is the *minimax decision procedure*. It assumes that nature is an active opponent who is out to get the decision maker. Consequently, the decision maker examines the maximum loss that would be incurred for each action, and selects the action with the smallest maximum loss. This is illustrated in Example 10.2.1.

EXAMPLE 10.2.1 Consider the decision problem with the loss table in Table 10.3. Note that if action a_1 is selected, a loss of 4, 7, or 3 units is incurred if the state of nature is θ_1, θ_2, or θ_3, respectively. Of course, the maximum loss in this case would be 7 units. Likewise, action a_2 would incur a maximum loss of 5 units; a_3, 10 units; and finally, a_4, 9 units. The decision maker then selects the action that would result in the smallest maximum loss, regardless of the true state of nature. In this case, the smallest maximum loss is 5, which corresponds to action a_2.

Table 10.3

Actions	States of nature			max $[l(a_i,\theta)]$
	θ_1	θ_2	θ_3	θ
a_1	4	7	3	7
a_2	5	2	4	⑤
a_3	8	6	10	10
a_4	3	1	9	9

$$\min_{A} \left\{ \max_{\theta} \left[l(A,\theta) \right] \right\} = 5$$

Generally, the minimax decision procedure should be used only when nature is an active opponent who is trying to maximize the decision maker's loss, or if the decision maker is interested only in keeping the maximum loss at a minimum, regardless of the state of nature.

10.3 BAYES DECISION PROCEDURE WITHOUT DATA

Suppose nature is not an active opponent. In this case, the decision maker would probably want to make a decision based on some type of expected loss. However, this would require that a probability be assigned to each state of nature. But how are the probabilities obtained? It would be most unusual if the decision maker did not have any information about the likelihood of the occurrence of each state of nature. Generally, the decision maker would at least have an intuitive feeling about the various states of nature. In any case, regardless of how the initial distribution of θ is obtained, the decision maker can use this distribution to calculate the expected loss for each action, and then select the action with the smallest expected loss. This is *Bayes decision procedure.* If the probabilities associated with the states of nature are available from previous experience and/or from intuition, the procedure for making a decision is called *Bayes decision procedure without data.* In this case, the probability distribution of the state of nature θ is called the *prior distribution* of θ. This prior distribution is used to obtain the expected loss for each action, and then the action is selected that has the smallest expected loss.

EXAMPLE 10.3.1 Consider the decision problem in Example 10.2.1. If the prior distribution of θ is

$$P_\theta(\theta_j) = P(\theta = \theta_j) = \begin{cases} \dfrac{1}{2} & \theta = \theta_1 \\[2mm] \dfrac{1}{3} & \theta = \theta_2 \\[2mm] \dfrac{1}{6} & \theta = \theta_3 \end{cases}$$

then the expected loss for action a_1 is

$$\underset{\theta}{E}[l(a_1, \theta)] = \frac{1}{2} l(a_1, \theta_1) + \frac{1}{3} l(a_1, \theta_2) + \frac{1}{6} l(a_1, \theta_3)$$

$$= \frac{1}{2}(4) + \frac{1}{3}(7) + \frac{1}{6}(3)$$

$$= \frac{29}{6}$$

For actions a_2, a_3, and a_4, the expected losses are

$$E_\theta[l(a_2, \theta)] = \frac{1}{2}(5) + \frac{1}{3}(2) + \frac{1}{6}(4)$$

$$= \frac{23}{6}$$

$$E_\theta[l(a_3, \theta)] = \frac{1}{2}(8) + \frac{1}{3}(6) + \frac{1}{6}(10)$$

$$= \frac{46}{6}$$

$$E_\theta[l(a_4, \theta)] = \frac{1}{2}(3) + \frac{1}{3}(1) + \frac{1}{6}(9)$$

$$= \frac{20}{6}$$

The complete analysis is given by Table 10.4. Thus, the Bayes decision procedure using the prior distribution of θ leads to the selection of action a_4 since it has the minimum expected loss.

EXAMPLE 10.3.2 Suppose an outdoor equipment store must determine the volume of ski equipment to order for use during a given ski season. Sales are primarily a function of the general ski conditions throughout the season in the local area. Based on past data, it is determined that ski conditions will be excellent, good, or poor with probability 0.5, 0.4, and 0.1, respectively. Management must decide whether to have a high, medium, or low volume of equipment on hand at the beginning of the season, since the delivery time to get additional equipment is approximately 2 months. The expected profit for each action and state of nature is given in Table 10.5 as an expected loss. For example, a loss of -20 units (profit of 20 units) is incurred if a high volume is stocked and ski conditions are excellent.

Table 10.4

	States of nature			
	θ_1	θ_2	θ_3	
Actions	$P(\theta = \theta_1) = \frac{1}{2}$	$P(\theta = \theta_2) = \frac{1}{3}$	$P(\theta = \theta_3) = \frac{1}{6}$	$E[l(a_i, \theta)]$
a_1	4	7	3	29/6
a_2	5	2	4	23/6
a_3	8	6	10	46/6
a_4	3	1	9	20/6

$$\min_A \left\{ E_\theta[l(A, \theta)] \right\} = \frac{20}{6}$$

Table 10.5 STATES OF NATURE (SKI CONDITIONS)

Action: volume on hand	θ_1 Excellent $P_{\theta_1} = 0.5$	θ_2 Good $P_{\theta_2} = 0.4$	θ_3 Poor $P_{\theta_3} = 0.1$	$\max_{\theta} [l(a_i,\theta)]$	$E[l(a_i,\theta)]$
a_1: high	-20	-12	-6	-6	-15.4
a_2: med	-16	-16	-8	-8	-15.2
a_3: low	-12	-12	-12	-12	-12.0

$$\min_A \left\{ \max_\theta [l(A,\theta)] \right\} = -12$$

$$\min_A \left\{ E[l(A,\theta)] \right\} = -15.4$$

The minimax decision procedure is to choose action a_3. This decision will result in a maximum profit of 12 units. Bayes decision procedure is to choose action a_1, from which an expected profit of 15.4 units will result.

10.3.1 Algorithm 10.1—Bayes Decision Procedure without Data

Assume the general decision table in Table 10.2, and let $P(\theta = \theta_j)$ be the prior distribution of the state of nature θ.

Step 1
Use the prior distribution of θ to calculate the expected loss for each action a_i with $i = 1, 2, \ldots, m$. That is, let

$$E_\theta[l(a_i, \theta)] = \sum_{j=1}^{n} l(a_i, \theta_j) \cdot P(\theta = \theta_j) \quad \text{for } i = 1, 2, \ldots, m$$

Step 2
Select the action that has the smallest expected loss. Stop.

10.4 BAYES DECISION PROCEDURE WITH DATA

The decision maker should always be aware of additional information that might be used to assist the decision-making process. There is usually good information and bad information available; hence, discretion must be used in selecting information. Quite often it is possible to obtain reliable information about the state of nature so that a more realistic estimate of the distribution of the state of nature can be obtained. For example, suppose we know the distribution of a random variable X that is a function of the state of nature θ. In particular, let $Q_X(x|\theta = \theta_j)$ be the conditional distribution of X, given that $\theta = \theta_j$. We can use this information and the prior distribution of θ to obtain an updated distribution of θ as a function of X. This updated distribution is called the *posterior distribution* of θ. The *Bayes decision procedure with data* is to obtain the posterior distribution of θ for a specific value of X, and then to choose the action which minimizes the expected loss using the posterior distribution.

In general, we assume the following information is known:

$$\theta = \text{random variable representing the state of nature}$$
$$X = \text{random variable that is related to } \theta$$
$$P_\theta(\theta_j) = \text{prior distribution of } \theta$$
$$Q_X(x|\theta = \theta_j) = \text{conditional distribution of } X, \text{ given } \theta = \theta_j$$

We want to determine

$$h_\theta(\theta_j|X = x) = \text{conditional distribution of } \theta, \text{ given } X = x$$

The distribution $h_\theta(\theta_j|X = x)$ is called the *posterior distribution* of θ. It is an updated distribution based on known information about X.

To determine $h_\theta(\theta_j|X = x)$, we define

$$g_X(x) = \text{marginal distribution of } X$$
$$f_{X\theta}(x,\theta_j) = \text{joint distribution of } X \text{ and } \theta$$

Both of these distributions are unknown, but can be used to determine $h_\theta(\theta_j|X = x)$. Specifically, $f_{X\theta}(x,\theta_j)$ and $g_X(x)$ can be written in terms of known distributions as follows:

$$f_{X\theta}(x, \theta_j) = Q_X(x|\theta = \theta_j)P_\theta(\theta_j) \tag{10.1}$$

$$g_X(x) = \sum_{j=1}^{n} f_{X\theta}(x, \theta_j)$$

$$= \sum_{j=1}^{n} Q_X(x|\theta = \theta_j)P_\theta(\theta_j) \tag{10.2}$$

Thus,

$$h_\theta(\theta_j|X = x) = \frac{f_{X\theta}(x, \theta_j)}{g_X(x)} \tag{10.3}$$

$$= \frac{Q_X(x|\theta = \theta_j)P_\theta(\theta_j)}{\sum_{k=1}^{n} Q_X(x|\theta = \theta_k)P_\theta(\theta_k)} \tag{10.4}$$

We now have a procedure to obtain a posterior distribution of θ for a specific value of the random variable X. The expected loss for each action a_i, based on this posterior distribution, is then

$$E_\theta[l(a_i, \theta)] = \sum_{j=1}^{n} h_\theta(\theta_j|X = x)l(a_i, \theta_j) \qquad i = 1, 2, \ldots, m \tag{10.5}$$

The action that results in the smallest expected loss, as calculated in Equation (10.5), is the Bayes decision with data. These concepts are illustrated in Example 10.4.1.

EXAMPLE 10.4.1 Suppose an outdoor equipment store must decide on whether to stock a high, medium, or low volume of ski equipment for the coming season. It is known from past data that the demand for ski equipment for a given season has a normal distribution with a variance of 10 and a mean of either 5, 10, or 15 units, depending on the ski conditions throughout the season. Thus, let

X = demand for ski equipment for a given season
θ = mean of the random variable X

The prior distribution of θ is determined to be

$$P_\theta(\theta_j) = \begin{cases} 0.2 & \theta = \theta_1 = 5 \\ 0.5 & \theta = \theta_2 = 10 \\ 0.3 & \theta = \theta_3 = 15 \end{cases}$$

Table 10.6 illustrates that the Bayes decision, based on the prior distribution of θ, is to stock a high volume of ski equipment. The decision yields a minimum expected loss of -13.6 units, which represents a maximum expected profit of 13.6 units.

If reliable information is available and can be used to update our thinking about θ, then certainly it should be used. In the present example, the conditional distribution of X, given $\theta = \theta_j$, is known to be

$$Q_X(x|\theta = \theta_j) = \frac{1}{\sqrt{2\pi}\sqrt{10}} e^{-1/2[(x-\theta_j)/\sqrt{10}]^2} \quad \text{for } \theta_j = 5, 10, 15$$

Hence, the posterior distribution of θ is

Table 10.6 BAYES DECISION WITHOUT DATA
STATES OF NATURE (MEAN DEMAND)

Actions: volume to stock	θ_1 $P_\theta(5) = 0.2$	θ_2 $P_\theta(10) = 0.5$	θ_3 $P_\theta(15) = 0.3$	$\underset{\theta}{E}[l(a_i,\theta)]$
a_1: high	-8	-12	-20	-13.6
a_2: medium	-10	-14	-14	-13.2
a_3: low	-12	-12	-12	-12.0
			$\underset{A}{\min}\left\{\underset{\theta}{E}[l(A,\theta)]\right\} =$	-13.6

$$h_\theta(\theta_j | X = x) = \frac{Q_X(x|\theta = \theta_j)P_\theta(\theta_j)}{\sum\limits_{k=1}^{3} Q_X(x|\theta = \theta_k)P_\theta(\theta_k)}$$

It is estimated from preseason research that the demand for the coming season will be 10 units. We want to combine this estimate with the prior distribution of the mean demand θ to obtain a posterior distribution of θ. That is, let

$$h_\theta(\theta_j | X = 10) = \frac{\dfrac{1}{\sqrt{2\pi}\sqrt{10}}\, e^{-1/2[(10-\theta_j)/\sqrt{10}]^2}\, P_\theta(\theta_j)}{\sum\limits_{k=1}^{3}\left\{\dfrac{1}{\sqrt{2\pi}\sqrt{10}}\, e^{-1/2[(10-\theta_k)/\sqrt{10}]^2}\, P_\theta(\theta_k)\right\}}$$

For $\theta = \theta_1 = 5$,

$$h_\theta(5 | X = 10) = \frac{\dfrac{1}{\sqrt{2\pi}\sqrt{10}}\, e^{-1/2[(10-5)/\sqrt{10}]^2}\, P_\theta(5)}{\dfrac{1}{\sqrt{2\pi}\sqrt{10}}\sum\limits_{k=1}^{3}\left\{e^{-1/2[(10-\theta_k)/\sqrt{10}]^2}\, P_\theta(\theta_k)\right\}}$$

$$= \frac{(0.2)e^{-1/2(2.5)}}{(0.2)e^{-1/2(2.5)} + (0.5) + (0.3)e^{-1/2(2.5)}}$$

$$= 0.089$$

For $\theta = \theta_2 = 10$,

$$h_\theta(10 | X = 10) = \frac{0.5}{(0.2)e^{-1/2(2.5)} + 0.5 + (0.3)e^{-1/2(2.5)}}$$

$$= 0.777$$

For $\theta = \theta_3 = 15$,

$$h_\theta(15 | X = 10) = \frac{(0.3)e^{-\frac{1}{2}(2.5)}}{(0.2)e^{-\frac{1}{2}(2.5)} + 0.5 + (0.3)e^{-\frac{1}{2}(2.5)}}$$

$$= 0.134$$

The posterior distribution of θ, given $X = 10$, is then

$$h_\theta(\theta_j | X = 10) = \begin{cases} 0.089 & \theta = 5 \\ 0.777 & \theta = 10 \\ 0.134 & \theta = 15 \end{cases}$$

Table 10.7 BAYES ANALYSIS WITH DATA

Actions: volume to stock	$\theta_1 = 5$ $h_\theta(5\|X=10)=0.089$	$\theta_2 = 10$ $h_\theta(10\|X=10)=0.777$	$\theta_3 = 15$ $h_\theta(15\|X=10)=0.134$	$E[l(a_i,\theta)]$ θ
a_1 : high	-8	-12	-20	-12.716
a_2 : medium	-10	-14	-14	-13.644
a_3 : low	-12	-12	-12	-12.000

$$\min_{A} \left\{ E[l(A,\theta)] \right\} = -13.644$$
$$\theta$$

The complete analysis is summarized in Table 10.7.

Thus, the Bayes decision procedure using the posterior distribution of θ, given $X = 10$, leads to the selection of action a_2 to stock a medium volume of ski equipment. The expected profit in this case would be 13.644 units. In summary, we see that Bayes procedure switched from action a_1 to action a_2 when additional information about the demand was provided.

10.4.1 Algorithm 10.2—Bayes Decision Procedure with Data

Assume the distributions

$$P_\theta(\theta_j) = \text{prior distribution of } \theta \quad j = 1, 2, \ldots, n$$
$$Q_X(x|\theta = \theta_j) = \text{conditional distribution of } X \text{ given } \theta = \theta_j$$

Step 1
Determine the posterior distribution of θ. That is, let

$$h_\theta(\theta_j|X = x) = \frac{Q_X(x|\theta = \theta_j)P_\theta(\theta_j)}{\displaystyle\sum_{k=1}^{n} [Q_X(x|\theta = \theta_k)P_\theta(\theta_k)]}$$

Step 2
Obtain a reliable value of the random variable X, say x^*.

Step 3
Use the posterior distribution $h_\theta(\theta_j|X = x^*)$ to calculate the expected loss for each action a_i with $i = 1, 2, \ldots, m$.

$$E_\theta[l(a_i,\theta)] = \sum_{j=1}^{n} h_\theta(\theta_j|X = x^*)l(a_i, \theta_j) \quad i = 1, 2, \ldots, m$$

Step 4
Select the action that has the smallest expected loss. Stop.

10.4.2 General Computer Program for Algorithms 10.1 and 10.2

This is a general computer program to carry out the Bayes decision procedure with and without data. As with all computer programs in this textbook, the comment cards at the beginning of the program explain what the program does and how to use it.

The conditional distribution of X, given $\theta = \theta_j$, is a statement function which is the first executable statement of the program. For example, if

$$Q_X(x|\theta = \theta_j) = \frac{1}{\sqrt{2\pi}\sqrt{10}} e^{-1/2[(x-\theta_j)/\sqrt{10}]^2}$$

the statement function would appear as:

$$Q(X,T)=EXP(-((X-T)/SQRT(10))**2/2)/SQRT(20*3.1416)$$

where T is a value of the random variable θ.

The program is set up for a maximum of 40 courses of action and 50 states of nature. To modify the program to handle larger problems with M courses of action and N states of nature, change the DIMENSION and INTEGER statements to

DIMENSION A(M,N),P(N),EL(M),HTHETA(N),ELPOST(M)

INTEGER XSTAR,THETA(N),TJ,X,T

The program as written occupies 48K bytes of core storage. The data and results for Example 10.3.1 and for Examples 10.3.2 and 10.4.1 follow the program listing.

```
C     ******************************************************************************
C     *                                                                            *
C     *            ***   ALGORITHMS  10.1 AND 10.2  ***                             *
C     *                                                                            *
C     *        BAYES DECISION PROCEDURE WITH AND WITHOUT DATA                       *
C     *                                                                            *
C     * THIS IS A GENERAL COMPUTER PROGRAM TO CARRY CUT THE BAYES DECISION          *
C     * PROCEDURE WITH AND WITHOUT DATA.                                            *
C     *                                                                            *
C     * THIS PROGRAM IS SET UP FOR A MAXIMUM OF 40 COURSES OF ACTION AND 50         *
C     * STATES OF NATURE.  TO MODIFY THE PROGRAM TO HANDLE LARGER PROBLEMS          *
C     * WITH  M  COURSES OF ACTION AND  N  STATES OF NATURE, CHANGE THE             *
C     * DIMENSION AND INTEGER STATEMENTS TO                                         *
C     *              DIMENSION A(M,N),P(N),EL(M),ELPOST(M),HTHETA(N)                *
C     *              INTEGER XSTAR, THETA(N), TJ, X, T                              *
C     *                                                                            *
C     * THE PROGRAM,AS WRITTEN, OCCUPIES 48 K BYTES OF CORE STORAGE.                *
C     *                                                                            *
C     * IT IS DESIGNED                                                             *
C     *                                                                            *
C     *     TO READ                                                                *
C     *        CARD 1    COLS  2-80   TITLE  DESCRIPTION OF THE PROBLEM USING       *
C     *                                      ANY CHARACTERS ON KEYPUNCH            *
C     *                                      ** COLUMN 1 MUST BE LEFT BLANK **     *
C     *        CARD 2    COLS  1- 5   NFLAG  FLAG TO INDICATE PRESENCE OR          *
C     *                                      ABSENCE OF DATA:  0  WITHOUT DATA     *
C     *                                                        1  WITH DATA (I5)   *
C     *        CARD 3    COLS  1- 5   M  # OF COURSES OF ACTION   (I5)             *
C     *                        6-10   N  # OF STATES OF NATURE    (I5)             *
C     *        CARDS 4 TO T   A(I,J)  LOSS MATRIX                                  *
C     *                               READ DATA ROWWISE IN 8F10.0 FORMAT          *
C     *                               IF  N>8, CONTINUE ON A NEW CARD             *
C     *                               START EACH NEW ROW ON A NEW CARD            *
C     *        CARD T+1  P(J)  PRIOR DISTRIBUTION OF THE STATES OF NATURE         *
C     *                        READ IN 8F10.0 FORMAT.  IF  N>8, CONTINUE          *
C     *                        ON A NEW CARD.                                     *
C     *        CARD T+2  THETA(J)  STATES OF NATURE  (8I10)                       *
C     *                        IF  N>8, CONTINUE ON A NEW CARD                    *
C     *        CARD T+3  COLS  1-10   XSTAR  SAMPLE VALUE OF X    (I10)           *
C     *              TO SOLVE MORE THAN ONE PROBLEM AT A TIME, REPEAT THE          *
C     *              READ SEQUENCE, AND STACK THE DATA ONE BEHIND THE OTHER        *
C     *                                                                            *
C     *     TO CALCULATE                                                          *
C     *        HTHETA(J)  POSTERIOR DISTRIBUTION OF THE STATE OF NATURE           *
C     *                   THETA(J)   (J=1,2,...,N)                                *
C     *        EL(I)      EXPECTED LOSS FOR EACH COURSE OF ACTION BASED ON        *
C     *                   PRIOR DISTRIBUTION  (I=1,2,...,M)                        *
C     *        SMALL      MINIMUM OF EL(I)                                         *
C     *        INDEX      ACTICN CORRESPONDING TO SMALL                            *
C     *        ELPOST(I)  EXPECTED LOSS FOR EACH COURSE OF ACTION BASED ON        *
C     *                   POSTERIOR DISTRIBUTION  (I=1,2,...,M)                    *
C     *        SMPOST     MINIMUM OF ELPOST(I)                                     *
C     *        INPOST     ACTION CORRESPONDING TO SMPOST                           *
C     *                                                                            *
C     *     TO PRINT                                                              *
C     *        ECHO CHECK OF DATA                                                  *
C     *        EL(I), SMALL, INDEX                                                 *
C     *        ELPOST(I), SMPOST, INPOST                                          *
C     *        HTHETA(J)                                                          *
C     *                                                                            *
C     ******************************************************************************
      DIMENSION A(40,50),P(50),EL(40),HTHETA(50),ELPOST(40)
      INTEGER XSTAR,THETA(50),TJ,X,T
      REAL*4 TITLE(20)
C DEFINE STATEMENT FUNCTICN TO BE USED LATER
      Q(X,T)=EXP(-((X-T)/SQRT(10.))**2/2)/SQRT(20.*3.1416)
C  READ IN DATA
    5 READ(5,10,END=200)TITLE
   10 FORMAT(20A4)
      WRITE(6,6)TITLE
    6 FORMAT('1',20A4,//)
```

```
      READ(5,15)NFLAG
   15 FORMAT(2I5)
      READ(5,15)M,N
      DO 20 I=1,M
   20 READ(5,25)(A(I,J),J=1,N)
   25 FORMAT(8F10.0)
      READ(5,25)(P(J),J=1,N)
      IF(NFLAG.EQ.0) GO TO 99
      READ(5,130)(THETA(J),J=1,N)
      READ(5,130)XSTAR
  130 FORMAT(8I10)
   99 WRITE(6,100)
  100 FORMAT(9X,'STATES OF NATURE'/' ACTIONS'/)
      DO 105 I=1,M
  105 WRITE(6,110)(A(I,J),J=1,N)
  110 FORMAT( 8F10.4)
      WRITE(6,111)(P(J),J=1,N)
  111 FORMAT( //'   PRIOR DISTRIBUTION OF STATES OF NATURE',/  8F10.4)
C     *******************************************************************
C     *                                                               *
C     *   STEPS 1,2                                                    *
C     *          CALCULATE THE EXPECTED LOSS FOR EACH ACTION BY USING THE *
C     *          PRIOR DISTRIBUTIONS OF THETA.                         *
C     *          SELECT THE ACTION HAVING THE SMALLEST EXPECTED LOSS   *
C     *******************************************************************
      SMALL=10.E10
      DO 30 I=1,M
      EL(I)=0.0
      DO 35 J=1,N
   35 EL(I)=EL(I) + P(J)*A(I,J)
      IF(EL(I).GE.SMALL) GO TO 30
      SMALL=EL(I)
      INDEX=I
   30 CONTINUE
C     *******************************************************************
C     *                                                               *
C     *   STEP 3                                                       *
C     *          IF PROBLEM HAS DATA, GO TO STEP 4.  OTHERWISE, PROBLEM IS *
C     *          COMPLETED, SO PRINT RESULTS                           *
C     *******************************************************************
      IF(NFLAG.EQ.0) GO TO 101
C     *******************************************************************
C     *   STEP 4    (STEP 1 - ALGORITHM 10.2)                          *
C     *          CALCULATE THE POSTERIOR DISTRIBUTION OF THE STATES OF NATURE *
C     *******************************************************************
      GX=0.0
      DO 150 J=1,N
      TJ=THETA(J)
  150 GX=GX+Q(XSTAR,TJ)*P(J)
      DO 160 J=1,N
      TJ=THETA(J)
  160 HTHETA(J)=Q(XSTAR,TJ)*P(J)/GX
      WRITE(6,112)XSTAR
  112 FORMAT( //'   SAMPLE VALUE OF X IS ',I10)
      WRITE(6,113)(THETA(J),J=1,N)
  113 FORMAT( // '  STATES OF NATURE', / 8I10)
      WRITE(6,115)(HTHETA(J),J=1,N)
  115 FORMAT(//'   POSTERIOR DISTRIBUTION OF STATES OF NATURE',/8F10.4)
C     *******************************************************************
C     *   STEP 5    (STEP 3,4 - ALGORITHM 10.2)                        *
C     *          CALCULATE THE EXPECTED LOSS FOR EACH ACTION USING THE *
C     *          POSTERIOR DISTRIBUTION                                *
C     *          SELECT ACTION HAVING SMALLEST EXPECTED LOSS           *
C     *******************************************************************
      SMPOST=10.E10
      DO 170 I=1,M
      ELPOST(I)=0.0
      DO 175 J=1,N
  175 ELPOST(I)=ELPOST(I)+HTHETA(J)*A(I,J)
      IF(ELPOST(I).GE.SMPOST) GO TO 170
      SMPOST=ELPOST(I)
      INPOST=I
  170 CONTINUE
```

```
C      **********************************************************************
C      *    STEP 6     PRINT RESULTS                                        *
C      **********************************************************************
  101 WRITE(6,114)
  114 FORMAT(///' RESULTS'/'+',    7('_')//)
      WRITE(6,40)(EL(I),I=1,M)
   40 FORMAT('    EXPECTED LOSS FOR EACH COURSE OF ACTION BASED ON PRIOR
     *DISTRIBUTION',/   8F10.4)
      WRITE(6,45)SMALL,INDEX
   45 FORMAT(//10X,'THE MINIMUM EXPECTED LOSS USING THE PRIOR DISTRIBUTI
     *ON OF'/10X,'THE STATE OF NATURE IS',F12.6//14X,'CHOOSE ACTION A(',
     *I2,')')
      IF(NFLAG.EQ.0) GO TO 5
      WRITE(6,180)(ELPOST(I),I=1,M)
  180 FORMAT( //'    EXPECTED LOSS FOR EACH COURSE OF ACTION BASED ON THE
     * POSTERIOR DISTRIBUTION',/  8F10.4)
      WRITE(6,185)SMPOST,INPOST
  185 FORMAT(//10X,'THE MINIMUM EXPECTED LOSS USING THE POSTERIOR DISTRI
     *BUTION'/10X,'OF THE STATE OF NATURE IS',F12.6,//14X,'CHOOSE ACTION
     * A(',I2,')')
      GO TO 5
  200 STOP
      END


/DATA

EXAMPLE 10.3.1
    0
    4      3
 4.           7.          3.
 5.           2.          4.
 8.           6.         10.
 3.           1.          9.
 0.5          0.333330    0.16667
EXAMPLES 10.3.2 AND 10.4.1
    1
    3      3
 -8.          -12.        -20.
 -10.         -14.        -14.
 -12.         -12.        -12.
 0.2          0.5         0.3
          5           10          15
         10
```

EXAMPLE 10.3.1

          STATES OF NATURE
ACTIONS

```
     4.0000     7.0000     3.0000
     5.0000     2.0000     4.0000
     8.0000     6.0000    10.0000
     3.0000     1.0000     9.0000
```


  PRIOR DISTRIBUTION OF STATES OF NATURE
```
  0.5000     0.3333     0.1667
```

RESULTS

EXPECTED LOSS FOR EACH COURSE OF ACTION BASED ON PRIOR DISTRIBUTION
  4.8333   3.8333   7.6667   3.3334

            THE MINIMUM EXPECTED LOSS USING THE PRIOR DISTRIBUTION OF
            THE STATE OF NATURE IS   3.333359

                CHOOSE ACTION A(4)

EXAMPLES 10.3.2 AND 10.4.1

            STATES OF NATURE
ACTIONS

  -8.0000   -12.0000   -20.0000
 -10.0000   -14.0000   -14.0000
 -12.0000   -12.0000   -12.0000

  PRIOR DISTRIBUTION OF STATES OF NATURE
    0.2000   C.5000   0.3000

  SAMPLE VALUE OF X IS   10

  STATES OF NATURE
        5   10   15

  POSTERIOR DISTRIBUTION OF STATES OF NATURE
    0.0891   0.7773   0.1336

RESULTS

  EXPECTED LOSS FOR EACH COURSE OF ACTION BASED ON PRIOR DISTRIBUTION
 -13.6000   -13.2000   -12.0000

            THE MINIMUM EXPECTED LOSS USING THE PRIOR DISTRIBUTION OF
            THE STATE OF NATURE IS   -13.599999

                CHOOSE ACTION A(1)

  EXPECTED LOSS FOR EACH COURSE OF ACTION BASED ON THE POSTERIOR DISTRIBUTION
 -12.7126   -13.6437   -12.0000

            THE MINIMUM EXPECTED LOSS USING THE POSTERIOR DISTRIBUTION
            OF THE STATE OF NATURE IS   -13.643685

                CHOOSE ACTION A(2)

10.5 REGRET FUNCTION VS. LOSS FUNCTION

The loss function used in the previous sections is only one measure of the consequences of choosing a certain action when the true state of nature is θ_j with $j = 1, 2, \ldots, n$. Another measure preferred by many is the regret function. It alleviates the situation in which a loss is incurred, even if the true state of nature is known and the best action is selected. Specifically, the regret for each action–state of nature combination is defined to be

$$r(a_i, \theta_j) = l(a_i, \theta_j) - \min_A l(a_k, \theta_j) \quad \begin{array}{l} i = 1, 2, \ldots, m \\ j = 1, 2, \ldots, n \end{array}$$

Thus, for each state of nature θ_j, some action will result in a regret of zero. That is, suppose

$$l(a_t, \theta_j) = \min_A [l(a_k, \theta_j)]$$

then for $i = t$,

$$r(a_t, \theta_j) = l(a_t, \theta_j) - l(a_t, \theta_j) = 0$$

For every other action $a_i \neq a_t$, an amount $r(a_i, \theta_j)$ will be *regretted* when the state of nature is θ_j.

It is easy to show that the loss and regret measures both lead to the same decision when Bayes decision procedure is used. However, the minimax decision procedure may lead to a different decision when the regret measure is used in place of the loss measure. This is illustrated in Example 10.5.1.

EXAMPLE 10.5.1 Consider the decision problem with the loss measures given in Table 10.8. The minimax decision is to select action a_4. The maximum loss would then be 6 units. The corresponding risk table is displayed in Table 10.9.

Hence, the minimax decision using the regret measure is to select action a_1. This decision will result in a maximum loss of 4 units of regret.

Table 10.8 LOSS TABLE

Actions	States of nature θ_1	θ_2	θ_3	max $[l(a_i,\theta)]$ θ
a_1	3	8	1	8
a_2	9	6	5	9
a_3	7	4	8	8
a_4	5	5	6	⑥

$$\min_A \left\{ \max_\theta [l(A,\theta)] \right\} = 6$$

Table 10.9 RISK TABLE

Actions	States of nature θ_1	θ_2	θ_3	max $[l(a_i,\theta)]$ θ
a_1	0	4	0	④
a_2	6	2	4	6
a_3	4	0	7	7
a_4	2	1	5	5

$$\min_A \left\{ \max_\theta [l(A,\theta)] \right\} = 4$$

In summary, if the regret measure is used, the decision maker can be assured that for every state of nature there is at least one action available that will result in no regret. However, when the Bayes procedure is used, it really does not matter whether the loss measure or the regret measure is used. Both will lead to the same decision. When the minimax procedure is used, there is general disagreement as to which measure should be used, since quite often each measure leads to a different decision.

SELECTED BIBLIOGRAPHY

1 Chernoff, H., and L. E. Moses: "Elementary Decision Theory," John Wiley & Sons, Inc., New York, 1959.
2 Hadley, G.: "Introduction to Probability and Statistical Decision Theory," Holden-Day, Inc., San Francisco, 1967.
3 Martin, J. J.: "Bayesian Decision Problems and Markov Chains," John Wiley & Sons, Inc., New York, 1967.
4 Newman, J. W.: "Management Applications of Decision Theory," Harper & Row Publishers, Inc., New York, 1971.
5 Pratt, J. W., H. Raiffa, and R. O. Schlaifer: "Introduction to Statistical Decision Theory," McGraw-Hill Book Company, New York, 1965.
6 Raiffa, H.: "Decision Analysis," Addison-Wesley Publishing Company, Inc., Reading, Mass., 1968.
7 Schlaifer, R.: "Analysis of Decisions under Uncertainty," McGraw-Hill Book Company, New York, 1969.
8 Weiss, L.: "Statistical Decision Theory," McGraw-Hill Book Company, New York, 1961.
9 Winkler, R. L.: "Introduction to Bayesian Inference and Decision," Holt, Rinehart and Winston, Inc., New York, 1972.

EXERCISES

10.1 Consider the decision problem with the loss table below. What is the minimax action?

A: actions	θ_1	θ_2	θ_3
a_1	5	3	5
a_2	8	6	3
a_3	9	4	2
a_4	8	3	4
a_5	7	1	10

θ: states of nature

10.2 Suppose a decision maker has obtained the following loss table:

	θ: states of nature		
A: actions	θ_1	θ_2	θ_3
a_1	3	2	1
a_2	2	1	9
a_3	6	3	7

(a) What is the minimax action?
(b) If the prior distribution of θ is

$$P(\theta = \theta_j) = \begin{cases} 0.4 & \theta = \theta_1 \\ 0.5 & \theta = \theta_2 \\ 0.1 & \theta = \theta_3 \end{cases}$$

What is the Bayes decision?

10.3 The first thing each morning a college student must make a decision; should he roll over and stay in bed, get up and go to class with an umbrella, or get up and go to class without an umbrella. The student has determined the loss corresponding to each decision and state of nature to be:

	States of nature	
	θ_1: rain	θ_2: no rain
a_1: skip class	4	4
a_2: go—take umbrella	2	5
a_3: go—do not take umbrella	5	0

The local weather report has predicted rain with probability 0.7.

(a) What is the minimax action?
(b) What is the Bayes decision?
(c) Suppose the weather report revises the forecast to indicate that the probability of rain is 0.6. What is the Bayes decision?

10.4 If the probability of excellent, good, or poor ski conditions is changed to 0.4, 0.5, or 0.1, respectively, in Example 10.3.2, what is the Bayes decision?

10.5 In Example 10.4.1, if the prior distribution of the mean demand for ski equipment is changed to

$$P(\theta = \theta_j) = \begin{cases} 0.4 & \theta = \theta_1 = 5 \\ 0.5 & \theta = \theta_2 = 10 \\ 0.1 & \theta = \theta_3 = 15 \end{cases}$$

what is the Bayes decision?

10.6 Use the general computer program for Algorithms 10.1 and 10.2 (Section 10.4.2) to find the posterior distribution of θ given $X = 13$ in Example 10.4.1. What is the Bayes decision using the obtained posterior distribution of θ?

10.7 Solve Exercise 10.6 using the prior distribution of θ given in Exercise 10.5.

10.8 In Example 10.4.1, suppose the conditional distribution of X, given $\theta = \theta_j$, is known to be the Poisson distribution

$$Q_X(x|\theta = \theta_j) = \frac{e^{-\theta_j}\theta_j^{\,x}}{x!} \qquad \begin{array}{l} x = 0, 1, 2, \ldots \\ \theta_j = 5, 10, 15 \end{array}$$

(a) Rework Example 10.4.1 using this new conditional distribution of X.
(b) Rework Exercise 10.6 using this new conditional distribution of X.
(c) Rework Exercise 10.7 using this new conditional distribution of X.

11

GAME THEORY

11.1 INTRODUCTION

We could consider the decision analysis problem in Chapter 10 as a game between a rational decision maker and nature. Since nature is generally not considered to be rational, the decision maker may choose to use something better than the most conservative strategy to try to maximize his gain. However, if the decision maker's opponent is also rational and is trying to maximize his gain, the problem becomes a decision problem involving conflict of interests. In this case, very conservative strategies must be used by both parties. The resolution of this conflict is the essence of game theory.

Although some games involve more than two players, we will restrict our attention to two-person games. Suppose we consider the decision problem in which two rational players, player I and player II, each have a set of possible actions available to them. Each player might be a football team, a company, an army, a building contractor, or a politician. A set of possible actions might be football plays, sites to locate a company, types of military gear to employ, etc. Suppose players I and II have m actions, $a_1, a_2, \ldots, a_m$, and n actions, $b_1, b_2, \ldots, b_n$, available, respectively. On each play of the game, each player selects a single action from his set of actions. The consequence of this decision by both players is a specific return or payoff. If the

**Table 11.1 PAYOFF MATRIX TWO–PERSON
ZERO–SUM GAME**

Player I, possible actions	Player II, possible actions					
	b_1	b_2	$\cdots$	b_j	$\cdots$	b_n
a_1	p_{11}	p_{12}	$\cdots$	p_{1j}	$\cdots$	p_{1n}
a_2	p_{21}	p_{22}	$\cdots$	p_{2j}	$\cdots$	p_{2n}
$\vdots$						
a_i	p_{i_1}	p_{i_2}	$\cdots$	p_{ij}	$\cdots$	p_{in}
$\vdots$						
a_m	p_{m1}	p_{m2}	$\cdots$	p_{mj}	$\cdots$	p_{mn}

payoff is nonzero, it represents a gain or loss to player I. We will only consider the case where player I's gain is player II's loss, and conversely. No units enter or leave the game. This type of game is called a *two-person zero-sum game*. Thus, without loss of generality, we can always consider the payoff as being from player II to player I. For example, if player I selects action a_2 and player II selects action b_3, the result may be that player I gains 4 units. Thus, the payoff from player II to player I is 4 units. Since player I's gain is player II's loss, and vice versa, the gain to player II in this case would be -4 units.

In general, we will let p_{ij} represent the payoff from player II to player I if player I chooses action a_i and player II chooses action b_j. The set of all possible payoffs is displayed in a table called the *payoff matrix*, which represents the payoff from player II to player I for all possible actions by both players. The payoff matrix in Table 11.1 could be considered player I's gain table, player II's loss table, or the negative of player II's gain table. If player I chooses action a_i, we will say that he plays row i. Likewise, if player II chooses action b_j, we will say that he plays column j.

A decision to play a certain row (column) with probability 1 and all other rows (columns) with probability 0 is called a *pure strategy* for player I (player II).

11.2 MINIMAX–MAXIMIN PURE STRATEGIES

Since each player knows that the other is rational and has the same objective, that is, to maximize the payoff from the other player, each might decide to use the conservative *minimax criterion* to select an action. That is, player I examines each row in the payoff matrix and selects the minimum element in each row, say p_{ij_i} with $i = 1$, $2, \ldots, m$. He then selects the maximum of these minimum elements, say p_{rs}. Mathematically,

$$\underline{v} = p_{rs} = \max_{i} \left[\min_{j} (p_{ij}) \right]$$

$$= \max_{i} (p_{ij_i})$$

The element p_{rs} is called the *maximin value of the game*, and the decision to play row *r* is called the *maximin pure strategy*. Likewise, player II examines each column in the payoff matrix to determine the maximum loss he would incur if he played that column. He then considers playing the column with the smallest maximum loss. Let

$$\bar{v} = p_{tu} = \min_{j} \left[\max_{i} (p_{ij}) \right]$$

Then p_{tu} is called the *minimax value of the game* and the decision to play column *u* is called the *minimax pure strategy*. It can be shown that the minimax value $\bar{v}$ is always greater than or equal to the maximin value $\underline{v}$. The value $\underline{v}$ represents a lower bound on a quantity called the *value of the game*, and $\bar{v}$ represents an upper bound on the value of the game. If the minimax value is equal to the maximin value, the common value is called a *saddle point*, and the minimax and maximin pure strategies are called *optimal minimax strategies*. Note that a saddle point is a minimum element in its row and a maximum element in its column.

If both players use their optimal minimax strategies, the resulting expected payoff is called the *value of the game*. When the optimal minimax strategies are pure strategies, then the expected payoff using these optimal minimax strategies is just the value of the saddle point.

EXAMPLE 11.2.1   Consider the game with the payoff matrix

$$
\begin{array}{cc}
 & \text{Player II} \quad \text{Row minimum} \\
\text{Player I} & \begin{bmatrix} 2 & 4 & 1 \\ \textcircled{3} & 5 & 4 \end{bmatrix} \begin{array}{l} 1 \\ 3 \longleftarrow \text{Maximin element} \end{array}
\end{array}
$$

Column maximum 3 5 4

↑

Minimax element

Player I knows that if he plays row 1, he may gain 2, 4, or 1 units, depending on which column player II plays. He also knows that he will gain at least the minimum of 2, 4, or 1 units, namely 1 unit, regardless of which column player II plays. In a similar manner, player I knows that he will gain at least 3 units if he plays row 2, regardless of what player II does. Thus, player I can be assured of at least 3 units if he plays the row that will maximize the minimum payoff, namely row 2. The payoff of 3 units is the *maximin value* or *lower bound on the value of the game*, and the decision to play row 2 is the *maximin pure strategy* in this case.

Player II wishes to minimize his maximum loss, so he examines each column to determine the maximum loss that would be incurred if he plays that column. That is, if column 1 is played, a maximum of 3 units would be lost. Likewise, a maximum of 5 and 4 units would be lost if columns 2 and 3 are played, respectively. Player II's *minimax pure strategy*, then, is to play the column that would result in the smallest maximum loss, namely column 1. The maximum payoff, or loss of 3 units, from playing column 1 is the *minimax value* of the game and represents an *upper bound on the value of the game*. Since

$$\text{Minimax value} = \text{maximin value} = 3$$

the value 3 represents a saddle point, in which case, the *value of the game* to player I is 3 units.

Thus, to determine if any pure strategies are optimal minimax strategies, it is only necessary to examine the minimum element in each row to see if it is also a maximum element in its column. If such an element exists, it is a saddle point, and the pure strategies to play the row and column it is in are optimal minimax strategies. In addition, the value of the game v is equal to the value of the saddle point.

The meaning of all of this is that if a saddle point exists, then the minimax and maximin pure strategies are optimal minimax strategies for players I and II. Player I can expect to gain at least an amount v if he uses his maximin pure strategy on each play of the game, and player II can expect to lose no more than v if he uses his minimax pure strategy on each play of the game. If player I deviates from his optimal minimax strategy, player II can possibly lose fewer than v units on each play of the game. In like manner, if player II deviates from his optimal minimax strategy, player I can possibly gain more than v units on each play of the game.

If players I and II use their maximin and minimax pure strategies, respectively, and if

$$\bar{v} = \text{minimax value} > \text{maximin value} = \underline{v}$$

then these strategies will not be optimal minimax strategies. For example, in the game with the payoff matrix

Player II

Player I $\begin{bmatrix} 1 & 4 \\ 3 & 2 \end{bmatrix}$ $\begin{matrix} 1 \\ 2 \end{matrix}$ ⟵———— Maximin element

$\begin{matrix} 3 & 4 \end{matrix}$

└—Minimax element

we have

$$\bar{v} = \text{minimax value} = 3 > 2 = \text{maximin value} = \underline{v}$$

Thus, each player has some latitude to try to gain some of the difference between $\bar{v}$ and $\underline{v}$, namely 1 unit. Player I wants to increase his expected gain as much as possible upward from $\underline{v} = 2$ units, while player II wants to decrease his expected loss as much as possible from $\bar{v} = 3$ units. Somewhere in between $\bar{v}$ and $\underline{v}$ (between 3 and 2 units) is a value v that represents the value of the game to player I. This value v is the minimum amount player I can expect to gain, regardless of what player II does. Clearly, playing the same pure strategy on each play of the game will not yield v. Consequently, player I might want to play one particular row on one play of the game, and other rows on successive plays of the game. But what proportion of the time should he play each row to maximize his expected payoff over the long run, regardless of what player II does?

Essentially we want to determine a strategy for player I that tells us what proportion of the time each row should be played to maximize the expected payoff to player I. Similar reasoning holds for player II. This leads to the use of mixed strategies.

11.3 MIXED STRATEGIES AND EXPECTED PAYOFF

Suppose player I does not want to play each row on each play of the game with probability 1 or 0, as was the case with pure strategies. Instead, suppose he decides to play row i with probability x_i with $i = 1, 2, \ldots, m$, where more than one x_i is greater than zero, and $\sum_{i=1}^{m} x_i = 1$. This decision, denoted by

$$X = \begin{bmatrix} x_1 \\ x_2 \\ \cdot \\ \cdot \\ \cdot \\ x_i \\ \cdot \\ \cdot \\ \cdot \\ x_m \end{bmatrix}$$

is called a *mixed strategy* for player I. In like manner, if player II decides to play column j with probability y_j with $j = 1, 2, \ldots, n$ where more than one y_j is greater than zero, and $\sum_{j=1}^{n} y_j = 1$, then

$$Y = [y_1 \quad y_2 \quad \cdots \quad y_j \quad \cdots \quad y_n]$$

is called a *mixed strategy* for player II.

Note that the row to use on a given play of the game could be considered a random variable, say R, which has values $\{1, 2, \ldots, m\}$, and takes on each of these values with probabilities $\{x_1, x_2, \ldots, x_m\}$, respectively. That is,

$$\Pr(R = i) = x_i \quad i = 1, 2, \ldots, m$$

If C is a random variable that represents the column to use on each given play of the game, then

$$\Pr(C = j) = y_j \quad j = 1, 2, \ldots, n$$

When player I decides to use a mixed strategy, a sample value from R must be selected for each play of the game, where row 1 is selected with probability x_1, row 2 is selected with probability x_2, etc. The details of how to sample from a distribution will be discussed in Chapter 14.

EXAMPLE 11.3.1   Consider the 2 × 2 game with payoff matrix

Player II

$$\text{Player I} \begin{bmatrix} 1 & 4 \\ 3 & 2 \end{bmatrix} \begin{matrix} 1 \\ 2 \end{matrix} \longleftarrow \text{Maximin element}$$

$$\begin{matrix} 3 & 4 \\ \uparrow \end{matrix}$$

Minimax element

Since the minimax element is greater than the maximin element, a saddle point does not exist, so no pure strategies will be optimal. Suppose player I decides to use the mixed strategy

$$X = \begin{bmatrix} x_1 \\ x_2 \end{bmatrix} = \begin{bmatrix} \dfrac{1}{3} \\ \dfrac{2}{3} \end{bmatrix}$$

and player II decides to use the mixed strategy

$$Y = [y_1 \quad y_2] = \begin{bmatrix} \dfrac{3}{4} & \dfrac{1}{4} \end{bmatrix}$$

If these strategies are used for many, many plays of the game, how much can player I expect to gain?

Since both players must select their strategies in advance of all plays of the game without knowledge of what strategy the other player selects, the probabilities are considered to be independent. Therefore, the *expected payoff* to player I is

$$\text{Expected payoff} = \left(\frac{1}{3}\right)\left(\frac{3}{4}\right)(1) + \left(\frac{1}{3}\right)\left(\frac{1}{4}\right)(4) + \left(\frac{2}{3}\right)\left(\frac{3}{4}\right)(3) + \left(\frac{2}{3}\right)\left(\frac{1}{4}\right)(2)$$

$$= \frac{29}{12}$$

In general, the expected payoff to player I is

$$\text{Expected payoff} = \sum_{i=1}^{m} \sum_{j=1}^{n} x_i y_j p_{ij} \qquad (11.1)$$

Both players would like to maximize their expected payoff. However, each player knows that the other is a rational being with the same objective as his, so he decides to play conservatively by selecting a strategy that will maximize the expected payoff to him, regardless of what the other player does. Such a strategy is called an *optimal minimax strategy*. Specifically, a strategy

$$X^* = \begin{bmatrix} x_1^* \\ x_2^* \\ \cdot \\ \cdot \\ \cdot \\ x_m^* \end{bmatrix}$$

such that the corresponding expected payoff

$$\sum_{i=1}^{m} \sum_{j=1}^{n} x_i^* y_j p_{ij}$$

is as large as possible, regardless of player II's strategy $Y = [y_1 \quad y_2 \quad \dots \quad y_n]$, is called an *optimal minimax strategy* for player I. Likewise, a strategy

$$Y^* = [y_1^* \quad y_2^* \quad \cdots \quad y_n^*]$$

such that the corresponding expected payoff to player I

$$\sum_{i=1}^{m} \sum_{j=1}^{n} x_i y_j^* p_{ij}$$

is as small as possible, regardless of player I's strategy

$$X = \begin{bmatrix} x_1 \\ \cdot \\ \cdot \\ \cdot \\ x_m \end{bmatrix}$$

is called an *optimal minimax strategy* for player II. It turns out that the expected payoff when player I uses an optimal minimax strategy X^* is always greater than or equal to a number v, and the expected payoff when player II uses an optimal minimax strategy Y^* is always less than or equal to the same number v. Thus X^* and Y^* are optimal minimax strategies for players I and II, respectively, if

$$\sum_{i=1}^{m} \sum_{j=1}^{n} x_i^* y_j p_{ij} \geqslant v \quad \text{for every strategy } Y = [y_1 \ \cdots \ y_n] \qquad (11.2)$$

$$\sum_{i=1}^{m} \sum_{j=1}^{n} x_i y_j^* p_{ij} \leqslant v \quad \text{for every strategy } X = \begin{bmatrix} x_1 \\ . \\ . \\ . \\ x_m \end{bmatrix} \qquad (11.3)$$

When players I and II both use optimal strategies, the expected payoff is equal to v, *the value of the game.* That is,

$$\text{Expected payoff} = \sum_{i=1}^{m} \sum_{j=1}^{n} x_i^* y_j^* p_{ij} = v \qquad (11.4)$$

Thus, when both players use optimal strategies, player I can expect to gain v units, and player II can expect to lose v units.

Although we can define optimal minimax strategies, it is not always easy to obtain them, or for that matter to verify whether a strategy is optimal or not, especially for large games. For 2 × 2 and 3 × 3 games certain algorithms have been developed to determine optimal minimax strategies. Also, optimal minimax strategies for 2 × n and m × 2 games can be obtained using a graphical procedure. However, for large games we must resort to linear programming or to an iterative procedure such as *Brown's algorithm.*

11.4 SOLUTION OF 2 × 2 GAMES

Consider a 2 × 2 game with the payoff matrix

Player II

$$\text{Player I} \begin{bmatrix} p_{11} & p_{12} \\ p_{21} & p_{22} \end{bmatrix}$$

Let x_i be the probability player I plays row i with $i = 1, 2$, and let y_j be the probability player II plays column j with $j = 1, 2$. Since $\Sigma_{i=1}^{2} x_i = 1$ and $\Sigma_{j=1}^{2} y_j = 1$, we can write

$$x_2 = 1 - x_1$$
$$y_2 = 1 - y_1$$

It can be shown that Algorithm 11.1 will yield optimal minimax strategies.

11.4.1 Algorithm 11.1—Solution of 2 X 2 Games

Step 1
Examine the payoff matrix for a saddle point. If one or more exist, the optimal minimax strategies are pure strategies. They are obtained by playing the row and column a saddle point is in with probability 1, and the other row and column with probability 0. The saddle point is necessarily the value of the game. If a saddle point does not exist, go to step 2.

Step 2
Let

$$x_1^* = \frac{p_{22} - p_{21}}{p_{11} + p_{22} - p_{12} - p_{21}} \qquad (11.5)$$

$$x_2^* = 1 - x_1^* \qquad (11.6)$$

$$y_1^* = \frac{p_{22} - p_{12}}{p_{11} + p_{22} - p_{12} - p_{21}} \qquad (11.7)$$

$$y_2^* = 1 - y_1^* \qquad (11.8)$$

These will be optimal minimax strategies for players I and II.

Step 3
The value of the game is

$$v = x_1^* y_1^* p_{11} + x_1^*(1 - y_1^*)p_{12} + (1 - x_1^*)y_1^* p_{21} + (1 - x_1^*)(1 - y_1^*)p_{22} \qquad (11.9)$$

The proof of step 2 can be found in Singleton and Tyndall [7].

EXAMPLE 11.4.1 In Section 11.2 we determined that the minimax and maximin pure strategies for the 2 X 2 game

Player II

Player I $\begin{bmatrix} 1 & 4 \\ 3 & 2 \end{bmatrix}$

were not optimal minimax strategies. Consequently, we must resort to mixed strategies since there are no saddle points.

$$\text{Let } x_1^* = \frac{2 - 3}{1 + 2 - 4 - 3} = \frac{1}{4}$$

$$x_2^* = 1 - x_1^* = \frac{3}{4}$$

$$y_1^* = \frac{2 - 4}{1 + 2 - 4 - 3} = \frac{1}{2}$$

$$y_2^* = 1 - y_1^* = \frac{1}{2}$$

The value of the game is

$$v = \sum_{i=1}^{2} \sum_{j=1}^{2} x_i^* y_j^* p_{ij}$$

$$= \left(\frac{1}{4}\right)\left(\frac{1}{2}\right)(1) + \left(\frac{1}{4}\right)\left(\frac{1}{2}\right)(4) + \left(\frac{3}{4}\right)\left(\frac{1}{2}\right)(3) + \left(\frac{3}{4}\right)\left(\frac{1}{2}\right)(2)$$

$$= 2\frac{1}{2}$$

Recall that the mixed strategies

$$X = \begin{bmatrix} \frac{1}{3} \\ \frac{2}{3} \end{bmatrix} \quad \text{and} \quad Y = \begin{bmatrix} \frac{3}{4} & \frac{1}{4} \end{bmatrix}$$

in Example 11.3.1 yielded an expected payoff of $\frac{29}{12}$, which is less than the value of the game.

11.5 RELEVANT ROWS AND COLUMNS

Given any strategy X with $x_i > 0$, then row i is said to be *relevant* for strategy X. Likewise, if $y_j > 0$ for some strategy Y, column j is said to be *relevant* for Y. We can make use of relevant rows in the following way: If X^* and Y^* are optimal minimax strategies for players I and II, respectively, then

$$\sum_{i=1}^{m} x_i^* p_{ij} = v \quad \text{for every } j \text{ such that } y_j^* > 0 \qquad (11.10)$$

$$\sum_{i=1}^{m} x_i^* p_{ij} \geq v \quad \text{for every } j \text{ such that } y_j^* = 0 \qquad (11.11)$$

$$\sum_{j=1}^{n} y_j^* p_{ij} = v \quad \text{for every } i \text{ such that } x_i^* > 0 \qquad (11.12)$$

$$\sum_{j=1}^{n} y_j^* p_{ij} \leq v \quad \text{for every } i \text{ such that } x_i^* = 0 \qquad (11.13)$$

and conversely.

EXAMPLE 11.5.1 The optimal minimax strategies for the game in Example 11.4.1 indicated that each row and column should be played with positive probability. Therefore,

$$\sum_{i=1}^{2} x_i^* p_{i1} = \left(\frac{1}{4}\right)(1) + \left(\frac{3}{4}\right)(3) = 2.5 = v$$

$$\sum_{i=1}^{2} x_i^* p_{i2} = \left(\frac{1}{4}\right)(4) + \left(\frac{3}{4}\right)(2) = 2.5 = v$$

$$\sum_{j=1}^{2} y_j^* p_{1j} = \left(\frac{1}{2}\right)(1) + \left(\frac{1}{2}\right)(4) = 2.5 = v$$

$$\sum_{j=1}^{2} y_j^* p_{2j} = \left(\frac{1}{2}\right)(3) + \left(\frac{1}{2}\right)(2) = 2.5 = v$$

This gives a quick way to calculate the value of the game when optimal minimax strategies are known.

11.6 DOMINANCE

Although 2 X 2 games can be solved quite easily, the solution of larger games usually requires different and longer techniques. Consequently, it is beneficial to reduce the size of a general $m \times n$ game before solving it, if possible. Simply stated, we say that row i *dominates* row k in the payoff matrix if

$$p_{ij} \geq p_{kj} \quad \text{for } j = 1, 2, \ldots, n \quad (11.14)$$

In this case, *row k* can be eliminated from further considerations. This says row k would not yield a larger payoff to player I than row i, regardless of what player II does, so eliminate it.

EXAMPLE 11.6.1 For the payoff matrix

$$\begin{bmatrix} 3 & 5 & 4 & 2 \\ 5 & 6 & 2 & 4 \\ 2 & 1 & 4 & 0 \\ 3 & 3 & 5 & 2 \end{bmatrix}$$

row 1 dominates row 3, since element by element

$$3 > 2 \quad 5 > 1 \quad 4 = 4 \quad 2 > 0$$

Therefore, row 3 can be eliminated and the payoff matrix reduced to

$$\begin{bmatrix} 3 & 5 & 4 & 2 \\ 5 & 6 & 2 & 4 \\ 3 & 3 & 5 & 2 \end{bmatrix}$$

With respect to columns, we say that column j dominates column k in the payoff matrix if

$$p_{ij} \geqslant p_{ik} \quad \text{for } i = 1, 2, \ldots, m \quad (11.15)$$

In this case, *column j* can be eliminated from further considerations. This is reasonable since player II would never want to play a column that would possibly yield a larger payoff to player I, regardless of which row player I plays.

EXAMPLE 11.6.2 In the reduced payoff matrix in Example 11.6.1, we see that column 2 dominates column 1, so column 2 can be eliminated to give

$$\begin{bmatrix} 3 & 4 & 2 \\ 5 & 2 & 4 \\ 3 & 5 & 2 \end{bmatrix}$$

Now, column 1 dominates column 3, so column 1 can be eliminated to give

$$\begin{bmatrix} 4 & 2 \\ 2 & 4 \\ 5 & 2 \end{bmatrix}$$

Finally, row 3 dominates row 1, so row 1 can be eliminated. Thus, the original game has been reduced to the 2 × 2 subgame

$$\begin{array}{cc} & y_3 \quad y_4 \\ \begin{array}{c} x_2 \\ x_4 \end{array} & \begin{bmatrix} 2 & 4 \\ 5 & 2 \end{bmatrix} \end{array}$$

Algorithm 11.1 yields the solution

$$x_2^* = \frac{3}{5} \quad x_4^* = \frac{2}{5}$$

$$y_3^* = \frac{2}{5} \quad y_4^* = \frac{3}{5}$$

Thus, the complete optimal minimax strategy for the original game is

$$X^* = \begin{bmatrix} x_1^* \\ x_2^* \\ x_3^* \\ x_4^* \end{bmatrix} = \begin{bmatrix} 0 \\ \frac{3}{5} \\ 0 \\ \frac{2}{5} \end{bmatrix} \qquad Y^* = \begin{bmatrix} 0 & 0 & \frac{2}{5} & \frac{3}{5} \end{bmatrix}$$

and the value of the game is

$$v = \frac{16}{5}$$

Note that columns 1 and 2 are not relevant, so

$$\sum_{i=1}^{4} x_i^* p_{i1} = (0)(3) + \left(\frac{3}{5}\right)(5) + (0)(2) + \left(\frac{2}{5}\right)(3) = \frac{21}{5} > \frac{16}{5} = v$$

$$\sum_{i=1}^{4} x_i^* p_{i2} = (0)(5) + \left(\frac{3}{5}\right)(6) + (0)(1) + \left(\frac{2}{5}\right)(3) = \frac{24}{5} > \frac{16}{5} = v$$

Since column 3 is relevant, we have

$$\sum_{i=1}^{4} x_i^* p_{i3} = (0)(4) + \left(\frac{3}{5}\right)(2) + (0)(4) + \left(\frac{2}{5}\right)(5) = \frac{16}{5} = v$$

The notion of dominance can be extended to the case in which a given row is dominated by a *convex combination* of the other rows and to the case in which a given column dominates a convex combination of the other columns. By convex combination, we mean a linear combination of the rows or columns where the coefficients sum to 1. Specifically, we say that row k is *dominated* if there exists a set of λ_i's such that

$$\sum_{\substack{i=1 \\ i \neq k}}^{m} \lambda_i p_{ij} \geq p_{kj} \qquad \text{for all } j = 1, 2, \ldots, n$$

where $\sum_{\substack{i=1 \\ i \neq k}}^{m} \lambda_i = 1$. In this case, row k can be eliminated.

EXAMPLE 11.6.3 In the 3 X 2 game

$$\begin{bmatrix} 2 & 4 \\ 5 & 1 \\ 3 & 2 \end{bmatrix}$$

the convex combination

$$\frac{1}{3} \text{ (row 1)} + \frac{2}{3} \text{ (row 2)} = \frac{1}{3} [2 \quad 4] + \frac{2}{3} [5 \quad 1]$$

$$= \begin{bmatrix} \frac{2}{3} & \frac{4}{3} \end{bmatrix} + \begin{bmatrix} \frac{10}{3} & \frac{2}{3} \end{bmatrix}$$

$$= \begin{bmatrix} \frac{12}{3} & \frac{6}{3} \end{bmatrix}$$

is greater than or equal to row 3, element by element, so row 3 can be eliminated.

Column k is said to dominate a convex combination of the other column if there exists a set of λ_j's such that

$$p_{ik} \geqslant \sum_{\substack{j=1 \\ j \neq k}}^{n} \lambda_j p_{ij} \qquad \text{for all } i = 1, 2, \ldots, m$$

where $\sum_{\substack{j=1 \\ j \neq k}}^{n} \lambda_j = 1$. In this case, column k can be eliminated.

EXAMPLE 11.6.4 In the 2 × 3 game

$$\begin{bmatrix} 1 & 6 & 3 \\ 6 & 2 & 5 \end{bmatrix}$$

column 3 is greater than or equal to the convex combination

$$\frac{3}{4} \text{ (col 1)} + \frac{1}{4} \text{ (col 2)} = \frac{3}{4} \begin{bmatrix} 1 \\ 6 \end{bmatrix} + \frac{1}{4} \begin{bmatrix} 6 \\ 2 \end{bmatrix}$$

$$= \begin{bmatrix} \frac{3}{4} \\ \frac{18}{4} \end{bmatrix} + \begin{bmatrix} \frac{6}{4} \\ \frac{2}{4} \end{bmatrix}$$

$$= \begin{bmatrix} \frac{9}{4} \\ \frac{20}{4} \end{bmatrix}$$

element by element, so column 3 can be eliminated.

11.7 SOLUTION OF 2 × n GAMES

EXAMPLE 11.7.1 Consider a 2 × 3 game with the payoff matrix

$$
\begin{array}{c}
\text{Player II}\\[4pt]
\begin{array}{ccc}
y_1 & y_2 & y_3
\end{array}\\[2pt]
\begin{array}{cc}
\text{Player I} \quad x_1\\
x_2 = 1 - x_1
\end{array}
\begin{bmatrix}
1 & 3 & 11\\
8 & 5 & 2
\end{bmatrix}
\end{array}
$$

If a saddle point exists, the pure strategies corresponding to the row and column it is in are played with probability 1, and the other row and columns are played with probability 0. In this case, a saddle point does not exist. The next step is to examine the columns for dominance. None of the columns dominates any of the others outright, and no obvious convex combination of two of the columns is dominated by the other column. Consequently, we move to a procedure that will solve $2 \times n$ games.

In the current example, three 2×2 subgames

$$
\begin{bmatrix} 1 & 3 \\ 8 & 5 \end{bmatrix} \quad
\begin{bmatrix} 1 & 11 \\ 8 & 2 \end{bmatrix} \quad
\begin{bmatrix} 3 & 11 \\ 5 & 2 \end{bmatrix}
$$

can be formed by using two different columns of the 2×3 game each time. The optimal minimax strategies for one of these subgames will also be optimal minimax strategies for the original game, where the column in the original game that is not in the subgame is played with probability 0. For example, consider the subgame

$$
\begin{array}{c}
\begin{array}{cc}
y_2 & y_3
\end{array}\\[2pt]
\begin{array}{c}
x_1\\
x_2
\end{array}
\begin{bmatrix}
3 & 11\\
5 & 2
\end{bmatrix}
\end{array}
$$

This subgame is formed by using the last two columns of the original 2×3 game. The optimal minimax strategies are:

$$
x_1^* = \frac{3}{11} \qquad y_2^* = \frac{9}{11}
$$

$$
x_2^* = \frac{8}{11} \qquad y_3^* = \frac{2}{11}
$$

with $v = \frac{49}{11}$. The corresponding complete solution for the original game is

$$
X = \begin{bmatrix} \dfrac{3}{11} \\[6pt] \dfrac{8}{11} \end{bmatrix}
\quad \text{and} \quad
Y = \begin{bmatrix} 0 & \dfrac{9}{11} & \dfrac{2}{11} \end{bmatrix}
$$

Since column 1 is not relevant ($y_1 = 0$), we see from constraint (11.11) that we must have

$$\sum_{i=1}^{2} x_i^* p_{i1} \geqslant \frac{49}{11} = v$$

if the above strategies are optimal for the original game. We have

$$\sum_{i=1}^{2} x_i^* p_{i1} = \left(\frac{3}{11}\right)(1) + \left(\frac{8}{11}\right)(8) = \frac{67}{11} > \frac{49}{11} = v$$

so the strategies

$$X = \begin{bmatrix} \dfrac{3}{11} \\ \dfrac{8}{11} \end{bmatrix} \quad \text{and} \quad Y = \begin{bmatrix} 0 & \dfrac{9}{11} & \dfrac{2}{11} \end{bmatrix}$$

are optimal for the original 2 × 3 game, and $v = \frac{49}{11}$.

For the 2 × 2 subgame

$$\begin{array}{c} \quad\quad y_1 \ \ y_3 \\ \begin{array}{c} x_1 \\ x_2 \end{array} \begin{bmatrix} 1 & 11 \\ 8 & 2 \end{bmatrix} \end{array}$$

the optimal minimax strategies are

$$x_1^* = \frac{6}{16} \quad y_1^* = \frac{9}{16}$$

$$x_2^* = \frac{10}{16} \quad y_3^* = \frac{7}{16}$$

with $v = \frac{86}{16}$. The corresponding complete solution for the original 2 × 3 game is

$$X = \begin{bmatrix} \dfrac{6}{16} \\ \dfrac{10}{16} \end{bmatrix} \quad \text{and} \quad Y = \begin{bmatrix} \dfrac{9}{16} & 0 & \dfrac{7}{16} \end{bmatrix}$$

Since column 2 is not relevant, we must have

$$\sum_{i=1}^{2} x_i^* p_{i2} \geqslant \frac{86}{16} = v$$

if the above strategies are optimal for the 2 × 3 game. But,

$$\sum_{i=1}^{2} x_i^* p_{i2} = \left(\frac{6}{16}\right)(3) + \left(\frac{10}{16}\right)(5) = \frac{68}{16} < \frac{86}{16} = v$$

Thus, the above strategies are not optimal for the original 2 × 3 game.

Finally, for the 2 × 2 subgame

$$
\begin{array}{cc}
 & \begin{array}{cc} y_1 & y_2 \end{array} \\
\begin{array}{c} x_1 \\ x_2 \end{array} &
\begin{bmatrix} 1 & 3 \\ 8 & 5 \end{bmatrix}
\end{array}
$$

the value 5 is a saddle point, so the pure strategies

$$
X^* = \begin{bmatrix} 0 \\ 1 \end{bmatrix} \quad \text{and} \quad Y^* = \begin{bmatrix} 0 & 1 \end{bmatrix}
$$

are optimal for the 2 × 2 subgame. The corresponding value of the game is $v = 5$. However,

$$
\sum_{i=1}^{2} x_i^* p_{i3} = (0)(11) + (1)(2) = 2 < 5
$$

Hence, the above pure strategies would not yield optimal minimax strategies for the original game.

Another approach to the solution of 2 × n games, which is generally preferable to examining every 2 × 2 subgame, is the graphic procedure. Suppose we look at how the graphic procedure would solve the 2 × 3 game in Example 11.7.1.

In constraint (11.2), note that in order for X^* to be an optimal minimax strategy, the corresponding expected payoff must be greater than or equal to the value of the game v for every strategy Y. That is, we must have

$$
\sum_{i=1}^{2} \sum_{j=1}^{3} x_i^* y_i p_{ij} \geq v \quad \text{for every strategy } Y = \begin{bmatrix} y_1 & \cdots & y_n \end{bmatrix} \quad (11.16)
$$

Consequently, if this condition must be true for every strategy, it must be true for each of the pure strategies $Y = \begin{bmatrix} 1 & 0 & 0 \end{bmatrix}$, $Y = \begin{bmatrix} 0 & 1 & 0 \end{bmatrix}$, and $Y = \begin{bmatrix} 0 & 0 & 1 \end{bmatrix}$. If we substitute these pure strategies in the optimality criterion in Equation (11.16) and plot v against x_1, we get a feasible region such that any values of x_1 and v in the region satisfy Equation (11.16). Player I wants to maximize v, so the value of x_1 that gives the largest value of v will yield the minimax optimal strategy for player I.

Note that in 2 × n games we can get a relationship between x_1 and v from Equation (11.16), and from the fact that $x_2 = 1 - x_1$. Thus, we find player I's optimal strategy first by maximizing v in the feasible region. For $m \times 2$ games, we get a relationship between y_1 and v, and minimize v in the feasible region to get player II's optimal minimax strategy.

For the 2 × 3 game

$$
\begin{bmatrix} 1 & 3 & 11 \\ 8 & 5 & 2 \end{bmatrix}
$$

we have

$$Y = [1 \quad 0 \quad 0]: \quad x_1 + 8(1 - x_1) = -7x_1 + 8 \geqslant v \quad \text{or} \quad v + 7x_1 \leqslant 8 \quad (11.17)$$
$$Y = [0 \quad 1 \quad 0]: \quad 3x_1 + 5(1 - x_1) = -2x_1 + 5 \geqslant v \quad \text{or} \quad v + 2x_1 \leqslant 5 \quad (11.18)$$
$$Y = [0 \quad 0 \quad 1]: \quad 11x_1 + 2(1 - x_1) = \quad 9x_1 + 2 \geqslant v \quad \text{or} \quad v - 9x_1 \leqslant 2 \quad (11.19)$$

To obtain the region described by constraints (11.17)–(11.19), we relax the inequalities to equalities, and plot the resulting equations

$$L_1: \quad v + 7x_1 = 8$$
$$L_2: \quad v + 2x_1 = 5$$
$$L_3: \quad v - 9x_1 = 2$$

as shown in Figure 11.1. Note that the region of feasible solutions is every (v, x_1) point below all three equations such that $0 \leqslant x_1 \leqslant 1$. Since the maximum value of v occurs at the intersection of L_2 and L_3, we can solve these two equations for x_1 and v. Namely,

$$v + 2x_1 = 5$$
$$v - 9x_1 = 2$$

or

$$x_1 = \frac{3}{11}$$

$$v = \frac{49}{11}$$

Thus, the optimal minimax strategy for player I is

$$x_1^* = \frac{3}{11} \qquad x_2^* = \frac{8}{11}$$

and the value of the game is $v = \frac{49}{11}$.

Every $2 \times n$ games contains a 2×2 subgame such that the optimal minimax strategies for the 2×2 subgame are also optimal minimax strategies for the $2 \times n$ game, with zero probability assigned to each column not in the 2×2 subgame. Graphically, the two columns that form the appropriate 2×2 subgame in this case are those corresponding to the two equations that intersect at the maximum value of v in Figure 11.1. Since lines L_2 and L_3 were formed from columns 2 and 3 in the original payoff matrix, the solution of the subgame

$$\begin{array}{cc} & y_2 \quad y_3 \\ \begin{array}{c} x_1 \\ x_2 \end{array} & \begin{bmatrix} 3 & 11 \\ 5 & 2 \end{bmatrix} \end{array}$$

using Algorithm 11.1 will yield the optimal minimax solution for the original game. Thus

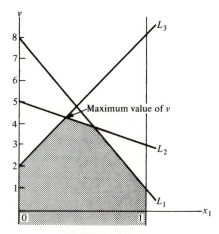

FIGURE 11.1
Graphic solution of 2 × 3 game.

$$y_2^* = \frac{2 - 11}{3 + 2 - 11 - 5} = \frac{9}{11}$$

$$y_3^* = 1 - y_1^* = \frac{2}{11}$$

therefore,

$$X^* = \begin{bmatrix} \dfrac{3}{11} \\ \dfrac{8}{11} \end{bmatrix} \quad \text{and} \quad Y^* = \begin{bmatrix} 0 & \dfrac{9}{11} & \dfrac{2}{11} \end{bmatrix} \qquad (11.20)$$

are optimal minimax strategies for the original game

$$\begin{bmatrix} 1 & 3 & 11 \\ 8 & 5 & 2 \end{bmatrix} \qquad (11.21)$$

Although we solved for X^* and v graphically, we could have obtained X^* by solving the subgame

$$\begin{bmatrix} 3 & 11 \\ 5 & 2 \end{bmatrix}$$

using Algorithm 11.1. Namely,

$$x_1^* = \frac{2 - 5}{3 + 2 - 11 - 5} = \frac{-3}{-11} = \frac{3}{11}$$

$$x_2^* = \frac{8}{11}$$

However, this would have required knowing that the last two columns were the ones that would yield an optimal solution for the original game. This is generally not known without some checking.

11.7.1 Algorithm 11.2—Solution of 2 × n Games

Given the 2 × n game with payoff matrix

$$
\begin{array}{c}
\text{Player II} \\
\begin{array}{cccc}
y_1 & y_2 & \cdots & y_n
\end{array} \\
\text{Player I}
\begin{array}{c}
x_1 \\
x_2 = 1 - x_1
\end{array}
\begin{bmatrix}
p_{11} & p_{12} & \cdots & p_{1n} \\
p_{21} & p_{22} & \cdots & p_{2n}
\end{bmatrix}
\end{array}
$$

a general algorithm to solve this game is:

Step 1
Check for a saddle point. If one or more exist, the optimal minimax strategies are pure strategies. They are obtained by playing the row and column a saddle point is in with probability 1, and the other row and columns with probability 0. The saddle point is the value of the game. If a saddle point does not exist, go to step 2.

Step 2
Check for column dominance. Eliminate every column that dominates some other column or that dominates an obvious convex combination of the other columns. This step is strictly to reduce the size of the game and is not essential for the graphic procedure to work. Go to step 3.

Step 3
Write out the constraints

$$
x_1 p_{1j} + (1 - x_1)p_{2j} \geqslant v \quad
\begin{array}{l}
\text{for those } j \text{ corresponding to} \\
\text{columns not eliminated in step 2}
\end{array}
$$

or $\qquad v - (p_{1j} - p_{2j})x_1 \leqslant p_{2j}$

Step 4
Write the constraints in step 3 as the equalities

$$
v - (p_{1j} - p_{2j})x_1 = p_{2j}
$$

Step 5
Plot the equations in step 4. These equations form an upper bound on the feasible region described by the constraints in step 3 for $0 \leqslant x_1 \leqslant 1$, if v is plotted as a function of x_1. Figure 11.2 illustrates the feasible region.

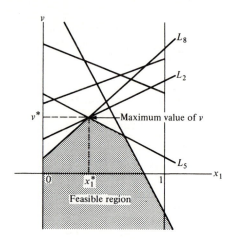

FIGURE 11.2
Feasible region for $2 \times n$ game.

The value of the game is the maximum value of v in the feasible region. This maximum value of v can occur at $x_1^* = 0$, $x_1^* = 1$, or anywhere in the interval $0 < x_1^* < 1$. The conclusions for the three cases are:

(*a*) If $x_1^* = 0$, $X^* = \begin{bmatrix} 0 \\ 1 \end{bmatrix}$ is optimal for player I, then the pure strategy involving the column corresponding to the equation that intersects v at $x_1^* = 0$ is optimal for player II.

(*b*) If $x_1^* = 1$, $X^* = \begin{bmatrix} 1 \\ 0 \end{bmatrix}$ is optimal for player I, then the pure strategy involving the column corresponding to the equation that intersects the perpendicular line at $x_1^* = 1$ is optimal for player II.

(*c*) If $0 < x_1^* < 1$, then the two columns corresponding to two of the equations with opposite slope, that intersect at the highest point in the feasible region, will yield optimal minimax strategies for players I and II. For example, in Figure 11.2, equations L_5 and L_8, which correspond to columns 5 and 8 in the original game, are of opposite slope, and they intersect at the highest point in the region of feasible solutions. Thus the 2×2 subgame

$$
\begin{array}{cc}
 & \begin{array}{cc} y_5 & y_8 \end{array} \\
\begin{array}{c} x_1 \\ x_2 = 1 - x_1 \end{array} & \begin{bmatrix} p_{15} & p_{18} \\ p_{25} & p_{28} \end{bmatrix}
\end{array}
$$

will yield the optimal minimax strategies for the original game when zero probabilities are assigned to all columns except 5 and 8. Note that L_2 and L_8 have the same slope, so columns 2 and 8 in the original game would not yield optimal strategies for the original game.

11.8 SOLUTION OF $m \times 2$ GAMES

The graphic procedure for solving $m \times 2$ games is quite similar to the solution of $2 \times n$ games. The exception is that v is plotted as a function of y_1 using the rows of the payoff matrix that have not been eliminated by dominance. A feasible region is constructed and the smallest value of v, say v^*, in the feasible region is the value of the game. Let y_1^* be the value of y_1 that yields the value of the game. The rows in the original game corresponding to two equations of opposite slope that intersect at (y_1^*, v^*) will yield optimal strategies for players I and II.

An example will illustrate this procedure.

EXAMPLE 11.8.1 In the 4×2 game

Player II

$$\text{Player I} \begin{bmatrix} 1 & 6 \\ 3 & 2 \\ 3 & 5 \\ 6 & 2 \end{bmatrix}$$

row 2 is dominated by row 3, so row 2 can be eliminated to give the reduced game

Player II

$$\begin{array}{cc} & y_1 \quad 1 - y_1 \end{array}$$

$$\text{Player I} \begin{array}{c} x_1 \\ x_3 \\ x_4 \end{array} \begin{bmatrix} 1 & 6 \\ 3 & 5 \\ 6 & 2 \end{bmatrix}$$

Form the three constraints

$$
\begin{array}{lll}
y_1 + 6(1 - y_1) \leqslant v & \text{or} & v \geqslant -5y_1 + 6 \\
3y_1 + 5(1 - y_1) \leqslant v & \text{or} & v \geqslant -2y_1 + 5 \\
6y_1 + 2(1 - y_1) \leqslant v & \text{or} & v \geqslant 4y_1 + 2
\end{array}
$$

and plot v as a function of y_1. The feasible region is displayed in Figure 11.3.

Lines L_2 and L_3 intersect at (y_1^*, v^*), so rows 3 and 4 in the original game which correspond to these lines form a 2×2 submatrix that will yield the optimal strategies. That is, optimal strategies for the subgame

$$\begin{array}{c} y_1 \quad y_2 \end{array}$$

$$\begin{array}{c} x_3 \\ x_4 \end{array} \begin{bmatrix} 3 & 5 \\ 6 & 2 \end{bmatrix}$$

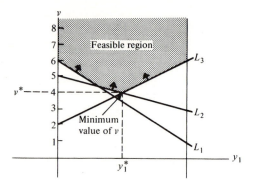

FIGURE 11.3
Feasible region for a 3 × 2 subgame.

are

$$x_3^* = \frac{2}{3} \qquad y_1^* = \frac{1}{2}$$

$$x_4^* = \frac{1}{3} \qquad y_2^* = \frac{1}{2}$$

and optimal strategies for the original game are

$$X^* = \begin{bmatrix} 0 \\ 0 \\ \dfrac{2}{3} \\ \dfrac{1}{3} \end{bmatrix} \quad \text{and} \quad Y^* = \begin{bmatrix} \dfrac{1}{2} & \dfrac{1}{2} \end{bmatrix}$$

with $v = 4$.

Another graphic procedure for solving $m \times 2$ games is:

(a) Let the columns of the game become the rows of a 2 × m game.
(b) Multiply each element in the new 2 × m game by -1.
(c) Solve the resulting 2 × m game using Algorithm 11.2.
(d) The value of the game for the $m \times 2$ game is just the negative of the value of the 2 × m game.
(e) Player I's optimal strategy for the original $m \times 2$ game is player II's optimal strategy for the 2 × m game.
(f) Player II's optimal strategy for the original $m \times 2$ game is player I's optimal strategy for the 2 × m game.

11.9 BROWN'S ALGORITHM

One of the most practical methods for solving games that are larger than a 3 X 3, 2 X n, or m X 2 is Brown's algorithm. It assumes that the past is the best guide to the future. That is, player I plays some row, say row 1, on the first play of the game, then player II plays the column that would minimize the payoff. Player I examines the column player II plays, and plays the row corresponding to the largest payoff. Player II sums element by element the rows player I has played, and plays the column corresponding to the *smallest sum element*. Player I then sums element by element the columns player II has played thus far, and plays the row corresponding to the *largest sum element*. This iterative process is continued until a decision to stop is made. At each play of the game, the *smallest sum element* selected by player II divided by the number of plays of the game is a *lower bound* on the value of the game. Likewise, the *largest sum element* selected by player I on each play of the game divided by the number of plays of the game is an *upper bound* on the value of the game. The proportion of the time column j is played is an approximation of y_j^* for $j = 1, 2, \ldots,$ n. Likewise, the proportion of the time row i is played is an approximation of x_i^* for $i = 1, 2, \ldots, m$.

EXAMPLE 11.9.1 Consider the 3 X 3 game

$$\begin{bmatrix} 1 & -2 & 3 \\ 1 & 3 & -2 \\ 4 & 2 & 1 \end{bmatrix}$$

Let $\underline{v}$ and $\bar{v}$ represent a lower and an upper bound, respectively, on the value of the game v. Suppose player I starts by playing row 2. The minimum element in row 2 is -2, so player II plays column 3. The maximum element in column 3 is 3 and is found in the first row, so player I plays row 1. The sum of the two rows played by player I is

$$\begin{array}{r} [1 \quad 3 \quad -2] \\ + [1 \quad -2 \quad 3] \\ = [2 \quad 1 \quad 1] \end{array}$$

Player II arbitrarily selects column 2 to play next since a minimum sum is in column 2. Player 1 now sums the two columns player II has played and finds that the largest sum is in row 3, namely

$$\begin{bmatrix} 3 \\ -2 \\ 1 \end{bmatrix} + \begin{bmatrix} -2 \\ 3 \\ 2 \end{bmatrix} = \begin{bmatrix} 1 \\ 1 \\ 3 \end{bmatrix}$$

Thus, he plays row 3 next. This process is repeated again and again. The results for the first 10 iterations are given below. The approximate optimal strategies for players I and II are

$$X^* \approx \begin{bmatrix} \dfrac{2}{10} \\ 0 \\ \dfrac{8}{10} \end{bmatrix} \quad \text{and} \quad Y^* \approx \begin{bmatrix} 0 & \dfrac{4}{10} & \dfrac{6}{10} \end{bmatrix}$$

Play of game			1	2	3	4	5	6	7	8	9	10	
1	−2	3	③	1	4	⑦	5	3	1	4	7	10	$\dfrac{2}{10}$
1	3	−2	−2	1	−1	−3	0	3	6	4	2	0	0
4	2	1	1	③	④	5	⑦	⑨	⑪	⑫	⑬	⑭	$\dfrac{8}{10}$

1	3	⊖2	Sum of the columns
2	①	1	player II has played
6	3	②	to date
10	5	③	
11	③	6	
15	⑤	7	Sum of the rows
19	⑦	8	player I has
23	9	⑨	played to date
27	11	⑩	
31	13	⑪	
0	$\dfrac{4}{10}$	$\dfrac{6}{10}$	

with an upper bound of $\frac{14}{10} = 1.4$ and a lower bound of $\frac{11}{10} = 1.1$ on the value of the game. Thus,

$$1.1 \leqslant v \leqslant 1.4$$

The optimal minimax strategies for the game are

$$X^* = \begin{bmatrix} \dfrac{1}{6} \\ 0 \\ \dfrac{5}{6} \end{bmatrix} \quad \text{and} \quad Y^* = \begin{bmatrix} 0 & \dfrac{1}{3} & \dfrac{2}{3} \end{bmatrix}$$

with $v = 1.33$. Hence, we see that the approximate solution after only 10 iterations is quite good.

This type of algorithm is well-suited for computer solution. Generally, approximations of the solution are quite good after only 200–500 iterations. Most games smaller than 50×50 can be solved in just a few seconds on most computers.

11.9.1 Algorithm 11.3—Brown's Algorithm for the Solution of $m \times n$ Games

Given an $m \times n$ game with the payoff matrix

Player II

$$
\text{Player I} \begin{bmatrix} p_{11} & p_{12} & \cdots & p_{1n} \\ p_{21} & p_{22} & \cdots & p_{2n} \\ \cdots & \cdots & \cdots & \cdots \\ p_{m1} & p_{m2} & \cdots & p_{mn} \end{bmatrix}
$$

Brown's algorithm is:

Step 1
Player I selects a row to play, and player II then plays the column corresponding to the minimum element in the row.

Step 2
Player I then selects the row to play that corresponds to the maximum element in the column selected by player II in step 1.

Step 3
Player II sums the rows player I has played thus far, and plays the column corresponding to a *minimum sum element*.

Step 4
Player I sums the columns player II has played thus far, and plays the row corresponding to a *maximum sum element*. If the desired number of iterations is satisfied, go to step 5; otherwise, return to step 3.

Step 5
Calculate an upper and lower bound, $\bar{v}$ and $\underline{v}$, respectively.

$$\bar{v} = \frac{\text{maximum sum element from step 4}}{\text{number of plays of the game thus far}}$$

$$\underline{v} = \frac{\text{minimum sum element from step 3}}{\text{number of plays of the game thus far}}$$

Step 6
Let x_i be the proportion of the time player I played row i with $i = 1, 2, \ldots, m$, and let y_j be the proportion of the time player II played column j with $j = 1, 2, \ldots, n$. These strategies approximate the optimal minimax strategies.

Upper and lower bounds on the value of the game are

$$\underline{v} \leqslant v \leqslant \bar{v}$$

where $\underline{v}$ and $\bar{v}$ are calculated in step 5. Stop.

11.9.2 Computer Program for Algorithm 11.3

This program uses Brown's algorithm to obtain approximate optimal minimax strategies for players I and II along with upper and lower bounds on the value of the game. The approximations are controlled by the number of iterations the user allows the program to run. The program as printed will handle matrix games with a maximum of 50 rows and 50 columns. The game need not have the same number of rows as columns. Larger games can be solved by changing the DIMENSION statement accordingly.

The program as written occupies 48K bytes of core storage. It solved 15 small games in the 3×3 to 5×5 range in 0.51 s on an IBM 370/168 computer.

```
C
C      ***********************************************************************
C      *                                                                     *
C      *             ***  BROWN'S ALGORITHM  ***                             *
C      *                          FOR                                        *
C      *       APPROXIMATING THE SOLUTION OF A FINITE MATRIX GAME            *
C      *                                                                     *
C      *  THIS PROGRAM IS DESIGNED TO HANDLE A MAXIMUM MATRIX SIZE OF 50 X 50 *
C      *  IT IS ALSO DESIGNED                                                *
C      *     TO READ                                                         *
C      *        CARD 1    COLS  2-80    TITLE   DESCRIPTION OF THE PROBLEM USING *
C      *                                        ANY CHARACTERS ON KEYPUNCH   *
C      *                                        ** COLUMN 1 MUST BE LEFT BLANK ** *
C      *        CARD 2    COLS  1- 5   M  NUMBER OF ROWS OF MATRIX A(I,J)  (I5) *
C      *                        6-10   N  NUMBER OF COLUMNS        "       (I5) *
C      *                       11-15   NUMIT  NUMBER OF ITERATIONS OR PLAYS  *
C      *                                       DESIRED AS A MAXIMUM  (I5)     *
C      *        CARDS 3 TO N   A(I,J)  DATA MATRIX                            *
C      *                               ELEMENTS ARE PUNCHED ROWWISE 8 PER CARD *
C      *                               IN FORMAT F10.4 .                      *
C      *              TO SOLVE MORE THAN ONE PROBLEM AT A TIME, REPEAT THE    *
C      *              READ SEQUENCE, AND STACK THE DATA ONE BEHIND THE OTHER  *
C      *                                                                     *
C      *     TO CALCULATE                                                    *
C      *        YHOLD(J)    SUM OF ELEMENTS OF ROWS PLAYED BY PLAYER I THUS FAR *
C      *        XHOLD(I)    SUM OF ELEMENTS OF COLUMNS PLAYED BY PLAYER II SO FAR *
C      *        YSMAL       COLUMN CORRESPONDING TO MINIMUM ELEMENT IN ROW    *
C      *        XLG         ROW CORRESPONDING TO MAXIMUM ELEMENT IN COLUMN    *
C      *        IXROW(I)    TOTAL NUMBER OF TIMES A ROW IS USED               *
C      *        JYCOL(J)    TOTAL NUMBER OF TIMES A COLUMN IS USED            *
C      *        LOWVAL      LOWER BOUND AT EACH PLAY OR ITERATION             *
C      *        UPVAL       UPPER BOUND AT EACH PLAY OR ITERATION             *
C      *        XOPT(I)     APPROXIMATE OPTIMAL STRATEGY FOR PLAYER I         *
C      *        YOPT(J)     APPROXIMATE OPTIMAL STRATEGY FOR PLAYER II        *
C      *                                                                     *
C      *     TO PRINT                                                        *
C      *        LOWVAL, UPVAL, XOPT(I), YOPT(I)                              *
C      *                                                                     *
C      ***********************************************************************
```

```
      DIMENSION YHOLD(50),XHOLD(50),JYCOL(50),IXROW(50),A(50,50),AMIN(50
     *),AMAX(50),LOCI(50),LOCJ(50),XOPT(50),YOPT(50)
      REAL*4 TITLE(20),LOWVAL
C READ IN DATA
   50 READ(5,6,END=500)TITLE
    6 FORMAT(20A4)
      WRITE(6,7)TITLE
    7 FORMAT('1',20A4,//)
      READ(5,100)M,N,NUMIT
  100 FORMAT(3I5)
      READ(5,101)((A(I,J),J=1,N),I=1,M)
  101 FORMAT(8F10.4)
      DO 1 I=1,M
    1 WRITE(6,101)(A(I,J),J=1,N)
      DO 18 J=1,N
      JYCOL(J)=0.0
   18 YHOLD(J)=0.0
      DO 19 I=1,M
      IXROW(I)=0.0
   19 XHOLD(I)=0.0
      IROW=1
      IX=180327419
C      ********************************************************************
C      * STEPS 1 TO 4 OF BROWN'S ALGORITHM ARE INCLUDED IN THE  DO 40  LOOP   *
C      *    STEPS 1 AND 2 ARE TAKEN CARE OF THE FIRST TIME THROUGH THE LOOP   *
C      ********************************************************************
      DO 40 K=1,NUMIT
      AK=K
C      ********************************************************************
C      * STEP 3                                                              *
C      *    PLAYER II SUMS THE ROWS PLAYER I HAS PLAYED ( YHOLD(I) ), AND     *
C      *    PLAYS THE COLUMN CORRESPONDING TO A MINIMUM SUM ELEMENT ( YSMAL ) *
C      ********************************************************************
      YHOLD(1)=YHOLD(1)+A(IROW,1)
      YSMAL=YHOLD(1)
      JCOL=1
      DO 20 J=2,N
      YHOLD(J)=YHOLD(J)+A(IROW,J)
      IF(YHOLD(J).GT.YSMAL) GO TO 20
      IF(YHOLD(J).EQ.YSMAL) GO TO 23
   22 YSMAL=YHOLD(J)
      JCOL=J
      GO TO 20
   23 IYY=IX*65539
      IX=IYY
      YY=IYY*.4656613E-9
      IF(YY.LT.0.0) GO TO 22
   20 CONTINUE
   28 JYCOL(JCOL)=JYCOL(JCOL)+1
C      ********************************************************************
C      * STEP 4                                                              *
C      *    PLAYER I SUMS THE COLUMNS PLAYER II HAS PLAYED ( XHOLD(I) ), AND  *
C      *    PLAYS THE ROW CORRESPONDING TO A MAXIMUM SUM ELEMENT ( XLG )      *
C      ********************************************************************
      IROW=1
      XHOLD(1)=XHOLD(1)+A(1,JCOL)
      XLG=XHOLD(1)
      DO 29 I=2,M
      XHOLD(I)=XHOLD(I)+A(I,JCOL)
      IF(XHOLD(I).LT.XLG) GO TO 29
      IF(XHOLD(I).EQ.XLG) GO TO 30
   31 XLG=XHOLD(I)
      IROW=I
      GO TO 29
   30 IXX=IX*65539
      IX=IXX
      XX=IXX*.4656613E-9
      IF(XX.LT.0.0) GO TO 31
   29 CONTINUE
   34 IXROW(IROW)=IXROW(IROW)+1
```

```
   40 CONTINUE
C     ****************************************************************************
C     *  STEP 5                                                                 *
C     *     CALCULATE THE UPPER AND LOWER BOUNDS                                *
C     ****************************************************************************
      UPVAL=XLG/AK
      LOWVAL=YSMAL/AK
C     ****************************************************************************
C     *  STEP 6                                                                 *
C     *     CALCULATE THE APPROXIMATE OPTIMAL MINIMAX STRATEGIES FOR PLAYER I   *
C     *     AND PLAYER II.  PRINT OUT THESE, AND THE UPPER AND LOWER BOUNDS     *
C     *     ON THE VALUE OF THE GAME.                                           *
C     ****************************************************************************
  666 DO 41 I=1,M
   41 XOPT(I)=IXROW(I)/AK
      DO 42 J=1,N
   42 YOPT(J)=JYCOL(J)/AK
      WRITE(6,210)K
  210 FORMAT(// 5X,'AT ITERATICN ',I4,//)
      I=1
      J=1
   62 WRITE(6,202)I,XOPT(I),J,YOPT(J)
  202 FORMAT(5X,'X(',I2,')=',F10.4,4X,'Y(',I2,')=',F10.4)
   66 I=I+1
      J=J+1
      IF(I-M)60,60,61
   60 IF(J-N)62,62,63
   61 IF(J-N)64,64,65
   63 WRITE(6,205)I,XOPT(I)
  205 FORMAT(5X,'X(',I2,')=',F10.4)
      GO TO 66
   64 WRITE(6,206)J,YOPT(J)
  206 FORMAT(25X,'Y(',I2,')=',F10.4)
      GO TO 66
   65 WRITE(6,203)LOWVAL
  203 FORMAT(// 10X,'LOWER BOUND ON V IS',F10.4,/)
      WRITE(6,204)UPVAL
  204 FORMAT(10X,'UPPER BCUND ON V IS',F10.4)
      GO TO 50
  500 STOP
      END

/DATA

EXAMPLE 11.9.1
    3     3   500     0
   1.       -2.         3.        1.        3.        -2.        4.        2.
     1.


EXAMPLE 11.9.1


    1.0000    -2.0000     3.0000
    1.0000     3.0000    -2.0000
    4.0000     2.0000     1.0000


   AT ITERATICN  500


   X( 1)=      0.1660     Y( 1)=      0.0
   X( 2)=      0.0020     Y( 2)=      0.3380
   X( 3)=      0.8320     Y( 3)=      0.6620


      LOWER BOUND ON V IS     1.3300

      UPPER BOUND ON V IS     1.3380
```

SELECTED BIBLIOGRAPHY

1 Davis, M. D.: "Game Theory: A Nontechnical Introduction," Basic Books, New York, 1970.
2 Dresher, M.: "Games of Strategy: Theory and Applications," Prentice-Hall, Inc., Englewood Cliffs, N.J., 1961.
3 Levin, R. L., and R. B. Desjardins: "Theory of Games and Strategies," International Textbook Company, Scranton, Pa., 1970.
4 McKinsey, J. C. C.: "Introduction of the Theory of Games," McGraw-Hill Book Company, New York, 1952.
5 Raiffa, R. D.: "Games and Decisions," John Wiley & Sons, Inc., New York, 1958.
6 Rapoport, A.: "Two Person Game Theory: The Essential Ideas," University of Michigan Press, Ann Arbor, Mich., 1966.
7 Singleton, R. R., and W. F. Tyndall: "Games and Programs," W. H. Freeman and Company, San Francisco, 1974.
8 Williams, J. D.: "The Compleat Strategyst," rev. ed., McGraw-Hill Book Company, New York, 1965.

EXERCISES

A matrix game is solved when optimal strategies for both players and the value of the game are determined.

11.1 Solve the following matrix games using an exact procedure.

(a) $\begin{bmatrix} 4 & -1 \\ -2 & 5 \end{bmatrix}$ (b) $\begin{bmatrix} 4 & 2 \\ 3 & 1 \end{bmatrix}$ (c) $\begin{bmatrix} 3 & 4 & 3 \\ -3 & 1 & -2 \\ 4 & 2 & 5 \end{bmatrix}$

(d) $\begin{bmatrix} 2 & 0 \\ 1 & 2 \end{bmatrix}$ (e) $\begin{bmatrix} 3 & 1 \\ 2 & 6 \end{bmatrix}$ (f) $\begin{bmatrix} 5 & 2 \\ 2 & 5 \end{bmatrix}$

(g) $\begin{bmatrix} 3 & 4 \\ 2 & 5 \end{bmatrix}$ (h) $\begin{bmatrix} 5 & 1 \\ 2 & 8 \end{bmatrix}$ (i) $\begin{bmatrix} 6 & 1 & 3 & 5 & 4 \\ 2 & 4 & 5 & 4 & 1 \end{bmatrix}$

11.2 Solve the following matrix games graphically.

(a) $\begin{bmatrix} 1 & 3 & 5 \\ 4 & 2 & 1 \end{bmatrix}$ (b) $\begin{bmatrix} 2 & 8 \\ 3 & 4 \\ 4 & 6 \\ 5 & 2 \end{bmatrix}$ (c) $\begin{bmatrix} -2 & 3 & 1 \\ 4 & 2 & 5 \end{bmatrix}$

(d)
$$\begin{bmatrix} 4 & 1 & 3 & 2 \\ 0 & 2 & 1 & 5 \end{bmatrix}$$

(e)
$$\begin{bmatrix} 2 & 5 & 4 & 1 \\ 3 & 1 & 2 & 6 \end{bmatrix}$$

(f)
$$\begin{bmatrix} 1 & -1 \\ 0 & 1 \\ 4 & -2 \\ -1 & 5 \end{bmatrix}$$

11.3 Consider the matrix game

$$\begin{bmatrix} 5 & 6 & 1 & 5 & 3 & 4 \\ 7 & 3 & 9 & 6 & 8 & 7 \end{bmatrix}$$

It has been determined that player I's optimal strategy is

$$X_0 = \begin{bmatrix} \dfrac{6}{11} \\ \dfrac{5}{11} \end{bmatrix}$$

Determine an optimal strategy for player II and the value of the game.

11.4 Given the strategies

$$X = \begin{bmatrix} \dfrac{3}{4} \\ \dfrac{1}{4} \end{bmatrix} \qquad Y = \begin{bmatrix} \dfrac{1}{3} & \dfrac{2}{3} \end{bmatrix}$$

for the matrix game

$$\begin{bmatrix} 4 & 2 \\ 1 & 5 \end{bmatrix}$$

(a) What is the expected payoff?
(b) Are the strategies optimal for players I and II? Why?

11.5 Carry out five iterations of Brown's algorithm on each of the following matrix games. For each problem, state the approximate optimal strategies for both players as well as the best available upper and lower bound on the value of the game.

(a)
$$\begin{bmatrix} 4 & 2 & 5 & 2 \\ 2 & 3 & 1 & 4 \\ 1 & 6 & 4 & 3 \end{bmatrix}$$

(b)
$$\begin{bmatrix} 2 & 4 & 5 & 2 \\ 2 & 1 & 4 & 5 \\ 3 & 2 & 6 & 1 \end{bmatrix}$$

(c)
$$\begin{bmatrix} 4 & 3 & 3 & 2 & 2 & 6 \\ 6 & 0 & 4 & 2 & 6 & 2 \\ 0 & 7 & 3 & 6 & 2 & 2 \end{bmatrix}$$

(d)
$$\begin{bmatrix} 4 & -3 & -2 \\ -3 & 4 & -2 \\ 0 & 0 & 1 \end{bmatrix}$$

11.6 Carry out 100, 200, and 500 iterations of Brown's algorithm on each of the matrix games in Exercise 11.5 using the computer program in Section 11.9.2.

11.7 Solve approximately the following matrix game using the computer program in Section 11.9.2.

$$
\begin{bmatrix}
4 & 8 & 7 & 0 & 0 & 0 & 0 & 0 & 0 \\
5 & 7 & 3 & 0 & 0 & 0 & 0 & 0 & 0 \\
4 & 1 & 8 & 0 & 0 & 0 & 0 & 0 & 0 \\
0 & 0 & 0 & 9 & 5 & 4 & 0 & 0 & 0 \\
0 & 0 & 0 & 2 & 3 & 8 & 0 & 0 & 0 \\
0 & 0 & 0 & 1 & 7 & 6 & 0 & 0 & 0 \\
0 & 0 & 0 & 0 & 0 & 0 & 7 & 4 & 1 \\
0 & 0 & 0 & 0 & 0 & 0 & 4 & 6 & 2 \\
0 & 0 & 0 & 0 & 0 & 0 & 8 & 3 & 8
\end{bmatrix}
$$

12
PERT

12.1 INTRODUCTION

The success of any large-scale project is very much dependent upon the quality of the planning, scheduling, and controlling of the various phases of the project. Unless some type of planning and coordinating tool is used, the number of phases does not need to be very large before management starts losing control. One such OR tool used on large-scale projects to aid management in expediting and controlling the utilization of personnel, materials, facilities, and time is the *program evaluation and review technique (PERT)*. This technique is used to pinpoint critical areas in a project so necessary adjustments can be made in order to meet the scheduled completion date of the project. PERT is most applicable to large-scale research and development projects which involve a high degree of uncertainty, such as new product development and marketing.

PERT was developed in 1958-1959 as a research and development tool for the U.S. Navy Polaris Missile program. Through its use, the Polaris program was completed 18-24 months ahead of the originally scheduled completion date. Since 1959, PERT has been used successfully in almost every type of large-scale industry. For example, PERT analyses have been used in a number of areas of the computer industry, in the motion picture industry, and in the military. In fact, a PERT analysis is required by the military for all large contracts.

The *critical-path method (CPM)* is another planning and coordinating tool. It was developed in the construction industry where previous experience was used to obtain time and cost estimates of the various phases of the project. Its development was jointly sponsored by E. I. du Pont de Nemours & Company and the Sperry-Rand Corporation. It was applied first to the construction of a chemical plant and then to the shutdown of the plant for overhaul and maintenance.

12.2 PERT NETWORK

The first phase of any PERT analysis is to identify the subprojects or tasks which must be accomplished before the overall project is completed. Each task, which is called an *activity*, requires time and resources. It represents work that must be done. Resources might be personnel, money, materials, facilities, and/or space. It should be clear that not all activities can be accomplished at the same time. Some cannot be started until others have been completed.

The relationship of all activities of a project can be represented by a network involving nodes and arrows. The arrows represent the various activities, and the nodes represent the start and completion of activities. Specifically, the tail of each arrow in Figure 12.1 represents the start of an activity, and the head represents the completion of an activity. The circles or nodes are called *events*. They represent the completion of all activities coming into the node, and the beginning of all activities leaving the node. Events do not require time or resources; they are milestones or points in time that signify the completion of some activities and the beginning of others. An event is said to be accomplished when all activities leading into that event are completed. Activities leading from a given event cannot begin until the event is accomplished. An activity that begins at event i and ends at event j will be referred to as *activity (i,j)*.

Event 1 in Figure 12.1 represents the start of the project, and event 6 represents the completion of the project. Event 3 is not accomplished until activities $(1,3)$ and

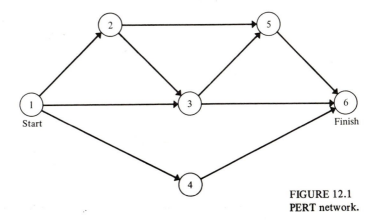

FIGURE 12.1
PERT network.

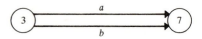

FIGURE 12.2
Two activities from event 3 to event 7.

(2,3) are both completed. Also, activity (3,6) cannot begin until event 3 is accomplished. The final event, event 6, is accomplished when activities (5,6), (3,6), and (4,6) are all completed.

The guidelines and rules for constructing a network to represent the inter-relationship of activities are:

1 Event 1 denotes the start of the project. All activities that are not preceded by other activities emanate from event 1.
2 Event M denotes the completion of the project, where M is the maximum number of events.
3 Activity (i,j) starts at event i and ends at event j.
4 For each activity (i,j), $i < j$.
5 For fixed j, all activities of the form (i,j) must be completed before event j is considered accomplished.
6 Each activity (i,j) must be unique.

Consider the implications of rule 6. If two or more activities need to start at event i and go to event j, dummy events and dummy activities with zero time are set up. For example, suppose two different activities, a and b, need to start at event 3 and end at event 7. This could not be represented as shown in Figure 12.2. Instead, a dummy event 6 and a dummy activity (6,7) are introduced. This is illustrated in Figure 12.3. The dashed line from event 6 to event 7 denotes the dummy activity. The dummy event 6 represents the completion of activity a, while event 7 represents the completion of both activities a and b.

With reference to rule 6 again, suppose a, b, c, and d are four activities that must be accomplished. Activities a and b must precede activity c, but only activity b precedes activity d. This is attained by adding a dummy activity as shown by the dashed line in Figure 12.4.

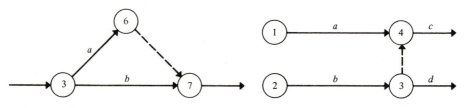

FIGURE 12.3
PERT network with dummy event and activity.

FIGURE 12.4
PERT network with dummy activity (3,4).

Table 12.1 HOUSE CONSTRUCTION ACTIVITIES

	Activities	Preceding activities
a	Start project	
b	Select building site	a
c	Dig basement and foundation	b
d	Purchase carpet	a
e	Purchase basic precut house	a
f	Construct basic precut house	e,t
g	Lay carpet	d,p
h	Finish plumbing	i
i	Lay flooring	j,l
j	Put on roof	f
k	Pour basement and foundation	q
l	Put stairs in basement	f
m	Put up guttering	n
n	Paint outside of house	j
p	Paint inside of house	w
q	Rough-in plumbing	c
r	Wire house for intercom and radio	i
s	Wire house for electricity	i
t	Finish preparation for house construction	k
u	Grade and landscape	m
v	Hang pictures	p
w	Finish walls and ceiling	h,r,s
x	Finish project	g

EXAMPLE 12.2.1 Consider the project of building a house. The activities involved are presented in Table 12.1. A complete PERT network is shown in Figure 12.5.

12.3 TIME ESTIMATES FOR ACTIVITIES (ET)

Time estimates for each activity in a PERT network must be supplied before the network is a useful planning and coordinating tool. In some cases, a single best possible estimate of each activity time is used. However, since PERT was developed primarily for research and development projects, three time estimates are normally used for each activity. These three estimates are:

a = optimistic time—the expected time if everything goes better than expected without delays

m = most likely time—the most realistic time available

b = pessimistic time—the expected time if just about everything goes wrong

Based on the three estimates a, m, and b, the mean completion time for each activity is estimated to be

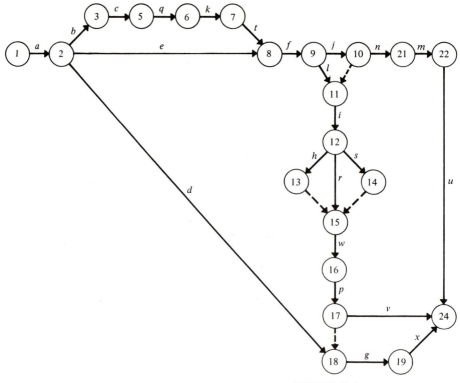

FIGURE 12.5
PERT network for Example 12.2.1.

$$ET = \frac{a + 4m + b}{6} \qquad (12.1)$$

Likewise, the variance of the completion time of each activity is estimated to be

$$\sigma_{ET}^2 = \left(\frac{b - a}{6}\right)^2 \qquad (12.2)$$

Theoretically, the distribution of the completion time of an activity might appear as in Figures 12.6–12.8. Note in each case that the highest point of the distribution occurs at the most likely completion time m. When the completion time of an activity has a distribution similar to the one in Figure 12.6, the probability is 0.5 that the activity will take less than m units of time to complete. Figure 12.7 illustrates the case for which the probability of completing the activity in less than m units of time is *greater than* 0.5, while Figure 12.8 illustrates the case for which the probability of completing the activity in less than m units of time is *less than* 0.5.

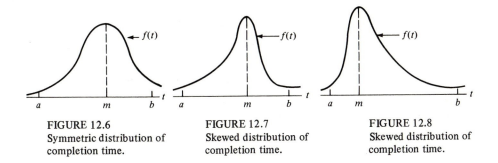

FIGURE 12.6
Symmetric distribution of
completion time.

FIGURE 12.7
Skewed distribution of
completion time.

FIGURE 12.8
Skewed distribution of
completion time.

The three time estimates for each activity are shown as $a - m - b$ above each arrow in Figure 12.9. Estimates of the mean and variance of the completion time of each activity are shown below each arrow. Event 1 is the starting event, and event 7 is the final event. The final event is also called the *sink of the network*.

12.4 EARLIEST EXPECTED COMPLETION TIME OF EVENTS (TE)

Each activity in a PERT network has an expected completion time ET, which is based on either a single best estimate or a composite estimate involving the estimates a, m, and b. Consequently, the expected activity times can be used to calculate the expected completion time of each event. Specifically, for each event the activity times are summed for each possible path leading from the starting event to the given event, and the largest sum is the earliest expected completion time for that event. Fortunately, it is not necessary to sum the activity times over each possible path for each event. Instead, we define:

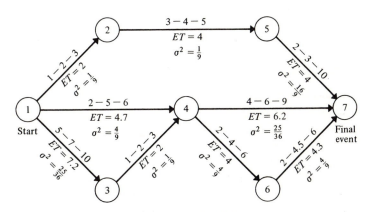

FIGURE 12.9
PERT network with time estimates.

$\text{ET}(I,J) = $ expected completion time of activity (I,J)

$\text{TE}(J) = $ earliest expected completion time of event J

Then for a fixed value of J, say J^*, $\text{TE}(J^*)$ is given by

$$\text{TE}(J^*) = \max_I \, [\text{TE}(I) + \text{ET}(I, J^*)] \qquad (12.3)$$

where I ranges over all activities of the form (I,J^*). For the events in Figure 12.9,

$$\text{TE}(1) = 0$$

$$\text{TE}(2) = \text{TE}(1) + \text{ET}(1,2) = 0 + 2 = 2$$

$$\text{TE}(3) = \text{TE}(1) + \text{ET}(1,3) = 0 + 7.2 = 7.2$$

$$\text{TE}(4) = \max \, \{[\text{TE}(1) + \text{ET}(1,4)], [\text{TE}(3) + \text{ET}(3,4)]\}$$

$$= \max \, [(0 + 4.7),(7.2 + 2)]$$

$$= 9.2$$

$$\text{TE}(5) = \text{TE}(2) + \text{ET}(2,5) = 2 + 4 = 6$$

$$\text{TE}(6) = \text{TE}(4) + \text{ET}(4,6) = 9.2 + 4 = 13.2$$

$$\text{TE}(7) = \max \, \{[\text{TE}(5) + \text{ET}(5,7)], [\text{TE}(4) + \text{ET}(4,7)],$$

$$[\text{TE}(6) + \text{ET}(6,7)]\}$$

$$= \max \, [(6 + 4), (9.2 + 6.2),(13.2 + 4.3)]$$

$$= 17.5$$

These TE values are shown in Figure 12.10. The TE time for each event represents the earliest time the event can be accomplished if each activity J on every path leading to the given event is completed in exactly ET(J) units of time. The path followed to calculate the TE value for the sink or final event is called the *critical path of the network*. The sum of the activity times for the critical path is greater than the sum of the activity times for any other path through the network.

12.5 LATEST ALLOWABLE EVENT COMPLETION TIME (TL)

Another measure that is associated with each event in the PERT network is the *latest allowable event completion time*. It is the latest allowable time an event can occur without delaying the scheduled completion date of the project if all succeeding events are completed as anticipated.

To calculate the latest allowable event completion time for a given event, the activity times are cumulatively subtracted from the scheduled project completion time along the various paths between the given event and the final event. The smallest result is the latest allowable event completion time for that event. Suppose we define

$\text{TL}(I) = $ latest allowable event completion time for event I then for a fixed value of I, say I^*, $TL(I^*)$ is given by

$$TL(I^*) = \min_J [TL(J) - ET(I^*, J)] \qquad (12.4)$$

where J is defined for all activities of the form (I^*, J). Thus, for M events, Equation (12.4) is a recursive equation from which we can calculate $TL(I)$, $I = M, M - 1, M - 2,$ ..., 1. In Figure 12.10, the latest allowable event completion time for event 7 is taken to be the same as the earliest expected completion time $TE(7)$. However, the TL for the final event is generally taken to be the scheduled completion time SD for the project. It may or may not be the same as the TE for that event.

The TL values shown in Figure 12.10 are calculated as follows:

$$TL(7) = TE(7) = 17.5$$
$$TL(6) = TL(7) - ET(6,7) = 17.5 - 4.3 = 13.2$$
$$TL(5) = TL(7) - ET(5,7) = 17.5 - 4.0 = 13.5$$
$$TL(4) = \min \{[TL(7) - ET(4,7)], [TL(6) - ET(4,6)]\}$$
$$= \min [(17.5 - 6.2), (13.2 - 4.0)]$$
$$= 9.2$$
$$TL(3) = TL(4) - ET(3,4) = 9.2 - 2.0 = 7.2$$
$$TL(2) = TL(5) - ET(2,5) = 13.5 - 4.0 = 9.5$$
$$TL(1) = \min \{[TL(2) - ET(1,2)], [TL(3) - ET(1,3)],$$
$$[TL(4) - ET(1,4)]\}$$
$$= \min [(9.5 - 2.0), (7.2 - 7.2), (9.2 - 4.7)]$$
$$= 0$$

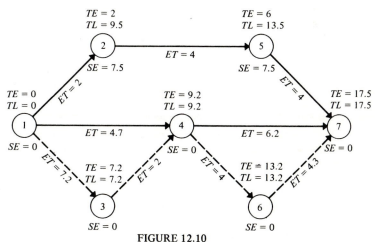

FIGURE 12.10
PERT network with *TE, TL,* and *SE* for each event.

12.6 EVENT SLACK TIMES (SE)

The event slack time SE for each event is the amount of time the event can be delayed without affecting the scheduled completion time for the project. Specifically, the slack time for event J is given by

$$SE(J) = TL(J) - TE(J) \qquad (12.5)$$

Events that have "small" slack times are considered to be "critical" and should be watched very closely. To assist events with "small" slack times, resources can be shifted from activities leading to events with rather large slack times to activities that affect the TE for events with "small" slack times. For example, in Figure 12.10, events 2 and 5 have rather large slack times, so we might want to consider shifting some resources from activities (1,2), (2,5), and/or (5,7) to activities on the critical path. This would tend to "speed up" the activities on the critical path and to "slow down" the activities between events 2, 5, and 7. In general, this procedure will decrease the earliest expected completion time for the project.

The slack time for each event in the example from Section 12.3 is shown in Figure 12.10.

12.7 CRITICAL PATH

The longest path through a PERT network is referred to as the *critical path*. It is the path that is followed to obtain the TE value for the final event.

To establish a reference point from which to calculate the TL value for each event, TL(M) is taken to be the scheduled completion time of the project SD(M). The corresponding slack time is given by

$$SE(M) = TL(M) - TE(M)$$

$$= SD(M) - TE(M) \qquad (12.6)$$

The slack time can be positive, negative, or zero. A positive, negative, or zero slack time indicates the project will be completed ahead of schedule, behind schedule, or on schedule, respectively.

Each event on the critical path will have a slack time equal to the slack time for the final event. Thus, if the final event is expected to be completed exactly on schedule, that is, if

$$TE(M) = SD(M) = TL(M)$$

then
$$SE(M) = TL(M) - TE(M) = 0$$

and each event on the critical path will have a zero slack time. This is the usual assumption made by most authors. However, it is quite possible that the earliest expected completion time of the project will be *less than* or *greater than* the scheduled completion time. If the scheduled project completion time cannot be met $[TE(M) > SD(M)]$, the SE(M) will be negative and each event on the critical path will have a negative slack time of SE(M) units. On the other hand, if current conditions indicate the project will be completed ahead of schedule $[TE(M) < SD(M)]$, SE(M) will be positive and the slack time for each event on the critical path will be SE(M).

What this all means is that if SE(M) is zero or negative, any activity on the critical path which requires time in excess of its expected completion time ET will delay the project completion time accordingly. Of course, this assumes all other activities on the critical path are completed as anticipated.

One of the main objectives of a PERT analysis is to pinpoint the critical path so resources from outside the system or from activities on noncritical paths can be supplied to activities on the critical path if needed. In connection with this, when the actual work begins on a project, the PERT network should be updated either weekly, monthly, or as needed, with all of the latest available information. This information might include scheduled dates, available resources, activity time estimates, actual activity completion times, etc.

The critical path for the example in Figure 12.10 is denoted by the symbol,

- - - - - - - - - - - ->

Since $TE(7) = TL(7)$, the slack time for each event on the critical path is zero. Note, however, that all events on the path $1 \rightarrow 4 \rightarrow 7$ have zero slack times, but the path is not a critical path. To be an activity on the critical path, an activity (I,J) must satisfy three conditions:

1 $TL(I) - TE(I) = SE(M)$
2 $TL(J) - TE(J) = SE(M)$
3 $TE(J) - TE(I) = TL(J) - TL(I) = ET(I,J)$

where SE(M) is the slack time for the final event. All activities on the path $1 \rightarrow 3 \rightarrow 4 \rightarrow 6 \rightarrow 7$ in Figure 12.10 satisfy these conditions, so the path is a critical path.

12.8 PROBABILITY OF COMPLETING EVENTS ON SCHEDULE

Many times scheduled completion times are provided for one or more of the events in a PERT network. In particular, a scheduled completion time is almost always given for the final event. These scheduled completion times can be used with the mean and variance of the completion time of each activity to determine the probability of completing events on schedule. The only necessary assumption is that the completion time of each event has a normal distribution with mean TE and variance σ_{TE}^2, where σ_{TE}^2 is the sum of the variances of those activity times on the path that is used to calculate TE. For example,

$$TE(4) = ET(1,3) + ET(3,4)$$
$$= 7.2 + 2.0$$
$$= 9.2$$

Thus,
$$\sigma^2_{TE(4)} = \sigma^2_{(1,3)} + \sigma^2_{(3,4)}$$
$$= \frac{25}{36} + \frac{1}{9}$$
$$= \frac{29}{36}$$

Note that $\sigma^2_{(1,3)}$ is the variance of the completion time for activity (1,3), and $\sigma^2_{(3,4)}$ is the variance of the completion time for activity (3,4).

For early events of a PERT network (events close to the beginning of the project) the normal distribution assumption may not be too valid; however, it is quite valid for late events (events further into the network). The completion time for a late event is the sum of several activity completion times, each having a certain mean and variance. Consequently, by the central limit theorem given in Section 8.5.2.1, the completion time for the event approaches the normal distribution.

We assume

$T =$ completion time of an event
$TE =$ expected value of T
$\sigma^2_{TE} =$ variance of T
$SD =$ scheduled completion time of an event

then
$$T \sim N(TE, \sigma^2_{TE})$$

It can be shown that

$$Z = \frac{T - TE}{\sigma_{TE}} \sim N(0,1)$$

Suppose we want the probability an event will be completed on or before the scheduled completion time. This probability is given by

$$P(T \leqslant SD) = \int_{-\infty}^{SD} N(TE, \sigma^2_{TE})\, dt = \int_{-\infty}^{(SD-TE)/\sigma_{TE}} N(0,1)\, dt$$

Consider the PERT network in Figure 12.11 and the input data in Table 12.2.

Suppose we want the probability of completing the project on or before the scheduled time. That is, for event 7, we want

$$P[T \leqslant SD(7)] = P(T \leqslant 25) = \int_{-\infty}^{25} N(25, 5.5)\, dt = \int_{-\infty}^{(25-25)/\sqrt{5.5}} N(0,1)\, dt$$
$$= 0.5$$

Table 12.2 INPUT DATA FOR NETWORK IN FIGURE 12.11

					Activities					
Estimates	$1 \rightarrow 2$	$1 \rightarrow 3$	$1 \rightarrow 4$	$2 \rightarrow 5$	$3 \rightarrow 4$	$3 \rightarrow 6$	$4 \rightarrow 5$	$4 \rightarrow 7$	$5 \rightarrow 7$	$6 \rightarrow 7$
a	2.20	1.51	5.00	6.00	2.00	5.51	1.76	4.00	5.00	2.51
m	2.45	6.12	9.90	7.50	5.00	10.21	4.06	8.16	10.38	5.62
b	6.00	10.00	15.39	12.00	8.00	14.00	6.00	11.35	13.49	11.00

Thus, there is a 50–50 chance of completing the project on schedule. Likewise, the probability of completing event 5 on or before the scheduled completion time of $SD(5) = 16$ is

$$P[T \leqslant SD(5)] = P(T \leqslant 16) = \int_{-\infty}^{16} N(15, 3.5)\, dt = \int_{-\infty}^{(16-15)/\sqrt{3.5}} N(0,1)\, dt$$

$$= \int_{-\infty}^{0.53} N(0,1)\, dt$$

$$= 1 - \int_{-\infty}^{-0.53} N(0,1)\, dt$$

$$= 1 - 0.2981$$

$$= 0.70$$

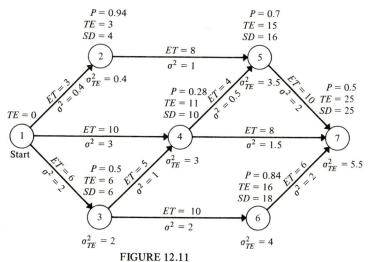

FIGURE 12.11
PERT network with probability of completing events before scheduled completion time.

Table 12.3 PROBABILITY OF COMPLETING EVENTS BEFORE SCHEDULED COMPLETION TIME

Event	TE	SD	σ^2_{TE}	$x = \dfrac{SD - TE}{\sigma_{TE}}$	$P(T \leqslant SD) = \int_{-\infty}^{x} N(0,1)dt$
2	3	4	0.4	1.58	0.94
3	6	6	2.0	0.0	0.50
4	11	10	3.0	−0.58	0.28
5	15	16	3.5	0.53	0.70
6	16	18	4.0	1.0	0.84
7	25	25	5.5	0.0	0.50

Table 12.3 presents the information needed to calculate the probability of completing events on or before the scheduled completion time for the example in Figure 12.11.

After calculating the probability of completing each event on schedule, events with low probabilities are noted and measures are taken to "speed up" the completion time of those activities leading up to the events in question.

12.9 COMPUTER PROGRAM FOR PERT ANALYSIS

Given the optimistic, most likely, and pessimistic completion times for each activity under consideration, this program is designed to calculate and print the

(a) Mean completion time for each activity
(b) Variance of the completion time for each activity
(c) Earliest expected completion time for each event
(d) Latest allowable event completion time for each event
(e) Slack time for each event
(f) Critical path
(g) Value $x(k)$ such that the integral of the $N(0,1)$ distribution from $-\infty$ to $x(k)$ is the probability of completing event k on or before the scheduled completion time

Note in (g) that $x(k)$ is the value such that

$$P[T(k) \leqslant SD(k)] = \int_{-\infty}^{x(k)} N(0,1)\, dt$$

where $T(k)$ is the completion time of event k. It is calculated using the formula

$$x(k) = \frac{SD(k) - TE(k)}{\sigma_{TE(k)}}$$

Once $x(k)$ is given, the user must find the area under the N(0,1) curve from $-\infty$ to $x(k)$ using the cumulative N(0,1) distribution in Table A.1. The value obtained is the probability of completing event k on or before the scheduled completion time.

The comment cards at the beginning of the program explain how to enter the data. The program is set up to handle a maximum of 100 activities. It can be expanded by changing the two DIMENSION statements and the INTEGER statement at the beginning of the program. The program as printed occupies 44K bytes of core storage.

The data and the PERT analysis for the problem in Figure 12.11 follow the computer program listing.

```
C     ************************************************************************
C     *                                                                    *
C     *                   ***  PERT  NETWORK  ***                          *
C     *                                                                    *
C     * THIS PROGRAM WILL DETERMINE THE CRITICAL PATH IN A PERT NETWORK AND *
C     * WILL PROVIDE THE INFORMATION NECESSARY TO DETERMINE THE PROBABILITY *
C     * OF COMPLETING EACH EVENT ON OR BEFORE THE SCHEDULED COMPLETION TIME. *
C     *                                                                    *
C     * TO CONSERVE STORAGE SPACE, THIS PROGRAM MAKES USE OF AN  N X 7      *
C     * MATRIX CALLED  C IN ORDER TO STORE                                 *
C     *         A(I,J)   ACTIVITY FROM EVENT I TO EVENT J                  *
C     *                     J IS STORED IN C(K,2)                          *
C     *                     I IS STORED IN C(K,1)    (K=1,2,...,N)         *
C     *         AT(I,J)  OPTIMISTIC COMPLETION TIME FOR ACTIVITY (I,J) IN C(K,3)*
C     *         MT(I,J)  MOST LIKELY COMPLETION TIME FOR ACTIVITY(I,J) IN C(K,4)*
C     *         BT(I,J)  PESSIMISTIC COMPLETION TIME FOR ACTIVITY(I,J) IN C(K,5)*
C     *         ET(I,J)  ESTIMATED MEAN COMPLETION TIME FOR ACTIVITY(I,J)  *
C     *                     IN C(K,6)                                      *
C     *         SIG(I,J) ESTIMATED VARIANCE OF COMPLETION TIME OF ACTIVITY(I,J) *
C     *                     IN C(K,7)                                      *
C     *                                                                    *
C     * THIS PROGRAM IS DESIGNED                                           *
C     *                                                                    *
C     *    TO READ                                                         *
C     *         CARD 1   COLS  2-80   TITLE  DESCRIPTION OF THE PROBLEM USING *
C     *                                      ANY CHARACTERS ON KEYPUNCH    *
C     *                                      ** COLUMN 1 MUST BE LEFT BLANK ** *
C     *         CARD 2   COLS  1- 5   M  MAXIMUM NUMBER OF EVENTS ON NETWORK(I5)*
C     *                        6-10   N  MAXIMUM NUMBER OF ACTIVITIES ON   *
C     *                                  NETWORK ( INCLUDING DUMMY)  (I5)  *
C     *         CARDS 3 TO N+2  COLS  1-10   C(K,1)   I OF A(I,J)          *
C     *                              11-20   C(K,2)   J OF A(I,J)          *
C     *                              21-30   C(K,3)   AT(I,J)             *
C     *                              31-40   C(K,4)   MT(I,J)             *
C     *                              41-50   C(K,5)   BT(I,J)             *
C     *                   PUNCH ONE CARD FOR EACH OF THE N ACTIVITIES  (5F10.0)*
C     *         CARD N+3   SD(J)   SCHEDULED COMLETION TIME FOR EVENT J    *
C     *                           (J=1,2,...,M)  PUNCH IN FORMAT(8F10.0)   *
C     *                           USING AS MANY CARDS AS NECESSARY.        *
C     *                           SET SD(1)=0.=SD(M).  PROPER VALUE FOR SD(M)*
C     *                           WILL BE FILLED IN BY PROGRAM.            *
C     *              TO SOLVE MORE THAN ONE PROBLEM AT A TIME, REPEAT THE  *
C     *              READ SEQUENCE, AND STACK THE DATA ONE BEHIND THE OTHER *
C     *                                                                    *
C     *    TO CALCULATE AND PRINT                                          *
C     *         ET(I,J)    MEAN COMPLETION TIME  (C(K,6))                  *
C     *         SIG(I,J)   VARIANCE OF COMPLETION TIME OF EACH ACTIVITY (C(K,7))*
C     *         TE(J)      EARLIEST EXPECTED COMPLETION TIME OF EVENT J    *
C     *         TL(I)      LATEST ALLOWABLE EVENT COMPLETION TIME FOR EVENT I*
C     *         SD         SCHEDULED COMPLETION TIME FOR ENTIRE PROJECT (TL(M))*
C     *         SE(J)      SLACK TIME FOR EACH EVENT  J                    *
C     *         SIGTE(J)   SUM OF VARIANCES OF ACTIVITY TIME IN PATH USED TO *
C     *                    CALCULATE TE(J)                                 *
C     *         CPATH(I)   CRITICAL PATH                                   *
C     *         X(K)       CRITICAL VALUE OF CUMULATIVE N(0,1) DISTRIBUTION *
C     *                    TO DETERMINE THE PROBABILITY OF COMPLETING EVENT K*
C     *                    CN OR BEFORE THE SCHEDULED COMPLETION TIME      *
C     *                                                                    *
C     ************************************************************************
      DIMENSION C(100,7),CPATH(100),SIGTE(100),SD(100)
      DIMENSION TE(100),TL(100),SE(100),X(100),TITLE(20)
      INTEGER CPATH,FLAG(100)
    5 READ(5,10,END=2000)TITLE
   10 FORMAT(20A4)
      WRITE(6,6)TITLE
    6 FORMAT('1',20A4 //)
      READ(5,15)M,N
   15 FORMAT(2I5)
      DO 25 I=1,N
      READ(5,20)(C(I,J),J=1,5)
```

```
   20 FORMAT(5F10.0)
      FLAG(I)=0
   25 CONTINUE
      READ(5,27)(SD(I),I=1,M)
   27 FORMAT(8F10.0)
C     ****************************************************************************
C     *   STEP 1                                                                *
C     *          CALCULATE ESTIMATED MEAN COMPLETION TIME OF ACTIVITY ET(I,J)   *
C     *          CALCULATE ESTIMATED VARIANCE OF COMPLETION TIME FOR EACH       *
C     *              EVENT   SIG(I,J)                                           *
C     ****************************************************************************
      DO 30 I=1,N
      C(I,6)=(C(I,3)+4*C(I,4)+C(I,5))/6
      C(I,7)=(C(I,5)*C(I,5)-2*C(I,5)*C(I,3)+C(I,3)*C(I,3))/36
   30 CONTINUE
      WRITE(6,35)
   35 FORMAT(9X,'I',9X,'J','   AT(I,J)    MT(I,J)    BT(I,J)    ET(I,J)    S
     *IG(I,J)'/)
      DO 40 I=1,N
   40 WRITE(6,45)(C(I,J),J=1,7)
   45 FORMAT(7F10.3)
C     ****************************************************************************
C     *   STEP 2                                                                *
C     *          CALCULATE EARLIEST EXPECTED COMPLETION TIME FOR EVENT J   TE(J)*
C     ****************************************************************************
      TE(1)=0.
      SIGTE(1)=0.
      DO 50 J=2,M
      TMAX=0.
      SIGMAX=0.
      DO 55 K=1,N
      IF(C(K,2).NE.J) GO TO 55
      TE(J)=TE(C(K,1))+C(K,6)
      SIGTE(J)=SIGTE(C(K,1))+C(K,7)
      IF(TE(J).LE.TMAX) GO TO 55
      TMAX=TE(J)
      SIGMAX=SIGTE(J)
   55 CONTINUE
      TE(J)=TMAX
      SIGTE(J)=SIGMAX
   50 CONTINUE
C     ****************************************************************************
C     *   STEP 3                                                                *
C     *          CALCULATE LATEST ALLOWABLE COMPLETION TIME FOR EVENT J   TL(J) *
C     ****************************************************************************
      TL(M)=TE(M)
      SD(M)=TL(M)
      DO 60 IF=2,M
      I=M-IF+1
      TMIN=100000.
      DO 65 KF=1,N
      K=N-KF+1
      IF(C(K,1).NE.I) GO TO 65
      TL(I)=TL(C(K,2))-C(K,6)
      IF(TL(I).GE.TMIN) GO TO 65
      TMIN=TL(I)
   65 CONTINUE
      TL(I)=TMIN
   60 CONTINUE
C     ****************************************************************************
C     *   STEP 4                                                                *
C     *          CALCULATE SLACK TIME FOR EACH EVENT J   SE(J)                  *
C     ****************************************************************************
      DO 70 J=1,M
   70 SE(J)=TL(J)-TE(J)
      WRITE(6,75)
   75 FORMAT(  // 5X,'EVENT J',10X,'TE(J)',10X,'TL(J)',10X,'SE(J)')
      DO 80 J=1,M
   80 WRITE(6,85)J,TE(J),TL(J),SE(J)
   85 FORMAT(/ 7X,I5,3F15.3)
```

```
C     ***********************************************************************
C     *    STEP 5                                                          *
C     *         FIND ACTIVITIES ON CRITICAL PATH                           *
C     ***********************************************************************
      DO 90 K=1,N
      I=C(K,1)
      J=C(K,2)
      IF(ABS(TL(I)-TE(I)-SE(M)).GT..0001) GO TO 90
      IF(ABS(TL(J)-TE(J)-SE(M)).GT..0001) GO TO 90
      IF(ABS(TE(J)-TE(I)-TL(J)+TL(I)).GT..0001.OR.ABS(TL(J)-TL(I)-C(K,6)
     *).GT..0001) GO TO 90
      FLAG(K)=1
   90 CONTINUE
      CPATH(1)=1
      KP=1
      DO 100 K=1,N
      I=C(K,1)
      J=C(K,2)
      IF(FLAG(K).EQ.0) GO TO 100
      IF(I.NE.CPATH(KP)) GO TO 100
      KP=KP+1
      CPATH(KP)=J
  100 CONTINUE
      WRITE(6,105)(CPATH(I),I=1,KP)
  105 FORMAT( // 5X,'CRITICAL PATH',15I4)
C     ***********************************************************************
C     *    STEP 6                                                          *
C     *         CALCULATE CRITICAL VALUE OF CUMULATIVE N(0,1) DISTRIBUTION *
C     *             TO DETERMINE PROBABILITY OF COMPLETING EVENT BEFORE     *
C     *             SCHEDULED COMPLETION TIME                              *
C     ***********************************************************************
      DO 110 K=2,M
  110 X(K)=(SD(K)-TE(K))/SQRT(SIGTE(K))
      WRITE(6,111)
  111 FORMAT(  // 5X,'EVENT',13X,'TE',13X,'SD',10X,'SIGTE',13X,'X')
      DO 115 K=2,M
  115 WRITE(6,120)K,TE(K),SD(K),SIGTE(K),X(K)
  120 FORMAT(/ 7X,I5,4F15.3)
      GO TO 5
 2000 STOP
      END


/DATA

EXAMPLE FROM TABLE 12.2 AND FIGURE 12.11
      7   10
           1.        2.        2.20      2.45      6.00
           1.        3.        1.51      6.12     10.00
           1.        4.        5.00      9.90     15.39
           2.        5.        6.00      7.50     12.00
           3.        4.        2.00      5.00      8.00
           3.        6.        5.51     10.12     14.00
           4.        5.        1.76      4.06      6.00
           4.        7.        4.00      8.16     11.35
           5.        7.        5.00     10.38     13.49
           6.        7.        2.51      5.62     11.00
           0.        4.        6.       10.       16.       18.       0.
```

EXAMPLE FROM TABLE 12.2 AND FIGURE 12.11

I	J	AT(I,J)	MT(I,J)	BT(I,J)	ET(I,J)	SIG(I,J)
1.000	2.000	2.200	2.450	6.000	3.000	0.401
1.000	3.000	1.510	6.120	10.000	5.998	2.002
1.000	4.000	5.000	9.900	15.390	9.998	2.999
2.000	5.000	6.000	7.500	12.000	8.000	1.000
3.000	4.000	2.000	5.000	8.000	5.000	1.000
3.000	6.000	5.510	10.120	14.000	9.998	2.002
4.000	5.000	1.760	4.060	6.000	4.000	0.499
4.000	7.000	4.000	8.160	11.350	7.998	1.501
5.000	7.000	5.000	10.380	13.490	10.002	2.002
6.000	7.000	2.510	5.620	11.000	5.998	2.002

EVENT J	TE(J)	TL(J)	SE(J)
1	0.0	-0.000	-0.000
2	3.000	6.998	3.998
3	5.998	5.998	-0.000
4	10.998	10.998	-0.000
5	14.998	14.998	-0.000
6	15.997	19.002	3.005
7	25.000	25.000	0.0

CRITICAL PATH   1   3   4   5   7

EVENT	TE	SD	SIGTE	X
2	3.000	4.000	0.401	1.579
3	5.998	6.000	2.002	0.001
4	10.998	10.000	3.002	-0.576
5	14.998	16.000	3.502	0.535
6	15.997	18.000	4.004	1.001
7	25.000	25.000	5.504	0.0

SELECTED BIBLIOGRAPHY

1 Archibald, R. D., and R. L. Villoria: "Network-based Management Systems (PERT/CPM)," John Wiley & Sons, Inc., New York, 1966.
2 Baker, B. N.: "An Introduction to PERT–CPM," Richard D. Irwin, Inc., Homewood, Ill., 1964.
3 Evarts, H. E.: "Introduction to PERT," Allyn and Bacon, Inc., Boston, 1964.
4 Levin, R., and C. A. Kirkpatrick: "Planning and Control with PERT/CPM," McGraw-Hill Book Company, New York, 1966.
5 Moder, Joseph J., and C. R. Phillips: "Project Management with CPM and PERT," 2d ed., D. Van Nostrand Company, Inc., New York, 1970.
6 Wiest, J. D., and F. Levy: "A Management Guide to PERT/CPM," Prentice-Hall, Inc., Englewood Cliffs, N.J., 1969.

EXERCISES

12.1   Consider the following PERT network and determine
   (*a*)   The earliest expected completion time for each event
   (*b*)   The latest allowable event completion time for each event
   (*c*)   The slack time for each event
   (*d*)   The critical path through the network

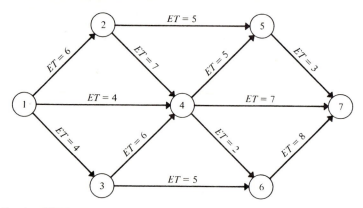

12.2   Given the following PERT network, determine
   (*a*)   Earliest expected completion time for each event
   (*b*)   Latest allowable completion time for each event
   (*c*)   Slack time for each event
   (*d*)   The critical path
   (*e*)   The probability the project will be completed on schedule if the scheduled completion time is 32
   (*f*)   The assumptions needed in (*e*)

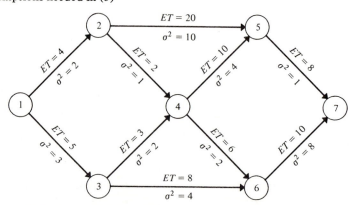

12.3   Rework Exercise 12.2 with the mean completion time for activity (2,5) changed to 8 and the variance of activity (2,5) changed to 3.
12.4   If event 4 in Exercise 12.2 is scheduled for completion at time 8, what is the probability it will be completed on or before the scheduled time?

12.5 If event 6 in Exercise 12.2 is scheduled for completion at time 12, what is the probability of completing it on or before the scheduled time?

12.6 The scheduled project completion time for the network in Exercise 12.2 has been moved back to time 36. What is the probability of completing the project on schedule?

12.7 Consider the optimistic, most likely, and pessimistic times for each activity that are given by Table 12.4. Use the computer program in Section 12.9 to carry out a complete PERT analysis.

Table 12.4

Activities	a	m	b
(1,2)	0	4	10
(2,3)	1	2	5
(2,7)	2	6	15
(2,17)	2	5	10
(3,4)	1	2	4
(4,5)	1	2	5
(5,6)	1	2	3
(6,7)	1	3	6
(7,8)	3	4	8
(8,9)	2	3	5
(8,10)	1	1	2
(9,10)	0	0	0
(9,19)	2	3	6
(10,11)	1	2	4
(11,12)	3	5	8
(11,13)	2	4	7
(11,14)	1	2	5
(12,14)	0	0	0
(13,14)	0	0	0
(14,15)	3	5	8
(15,16)	3	6	10
(16,17)	0	0	0
(16,21)	0.1	0.5	1
(17,18)	2	3	5
(18,21)	0	0	0
(19,20)	0.5	1	2
(20,21)	2	4	10

QUEUEING THEORY

13.1 INTRODUCTION

Queueing theory deals with all aspects of a situation in which customers must wait for a given service. Typical queueing situations are:

Students waiting to register for classes
Airplanes waiting to land
Machines waiting to be repaired
People waiting in a doctor's office
People waiting for gasoline at a service station
Students waiting for their computer results
People waiting at a stop light

Waiting lines (queues) are a part of everyone's daily life. They form when the current demand for a given service exceeds the capacity to provide the service. In most cases, additional service facilities could be provided to decrease queues or to prevent queues from forming; however, the cost to provide the additional service may cause the margin of profit to drop below an acceptable level. On the other hand, excessively long waiting lines result in lost sales and lost customers. Hence, problems arise because of

Too much demand (excessive waiting by customers)
Too little demand (excessive idle time at the service facility)

The problem faced by management is how to balance the cost associated with waiting against the cost associated with the prevention of waiting in order to maximize profits. An analysis of queueing systems will provide the answer to this problem under fairly general conditions. However, before looking at how queueing problems can be solved, consider the general framework of a queueing system.

A queueing system involves customers (students, airplanes, machines, etc.) arriving at a constant or variable rate for service at a service facility. If arriving customers can enter the service facility, they do so. If they must wait for service, they join or begin a queue, and remain in the queue until they can be serviced. They are then serviced at a constant or variable rate and leave the system. The queueing system involves both the waiting line and the service facility as shown in Figure 13.1.

There are many types of queueing systems, but all can be classified according to the following characteristics:

1 The input or arrival process This includes the distribution of the number of arrivals per unit of time, the number of queues that are permitted to form, the maximum queue length, and the maximum number of customers desiring service (source).

2 The service process This includes the distribution of the time to service a customer, the number of servers, and the arrangement of servers (in parallel, in series, etc.).

3 Queue discipline This is the manner in which customers form a queue [first come, first served (FIFO), last come, first served (LIFO), random selection, priority selection, etc.].

The framework of several typical queueing systems is illustrated in Figures 13.2–13.5.

13.2 NOTATION AND ASSUMPTIONS

In this chapter we assume

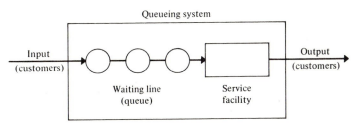

FIGURE 13.1

Single queue, single-server queueing system.

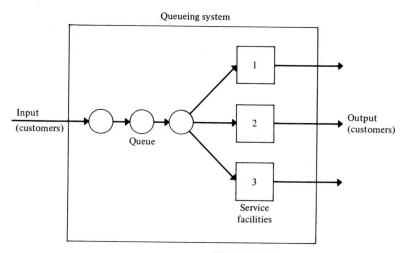

FIGURE 13.2

Single queue, multiple servers in parallel.

(*a*) Service is provided on a first come, first served (FIFO) basis.

(*b*) Customers arrive completely at random but at a certain average rate.

(*c*) The queueing system is in a steady-state condition.

These three assumptions are valid in many realistic queueing systems and will serve to illustrate the use of queueing theory. Assumption (*a*) says that a customer who arrives first will be serviced first regardless of whether he joins a queue or not. Assumption (*b*) says that an arrival is equally likely to occur at any time and is independent of the time that has elapsed since the last arrival. This is equivalent to saying that the number of arrivals per unit of time is a random variable with a Poisson distribution. That is, if

X = number of arrivals per unit of time

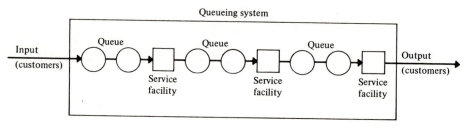

FIGURE 13.3

Single queue, multiple servers in series.

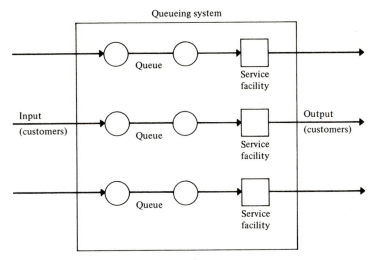

FIGURE 13.4

Multiple queues, multiple servers.

then

$$f(x) = P(X = x) = \frac{e^{-\lambda}\lambda^x}{x!} \quad \begin{array}{l} x = 0, 1, 2, \ldots \\ \lambda > 0 \end{array} \quad (13.1)$$

$$E(X) = \lambda$$

where λ is the average number of arrivals per unit of time. Another interesting result of assumption (*b*) is that the time between consecutive arrivals T (also called the *interarrival time*) has an exponential distribution with the same parameter λ. This result is derived in Appendix B. Thus, if

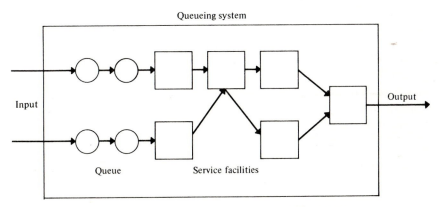

FIGURE 13.5

Multiple queues, multiple servers.

T = time between consecutive arrivals

then

$$g(t) = \lambda e^{-\lambda t} \quad \begin{matrix} t > 0 \\ \lambda > 0 \end{matrix} \quad (13.2)$$

$$E(T) = \frac{1}{\lambda}$$

In summary, if the number of arrivals per unit of time has a Poisson distribution with mean λ, then the time between consecutive arrivals has an exponential distribution with mean $1/\lambda$. The queueing system in this situation is said to have a *Poisson input*, and customers are said to arrive according to a *Poisson process*.

EXAMPLE 13.2.1 Suppose cars arrive at a single-pump service station completely at random with an average of 5 min between arrivals. An hour is selected as the unit of time since the unit of time is purely arbitrary. Thus, cars arrive according to a Poisson process with an average of $\lambda = 12$ cars/hr. The distribution of the number of arrivals per hour X is

$$f(x) = P(X = x) = \frac{e^{-\lambda}\lambda^x}{x!} = \frac{e^{-12}12^x}{x!} \quad x = 0, 1, 2, \ldots$$

$$E(X) = 12 \text{ cars/hr}$$

The distribution of the time between consecutive arrivals T is

$$g(t) = 12e^{-12t} \quad t > 0$$

$$E(T) = \frac{1}{12} \text{ hr between arrivals}$$

Assumption (c) means the queueing system has been operating long enough to be independent of the initial state of the system and is independent of time. That is, the system has reached a state of equilibrium with respect to time. The distribution of the number of arrivals per unit of time and the distribution of the service time do not change with time.

The development of important quantities for many queueing models is based on the probability of n customers (arrivals) in the system at any point in time. Likewise, the distribution of the number of arrivals per unit of time and the distribution of service time are often dependent upon the number of customers in the system. For example, it may be that servers in the service facility will work faster as the waiting line becomes longer.

Suppose we let

S_n = number of customers in the system
$P_n(t)$ = probability of n customers in the system at time t
λ_n = average arrival rate when n customers are in the system (both waiting and being served)
μ_n = average service rate when n customers are in the system

The system being in steady-state does not imply that the arrival rate and service rate are independent of the number of customers in the system. For finite queue, limited source, and multiple-server models, λ_n and μ_n will be functions of the number of customers in the system. In steady-state, we will use the notation

P_n = probability of n customers in the system at any point in time

13.3 QUEUEING MODELS WITH POISSON INPUT—EXPONENTIAL SERVICE

In this section we assume

(a) Arrivals to the system occur completely at random.
(b) Arrivals form a single queue.
(c) First in, first out queue discipline (FIFO).
(d) Departures from the system occur completely at random.
(e) The probability of an arrival in the interval t to $t + \Delta t$, for Δt sufficiently small, when the system is in state S_n at time t is $\lambda_n \Delta t$.
(f) The probability of a departure in the interval t to $t + \Delta t$, for Δt sufficiently small, when the system is in state S_n at time t is $\mu_n \Delta t$.
(g) The probability of more than one arrival and/or departure in the interval t to $t + \Delta t$, for Δt sufficiently small, when the system is in state S_n at time t is "0" $\cdot \Delta t$, where "0" denotes a negligible term.

With these basic assumptions, we can derive a set of differential equations, which, when solved, will yield $P_n(t)$. In steady-state the differential equations become the difference equations

$$\lambda_{n-1}P_{n-1} + \mu_{n+1}P_{n+1} - (\lambda_n + \mu_n)P_n = 0 \qquad n > 0 \qquad (13.3)$$
$$-\lambda_0 P_0 + \mu_1 P_1 = 0 \qquad n = 0 \qquad (13.4)$$

These equations are derived in Appendix B. Equations (13.3) and (13.4) may be solved by successive substitution to yield P_1, P_2, ... as functions of P_0, λ_i, and μ_i for $i = 1$, 2, ... That is,

$$P_1 = \frac{\lambda_0}{\mu_1} P_0 \qquad \text{from Equation (13.4)}$$

$$P_2 = \frac{(\lambda_1 + \mu_1)P_1 - \lambda_0 P_0}{\mu_2} = \frac{(\lambda_1 + \mu_1)\left(\dfrac{\lambda_0}{\mu_1}\right)P_0 - \lambda_0 P_0}{\mu_2}$$

$$P_2 = \frac{\lambda_0 \lambda_1}{\mu_1 \mu_2} P_0$$

$$P_3 = \frac{\lambda_0 \lambda_1 \lambda_2}{\mu_1 \mu_2 \mu_3} P_0$$

. . . .

$$P_n = \frac{\lambda_0 \lambda_1 \cdots \lambda_{n-1}}{\mu_1 \mu_2 \cdots \mu_n} P_0 = \left(\frac{\prod_{i=0}^{n-1} \lambda_i}{\prod_{i=1}^{n} \mu_i} \right) P_0 \qquad \text{for } n = 1, 2, \ldots \qquad (13.5)$$

We can now make use of the fact that

$$\sum_{n=0}^{\infty} P_n = 1$$

to determine P_0. When P_0 is determined, all other P_n's can be determined. Thus, from Equation (13.5)

$$\sum_{n=0}^{\infty} P_n = P_0 + \sum_{n=1}^{\infty} \left(\frac{\prod_{i=0}^{n-1} \lambda_i}{\prod_{i=1}^{n} \mu_i} \right) P_0 = 1$$

Hence,

$$P_0 = \frac{1}{1 + \sum_{n=1}^{\infty} \left(\frac{\prod_{i=0}^{n-1} \lambda_i}{\prod_{i=1}^{n} \mu_i} \right)} \qquad (13.6)$$

Equations (13.5) and (13.6) provide the basis for the development of important quantities for the queueing models in Sections 13.3.1–13.3.6.

13.3.1 Infinite Queue–Infinite Source, Single-Server Model

Assume

  (a) The average arrival rate is constant; $\lambda_n = \lambda$ for all n.
  (b) The average service rate is constant; $\mu_n = \mu$ for all n.
  (c) The average arrival rate is less than the average service rate; $\lambda < \mu$. This assures that an infinite queue will not build up.

With these assumptions, we can determine $P_0, P_1, P_2, \ldots$ as follows:

$$\sum_{n=0}^{\infty} \left(\frac{\lambda}{\mu} \right)^n = \frac{1}{1 - \frac{\lambda}{\mu}} \qquad \text{since } \frac{\lambda}{\mu} < 1$$

$$\sum_{n=0}^{\infty} P_n = 1$$

Therefore,
$$\sum_{n=0}^{\infty} P_n = \sum_{n=0}^{\infty} \left(\frac{\lambda}{\mu}\right)^n P_0 = \frac{P_0}{1 - \lambda/\mu} = 1$$

Thus,
$$P_0 = 1 - \frac{\lambda}{\mu} \qquad (13.7)$$

$$P_n = \left(\frac{\lambda}{\mu}\right)^n \left(1 - \frac{\lambda}{\mu}\right) \qquad n = 1, 2, \ldots \qquad (13.8)$$

For this model, let

$\quad X =$ number of arrivals per unit of time

then
$$f(x) = \frac{e^{-\lambda}\lambda^x}{x!} \qquad \begin{matrix} x = 0, 1, 2, \ldots \\ \lambda > 0 \end{matrix}$$

$$E(X) = \lambda$$

The parameter λ, then, is the average arrival rate per unit of time. Also, let

$\quad T =$ time to service a customer

then
$$g(t) = \mu e^{-\mu t} \qquad \begin{matrix} t > 0 \\ \mu > 0 \end{matrix}$$

$$E(T) = \frac{1}{\mu}$$

We noted earlier that if the number of arrivals per unit of time has a Poisson distribution with parameter λ, then the interarrival time (the time between consecutive arrivals) has an exponential distribution with the same parameter λ. Likewise, if the service time has an exponential distribution with parameter μ (completely random departures), then the number of customers serviced per unit of time has a Poisson distribution with parameter μ. Thus, if

$\quad X_s =$ number of customers serviced per unit of time

then
$$f(x_s) = \frac{e^{-\mu}\mu^{x_s}}{x_s!} \qquad \begin{matrix} x_s = 0, 1, 2, \ldots \\ \mu > 0 \end{matrix}$$

$$E(X_s) = \mu$$

In general, the parameter λ is referred to as the *arrival rate* and the parameter μ is referred to as the *service rate*.

One is generally interested in modeling a given queueing system and then in studying certain interesting characteristics to determine if measures should be taken to modify the queueing system. Modifications might take the form of adding additional servers to the service facility, providing more space in the queueing area, or buying a new piece of equipment to increase the service rate. Most decisions are based on several useful quantities which can be obtained through the use of Equations (13.7) and (13.8); namely,

$$L = \frac{\lambda}{\mu - \lambda} = \text{average number of customers in the system} \qquad (13.9)$$

Que length $$L_q = \frac{\lambda^2}{\mu(\mu - \lambda)} = \text{average number of customers in the queue} \qquad (13.10)$$

$$L_w = \frac{\mu}{\mu - \lambda} = \text{average number of customers in nonempty} \qquad (13.11)$$
$$\text{queues}$$

$$W = \frac{1}{\mu - \lambda} = \text{average time a customer spends in the system} \qquad (13.12)$$

$$W_q = \frac{\lambda}{\mu(\mu - \lambda)} = \text{average time a customer spends in the queue} \qquad (13.13)$$

$$W_w = \frac{1}{\mu - \lambda} = \text{average time a customer spends in the} \qquad (13.14)$$
$$\text{queue if he must wait}$$

$$P(n > k) = \left(\frac{\lambda}{\mu}\right)^{k+1} = \text{probability of more than } k \text{ customers} \qquad (13.15)$$
$$\text{in the system}$$

$$P(T > t) = e^{-\mu(1 - \lambda/\mu)t} = \text{probability the time in the system is} \qquad (13.16)$$
$$\text{greater than } t$$

Several of these quantities are derived in Appendix B. If any one of the quantities L, L_q, W, or W_q can be determined, the others can be determined from the relationships

$$L = \lambda W$$

$$L_q = \lambda W_q$$

$$W = W_q + \frac{1}{\mu}$$

$$L = L_q + \frac{\lambda}{\mu}$$

With the exception of the finite queue and limited source models, these relationships hold for all of the models described in this book.

EXAMPLE 13.3.1 Customers arrive at a one-person barber shop according to a Poisson process with a mean interarrival time of 20 min. Customers spend an average of 15 min in the barber chair. Thus, if an hour is used as a unit of time,

$\lambda = 3$ customers/hr
$\mu = 4$ customers/hr

(*a*) What is the probability a customer will not have to wait for a haircut? The customer will not have to wait if there are no customers in the barber shop. Thus

$$P_0 = 1 - \frac{\lambda}{\mu}$$

$$= 1 - \frac{3}{4}$$

$$= 0.25$$

(b) What is the expected number of customers in the barber shop?

L = expected number of customers in the barber shop

$$= \frac{\lambda}{\mu - \lambda}$$

$$= \frac{3}{4 - 3}$$

$$= 3 \text{ customers}$$

(c) How much time can a customer expect to spend in the barber shop?

W = expected time in the shop

$$= \frac{1}{\mu - \lambda}$$

$$= \frac{1}{4 - 3}$$

$$= 1 \text{ hr}$$

(d) Management will put in another chair and hire another barber when a customer's average time in the shop exceeds 1.25 hr. How much must the average rate of arrivals increase to warrant a second barber? We want the value of λ such that

$$W = \frac{1}{4 - \lambda} = 1.25$$

Thus,
$$1.25(4 - \lambda) = 1$$

$$\lambda = 3.2 \text{ customers/hr}$$

The arrival rate must be increased 0.2 customers/hr to warrant a second barber. Other quantities that can be determined are

$$L_q = \frac{\lambda^2}{\mu(\mu - \lambda)}$$

$$= \frac{(3)^2}{4(4 - 3)}$$

$$= 2.25 \text{ customers} \quad \text{average number of customers in the queue}$$

$$W_q = \frac{\lambda}{\mu(\mu - \lambda)}$$

$$= \frac{3}{4(4 - 3)}$$

$$= 0.75 \text{ hr} \qquad \text{average time customers spend in the queue}$$

$$P(n > 3) = \left(\frac{\lambda}{\mu}\right)^4$$

$$= \left(\frac{3}{4}\right)^4$$

$$\approx 0.32 \qquad \text{probability of more than 3 customers in the system}$$

$$P(T > t) = e^{-\mu(1 - \lambda/\mu)t}$$

$$= e^{-4(1 - 3/4)t}$$

$$= e^{-t}$$

$$(P(T > 0.5 \text{ hr}) = e^{-0.5}$$

$$\approx 0.61 \qquad \text{probability that the time in the}$$

$$\text{system is greater than } \frac{1}{2} \text{ hr}$$

$$P(T > 1 \text{ hr}) = e^{-1}$$

$$\approx 0.37$$

$$P(T > 2 \text{ hr}) = e^{-2}$$

$$\approx 0.14$$

In Example 13.3.1 we could have determined

$$L = \frac{\lambda}{\mu - \lambda} = 3$$

and then calculated

$$L_q = L - \frac{\lambda}{\mu}$$

$$= 3 - \frac{3}{4}$$

$$= 2.25$$

$$W = \frac{L}{\lambda}$$

$$= \frac{3}{3}$$

$$= 1 \text{ hr}$$

$$W_q = \frac{L_q}{\lambda}$$

$$= \frac{2.25}{3}$$

$$= 0.75 \text{ hr}$$

EXAMPLE 13.3.2 Suppose people arrive to purchase tickets for a basketball game at the average rate of 1/min. It takes an average of 20 s to purchase a ticket.

(a) If a sports fan arrives 2 min before the game starts and if it takes exactly $1\frac{1}{2}$ min to reach the correct seat after the fan purchases a ticket, can the sports fan expect to be seated for the tip-off? If a minute is used as a unit of time,

$$\lambda = 1 \text{ arrival/min}$$

$$\mu = 3 \text{ arrivals/min}$$

$$W = \frac{1}{\mu - \lambda}$$

$$= \frac{1}{3 - 1}$$

$$= \frac{1}{2} \text{ min}$$

The average time to get the ticket and the time to reach the correct seat total 2 min exactly, so the sports fan can expect to be seated for the tip-off.

(b) What is the probability the sports fan will be seated for the start of the game? This is equivalent to the probability the fan can obtain a ticket in less than or equal to $\frac{1}{2}$ min.

$$P\left(T < \frac{1}{2}\right) = 1 - P\left(T > \frac{1}{2}\right)$$

$$= 1 - e^{-3\left(1 - \frac{1}{3}\right)\left(\frac{1}{2}\right)}$$

$$= 1 - e^{-1}$$

$$\approx 0.63$$

(c) How early must the fan arrive in order to be 99 percent sure of being seated for the start of the game? For this problem, we need to determine t such that

$$P(T > t) = e^{-3\left(1 - \frac{1}{3}\right)t} = 0.01$$

$$e^{-2t} = 0.01$$

Table 13.1 QUEUEING STATISTICS FOR $\mu = 3$ AND $1 \leqslant \lambda \leqslant 2.999$ (UNIT OF TIME = 1 MIN)

λ	L $\dfrac{\lambda}{\mu-\lambda}$	L_q $\dfrac{\lambda^2}{\mu(\mu-\lambda)}$	W $\dfrac{1}{\mu-\lambda}$	W_q $\dfrac{\lambda}{\mu(\mu-\lambda)}$	P_0 $1-\dfrac{\lambda}{\mu}$	$P(T>4)$ $e^{-3(1-\lambda/3)4}$
1.0	0.5	0.167	0.50	0.167	0.667	0.0003
1.5	1.0	0.500	0.67	0.333	0.500	0.0025
2.0	2.0	1.333	1.0	0.667	0.333	0.0183
2.5	5.0	4.167	2.0	1.667	0.167	0.1353
2.75	11.0	10.083	4.0	3.667	0.083	0.3679
2.90	29.0	28.033	10.0	9.667	0.033	0.6703
2.95	59.0	58.017	20.0	19.667	0.017	0.8187
2.99	299.0	298.003	100.0	99.667	0.003	0.9608
2.999	2999.0	2998.000	1000.0	999.667	0.000	0.9960

$$-2t = \ln 0.01$$

$$t = -\frac{1}{2} \ln 0.01$$

$$= 2.3 \text{ min}$$

That is,
$$P(T > 2.3) = 0.01$$
$$P(T < 2.3) = 0.99$$

Thus, the fan can be 99 percent sure of spending less than 2.3 min obtaining a ticket (waiting for and purchasing a ticket). Since it takes exactly 1.5 min to reach the correct seat after purchasing a ticket, the fan must arrive 3.8 min ($2.3 + 1.5 = 3.8$) early to be 99 percent of seeing the tip-off.

Table 13.1 illustrates what happens to L, L_q, W, W_q, P_0, and $P(T>4)$ in this example as the arrival rate approaches the service rate.

EXAMPLE 13.3.3 Patients arrive at the local hospital for emergency service at the rate of one every hour. Currently, only one emergency case can be handled at a time. Patients spend an average of 20 min receiving emergency care. Consider the following vital information that is available:

$$\lambda = 1/\text{hr}$$
$$\mu = 3/\text{hr}$$
$$P_n = \left(\frac{1}{3}\right)^n \left(\frac{2}{3}\right)$$
$$P(T > t) = e^{-3(2/3)t}$$

$$= e^{-2t}$$

$$L = \frac{1}{3-1}$$

$$= 0.5$$

$$L_q = L - \frac{1}{3}$$

$$= 0.1667$$

$$W = \frac{L}{1}$$

$$= 0.5 \text{ hr}$$

$$W_q = \frac{L_q}{1}$$

$$= 0.1667 \text{ hr}$$

$$P_0 = \text{fraction of the time there are no patients}$$

$$= 1 - \frac{\lambda}{\mu}$$

$$= 0.6667$$

$$P_2 = \left(\frac{1}{3}\right)^2 \left(\frac{2}{3}\right)$$

$$\approx 0.074$$

$$P(n > 2) = \left(\frac{1}{3}\right)^3$$

$$\approx 0.04$$

How much would the average service time need to be decreased to keep the average time in the system (waiting and receiving service) less than 25 min? We want to determine μ such that

$$W = \frac{1}{\mu - \lambda} < \frac{25}{60} \text{ hr}$$

or

$$\frac{1}{\mu - 1} < 0.416667 \text{ hr}$$

$$\mu > 3.4 \text{ patients/hr}$$

$$\frac{1}{\mu} < 0.294 \text{ hr/patient}$$

$$\frac{1}{\mu} < 17.65 \text{ min/patient}$$

Therefore, the average service time must be decreased 2.35 min/patient.

EXAMPLE 13.3.4 A departmental secretary receives an average of 8 jobs/hr. Many are short jobs, while others are quite long. Assume, however, that the time to perform a job has an exponential distribution with a mean of 6 min.

(a) What is the average elapsed time from the time the secretary receives a job until it is completed?

$$\lambda = 8 \text{ jobs/hr}$$

$$\mu = 10 \text{ jobs/hr}$$

$$W = \frac{1}{10 - 8} = \frac{1}{2} \text{ hr}$$

(b) Calculate other important quantities.

$$L = \lambda W$$

$$= 8\left(\frac{1}{2}\right)$$

$$= 4$$

$$W_q = W - \frac{1}{\mu}$$

$$= \frac{1}{2} - \frac{1}{10}$$

$$= \frac{2}{5} \text{ hr}$$

$$= 24 \text{ min}$$

$$P\left(T > \frac{1}{2}\right) = e^{-10(1 - 8/10)(1/2)}$$

$$\approx 0.37$$

$$P(T > 1) = e^{-10(2/10)(1)}$$

$$\cong 0.14$$

$$P(T > 2) = e^{-10(2/10)(2)}$$

$$\approx 0.02$$

Thus, the probability a job will be completed in less than 2 hr is 0.98.

$$\rho_0 = \text{fraction of the time the secretary is busy}$$

$$= \frac{\lambda}{\mu}$$

$$= 0.8$$

$$P(n > 5) = \text{probability of more than five jobs in the system}$$

$$= \left(\frac{\lambda}{\mu}\right)^6$$

$$= (0.8)^6$$

$$\approx 0.262$$

13.3.2 Infinite Queue–Infinite Source, Multiple-Server Model

Many realistic queueing systems have more than one server providing the service in the service facility. Figure 13.6 illustrates a single queue, multiple-server queueing system we will study in this section.

We assume

(a) s servers
(b) Each server provides service at the same constant average rate μ
(c) The average arrival rate is constant; $\lambda_n = \lambda$ for all n
(d) $\lambda < s\mu$

With these assumptions, we have

$$P_n = \frac{1}{n!}\left(\frac{\lambda}{\mu}\right)^n P_0 \qquad n = 0, 1, \ldots, s - 1 \qquad (13.17)$$

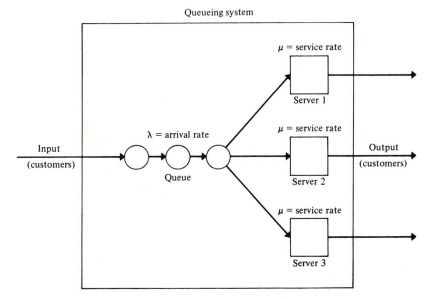

FIGURE 13.6
Single queue, multiple servers in parallel.

$$P_n = \frac{1}{s!s^{n-s}}\left(\frac{\lambda}{\mu}\right)^n P_0 \qquad n \geqslant s \tag{13.18}$$

$P(n \geqslant s)$ = probability an arrival has to wait for service

= probability of at least s customers in the system

$$= \sum_{n=s}^{\infty} P_n$$

$$= \frac{(\lambda/\mu)^s P_0}{s!(1 - \lambda/\mu s)} \tag{13.19}$$

$$P_0 = \frac{1}{\left\{\left[\sum_{n=0}^{s-1}\frac{1}{n!}\left(\frac{\lambda}{\mu}\right)^n\right] + \frac{1}{s!(1 - \lambda/\mu s)}\left(\frac{\lambda}{\mu}\right)^s\right\}} \tag{13.20}$$

$$L_q = \frac{\left(\frac{\lambda}{\mu}\right)^{s+1} P_0}{s \cdot s!(1 - \lambda/\mu s)^2} \tag{13.21}$$

$$L = L_q + \frac{\lambda}{\mu} \tag{13.22}$$

$$W = \frac{L}{\lambda} \tag{13.23}$$

$$W_q = \frac{L_q}{\lambda} \tag{13.24}$$

$$P(T > t) = e^{-\mu t}\left\{1 + \frac{(\lambda/\mu)^s P_0 [1 - e^{-\mu t(s-1-\lambda/\mu)}]}{s!(1 - \lambda/\mu s)(s - 1 - \lambda/\mu)}\right\} \tag{13.25}$$

EXAMPLE 13.3.5   Suppose there are three typists in a typing pool. Each typist can type an average of 6 letters/hr. If letters arrive to be typed at the rate of 15 letters/hr, (a) What fraction of the time are all three typists busy? We know that

$\lambda = 15$ letters/hr
$\mu = 6$ letters/hr
$s = 3$

Thus, we want $P(n \geqslant 3)$. To get this we need P_0.

$$P_0 = \frac{1}{\left[1 + (\lambda/\mu) + \frac{1}{2}(\lambda/\mu)^2 + \frac{1}{6}(\lambda/\mu)^3 (1/(1 - \lambda/3\mu))\right]}$$

$$= \cfrac{1}{\left[1 + \cfrac{15}{6} + \cfrac{1}{2}\left(\cfrac{15}{6}\right)^2 + \cfrac{1}{6}\left(\cfrac{15}{6}\right)^3\left(\cfrac{1}{1 - \cfrac{15}{18}}\right)\right]}$$

$$= 0.044944$$

Therefore,
$$P(n \geqslant 3) = \cfrac{\left(\cfrac{15}{6}\right)^3 (0.044944)}{6\left(1 - \cfrac{15}{18}\right)}$$

$$= 0.70225$$

Note also that the probability of one letter in the system (none waiting to be typed and one being typed) is

$$P_1 = \cfrac{1}{1!}\left(\cfrac{15}{6}\right)^1 (0.044944)$$

$$= 0.11236$$

(b) What is the average number of letters waiting to be typed?

$$L_q = \cfrac{\left(\cfrac{15}{6}\right)^4 (0.044944)}{(3)(6)\left(1 - \cfrac{15}{18}\right)^2}$$

$$= 3.51124$$

(c) What is the average time a letter spends in the system (waiting and being typed)? We first need the average number of letters in the system.

$$L = L_q + \cfrac{\lambda}{\mu}$$

$$= 3.51124 + \cfrac{15}{6}$$

$$= 6.01124$$

Therefore,
$$W = \cfrac{L}{\lambda}$$

$$= \cfrac{6.01124}{15}$$

$$= 0.40075 \text{ hr}$$

$$\approx 24 \text{ min}$$

(*d*) What is the probability a letter will take longer than 20 min waiting to be typed and being typed?

$$P\!\left(T > \frac{1}{3}\,\mathrm{hr}\right) = e^{-6(1/3)}\left[1 + \frac{\left(\frac{15}{6}\right)^{3}(0.044944)\left(1 - e^{-6(1/3)(3-1-15/6)}\right)}{6\left(1 - \frac{15}{18}\right)\left(3 - 1 - \frac{15}{6}\right)}\right]$$

$$= 0.46198$$

(*e*) Suppose each individual typist receives letters at the average rate of 5/hr. Assume each typist can type at the average rate of 6 letters/hr. The queueing system would appear as in Figure 13.7.

What is the average time a letter spends in the system (waiting and being typed)? Each queue and server can be treated as a separate single queue, single-server system. Thus,

$$W = \frac{1}{\mu - \lambda}$$

$$= \frac{1}{6 - 5}$$

$$= 1 \,\mathrm{hr}$$

Note that the time in the system increases $2\frac{1}{2}$ times when separate queues feed the three servers as opposed to a single queue feeding the three servers. This is illustrated in Table 13.2.

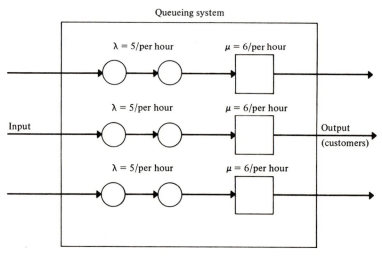

Queueing system

$\lambda = 5$/per hour $\mu = 6$/per hour

$\lambda = 5$/per hour $\mu = 6$/per hour

Input   Output (customers)

$\lambda = 5$/per hour $\mu = 6$/per hour

FIGURE 13.7
Multiple queues, multiple servers [Example 13.3.5(*e*)].

Table 13.2 COMPARISONS OF SYSTEM TIMES USING DIFFERENT NUMBER OF QUEUES

Number of queues	$\mu = 6$ letters/hr both systems
	W
One queue $\lambda = 15$/hr	24 min
Three queues $\lambda = 5$/hr each queue	60 min

13.3.2.1 Computer program for infinite-queue–infinite-source, multiple-server model
This program obtains the quantities in Equations (13.17)–(13.25) for any number of service facilities. The comment cards at the beginning of the program explain exactly what the program is designed to do. The input data and results for Example 13.3.5 follow the program listing.

```
C     **********************************************************************
C     *                                                                    *
C     *            **   QUEUEING PROGRAM 13.3.2.1    **                     *
C     *      **   INFINITE SOURCE, INFINITE QUEUE, MULTIPLE SERVERS   **    *
C     *                                                                    *
C     * WE ASSUME
C     *      ARRIVALS FORM A SINGLE QUEUE                                   *
C     *      INFINITE SOURCE AND INFINITE QUEUE                            *
C     *      FIFO QUEUE DISCIPLINE                                         *
C     *      THERE ARE MULTIPLE SERVERS WITH EXPONENTIAL SERVICE TIME      *
C     *      DEPARTURES FROM SYSTEM OCCUR COMPLETELY AT RANDOM             *
C     *                                                                    *
C     * THIS PROGRAM IS DESIGNED                                           *
C     *      TO READ                                                       *
C     *            CARD 1    COLS  2-80    TITLE  DESCRIPTION OF THE PROBLEM USING  *
C     *                                           ANY CHARACTERS ON KEYPUNCH        *
C     *                                           ** COLUMN 1 MUST BE LEFT BLANK ** *
C     *            CARD 2    COLS  1-10    LAMBDA  PARAMETER IN THE INPUT   *
C     *                                           DISTRIBUTION  (F10.0)    *
C     *                          11-20    MU      PARAMETER IN THE SERVICE *
C     *                                           TIME DISTRIBUTION  (F10.0) *
C     *            CARD 3    COLS  1-10    N  USED TO FIND PROBABILITY OF N CUSTOMERS *
C     *                                       IN SYSTEM AT ANY ONE TIME (F10.0)      *
C     *                          11-20    S  NUMBER OF SERVICE FACILITIES  (F10.0)   *
C     *                          21-30    T  USED TO FIND PROBABILITY THAT TIME IN   *
C     *                                       THE SYSTEM IS GREATER THAN T  (F10.0)  *
C     *                                                                    *
C     *            TO SOLVE MORE THAN ONE PROBLEM AT A TIME, REPEAT THE    *
C     *            READ SEQUENCE, AND STACK THE DATA ONE BEHIND THE OTHER  *
C     *                                                                    *
C     *      TO CALCULATE AND PRINT                                        *
C     *      L        AVERAGE # OF CUSTOMERS IN THE SYSTEM                 *
C     *      LQ       AVERAGE # OF CUSTOMERS IN QUEUE                      *
C     *      W        AVERAGE TIME CUSTOMER SPENDS IN SYSTEM              *
C     *      WQ       AVERAGE TIME CUSTOMER SPENDS IN QUEUE               *
C     *      PT       PROBABILITY THAT TIME IN THE SYSTEM IS GREATER THAN T *
C     *      PN       PROBABILITY OF N CUSTOMERS IN SYSTEM AT ANY POINT IN TIME *
C     *      PZERO    PROBABILITY OF NO CUSTOMERS IN THE SYSTEM           *
C     *      PS       PROBABILITY OF AT LEAST S CUSTOMERS IN THE SYSTEM   *
C     *                                                                    *
C     **********************************************************************
      REAL*4 TITLE(20),LAMBDA,MU,N,L,LQ,NFACT
    5 READ(5,10,END=2000)TITLE
   10 FORMAT(20A4)
      WRITE(6,11)TITLE
   11 FORMAT('1',20A4,//)
      READ(5,20)LAMBDA,MU
   20 FORMAT(3F10.0)
      READ(5,20)N,S,T
      IF(LAMBDA.GE.S*MU) GO TO 700
C     **********************************************************************
C     *            CALCULATE PZERO                                         *
C     **********************************************************************
      NS=S
      SUM=0.0
      DO 205 NK=1,NS
      SK=NK-1
      CALL FACT(SK,NFACT)
      SUM=SUM+(1/NFACT)*(LAMBDA/MU)**SK
  205 CONTINUE
      CALL FACT(S,SFACT)
      PZERO=1/(SUM+(1/(SFACT*(1-LAMBDA/(MU*S)))))*(LAMBDA/MU)**S)
C     **********************************************************************
C     *            CALCULATE PN                                            *
C     **********************************************************************
      IF(N.GE.S) GO TO 210
      CALL FACT(N,NFACT)
      PN=(1/NFACT)*((LAMBDA/MU)**N)*PZERO
      GO TO 215
  210 CALL FACT(S,SFACT)
```

```
      PN=(1/(SFACT*S**(N-S)))*((LAMBDA/MU)**N)*PZERO
C     ***************************************************************************
C     *            CALCULATE  PS, PT, L, LQ, W, WQ                             *
C     ***************************************************************************
  215 CALL FACT(S,SFACT)
      PS=(((LAMBDA/MU)**S)*PZERO)/(SFACT*(1-LAMBDA/(MU*S)))
      PTN=((LAMBDA/MU)**S)*PZERO*(1-EXP(-MU*T*(S-1-LAMBDA/MU)))
      PTD=SFACT*(1-LAMBDA/(MU*S))*(S-1-LAMBDA/MU)
      PT=EXP(-MU*T)*(1+PTN/PTD)
      LQ=(((LAMBDA/MU)**(S+1))*PZERO)/(S*SFACT*(1-LAMBDA/(MU*S))**2)
      L=LQ+LAMBDA/MU
      W=L/LAMBDA
      WQ=LQ/LAMBDA
C     ***************************************************************************
C     *            PRINT RESULTS                                               *
C     ***************************************************************************
      WRITE(6,100)LAMBDA,MU,N,S,T,L,LQ,W,WQ,PT,PN,PZERO,PS
  100 FORMAT(' LAMBDA =',F10.5/' MU      =',F10.5/' N       =',F10.5/' S
     *      =',F10.5/' T      =',F10.5/' L      =',F10.5/' LQ     =',F10.5
     */' W      =',F10.5/' WQ     =',F10.5/' PT      =',F10.5/' PN      ='
     *,F10.5/' PZERO  =',F10.5/' PS      =',F10.5)
      GO TO 5
  700 WRITE(6,705)
  705 FORMAT(' QUEUEING SYSTEM NOT VALID BECAUSE LAMBDA ¬< S*MU')
      GO TO 5
 2000 STOP
      END

      SUBROUTINE FACT(P,PROD)
      NUM=P
      PROD=1.
      IF(NUM.EQ.0) GO TO 20
      DO 10 K=1,NUM
   10 PROD=PROD*K
   20 RETURN
      END


/DATA

   EXAMPLE 13.3.5     SINGLE QUEUE - MULTIPLE SERVER MODEL
   15.       6.
   1.        3.          .3333



   EXAMPLE 13.3.5     SINGLE QUEUE - MULTIPLE SERVER MODEL


LAMBDA =    15.00000
MU     =     6.00000
N      =     1.00000
S      =     3.00000
T      =     0.33330
L      =     6.01124
LQ     =     3.51124
W      =     0.40075
WQ     =     0.23408
PT     =     0.46198
PN     =     0.11236
PZERO  =     0.04494
PS     =     0.70225
```

13.3.3   Finite Queue–Infinite Source, Single-Server Model

This is the situation in which the waiting line can accommodate only a finite number of arrivals. If a customer arrives and the queue is full, the customer leaves without joining the queue. Typical situations are:

> Limited space for cars that arrive at a single-window drive-in bank
> Limited space for cars that arrive at a do-it-yourself car wash
> Limited waiting space in a one-barber barber shop

> Let M = maximum number of customers that can get in the system at any one time.

For this case, λ need not be less than μ since the queue cannot build up without bound.

The difference equations in Section 13.3 [Equations (13.3) and (13.4)] are valid in this case, with

$$\mu_n = \mu \quad \text{for } n = 1, 2, 3, \ldots \tag{13.26}$$

$$\lambda_n = \begin{cases} \lambda & \text{for } n = 0, 1, 2, \ldots, M-1 \\ \\ 0 & \text{for } n = M, M+1, \ldots \end{cases} \tag{13.27}$$

Thus, if we substitute Equations (13.26) and (13.27) in Equation (13.6), we get

$$P_0 = \frac{1}{\left[1 + \sum_{n=1}^{M} (\lambda/\mu)^n\right]}$$

$$= \frac{1}{\left[\dfrac{1 + (\lambda/\mu)^{M+1}}{1 - \lambda/\mu}\right]}$$

$$= \frac{1 - \lambda/\mu}{1 - (\lambda/\mu)^{M+1}} \quad \text{for } \lambda \neq \mu \tag{13.28}$$

$$= \frac{1}{M+1} \quad \text{for } \lambda = \mu \tag{13.29}$$

Likewise,
$$P_n = \left(\frac{\lambda}{\mu}\right)^n P_0 \quad \text{for } n = 0, 1, 2, \ldots, M \tag{13.30}$$
$$\lambda \neq \mu$$

$$= P_0 \quad \text{for } \lambda = \mu \tag{13.31}$$

$$L = \frac{\lambda}{\mu - \lambda} - \frac{(M+1)(\lambda/\mu)^{M+1}}{1 - (\lambda/\mu)^{M+1}} \quad \text{for } \lambda \neq \mu \tag{13.32}$$

$$= \frac{M}{2} \qquad\qquad \text{for } \lambda = \mu \quad (13.33)$$

$$L_q = L - (1 - P_0) \qquad\qquad (13.34)$$

The average arrival rate is λ as long as there is a vacant space in the queue; however, when the system becomes full, the arrival rate is zero. Consequently, it would be meaningful to know the overall effective arrival rate λ_{eff}.

From

$$L_q = L - \frac{\lambda_{\text{eff}}}{\mu}$$

we get

$$\lambda_{\text{eff}} = \mu(L - L_q)$$

Since P_0 and L_q are given in Equations (13.28), (13.29), and (13.34),

$$\lambda_{\text{eff}} = \mu\{L - [L - (1 - P_0)]\}$$
$$= \mu(1 - P_0) \qquad\qquad (13.35)$$

Then,

$$W = \frac{L}{\lambda_{\text{eff}}} \qquad (13.36)$$

$$W_q = \frac{L_q}{\lambda_{\text{eff}}} \qquad (13.37)$$

EXAMPLE 13.3.6 A one-person barber shop has six chairs to accommodate people waiting for a haircut. Assume customers who arrive when all six chairs are full leave without entering the barber shop. Customers arrive at the average rate of 3/hr and spend an average of 15 min in the barber chair. Thus,

M = maximum number in the system
  $= 7$
$\lambda = 3/\text{hr}$
$\mu = 4/\text{hr}$

(a) What is the probability a customer can get directly into the barber chair upon arrival? This is the same as the probability of no one in the barber shop.

$$P_0 = \frac{1 - \dfrac{3}{4}}{1 - \left(\dfrac{3}{4}\right)^8}$$

$$= 0.2778$$

(b) What is the expected number of customers waiting for a haircut?

$$L = \frac{\frac{3}{4}}{1 - \frac{3}{4}} - \frac{(8)\left(\frac{3}{4}\right)^8}{1 - \left(\frac{3}{4}\right)^8}$$

$$= 2.11$$

then,

$$L_q = L - (1 - P_0)$$
$$= 2.11 - (1 - 0.2778)$$
$$= 1.39$$

(c) What is the effective arrival rate?

$$\lambda_{\text{eff}} = \mu(1 - P_0)$$
$$= 4(1 - 0.2778)$$
$$= 2.89/\text{hr}$$

(d) How much time can a customer expect to spend in the barber shop?

$$W = \frac{L}{\lambda_{\text{eff}}}$$
$$= \frac{2.11}{2.89}$$
$$= 0.73 \text{ hr}$$
$$= 43.8 \text{ min}$$

(e) What fraction of potential customers are turned away?

$$P(7 \text{ in the system}) = P_7 = \left(\frac{\lambda}{\mu}\right)^7 \left[\frac{1 - \lambda/\mu}{1 - (\lambda/\mu)^8}\right]$$

$$= \left(\frac{3}{4}\right)^7 \left(\frac{1 - \frac{3}{4}}{1 - \left(\frac{3}{4}\right)^8}\right)$$

$$\approx 0.037$$
$$\approx 3.7 \text{ percent}$$

(f) If the arrival rate is such that 10 percent of the potential customers are turned away, the barber will put in additional chairs for waiting. What must the new arrival rate be to warrant more chairs for waiting?

We want the value of λ such that $P_7 = 0.10$. Since P_7 involves a very complicated function of λ, we could use a root-finding technique such as the

Table 13.3 P_7 FOR TRIAL VALUES OF λ

λ	P_7
3.0000	0.03700
3.5000	0.07478
3.7000	0.09365
3.7500	0.09864
3.7634	0.10000

Newton-Raphson method or the Bairstow method. However, for now we will just use successive approximations of λ. Table 13.3 gives the values of P_7 for several trial values of λ. Thus, the arrival rate must be increased from 3/hr to 3.7634 arrivals/hr before 10 percent of the potential customers will be turned away.

Table 13.4 compares the results for the barber shop example when the queue is finite and when it is infinite.

13.3.4 Finite Queue–Infinite Source, Multiple-Server Model

This model represents the situation where the waiting space is limited and more than one server is servicing customers. A typical situation is a barber shop with a fixed number of chairs for waiting customers and more than one barber.

Let s = number of servers

M = maximum number of customers that can be in the system at any one time

$$\lambda_n = \begin{cases} \lambda & \text{for } n = 0, 1, \ldots, M-1 \\ 0 & \text{for } n = M, M+1, \ldots \end{cases} \tag{13.38}$$

$$\mu_n = \begin{cases} n\mu & \text{for } n = 0, 1, \ldots, s \\ s\mu & \text{for } n = s+1, s+2, \ldots \end{cases} \tag{13.39}$$

Assume $1 < s < M$. It follows from Equations (13.38), (13.39), and (13.6) that

Table 13.4   INFINITE QUEUE VS. FINITE QUEUE–EXAMPLE 13.3.6

$\lambda = 3/\text{hr}, \mu = 4/\text{hr}$	L	L_q	W	W_q	P_0	Fraction of potential customers turned away
Finite queue, $M = 7$	2.11	1.39	0.73	0.48	0.278	0.037
Infinite queue	3.0	2.25	1.0	0.75	0.250	0

$$P_0 = \cfrac{1}{\sum_{n=0}^{s}(1/n!)(\lambda/\mu)^n + (1/s!)(\lambda/\mu)^s \sum_{n=s+1}^{M}(\lambda/\mu s)^{n-s}} \tag{13.40}$$

$$P_n = \begin{cases} \dfrac{1}{n!}\left(\dfrac{\lambda}{\mu}\right)^n P_0 & \text{for } n \leqslant s \\[2ex] \dfrac{1}{s!s^{n-s}}\left(\dfrac{\lambda}{\mu}\right)^n P_0 & \text{for } s < n \leqslant M \\[2ex] 0 & \text{for } n > M \end{cases} \tag{13.41}$$

$$L_q = \frac{P_0(\lambda/\mu)^s(\lambda/\mu s)}{s!(1 - \lambda/\mu s)^2}\left[1 - \left(\frac{\lambda}{\mu s}\right)^{M-s} - (M - s)\left(\frac{\lambda}{\mu s}\right)^{M-s}\left(1 - \frac{\lambda}{\mu s}\right)\right] \tag{13.42}$$

$$L = L_q + s - \sum_{n=0}^{s-1}(s - n)P_n \tag{13.43}$$

$$\lambda_{\text{eff}} = \mu\left[s - \sum_{n=0}^{s-1}(s - n)P_n\right] \tag{13.44}$$

$$W_q = \frac{L_q}{\lambda_{\text{eff}}} \tag{13.45}$$

$$W = \frac{L}{\lambda_{\text{eff}}} \tag{13.46}$$

EXAMPLE 13.3.7 A two-person barber shop has five chairs to accommodate waiting customers. Potential customers who arrive when all five chairs are full leave without entering the barber shop. Customers arrive at the average rate of 3.7634/hr and spend an average of 15 min in the barber chair.

For this example, assume

$M = 7$
$\lambda = 3.7634/\text{hr}$
$\mu = 4/\text{hr}$
$s = 2$ servers

Answer questions (a)–(e) in Example 13.3.6 using this model.

$$P_0 = \cfrac{1}{\sum_{n=0}^{2}(1/n!)(3.7634/4)^n + \frac{1}{2}(3.7634/4)^2 \sum_{n=3}^{7}(3.7634/4 \cdot 2)^{n-2}}$$

$$= 0.36133$$

$$L_q = \frac{(0.36133)(3.7634/4)^2(3.7634/4 \cdot 2)}{2![1 - (3.7634/4 \cdot 2)]^2}$$

$$\left[1 - \left(\frac{3.7634}{4 \cdot 2}\right)^{7-2} - (7 - 2)\left(\frac{3.7634}{4 \cdot 2}\right)^{7-2}\left(1 - \frac{3.7634}{4 \cdot 2}\right)\right]$$

$$= 0.2457$$

$$P_{\cdot} = \frac{1}{1}\left(\frac{3.7634}{4}\right)^1 P_0$$

$$= 0.339957$$

$$\lambda_{\text{eff}} = 4(2 - 2P_0 - P_1)$$

$$= 4[2 - 2(0.36133) - 0.339957]$$

$$= 3.7495$$

$$W = \frac{L}{\lambda_{\text{eff}}} = \frac{L_q + (2 - 2P_0 - P_1)}{\lambda_{\text{eff}}}$$

$$= \frac{1.183083}{3.7495}$$

$$= 0.3155 \text{ hr}$$

$$\cong 19 \text{ min}$$

$$P_7 = \frac{1}{2!2^{7-2}}\left(\frac{3.7634}{4}\right)^7(0.36133)$$

$$= 0.00368$$

$$= 0.3 \text{ percent}$$

Thus, only 0.3 percent of the potential customers will be turned away.

13.3.4.1 Computer program for finite queue–infinite source multiple-server model

This program calculates the quantities in Equations (13.40)–(13.47). The details of the program are explained by the comment cards at the beginning of the program.

The input data and results from Example 13.3.7 follow the program listing.

```
C     ***********************************************************************
C     *                                                                     *
C     *       **    INFINITE SOURCE, FINITE QUEUE, MULTIPLE SERVERS   **     *
C     *          **   QUEUEING PROGRAM 13.3.4.1    **                       *
C     *                                                                     *
C     * WE ASSUME                                                           *
C     *    ARRIVALS TO SYSTEM ARE COMPLETELY AT RANDOM - POISSON INPUT      *
C     *    ARRIVALS FORM A SINGLE QUEUE                                     *
C     *    INFINITE SOURCE AND FINITE QUEUE                                 *
C     *    FIFO QUEUE DISCIPLINE                                            *
C     *    THERE ARE MULTIPLE SERVERS WITH EXPONENTIAL SERVICE TIME         *
C     *    DEPARTURES FROM SYSTEM OCCUR COMPLETELY AT RANDOM                *
C     *                                                                     *
C     * THIS PROGRAM IS DESIGNED                                            *
C     *    TO READ                                                          *
C     *       CARD 1    COLS  2-80   TITLE  DESCRIPTION OF THE PROBLEM USING *
C     *                                     ANY CHARACTERS ON KEYPUNCH      *
C     *                                     ** COLUMN 1 MUST BE LEFT BLANK ***
C     *       CARD 2    COLS  1-10   LAMBDA PARAMETER IN THE INPUT          *
C     *                                     DISTRIBUTION  (F10.0)           *
C     *                       11-20  MU     PARAMETER IN THE SERVICE        *
C     *                                     TIME DISTRIBUTION (F10.0)       *
C     *       CARD 3    COLS  1-10   N  USED TO FIND PROBABILITY OF N CUSTOMERS *
C     *                                     IN SYSTEM AT ANY ONE TIME (F10.0)*
C     *                       11-20  M  MAXIMUM # OF CUSTOMERS THAT CAN GET *
C     *                                     INTO SYSTEM AT ONE TIME (F10.0) *
C     *                       21-30  S  NUMBER OF SERVICE FACILITIES (F10.0)*
C     *              TO SOLVE MORE THAN ONE PROBLEM AT A TIME, REPEAT THE   *
C     *              READ SEQUENCE, AND STACK THE DATA ONE BEHIND THE OTHER *
C     *                                                                     *
C     *    TO CALCULATE AND PRINT                                           *
C     *       L       AVERAGE # OF CUSTOMERS IN THE SYSTEM                  *
C     *       LQ      AVERAGE # OF CUSTOMERS IN QUEUE                       *
C     *       PN      PROBABILITY OF N CUSTOMERS IN SYSTEM AT ANY POINT IN TIME *
C     *       PZERO   PROBABILITY OF NO CUSTOMERS IN THE SYSTEM            *
C     *       W       AVERAGE TIME CUSTOMER SPENDS IN SYSTEM               *
C     *       WQ      AVERAGE TIME CUSTOMER SPENDS IN QUEUE                *
C     *       LAMEFF  OVERALL EFFECTIVE ARRIVAL RATE FOR FINITE QUEUE WITH *
C     *                 INFINITE SOURCE                                     *
C     *                                                                     *
C     ***********************************************************************
      REAL*4 TITLE(20),LAMBDA,MU,N,M,L,LQ,LAMEFF
    5 READ(5,10,END=2000)TITLE
   10 FORMAT(20A4)
      WRITE(6,11)TITLE
   11 FORMAT('1',20A4,//)
      READ(5,20)LAMBDA,MU
   20 FORMAT(3F10.0)
      READ(5,20)N,M,S
C     ***********************************************************************
C     *              CALCULATE PZERO                                        *
C     ***********************************************************************
      IS=S+1
      SUM=0.0
      DO 405 NK=1,IS
      SK=NK-1
      CALL FACT(SK,TFACT)
      SUM=SUM+(1/TFACT)*(LAMBDA/MU)**SK
  405 CONTINUE
      SUM2=0.0
      NM=M
      DO 410 NK=IS,NM
      SUM2=SUM2+(LAMBDA/(MU*S))**(NK-S)
  410 CONTINUE
      CALL FACT(S,SFACT)
      PZERO=1/(SUM+(1/SFACT)*((LAMBDA/MU)**S)*SUM2)
C     ***********************************************************************
C     *              CALCULATE PN AND LQ                                    *
C     ***********************************************************************
      IF(N.LE.S) GO TO 415
      IF(N.GT.M) GO TO 420
      PN=(1/(SFACT*S**(N-S)))*((LAMBDA/MU)**N)*PZERO
```

```
        GO TO 425
  415 CALL FACT(N,TFACT)
      PN=(1/TFACT)*((LAMBDA/MU)**N)*PZERO
      GO TO 425
  420 PN=0.0
  425 LQ=((((LAMBDA/MU)**(S+1)*PZERO)*(1-(LAMBDA/(MU*S))**(M-S)-(M-S)*((L
     *AMBDA/(MU*S))**(M-S))*(1-LAMBDA/(MU*S))))/(S*SFACT*(1-LAMBDA/(MU*S
     *))**2)
C     **********************************************************************
C     *            CALCULATE LAMEFF, L, W, WQ                             *
C     **********************************************************************
      NS=S
      SUM=0
      DO 560 NK=1,NS
      KK=NK-1
      SKK=KK
      CALL FACT(SKK,AFACT)
      SUM=SUM+(S-KK)*PZERO*(1/AFACT)*(LAMBDA/MU)**KK
  560 CONTINUE
      LAMEFF=MU*(S-SUM)
      L=LQ+LAMEFF/MU
      W=L/LAMEFF
      WQ=LQ/LAMEFF
C     **********************************************************************
C     *            PRINT RESULTS                                          *
C     **********************************************************************
      WRITE(6,810)LAMBDA,MU,L,LQ,N,PN,PZERO,W,WQ,LAMEFF
  810 FORMAT(' LAMBDA =',F10.5/' MU      =',F10.5/' L       =',F10.5/' LQ
     *      =',F10.5/' N       =',F10.5/' PN      =',F10.5/' PZERO   =',F10.5
     */' W       =',F10.5/' WQ      =',F10.5/' LAMEFF  =',F10.5)
      GO TO 5
 2000 STOP
      END

      SUBROUTINE FACT(P,PROD)
      NUM=P
      PROD=1.
      IF(NUM.EQ.0) GO TO 20
      DO 10 K=1,NUM
   10 PROD=PROD*K
   20 RETURN
      END


/DATA

  EXAMPLE 13.3.7  WITH N=1
   3.7634     4.
   1.         7.        2.




   EXAMPLE 13.3.7  WITH N=1


LAMBDA =    3.76340
MU     =    4.00000
L      =    1.18309
LQ     =    0.24571
N      =    1.00000
PN     =    0.33996
PZERO  =    0.36133
W      =    0.31553
WQ     =    0.06553
LAMEFF =    3.74953
```

13.3.5 Finite Source, Multiple-Server Model

In this model, the number of customers desiring service is finite. Consequently, the effective arrival rate is a function of the service rate of each server, the number of servers, the number of customers in the calling population, and the distribution of "the time until service is needed" for each customer. Thus, we assume *each* customer arrives for service according to a Poisson process at the average rate of λ per hour. This is in contrast to the total population of customers arriving at an average rate of λ per hour, as was the case with an infinite population. Hence, the information in Section 13.3.1 would not be valid in general. We say "in general" because there are finite source models that can be treated as infinite source models if the arrival rate of the total calling population (source) is not seriously affected by the fact that there is only a finite number of potential customers. Every queueing system has a finite source, but the source is generally large enough to assume the customers come from an infinite source. How large, then, must the calling population be to justify using an infinite source model? There is no single answer to this question because it is a function of the arrival rate and the service rate.

Typical situations in which a finite source model is applicable are

1 s repairers are assigned to N machines that break down periodically
2 N graduate students are given sole access to s keypunch machines
3 N faculty members are given sole access to a single computer terminal

For situation 1, a machine joins the queueing system when it breaks down. It is out of service and is not a candidate to break down again until it is repaired. For situations 2 and 3, the graduate students and faculty members are the calling population in each case, respectively.

Assume service by each server is provided according to an exponential distribution. Let

N = number of potential customers
s = number of servers
λ = arrival rate of *each* customer
μ = service rate of *each* server

The usual statistics are

$$P_0 = \cfrac{1}{\displaystyle\sum_{n=0}^{s-1} \binom{N}{n}\left(\frac{\lambda}{\mu}\right)^n + \sum_{n=s}^{N} \frac{n!}{s!\,s^{n-s}} \binom{N}{n}\left(\frac{\lambda}{\mu}\right)^n} \qquad (13.47)$$

$$P_n = \begin{cases} P_0 \binom{N}{n}\left(\dfrac{\lambda}{\mu}\right)^n & 0 \leqslant n \leqslant s \\[3ex] P_0 \dfrac{n!}{s!\,s^{n-s}} \binom{N}{n}\left(\dfrac{\lambda}{\mu}\right)^n & s < n \leqslant N \end{cases} \qquad (13.48)$$

$$L_q = \sum_{n=s+1}^{N} (n - s)P_n \tag{13.49}$$

$$L = L_q + \left[s - \sum_{n=0}^{s} (s - n)P_n \right] \tag{13.50}$$

$$= L_q + \frac{\lambda_{\text{eff}}}{\mu} \tag{13.51}$$

$$\lambda_{\text{eff}} = \mu \left[s - \sum_{n=0}^{s} (s - n)P_n \right] \tag{13.52}$$

$$= \lambda(N - L) \tag{13.53}$$

$$W_q = \frac{L_q}{\lambda_{\text{eff}}} \tag{13.54}$$

$$W = \frac{L}{\lambda_{\text{eff}}} \tag{13.55}$$

EXAMPLE 13.3.8 Suppose two repairers have the sole responsibility of keeping five sensitive machines running. Each machine breaks down at the average rate of once every hour. In addition, both repairers can repair the machines at the same average rate of 4/hr. Thus,

$N = 5$
$\lambda = 1/\text{hr}$
$\mu = 4/\text{hr}$
$s = 2$

(a) Find the average number of machines waiting to be repaired L_q. From Equation (13.47) we have

$$P_0 = \left[\binom{5}{0}\left(\frac{1}{4}\right)^0 + \binom{5}{1}\left(\frac{1}{4}\right) + \left(\frac{2!}{2!2^0}\right)\binom{5}{2}\left(\frac{1}{4}\right)^2 + \left(\frac{3!}{2!2}\right)\binom{5}{3}\left(\frac{1}{4}\right)^3 \right.$$
$$\left. + \left(\frac{4!}{2!2^2}\right)\binom{5}{4}\left(\frac{1}{4}\right)^4 + \left(\frac{5!}{2!2^3}\right)\binom{5}{5}\left(\frac{1}{4}\right)^5 \right]^{-1}$$
$$= (1 + 1.25 + 0.625 + 0.234375 + 0.058594 + 0.007324)^{-1}$$
$$= 0.314932$$

Table 13.5 illustrates P_n for $n = 0, 1, \ldots, 5$. Thus,

$$L_q = P_3 + 2P_4 + 3P_5 = 0.118$$

Table 13.5 PROBABILITY OF
n IN THE SYSTEM—
EXAMPLE 13.3.8

n	P_n
0	0.315
1	0.394
2	0.197
3	0.074
4	0.018
5	0.002

(b) Find the average number of machines that are out of service L.

$$L = L_q + s - 2P_0 - P_1$$
$$= 0.118 + 2 - 0.63 - 0.394$$
$$= 1.094$$

(c) What is the effective breakdown rate when considering all five machines?
From Equation (13.52)

$$\lambda_{\text{eff}} = 4(2 - 2P_0 - P_1)$$
$$= 4(2 - 2(0.315) - 0.394)$$
$$= 3.904$$

From Equation (13.53), the effective arrival rate is

$$\lambda_{\text{eff}} = 1(5 - 1.094)$$
$$= 3.906$$

We see that the two answers are off in the third decimal place due to round-off error. $\lambda_{\text{eff}} = 3.906$ means that on the average, 3.906 machines break down every hour.
The average time in the queue and the average time in the system are given by

$$W_q = \frac{0.118}{3.906} = 0.03 \text{ hr}$$

$$W = \frac{1.094}{3.906} = 0.28 \text{ hr}$$

13.4 QUEUEING MODELS WITH POISSON INPUT—ARBITRARY SERVICE TIME

In this section we assume

(a) Infinite queue and infinite source.
(b) Arrivals to the system occur completely at random.
(c) Arrivals form a single queue.
(d) FIFO queue discipline.
(e) There is a single server in the service facility; $s = 1$.
(f) The service time T has an arbitrary distribution with mean $E(T)$ and variance var (T).
(g) $\frac{1}{\lambda} > E(T)$ the average time between arrivals is greater than the expected (average) service time.

With these basic assumptions and (e) changed to any number of servers in the service facility, the following relationships hold:

$$L = \lambda W$$

$$L_q = \lambda W_q$$

$$W_q = W - \frac{1}{\mu}$$

$$L_q = L - \frac{\lambda}{\mu}$$

The embedded Markov-chain technique can be used to obtain

$$P_0 = 1 - \lambda E(T) \tag{13.56}$$

$$L = \lambda E(T) + \frac{\lambda^2 \text{ var } (T) + [\lambda E(T)]^2}{2[1 - \lambda E(T)]} \tag{13.57}$$

$$L_q = L - \lambda E(T) \tag{13.58}$$

$$W = \frac{L}{\lambda} \tag{13.59}$$

$$W_q = \frac{L_q}{\lambda} \tag{13.60}$$

Note that when the service time T has an exponential distribution with parameter μ,

$$E(T) = \frac{1}{\mu}$$

$$\text{var } (T) = \frac{1}{\mu^2}$$

Thus,
$$L = \frac{\lambda}{\mu} + \frac{\lambda^2(1/\mu^2) + (\lambda/\mu)^2}{2(1 - \lambda/\mu)}$$

$$= \frac{\lambda}{\mu - \lambda}$$

This result agrees with Equation (13.9) in Section 13.3.1. The corresponding results for L_q, W, and W_q follow immediately.

13.4.1 Constant Service Time

Many practical queueing systems are such that the service time is constant for all customers. For example, the time to perform a certain task in an assembly line operation is quite often a constant. This means that the variance, var (T), is zero. Hence, from Equations (13.56)–(13.60)

$$P_0 = 1 - \lambda E(T) \tag{13.61}$$

$$L = \lambda E(T) + \frac{[\lambda E(T)]^2}{2[1 - \lambda E(T)]} \tag{13.62}$$

$$L_q = L - \lambda E(T) = \frac{[\lambda E(T)]^2}{2[1 - \lambda E(T)]} \tag{13.63}$$

$$W = \frac{L}{\lambda} \tag{13.64}$$

$$W_q = \frac{L_q}{\lambda} \tag{13.65}$$

Recall that $E(T) = 1/\mu$ for the exponential distribution. Thus, L_q for the exponential service time [Equation (13.10)] becomes

$$L_q = \frac{\lambda^2}{\mu(\mu - \lambda)}$$

$$= \frac{\lambda^2}{[1/E(T)]\{[1/E(T)] - \lambda\}}$$

$$= \frac{[\lambda E(T)]^2}{[1 - \lambda E(T)]}$$

Hence, note that L_q using constant service time [Equation (13.63)] is exactly half the value it is when exponential service time is used. A similar statement holds for W_q; however, L and W will be slightly larger than one-half of the values they would be for exponential service time.

13.4.2 Erlang Service Time

The *Erlang* distribution is a two-parameter family of distributions which is a special case of the more general *gamma* distribution. It permits more latitude in selecting a service-time distribution than the one-parameter exponential distribution. In fact, the exponential service-time and constant service-time situations are special cases of the Erlang service time. In practical situations, the exponential distribution is unduly restrictive because it assumes that small service times are more probable than large service times. On the other hand, the Erlang distribution permits the flexibility of approximating almost any realistic service-time distribution. Even some normal distributions can be approximated adequately with an Erlang distribution.

Consider the general two-parameter Erlang distribution

$$f(t;\mu,k) = \frac{(\mu k)^k t^{k-1} e^{-\mu k t}}{(k-1)!} \qquad \begin{matrix} t > 0 \\ \mu > 0 \\ k = 1, 2, 3, \ldots \end{matrix} \qquad (13.66)$$

with
$$E(T) = \frac{1}{\mu} \qquad \text{for every } k = 1, 2, 3, \ldots$$

$$\text{var}\,(T) = \frac{1}{k\mu^2}$$

The mean remains the same for each k, but the variance *decreases* as k *increases*. Note that for $k = 1$, the Erlang reduces to the exponential distribution. Also, as k becomes large,

$$\text{var}\,(T) = \frac{1}{k\mu^2}$$

becomes very small and service-time clusters closer and closer to the mean $1/\mu$. As k approaches ∞, the variance approaches zero. This implies the service time is approaching a constant. Thus, for $k = \infty$, the variance is equal to zero, which says that service time is no longer a random variable but is now a constant.

Erlang distributions are displayed in Figure 13.8 for several values of k.

Since this model is a special case of the model in Section 13.4, substituting

$$E(T) = \frac{1}{\mu} \quad \text{and} \quad \text{var}\,(T) = \frac{1}{k\mu^2}$$

in Equation (13.57) yields

$$\begin{aligned} L &= \frac{\lambda}{\mu} + \frac{\lambda^2(1/k\mu^2) + (\lambda/\mu)^2}{2(1 - \lambda/\mu)} \\ &= \frac{\lambda}{\mu} + \frac{[(k+1)/k](\lambda^2/\mu^2)}{[2(\mu - \lambda)]/\mu} \\ &= \left(\frac{k+1}{2k}\right)\left(\frac{\lambda^2}{\mu(\mu - \lambda)}\right) + \frac{\lambda}{\mu} \qquad (13.67) \end{aligned}$$

Also,
$$L_q = \left(\frac{k+1}{2k}\right)\left(\frac{\lambda^2}{\mu(\mu - \lambda)}\right) \qquad (13.68)$$

$$W = \frac{L}{\lambda} \qquad (13.69)$$

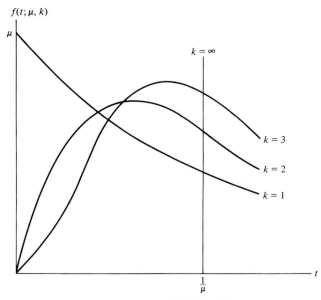

FIGURE 13.8
Erlang distribution for $k = 1,2,3$.

$$W_q = \frac{L_q}{\lambda} \tag{13.70}$$

Equations (13.67)-(13.70) hold for $\lambda < \mu$.

We mentioned that the Erlang distribution is important because it provides a whole family of distributions to choose from in approximating an observed service-time distribution. In fact, for large k, say $k \geqslant 10$, the Erlang distribution does a good job of approximating the normal distribution with the same mean and variance.

The Erlang distribution has a second important property. Namely, if an arrival must pass through k stations in the service facility, where the service time T_i at each station is independent of the service times at the other stations and has an exponential distribution with mean $1/k\mu$, then the sum of the service times

$$T = \sum_{i=1}^{k} T_i$$

has an Erlang distribution with mean $1/\mu$ and variance $1/k\mu^2$. Of course, this assumes a customer must complete service at all k stations before another customer can enter the service facility. Equations (13.67)-(13.70) hold for this situation.

EXAMPLE 13.4.1 Suppose a one-person tailor shop is in the business of making men's suits. Each suit requires four distinct tasks to be performed before it is completed. Assume all four tasks must be completed on each suit before another suit is started. The time to perform each task has an exponential distribution with a mean of 2 hr. For this example, let

T_i = time to perform task i where $i = 1, 2, 3, 4$
$k = 4$
$\frac{1}{k\mu} = \frac{1}{4\mu} = 2$

then

$$f(t_i) = k\mu e^{-k\mu t_i}$$

$$= \frac{1}{2} e^{-t_i/2}$$

$$E(T_i) = \frac{1}{k\mu} = 2 \text{ hr}$$

Let

$$T = \sum_{i=1}^{4} T_i$$

then

$$g(t) = \frac{(k\mu)^k t^{k-1} e^{-k\mu t}}{(k-1)!}$$

$$= \frac{(1/2)^4 t^3 e^{-t/2}}{3!}$$

$$E(T) = \frac{1}{\mu}$$

$$= 8 \text{ hr}$$

If orders for a suit come in at the average rate of 5.5/week (assume an 8-hr day, 6-day week), how long can a customer expect to wait to have a suit made?

Suppose we use an hour as a unit of time, then

$$\lambda = \frac{5.5}{48} \text{ orders/hr}$$

The service time for each task is

$$\frac{1}{4\mu} = 2 \text{ hr}$$

thus,

$$\mu = \frac{1}{8} \text{ order/hr}$$

Note that the average service rate μ is the average service rate to complete a suit.

To determine the average time to have a suit made, we could calculate

$$L = \frac{5}{8} \frac{(5.5/48)^2}{\left(\frac{1}{8}\right)\left(\frac{1}{8} - 5.5/48\right)} + \frac{(5.5/48)}{\frac{1}{8}}$$

$$= 7.2188$$

then
$$W = \frac{7.2188}{5.5/48}$$

$$= 63 \text{ hr}$$

$$\approx 1.3 \text{ weeks}$$

Note that we could have used 1 week as a unit of time, then

$$\lambda = 5.5 \text{ orders/week}$$

$$\mu = 6 \text{ orders/week}$$

$$L = \frac{5}{8} \frac{(5.5)^2}{6(6 - 5.5)} + \frac{5.5}{6}$$

$$= 7.2188$$

$$W = \frac{7.2188}{5.5}$$

$$= 1.3 \text{ weeks}$$

13.4.3   Computer Program for Poisson Input—Arbitrary Service Time

This program will calculate the quantities in Equations (13.56)–(13.60). The user must supply the parameter for the exponentially distributed time between consecutive arrivals, the mean service time, and the variance of the service time. The input data and results from Example 13.4.1 follow the program listing. This example uses Erlang service time.

The details of the program are explained by the comment cards at the beginning of the program.

```
C     *****************************************************************************
C     *                                                                         *
C     *            **    QUEUEING PROGRAM 13.4.1    **                           *
C     *        **   ARBITRARY DISTRIBUTION OF SERVICE TIME    **                 *
C     *                                                                         *
C     * WE ASSUME                                                               *
C     *     ARRIVALS TO SYSTEM ARE COMPLETELY AT RANDOM - POISSON INPUT         *
C     *     ARRIVALS FORM A SINGLE QUEUE                                         *
C     *     INFINITE SOURCE AND INFINITE QUEUE                                   *
C     *     FIFO QUEUE DISCIPLINE                                                *
C     *     THERE IS A SINGLE SERVER IN THE SERVICE FACILITY                     *
C     *     SERVICE TIME (T) HAS AN ARBITRARY DISTRIBUTION WITH MEAN ETIM        *
C     *        AND VARIANCE VARTIM                                               *
C     *     1/LAMBDA > ETIM                                                      *
C     *                                                                         *
C     * THIS PROGRAM IS DESIGNED                                                 *
C     *     TO READ                                                              *
C     *         CARD 1    COLS  2-80    TITLE  DESCRIPTION OF THE PROBLEM USING  *
C     *                                        ANY CHARACTERS ON KEYPUNCH        *
C     *                                        ** COLUMN 1 MUST BE LEFT BLANK ** *
C     *         CARD 2    COLS  1-10    LAMBDA PARAMETER IN THE INPUT            *
C     *                                        DISTRIBUTION  (F10.0)             *
C     *                         11-20   ETIM   MEAN OF SERVICE TIME  (F10.0)     *
C     *                         21-30   VARTIM VARIANCE OF SERVICE TIME  (F10.0) *
C     *                                        (IF SERVICE TIME IS CONSTANT,     *
C     *                                        VARTIM=0)                         *
C     *             TO SOLVE MORE THAN ONE PROBLEM AT A TIME, REPEAT THE         *
C     *             READ SEQUENCE, AND STACK THE DATA ONE BEHIND THE OTHER       *
C     *                                                                         *
C     *     TO CALCULATE AND PRINT                                              *
C     *         L       AVERAGE # OF CUSTOMERS IN THE SYSTEM                     *
C     *         LQ      AVERAGE # OF CUSTOMERS IN QUEUE                          *
C     *         W       AVERAGE TIME CUSTOMER SPENDS IN SYSTEM                   *
C     *         WQ      AVERAGE TIME CUSTOMER SPENDS IN QUEUE                    *
C     *         PZERO   PROBABILITY OF NO CUSTOMERS IN THE SYSTEM               *
C     *                                                                         *
C     *****************************************************************************
      REAL*4 TITLE(20),L,LQ,LAMBDA
    5 READ(5,10,END=2000)TITLE
   10 FORMAT(20A4)
      WRITE(6,11)TITLE
   11 FORMAT('1',20A4,//)
      READ(5,20)LAMBDA,ETIM,VARTIM
   20 FORMAT(3F10.0)
      IF(1/LAMBDA.LE.ETIM) GO TO 40
C     *****************************************************************************
C     *            CALCULATE QUANTITIES AND PRINT RESULTS                        *
C     *****************************************************************************
      PROD=LAMBDA*ETIM
      PZERO=1-PROD
      L=PROD+(LAMBDA*LAMBDA*VARTIM+PROD*PROD)/(2*PZERO)
      LQ=L-PROD
      W=L/LAMBDA
      WQ=LQ/LAMBDA
      WRITE(6,30)LAMBDA,ETIM,VARTIM,L,LQ,W,WQ,PZERO
   30 FORMAT(' LAMBDA =',F10.5/' ETIM   =',F10.5/' VARTIM =',F10.5/' L
     *     =',F10.5/' LQ     =',F10.5/' W      =',F10.5/' WQ      =',F10.5
     */' PZERO  =',F10.5)
      GO TO 5
   40 WRITE(6,45)
   45 FORMAT(' PROBLEM NOT VALID BECAUSE 1/LAMBDA -> ETIM')
      GO TO 5
 2000 STOP
      END


/DATA

      EXAMPLE 13.4.1 - ERLANG SERVICE TIME
      .114583        8.        16.
```

```
      EXAMPLE 13.4.1 - ERLANG SERVICE TIME

LAMBDA  =    0.11458
ETIM    =    8.00000
VARTIM  =   16.00000
L       =    7.21852
LQ      =    6.30185
W       =   62.99812
WQ      =   54.99812
PZERO   =    0.08334
```

13.5 SUMMARY

In this chapter we have analyzed simple queueing systems with Poisson arrivals and arbitrary service time. One system had a finite source while another had an infinite source. In addition, systems were examined that had

>   Limited waiting area
>   Unlimited waiting area
>   Single server
>   Multiple servers

There are other systems that can be analyzed analytically; however, the system need not be very complex before analytical solutions are no longer available, in which case we must resort to simulation. For example, customers arriving at a multiple queue, multiple-server queueing system

>   May see that all lines are too long, so they leave without being served
>   May jump from one line to another
>   May arrive according to a non-Poisson process
>   May be given a certain priority

In addition, one or more servers

>   May be servicing at different rates depending on the type of customer
>   May shut down for a break or lunch
>   May be interrupted by the manager occasionally
>   May service faster as the queue becomes longer

In this case, simulation (to be discussed in Chapter 14) may be the only means of analyzing the system.

SELECTED BIBLIOGRAPHY

1 Cooper, Robert B.: "Introduction to Queueing Theory," The Macmillan Company, New York, 1972.
2 Gross, D., and C. M. Harris: "Fundamentals of Queueing Theory," Wiley-Interscience, New York, 1974.

3 Lee, A. M.: "Applied Queueing Theory," The Macmillan Company, London, 1966.

4 Morse, P. M.: "Queues, Inventories, and Maintenance," John Wiley & Sons, Inc., New York, 1958.

5 Panico, J. A.: "Queueing Theory: A Study of Waiting Lines for Business, Economics, and Science," Prentice-Hall, Inc., Englewood Cliffs, N.J., 1969.

6 Prabhu, N. U.: "Queues and Inventories," John Wiley & Sons, Inc., New York, 1965.

7 Ruiz-Pala, E., C. Avila-Beloso, and W. W. Hines: "Waiting-Line Models, An Introduction to Their Theory and Applications," Reinhold Publishing Company, New York, 1967.

EXERCISES

13.1 The local DR Service Station expects a customer every 4 min on the average. Service takes, on the average, 3 min. Assume Poisson input and exponential service.

(*a*) What is the average number of customers waiting for service?

(*b*) How long can a customer expect to wait for service?

(*c*) What is the probability a customer will spend less than 15 min waiting for and getting service?

(*d*) What is the probability a customer will spend longer than 10 min waiting for and getting service?

13.2 Assume an average of 9 customers arrive every 5 min according to a Poisson process and the service facility can service customers at an average rate of 10 customers every 5 min. Service time is exponential.

(*a*) What is the average number of customers waiting for service?

(*b*) What is the average waiting time in the queue?

(*c*) How are the answers to (*a*) and (*b*) affected if the service rate is doubled?

13.3 If customers arrive for service according to a Poisson distribution at the average rate of 5/day, how fast must they be serviced on the average (assume exponential service time) in order to keep the average number in the system less than 4?

13.4 Consider a queueing system with Poisson input. The average arrival rate is 4/hr. The average time in the system must not exceed 1 hr. What is the minimum constant service rate that must be provided?

13.5 A duplicating machine maintained for office use is operated by a student assistant who earns $3 per hour. The time to complete each job varies according to an exponential distribution with mean 6 min. Assume a Poisson input with an average arrival rate of 5 jobs/hr. If an 8-hr day is used as a base, determine

(*a*) The percent idle time of the machine

(*b*) The average time a job is in the system

(*c*) The average cost/day for the student assistant to operate the duplicating machine

13.6 During deer season deer are brought to a check-in station at an average rate of 10/hr. What must be the minimum check-in rate to assure a hunter that the average time at the station (waiting and checking in) will not be longer than 20 min, when check-in time is

(a) Constant

(b) Exponential

Assume arrivals occur completely at random.

13.7   In Exercise 13.6, what fraction of the time will the check-in station be busy?

13.8   Arrivals at a telephone booth are considered to occur completely at random with an average of 12 min between arrivals. The length of a telephone call is assumed to be exponentially distributed with a mean of 3 min. What is the probability a person arriving at the booth will have to wait?

13.9   A dress shop has four salespeople. Assume Poisson arrivals with an average of 10 min between arrivals. Also assume any salesperson can provide the desired service for any customer. If the time to provide service for a customer is exponentially distributed with a mean of 20 min/customer, calculate L, L_q, W, W_q, and P_n for $n = 0, 1, 2$.

13.10 Consider the information in Example 13.3.5. Use the computer program in Section 13.3.2.1 to determine the number of typists needed to reduce the average time in the system to 15 min.

13.11 The local one-person barber shop can accommodate a maximum of five people at a time (four waiting and one getting a haircut). Customers arrive according to a Poisson distribution with mean $\lambda = 5/\text{hr}$. The barber cuts hair at an average rate of 4/hr (exponential service time).

(a) What percent of the time is the barber idle?

(b) What is the effective arrival rate of customers?

(c) What fraction of the potential customers are turned away?

(d) What is the expected number of customers waiting for a haircut?

(e) How much time can a customer expect to spend in the barber shop?

13.12 Use the computer program in Section 13.3.4.1 to calculate P_0, L_q, L, W, W_q, and λ_{eff} for Example 13.3.7 if there are 3 barbers and 10 chairs. Use the same arrival and service rates.

13.13 An office has a single telephone line. Calls are made (in and out) at a rate of 10/hr (Poisson input). The average call takes 3 min with a variance of 2 min. What is the probability the line will be busy at any given time?

13.14 Jobs arrive at a service facility according to a Poisson distribution with a mean of 10 min between jobs. Each job must pass through three preparation phases and a final assembly phase. The time spent in each phase is independent of the times spent in the other phases and is assumed to be negative exponential with mean 2 min. Determine:

(a) The average time in the system

(b) The average number waiting to be serviced

14
SIMULATION

14.1 INTRODUCTION

Simulation is one of the most important OR tools in use today. It has been used successfully to analyze any number of systems, such as

Telephone systems
Job shop operations
Sawmill operations
Computer time-sharing systems
Drive-in bank operations
Lead mine operations
Production scheduling systems

The list goes on and on. The use of simulation has become so widespread that almost every industry has benefitted in some way through the use of simulation.

So what is simulation? Basically, it is a technique for conducting experiments on a model of a system. Recall that we defined a model as "a representation of a system," regardless of whether the system is continuous or discrete. For example, a model of a single queue, single-server queueing system might be

    1 Poisson service time with parameter λ
    2 Exponential service time with parameter μ
    3 FIFO queue discipline
    4 Steady-state with respect to time
    5 Infinite calling population
    6 Unlimited waiting area

We showed in Chapter 13 that this queueing system can be analyzed analytically. However, if the distribution of arrivals is not Poisson, and if it changes several times throughout the day, and/or if several queues form in front of several servers who service at different rates, analytical methods are no longer applicable. In fact, realistic queueing systems are seldom well-behaved enough for the use of analytical methods. Consequently, simulation is widely used to analyze queueing systems.

    In order to study a system once it is defined, two alternatives are available. One is to study the actual system itself; the other is to construct a model of the system and study the model. Generally, a study of the actual system has the disadvantages of being overly time-consuming, expensive, and/or outright impossible. For example, in a sawmill operation, it would be extremely time-consuming and costly to try every possible way of cutting logs to maximize profit. Likewise, it would be impossible to study a proposed system without constructing some type of model. Consequently, models of most existing or proposed systems are constructed, and then the models are analyzed to determine how the actual system will react to change. For example, linear programming models have been constructed to optimize product mix problems, transportation problems, etc. Other OR models that can be solved analytically or numerically to provide answers to questions about the real systems are:

    1 Dynamic programming models
    2 Integer programming models
    3 Regression models
    4 Queueing models
    5 PERT models

However, many realistic systems cannot be modeled for solution by standard OR methods. Hence, some form of simulation must be used to provide the solution.

    There are several types of simulation, but we will restrict our attention to the simulation of mathematical models of systems in which the variables involved are subject to random variation. Since many systems can be modeled as a queueing system, a single queue, single-server queueing system will be modeled and simulated to illustrate the general simulation process. The simulated results will be compared to the exact analytical results to validate the simulation model and computer program. The simulation concepts illustrated in the example can readily be extended to more complex queueing systems involving multiple queues, multiple servers, priority queue discipline, non-Poisson input, etc.

Before considering the illustrative example, consider some definitions that will be of interest.

Definition 14.1 Entity   An object of interest in the system.
An entity could be customers or servers in a queueing system.   ////

Definition 14.2 Attribute   A property of an entity.
If a customer at a supermarket is an entity, then the number of items desired by the customer would be an attribute. If a server is an entity, the number of servers would be an attribute.   ////

Definition 14.3 Activity   Any process that causes a change in the system.
If a customer is an entity who is checking out at a supermarket, then checking out is an activity. Activities in simulation correspond to activities in a PERT network.   ////

Definition 14.4 Event   The start or completion of an activity; the occurrence of a change at a point in time.
The moment a customer starts to check out at a supermarket is an event. The moment a customer leaves the store is another event.   ////

14.2 SIMULATION OF A SINGLE QUEUE, SINGLE-SERVER QUEUEING SYSTEM

Suppose the faculty in a small academic department are unhappy with the supposedly slow turnaround time they get when they submit letters to the departmental secretary to be typed. To study this situation, the department head asks the secretary to record for the next 8 hr the time each letter is received and the time it takes to type each letter. Table 14.1 illustrates these times.

The purpose of the study is to determine

Maximum number of letters waiting to be typed (maximum queue length)
Average time a letter spends waiting to be typed (average waiting time)
Average time a letter spends waiting to be typed and being typed (average time in the system)
Percent of the time the secretary is busy
Average waiting time for letters that must wait to be typed

The first step in any simulation project is to construct a simulation model. In this example, the model consists of the distribution of the time between consecutive arrivals and the distribution of service time, such that customers arrive from an infinite population and enter a single queue with an unlimited area on a FIFO basis. The next step is determine how to generate arrivals to the system and how to generate service times.

Table 14.1   QUEUEING DATA–SECRETARY EXAMPLE

Letter number	Time received	Time started to type	Time finished typing	Time since last arrival	Service time
1	8:07	8:07	8:17	7	10
2	8:38	8:38	9:07	31	29
3	8:39	9:07	9:27	1	20
4	8:44	9:27	9:44	5	17
5	9:22	9:44	9:53	38	9
6	9:25	9:53	10:09	3	16
7	9:28	10:09	10:26	3	17
8	9:49	10:26	10:30	21	4
9	10:06	10:30	10:39	17	9
10	10:22	10:39	10:47	16	8
11	10:25	10:47	10:55	3	8
12	11:03	11:03	11:23	38	20
13	12:24	12:24	12:42	81	18
14	12:29	12:42	12:52	5	10
15	12:43	12:52	1:16	14	24
16	12:44	1:16	1:21	1	5
17	1:04	1:21	1:32	20	11
18	1:16	1:32	1:44	12	12
19	3:06	3:06	3:21	94	15
20	3:50	3:50	4:37	44	47

14.2.1   Generation of Simulation Data

At least three approaches can be used to generate input data for the system under consideration. First, the actual data could be used to calculate the desired statistics and then further experimentation could be done with other queueing models using the same actual data. For example, a second secretary could be hired or a priority could be assigned to each letter as it is received. The same desired statistics could then be recalculated using the same arrival times and the new conditions on service. This approach has the advantage of using the same actual input data while experimenting with the system. In addition, the simulation model can be validated by comparing the results from the simulation with the results from the actual system. Generally, this approach is valid only when there are sufficient data to be assured that there are no "holes" in the data; that is, essentially all of the possible conditions are represented in the data.

A second approach that can be used to generate input data for simulation is to plot histograms of the cumulative distribution of the arrival times and the cumulative distribution of the service times, and then to generate sample arrival and service times using these distributions. Figures 14.1 and 14.2 illustrate these distributions for the data in Table 14.1.

Figure 14.1 is constructed by noting that 20 letters arrived to be typed and that 2 letters arrived *1 min* apart, 3 letters arrived *3 min* apart, 2 letters arrived *5 min* apart, etc. Figure 14.2 is constructed in a similar fashion using service time.

If we had a way of generating equally likely decimal numbers between 0 and 1, we could locate these numbers on the $F(t)$ axis, project horizontally until $F(t)$ or a discontinuity of $F(t)$ is intersected, and then read off the corresponding value of t. For example, if the random number 0.27 is selected, find 0.27 on the $F(t)$ axis in Figure 14.1 and move to the right until the discontinuity of $F(t)$ is intersected. The corresponding value $t = 5$ is selected as the time until the next arrival.

Note that 2 of the 20 letters (10 percent of the letters) arrive 5 min apart. Since every decimal number between 0 and 1 on the $F(t)$ axis is equally likely, 10 percent of the time a number between 0.25 and 0.35 will be selected, which implies that the time $t = 5$ will occur 10 percent of the time in the simulation. But how are the decimal numbers between 0 and 1 generated? For hand calculations, a random number can be selected from a table such as Table 14.2. To select a number from a random number table, merely close your eyes and drop the point of your pencil on the table. The nearest number is selected as the random number. Place a decimal in front of the number and the result will be a random number between 0 and 1. For additional

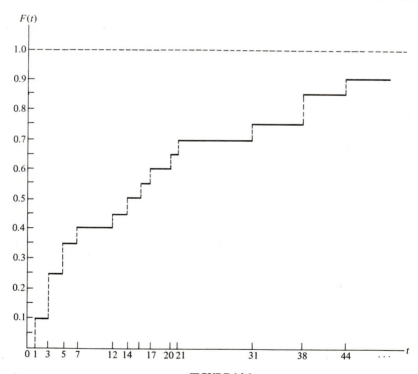

FIGURE 14.1
Cumulative distribution of time between arrivals.

random numbers, start at the first number selected and move down the column, up the column, or across the row.

A third approach that can be used to generate input data for the simulation is to assume the actual data are values from a certain theoretical distribution, and then sample from the theoretical distribution. This is probably the preferred approach in most cases. To determine a theoretical distribution that would be a good approximation of the actual data, several possible distributions could be considered as candidates, and then the chi-square and/or Kolmogorov-Smirnov tests in Chapter 8 could be used to determine the "best" distribution to use. Many times arrivals occur completely at random, so the distribution of the number of arrivals per unit of time is some form of the Poisson distribution. This implies that the time between consecutive arrivals would have an exponential distribution with the same parameter as the Poisson, and the mean of the actual time between consecutive arrivals could be used to approximate this parameter. Although tests should be run to determine the distribution of the time between consecutive arrivals, we will assume an exponential in this example. Since the mean time between consecutive arrivals is $\bar{t}_a = 22.7$, the distribution of the time between consecutive arrivals is assumed to be

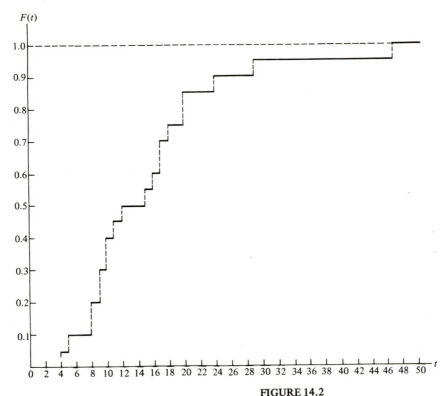

FIGURE 14.2
Cumulative distribution of service time.

Table 14.2 RANDOM NUMBER TABLE

40798	69214	48103	65691	61216	76075	5502	48338	40504	7981
83349	28264	19442	62277	98679	31578	1356	23937	31412	73041
55531	75816	55117	48354	94068	29219	28705	9253	97177	99777
24070	46423	61908	53640	64663	5215	49320	48982	50004	59187
5083	97814	41129	66447	23524	73116	81977	33817	65106	86278
31718	13802	97345	59854	83011	59378	9171	20624	41202	61589
98714	37982	39466	94955	14536	32618	64877	95700	90304	80527
70420	97779	52889	37325	47943	51733	78913	7876	37039	51347
74727	86237	44876	93120	54832	90908	51955	93554	93732	20399
78807	89249	26226	54112	88637	44814	71142	23529	892	93589
53503	78717	90773	36183	132	75146	49689	21817	83695	5816
81638	37488	90182	3697	10536	29942	84827	39487	73473	85453
51460	39676	74920	92430	80299	49925	76858	11818	79187	68757
99857	80329	83253	76562	10088	71469	38022	84912	67267	39393
30956	31192	8548	70561	46432	43539	43344	68211	19167	1099
34089	94645	61066	14588	37937	96326	36519	52179	84400	36789
61132	35685	63921	62364	98891	32067	2386	25708	32772	65254
96574	92158	83781	73263	85542	53886	53437	35647	32951	76874
64686	96251	95326	5700	76261	6268	51258	51133	45472	12631
66538	85547	14437	16694	70232	71140	94751	28242	16693	45971
25591	39805	8509	92807	80258	46286	55393	15782	96158	34905
44003	49875	3222	7C451	93707	28188	25757	849	73282	32047
32743	8040	53545	48913	11564	29169	70938	63103	40171	73095
77030	4327	32691	57198	48970	79034	33471	89519	35874	9571
34556	21193	16150	6161	91609	94207	40757	96680	13264	9463
37405	39262	98920	40163	50695	42705	99974	15492	93189	19697
79485	99632	82422	97847	45282	91066	38856	13535	31507	67221
19760	13573	3593	99396	64041	89675	61684	63026	22998	70745
17492	68244	52028	97974	19587	35757	38261	7746	2127	43046
39131	47369	32030	65861	6892	48602	29576	40042	74065	84007
37452	68648	74824	31108	13228	99396	77322	69365	20284	97418
1953	34956	92154	38323	548	58378	45330	46582	71516	9855
15485	4214	85914	77562	92142	54791	99464	3660	26784	27759
25496	3143	89391	8059	43839	90496	48424	76077	20644	39174
49243	42889	14147	98881	65960	5835	41364	95669	1737	49394
80734	39852	12508	16377	85687	66724	29157	74430	84161	35094
53116	2849	39047	8639	410	24712	44578	45058	69140	9320
33655	18048	5397	69947	71102	97090	42621	81911	7874	10044
89391	45952	71188	13558	40658	21920	65597	96298	87411	57784
60006	39973	99783	38945	35616	63190	58596	82864	69816	73113
10338	4008	31002	49933	20584	74100	59343	89156	848	2685
8477	26696	83880	63013	23152	71794	22395	88225	27793	72730
86239	62863	1022	40367	32997	34680	11102	54493	27035	71773
87324	77983	81980	90025	2334	3774	1638	75856	40392	59646
94351	29289	26571	95822	35790	52335	91899	80378	55180	7675
49424	27466	19978	72673	56234	83347	93968	13687	36404	95241
43812	5697	39878	87988	69024	22254	12300	73516	30395	20722
50773	18133	51843	47857	20555	92617	70705	90675	7702	30133
11475	97653	82638	16951	57963	95223	49665	40983	98907	24598
57419	23131	22013	23894	45250	56447	31434	80576	548	78105

$$f(t_a) = \frac{1}{22.7}\ e^{-(t_a/22.7)} \qquad t_a > 0 \qquad (14.1)$$

$$= 0.044053e^{-0.044053t_a}$$

$$E(T_a) = 22.7 \text{ min}$$

Generally, some form of the Erlang distribution will be a good approximation of the actual service time, so the tests in Chapter 8 can be used to determine the best value of k to use in the Erlang distribution. For our purposes in the current example, we will assume that an Erlang with $k = 1$ is a good approximation of the actual service-time distribution. This, of course, is the exponential distribution. The mean of the actual service times in Table 14.1 is $\bar{t}_s = 15.45$. This value can be used to approximate the parameter in the exponential distribution of service time. Thus, the service-time distribution is assumed to be

$$g(t_s) = \frac{1}{15.45} e^{-(t_s/15.45)} \qquad t_s > 0$$

$$= 0.064725 e^{-0.064725 t_s} \qquad (14.2)$$

$$E(T_s) = 15.45 \text{ min}$$

To sample from $f(t_a)$ and $g(t_s)$, we could plot the cumulative distributions of T_a and T_s, and repeat the same process as we did to obtain sample values using the cumulative distribution of the actual data, where T_a and T_s are random variables with distributions $f(t_a)$ and $g(t_s)$, respectively. The cumulative distribution of T_a is

$$F(t_a) = P(T_a \leqslant t_a) = \int_0^{t_a} 0.044053 e^{-0.044053x} \, dx$$

$$= -e^{-0.044053x} \Big|_0^{t_a}$$

$$= 1 - e^{-0.044053 t_a} \qquad (14.3)$$

Figure 14.3 illustrates $F(t_a)$.

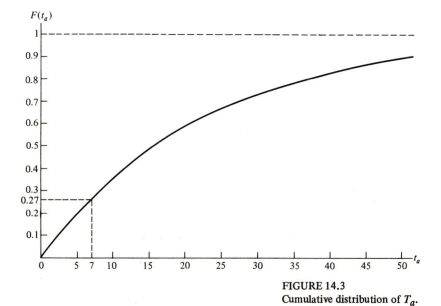

FIGURE 14.3
Cumulative distribution of T_a.

To sample from $f(t_a)$, the usual procedure is to set

$$r = F(t_a) = 1 - e^{-0.044053t_a}$$

where r is a random number between 0 and 1, and then to do an inverse transformation to obtain t_a. That is, solve for t_a in terms of r. Thus,

$$r = 1 - e^{-0.044053t_a}$$

$$e^{-0.044053t_a} = 1 - r$$

$$-0.044053t_a = \ln(1 - r)$$

$$t_a = -\frac{1}{0.044053} \ln(1 - r)$$

$$= -22.7 \ln(1 - r) \qquad (14.4)$$

For r equal to any value in the range $0 \leqslant r < 1$, this actually answers the question, "What value of t_a will yield the cumulative distribution value $F(t_a) = r$?"

If the random number $r = 0.27$ is selected, a sample value of the time until the next arrival is

$$t_a = -22.7 \ln(1 - 0.27)$$

$$= -22.7(-0.314711)$$

$$= 7.1439 \text{ min} \qquad (14.5)$$

If whole minutes are used, the next arrival is selected to arrive 7 min hence. This compares rather closely with the 5 min that would have been selected had we used the cumulative distribution of the actual data in Figure 14.1.

It should be emphasized that the amount of data collected for this example is somewhat less than minimal, so we would not expect it to be representative of the actual system. However, it will suffice to illustrate the simulation procedure. To be representative, data should be collected for 2 or 3 weeks.

Service times can be obtained by using the formula

$$t_s = -15.45 \ln(1 - r) \qquad (14.6)$$

The random numbers r and $1 - r$ are equally likely since $0 < r < 1$, so arrival times and service times can be generated using

$$t_a = -22.7 \ln r \qquad (14.7)$$

$$t_s = -15.45 \ln r \qquad (14.8)$$

Of course, one value of r is used to obtain t_a and another value is used to obtain t_s.

Regardless of which approach is used to generate data for a simulation study, it is essential that the actual data collected be representative of the population from which it came. For example, if we were to simulate the operation of a supermarket, we would not collect data only during the first hour the store is open and expect it to be representative of the daily operation. Likewise, we would not collect data only at the peak periods or slack periods. Hence, a great deal of effort should go into the collection of data to assure that it is representative. Remember, the results from a properly designed simulation study are only as good as the input data.

14.2.2 Generation of Random Numbers

One concern in a simulation study is how to generate variates (values) from a uniform distribution defined on the interval $[0,1]$. The primary reason for the concern is that the generation of variates from many distribution functions is highly dependent on being able to generate *random numbers* (values from a uniform distribution defined on the interval $[0,1]$). This was illustrated in Section 14.2.1 with the exponential distribution. Namely,

$$t_a = -22.7 \ln r$$

is a sample value from an exponential distribution with mean 22.7, where r is a random number.

A great deal of research has gone into the development of good random number generators. Since a random number generator may be called upon several thousand times during a simulation run, it is essential that it be

Fast
Recursive
Nondegenerate
Algorithmic in nature

For hand simulations, random numbers can be taken from a table (see Table 14.2); however, this is not practical for computer simulations. Rather than go into the theory of generating random numbers, we will merely state that all computer systems have a subroutine available for generating random numbers. The subroutine available with the IBM 360 system is

```
        SUBROUTINE RANDU(IX, IY, YFL)
        IY = IX*65539
        IF(IY)5,6,6
     5  IY = IY + 2147483647 + 1
     6  YFL = IY
        YFL = YFL*.4656613E − 9
        RETURN
        END
```

The variables in the argument of RANDU are defined as follows:

IX = any number with nine or fewer digits supplied by the user. It is preferable that IX be an odd number. IX is set equal to IY each time after the subroutine is called.

IY = a resultant integer random number between 0 and 2^{31}.

YFL = the desired random number between 0 and 1.

An example of how to use the subroutine is

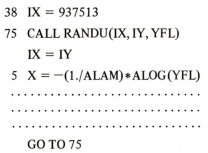

38   IX = 937513

75   CALL RANDU(IX, IY, YFL)

       IX = IY

  5   X = −(1./ALAM)∗ALOG(YFL)

       ....
       ....
       ....

              GO TO 75

The program should never return to statement 38; otherwise, the random number generator will be reinitialized and will produce the same values over again.

The subroutine RANDU has the feature that it will produce exactly the same set of random numbers for each simulation run if it is initialized with the same IX value each time. Thus, many different systems can be analyzed using the same set of generated data.

14.2.3   Fixed-Time-Increment Model vs. Next-Event-Oriented Model

Once a simulation model has been constructed, a means for carrying out the actual simulation must be selected. Basically, there are two approaches that are used. Either the simulation model can be updated at very small increments of time, or it can be updated only when the next event occurs. A simulation model which uses the first approach is called a *fixed-time-increment model*, while the model which uses the second approach is called a *next-event-oriented model*. Both approaches have some advantages and disadvantages; however, we will select the next-event-oriented model for further study since it is usually preferable. For the secretary example, there are only two events which can occur: a letter can arrive to be typed or the secretary can finish typing a letter. A general algorithm for the simulation of a single queue, single-server queueing system will be presented and then the algorithm will be illustrated with the secretary example.

14.2.4   Algorithm 14.1—Simulation of a Single Queue, Single-Server
Queueing System

The purpose of this algorithm is to illustrate how to simulate a single queue, single-server queueing system in order to determine statistics such as

Maximum queue length
Average time in the queue
Average time in the service facility
Average time in the system
Average time in the system for those who must wait
Percentage of time the service facility is busy

The necessary assumptions are

The first customer arrives at time zero
FIFO queue discipline
Infinite calling population
Unlimited waiting area
Next-event-oriented model

The following notation will be used

$$AT = \text{time of next arrival}$$
$$ST = \text{time of next departure from service facility}$$
$$CLOCK = \text{current clock time (time since the simulation started)}$$
$$MAXCT = \text{maximum time to run simulation}$$
$$NQUE = \text{current number in the queue}$$
$$TIDT = \text{total time service facility has been idle}$$
$$NTOTQ = \text{total number of arrivals who enter the queue}$$
$$TWT = \text{total waiting time for all arrivals}$$
$$TISF = \text{total time all arrivals have been in the service facility}$$
$$TIS = \text{total time all arrivals have been in the system}$$
$$NARRV = \text{total number of arrivals}$$
$$MAXQUE = \text{maximum queue length}$$

Step 1
Read in the maximum simulation time and the input data to generate arrivals and departures.

Step 2
Set the initial conditions:

$$CLOCK = 0$$
$$AT = 0$$
$$NQUE = 0$$
$$NTOTQ = 0$$
$$TWT = 0$$
$$TIDT = 0$$
$$NARRV = 1$$
$$MAXQUE = 0$$

Step 3
Generate the time of the next departure ST.

Step 4
Generate the time of the next arrival AT.

Step 5
If the next event is a departure (ST < AT), go to step 6; otherwise go to step 15.

Step 6
If the queue is empty, go to step 7; otherwise, go to step 11.

Step 7
Update the clock to the time of the next event (departure).

$$CLOCK = ST$$

Step 8
Update the total idle time of the service facility.

$$TIDT = TIDT + (AT - CLOCK)$$

Step 9
Update the clock to the time of the next event (arrival).

$$CLOCK = AT$$

Increase the number of arrivals by 1.

Step 10
If the current clock time exceeds the maximum simulation time, go to step 22; otherwise, return to step 3.

Step 11
Update the total waiting time of all arrivals

$$TWT = TWT + NQUE(ST - CLOCK)$$

Step 12
Update the clock to the time of the next event (departure).

$$CLOCK = ST$$

Step 13
Decrease the number in the queue by 1 and generate the time of the next departure.

Step 14
If the current clock time exceeds the maximum simulation time, go to step 22; otherwise, return to step 5.

Step 15
Update the total waiting time of all arrivals.

$$TWT = TWT + NQUE(AT - CLOCK)$$

Step 16
Update the clock to the time of the next event (arrival).

$$CLOCK = AT$$

Increase the number of arrivals by 1.

Step 17
If the next event is both a departure and an arrival $(ST = AT)$, go to step 10; otherwise, go to step 18.

Step 18
Increase the number in the queue by 1.

Step 19
If the current number in the queue (NQUE) exceeds the longest queue length to date (MAXQUE), set

$$MAXQUE = NQUE$$

and go to step 20; otherwise, go directly to step 20.

Step 20
Increase the total number of arrivals who wait (NTOTQ) by 1.

Step 21
If the current clock time exceeds the maximum simulation time, go to step 22; otherwise, return to step 4.

Step 22
Calculate and print the desired statistics:

$$TISF = CLOCK - TIDT$$
$$TIS = TISF + TWT$$
$$ATIS = \text{average time in system}$$
$$= TIS/NARRV$$
$$ATISF = \text{average time in service facility}$$
$$= TISF/NARRV$$
$$ATIQ = \text{average time in queue}$$
$$= TWT/NARRV$$
$$ATNEQ = \text{average time in queue for those who wait}$$
$$= TWT/NTOTQ$$

POTB = percentage of time service facility is busy

= TISF/CLOCK

A flowchart for Algorithm 14.1 is shown in Figure 14.4.

14.2.5 Application of Algorithm 14.1

For the secretary example, we assume the time between consecutive arrivals can be approximated with an exponential distribution with parameter ALAM = 1/22.7 = 0.044053. Likewise, service time is assumed to be exponentially distributed with parameter AMU = 1/15.45 = 0.064725.

Suppose we want to run the simulation for 1000 min. Thus, in step 1 of Algorithm 14.1, we would read in

$$ALAM = 0.044053$$

$$AMU = 0.064725$$

$$MAXCT = 1000 \text{ min}$$

Note that the same time unit must be used for the time between arrivals, service time, and maximum simulation time.

We assume

The first arrival occurs at time zero
The initial conditions have been set
The variable IX has been initialized at the beginning of the program

The time of the first departure is then generated with the statements

CALL RANDU(IX, IY, YFL)

IX = IY

ST = CLOCK + (−1./AMU) * ALOG(YFL)

The time of the second arrival is generated with the statements

CALL RANDU(IX, IY, YFL)

IX = IY

AT = CLOCK + (−1./ALAM) * ALOG(YFL)

The process then follows Algorithm 14.1 step by step until the current clock time exceeds the maximum simulation time.

The results from repeating the simulation using maximum simulation times of 25,000, 50,000, and 100,000 min are shown in Table 14.3.

With reference to Table 14.3, an average turnaround time of approximately 48 min seems reasonable, so the faculty's unhappiness is apparently not caused by slow typing service.

Table 14.3 SIMULATION AND ANALYTICAL RESULTS (SECRETARY
EXAMPLE) ALAM = 0.044053, AMU = 0.064725

	Maximum simulation time, minutes			Analytical results
	25,000	50,000	100,000	
MAXQUE	14.00	14.00	20.00	
$W = $ ATIS	40.81	45.10	46.46	48.37
$W_q = $ ATIQ	25.82	29.86	31.44	32.92
$W_w = $ ATNEQ	39.73	44.82	47.44	48.37
$1/$AMU $= $ ATISF	15.00	15.25	15.03	15.45
ALAM/AMU $= $ POTB	64%	69%	66%	68%

14.2.6 Computer Program for Algorithm 14.1

Although Algorithm 14.1 is designed to simulate a single queue, single-server queueing system with any input and service-time distributions, this program assumes the time between consecutive arrivals is exponential with mean 1/ALAM and the service time is exponential with mean 1/AMU. The user specifies the values of ALAM, AMU, and the maximum simulation time MAXCT. To use any other input and service-time distributions, statement 1 would need to be changed accordingly to read in the desired distributions. Likewise, statements 3, 4, and 25, as well as the two cards after each of them, must be changed to generate the arrival time and the service times from the given distributions.

The program simulated the secretary example in Section 14.2.5 for 25,000, 50,000, and 100,000 min. The results are printed after the program and in Table 14.3.

The program follows the general flowchart in Figure 14.4. The comment cards throughout the program relate to the numbers on the boxes in the flowchart. As printed, the program occupies 36K bytes of core storage. The total simulation time for the secretary example was 1.78 s on an IBM 370/168 computer.

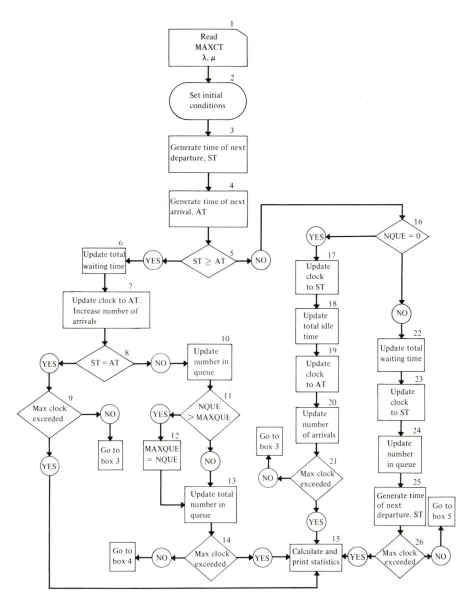

FIGURE 14.4
Flowchart for single queue, single-server queueing system.

```
C     ******************************************************************************
C     *                                                                          *
C     *          *** SIMULATION OF A SINGLE QUEUE-SINGLE SERVER ***              *
C     *                         QUEUEING SYSTEM                                   *
C     *                                                                          *
C     * THIS PROGRAM IS DESIGNED TO SIMULATE A SINGLE QUEUE-SINGLE SERVER        *
C     * QUEUEING SYSTEM WITH EXPONENTIAL INPUT AND SERVICE TIME. THE USER        *
C     * SPECIFIES THE VALUES OF THE PARAMETERS FOR THE INPUT AND SERVICE         *
C     * TIME DISTRIBUTIONS AS WELL AS THE MAXIMUM TIME THE SIMULATION IS         *
C     * TO RUN AS FOLLOWS:                                                        *
C     *     READ                                                                  *
C     *          CARD 1   COLS  2-80   TITLE  DESCRIPTION OF THE PROBLEM USING   *
C     *                                       ANY CHARACTERS ON KEYPUNCH          *
C     *                                       ** COLUMN 1 MUST BE LEFT BLANK **   *
C     *          CARD 2   COLS  1-10   ALAM   PARAMETER IN THE EXPONENTIAL INTER- *
C     *                                       ARRIVAL TIME DISTRIBUTION  (F10.0)  *
C     *                         11-20  AMU    PARAMETER IN THE EXPONENTIAL SERVICE*
C     *                                       TIME DISTRIBUTION  (F10.0)          *
C     *                         21-30  MAXCT  MAXIMUM SIMULATION TIME  (I10)      *
C     *          TO SIMULATE MORE THAN ONE PROBLEM AT A TIME, REPEAT THE READ    *
C     *          SEQUENCE AND STACK THE DATA ONE BEHIND THE OTHER.               *
C     *                                                                          *
C     *     CALCULATE                                                            *
C     *          NARRV      NUMBER OF ARRIVALS TO SYSTEM                         *
C     *          NTOTQ      TOTAL NUMBER THAT JOINED THE QUEUE                   *
C     *          TISF       TIME IN SERVICE FACILITY                            *
C     *          TIS        TIME IN SYSTEM                                       *
C     *          ATIS       AVERAGE TIME IN SYSTEM                              *
C     *          ATISF      AVERAGE TIME IN SERVICE FACILITY                    *
C     *          ATIQ       AVERAGE TIME IN QUEUE                               *
C     *          ATNEQ      AVERAGE TIME FOR THOSE WHO WAIT                     *
C     *          TIDT       TOTAL IDLE TIME                                      *
C     *          POTB       PERCENT OF TIME SERVICE FACILITY WAS BUSY           *
C     *          TWT        TOTAL WAITING TIME                                   *
C     *          MAXQUE     MAXIMUM QUEUE LENGTH                                 *
C     *                                                                          *
C     *     PRINT                                                                *
C     *          ALAM, AMU, MAXCT, TISF, TIS, ATIS, ATISF, ATIQ, ATNEQ,         *
C     *          TIDT, POTB, MAXQUE                                             *
C     *                                                                          *
C     ******************************************************************************
      REAL*4 TITLE(20)
      IX=973253
C READ DATA
   95 READ(5,102,END=2000)TITLE
  102 FORMAT(20A4)
      WRITE(6,103)TITLE
  103 FORMAT('1',20A4,//)
    1 READ(5,100) ALAM,AMU,MAXCT
  100 FORMAT(2F10.0,I10)
C     ******************************************************************************
C     *              SET INITIAL CONDITIONS                                      *
C     ******************************************************************************
      CLOCK=0.0
      AT=0.0
      NQUE=0.0
      NTOTQ=0.0
      TWT=0.0
      TIDT=0.0
      NARRV=1
      MAXQUE=0
C     ******************************************************************************
C     *              GENERATE TIME OF NEXT DEPARTURE                             *
C     ******************************************************************************
    3 CALL RANDU(IX,IY,YFL)
      IX=IY
      ST=CLOCK+(-1./AMU)*ALOG(YFL)
C     ******************************************************************************
C     *              GENERATE TIME OF NEXT ARRIVAL                               *
C     ******************************************************************************
```

```
    4 CALL RANDU(IX,IY,YFL)
      IX=IY
      AT=CLOCK+(-1./ALAM)*ALOG(YFL)
C     **************************************************************************
C     *            IF NEXT EVENT IS AN ARRIVAL, GO TO STATEMENT 6; OTHERWISE, *
C     *            GO TO STATEMENT 16.                                        *
C     **************************************************************************
    5 IF(ST-AT)16,6,6
C     **************************************************************************
C     *            UPDATE TOTAL WAITING TIME, CLOCK, AND THE NUMBER OF ARRIVALS. *
C     **************************************************************************
    6 TWT=TWT+NQUE*(AT-CLOCK)
      CLOCK=AT
      NARRV=NARRV+1
C     **************************************************************************
C     *            IF NEXT EVENT IS BOTH AN ARRIVAL AND A DEPARTURE, GO TO    *
C     *            STATEMENT 9; OTHERWISE, GO TO STATEMENT 10.                *
C     **************************************************************************
    8 IF(ST-AT)10,9,10
C     **************************************************************************
C     *            UPDATE NUMBER IN QUEUE, MAXIMUM QUEUE LENGTH, AND TOTAL    *
C     *            NUMBER IN QUEUE.                                           *
C     **************************************************************************
   10 NQUE=NQUE+1
   11 IF(NQUE-MAXQUE)13,13,12
   12 MAXQUE=NQUE
   13 NTOTQ=NTOTQ+1
C     **************************************************************************
C     *            IF MAXIMUM CLOCK TIME IS EXCEEDED, GO TO STATEMENT 15;     *
C     *            OTHERWISE, RETURN TO STATEMENT 4 TO GENERATE NEXT ARRIVAL. *
C     **************************************************************************
   14 IF(MAXCT-CLOCK)15,15,4
C     **************************************************************************
C     *            IF MAXIMUM CLOCK TIME IS EXCEEDED, GO TO STATEMENT 15;     *
C     *            OTHERWISE, RETURN TO STATEMENT 3 TO GENERATE THE TIME      *
C     *            OF THE NEXT DEPARTURE.                                     *
C     **************************************************************************
    9 IF(MAXCT-CLOCK)15,15,3
C     **************************************************************************
C     *            IF THE QUEUE IS EMPTY, GO TO STATEMENT 17; OTHERWISE,      *
C     *            GO TO STATEMENT 22.                                        *
C     **************************************************************************
   16 IF(NQUE)22,17,22
C     **************************************************************************
C     *            UPDATE CLOCK, TOTAL WAITING TIME, NUMBER OF ARRIVALS.      *
C     **************************************************************************
   17 CLOCK=ST
      TIDT=TIDT+(AT-CLOCK)
      CLOCK=AT
      NARRV=NARRV+1
C     **************************************************************************
C     *            IF MAXIMUM CLOCK TIME IS EXCEEDED, GO TO STATEMENT 15;     *
C     *            OTHERWISE, RETURN TO STATEMENT 3.                          *
C     **************************************************************************
   21 IF(MAXCT-CLOCK)15,15,3
C     **************************************************************************
C     *            UPDATE CLOCK, TOTAL WAITING TIME, NUMBER IN QUEUE.         *
C     **************************************************************************
   22 TWT=TWT+NQUE*(ST-CLOCK)
      CLOCK=ST
      NQUE=NQUE-1
C     **************************************************************************
C     *            GENERATE TIME OF NEXT DEPARTURE                           *
C     **************************************************************************
   25 CALL RANDU(IX,IY,YFL)
      IX=IY
      ST=CLOCK+(-1./AMU)*ALOG(YFL)
C     **************************************************************************
C     *            IF MAXIMUM CLOCK TIME IS EXCEEDED, GO TO STATEMENT 15;     *
C     *            OTHERWISE, RETURN TO STATEMENT 5.                          *
C     **************************************************************************
```

```
   26 IF(MAXCT-CLOCK)15,15,5
C      *****************************************************************
C      *            CALCULATE AND PRINT STATISTICS.                   *
C      *****************************************************************
   15 TISF=CLOCK-TIDT
      TIS=TISF+TWT
      ATIS=TIS/NARRV
      ATISF=TISF/NARRV
      ATIQ=TWT/NARRV
      ATNEQ=TWT/NTOTQ
      POTB=TISF/CLOCK
      WRITE(6,101)ALAM,AMU,MAXCT,TISF,TIS,ATIS,ATISF,ATIQ,ATNEQ,TIDT,
     *POTB,MAXQUE
  101 FORMAT(' ALAM  =',F12.4/' AMU   =',F12.4/' MAXCT =',I12/
     *' TISF  =',F12.4/' TIS   =',F12.4/' ATIS  =',F12.4/
     *' ATISF =',F12.4/' ATIQ  =',F12.4/' ATNEQ =',F12.4/
     *' TIDT  =',F12.4/' POTB  =',F12.4/' MAXQUE =',I12)
      GO TO 95
 2000 STOP
      END

      SUBROUTINE RANDU(IX,IY,YFL)
      IY=IX*65539
      IF(IY)5,6,6
    5 IY=IY+2147483647+1
    6 YFL=IY
      YFL=YFL*.4656613E-9
      RETURN
      END


/DATA

    SECRETARY EXAMPLE FROM SECTION 14.2.5  - MAXCT=100000
    .044053   .064725    100000


    SECRETARY EXAMPLE FROM SECTION 14.2.5  - MAXCT=100000

ALAM   =       0.0441
AMU    =       0.0647
MAXCT  =       100000
TISF   =   66105.8750
TIS    =  204432.125
ATIS   =      46.4618
ATISF  =      15.0250
ATIQ   =      31.4369
ATNEQ  =      47.4356
TIDT   =   33896.9453
POTB   =       0.6611
MAXQUE =           20
```

14.3 GENERATION OF RANDOM VARIATES

A *random variate* is defined to be a value of a random variable. We now want to consider how to generate random variates from a number of different distribution functions. In Section 14.2 we examined a method for generating random variates using the cumulative distribution function of a random variable. In particular, we examined how to select a random variate using the cumulative distribution of actual arrival and service times. We also examined how to select a random variate from an exponential distribution. The method used is called the *inverse transformation method.*

Quite often departures from a service facility are not completely at random, so the service time does not have an exponential distribution. Hence, it is desirable to be able to generate random variates from many different distribution functions.

14.3.1 Inverse Transformation Method

This method can be used to generate random variates either from empirical distributions based on actual data or from many theoretical distributions. If the distribution function is discrete, the procedure to generate a random variate from $f(x)$ is:

1 Plot $F(x)$, the cumulative distribution of the random variable X.
2 Choose a random number r from a random number table; $0 < r < 1$.
3 Locate the random number on the $F(x)$ axis and project horizontally until the projected line intersects $F(x)$ or a discontinuity of $F(x)$.
4 Write down the value of x corresponding to the point of intersection. The value of x is a random variate from $f(x)$.

EXAMPLE 14.3.1 Suppose we have the following demands with their corresponding probabilities:

X = demand	0	10	20	30	40
$f(x) = \mathrm{P}(X = x)$	$\frac{1}{8}$	$\frac{1}{4}$	$\frac{1}{2}$	$\frac{1}{16}$	$\frac{1}{16}$

Plot $F(x)$. (See Figure 14.5.)

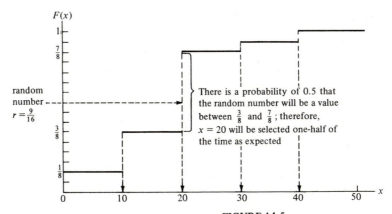

FIGURE 14.5
Cumulative distribution of demand.

Random numbers are selected from a random number table and the corresponding values of x are determined. For $r = \frac{9}{16}$, the projected line intersects the discontinuity of $F(x)$ at $x = 20$. Therefore, $x = 20$ is selected as the random variate.

If a computer is used to select a value from a discrete distribution, the cumulative distribution is examined using successive values of x until a value is found that is greater than or equal to r. The corresponding value of X is then selected as the random variate.

If $f(x)$ is a continuous distribution function, the inverse transformation procedure is to write

$$r = F(x) = P(X \leqslant x)$$

and solve for x in terms of r. For the exponential distribution

$$r = F(x) = \int_0^x \mu e^{-\mu y}\, dy = 1 - e^{-\mu x}$$

$$e^{-\mu x} = 1 - r$$

$$-\mu x = \ln(1 - r)$$

$$x = -\frac{1}{\mu} \ln(1 - r)$$

or

$$x = -\frac{1}{\mu} \ln r \tag{14.9}$$

However, it is not always possible to write down the cumulative distribution of a random variable and solve for x in terms of the random number r. The normal distribution is an example. However, there are methods available that can be used to generate normal random variates.

14.3.2 Normal Random Variates

A number of procedures for generating random variates from a normal distribution are available. We will develop the one which makes use of the central limit theorem. Recall from Chapter 8 that the central limit theorem essentially states that the probability distribution of the sum of N independently and identically distributed random variables R_i with mean μ_i and variance σ_i^2 with $i = 1, 2, \ldots, N$ approaches the normal distribution with mean $\Sigma_{i=1}^{N} \mu_i$ and variance $\Sigma_{i=1}^{N} \sigma_i^2$ asymptotically as N becomes large. Hence, we can let R_i with $i = 1, 2, \ldots, N$ be random variables with the uniform distribution on the interval $[0,1]$. That is, let

$$f(r_i) = 1 \qquad 0 \leqslant r_i \leqslant 1 \tag{14.10}$$

$$\mu_i = E(R_i) = \int_0^1 x\, 1\, dx = \frac{1}{2} \tag{14.11}$$

$$\sigma_i^2 = \text{var}(R_i) = \int_0^1 [(x - E(x)]^2 \, 1 \, dx = \frac{1}{12} \qquad (14.12)$$

As N becomes large,

$$\sum_{i=1}^{N} R_i \overset{\cdot}{\sim} N\left(\sum_{i=1}^{N} \mu_i, \sum_{i=1}^{N} \sigma_i^2\right) \qquad (14.13)$$

$$\overset{\cdot}{\sim} N\left(\sum_{i=1}^{N} \frac{1}{2}, \sum_{i=1}^{N} \frac{1}{12}\right)$$

$$\overset{\cdot}{\sim} N(N/2, N/12) \qquad (14.14)$$

where $\overset{\cdot}{\sim}$ denotes "is distributed approximately as." Thus, $\Sigma_{i=1}^{N} R_i$ has approximately a normal distribution with mean $N/2$ and variance $N/12$ as N becomes large. The value of N does not have to be very large to give a good approximation. In fact, the approximation is quite good even for N as small as 12.

To generate a random variate from a normal distribution with mean 0 and variance 1, we note that

$$Z = \frac{\sum_{i=1}^{N} R_i - N/2}{\sqrt{N/12}} \overset{\cdot}{\sim} N(0, 1) \qquad \text{for large } N \qquad (14.15)$$

For $N = 12$,

$$Z = \left(\sum_{i=1}^{12} R_i - 6\right) \overset{\cdot}{\sim} N(0, 1) \qquad (14.16)$$

Hence, we can generate 12 random numbers (values of R_i with $i = 1, 2, \ldots, 12$) and subtract 6 from the sum of the 12 values to get a sample value from a normal distribution with mean 0 and variance 1. That is, let

$$z = \sum_{i=1}^{12} r_i - 6 \qquad (14.17)$$

where r_i is a value of R_i with $i = 1, 2, \ldots, 12$.

To generate a random variate from a normal distribution with mean μ and variance σ^2, note that if

$$X \sim N(\mu, \sigma^2) \qquad (14.18)$$

$$\sum_{i=1}^{N} R_i \overset{\cdot}{\sim} N\left(\sum_{i=1}^{N} \mu_i, \sum_{i=1}^{N} \sigma_i^2\right) \qquad (14.19)$$

then
$$Y = \frac{X - \mu}{\sigma} \sim N(0,1) \qquad (14.20)$$

$$Z = \frac{\sum\limits_{i=1}^{N} R_i - N/2}{\sqrt{N/12}} \overset{\cdot}{\sim} N(0,1) \qquad (14.21)$$

Therefore, since Y and Z are both distributed normally with mean 0 and variance 1, we can set Y equal to Z and solve for X.

$$\frac{X - \mu}{\sigma} = \frac{\sum\limits_{i=1}^{N} R_i - N/2}{\sqrt{N/12}} \qquad (14.22)$$

$$X = \mu + \sigma \frac{\sum\limits_{i=1}^{N} R_i - N/2}{\sqrt{N/12}} \qquad (14.23)$$

For $N = 12$, generate a value of z from Equation (14.17), multiply the result by σ and add the new result to μ. The value obtained will be a sample value of X.

A subroutine to generate random variates from a normal distribution with mean AMU and standard deviation SIGMA (square root of the variance) is

```
            SUBROUTINE NORMAL(IX, AMU, SIGMA, Y)
            SUM = 0.0
            DO 14 I = 1,12
            CALL RANDU(IX, IY, YFL)
            IX = IY
        14  SUM = SUM + YFL
            Y = AMU + SIGMA*(SUM − 6.)
            RETURN
            END
```

This subroutine assumes

$N = 12$ in Equation (14.23).
IX has been initialized before the subroutine is called the first time.
The subroutine RANDU in Section 14.2.2 is part of the source program.

The subroutine will return a sample value of Y.

14.3.3 Uniform Random Variates on the Interval [a,b]

Suppose X has the distribution

$$f(x) = \frac{1}{b-a} \qquad a \leqslant x \leqslant b \qquad (14.24)$$

then

$$r = F(x) = \int_a^x \frac{dt}{b-a} = \frac{x-a}{b-a}$$

$$x = a + (b-a)r \qquad (14.25)$$

14.3.4 Erlang Random Variates

Quite often service time in a queueing system has a distribution that can be approximated with some form of an Erlang distribution. Recall from Chapter 13 that if k independent random variables T_i with $i = 1, 2, \ldots, k$ each have the same exponential distribution

$$f(t_i) = \mu k e^{-\mu k t_i} \qquad \begin{matrix} t_i > 0 \\ \mu > 0 \\ k = \text{positive integer} \end{matrix} \qquad (14.26)$$

then $T = \Sigma_{i=1}^k T_i$ has the Erlang distribution. Thus, to generate random variates from the Erlang distribution

$$f(t) = \frac{(\mu k)^k t^{k-1} e^{-\mu k t}}{(k-1)!} \qquad \begin{matrix} t > 0 \\ \mu > 0 \\ k = \text{positive integer} \end{matrix} \qquad (14.27)$$

we generate k random variates from the exponential distribution in Equation (14.26), and then sum these k random variates to obtain a random variate from the Erlang distribution in Equation (14.27). That is, if

$$t_i = -\frac{1}{\mu k} \ln r_i \qquad i = 1, 2, \ldots, k \qquad (14.28)$$

then

$$t = \sum_{i=1}^k t_i = \sum_{i=1}^k \left(-\frac{1}{\mu k}\right) \ln r_i$$

$$= -\frac{1}{\mu k} \sum_{i=1}^k \ln r_i$$

$$= -\frac{1}{\mu k} \ln \prod_{i=1}^k r_i \qquad (14.29)$$

where r_i with $i = 1, 2, \ldots, k$ are k random numbers.

A computer subroutine to generate random variates from an Erlang distribution with parameters K and μ is

> SUBROUTINE ERLANG(IX,K,AMU,T)
>
> AK = K
>
> PROD = 1.0
>
> DO 25 I = 1, K
>
> CALL RANDU(IX, IY, YFL)
>
> IX = IY
>
> 25 PROD = PROD * YFL
>
> T = (−1./(AMU * AK)) * ALOG(PROD)
>
> RETURN
>
> END

This subroutine assumes

> K has been given a value before the subroutine is called
> IX has been initialized before the subroutine is called the first time
> The subroutine RANDU in Section 14.2.2 is part of the source program
> The parameter μ is represented by AMU

The subroutine will return a sample value of T.

14.3.5 Binomial Random Variates

To generate a random variate from the binomial distribution

$$f(x) = \binom{n}{x} p^x (1 - p)^{n-x} \qquad \begin{matrix} x = 0, 1, 2, \ldots, n \\ 0 < p < 1 \end{matrix} \qquad (14.30)$$

generate n random numbers, r_i with $i = 1, 2, \ldots, n$, and let x be the number of r_i's that are less than or equal to p. Recall that x represents the number of successes in n independent trials in which p is the probability of a success on each trial and $1 - p$ is the probability of a failure on each trial. Essentially, we conduct n independent trials by selecting a random number on each trial. Consequently, if an r_i is less than or equal to p, we record it as a success since it occurs with probability p. The total number of r_i's that are less than or equal to p is the desired sample value of X.

A computer subroutine to generate a random variate from a binomial distribution with parameters N and P is

> SUBROUTINE BINOM(IX, N, P, X)
>
> X = 0.0

```
          DO 12 I = 1, N
          CALL RANDU(IX, IY, YFL)
          IX = IY
          IF (YFL. LE. P)X = X + 1.
     12   CONTINUE
          RETURN
          END
```

This subroutine assumes

> IX has been initialized before the subroutine is called the first time
> N = number of trials (supplied to subroutine)
> P = probability of success on each trial (supplied to subroutine)
> The subroutine RANDU is part of the source program

The subroutine returns a sample value of X.

14.4 SIMULATION LANGUAGES

Most realistic simulation projects are of the nature that a separate computer program is required for each project. Consequently, one of the main objectives is to get a fairly efficient executable program running in a short period of time. Obviously, the program should not be written in machine language or assembly language, but what about a general-purpose language such as FORTRAN or PL/1? Both of these languages are very general in nature and can be used for any simulation project. In fact, FORTRAN is used quite often because it is

> Well-known
> Available on almost all computer systems
> Generally more efficient in time as well as in storage

However, most realistic projects are sufficiently complex so that the bookkeeping gets out of hand quite rapidly, so programming in FORTRAN becomes very time-consuming. Hence, there is a definite need for simulation languages that automatically take care of the intricate details as the actual simulation is carried out by the computer. Some of these details can be handled with PL/1 since it has list-processing capabilities. However, simulation languages have other desirable time-saving features.

Simulation languages such as GASP and SIMSCRIPT are general in nature and can be used to do anything that can be done in FORTRAN or PL/1. In fact, GASP is a FORTRAN-compiled set of subroutines and function subprograms which is controlled by the main program, the GASP EXECUTIVE. SIMSCRIPT is also based on FORTRAN and requires a knowledge of computer programming. Both languages relieve the user of all bookkeeping chores and decrease the actual programming time required using FORTRAN. However, the user must still be involved with some of the programming details.

The most widely used simulation language is GPSS (general-purpose simulation system), which was developed by IBM. The latest version is GPSS/360. GPSS is a problem-oriented language, but it has a wide range of applications. It is a variable-time-increment language which carries out simulations in integral time units. This is extremely important since all calculations are performed using integer arithmetic; thus, round-off errors are minimized.

The GPSS user writes down the general flow of what is to be simulated in block diagram form and then the blocks are written as GPSS statements. GPSS automatically performs all bookkeeping chores, and also calculates and prints many important statistics. Once the language is learned, a program to simulate complex projects can be written in a very short period of time.

As with any high-level language, the use of a simulation language generally decreases programming time but increases the computer running time and core storage requirements. Consequently, care should be used in deciding whether to use a general-purpose language such as FORTRAN or PL/1, or whether to use a simulation language such as GASP, GPSS, or SIMSCRIPT. Some of the many other simulation languages which have been developed are DYNAMO, CSMP, SIMPAC, SIMULATE, GSP, SIMULA, ESP, and CSL. However, GPSS and SIMSCRIPT are the most widely used simulation languages.

SELECTED BIBLIOGRAPHY

1 Butler, E. L.: Algorithm 370, General Random Number Generator [G5], *Comm. ACM*, vol. 13, pp. 49–52, 1970.

2 Chorafas, D. N.: "Systems and Simulation," Academic Press, Inc., New York, 1965.

3 Gordon, G.: "Systems Simulation," Prentice-Hall, Inc., Englewood Cliffs, N.J., 1969.

4 Harbaugh, J. W., and G. Bonham-Carter: "Computer Simulation in Geology," John Wiley & Sons, Inc., New York, 1970.

5 Maisel, H., and G. Gnugnoli: "Simulation of Discrete Stochastic Systems," Science Research Associates, Inc., Chicago, 1972.

6 Markowitz, H., B. Hauser, and H. Karr: "SIMSCRIPT: A Simulation Programming Language," Prentice-Hall, Inc., Englewood Cliffs, N.J., 1965.

7 Martin, F. F.: "Computer Modeling and Simulation," John Wiley & Sons, Inc., New York, 1968.

8 McLeod, J. (ed.): "Simulation," McGraw-Hill Book Company, New York, 1968.

9 Mier, R. C., W. T. Newell, and H. L. Pazer: "Simulation in Business and Economics," Prentice-Hall, Inc., Englewood Cliffs, N.J., 1969.

10 Mihram, G. Arthur: "Simulation: Statistical Foundations and Methodology," Academic Press, Inc., New York, 1972.

11 Naylor, T. H., J. L. Balintfy, D. S. Burdick, and K. Chu: "Computer Simulation Techniques," John Wiley & Sons, Inc., New York, 1966.

12 Naylor, T.: "Computer Simulation Experiments with Models of Economic Systems," John Wiley & Sons, Inc., New York, 1971.

13 Schmidt, J. W., and R. E. Taylor: "Simulation and Analysis of Industrial Systems," Richard D. Irwin, Inc., Homewood, Ill., 1970.

14 Schriber, Thomas J.: "Simulation Using GPSS," John Wiley & Sons, Inc., New York, 1974.

15 Wyman, F. P.: "Simulation Modeling: A Guide to Using SIMSCRIPT," John Wiley & Sons, Inc., New York, 1970.

EXERCISES

14.1 Generate 300 random numbers using the subroutine in Section 14.2.2.
  (*a*) Calculate and print the mean.
  (*b*) Use the chi-square and Kolmogorov-Smirnov tests from Chapter 8 to test whether the hypothesis that the data came from a uniform distribution on the interval [0,1] can be rejected at the 95 percent confidence level. Use 10 equally spaced subintervals in each case.

14.2 Write a computer program to generate 100 random variates as follows:

$$Y = X + Z$$

X has a Poisson distribution with a mean of 3 and Z has a normal distribution with mean 0 and variance 1. Use the chi-square and Kolmogorov-Smirnov tests to test the hypothesis that the generated data came from a normal distribution with a mean of 3 and variance 1. Test at the 95 percent significance level.

14.3 Use the chi-square and Kolmogorov-Smirnov tests to test the hypothesis that the following data came from a Poisson distribution. (Test at the 95 percent level.)

$$5, 4, 6, 2, 10, 7, 4, 5, 3, 4, 2, 3, 7, 3, 5, 2, 6, 9, 5$$

Hint: Use the mean of the data to estimate the parameter in the Poisson distribution.

14.4 Generate and print 100 sample values from an exponential distribution with a mean of 5.

14.5 Use simulation to approximate the value of $\int_0^1 e^{-x} dx$.

14.6 Describe how to generate a random variate from the distribution function

$$f(x) = \frac{1}{10} \quad -4 \leqslant x \leqslant 6$$

14.7 Describe how to generate a random variate from the distribution function

$$f(x) = \frac{3}{7} x^2 \quad 1 \leqslant x \leqslant 2$$

14.8 Suppose a random variable X has the following distribution function:

x	2	5	7	9	10
$f(x)$	0.2	0.2	0.2	0.3	0.1

(*a*) Plot the cumulative distribution of X.

(*b*) What value of X corresponds to the uniform variate (on the interval [0,1]), 0.68?

14.9 Simulate a single queue, single-server queueing system until four arrivals have been processed through the system. The distribution of the time between arrivals is:

T	1	2	3
$f(t)$	$\frac{1}{4}$	$\frac{1}{2}$	$\frac{1}{4}$

The distribution of the time to service an arrival is:

S	1	2	3
$f(s)$	$\frac{1}{2}$	$\frac{1}{4}$	$\frac{1}{4}$

(*a*) Plot the cumulative distribution of T and S and then use the random digits 14, 24, 94, 47 to generate the arrivals and the random digits 60, 82, 20, 41 to generate the corresponding service times for the arrivals.

(*b*) Complete the following table:

Arrival number	Arrival time	Time in service	Time out service	Waiting time in queue
1				
2				
3				
4				

(*c*) What is the average waiting time in the queue per arrival?

14.10 Modify the simulation program in Section 14.2.6 to generate arrival and service times using the cumulative distributions developed from the secretary data in Table 14.1. Use the new program to simulate the secretary example for 25,000 min. Compare your results with the results in Table 14.3.

14.11 Modify the computer program in Section 14.2.6 to permit a maximum queue length of five customers.

14.12 The time between arrivals (customers) at a one-chair barber shop is uniformly distributed between 12 and 24 min. The time per haircut is normally distributed with mean 15 and variance 4. If more than two people are waiting to get a haircut, the arrival leaves.

1 Design a next-event simulation model of the barber shop operation.

2 Write a computer program to carry out the simulation.

3 Use the program to simulate the operation of the shop for 500 hr.

4 Determine the simulated values for:
  (*a*) Percentage of idle time of the barber
  (*b*) The average waiting time of the customers
  (*c*) The maximum length of the waiting line
  (*d*) The average number of customers in the shop
  (*e*) The average time a customer spent in the shop
  (*f*) The number of lost customers

14.13 Modify the simulation program in Section 14.2.6 to generate arrival and
service times from these two distributions:

AT	1	2	3	4	5	6
f(AT)	0.05	0.10	0.20	0.0	0.50	0.15

ST	1	2	3	4
g(ST)	0.20	0.35	0.27	0.18

15

PROBABILISTIC INVENTORY MODELS

15.1 INTRODUCTION

In Chapter 6 we introduced inventory models in which the demand for a single product and the lead time to replenish inventory were known constants. Consequently, the analysis was fairly straightforward. In this chapter some basic approaches to the analysis of single-period models with random demand and multiperiod models with random demand and random lead time will be developed and demonstrated. Since it is virtually impossible to present a model of every inventory situation, the discussion will be primarily restricted to *single-period models* and *fixed-reorder-point, fixed-reorder-quantity models*.

In the *single-period* model, the problem is to determine *how much* of a single product to have on hand at the beginning of a single time period to minimize the total purchase cost, stockout cost, and ending inventory holding cost. When demand is a random variable, the problem reduces to minimizing the *expected* total inventory cost. Two basic single-period models will be discussed: a model with no setup or ordering cost and a model with a setup cost. In Section 15.2.5, a computer program is presented to determine the optimal starting inventory level when the distribution of demand is discrete and known.

The *multiperiod* inventory model to be discussed is the *fixed-reorder-point, fixed-reorder-quantity model*. In this model, the inventory level is reviewed after each transaction (sale or use) and an order is placed for a fixed, predetermined amount of the product (fixed reorder quantity) when the inventory level reaches a fixed, predetermined level (fixed reorder point). The objective is to determine the optimal reorder point and the optimal reorder quantity under certain assumptions (including the assumption that demand and lead time are random variables).

Another multiperiod inventory model that is used extensively, but will not be discussed, is the *fixed-review-period model*. Basically, in this model the inventory level is reviewed at fixed points in time and one of two policies is used:

1 An order is placed to raise the inventory to a fixed level.
2 If the inventory level is below a certain quantity, an order is placed to raise the inventory to a fixed level.

Variations of the basic fixed-reorder-point and fixed-review-period models can be constructed to adequately represent many realistic inventory situations.

The computer program in Section 15.3.3.1 can be used to calculate the distribution of the demand during lead time and the optimal reorder point and reorder quantity in the fixed-reorder-point model.

15.2 SINGLE-PERIOD MODELS

Consider the situation in which a product must be produced or purchased for use or sale during a single time period. Some examples of realistic situations that can be formulated as a single-period model are:

Stocking of seasonal products, such as ski equipment, fireworks, Christmas trees, bathing suits, easter eggs, or garden seed
Stocking of short-lived perishable items, such as donuts, bread, vegetables, or newspapers

In each case, the demand for the product is considered to be a random variable with a distribution function that is known or can be approximated. The problem is to determine *how much* of the product to have on hand at the beginning of the period to minimize the sum of the

Cost to purchase or produce enough of the product to bring the inventory up to a certain level
Cost of stockouts (unfilled demands)
Cost of holding ending inventory

Since the demand for the product is a random variable, the number of stockouts encountered and the number of units in ending inventory are also random variables, since they are both functions of the demand. Hence, the total inventory cost associated with starting the period with a given inventory level is a random variable. In this light, we can only hope to determine the starting inventory level that will minimize the *expected value* of the three costs that make up the total inventory cost.

Consider the notation to be used in this section:

X = demand for the product during the given period

$f(x)$ = distribution function of demand

$F(x)$ = cumulative distribution function of demand

Q = order quantity (amount to order)

c_0 = ordering cost/order

c_1 = inventory holding cost/unit of ending inventory

c_3 = cost/item purchased or produced

c_4 = stockout cost/item out-of-stock

DIL = desired inventory level at the start of the period

IOH = initial inventory on hand before placing an order

TIC(X,DIL) = total inventory cost as a function of demand and the desired inventory level

TIC(X,DIL,c_0) = total inventory cost as a function of demand, desired inventory level, and setup cost c_0

In the next two sections, we will take the expected value of the total inventory cost with respect to the demand X, and then determine the value of DIL that will minimize the expected total inventory cost. In each section, we assume no backordering is permitted (unfilled demands are lost sales), the delivery rate is infinite, and lead time is zero.

15.2.1 Single-Period Model with Zero Ordering Cost

In this section, we assume there is no cost associated with placing an order or setting up to produce an order, as the case may be. We start by assuming the distribution of demand is continuous. The *total inventory cost* is given by

$$\text{TIC}(X,\text{DIL}) = \begin{cases} c_3(\text{DIL} - \text{IOH}) + c_1(\text{DIL} - X) & X < \text{DIL} \\ c_3(\text{DIL} - \text{IOH}) + c_4(X - \text{DIL}) & X \geqslant \text{DIL} \end{cases} \tag{15.1}$$

Note that if the demand during the period turns out to be less than the inventory level at the start of the period (after order is received if one was placed), then the total inventory cost consists of the cost to order $Q = \text{DIL} - \text{IOH}$ items, namely,

$$c_3 Q = c_3(\text{DIL} - \text{IOH})$$

plus the cost of holding one unit in inventory, times the number of items that will be in inventory at the end of the period, namely, $c_1(\text{DIL} - X)$. On the other hand, if the demand is greater than or equal to the desired inventory level, the total inventory cost consists of the cost to order DIL − IOH items, plus the cost of a stockout, times the total number of stockouts.

The *expected total inventory cost* can be expressed as

$$\mu_I(\text{DIL}) = \underset{X}{E}\, [\text{TIC}(X, \text{DIL})] = \int_{-\infty}^{\infty} \text{TIC}(x, \text{DIL}) f(x)\, dx$$

$$= \int_{-\infty}^{\text{DIL}} [c_3(\text{DIL} - \text{IOH}) + c_1(\text{DIL} - x)]\, f(x)\, dx$$

$$+ \int_{\text{DIL}}^{\infty} [c_3(\text{DIL} - \text{IOH}) + c_4(x - \text{DIL})]\, f(x)\, dx$$

$$= c_3(\text{DIL} - \text{IOH}) \int_{-\infty}^{\infty} f(x)\, dx + c_1 \int_{-\infty}^{\text{DIL}} (\text{DIL} - x) f(x)\, dx$$

$$+ c_4 \int_{\text{DIL}}^{\infty} (x - \text{DIL}) f(x)\, dx$$

$$= \underbrace{c_3(\text{DIL} - \text{IOH})}_{\text{Cost of } Q \text{ items}} + \underbrace{c_1 \int_{-\infty}^{\text{DIL}} (\text{DIL} - x) f(x)\, dx}_{\text{Expected holding cost}} + \underbrace{c_4 \int_{\text{DIL}}^{\infty} (x - \text{DIL}) f(x)\, dx}_{\text{Expected stockout cost}}$$

$$(15.2)$$

Since the expected total inventory cost is not a function of the demand, we can take its derivative with respect to DIL, set the result equal to zero, and solve for the optimal DIL. That is,

$$\frac{d[\mu_I(\text{DIL})]}{d(\text{DIL})} = c_3 + c_1 \int_{-\infty}^{\text{DIL}} f(x)\, dx - c_4 \int_{\text{DIL}}^{\infty} f(x)\, dx = 0 \qquad (15.3)$$

Thus,

$$c_3 + c_1 F(\text{DIL}) - c_4[1 - F(\text{DIL})] = 0$$

$$(c_1 + c_4) F(\text{DIL}) = c_4 - c_3$$

$$F(\text{DIL}) = \frac{c_4 - c_3}{c_1 + c_4} \qquad (15.4)$$

The inventory level that will minimize the expected total inventory cost is the value of DIL such that

$$P(X \leqslant \text{DIL}) = F(\text{DIL}) = \frac{c_4 - c_3}{c_1 + c_4} \qquad (15.5)$$

Note in Equation (15.5) that $(c_4 - c_3)/(c_1 + c_4)$ represents the probability of no stockouts when the given product is stocked at the optimal DIL. Likewise,

$$P(X > \text{DIL}) = 1 - F(\text{DIL}) = 1 - \frac{c_4 - c_3}{c_1 + c_4} \qquad (15.6)$$

represents the probability of at least one stockout (demand X exceeds DIL).

EXAMPLE 15.2.1   An outdoor equipment shop in Idaho is interested in determining how many pairs of touring skis of type SK009 should be in stock at the beginning of the upcoming tour-skiing season. Assume reordering cannot be done because of the long delay in delivery. Last season was a light year, so the store still has 10 pairs of type SK009 skis on hand. If

   1   The cost of each pair of skis is $60.
   2   The retail price is $90.
   3   The inventory holding cost is $10 per year minus the end-of-season discount price of $50.
   4   The stockout cost is $125 per stockout.
   5   The demand can be approximated with a normal random variable that has a mean of 20 and a variance of 25; $X \sim N(20,25)$.

how many pairs of touring skis of type SK009 should be stocked at the start of the season to minimize the expected total inventory cost?

From the given information

$$c_1 = \$10 - \$50 = -\$40$$
$$c_3 = \$60$$
$$c_4 = \$125$$

We want the value of DIL such that

$$P(X \leqslant \text{DIL}) = F(\text{DIL}) = \frac{c_4 - c_3}{c_1 + c_4} = \frac{125 - 60}{-40 + 125} = 0.7647$$

or $$F(\text{DIL}) = \int_{-\infty}^{\text{DIL}} f(x)\, dx = \int_{-\infty}^{\text{DIL}} \frac{1}{5\sqrt{2\pi}}\, e^{-\frac{1}{2}[(x-20)/5]^2}\, dx = 0.7647$$

That is, we want the value of DIL such that the area under the normal curve with mean 20 and variance 25 from $-\infty$ to DIL is equal to 0.7647. This is illustrated in Figure 15.1.

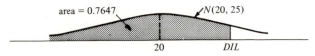

FIGURE 15.1
Normal distribution with mean 20 and variance 25.

The cumulative distribution of every normal random variable is not readily available; however, the cumulative distribution of a normal random variable with mean 0 and variance 1 is available in Appendix A. Recall from Chapter 8 that if the random variable X has a normal distribution with mean μ and variance σ^2, denoted by $X \sim N(\mu, \sigma^2)$, then

$$Z = \frac{X - \mu}{\sigma} \sim N(0,1)$$

Thus,

$$F(\mathrm{DIL}) = \int_{-\infty}^{\mathrm{DIL}} N(20,25)\, dx = \int_{-\infty}^{z=(\mathrm{DIL}-20)/5} N(0,1)\, dz = 0.7647$$

From the cumulative normal $(0,1)$ table in Appendix A, Table A.1, we see that the value of z such that

$$\int_{-\infty}^{z=(\mathrm{DIL}-20)/5} N(0,1)\, dz = 0.7647$$

is $z = 0.72$. Thus,

$$\frac{\mathrm{DIL} - 20}{5} \approx 0.72$$

$$\mathrm{DIL} \approx 23.6$$

Choose $\mathrm{DIL} = 24$. Since $\mathrm{IOH} = 10$, order $Q = 14$ more pairs of type SK009 skis.

If management wants to be $100(1 - \alpha)$ percent confidence that no demands will go unfilled (no stockouts), what must DIL be? We want DIL such that

$$P(X \leqslant \mathrm{DIL}) = F(\mathrm{DIL}) = \int_{-\infty}^{\mathrm{DIL}} f(x)\, dx = 1 - \alpha \qquad (15.7)$$

EXAMPLE 15.2.2 Assume the data in Example 15.2.1. What value of DIL will let management be at least 95 percent confident that no demands will go unfilled? We want DIL such that

$$P(X \leqslant \mathrm{DIL}) = \int_{-\infty}^{\mathrm{DIL}} N(20, 25)\, dx = \int_{-\infty}^{z=(\mathrm{DIL}-20)/5} N(0,1)\, dz = 0.95 \qquad (15.8)$$

From the cumulative normal $(0,1)$ table, $z = 1.645$. Therefore,

$$\frac{\mathrm{DIL} - 20}{5} = 1.645$$

$$\mathrm{DIL} = 28.225$$

Hence, the inventory level must be 29 units at the start of the period in order to be at least 95 percent confident that no demands will go unfilled.

It can be shown that if the demand is a discrete random variable, then the optimal desired inventory level is the smallest value of DIL such that

$$F(\text{DIL}) = P(X \leqslant \text{DIL}) \geqslant \frac{c_4 - c_3}{c_1 + c_4} \qquad (15.9)$$

EXAMPLE 15.2.3 Suppose the demand for touring skis in Example 15.2.1 has the discrete probability distribution function and cumulative distribution function as given in Table 15.1. Assume all other conditions are the same as in Example 15.2.1, so

$$c_1 = -\$40$$
$$c_3 = \$60$$
$$c_4 = \$125$$

We want the smallest integer value of DIL such that

$$F(\text{DIL}) \geqslant \frac{c_4 - c_3}{c_1 + c_4} = \frac{125 - 60}{-40 + 125} = 0.7647$$

From Table 15.1,

$$F(21) = 0.74 < 0.7647$$
$$F(22) = 0.88 > 0.7647$$

Therefore, the optimal value of DIL is $\text{DIL}^* = 22$.

15.2.2 Single-Period Model with Ordering Cost

In most realistic systems there is a cost associated with placing an order or setting up for production. Suppose a single, one-time order is placed at a cost of c_0. The *total inventory cost* will be

$$\text{TIC}(X, \text{DIL}, c_0) = \begin{cases} c_0 + c_3(\text{DIL} - \text{IOH}) + c_1(\text{DIL} - X) & X < \text{DIL} \\ c_0 + c_3(\text{DIL} - \text{IOH}) + c_4(X - \text{DIL}) & X \geqslant \text{DIL} \end{cases} \qquad (15.10)$$

Table 15.1 PROBABILITY DISTRIBUTION FUNCTION AND CUMULATIVE DISTRIBUTION FUNCTION OF DEMAND

X	17	18	19	20	21	22	23	24
$f(x)$	0.02	0.06	0.12	0.34	0.20	0.14	0.08	0.04
$F(x)$	0.02	0.08	0.20	0.54	0.74	0.88	0.96	1.00

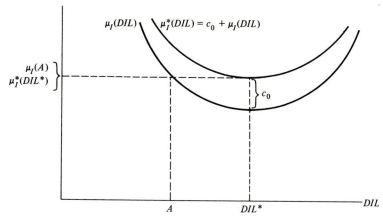

FIGURE 15.2
Graph of $\mu_I(\text{DIL})$ and $\mu_I^*(\text{DIL})$.

If demand is a continuous random variable, the *expected total inventory cost* will be

$$\mu_I^*(\text{DIL}) = \underset{X}{E}[\text{TIC}(X, \text{DIL}, c_0)] = c_0 + c_3(\text{DIL} - \text{IOH})$$

$$+ c_1 \int_{-\infty}^{\text{DIL}} (\text{DIL} - x)f(x)\, dx + c_4 \int_{\text{DIL}}^{\infty} (x - \text{DIL})f(x)\, dx$$

$$\mu_I^*(\text{DIL}) = c_0 + \mu_I(\text{DIL}) \tag{15.11}$$

The graph of $\mu_I(\text{DIL})$ and $\mu_I^*(\text{DIL})$ are shown in Figure 15.2.

Since c_0 is not a function of DIL, the derivative of $\mu_I^*(\text{DIL})$ with respect to DIL will be the same as Equation (15.3). Thus, the optimal DIL is the value of DIL, say DIL^*, such that Equation (15.5) is satisfied. That is, the optimal DIL value satisfies

$$P(X \leqslant \text{DIL}) = F(\text{DIL}) = \frac{c_4 - c_3}{c_1 + c_4} \tag{15.12}$$

Likewise, if demand is a discrete random variable, the optimal DIL value, DIL^*, is the smallest integer value of DIL such that

$$P(X \leqslant \text{DIL}) = F(\text{DIL}) \geqslant \frac{c_4 - c_3}{c_1 + c_4} \tag{15.13}$$

Note in Figure 15.2 that DIL^* is the optimal inventory level in that it minimizes the expected total inventory cost. However, if the initial inventory level before ordering (IOH) is greater than A, then

$$\mu_I(\text{IOH}) < \mu_I^*(\text{DIL}^*) \tag{15.14}$$

so an order should not be placed to bring the beginning inventory up to DIL^*. On the other hand, if $\text{IOH} < A$,

$$\mu_I(\text{IOH}) > \mu_I^*(\text{DIL}^*) \qquad (15.15)$$

Thus, an order for $Q = \text{DIL}^* - \text{IOH}$ units should be placed.

Figure 15.2 illustrates that A is the smallest value of DIL that satisfies the equation

$$\mu_I(\text{DIL}) = \mu_I^*(\text{DIL}^*) = c_0 + \mu_I(\text{DIL}^*) \qquad (15.16)$$

The optimal policy then is to order up to DIL^* if $\text{IOH} < A$ and not to order anything if $\text{IOH} > A$.

EXAMPLE 15.2.4 Assume the data in Example 15.2.1 with the exception that demand has a uniform distribution on the interval [18,24]. In addition, suppose an ordering cost of $50 is incurred if an order is placed. What is the optimal beginning inventory level and how many pairs of skis should be ordered?

$$\text{IOH} = 10$$
$$c_0 = \$50$$
$$c_1 = -\$40$$
$$c_3 = \$60$$
$$c_4 = \$125$$
$$X = \text{demand}$$
$$f(x) = \frac{1}{6} \quad \text{for } 18 \leqslant x \leqslant 24$$

The optimal beginning inventory level is the value of DIL such that

$$P(X \leqslant \text{DIL}) = F(\text{DIL}) = \int_{18}^{\text{DIL}} \frac{1}{6}\, dx = \frac{c_4 - c_3}{c_1 + c_4} = \frac{125 - 60}{-40 + 125} = 0.7647$$

Now,

$$\int_{18}^{\text{DIL}} \frac{1}{6}\, dx = \frac{x}{6}\Big|_{18}^{\text{DIL}} = \frac{1}{6}(\text{DIL} - 18) = 0.7647$$

$$\text{DIL} = 6(0.7647) + 18$$
$$= 22.58$$

Thus, select $\text{DIL}^* = 23$.

The critical A is determined as follows:

$$\mu_I(A) = \mu_I^*(\text{DIL}^*) = c_0 + \mu_I(\text{DIL}^*) \qquad (15.17)$$

or
$$c_3(A - 10) + c_1 \int_{18}^{A} (A - x)f(x)\, dx + c_4 \int_{A}^{24} (x - A)f(x)\, dx$$

$$= c_0 + c_3(23 - 10) + c_1 \int_{18}^{23} (23 - x)f(x)\, dx$$

$$+ c_4 \int_{23}^{24} (x - 23)f(x)\, dx$$

or
$$7.0833A^2 - 320A + 3562.92 = 0$$
$$A = 19.8998$$

Thus, since IOH $= 10$, order 13 pairs of skis. If IOH were 20 or greater, then no order should be placed. This concept is illustrated in Figure 15.3.

For IOH $= 21$, $\mu_I(21) < \mu_I^*(23) = \$807.08$. That is, if IOH $= 21$, it would cost less to start the period with a nonoptimal number of skis (21 pairs) than it would to order 2 pairs of skis so the period could be started with the optimal number (23 pairs).

If demand is a discrete random variable, then the optimal starting inventory level DIL* is the smallest value of DIL such that

$$P(X \leqslant \text{DIL}) = F(\text{DIL}) \geqslant \frac{c_4 - c_3}{c_1 + c_4} \qquad (15.18)$$

The corresponding expected total inventory cost is given by

$$\mu_I^*(\text{DIL}) = \underset{X}{E}[\text{TIC}(X, \text{DIL}, c_0)] = c_0 + c_3(\text{DIL} - \text{IOH})$$

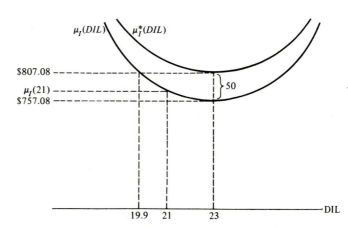

FIGURE 15.3
Graph of $\mu_I(\text{DIL})$ and $\mu_I^*(\text{DIL})$–Example 15.2.4.

$$+ c_1 \sum_{x=-\infty}^{\text{DIL}} (\text{DIL} - x)f(x) + c_4 \sum_{x=\text{DIL}}^{\infty} (x - \text{DIL})f(x)$$

$$= c_0 + \mu_I(\text{DIL}) \tag{15.19}$$

The critical value A for determining if an order should be placed is obtained by solving the equation

$$\mu_I(A) = \mu_I^*(\text{DIL}^*) = c_0 + \mu_I(\text{DIL}^*) \tag{15.20}$$

$$c_3(A - \text{IOH}) + c_1 \sum_{x=-\infty}^{A} (A - x)f(x) + c_4 \sum_{x=A}^{\infty} (x - A)f(x)$$

$$= c_0 + c_3(\text{DIL}^* - \text{IOH}) + c_1 \sum_{x=-\infty}^{\text{DIL}^*} (\text{DIL}^* - x)f(x)$$

$$+ c_4 \sum_{x=\text{DIL}^*}^{\infty} (x - \text{DIL}^*)f(x) \tag{15.21}$$

The computer program for Algorithm 15.2 solves for DIL^* and the critical A value.

EXAMPLE 15.2.5 Consider the data in Example 15.2.3 with the setup cost, $c_0 = \$50$. We determined that $\text{DIL}^* = 22$. The critical A value is determined by substituting the probability distribution function from Table 15.1 into Equation (15.21) and solving for A.

$$60(A - 10) - 40 \sum_{x=17}^{A} (A - x)f(x) + 125 \sum_{x=A}^{24} (x - A)f(x)$$

$$= 50 + 60(22 - 10) - 40 \sum_{x=17}^{22} (22 - x)f(x)$$

$$+ 125 \sum_{x=22}^{24} (x - 22)f(x) \tag{15.22}$$

Since the unknown A is a limit on each of the sums on the left side of the equality, an iterative procedure must be used to determine the value of A. The left side of the equality is

$$\mu_I(A) = 60(A - 10) - 40 \sum_{x=17}^{A} (A - x)f(x) + 125 \sum_{x=A}^{24} (x - A)f(x) \tag{15.23}$$

and the right side is

$$\mu_I^*(\text{DIL}^*) = \mu_I^*(22) = 50 + 60(22 - 10) - 40 \sum_{x=17}^{22} (22 - x)f(x)$$

$$+ 125 \sum_{x=22}^{24} (x - 22)f(x)$$

$$= 726.80$$

The basic procedure to determine the largest value of A such that $A < DIL^* = 22$ and

$$\mu_I(A) \geqslant \mu_I^*(22) = 726.80$$

is

(a) Set $A = DIL^* - 1 = 21$.
(b) Evaluate Equation (15.23) using the current value of A.
(c) If $\mu_I(A) < 726.80$, decrease A by 1 and return to step (b); otherwise, go to step (d).
(d) If $IOH > A$, do not order; otherwise, order $Q = DIL^* - IOH$ units.

The results from evaluating Equation (15.23) at $A = 22$, 21, 20, and 19 appear in Table 15.2.

The largest value of A such that

$$\mu_I(A) > \mu_I^*(22) = \$726.80$$

is $A = 19$. Thus if

$$IOH > 19 \quad \text{do not order}$$

$$IOH \leqslant 19 \quad \text{order } Q = 22 - IOH \text{ units}$$

Since $IOH = 10$ in this example, order $Q = 12$ units.

15.2.3 Algorithm 15.1–Single-Period Model with Continuous Demand Distribution

Assume the notation used in Section 15.2 with demand considered to be a continuous random variable. The step-by-step procedure to determine DIL^* and A is:

Table 15.2 EVALUATION OF EQUATION (15.23)– EXAMPLE 15.2.5

A	$\mu_I(A)$
22	$676.80
21	$678.90
20	$698.00
19	$746.00

Step 1
Calculate

$$c = \frac{c_4 - c_3}{c_1 + c_4}$$

Step 2
DIL* is the value of DIL such that

$$P(X \leqslant \text{DIL}) = F(\text{DIL}) = \int_{-\infty}^{\text{DIL}} f(x)\,dx = c$$

Step 3
If $c_0 = 0$, set $A = \text{DIL}^*$ and go to step 6; otherwise, go to step 4.

Step 4
Calculate

$$\mu_I^*(\text{DIL}^*) = c_0 + c_3(\text{DIL}^* - \text{IOH}) + c_1 \int_{-\infty}^{\text{DIL}^*} (\text{DIL}^* - x)f(x)\,dx$$

$$+ c_4 \int_{\text{DIL}^*}^{\infty} (x - \text{DIL}^*)f(x)\,dx$$

Step 5
Determine the smallest value of A such that

$$\mu_I(A) = c_3(A - \text{IOH}) + c_1 \int_{-\infty}^{A} (A - x)f(x)\,dx + c_4 \int_{A}^{\infty} (x - A)f(x)\,dx$$

$$= \mu_I^*(\text{DIL}^*)$$

Step 6
If

$$\text{IOH} < A \qquad \text{order } Q = \text{DIL}^* - \text{IOH units}$$
$$\text{IOH} \geqslant A \qquad \text{do not order}$$

Stop.

15.2.4 Algorithm 15.2—Single-Period Model with Discrete Demand Distribution

Assume the notation in Section 15.2 with demand considered to be a discrete random variable. The general procedure to determine DIL* and A is:

Step 1
Calculate

$$c = \frac{c_4 - c_3}{c_1 + c_4}$$

Step 2
DIL^* is the smallest value of DIL such that

$$P(X \leqslant DIL) = F(DIL) = \sum_{x=-\infty}^{DIL} f(x) \geqslant c$$

Step 3
If $c_0 = 0$, set $A = DIL^*$ and go to step 8; otherwise, go to step 4.

Step 4
Calculate

$$\mu_I^*(DIL^*) = c_0 + c_3(DIL^* - IOH) + c_1 \sum_{x=-\infty}^{DIL^*} (DIL^* - x)f(x)$$

$$+ c_4 \sum_{x=DIL^*}^{\infty} (x - DIL^*)f(x)$$

Steps 5-7 determine the largest value of A such that $A < DIL^*$ and $\mu_I(A) > \mu_I^*(DIL^*)$.

Step 5
Set $A = DIL^* - 1$.

Step 6
Evaluate

$$\mu_I(A) = c_3(A - IOH) + c_1 \sum_{x=-\infty}^{A} (A - x)f(x) + c_4 \sum_{x=A}^{\infty} (x - A)f(x)$$

Step 7
If $\mu_I(A) < \mu_I^*(DIL^*)$ and $A > 0$, decrease A by 1 and return to step 6; otherwise, go to step 8.

Step 8
If $A > 0$ and

$$IOH \leqslant A \quad \text{order } Q = DIL^* - IOH \text{ units}$$
$$IOH > A \quad \text{do not order}$$

otherwise, $A = 0$, so do not order. Stop.

15.2.5 Computer Program for Algorithm 15.2

This program is designed to read in the discrete probability distribution of the demand along with c_0, c_1, c_3, c_4, and IOH and to calculate and print values for DIL^* and A, if applicable. If $c_0 = 0$, Q and DIL^* are calculated and printed; otherwise, Q, DIL^*, and A are calculated and printed.

The data used in Example 15.2.5 were entered as sample data. The solution was obtained in 0.08 s of IBM 370/168 time.

The program utilizes 36K bytes of core storage. It is set up to handle a maximum of 100 values of the discrete probability distribution of demand. The comment cards at the beginning of the program explain how to enter the data.

```
C    ****************************************************************************
C    *                                                                        *
C    *          **   ALGORITHM 15.2        PROBABILISTIC INVENTORY   **        *
C    *                                                                        *
C    * THIS PROGRAM IS DESIGNED                                               *
C    *                                                                        *
C    *    TO READ                                                             *
C    *       CARD 1    COLS  2-80    TITLE  DESCRIPTION OF THE PROBLEM USING   *
C    *                                      ANY CHARACTERS ON KEYPUNCH        *
C    *                                      ** COLUMN 1 MUST BE LEFT BLANK **  *
C    *       CARD 2    COLS  1-10    CO  ORDERING COST/ORDER   (F10.0)         *
C    *                      11-20    C1  INVENTORY HOLDING COST/UNIT           *
C    *                                   OF ENDING INVENTORY  (F10.0)          *
C    *                      21-30    C3  COST/ITEM PURCHASED OR PRODUCED (F10.0)*
C    *                      31-40    C4  STOCKOUT COST/ITEM OUT OF STOCK (F10.0)*
C    *       CARD 3    COLS  1-10    IOH  INITIAL INVENTORY ON HAND  (I10)      *
C    *                      11-20    LOWX  LOWEST POSSIBLE DEMAND   (I10)       *
C    *                      21-30    HIGHX  HIGHEST POSSIBLE DEMAND  (I10)      *
C    *       CARDS 4 TO ?   COLS  1-10    PDF(I)  PROBABILITY DISTRIBUTION      *
C    *                                           FUNCTION OF DEMAND   (F10.0)   *
C    *                      11-20    CDF(I)  CUMULATIVE DISTRIBUTION            *
C    *                                       FUNCTION OF DEMAND   (F10.0)       *
C    *                           ( I=LOWX, LOWX+1, ..., HIGHX-1, HIGHX)        *
C    *              TO SOLVE MORE THAN ONE PROBLEM AT A TIME, REPEAT THE       *
C    *              READ SEQUENCE, AND STACK THE DATA ONE BEHIND THE OTHER     *
C    *                                                                        *
C    *    TO CALCULATE                                                        *
C    *       DIL         DESIRED INVENTORY LEVEL                              *
C    *       A           CRITICAL VALUE FOR DETERMINING IF AN ORDER SHOULD    *
C    *                   BE PLACED                                            *
C    *       DILSTR      OPTIMAL INTEGER INVENTORY LEVEL                      *
C    *       Q           NUMBER OF ITEMS TO ORDER, IF AN ORDER SHOULD BE PLACED *
C    *                                                                        *
C    *    TO PRINT                                                            *
C    *       DILSTR, A, Q                                                     *
C    *                                                                        *
C    ****************************************************************************
     DIMENSION PDF(100),CDF(100),TITLE(20)
     INTEGER DIL,DILSTR,A,Q,HIGHX
   5 READ(5,10,END=2000)TITLE
  10 FORMAT(20A4)
     WRITE(6,11)TITLE
  11 FORMAT('1',20A4,//)
     READ(5,15)CO,C1,C3,C4
  15 FORMAT(4F10.0)
     READ(5,20)IOH,LOWX,HIGHX
  20 FORMAT(3I10)
     DO 25 I=LOWX,HIGHX
  25 READ(5,30)PDF(I),CDF(I)
  30 FORMAT(2F10.2)
C    ****************************************************************************
C    *    STEPS 1,2                                                           *
C    *          CALCULATE THE OPTIMAL DESIRED INVENTORY LEVEL,DILSTR.         *
C    ****************************************************************************
     CCAL=(C4-C3)/(C1+C4)
     DO 200 DIL=LOWX,HIGHX
     IF(CDF(DIL).GE.CCAL) GO TO 210
 200 CONTINUE
 210 DILSTR=DIL
```

```
C     ************************************************************************
C     *     STEP 3                                                          *
C     *           IF THE SETUP COST IS ZERO, SET A=DILSTR AND GO TO STEP 8; *
C     *              OTHERWISE, GO TO STEP 4.                               *
C     ************************************************************************
      IF(CO.NE.0.) GO TO 400
      A=DILSTR
      GO TO 800
C     ************************************************************************
C     *     STEP 4                                                          *
C     *           CALCULATE THE OPTIMAL MEAN INVENTORY COST USING DILSTR    *
C     *              AND SETUP COST.                                        *
C     ************************************************************************
  400 SUM1=0.
      DO 410 I=LOWX,DILSTR
  410 SUM1=SUM1+(DILSTR-I)*PDF(I)
      SUM2=0.
      DO 420 I=DILSTR,HIGHX
  420 SUM2=SUM2+(I-DILSTR)*PDF(I)
      STARMU=CO+C3*(DILSTR-IOH)+C1*SUM1+C4*SUM2
C     ************************************************************************
C     *     STEPS 5,6,7                                                     *
C     *           DETERMINE THE LARGEST VALUE OF A SUCH THAT A IS LESS THAN *
C     *              DILSTR AND SUCH THAT THE MEAN INVENTORY COST USING A AND*
C     *              NO SETUP COST IS GREATER THAN THE MEAN INVENTORY COST  *
C     *              USING DILSTR AND SETUP COST.                           *
C     ************************************************************************
      A=DILSTR-1
  600 SUM1=0.
      DO 610 I=LOWX,A
  610 SUM1=SUM1+( A  -I)*PDF(I)
      SUM2=0.
      DO 620 I= A  ,HIGHX
  620 SUM2=SUM2+(I- A  )*PDF(I)
      TESTMU=C3*( A  -IOH)+C1*SUM1+C4*SUM2
      IF(TESTMU.GE.STARMU.OR. A  .LE.0) GO TO 800
      A=A-1
      GO TO 600
C     ************************************************************************
C     *     STEP 8                                                          *
C     *           IF A FROM STEPS 5 TO 7 IS GREATER THAN ZERO AND           *
C     *              1)INVENTORY ON HAND, IOH, IS LESS THAN OR EQUAL TO A,  *
C     *                 ORDER (DILSTR-IOH) UNITS.                           *
C     *              2)IOH IS GREATER THAN A, DO NOT ORDER.                 *
C     *              OTHERWISE, A=0, SO DO NOT ORDER.                       *
C     ************************************************************************
  800 IF(A.EQ.0) GO TO 810
      IF(A.LT.0) GO TO 820
      IF(IOH.GT.A) GO TO 830
      Q=DILSTR-IOH
      GO TO 840
  810 WRITE(6,815)
  815 FORMAT(//5X,'DO NOT ORDER BECAUSE A=0')
      GO TO 840
  820 WRITE(6,825)
  825 FORMAT(//5X,'ERROR  A < 0')
      GO TO 5
  830 WRITE(6,835)
  835 FORMAT(//5X,'DO NOT ORDER BECAUSE IOH > A'/)
  840 WRITE(6,845) Q,DILSTR
  845 FORMAT(/' NUMBER OF UNITS TO ORDER',I5//' OPTIMAL STARTING INVENTO
     *RY LEVEL',I5/)
      IF(CO.EQ.0.) GO TO 5
      WRITE(6,806)A
  806 FORMAT(' A (CRITICAL VALUE FOR DETERMINING IF AN ORDER SHOULD BE P
     *LACED) =',I5/)
      GO TO 5
 2000 STOP
      END
```

```
/DATA

EXAMPLE 15.2.5      CO=50
         50.          -40.        60.         125.
         10            17          24
         .02           .02
         .06           .08
         .12           .20
         .34           .54
         .20           .74
         .14           .88
         .08           .96
         .04          1.00


  EXAMPLE 15.2.5      CO=50


NUMBER OF UNITS TO ORDER     12

OPTIMAL STARTING INVENTORY LEVEL     22

A (CRITICAL VALUE FOR DETERMINING IF AN ORDER SHOULD BE PLACED) =     19
```

15.3 MULTIPERIOD MODELS

In this section, inventory situations which involve a product that must be reordered periodically are analyzed. There are basically two types of multiperiod models: fixed-review-period models and fixed-reorder-point, fixed-reorder-quantity models as discussed in Section 15.1. However, the remaining sections in this chapter will be devoted to a model of the latter type in which the demand for a single product and the lead time are both discrete random variables with known probability distribution functions.

In order to discuss the distributions of demand and lead time, a unit of time must be established. For items with a daily demand, such as light bulbs or steel for fan blade assemblies, 1 day can be used as a unit of time. However, it might be more appropriate to use 1 week or 1 month as a unit of time for other products, such as automobiles, mobile homes, or farm equipment. In the analysis of the inventory model in this section, the *demand* represents the number of units of the product desired by customers *per unit of time*, whereas the *lead time* represents the *number of units of time* from the time a replenishment order is placed until it is received. It is imperative that the same unit of time be used for both demand and lead time. Although demand and lead time are random variables, we assume their distributions remain the same from cycle to cycle, where a *cycle* is defined to be the number of units of time between the receipt of two consecutive replenishment orders. Since cycle time is a function of demand and lead time, it will also be a random variable. When one or both of the distributions (demand and/or lead time) fluctuate with the seasons, the corresponding inventory model can be formulated and analyzed using dynamic programming.

15.3.1 Fixed-Reorder-Point, Fixed-Reorder-Quantity Inventory Model

In this section we assume

1 A fixed-reorder-point, fixed-reorder-quantity model.
2 Demand and lead time are discrete random variables with known probability distribution functions.
3 The demand and lead time distributions do not change from cycle to cycle.
4 Cycle time is the number of units of time between the receipt of two consecutive orders.
5 A planning period of 1 year.
6 Infinite delivery rate (a complete order is received at one time).
7 Backordering is allowed.
8 An annual expected demand is given.
9 Costs are associated with placing an order, holding inventory, and stockouts.

Units of the product that are requested after the inventory level reaches zero are called *stockouts*. These units are backordered in the sense that they will supply the unfilled demands when the next replenishment order is received. The notation to be used is

$$LT = \text{lead time}$$
$$g(lt) = \text{distribution of lead time}$$
$$X = \text{demand}$$
$$f(x) = \text{distribution of demand}$$
$$Y = \text{demand during lead time}$$
$$P(Y = y) = h(y) = \text{distribution of demand during lead time}$$
$$H(y) = \text{cumulative distribution of } Y$$
$$c_0 = \text{order cost/order}$$
$$c_1 = \text{annual inventory holding cost/unit}$$
$$c_3 = \text{cost/item}$$
$$c_4 = \text{stockout cost/unit out-of-stock}$$
$$ROP = \text{reorder point (level of inventory when a reorder is placed)}$$
$$Q = \text{reorder quantity}$$
$$D = \text{expected annual demand}$$
$$\frac{D}{Q} = \text{number of cycles/year}$$

Figure 15.4 illustrates a fixed-reorder-point, fixed-reorder-quantity model with random demand and lead time.

Since there are costs associated with placing an order, stockouts, and holding items in inventory, the objective is to determine when to order (optimal ROP) and how much to order (optimal Q) to minimize the total annual inventory cost. If Q is "large" as opposed to "small," fewer orders would be placed and fewer stockouts would occur (smaller stockout cost), since a stockout can occur only during lead time

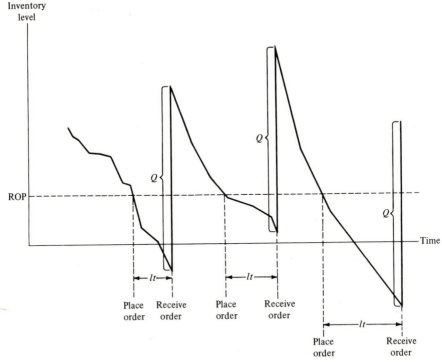

FIGURE 15.4
Inventory model with random demand and lead time.

and there would be fewer lead times; however, more inventory would need to be carried which would increase the annual inventory holding cost. On the other hand, if Q is "small" as opposed to "large," the inventory cost would decrease but the stockout cost would increase, since more stockouts would occur (more orders would be placed). As ROP increases, more orders are received when the inventory level is above zero, which implies that the average inventory level increases and stockouts decrease. The converse is true when ROP decreases.

Thus, it should be clear that the total annual inventory cost is a function of both ROP and Q. Hence, we would like to simultaneously determine ROP and Q to minimize the total annual inventory cost. However, ROP and Q are both functions of demand and lead time (random variables), so generally, we must be satisfied to determine ROP and Q to minimize the *expected* total annual inventory cost.

The expected total annual inventory cost ETAIC(ROP,Q) can be expressed as the sum of three costs, namely,

$$\text{AOC} = \text{annual ordering cost}$$

$$= c_0 \, \frac{D}{Q} \tag{15.24}$$

$$\text{EASC} = \text{expected annual stockout cost}$$

$$= c_4 \frac{D}{Q} \text{ (expected number of stockouts/cycle)} \quad (15.25)$$

$$\text{EAIHC} = \text{expected annual inventory holding cost}$$

$$= c_1 \text{ (expected inventory level/cycle)} \quad (15.26)$$

To determine the expected number of stockouts/cycle in Equation (15.25), note that a stockout occurs when the demand during lead time exceeds ROP. Thus, the expected number of stockouts/cycle is a function of ROP and is given by

$$\text{ENS(ROP)} = \sum_{y=\text{ROP}}^{\infty} (y - \text{ROP})h(y) = \sum_{y=\text{ROP}}^{\infty} (y - \text{ROP})P(Y = y) \quad (15.27)$$

For example, if the demand during lead time Y has the distribution

Y	0	1	2	3	4
$h(y)$	$\frac{1}{12}$	$\frac{1}{12}$	$\frac{1}{6}$	$\frac{1}{3}$	$\frac{1}{3}$

and ROP $= 2$, the expected number of stockouts/cycle would be

$$\text{ENS}(2) = (2 - 2)h(2) + (3 - 2)h(3) + (4 - 2)h(4)$$

$$= 0\left(\frac{1}{6}\right) + 1\left(\frac{1}{3}\right) + 2\left(\frac{1}{3}\right)$$

$$= 1$$

On the other hand, if ROP $= 3$,

$$\text{ENS}(3) = (3 - 3)h(3) + (4 - 3)h(4)$$

$$= 0\left(\frac{1}{3}\right) + 1\left(\frac{1}{3}\right)$$

$$= \frac{1}{3}$$

To determine the expected inventory level/cycle in Equation (15.26), note that the expected inventory level/cycle would be

$$\text{ROP} + \frac{Q}{2} \quad (15.28)$$

if lead time were zero. That is, suppose Q units are ordered and received immediately when the inventory level reaches the reorder point ROP. The average inventory level would consist of ROP units plus one-half of what is ordered each time. This is illustrated in Figure 15.5.

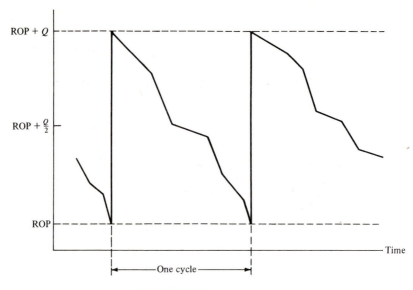

FIGURE 15.5
Expected inventory level per cycle when lead time is zero.

Since lead time is not zero but is a random variable, the demand for the product during lead time may occur, so the *expected* inventory level will be reduced by an amount equal to the *expected* demand during lead time. Let

Y = random variable representing the demand during lead time
$h(y)$ = distribution of Y
$E(Y)$ = expected demand during lead time

Note that Y is a function of both the demand X and the lead time LT. The expected inventory level/cycle is then given by

$$\text{EIV}(\text{ROP}, Q) = \text{ROP} + \frac{Q}{2} - E(Y) \qquad (15.29)$$

The distribution of Y may be available from past data, or it may be necessary to calculate it from the distribution of X and LT. If the distribution of Y is not given, one of the best ways to calculate it is by simulation. The procedure for simulating the distribution of Y is set forth in Algorithm 15.3.

15.3.2 Algorithm 15.3—Simulation of the Distribution of the Demand During Lead Time Y

The notation at the beginning of Section 15.3.1 is assumed.

Step 1
Select a sample value of LT, say t.

Step 2
Select t sample values of X, say $x_1, x_2, \ldots, x_t$.

Step 3
Let $y = \Sigma_{i=1}^{t} x_i$ be a sample value of the demand during lead time Y.

Step 4
Increase by one the number of times the value y has occurred.

Step 5
If the process has simulated a large number of Y values, say 25,000 values, go to step 6; otherwise, return to step 1.

Step 6
The proportion of the time each value of Y occurs is taken as the probability distribution of the demand during lead time Y.

   Stop.

   The computer program for Algorithm 15.3 is part of the general program in Section 15.3.3.1 which determines the optimal ROP and Q values.

   The expected total annual inventory cost can now be expressed as

$$
\begin{aligned}
\text{ETAIC}(\text{ROP}, Q) &= \text{AOC} + \text{EASC} + \text{EAIHC} \\
&= c_0 \frac{D}{Q} + c_4 \frac{D}{Q}\left[\text{ENS}(\text{ROP})\right] + c_1 \left[\text{EIV}(\text{ROP}, Q)\right] \\
&= c_0 \frac{D}{Q} + c_4 \frac{D}{Q}\left[\sum_{y=\text{ROP}}^{\infty} (y - \text{ROP})P(Y = y)\right] \\
&\quad + c_1\left[\text{ROP} + \frac{Q}{2} - E(Y)\right]
\end{aligned}
\tag{15.30}
$$

Two basic approaches for finding the optimal ROP and Q values are:

1 Calculate ETAIC(ROP,Q) for $Q = 1, 2, \ldots, D$ and ROP $= 1, 2, \ldots, Q$. Select the value of ROP and Q that yields the minimum ETAIC. In reality, only a subset of the possible ETAIC need to be calculated.
2 Take the partial derivative of ETAIC(ROP,Q) with respect to ROP and Q, set the results equal to zero, and solve the resulting equations iteratively until convergence is achieved.

To use the second approach, note that

$$\frac{\partial ETAIC(ROP,Q)}{\partial(ROP)} = -c_4 \frac{D}{Q}\left[\sum_{y=ROP}^{\infty} P(Y=y)\right] + c_1 = 0$$

or

$$-c_4 \frac{D}{Q}[1 - H(ROP)] = -c_1$$

$$P(Y > ROP) = 1 - H(ROP) = \frac{c_1 Q}{c_4 D} \qquad (15.31)$$

The optimal ROP and Q values must be such that the probability the demand during lead time is greater than ROP is $(c_1 Q)/(c_4 D)$. Of course, this assumes $c_1 Q \leqslant c_4 D$ since the quotient $(c_1 Q)/(c_4 D)$ represents a probability. Also,

$$\frac{\partial ETAIC(ROP,Q)}{\partial Q} = -\frac{c_0 D}{Q^2} - \frac{c_4 D[ENS(ROP)]}{Q^2} + \frac{c_1}{2} = 0$$

or

$$\frac{c_1 Q^2}{2} = c_0 D + c_4 D[ENS(ROP)]$$

$$Q = \sqrt{\frac{2\{c_0 D + c_4 D[ENS(ROP)]\}}{c_1}} \qquad (15.32)$$

The optimal values of ROP and Q must satisfy Equations (15.31) and (15.32) simultaneously. Since ROP and Q are integers when demand is a discrete random variable, Equations (15.31) and (15.32) cannot be satisfied exactly, so an algorithm to handle this situation will be presented.

15.3.3 Algorithm 15.4—Optimal ROP and Q to Minimize the Expected Total Annual Inventory Cost

The notation at the beginning of Section 15.3.1 is assumed.

Step 1
If the probability distribution of the demand during lead time $h(y)$ is known, go to step 2; otherwise, use Algorithm 15.3 to determine $h(y)$ by simulation, then go to step 2.

Step 2
Calculate the expected demand during lead time

$$E(Y) = \sum_{y=0}^{M^*} yh(y) = \sum_{y=0}^{M^*} yP(Y=y) \qquad (15.33)$$

where M^* is the maximum demand during lead time.

Step 3
Calculate the expected number of stockouts for ROP = 1, 2, ... , M^*.

$$\text{ENS(ROP)} = \sum_{y=\text{ROP}}^{M^*} (y - \text{ROP})h(y) = \sum_{y=\text{ROP}}^{M^*} (y - \text{ROP})P(Y = y) \qquad (15.34)$$

Step 4
Calculate the probability that the demand during lead time will exceed the reorder point ROP, for ROP = 1, 2, ... , M^*. That is, calculate $P(Y > \text{ROP})$ for ROP = 1, 2, ... , M^*.

Step 5
Let ROP = M^*, then the expected number of stockouts ENS(ROP) will be zero.

Step 6
Calculate

$$Q = \sqrt{\frac{2D\{c_0 + c_4 [\text{ENS(ROP)}]\}}{c_1}} \qquad (15.35)$$

Let Q^* be the largest integer less than or equal to Q.

Step 7
Calculate

$$c = \frac{c_1 Q^*}{c_4 D} \qquad (15.36)$$

Step 8
Let ROP^* be the smallest integer value of Z such that

$$P(Y > Z) \leqslant c \qquad (15.37)$$

Step 9
If ROP^* is equal to ROP, go to step 10; otherwise, set ROP = ROP^* and return to step 6. *Note:* If the algorithm does not converge in 50 iterations, go to step 10.

Step 10
The integers ROP^* and Q^* are only approximations of the continuous optimal values, so calculate ETAIC(ROP,Q) for ROP = $\text{ROP}^* - 1$, ROP^*, $\text{ROP}^* + 1$ and $Q = Q^* - 1$, Q^*, $Q^* + 1$. This will assure that the minimum ETAIC is attained.

$$\text{ETAIC(ROP}, Q) = c_0 \frac{D}{Q} + c_4 \frac{D}{Q} [\text{ENS(ROP)}] + c_1 \left[\text{ROP} + \frac{Q}{2} - E(Y) \right] \qquad (15.38)$$

Step 11
Print the minimum ETAIC with the corresponding optimal ROP and Q from step 10.
   Stop.

Table 15.3

X: demand, pairs/week	0	1	2	3	4
$f(x) = P(X = x)$	0.3	0.4	0.15	0.1	0.05

EXAMPLE 15.3.1 The weekly demand for hiking boots of type D6490 at an outdoor equipment store has the distribution given in Table 15.3. A replenishment order usually takes 3 weeks, but varies from order to order. In fact, it has been determined that the lead time has the distribution given in Table 15.4.

Each time a replenishment order is placed, a cost of $20 is incurred. Space is limited so the annual inventory holding cost/pair is $15. Backpackers usually plan well in advance. Hence, unfilled orders can be backordered, but the loss of good will and loss of additional customers is estimated to cost $50 per stockout. Each pair of boots costs $24.75 and sells for $44. The expected demand per year is 60 pairs.

Based on the above data, what is the optimal reorder point and optimal reorder quantity to minimize the expected total annual inventory cost? Note that

$$c_0 = \$20$$
$$c_1 = \$15$$
$$c_4 = \$50$$

The solution will be obtained by following Algorithm 15.4 step by step.

Step 1
Since the distribution of demand during lead time is not given, it must be calculated using simulation. See Algorithm 15.3. The subroutine DDDLT in Section 15.3.3.1 yielded the distribution in Table 15.5 after 25,000 sample lead times.

Step 2
The expected demand during lead time is

$$E(Y) = \sum_{y=0}^{15} yh(y)$$

Table 15.4

LT: lead time, weeks	1	2	3	4	5
$g(lt)$	0.05	0.15	0.6	0.15	0.05

Table 15.5 **PROBABILITY DISTRIBUTION,
CUMULATIVE DISTRIBUTION,
AND ONE MINUS THE CUMULATIVE
DISTRIBUTION OF DEMAND DURING
LEAD TIME**

y	$h(y)$	$H(y)$	$P(Y > y)$
0	0.04420	0.04420	0.95580
1	0.13000	0.17420	0.82580
2	0.17436	0.34856	0.65144
3	0.17568	0.52424	0.47576
4	0.16212	0.68636	0.31364
5	0.13048	0.81684	0.18316
6	0.08172	0.89856	0.10144
7	0.04932	0.94788	0.05212
8	0.02876	0.97664	0.02336
9	0.01244	0.98908	0.01092
10	0.00620	0.99528	0.00472
11	0.00264	0.99792	0.00208
12	0.00128	0.99920	0.00080
13	0.00048	0.99968	0.00032
14	0.00028	0.99996	0.00004
15	0.00004	1.00000	0.00000
16	0.00000	1.00000	0.00000

$$= 0(0.04420) + 1(0.13000) + 2(0.17436)$$
$$+ \cdots + 15(0.00004)$$
$$= 3.6014$$

Step 3
The expected number of stockouts for

$$\text{ROP} = 1 \quad \text{ENS}(1) = \sum_{y=1}^{15} (y - 1)h(y)$$

$$= 0(0.13000) + 1(0.17436) + \cdots + 14(0.00004)$$

$$= 2.64559$$

$$\text{ROP} = 2 \quad \text{ENS}(2) = \sum_{y=2}^{15} (y - 2)h(y)$$

$$= 0(0.17436) + 1(0.17568) + \cdots + 13(0.00004)$$

$$= 1.8198$$

The complete set of ENS(ROP) values for ROP $= 0, 1, 2, \ldots, 20$ are printed after the computer listing in Section 15.3.3.1.

Step 4
The probability the demand during lead time will exceed the reorder point ROP for ROP = 0, 1, 2, ..., 20 is printed after the computer listing in Section 15.3.3.1.

Step 5
Let ROP = 20, then ENS(20) = 0.

Step 6

$$Q = \sqrt{\frac{2Dc_0}{c_1}}$$

$$= \sqrt{\frac{2(60)(20)}{15}}$$

$$= 12.649$$

Let $Q^* = 12$.

Step 7

$$c = \frac{c_1 Q^*}{c_4 D}$$

$$= \frac{15(12)}{50(60)}$$

$$= 0.06$$

Step 8
Note that

$$P(Y > 6) = 0.10144$$
$$P(Y > 7) = 0.05212$$

Therefore, the smallest integer Z such that

$$P(Y > Z) \leqslant 0.06$$

is $Z = 7$. Thus let $\text{ROP}^* = 7$.

Step 9
$\text{ROP}^* \neq \text{ROP}$, so let $\text{ROP} = \text{ROP}^* = 7$ and return to step 6.

Step 6A

$$Q = \sqrt{\frac{2(60)[(20 + 50\text{ENS}(7)]}{15}}$$

$$= \sqrt{\frac{2(60)[20 + 50(0.09436)]}{15}}$$

$$= 14.06$$

Therefore, $Q^* = 14$.

Step 7A

$$c = \frac{15(14)}{50(60)} = 0.07$$

Step 8A
The smallest integer Z such that

$$P(Y > Z) \leqslant 0.07$$

is $Z = 7$. Hence, let $ROP^* = 7$.

Step 9A
Since $ROP^* = ROP = 7$, go to step 10.

Step 10
Use Equation (15.38) to calculate ETAIC(ROP,Q) for ROP = 6, 7, 8 and Q = 13, 14, 15.

ROP	Q	ETAIC(ROP,Q)
6	13	270.97
6	14	268.65
6	15	267.64
7	13	262.56
7	14	261.91 ⟵
7	15	262.35
8	13	265.53
8	14	265.74
8	15	266.93

Step 11
The minimum ETAIC occurs with ROP = 7 and Q = 14. Thus, 14 pairs of type D6490 hiking boots should be ordered when the inventory level reaches 7 pairs.

15.3.3.1 Computer program for Algorithm 15.4 This computer program contains the option of reading in the distribution of the demand during lead time or of reading in the demand distribution and the lead time distribution. In the latter case, the subroutine DDDLT simulates the distribution of the demand during lead time. The program is set up to handle a maximum of 20 values of demand, 20 values of lead time, and 50 values of demand during lead time. The program assumes that the number of demands during lead time Y will be 0, 1, 2, ... (maximum demand during lead time). It prints out the distribution of Y, the cumulative distribution of Y, and the expected value of Y. It also prints the expected number of stockouts for a given reorder point ROP, and the probability Y will exceed ROP, for ROP = 0, 1, 2, ... Finally, the value of Q^* and ROP^* at each iteration and the minimum expected total annual inventory cost are printed.

The program occupies 40K bytes of core storage. The data for Example 15.3.1 follow the listing of the program.

```
C
C     ****************************************************************************
C     *                                                                        *
C     *        **    ALGORITHM 15.4        PROBABILISTIC INVENTORY    **        *
C     *                                                                        *
C     * THIS PROGRAM IS DESIGNED                                               *
C     *                                                                        *
C     *    TO READ                                                             *
C     *        CARD 1    COLS   2-80   TITLE   DESCRIPTION OF THE PROBLEM USING *
C     *                                        ANY CHARACTERS ON KEYPUNCH      *
C     *                                        ** COLUMN 1 MUST BE LEFT BLANK ***
C     *        CARD 2    COLS  1-10    CO  ORDERING COST/ORDER   (F10.0)        *
C     *                               11-20   C1  INVENTORY HOLDING COST/UNIT   *
C     *                                        OF ENDING INVENTORY  (F10.0)     *
C     *                               21-30   C3  COST/ITEM PURCHASED OR PRODUCED (F10.0)*
C     *                               31-40   C4  STOCKOUT COST/ITEM OUT OF STOCK (F10.0)*
C     *                               41-50   D   EXPECTED DEMAND PER YEAR  (F10.0) *
C     *        CARD 3    COLS  1- 5    KNTY  # OF DIFF.DEM.DUR.LEAD TIME   (I5)  *
C     *                               6-10   KNOWN  0 IF DIST.OF DEM.DUR.LEAD TIME *
C     *                                         IS NOT KNOWN                    *
C     *                                       1   IF DIST. IS KNOWN  (I5)       *
C     *                                                                        *
C     *    IF KNOWN=0, INSERT ALL THE CARDS DESCRIBED IN SUBROUTINE DDDLT      *
C     *    WHICH FOLLOWS THIS PROGRAM, AND OMIT THE FOLLOWING.                 *
C     *    IF KNOWN = 1, USE THE FOLLOWING.                                    *
C     *                                                                        *
C     *        CARD 4    HSMALL(I)  DISTRIBUTION OF DEMAND DURING LEAD TIME     *
C     *                               I=1 TO KNTY                              *
C     *                               PUNCH 8 TO A CARD IN 8F10.0 FORMAT.       *
C     *                               IF KNTY > 8, CONTINUE ON NEXT CARD.       *
C     *         TO SOLVE MORE THAN ONE PROBLEM AT A TIME, REPEAT THE           *
C     *         READ SEQUENCE, AND STACK THE DATA ONE BEHIND THE OTHER         *
C     *                                                                        *
C     *    TO CALCULATE AND PRINT                                              *
C     *        EXPECY          EXPECTED DEMAND DURING LEAD TIME                 *
C     *        HSMALL(I)       PROBABILITY DISTRIBUTION OF DEMAND DURING        *
C     *                        LEAD TIME (IF APPLICABLE)                        *
C     *        HLARGE(I)       CUMULATIVE DISTRIBUTION OF DEMAND DURING         *
C     *                        LEAD TIME                                        *
C     *        PYGROP(ROP)     PROBABILITY, Y, THAT THE DEMAND DURING LEAD      *
C     *                        TIME IS GREATER THAN ROP, THE REORDER POINT      *
C     *        ENS(ROP)        EXPECTED NUMBER OF STOCKOUTS IF ROP=0,1,2,...    *
C     *        OPTROP          OPTIMAL REORDER POINT                            *
C     *        OPTQ            OPTIMAL AMOUNT TO REORDER                        *
C     *        ETAIC(I,J)      OPTIMAL EXPECTED ANNUAL INVENTORY COST           *
C     *                                                                        *
C     ****************************************************************************
      COMMON KNTY,MSTAR,HSMALL(50),HLARGE(50),Y(50),KY(50)
      DIMENSION ENS(50),TITLE(20),PYGROP(50),ETAIC(3,3)
      INTEGER OPTQ,OPTROP, ROP,QSTAR,ROPSTR,Y
C READ TITLE AND DATA
    5 READ(5,10,END=2000)TITLE
   10 FORMAT(20A4)
      WRITE(6,11)TITLE
   11 FORMAT('1',20A4,//)
      READ(5,15)CO,C1,C3,C4,D
   15 FORMAT(5F10.0)
      READ(5,20)KNTY,KNOWN
   20 FORMAT(2I5)
      DO 21 I=1,KNTY
      II=I-1
      Y(I)=II
```

```
   21 KY(I)=0
C     ****************************************************************
C     *    STEP 1                                                   *
C     *         IF THE DISTRIBUTION OF DEMAND DURING LEAD TIME IS KNOWN, READ  *
C     *         IT IN; OTHERWISE, CALL SUBROUTINE DDDLT TO SIMULATE IT.  *
C     ****************************************************************
      IF(KNOWN.EQ.1) GO TO 100
      CALL DDDLT
      GO TO 200
  100 READ(5,110)(HSMALL(I),I=1,KNTY)
  110 FORMAT(8F10.0)
      SUMY=0.
      DO 120 I=1,KNTY
      SUMY=SUMY+HSMALL(I)
  120 HLARGE(I)=SUMY
      MSTAR=Y(KNTY)
C     ****************************************************************
C     *    STEP 2                                                   *
C     *         CALCULATE EXPECTED DEMAND DURING LEAD TIME          *
C     ****************************************************************
  200 EXPECY=0.
      DO 210 NEWI=1,KNTY
  210 EXPECY=EXPECY+(NEWI-1)*HSMALL(NEWI)
      WRITE(6,220)EXPECY
  220 FORMAT(/5X,'EXPECY=',F10.5/)
C     ****************************************************************
C     *    STEP 3                                                   *
C     *         CALCULATE EXPECTED NUMBER OF STOCKOUTS              *
C     ****************************************************************
      DO 300 ROP=1,KNTY
      ENS(ROP)=0
      DO 300 IY=ROP,KNTY
      ENS(ROP)=ENS(ROP)+(IY-ROP)*HSMALL(IY)
  300 CONTINUE
C     ****************************************************************
C     *    STEP 4                                                   *
C     *         CALCULATE THE PROBABILITY THAT DEMAND DURING LEAD TIME WILL  *
C     *             EXCEED THE REORDER POINT                        *
C     ****************************************************************
      DO 400 ROP=1,KNTY
  400 PYGROP(ROP)=1.-HLARGE(ROP)
      WRITE(6,1500)
 1500 FORMAT(///5X,'Y    HSMALL(Y)   HLARGE(Y)',12X,'ROP   ENS(ROP)   PYG
     *ROP(ROP)')
      DO 1515 I=1,KNTY
 1515 WRITE(6,1510)Y(I),HSMALL(I),HLARGE(I),Y(I),ENS(I),PYGROP(I)
 1510 FORMAT(I6,2F12.5,I15,2F12.5)
      WRITE(6,1560)
 1560 FORMAT(/////)
C     ****************************************************************
C     *    STEP 5                                                   *
C     *         INITIALIZE REORDER POINT AT MAXIMUM DEMAND DURING LEAD TIME  *
C     ****************************************************************
      NROP=MSTAR+1
      ITKT=1
C     ****************************************************************
C     *    STEP 6                                                   *
C     *         CALCULATE THE OPTIMAL REORDER QUANTITY FROM THE GIVEN  *
C     *             REORDER POINT                                   *
C     ****************************************************************
  600 Q=SQRT((2*D*(CO+C4*ENS(NROP)))/C1)
      QSTAR=Q
C     ****************************************************************
C     *    STEPS 7,8                                                *
C     *         CALCULATE THE OPTIMAL REORDER POINT FROM THE GIVEN  *
C     *             REORDER QUANTITY                                *
C     ****************************************************************
      CCAL=(C1*QSTAR)/(C4*D)
      DO 800 ROP=1,KNTY
      IF(PYGROP(ROP).LE.CCAL) GO TO 810
```

```
  800 CONTINUE
  810 ROPSTR=ROP
C     ***********************************************************************
C     *    STEP 9                                                          *
C     *         CHECK TO SEE IF CONVERGENCE HAS BEEN OBTAINED              *
C     ***********************************************************************
      IF(ROPSTR.EQ.NROP) GO TO 1000
      IF(ITKT.EQ.50) GO TO 1000
      ITKT=ITKT+1
      NROP=ROPSTR
      GO TO 600
C     ***********************************************************************
C     *    STEP 10                                                         *
C     *         BASED ON THE APPROXIMATE OPTIMAL REORDER QUANTITY AND OPTIMAL *
C     *         REORDER POINT CALCULATE THE ACTUAL OPTIMAL REORDER POINT   *
C     *         AND QUANTITY BY EXAMINING THE EXPECTED TOTAL ANNUAL INVENTORY *
C     *         COST AT POINTS AROUND THE APPROXIMATE OPTIMAL REORDER POINT *
C     *         AND QUANTITY.                                              *
C     ***********************************************************************
 1000 EMIN=1000000.
      MINR=ROPSTR-3
      DO 1010 I=1,3
      MINR=MINR+1
      MINQ=QSTAR-2
      DO 1010 J=1,3
      MINQ=MINQ+1
      NEWR=MINR+1
      ETAIC(I,J)=CO*(D/MINQ)+C4*(D/MINQ)*ENS(NEWR)+C1*(MINR+MINQ/2.-EXPE
     *CY)
      EMIN=AMIN1(ETAIC(I,J),EMIN)
      IF(EMIN.NE.ETAIC(I,J))GO TO 1010
      OPTROP=MINR
      OPTQ=MINQ
      ISAVE=I
      JSAVE=J
 1010 CONTINUE
C     ***********************************************************************
C     *    STEP 11                                                         *
C     *         PRINT THE OPTIMAL EXPECTED ANNUAL INVENTORY COST WITH THE  *
C     *         CORRESPONDING OPTIMAL REORDER POINT AND QUANTITY.          *
C     ***********************************************************************
      WRITE(6,1100)ETAIC(ISAVE,JSAVE),OPTQ,OPTROP
 1100 FORMAT(//5X,'THE EXPECTED ANNUAL INVENTORY COST IS',F8.2//12X,'THE
     * OPTIMAL AMOUNT TO ORDER IS',I8//14X,'THE OPTIMAL REORDER POINT IS
     *',I8)
      GO TO 5
 2000 STOP
      END
```

```
      SUBROUTINE DDDLT
C     *******************************************************************
C     *                                                                 *
C     *                 *** ALGORITHM 15.3 ***                          *
C     *                                                                 *
C     *     SIMULATION OF DISTRIBUTION OF DEMAND DURING LEAD TIME       *
C     *                                                                 *
C     *    THIS SUBROUTINE IS DESIGNED                                  *
C     *      TO READ                                                    *
C     *         CARD 1    COLS  1- 5   MINLT  MINIMUM LEAD TIME   (I5)  *
C     *                         6-10   MAXLT  MAXIMUM LEAD TIME   (I5)  *
C     *                        11-15   KNTLT  # OF DIFF. POSSIBLE LEAD TIMES (I5) *
C     *         CARD 2    GSMALL(I), I=1,KNTLT  DISTRIBUTION OF LEAD TIME *
C     *                        PUNCH 8 TO A CARD IN 8F10.0 FORMAT.      *
C     *                        IF KNTLT > 8, CONTINUE ON NEXT CARD.     *
C     *         CARD N    COLS  1- 5   MINX   MINIMUM DEMAND   (I5)     *
C     *                         6-10   MAXX   MAXIMUM DEMAND   (I5)     *
C     *                        11-15   KNTX   # OF POSS. DEMANDS   (I5) *
C     *         CARD N+1  FSMALL(I), I=1,KNTX  DISTRIBUTION OF DEMAND   *
C     *                        PUNCH 8 TO A CARD IN 8F10.0 FORMAT.      *
C     *                        IF KNTX > 8, CONTINUE ON NEXT CARD.      *
C     *                                                                 *
C     *      TO CALCULATE                                               *
C     *         GLARGE(I)         CUMULATIVE DISTRIBUTION OF LEAD TIME  *
C     *         FLARGE(I)         CUMULATIVE DISTRIBUTION OF DEMAND     *
C     *         HSMALL(I)         PROBABILITY DIST. OF DEMAND DURING LEAD TIME *
C     *         HLARGE(I)         CUMULATIVE DIST. OF DEMAND DURING LEAD TIME  *
C     *                                                                 *
C     *******************************************************************
      COMMON KNTY,MSTAR,HSMALL(50),HLARGE(50),Y(50),KY(50)
      DIMENSION FSMALL(20),FLARGE(20),GSMALL(20),GLARGE(20),LT(20)
      DIMENSION KLT(20)
      INTEGER X(20),Y,T
C READ IN DATA
      READ(5,20)MINLT,MAXLT,KNTLT
   20 FORMAT(3I5)
      DO 25 I=1,KNTLT
      II=I-1
      KLT(I)=0
   25 LT(I)=MINLT+II
      READ(5,40)(GSMALL(I),I=1,KNTLT)
   40 FORMAT(8F10.0)
      READ(5,20)MINX,MAXX,KNTX
      DO 30 I=1,KNTX
      II=I-1
   30 X(I)=MINX+II
      READ(5,40)(FSMALL(I),I=1,KNTX)
C CALCULATE CDF FOR LT AND X
      SUMLT=0.
      DO 100 I=1,KNTLT
      SUMLT=SUMLT+GSMALL(I)
      GLARGE(I)=SUMLT
  100 CONTINUE
      SUMX=0.
      DO 110 I=1,KNTX
      SUMX=SUMX+FSMALL(I)
      FLARGE(I)=SUMX
  110 CONTINUE
C LOOP 25000 TIMES FOR THE SIMULATION
      IN=180327418
      DO 199 LOOP=1,25000
C     *******************************************************************
C     *  STEP 1                                                         *
C     *          SELECT SAMPLE VALUE OF LEAD TIME                       *
C     *******************************************************************
      NUMBER=IN*65539
      IF(NUMBER.GT.0) GO TO 114
      NUMBER=NUMBER+2147483647+1
  114 RANDOM=NUMBER*.4656613E-9
      IN=NUMBER
```

```
            DO 115 I=1,KNTLT
            IF(RANDOM.LE.GLARGE(I)) GO TO 116
    115 CONTINUE
    116 T=LT(I)
            KLT(I)=KLT(I)+1
C     **********************************************************************
C     *     STEPS 2,3                                                     *
C     *             SELECT SAMPLE VALUE OF DEMAND DURING LEAD TIME        *
C     **********************************************************************
            NEWY=0
            DO 120 NEWX=1,T
            NUMBER=IN*65539
            IF(NUMBER.GT.0) GO TO 124
            NUMBER=NUMBER+2147483647+1
    124 RANDOM=NUMBER*.4656613E-9
            IN=NUMBER
            DO 121 I=1,KNTX
            IF(RANDOM.LE.FLARGE(I)) GO TO 122
    121 CONTINUE
    122 NEWY=NEWY+X(I)
    120 CONTINUE
C     **********************************************************************
C     *     STEP 4                                                        *
C     *             UPDATE NUMBER OF TIMES CURRENT DEMAND DURING LEAD TIME*
C     *             HAS OCCURRED                                          *
C     **********************************************************************
            DO 125 J=1,KNTY
            IF(NEWY.EQ.Y(J)) GO TO 126
    125 CONTINUE
    126 KY(J)=KY(J)+1
C     **********************************************************************
C     *     STEP 5                                                        *
C     *             HAVE WE SIMULATED LONG ENOUGH?  IF YES, GO TO STEP 6. *
C     **********************************************************************
    199 CONTINUE
C     **********************************************************************
C     *     STEP 6                                                        *
C     *             CALCULATE PDF AND CDF OF DEMAND DURING LEAD TIME AND THE *
C     *             PROPORTION OF TIME EACH DEMAND DURING LEAD TIME HAS OCCURRED *
C     **********************************************************************
            HSUM=0.
            DO 130 I=1,KNTY
            HSMALL(I)=KY(I)/25000.
            HSUM=HSUM+HSMALL(I)
            HLARGE(I)=HSUM
    130 CONTINUE
            MSTAR=Y(KNTY)
            RETURN
            END




/DATA

EXAMPLE 15.3.1
        20.         15.     24.75       50.         60.
    21      0
     1      5     5
          .05         .15         .60         .15         .05
     0      4     5
          .30         .40         .15         .10         .05
```

EXAMPLE 15.3.1

EXPECY=   3.60139

Y	HSMALL(Y)	HLARGE(Y)	ROP	ENS(ROP)	PYGROP(ROP)
0	0.04420	0.04420	0	3.60139	0.95580
1	0.13000	0.17420	1	2.64559	0.82580
2	0.17436	0.34856	2	1.81980	0.65144
3	0.17568	0.52424	3	1.16836	0.47576
4	0.16212	0.68636	4	0.69260	0.31364
5	0.13048	0.81684	5	0.37896	0.18316
6	0.08172	0.89856	6	0.19580	0.10144
7	0.04932	0.94788	7	0.09436	0.05212
8	0.02876	0.97664	8	0.04224	0.02336
9	0.01244	0.98908	9	0.01888	0.01092
10	0.00620	0.99528	10	0.00796	0.00472
11	0.00264	0.99792	11	0.00324	0.00208
12	0.00128	0.99920	12	0.00116	0.00080
13	0.00048	0.99968	13	0.00036	0.00032
14	0.00028	0.99996	14	0.00004	0.00004
15	0.00004	1.00000	15	0.0	0.00000
16	0.0	1.00000	16	0.0	0.00000
17	0.0	1.00000	17	0.0	0.00000
18	0.0	1.00000	18	0.0	0.00000
19	0.0	1.00000	19	0.0	0.00000
20	0.0	1.00000	20	0.0	0.00000

THE EXPECTED ANNUAL INVENTORY COST IS   261.91

THE OPTIMAL AMOUNT TO ORDER IS   14

THE OPTIMAL REORDER POINT IS   7

15.4 SUMMARY

Single-period models with and without a setup or ordering cost were analyzed to determine the optimal beginning inventory level when the demand is a continuous or discrete random variable. The computer program in Section 15.2.5 can be used to determine the optimal beginning inventory level when the probability distribution of demand is discrete and known.

Section 15.3 was devoted to the multiperiod, fixed-reorder-point, fixed-reorder-quantity model in which the demand and lead time were discrete random variables. However, the analysis would be virtually the same if they were continuous random variables. The only change would be to replace the summation symbols with integrals. In most cases the continuous case is much harder to analyze, since the expected number of stockouts as a function of the reorder point is usually quite difficult to calculate analytically. Generally, one must resort to numerical integration.

If management wants the optimal values of ROP and Q such that the probability of a stockout is kept below a certain quantity α, it is a simple matter to consult the $P(Y > \text{ROP})$ table, find the smallest value of ROP such that $P(Y > \text{ROP}) \leqslant \alpha$, and then use the value of ROP obtained to find the corresponding value of Q using Equation (15.32). Note that $P(Y > \text{ROP})$ is the probability the demand during lead time exceeds ROP, which is the same as the probability of a stockout.

If the distribution of the demand during lead time is known, it is unimportant whether lead time is a random variable or not. In fact, the demand and lead time distributions would not be needed.

When backordering is not allowed (unfilled demands are lost), the solution of Equations (15.31) and (15.32) usually provides a good approximation of the optimal reorder point and optimal reorder quantity. This is especially true when the stockout cost is quite large compared to the inventory cost.

SELECTED BIBLIOGRAPHY

1 Buchan, J., and E. Koenigsberg: "Scientific Inventory Management," Prentice-Hall, Inc., Englewood Cliffs, N.J., 1963.
2 Buffa, E. S., and W. H. Taubert: "Production Inventory Systems: Planning and Control," rev. ed., Richard D. Irwin, Inc., Homewood, Ill., 1972.
3 Hadley, G., and T. M. Whitin: "Analysis of Inventory Systems," Prentice-Hall, Inc., Englewood Cliffs, N.J., 1963.
4 Hanssmann, Fred: "Operations Research in Production and Inventory Control," John Wiley & Sons, Inc., New York, 1962.
5 Magee, J. F., and D. M. Boodman: "Production Planning and Inventory Control," 2d ed., McGraw-Hill Book Company, New York, 1967.
6 Naddor, Eliezer: "Inventory Systems," John Wiley & Sons, Inc., New York, 1966.

EXERCISES

15.1 If the stockout cost is reduced to $72 per stockout in Example 15.2.1 and if the corresponding mean demand is reduced to 15, what is the new desired inventory level at the start of the season? What must the desired inventory level be in order to be 95 percent confident that no demands will go unfilled?

15.2 If the demand for skis of type SK009 in Example 15.2.1 has a Poisson distribution with a mean of 25, what is the optimal DIL? What must DIL be in order to be 90 percent confident that no demands will go unfilled?

15.3 Work through the details of Example 15.2.5 using $c_0 = \$100$.

15.4 Use the computer program in Section 15.2.5 to solve for the optimal DIL and critical A value when c_0 is increased to $100 and c_4 is reduced to $55 in Example 15.2.5.

15.5 Consider the single-period inventory problem with

$$c_0 = \$10$$
$$c_1 = -2$$
$$c_3 = \$23$$
$$c_4 = \$15$$

The demand for the product has a Poisson distribution with a mean of 125. Modify the computer program in Section 15.2.5 to handle this demand distribution. What is the optimal DIL and critical A value?

Exercises 15.6–15.8 assume the fixed-reorder-point, fixed-reorder-quantity inventory model in Section 15.3.1.

15.6 The demand for a certain product has the distribution:

X: demand	0	1	2	3	4	5
f(x)	0.05	0.05	0.1	0.4	0.35	0.05

The distribution of the lead time is:

LT: lead time	2	3	4
g(lt)	0.3	0.5	0.2

Assume

$$c_0 = \$30$$
$$c_1 = \$10$$
$$c_4 = \$60$$
$$D = 160$$

(a) Use the subroutine DDDLT in Section 15.3.3.1 to simulate the distribution of the demand during lead time.
(b) Calculate the expected demand during lead time.
(c) Use the computer program in Section 15.3.3.1 to calculate the expected number of stockouts for ROP = 0, 1, 2, . . . , 20.
(d) Calculate the optimal ROP and Q by hand using Algorithm 15.4.

15.7 Modify the program in Section 15.3.3.1 to handle the Poisson distribution as the distribution of demand during lead time.

15.8 Rework Example 15.3.1 using a Poisson demand during lead time with a mean of 4.

16

MARKOV CHAINS

16.1 INTRODUCTION

Consider a system that can be in one and only one of a finite number of possible states at every point in time. For example, if the system is a piece of equipment that is producing parts for fan blade assemblies, the system may be in excellent condition (represented by state 0), average condition (represented by state 1), or poor condition (represented by state 2). Likewise, the system could be a customer interested in a certain product, such as freeze-dried dinners. The customer has the option of selecting any one of a finite number of brands. If the customer selects brand RM, we might say the system is in state 0. If the customer selects brand MH, we might say the system is in state 1, etc. Finally, the system might be the inventory level of a given product. A zero inventory could be denoted by state 0, one unit of inventory could be denoted by state 1, etc.

Some questions we want to consider are:

1 If the system is currently in state r, what is the probability it will be in state s n steps from now?
2 After a large number of steps, what is the probability the system will be in state s?

3 If a company currently has a certain share of the market, what share of the market will it have *n* steps from now?

4 Will each competitor's share of the market stabilize in the future?

Markov chains can be used to answer these and many other questions relative to dynamic systems. In particular, Markov chains have been used to analyze inventory problems, brand-switching problems, equipment replacement problems, population growth problems, accounting problems, plant location problems, and other problems involving dynamic systems.

We will be interested in analyzing systems in which the next state of the system is dependent on the current state and is completely independent of the previous states of the system.

16.2 FORMULATION OF MARKOV CHAINS

Let X_i be a random variable that represents the state of a given system at step i, $i = 1$, $2, \ldots$, where $X_i = 0, 1, 2, \ldots, N$. Quite often "step i" means "at time i" or "i time units from time zero." For example, in an inventory system, X_1 might represent the inventory level of a product after the first week, X_2 the inventory level after the second week, etc. On the other hand, "step i" might mean "when the ith transaction occurs." For example, in the brand-switching problem to be discussed later, a customer may have just purchased brand A and we may want to know which brand that customer will purchase next time (the state of the system at step 1), or we may want to know which brand that customer will purchase time after next (the state of the system at step 2).

Definition 16.2.1 Stochastic process The indexed collection of random variables $\{X_i\}$ is called a stochastic process, where i ranges through some set I.

////

The set I may be finite or it may be the set of positive integers. Quite often the index set I represents points in time. For example, X_1 might represent the state of the system at the end of the first hour, X_2 the state of the system at the end of the second hour, etc. Note that each random variable X_i has its own probability distribution function.

Definition 16.2.2 First-order markovian property If the conditional probability distribution of X_{i+1} is independent of the states the system is in at steps 0, $1, 2, \ldots, i - 1$ and is dependent only on the state the system is in at step i, then the stochastic process $\{X_i\}$ is said to have the first-order markovian property.

////

That is, the stochastic process $\{X_i\}$ has the markovian property if

$$P(X_{i+1} = s | X_0 = t_0, X_1 = t_1, \ldots, X_{i-1} = t_{i-1}, X_i = r)$$
$$= P(X_{i+1} = s | X_i = r)$$

The quantity $P(X_{i+1} = s | X_i = r)$ is called the *one-step transition probability* of going from state r at step i to state s at step $i + 1$. Thus, the one-step transition probabilities represent the conditional probability of X_{i+1} given X_i.

Definition 16.2.3 One-step stationary transition probabilities If for each r and s,

$$P(X_{i+1} = s | X_i = r) = P(X_1 = s | X_0 = r) = p_{rs} \qquad (16.1)$$

for all i, then the one-step transition probabilities are said to be stationary.

////

Thus, the probability of going from state r at the current step to state s at the next step is independent of the current step number. It should be emphasized that this says that the one-step stationary transition probabilities remain constant throughout the entire period of analysis.

Definition 16.2.4 First-order, finite-state Markov chain A stochastic process $\{X_i\}$ is said to be a first-order, finite-state Markov chain if it has the first-order markovian property, a finite number of states, a set of stationary transition probabilities, and a set of initial probabilities $P(X_0 = r)$, for all r. ////

The remainder of the chapter will be devoted to the analysis of systems that can be formulated as a first-order, finite-state Markov chain.

EXAMPLE 16.2.1 *Brand switching* A market survey indicates that the RM brand of freeze-dried dinners has 35 percent of the market, the MH brand has 30 percent of the market, and all "other" brands have the remaining 35 percent of the market. It is estimated that the RM and MH brands retain 90 and 87 percent of their customers at each step, respectively, while all "other" brands combined retain only 73 percent of their customers at each step. If a customer has just bought a freeze-dried dinner, let X_0 denote the brand bought. Since the brand is qualitative, let

$$X_0 = \begin{cases} 0 & \text{if brand RM is purchased} \\ 1 & \text{if brand MH is purchased} \\ 2 & \text{if brand "other" is purchased} \end{cases}$$

In general, let

$$X_i = \begin{cases} 0 & \text{if brand RM is purchased at step } i \\ 1 & \text{if brand MH is purchased at step } i \\ 2 & \text{if brand "other" is purchased at step } i \end{cases}$$

Thus, the system (customers purchasing a freeze-dried dinner) is in one of three different states (0, 1, or 2) at each step. Each time the customer purchases a freeze-dried dinner a transaction or step occurs that leaves the system in state 0, 1, or 2. Note that by Definition 16.2.1, the set $\{X_i\}$ is a stochastic process.

The one-step stationary transition probabilities in Table 16.1 are based on the retention rate of each brand at each step and market estimates of the *gains from* and *losses to* other brands.

In Table 16.1, we assume the first-order markovian property holds and that the transition probabilities are stationary. Thus, p_{rs} represents the probability of going from state r to state s in one step. Note, for example, that

p_{00} = probability that a customer who has just purchased brand RM will buy brand RM next time a freeze-dried dinner is bought
= 0.90

p_{01} = probability that a customer who has just purchased brand RM will switch to brand MH the next time a freeze-dried dinner is bought
= 0.02

Likewise,

p_{12} = probability that a customer who has just purchased brand MH will switch to brand "other" the next time a freeze-dried dinner is bought
= 0.09

If we assume

$$P(X_0 = 0) = P(X_0 = 1) = 0$$
$$P(X_0 = 2) = 1$$

the stochastic process is a first-order, finite-state Markov chain.

Table 16.1 **ONE–STEP STATIONARY TRANSITION PROBABILITIES, FREEZE–DRIED DINNERS**

	To state		
	RM	MH	"Other"
From state	0	1	2
RM: 0	0.90	0.02	0.08
MH: 1	0.04	0.87	0.09
"Other": 2	0.15	0.12	0.73

If no changes are made in the current stationary transition probabilities, the information in Table 16.1 can be used to determine

1 RM's and MH's shares of the market in the future
2 If the market will reach a point of equilibrium where each brand will have a constant share of the market
3 The rate at which RM's and MH's shares of the market increase or decrease
4 The strategy that should be used by the various companies to corner a larger share of the market

If a company decides to improve its product drastically or to do extensive advertising in an attempt to corner a larger share of the market, a complete new analysis would need to be conducted.

Consider now how a Markov-chain analysis can be useful in solving the problem at hand. The first question we might want answered is, "What will each competitor's share of the market be one step from now (at step 1)?"

$$
\begin{pmatrix} \text{RM's share} \\ \text{at step 1} \end{pmatrix} = \begin{pmatrix} \text{RM's share} \\ \text{at step 0} \end{pmatrix} \begin{pmatrix} \text{fraction of current RM} \\ \text{customers who will buy} \\ \text{brand RM at step 1} \end{pmatrix}
$$

$$
+ \begin{pmatrix} \text{MH's share} \\ \text{at step 0} \end{pmatrix} \begin{pmatrix} \text{fraction of current MH} \\ \text{customers who will buy} \\ \text{brand RM at step 1} \end{pmatrix}
$$

$$
+ \begin{pmatrix} \text{"others" share} \\ \text{at step 0} \end{pmatrix} \begin{pmatrix} \text{fraction of current} \\ \text{"other" customers} \\ \text{who will buy brand} \\ \text{RM at step 1} \end{pmatrix}
$$

$$
= (0.35)p_{00} + (0.30)p_{10} + (0.35)p_{20}
$$

$$
= (0.35)(0.90) + (0.30)(0.04) + (0.35)(0.15)
$$

$$
= 0.3795
$$

Note that the fraction of the current RM customers who will buy brand RM at step 1 is just the probability of remaining in state 0 from step 0 to step 1, namely, p_{00}.

$$
\begin{pmatrix} \text{MH's share} \\ \text{at step 1} \end{pmatrix} = \begin{pmatrix} \text{RM's share} \\ \text{at step 0} \end{pmatrix} \begin{pmatrix} \text{fraction of current RM} \\ \text{customers who will buy} \\ \text{brand MH at step 1} \end{pmatrix}
$$

$$
+ \begin{pmatrix} \text{MH's share} \\ \text{at step 0} \end{pmatrix} \begin{pmatrix} \text{fraction of current MH} \\ \text{customers who will buy} \\ \text{brand MH at step 1} \end{pmatrix}
$$

$$
+ \begin{pmatrix} \text{"others" share} \\ \text{at step 0} \end{pmatrix} \begin{pmatrix} \text{fraction of current} \\ \text{"other" customers} \\ \text{who will buy brand} \\ \text{MH at step 1} \end{pmatrix}
$$

$$= (0.35)p_{01} + (0.30)p_{11} + (0.35)p_{21}$$
$$= (0.35)(0.02) + (0.30)(0.87) + (0.35)(0.12)$$
$$= 0.3100$$

$$\begin{pmatrix} \text{``Others'' share} \\ \text{at step 1} \end{pmatrix} = \begin{pmatrix} \text{RM's share} \\ \text{at step 0} \end{pmatrix} \begin{pmatrix} \text{fraction of RM} \\ \text{customers who will} \\ \text{buy brand ``other'' at} \\ \text{step 1} \end{pmatrix}$$

$$+ \begin{pmatrix} \text{MH's share} \\ \text{at step 0} \end{pmatrix} \begin{pmatrix} \text{fraction of MH} \\ \text{customers who will} \\ \text{buy brand ``other''} \\ \text{at step 1} \end{pmatrix}$$

$$+ \begin{pmatrix} \text{``others'' share} \\ \text{at step 0} \end{pmatrix} \begin{pmatrix} \text{fraction of} \\ \text{``other'' customers} \\ \text{who will buy} \\ \text{brand ``other'' at} \\ \text{step 1} \end{pmatrix}$$

$$= (0.35)p_{02} + (0.30)p_{12} + (0.35)p_{22}$$
$$= (0.35)(0.08) + (0.30)(0.09) + (0.35)(0.73)$$
$$= 0.3105$$

Table 16.2 illustrates the change in the share of the market from step 0 to step 1.

EXAMPLE 16.2.2 *Equipment maintenance* Consider a truck that can be in one of five states of deterioration as given in Table 16.3. The truck is inspected each week and is classified as being in one of the five states given in Table 16.3. If the truck is in state 0, 1, 2, 3, or 4, the owner's profit from the past week is $500, $400, $300, $200, or $0, respectively. If the truck is in state 4 (not running), it is repaired at an average cost of $300. Assume the repair work can be done during the weekend, so the truck will be ready to roll on Monday of the next week. After each repair, the truck is restored to state 1 (87–94 percent efficient).

Table 16.2 SHARE OF MARKET FROM STEP 0 TO STEP 1

Step	Competitor		
	RM	MH	"Other"
0	0.3500	0.3000	0.3500
1	0.3795	0.3100	0.3105

Table 16.3 STATES OF DETERIORATION

States	0	1	2	3	4
Operating efficiency, percent	95–100	87–94	79–86	70–78	Not running

Let $X_i = \{0,1,2,3,4\}$ represent the state of deterioration of the truck at the end of the ith week. The one-step stationary transition probabilities given in Table 16.4 were determined on the basis of past data. Note that $p_{00} = 0.50$ means that a truck in state 0 at the end of a given week has a 50 percent chance of being in state 0 at the end of the next week. Likewise, $p_{13} = 0.03$ means there is a 3 percent chance that a truck in state 1 at the end of a given week will be in state 3 at the end of the next week. The probability $p_{41} = 1$ means that a truck which is broken down at the end of a given week will always be in state 1 at the end of the next week.

16.2.1 *n*-Step Stationary Transition Probabilities

Since the type of system under consideration must be in one and only one state at each point in time, a system that is currently in state r must be in some state n steps from now. Under fairly general conditions, if the one-step stationary transition probabilities are available, we can determine

1 The probability of going from state r to state s in n steps (for all states r and s)

2 The probability of going from state r to state s for the first time in n steps (for all states r and s)

3 The expected number of steps to go from state r to state s for the first time (for all states r and s)

4 The probability of being in state s after a large number of steps (for all states s)

Table 16.4 ONE–STEP STATIONARY TRANSITION
PROBABILITIES–TRUCK EXAMPLE

From state	To state				
	0	1	2	3	4
0	0.50	0.45	0.03	0.02	0
1	0	0.56	0.40	0.03	0.01
2	0	0	0.45	0.50	0.05
3	0	0	0	0.60	0.40
4	0	1.0	0	0	0

Definition 16.2.5 *n*-step stationary transition probabilities The *n*-step stationary transition probabilities are defined to be

$$p_{rs}^{(n)} = P(X_{i+n} = s | X_i = r) = P(X_n = s | X_0 = r) \qquad (16.2)$$

where $\qquad p_{rs}^{(n)} \geq 0 \qquad$ for all states r and $s; n = 1, 2, \ldots \qquad (16.3)$

$$\sum_{s=0}^{N} p_{rs}^{(n)} = 1 \qquad \text{for all states } r; n = 1, 2, \ldots \qquad (16.4)$$

////

Equation (16.4) assumes there are $N + 1$ possible states. Note that if the system
is currently in state r, it must be in some state n steps from now. Thus,

$$\sum_{s=0}^{N} p_{rs}^{(n)} = 1$$

In general, the *n*-step stationary transition probabilities can be calculated as
follows:

$$p_{rs}^{(n)} = \sum_{j=0}^{N} p_{rj} p_{js}^{(n-1)} \qquad (16.5)$$

where the possible states are $0, 1, 2, \ldots, N$. That is, the probability of going from
state r to state s in n steps is the probability of going from state r to state j in one step,
times the probability of going from state j to state s in $n - 1$ steps, summed over all
$j = 0, 1, 2, \ldots, N$.

EXAMPLE 16.2.3 For the brand-switching problem in Example 16.2.1, suppose we
want the probability that someone who has just purchased brand MH (system is in
state 1) will buy brand MH two steps from now (system will be in state 1 two steps
from now). Given that a person has just bought brand MH, the event that the person
will buy brand MH again two steps from now can occur in three mutually exclusive
ways; namely, the person can

(*a*) Buy brand RM one step from now (step 1) and then switch back to brand
MH two steps from now (step 2).
(*b*) Buy brand MH at step 1 and then buy brand MH again at step 2.
(*c*) Buy brand "other" at step 1 and then switch back to brand MH at step 2.

This is illustrated in Figure 16.1.
From Table 16.1 we see that

$$\text{Prob } (a) = p_{10} p_{01} = (0.04)(0.02) = 0.0008$$
$$\text{Prob } (b) = p_{11} p_{11} = (0.87)(0.87) = 0.7569$$
$$\text{Prob } (c) = p_{12} p_{21} = (0.09)(0.12) = 0.0108$$

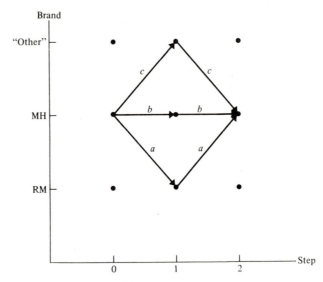

FIGURE 16.1
Ways to go from brand MH to brand MH in two steps.

Thus,

$$p_{11}{}^{(2)} = \text{Prob }(a) + \text{Prob }(b) + \text{Prob }(c)$$
$$= p_{10}p_{01} + p_{11}p_{11} + p_{12}p_{21}$$
$$= 0.0008 + 0.7569 + 0.0108$$
$$= 0.7685$$

Likewise,

$$p_{20}{}^{(2)} = p_{20}p_{00} + p_{21}p_{10} + p_{22}p_{20}$$
$$= (0.15)(0.90) + (0.12)(0.04) + (0.73)(0.15)$$
$$= 0.1350 + 0.0048 + 0.1095$$
$$= 0.2493$$

The quantity $p_{20}{}^{(2)}$ is the probability that a customer who has just bought brand "other" (system is in state 2 at step 0) will buy brand RM time after next (system is in state 0 at step 2). Figure 16.2 illustrates the possible ways a customer who is currently in state 2 can be in state 0 two steps from now.

From the pattern followed in calculating $p_{11}{}^{(2)}$ and $p_{20}{}^{(2)}$, note that the general two-step stationary transition probability $p_{rs}{}^{(2)}$ is given by

$$p_{rs}{}^{(2)} = p_{r0}p_{0s} + p_{r1}p_{1s} + p_{r2}p_{2s} \qquad (16.6)$$

for all states r and s. The complete set of two-step stationary transition probabilities is shown in Table 16.5. Consider each competitor's share of the market after two transactions (at step 2).

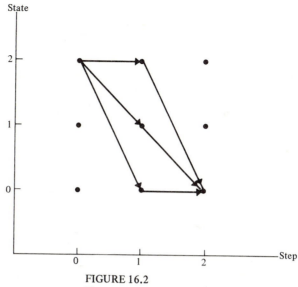

FIGURE 16.2
Ways to go from state 2 to state 0 in two steps.

$$\begin{pmatrix} \text{RM's share} \\ \text{at step 2} \end{pmatrix} = \begin{pmatrix} \text{RM's share} \\ \text{at step 0} \end{pmatrix} \begin{pmatrix} \text{fraction of current RM} \\ \text{customers who will buy} \\ \text{brand RM at step 2} \end{pmatrix}$$

$$+ \begin{pmatrix} \text{MH's share} \\ \text{at step 0} \end{pmatrix} \begin{pmatrix} \text{fraction of current MH} \\ \text{customers who will buy} \\ \text{brand RM at step 2} \end{pmatrix}$$

$$+ \begin{pmatrix} \text{"others" share} \\ \text{at step 0} \end{pmatrix} \begin{pmatrix} \text{fraction of current} \\ \text{"other" customers} \\ \text{who will buy brand} \\ \text{RM at step 2} \end{pmatrix}$$

$$= (0.35)p_{00}^{(2)} + (0.30)p_{10}^{(2)} + (0.35)p_{20}^{(2)}$$

Table 16.5 TWO–STEP STATIONARY TRANSITION PROBABILITIES, FREEZE–DRIED DINNERS

States	0	1	2
0	0.8228	0.0450	0.1322
1	0.0843	0.7685	0.1472
2	0.2493	0.1950	0.5557

$$= (0.35)(0.8228) + (0.30)(0.0843) + (0.35)(0.2493)$$

$$= \underbrace{0.28798}_{\substack{\text{From original} \\ \text{RM customers}}} + \underbrace{0.02529}_{\substack{\text{From original} \\ \text{MH customers}}} + \underbrace{0.08726}_{\substack{\text{From original} \\ \text{"other"} \\ \text{customers}}}$$

$$= 0.4005$$

This says that brand RM will have 40.05 percent of the market after two steps. Note that 28.80 percent of the market will come from retaining original customers, 2.53 percent will come from original MH customers, and 8.73 percent will come from original "other" customers.

$$\text{MH's share at step 2} = (0.35)p_{01}^{(2)} + (0.30)p_{11}^{(2)} + (0.35)p_{21}^{(2)}$$

$$= (0.35)(0.0450) + (0.30)(0.7685) + 0.35(0.1950)$$

$$= \underbrace{0.01575}_{\substack{\text{From original} \\ \text{RM customers}}} + \underbrace{0.23055}_{\substack{\text{From original} \\ \text{MH customers}}} + \underbrace{0.06825}_{\substack{\text{From original} \\ \text{"other"} \\ \text{customers}}}$$

$$= 0.3145$$

$$\text{"Others" share at step 2} = (0.35)p_{02}^{(2)} + (0.30)p_{12}^{(2)} + (0.35)p_{22}^{(2)}$$

$$= (0.35)(0.1322) + (0.30)(0.1472) + (0.35)(0.5557)$$

$$= \underbrace{0.04627}_{\substack{\text{From original} \\ \text{RM customers}}} + \underbrace{0.04416}_{\substack{\text{From original} \\ \text{MH customers}}} + \underbrace{0.19449}_{\substack{\text{From original} \\ \text{"other"} \\ \text{customers}}}$$

$$= 0.2849$$

Table 16.6 illustrates the change in the share of the market from step 0 to step 20.

Note in Table 16.7 that after 33 steps, the probability of being in a given state is independent of the starting state. This means that brand RM will eventually have 47 percent of the market, brand MH will have 29 percent of the market, and all "other" brands will have 24 percent of the market.

Note in Table 16.7 that the probability of being in state 0 after 33 steps is 0.47 regardless of the state at step 0, that is, $p_{i0}^{(33)} = 0.47$ for $i = 0, 1, 2$. Likewise, $p_{i1}^{(33)} = 0.29$ and $p_{i2}^{(33)} = 0.24$ for $i = 0, 1, 2$. This information can be used to show that each competitor's eventual (long-run) share of the market is independent of each competitor's initial share. Let S_0 represent RM's initial share of the market; S_1, MH's share; and S_2, "others" share. Then each competitor's long-run share is given by

$$\text{RM's eventual share} = S_0 p_{00}^{(33)} + S_1 p_{10}^{(33)} + S_2 p_{20}^{(33)}$$

$$= S_0(0.47) + S_1(0.47) + S_2(0.47)$$

Table 16.6 SHARE OF THE MARKET AFTER 0, 1, . . . , 20 STEPS

Steps	Competitor		
	RM	MH	"Other"
0	0.35	0.30	0.35
1	0.38	0.31	0.31
2	0.40	0.31	0.28
3	0.42	0.32	0.27
4	0.43	0.32	0.26
5	0.44	0.31	0.25
6	0.44	0.31	0.25
7	0.45	0.31	0.24
8	0.45	0.31	0.24
9	0.45	0.31	0.24
10	0.46	0.30	0.24
11	0.46	0.30	0.24
12	0.46	0.30	0.24
13	0.46	0.30	0.24
14	0.46	0.30	0.24
15	0.47	0.30	0.24
16	0.47	0.30	0.24
17	0.47	0.30	0.24
18	0.47	0.29	0.24
19	0.47	0.29	0.24
20	0.47	0.29	0.24

Table 16.7 n-STEP STATIONARY TRANSITION PROBABILITIES FOR n = 2, 3, 5, 10, 20, 30, 32, 33 BRAND–SWITCHING PROBLEM

Step	States	0	1	2
2	0	0.82	0.04	0.13
	1	0.08	0.77	0.15
	2	0.25	0.19	0.56
3	0	0.76	0.07	0.17
	1	0.13	0.69	0.18
	2	0.32	0.24	0.44
5	0	0.67	0.12	0.20
	1	0.21	0.57	0.22
	2	0.39	0.29	0.32
10	0	0.56	0.21	0.23
	1	0.35	0.41	0.24
	2	0.45	0.30	0.25
20	0	0.49	0.27	0.24
	1	0.45	0.32	0.24
	2	0.47	0.29	0.24
30	0	0.48	0.29	0.24
	1	0.47	0.30	0.24
	2	0.47	0.29	0.24
32	0	0.47	0.29	0.24
	1	0.47	0.30	0.24
	2	0.47	0.29	0.24
33	0	0.47	0.29	0.24
	1	0.47	0.29	0.24
	2	0.47	0.29	0.24

$$= (0.47)(S_0 + S_1 + S_2)$$
$$= 0.47$$

since $S_0 + S_1 + S_2 = 1$.

$$\text{MH's eventual share} = S_0\, p_{01}^{(33)} + S_1\, p_{11}^{(33)} + S_2\, p_{21}^{(33)}$$
$$= S_0(0.29) + S_1(0.29) + S_2(0.29)$$
$$= 0.29$$
$$\text{"Others" eventual share} = S_0 p_{02}^{(33)} + S_1 p_{12}^{(33)} + S_2 p_{22}^{(33)}$$
$$= S_0(0.24) + S_1(0.24) + S_2(0.24)$$
$$= 0.24$$

EXAMPLE 16.2.4 Consider the n-step stationary transition probabilities for the truck problem in Example 16.2.2. These probabilities are given in Table 16.8 for steps 1, 5, 10, and 15.

16.2.2 Steady-State Stationary Transition Probabilities

Suppose a given system has $N + 1$ states, $0, 1, 2, \ldots, N$. If for some value of n,

Table 16.8 n-STEP STATIONARY TRANSITION PROBABILITIES FOR $n = 1, 5, 10, 15$–TRUCK PROBLEM

Step	States	0	1	2	3	4
	0	0.5000	0.4500	0.0300	0.0200	0
	1	0	0.5600	0.4000	0.0300	0.0100
1	2	0	0	0.4500	0.5000	0.0500
	3	0	0	0	0.6000	0.4000
	4	0	1.0000	0	0	0
	0	0.0313	0.2830	0.2584	0.3086	0.1188
	1	0	0.2931	0.1984	0.3452	0.1633
5	2	0	0.3773	0.2120	0.2742	0.1366
	3	0	0.3322	0.2791	0.2795	0.1092
	4	0	0.2399	0.2276	0.3737	0.1588
	0	0.0010	0.3203	0.2321	0.3088	0.1378
	1	0	0.3146	0.2337	0.3131	0.1386
10	2	0	0.3144	0.2274	0.3160	0.1422
	3	0	0.3217	0.2279	0.3101	0.1402
	4	0	0.3184	0.2363	0.3090	0.1363
	0	0	0.3174	0.2305	0.3123	0.1397
	1	0	0.3177	0.2309	0.3120	0.1395
15	2	0	0.3170	0.2311	0.3123	0.1395
	3	0	0.3170	0.2306	0.3126	0.1398
	4	0	0.3178	0.2305	0.3120	0.1397

$$p_{rs}^{(n)} > 0 \qquad \text{for } r = 0, 1, 2, \dots, N \qquad (16.7)$$
$$s = 0, 1, 2, \dots, N$$

and if

$$p_{rr} > 0 \qquad \text{for } r = 0, 1, 2, \dots, N \qquad (16.8)$$

then

$$\lim_{n \to \infty} p_{rs}^{(n)} = a_s \qquad \text{for } s = 0, 1, 2, \dots, N \qquad (16.9)$$

The quantity a_s is the steady-state stationary transition probability of being in state s after a large number of steps. That is to say, if every state can eventually be reached from every other state (possibly in a large number of steps), and if the system can be in any given state on two consecutive steps, then the probability of being in any given state after a large number of steps is a constant. This constant is called the *steady-state probability* for the given state.

The $N + 1$ steady-state probabilities satisfy the $N + 2$ linear steady-state equations

$$a_s = \sum_{r=0}^{N} a_r p_{rs} \qquad \text{for } s = 0, 1, 2, \dots, N \qquad (16.10)$$

$$\sum_{s=0}^{N} a_s = 1 \qquad (16.11)$$

Thus, if we form a system of $N + 1$ linear equations in $N + 1$ unknowns by using any N of the equations in (16.10) and Equation (16.11), the solution of the system will be the $N + 1$ steady-state probabilities. Equation (16.11) must be one of the $N + 1$ equations to assure that the steady-state probabilities sum to 1.

EXAMPLE 16.2.5   In Example 16.2.1, $p_{rs} > 0$ for all states r and s (see Table 16.1). Hence, inequalities (16.7) are satisfied for $n = 1$ and inequalities (16.8) are satisfied for $r = 0, 1, 2$. Thus, the steady-state probabilities can be calculated immediately by using any two of the equations in (16.10) and Equation (16.11). Suppose we use the last two equations in (16.10) and Equation (16.11), then

$$a_1 = a_0 p_{01} + a_1 p_{11} + a_2 p_{21}$$
$$a_2 = a_0 p_{02} + a_1 p_{12} + a_2 p_{22} \qquad (16.12)$$
$$1 = a_0 \quad + a_1 \quad + a_2$$

When the p_{rs} values from Table 16.1 are substituted in Equations (16.12) we get

$$a_1 = (0.02)a_0 + (0.87)a_1 + (0.12)a_2$$

$$a_2 = (0.08)a_0 + (0.09)a_1 + (0.73)a_2 \quad (16.13)$$
$$1 = a_0 + a_1 + a_2$$

The computer program in Section 16.4 yielded the solution

$$a_0 = 0.4718$$
$$a_1 = 0.2913$$
$$a_2 = 0.2369$$

This says that each potential customer will be selecting brands RM, MH, and "other" with probabilities 0.47, 0.29, and 0.24, respectively, after a large number of steps if the one-step stationary transition probabilities do not change.

EXAMPLE 16.2.6 For the truck problem in Example 16.2.2, note that if the truck starts out in state 0 and eventually leaves that state, it will never return. Thus, $p_{10}^{(n)} = p_{20}^{(n)} = p_{30}^{(n)} = p_{40}^{(n)} = 0$ for all n. This means that state 0 can be ignored and steady-state probabilities calculated for the last four states since these states satisfy inequalities (16.7) and (16.8). Hence,

$$a_1 = a_1 p_{11} + a_2 p_{21} + a_3 p_{31} + a_4 p_{41}$$
$$a_2 = a_1 p_{12} + a_2 p_{22} + a_3 p_{32} + a_4 p_{42}$$
$$a_3 = a_1 p_{13} + a_2 p_{23} + a_3 p_{33} + a_4 p_{43} \quad (16.14)$$
$$a_4 = a_1 p_{14} + a_2 p_{24} + a_3 p_{34} + a_4 p_{44}$$
$$1 = a_1 + a_2 + a_3 + a_4$$

If the last four equations in (16.14) and the one-step stationary transition probabilities from Table 16.4 are used, we have

$$a_2 = 0.40a_1 + 0.45a_2$$
$$a_3 = 0.03a_1 + 0.50a_2 + 0.60a_3$$
$$a_4 = 0.01a_1 + 0.05a_2 + 0.40a_3$$
$$1 = a_1 + a_2 + a_3 + a_4$$

The computer program in Section 16.4 yielded the solution

$$a_1 = 0.3178$$
$$a_2 = 0.2305$$
$$a_3 = 0.3120$$
$$a_3 = 0.1397$$

Of course $a_0 = 0$.

Based on the data in Example 16.2.2, the trucker's expected profit per week will eventually be

$$\begin{aligned}
\text{Expected} \atop \text{profit/week} &= \$500a_0 + \$400a_1 + \$300a_2 + \$200a_3 - \$300a_4 \\
&= \$500(0) + \$400(0.3178) + \$300(0.2305) \\
&\quad + \$200(0.3120) - \$300(0.1397) \\
&= \$216.76
\end{aligned}$$

EXAMPLE 16.2.7 *Brand switching under two potential plans* The manufacturer of brand MH (freeze-dried dinners) is not satisfied with eventually having only 29 percent of the market. Therefore, two potential plans are being considered.

Plan A
The manufacturer of brand MH can launch a campaign to retain 6 percent more of its own customers at each step. MH's loss to brand RM and "other" is reduced to 2 and 5 percent, respectively.

Plan B
The manufacturer of brand MH can launch a campaign to attract 18 percent of "others" losses at each step, rather than the current 12 percent.

Which plan will result in a long-run larger share of the market for brand MH?
The new transition probabilities under plan A are given in Table 16.9.
Since $p_{rs} > 0$ for all states r and s, the steady-state probabilities exist and will yield the new long-run share of the market for each competitor. The steady-state equations are given by

$$\begin{aligned}
a_0 &= 0.90a_0 + 0.02a_1 + 0.15a_2 \\
a_1 &= 0.02a_0 + 0.93a_1 + 0.12a_2 \\
a_2 &= 0.08a_0 + 0.05a_1 + 0.73a_2 \\
1 &= a_0 + a_1 + a_2
\end{aligned}$$

The solution of the last three equations is

Table 16.9 ONE–STEP STATIONARY TRANSITION PROBABILITIES–PLAN A

States	0	1	2
0	0.90	0.02	0.08
1	0.02	0.93	0.05
2	0.15	0.12	0.73

Table 16.10 ONE–STEP STATIONARY TRANSITION PROBABILITIES–PLAN B

States	0	1	2
0	0.90	0.02	0.08
1	0.04	0.87	0.09
2	0.09	0.18	0.73

$$a_0 = 0.3740$$
$$a_1 = 0.4347$$
$$a_2 = 0.1913$$

Thus, brand MH could increase its long-run share of the market from 29 to 43 percent with plan A.

The transition probabilities for plan B are given in Table 16.10.

The steady-state equations are given by

$$a_0 = 0.90a_0 + 0.04a_1 + 0.09a_2$$
$$a_1 = 0.02a_0 + 0.87a_1 + 0.18a_2$$
$$a_2 = 0.08a_0 + 0.09a_1 + 0.73a_2$$
$$1 = a_0 + a_1 + a_2$$

The solution is

$$a_0 = 0.3711$$
$$a_1 = 0.3892$$
$$a_2 = 0.2397$$

Plan A is superior since MH can eventually have 43 percent of the market using it, whereas MH would eventually only have approximately 39 percent of the market under plan B. Of course, both plans are superior to the original operation.

16.3 FIRST-PASSAGE TIME

Quite often it is of interest to know something about the transition times in a Markov chain. Information about transition times is usually defined in terms of first-passage times.

Definition 16.3.1 First-passage time The number of transitions (steps) needed to go from state r to state s for the first time is defined to be the first-passage time from state r to state s. It is denoted by T_{rs}. ////

If the probability of the system going from state r to state s eventually (possibly in a large number of steps) is 1, the corresponding first-passage time T_{rs} is a random variable; otherwise, it is infinity. For example, if the one-step stationary transition probabilities are given by:

States	0	1	2
0	0	$\frac{1}{2}$	$\frac{1}{2}$
1	$\frac{1}{2}$	$\frac{1}{2}$	0
2	0	$\frac{1}{2}$	$\frac{1}{2}$

then the first-passage time between any two states is a random variable. More specifically, the probability of never getting to a given state is always zero.

If the one-step stationary transition probabilities are given by:

States	0	1	2
0	0	$\frac{1}{2}$	$\frac{1}{2}$
1	$\frac{1}{2}$	$\frac{1}{2}$	0
2	0	0	1

there is a positive probability the system will leave state 0 and never return. For example, if it goes to state 2 (it will eventually), it will never return. Thus, T_{00} and T_{01} are not random variables. Likewise, T_{10}, T_{11}, T_{20}, T_{21}, and T_{22} are not random variables. However, the variables T_{02} and T_{12} *are* random variables since the system will eventually be in state 2.

If T_{rs} is a random variable, let $g_{rs}(t)$ be the corresponding probability distribution function, where t represents the values T_{rs} can take on, namely, $t = 1, 2, 3, \ldots$. Note that

$$g_{rs}(1) = \text{probability of going from state } r \text{ to state } s$$
$$\text{for the first time in one step}$$

$$= p_{rs}$$
$$g_{rs}(2) = \text{probability of going from state } r \text{ to state } s$$
$$\text{for the first time in two steps}$$

$$= p_{rs}^{(2)} - p_{rs}p_{ss}$$
$$= p_{rs}^{(2)} - g_{rs}(1)p_{ss}$$

$$g_{rs}(n) = p_{rs}^{(n)} - \sum_{t=1}^{n-1} g_{rs}(t)p_{ss}^{n-t}$$

(16.15)

Since T_{rs} is a random variable,

$$\sum_{t=1}^{\infty} g_{rs}(t) = 1$$

Also, note that the expected value of T_{rs} (expected first-passage time from state r to state s) is

$$\mu_{rs} = E(T_{rs}) = \sum_{t=1}^{\infty} t g_{rs}(t)$$

If $r = s$, the expected first-passage time is called the *expected recurrence time* for state r. The expected recurrence time for state r is the reciprocal of the steady-state probability of being in state r.

In general, if the variables T_{is} where $i = 0, 1, \ldots, s-1, s+1, \ldots, N$ are random variables, the expected first-passage time from state r to state s $(r \neq s)$ can be obtained by solving the system of linear equations given by Equations (16.16).

$$\mu_{0s} = 1 + \sum_{\substack{i=0 \\ i \neq s}}^{N} p_{0i} \mu_{is}$$

$$\mu_{1s} = 1 + \sum_{\substack{i=1 \\ i \neq s}}^{N} p_{1i} \mu_{is}$$

$$\cdots \cdots \cdots \cdots \cdots \cdots$$

$$\mu_{s-1,s} = 1 + \sum_{\substack{i=0 \\ i \neq s}}^{N} p_{s-1,i} \mu_{is} \qquad (16.16)$$

$$\mu_{s+1,s} = 1 + \sum_{\substack{i=0 \\ i \neq s}}^{N} p_{s+1,i} \mu_{is}$$

$$\cdots \cdots \cdots \cdots \cdots \cdots$$

$$\mu_{N,s} = 1 + \sum_{\substack{i=0 \\ i \neq s}}^{N} p_{Ni} \mu_{is}$$

Note that in the process of obtaining μ_{rs}, the solution of Equations (16.16) yields μ_{is} where $i = 0, 1, \ldots, s-1, s+1, \ldots, N$.

EXAMPLE 16.3.1   For the brand-switching problem in Example 16.2.1, all $p_{rs} > 0$, so the first-passage time from state r to state s is a random variable $(r,s = 0, 1, 2)$. Hence, the probability distribution function can be defined for each T_{rs}. Consider the probability distribution function for the first-passage time from state 1 to state 2.

$$g_{12}(1) = \text{probability of going from state 1 to state 2}$$
$$\text{for the first time in one step}$$

$$= p_{12}$$

$$= 0.09$$

$$g_{12}(2) = \text{probability of going from state 1 to state 2}$$
$$\text{for the first time in two steps}$$

$$= p_{12}^{(2)} - g_{12}(1)p_{22}$$

$$= 0.1472 - (0.09)(0.73)$$

$$= 0.0815$$

$$g_{12}(3) = p_{12}^{(3)} - g_{12}(1)p_{22}^{(2)} - g_{12}(2)p_{22}$$

$$= 0.1834 - (0.09)(0.5557) - (0.0815)(0.73)$$

$$= 0.07389$$

etc.

For the case at hand, Equations (16.16) can be solved to obtain the desired expected first-passage time from state 1 to state 2. That is, to obtain $\mu_{12} = E(T_{12})$, set up the two linear equations

$$\mu_{02} = 1 + p_{00}\mu_{02} + p_{01}\mu_{12}$$
$$\mu_{12} = 1 + p_{10}\mu_{02} + p_{11}\mu_{12}$$

Substitute the p_{rs} values from Table 16.1 to get

$$\mu_{02} = 1 + 0.90\mu_{02} + 0.02\mu_{12}$$
$$\mu_{12} = 1 + 0.04\mu_{02} + 0.87\mu_{12}$$

or

$$0.10\mu_{02} - 0.02\mu_{12} = 1$$
$$-0.04\mu_{02} + 0.13\mu_{12} = 1$$

Thus,

$$\mu_{02} = 12.295$$
$$\mu_{12} = 11.475$$

This indicates that the expected first-passage time from state 0 to state 2 is approximately 12 steps and from state 1 to state 2 is approximately 11 steps. In Example 16.2.5, it was determined that the steady-state probability of being in state 2 is $a_2 = 0.2369$. Hence, the expected recurrence time for state 2 is

$$\mu_{22} = \frac{1}{a_2} = \frac{1}{0.2369} = 4.2212$$

Table 16.11 **EXPECTED FIRST-PASSAGE AND RECURRENCE TIMES– EXAMPLE 16.2.5**

States	0	1	2
0	2.1197	23.3333	12.2951
1	14.8148	3.4326	11.4754
2	10.2881	16.6666	4.2213

Likewise, the expected recurrence times for states 0 and 1 are

$$\mu_{00} = \frac{1}{a_0} = \frac{1}{0.4718} = 2.1195$$

$$\mu_{11} = \frac{1}{a_1} = \frac{1}{0.2913} = 3.4329$$

The computer program in Section 16.4 yielded the expected first-passage and recurrence times given in Table 16.11. The elements in Table 16.11 are the μ_{ij}'s where $i = 0, 1, 2; j = 0, 1, 2$.

16.4 COMPUTER PROGRAM FOR MARKOV ANALYSIS

This program calculates the n-step probabilities successively until the system reaches steady-state or until $n = 100$, whichever occurs first. If steady-state cannot be reached, a message stating such is printed. The first, last, and several intermediate n-step stationary transition probability tables are printed regardless of whether steady-state can be reached or not.

Given the initial probability of being in state i for $i = 0, 1, \ldots, N$, the program prints out the probability of being in state i for $i = 0, 1, 2, \ldots, N$ after $n = 1, 2, \ldots$ steps.

Finally, if steady-state probabilities exist, the expected first-passage and recurrence times are calculated and printed.

The data and results from Example 16.2.1 follow the computer listing. The program occupies 56K bytes of core storage. It took 0.42 s of IBM 370/168 time to solve five problems comparable to Examples 16.2.1 and 16.2.2. Problems with a maximum of 20 states can be solved without changing the DIMENSION statement at the start of the program.

```
C     *******************************************************************************
C     *                                                                            *
C     *               ***  MARKOV CHAIN ANALYSIS  ***                              *
C     *                                                                            *
C     * THIS PROGRAM IS DESIGNED                                                   *
C     *     TO READ                                                                *
C     *         CARD 1    COLS  2-80   TITLE  DESCRIPTION OF THE PROBLEM USING     *
C     *                                       ANY CHARACTERS ON KEYPUNCH           *
C     *                                       ** COLUMN 1 MUST BE LEFT BLANK **    *
C     *         CARD 2    COLS  1- 5   NP  NUMBER OF STATES  (I5)                  *
C     *         CARDS 3 TO T   PR(XO=I)  PROBABILITY OF BEING IN STATE I           *
C     *                                  INITIALLY.  PUNCH 8 PER CARD IN           *
C     *                                  8F10.0 FORMAT.  IF I>8, CONTINUE          *
C     *                                  ON THE NEXT CARD.                         *
C     *         CARDS T+1 TO R   P(I,J)  ONE-STEP STATIONARY TRANSITION            *
C     *                                  PROBABILITIES.  PUNCH DATA ROWWISE        *
C     *                                  IN 8F10.0 FORMAT.  EACH NEW ROW           *
C     *                                  BEGINS ON A NEW CARD.                     *
C     *           TO SOLVE MORE THAN ONE PROBLEM AT A TIME, REPEAT THE            *
C     *           READ SEQUENCE, AND STACK THE DATA ONE BEHIND THE OTHER          *
C     *                                                                            *
C     *     TO CALCULATE AND PRINT                                                 *
C     *         PNEW(I,J)    N-STEP STATIONARY TRANSITION PROBABILITIES            *
C     *                      FOR N=1,2,...                                         *
C     *         PNEW(NP,J)   STEADY-STATE TRANSITION PROBABILITIES                 *
C     *         TABLE(I,J)   PROBABILITY OF BEING IN STATE J AFTER I STEPS         *
C     *         EXTIME(I,J)  EXPECTED FIRST PASSAGE TIME FROM STATE I TO STATE J   *
C     *                                                                            *
C     *******************************************************************************
      DIMENSION P(20,20),PNEW(20,20),PTEMP(20,20),PR(20),TEMP(20),
     *          TABLE(102,20),A(20,20),EXTIME(20,20),TITLE(20)
   50 READ(5,55,END=2000)TITLE
   55 FORMAT(20A4)
      WRITE(6,60)TITLE
   60 FORMAT('1',20A4,//)
C     *******************************************************************************
C     *  STEP 1                                                                    *
C     *        READ DATA                                                           *
C     *******************************************************************************
      READ(5,10)NP
   10 FORMAT(I5)
      N=NP-1
      READ(5,20)(PR(J),J=1,NP)
   20 FORMAT(8F10.0)
      DO 15 I=1,NP
   15 READ(5,20)(P(I,J),J=1,NP)
C     *******************************************************************************
C     *  STEP 2                                                                    *
C     *        CALCULATE POWERS OF MATRIX P                                        *
C     *******************************************************************************
   25 DO 30 I=1,NP
      DO 30 J=1,NP
   30 PNEW(I,J)=P(I,J)
      DO 35 J=1,NP
   35 TABLE(1,J)=PR(J)
      KOUNT=1
      DO 100 KK=1,101
      NFINAL=0
      IF(KK.EQ.1)GO TO 42
      DO 200 I=1,NP
      DO 211 J=1,NP
      PTEMP(I,J)=0
      DO 211 M=1,NP
  211 PTEMP(I,J)=PTEMP(I,J)+P(I,M)*PNEW(M,J)
  200 CONTINUE
      DO 212 I=1,NP
      DO 212 J=1,NP
  212 PNEW(I,J)=PTEMP(I,J)
C TEST FOR LAST TIME
      DO 230 J=1,NP
```

```
          DO 235 I=1,N
          IP=I+1
          DO 235 K=IP,NP
          DIFF=PNEW(I,J)-PNEW(K,J)
          IF(ABS(DIFF).GT..001) GO TO 45
    235 CONTINUE
    230 CONTINUE
          NFINAL=1
          GO TO 42
     45 ITEST=KK/5
          IF(ITEST*5.NE.KK) GO TO 47
     42 WRITE(6,40)KK
     40 FORMAT(' MATRIX RAISED TO POWER ',I3,/)
          DO 270 I=1,NP
    270 WRITE(6,280)(PNEW(I,J),J=1,NP)
    280 FORMAT(8F9.4)
          WRITE(6,275)
    275 FORMAT(/)
     47 DO 250 J=1,NP
          TEMP(J)=0
          DO 251 I=1,NP
    251 TEMP(J)=TEMP(J)+PR(I)*PNEW(I,J)
    250 CONTINUE
          KOUNT=KOUNT+1
          DO 41 J=1,NP
     41 TABLE(KOUNT,J)=TEMP(J)
          IF(NFINAL.EQ.1) GO TO 48
    100 CONTINUE
          WRITE(6,80)
     80 FORMAT(' STEADY-STATE PROBABILITIES HAVE NOT BEEN OBTAINED IN 100
         *STEPS')
          GO TO 50
C     **********************************************************************
C     *    STEP 3                                                         *
C     *           PRINT STEADY-STATE PROBABILITIES                        *
C     **********************************************************************
     48 WRITE(6,152)
    152 FORMAT(//' THE STEADY-STATE PROBABILITY OF BEING IN')
          DO 151 J=1,NP
          JM=J-1
    151 WRITE(6,153)JM,PNEW(NP,J)
    153 FORMAT('    STATE ',I4,' IS',F10.4)
C     **********************************************************************
C     *    STEP 4                                                         *
C     *           CALCULATE PRABABILITY OF BEING IN STATE J AFTER I STEPS *
C     **********************************************************************
          WRITE(6,155)
    155 FORMAT('1','PROBABILITY OF BEING IN STATE J AFTER I STEPS'//'
         *|J=',4X,'1',9X,'2',9X,'3',9X,'...'/'    I|')
          KK=KK+1
          DO 150 I=1,KK
          NI=I-1
          WRITE(6,160)NI,(TABLE(I,J),J=1,NP)
    160 FORMAT(I5,7F10.4,(/5X,7F10.4))
    150 CONTINUE
C     **********************************************************************
C     *    STEPS 5,6                                                      *
C     *           CALCULATE TABLE OF EXPECTED FIRST PASSAGE TIMES AND     *
C     *           RECURRENCE TIMES                                        *
C     **********************************************************************
          DO 500 KS=1,NP
          INR=0
          DO 510 KSS=1,NP
          IF(KSS.EQ.KS) GO TO 510
          INC=0
          INR=INR+1
          DO 520 I=1,NP
          IF(I.EQ.KS) GO TO 520
          INC=INC+1
          A(INR,INC)=-P(KSS,I)
          IF(KSS.EQ.I) A(INR,INC)=1+A(INR,INC)
```

```
   520 CONTINUE
   510 CONTINUE
       DO 540 KOUNT=1,N
   540 A(KOUNT,NP)=1
       CALL GSJOR(N,NP,A)
       NEWI=1
       DO 600 NEWJ=1,NP
       IF(NEWJ.EQ.KS) GO TO 610
       EXTIME(NEWJ,KS)=A(NEWI,NP)
       NEWI=NEWI+1
       GO TO 600
   610 EXTIME(NEWJ,KS)=1/PNEW(NP,KS)
   600 CONTINUE
   500 CONTINUE
       WRITE(6,700)
   700 FORMAT(//' TABLE OF EXPECTED FIRST PASSAGE TIMES AND RECURRENCE TI
      *MES'/8X,'TO')
       NONE=0
       WRITE(6,706)NONE,(I,I=1,N)
   706 FORMAT(3X,6(9X,I3))
       WRITE(6,707)
   707 FORMAT(' FROM')
       DO 710 I=1,NP
       IMINUS=I-1
   710 WRITE(6,720)IMINUS,(EXTIME(I,J),J=1,NP)
   720 FORMAT(I6,6F12.4,(/6X,6F12.4))
       GO TO 50
  2000 STOP
       END



       SUBROUTINE GSJOR(N,M,A)
       DIMENSION A(20,20)
       DO 16 K=1,N
       KP1=K+1
       DO 9 J=KP1,M
     9 A(K,J)=A(K,J)/A(K,K)
       DO 12 I=1,N
       IF(I.EQ.K) GO TO 12
       DO 14 J=KP1,M
    14 A(I,J)=A(I,J)-A(I,K)*A(K,J)
    12 CONTINUE
    16 CONTINUE
    13 RETURN
       END


/DATA

   EXAMPLE USING TABLE 16.1
      3
       .35        .30        .35
       .9         .02        .08
       .04        .87        .09
       .15        .12        .73
```

EXAMPLE USING TABLE 16.1

MATRIX RAISED TO POWER   1

```
0.9000    0.0200    0.0800
0.0400    0.8700    0.0900
0.1500    0.1200    0.7300
```

MATRIX RAISED TO POWER   5

```
0.6746    0.1217    0.2037
0.2096    0.5702    0.2202
0.3904    0.2861    0.3235
```

MATRIX RAISED TO POWER   10

```
0.5601    0.2097    0.2301
0.3469    0.4136    0.2395
0.4496    0.3032    0.2472
```

MATRIX RAISED TO POWER   15

```
0.5117    0.2536    0.2347
0.4142    0.3466    0.2392
0.4634    0.2983    0.2383
```

MATRIX RAISED TO POWER   20

```
0.4900    0.2740    0.2360
0.4455    0.3165    0.2381
0.4682    0.2946    0.2372
```

MATRIX RAISED TO POWER   25

```
0.4801    0.2834    0.2365
0.4598    0.3028    0.2374
0.4702    0.2928    0.2370
```

MATRIX RAISED TO POWER   30

```
0.4756    0.2877    0.2367
0.4663    0.2965    0.2371
0.4711    0.2920    0.2369
```

MATRIX RAISED TO POWER   35

```
0.4736    0.2896    0.2368
0.4693    0.2937    0.2370
0.4715    0.2916    0.2369
```

MATRIX RAISED TO POWER   40

```
0.4726    0.2905    0.2369
0.4707    0.2924    0.2369
0.4717    0.2914    0.2369
```

MATRIX RAISED TO POWER   45

```
0.4722    0.2909    0.2369
0.4713    0.2918    0.2369
0.4718    0.2913    0.2369
```

```
THE STEADY-STATE PROBABILITY OF BEING IN
   STATE   0  IS    0.4718
   STATE   1  IS    0.2913
   STATE   2  IS    0.2369
```

PROBABILITY OF BEING IN STATE J AFTER I STEPS

I | J=	1	2	3	...
0	0.3500	0.3000	0.3500	
1	0.3795	0.3100	0.3105	
2	0.4005	0.3145	0.2849	
3	0.4158	0.3159	0.2683	
4	0.4271	0.3153	0.2576	
5	0.4356	0.3138	0.2506	
6	0.4422	0.3118	0.2460	
7	0.4474	0.3096	0.2430	
8	0.4515	0.3075	0.2411	
9	0.4548	0.3055	0.2398	
10	0.4575	0.3036	0.2389	
11	0.4597	0.3020	0.2383	
12	0.4616	0.3005	0.2379	
13	0.4631	0.2992	0.2377	
14	0.4644	0.2981	0.2375	
15	0.4655	0.2971	0.2373	
16	0.4665	0.2963	0.2372	
17	0.4673	0.2956	0.2372	
18	0.4679	0.2950	0.2371	
19	0.4685	0.2944	0.2371	
20	0.4690	0.2940	0.2370	
21	0.4694	0.2936	0.2370	
22	0.4698	0.2932	0.2370	
23	0.4701	0.2930	0.2370	
24	0.4703	0.2927	0.2370	
25	0.4705	0.2925	0.2370	
26	0.4707	0.2923	0.2369	
27	0.4709	0.2922	0.2369	
28	0.4710	0.2920	0.2369	
29	0.4711	0.2919	0.2369	
30	0.4712	0.2918	0.2369	
31	0.4713	0.2917	0.2369	
32	0.4714	0.2917	0.2369	
33	0.4715	0.2916	0.2369	
34	0.4715	0.2916	0.2369	
35	0.4716	0.2915	0.2369	
36	0.4716	0.2915	0.2369	
37	0.4716	0.2914	0.2369	
38	0.4717	0.2914	0.2369	
39	0.4717	0.2914	0.2369	
40	0.4717	0.2914	0.2369	
41	0.4717	0.2914	0.2369	
42	0.4718	0.2913	0.2369	
43	0.4718	0.2913	0.2369	
44	0.4718	0.2913	0.2369	
45	0.4718	0.2913	0.2369	

TABLE OF EXPECTED FIRST PASSAGE TIMES AND RECURRENCE TIMES

FROM \ TO	0	1	2
0	2.1197	23.3333	12.2951
1	14.8148	3.4326	11.4754
2	10.2881	16.6666	4.2213

16.5 SUMMARY

In this chapter we have limited our discussion to the analysis of first-order, finite-state Markov chains. We have seen that the one-step stationary transition probabilities form the basis for every Markov analysis. If these probabilities are given or can be calculated, the n-step stationary transition probabilities can then be calculated. In the brand-switching problem we used these probabilities to calculate each competitor's share of the market after 0, 1, 2, ..., 20 steps. We also noted that the n-step stationary transition probabilities settled down to a steady-state after 33 steps. That is, the probability of being in any given state after 33 steps was a constant (to two decimal places) and represented each competitor's eventual share of the market.

When each state can be reached from every state of the system [inequalities (16.7) are satisfied], the first-passage time from any given state to any state can be expressed as a random variable with a certain probability distribution function. To determine the expected first-passage time for each pair of states, the system of equations in (16.16) can be solved using the computer program in Section 16.4.

If each state can be reached from every state of the system [inequalities (16.7) are satisfied] and if the system can be in state r at steps i and $i + 1$, for all possible states [inequalities (16.8) are satisfied], then the system will eventually reach steady-state. In steady-state, the probability of being in any given state is a constant, regardless of the starting state at step 0. The steady-state probabilities can be determined either by calculating $p_{rs}^{(n)}$ successively for all states r and s until the probability of being in state s is constant for all r or by solving a system of $N + 1$ linear equations in $N + 1$ unknowns [see Equations (16.10) and (16.11)].

The computer program in Section 16.4 will calculate the n-step stationary transition probabilities, the steady-state probabilities (if they exist), and the expected first-passage times (if they exist) for any given system.

SELECTED BIBLIOGRAPHY

1   Bhat, U. N.: "Elements of Applied Stochastic Processes," John Wiley & Sons, Inc., New York, 1972.
2   Chung, K. L.: "Markov Chains," Springer-Verlag, New York, 1967.
3   Clarke, A. B., and R. L. Disney: "Probability and Random Processes for Engineers and Scientists," John Wiley & Sons, Inc., New York, 1970.
4   Derman, C.: "Finite State Markov Decision Processes," Academic Press, New York, 1970.
5   Kemeny, J. G., J. L. Snell, and G. L. Thompson: "Finite Markov Chains," Prentice-Hall, Inc., Englewood Cliffs, N.J., 1960.

EXERCISES

16.1 Given the one-step stationary transition probabilities:

	To state		
From state	0	1	2
0	0.5	0.5	0
1	0	0.5	0.5
2	0.5	0	0.5

(*a*) Calculate the three-step stationary transition probabilities.

(*b*) If $P(X_0 = 0) = P(X_0 = 1) = 0$ and $P(X_0 = 2) = 1$, what is the probability of being in state 1 after three steps?

(*c*) Do steady-state probabilities exist in this case? If so, what are they? If not, why not?

16.2 Calculate the expected first-passage time from state 0 to state 1 if the one-step stationary transition probabilities are given by:

	To state	
From state	0	1
0	0.25	0.75
1	0.50	0.50

16.3 What are the steady-state equations for the Markov chain with the one-step stationary probabilities:

	To state		
From state	0	1	2
0	0	0.5	0.5
1	0.75	0.25	0
2	0	1	0

16.4 In Exercise 16.3, what are the steady-state probabilities for each state?

16.5 Calculate the expected recurrence time for state 0 and state 1 using the one-step stationary transition probabilities:

	To state	
From state	0	1
0	0.25	0.75
1	0.50	0.50

16.6 Use the computer program in Section 16.4 to carry out a complete Markov analysis when the one-step stationary transition probabilities are given by:

| | To state | | | | |
From state	0	1	2	3	4
0	0.1	0	0	0.4	0.5
1	0	0.5	0.2	0.2	0.1
2	0.1	0	0	0.2	0.7
3	0	0	0.6	0.2	0.2
4	0	0.6	0.2	0.1	0.1

Assume:

x	0	1	2	3	4
$P(X_0 = x)$	0.1	0.2	0.4	0.1	0.2

16.7 Suppose the one-step stationary transition probabilities for the truck problem (Example 16.2.2) have been updated and are given by:

| | To state | | | | |
From state	0	1	2	3	4
0	0.6	0.4	0	0	0
1	0	0.6	0.3	0.1	0
2	0	0	0.6	0.3	0.1
3	0	0	0	0.5	0.5
4	0	1.0	0	0	0

Use the computer program in Section 16.4 to do a complete Markov analysis. Assume:

x	0	1	2	3	4
$P(X_0 = x)$	1	0	0	0	0

16.8 When is the first-passage time from state i to state j a random variable? In a practical sense, how can we determine whether or not the first-passage time is a random variable?

Table A.1 CUMULATIVE NORMAL DISTRIBUTION FUNCTION*

Y	.00	.01	.02	.03	.04	.05	.06	.07	.08	.09
0.0	.5000	.5040	.5080	.5120	.5160	.5199	.5239	.5279	.5319	.5359
0.1	.5398	.5438	.5478	.5517	.5557	.5596	.5636	.5675	.5714	.5753
0.2	.5793	.5832	.5871	.5910	.5948	.5987	.6026	.6064	.6103	.6141
0.3	.6179	.6217	.6255	.6293	.6331	.6368	.6406	.6443	.6480	.6517
0.4	.6554	.6591	.6628	.6664	.6700	.6736	.6772	.6808	.6844	.6879
0.5	.6915	.6950	.6985	.7019	.7054	.7088	.7123	.7157	.7190	.7224
0.6	.7257	.7291	.7324	.7357	.7389	.7422	.7454	.7486	.7517	.7549
0.7	.7580	.7611	.7642	.7673	.7703	.7734	.7764	.7793	.7823	.7852
0.8	.7881	.7910	.7939	.7967	.7995	.8023	.8051	.8078	.8106	.8133
0.9	.8159	.8186	.8212	.8238	.8264	.8289	.8315	.8340	.8365	.8389
1.0	.8413	.8438	.8461	.8485	.8508	.8531	.8554	.8577	.8599	.8621
1.1	.8643	.8665	.8686	.8708	.8729	.8749	.8770	.8790	.8810	.8830
1.2	.8849	.8869	.8888	.8906	.8925	.8943	.8962	.8980	.8997	.9015
1.3	.9032	.9049	.9066	.9082	.9099	.9115	.9131	.9147	.9162	.9177
1.4	.9192	.9207	.9222	.9236	.9251	.9265	.9279	.9292	.9306	.9319
1.5	.9332	.9345	.9357	.9370	.9382	.9394	.9406	.9418	.9429	.9441
1.6	.9452	.9463	.9474	.9484	.9495	.9505	.9515	.9525	.9535	.9545
1.7	.9554	.9564	.9573	.9582	.9591	.9599	.9608	.9616	.9625	.9633
1.8	.9641	.9649	.9656	.9664	.9671	.9678	.9686	.9693	.9699	.9706
1.9	.9713	.9719	.9726	.9732	.9738	.9744	.9750	.9756	.9761	.9767
2.0	.9772	.9778	.9783	.9788	.9793	.9798	.9803	.9808	.9812	.9817
2.1	.9821	.9826	.9830	.9834	.9838	.9842	.9846	.9850	.9854	.9857
2.2	.9861	.9864	.9868	.9871	.9875	.9878	.9881	.9884	.9887	.9890
2.3	.9893	.9896	.9898	.9901	.9904	.9906	.9909	.9911	.9913	.9916
2.4	.9918	.9920	.9922	.9925	.9927	.9929	.9931	.9932	.9934	.9936
2.5	.9938	.9940	.9941	.9943	.9945	.9946	.9948	.9949	.9951	.9952
2.6	.9953	.9955	.9956	.9957	.9959	.9960	.9961	.9962	.9963	.9964
2.7	.9965	.9966	.9967	.9968	.9969	.9970	.9971	.9972	.9973	.9974
2.8	.9974	.9975	.9976	.9977	.9977	.9978	.9979	.9979	.9980	.9981
2.9	.9981	.9982	.9982	.9983	.9984	.9984	.9985	.9985	.9986	.9986
3.0	.9987	.9987	.9987	.9988	.9988	.9989	.9989	.9989	.9990	.9990
3.1	.9990	.9991	.9991	.9991	.9992	.9992	.9992	.9992	.9993	.9993
3.2	.9993	.9993	.9994	.9994	.9994	.9994	.9994	.9995	.9995	.9995
3.3	.9995	.9995	.9995	.9996	.9996	.9996	.9996	.9996	.9996	.9997
3.4	.9997	.9997	.9997	.9997	.9997	.9997	.9997	.9997	.9997	.9998

*This table gives the area to the left of y under a standard normal curve, for $y = 0.0$, 0.01, 0.02, ..., 3.49. For $y = 0.02$,

$$F(0.02) = \int_{-\infty}^{0.02} N(0,1)\, dx = 0.5080$$

Table A.2 CRITICAL VALUES FOR CHI–SQUARE TEST*

Degrees of freedom	Level of significance $= \alpha$	
	.05	.01
1	3.84	6.63
2	5.99	9.21
3	7.82	11.34
4	9.49	13.28
5	11.07	15.09
6	12.59	16.81
7	14.07	18.48
8	15.51	20.09
9	16.92	21.67
10	18.31	23.21
11	19.68	24.72
12	21.03	26.22
13	22.36	27.69
14	23.68	29.14
15	25.00	30.58
16	26.30	32.00
17	27.59	33.41
18	28.87	34.80
19	30.14	36.19
20	31.41	37.57
21	32.67	38.93
22	33.92	40.29
23	35.17	41.64
24	36.42	42.98
25	37.65	44.31
26	38.88	45.64
27	40.11	46.96
28	41.34	48.28
29	42.56	49.59
30	43.77	50.89

*This table gives the critical values for a chi-square test, for various degrees of freedom and levels of significance α. For $n = 10$ and $\alpha = 0.05$,

$$\int_{18.31}^{\infty} \chi^2(10)\, d\chi^2 = 0.05$$

From "Vital Statistics" by Michael Orkin and Richard Drogin. Copyright 1975, McGraw-Hill Book Company. Used with permission of McGraw-Hill Book Company.

Table A.3 CRITICAL VALUES OF D IN THE KOLMOGOROV–SMIRNOV ONE–SAMPLE TEST

Sample size (N)	Level of significance for D = maximum $\|F_0(X) - S_N(X)\|$				
	.20	.15	.10	.05	.01
1	.900	.925	.950	.975	.995
2	.684	.726	.776	.842	.929
3	.565	.597	.642	.708	.828
4	.494	.525	.564	.624	.733
5	.446	.474	.510	.565	.669
6	.410	.436	.470	.521	.618
7	.381	.405	.438	.486	.577
8	.358	.381	.411	.457	.543
9	.339	.360	.388	.432	.514
10	.322	.342	.368	.410	.490
11	.307	.326	.352	.391	.468
12	.295	.313	.338	.375	.450
13	.284	.302	.325	.361	.433
14	.274	.292	.314	.349	.418
15	.266	.283	.304	.338	.404
16	.258	.274	.295	.328	.392
17	.250	.266	.286	.318	.381
18	.244	.259	.278	.309	.371
19	.237	.252	.272	.301	.363
20	.231	.246	.264	.294	.356
25	.21	.22	.24	.27	.32
30	.19	.20	.22	.24	.29
35	.18	.19	.21	.23	.27
Over 35	$\dfrac{1.07}{\sqrt{N}}$	$\dfrac{1.14}{\sqrt{N}}$	$\dfrac{1.22}{\sqrt{N}}$	$\dfrac{1.36}{\sqrt{N}}$	$\dfrac{1.63}{\sqrt{N}}$

Adapted from F. J. Massey, Jr. The Kolmogorov-Smirnov test for goodness of fit. *J. Amer. Statist. Ass.*, vol. 46, p. 70, 1951, with the kind permission of the publisher.

Table A.4 CRITICAL VALUES FOR F TEST WITH α = 0.05*

ν_1 / ν_2	1	2	3	4	5	6	7	8	9	10	15	20	30	40	60	∞
1	161	200	216	225	230	234	237	239	241	242	246	248	250	251	252	254
2	18.5	19.0	19.2	19.2	19.3	19.3	19.4	19.4	19.4	19.4	19.4	19.4	19.5	19.5	19.5	19.5
3	10.1	9.55	9.28	9.12	9.01	8.94	8.89	8.85	8.81	8.79	8.70	8.66	8.62	8.59	8.57	8.53
4	7.71	6.94	6.59	6.39	6.26	6.16	6.09	6.04	6.00	5.96	5.86	5.80	5.75	5.72	5.69	5.63
5	6.61	5.79	5.41	5.19	5.05	4.95	4.88	4.82	4.77	4.74	4.62	4.56	4.50	4.46	4.43	4.37
6	5.99	5.14	4.78	4.53	4.39	4.28	4.21	4.15	4.10	4.06	3.94	3.87	3.81	3.77	3.74	3.67
7	5.59	4.74	4.35	4.12	3.97	3.87	3.79	3.73	3.68	3.64	3.51	3.44	3.38	3.34	3.30	3.23
8	5.32	4.46	4.07	3.84	3.69	3.58	3.50	3.44	3.39	3.35	3.22	3.15	3.08	3.04	3.01	2.93
9	5.12	4.26	3.86	3.63	3.48	3.37	3.29	3.23	3.18	3.14	3.01	2.94	2.86	2.83	2.79	2.71
10	4.96	4.10	3.71	3.48	3.33	3.22	3.14	3.07	3.02	2.98	2.85	2.77	2.70	2.66	2.62	2.54
11	4.84	3.98	3.59	3.36	3.20	3.09	3.01	2.95	2.90	2.85	2.72	2.65	2.57	2.53	2.49	2.40
12	4.75	3.89	3.49	3.26	3.11	3.00	2.91	2.85	2.80	2.75	2.62	2.54	2.47	2.43	2.38	2.30
13	4.67	3.81	3.41	3.18	3.03	2.92	2.83	2.77	2.71	2.67	2.53	2.46	2.38	2.34	2.30	2.21
14	4.60	3.74	3.34	3.11	2.96	2.85	2.76	2.70	2.65	2.60	2.46	2.39	2.31	2.27	2.22	2.13
15	4.54	3.68	3.29	3.06	2.90	2.79	2.71	2.64	2.59	2.54	2.40	2.33	2.25	2.20	2.16	2.07
16	4.49	3.63	3.24	3.01	2.85	2.74	2.66	2.59	2.54	2.49	2.35	2.28	2.19	2.15	2.11	2.01
17	4.45	3.59	3.20	2.96	2.81	2.70	2.61	2.55	2.49	2.45	2.31	2.23	2.15	2.10	2.06	1.96
18	4.41	3.55	3.16	2.93	2.77	2.66	2.58	2.51	2.46	2.41	2.27	2.19	2.11	2.06	2.02	1.92
19	4.38	3.52	3.13	2.90	2.74	2.63	2.54	2.48	2.42	2.38	2.23	2.16	2.07	2.03	2.98	2.88
20	4.35	3.49	3.10	2.87	2.71	2.60	2.51	2.45	2.39	2.35	2.20	2.12	2.04	1.99	1.95	1.84
21	4.32	3.47	3.07	2.84	2.68	2.57	2.49	2.42	2.37	2.32	2.18	2.10	2.01	1.96	1.92	1.81
22	4.30	3.44	3.05	2.82	2.66	2.55	2.46	2.40	2.34	2.30	2.15	2.07	1.98	1.94	1.89	1.78
23	4.28	3.42	3.03	2.80	2.64	2.53	2.44	2.37	2.32	2.27	2.13	2.05	1.96	1.91	1.86	1.76
24	4.26	3.40	3.01	2.78	2.62	2.51	2.42	2.36	2.30	2.25	2.11	2.03	1.94	1.89	1.84	1.73
25	4.24	3.39	2.99	2.76	2.60	2.49	2.40	2.34	2.28	2.24	2.09	2.01	1.97	1.87	1.82	1.71
30	4.17	3.32	2.92	2.69	2.53	2.42	2.33	2.27	2.21	2.16	2.01	1.93	1.84	1.79	1.74	1.62
40	4.08	3.23	2.84	2.61	2.45	2.34	2.25	2.18	2.12	2.08	1.92	1.84	1.74	1.69	1.64	1.51
60	4.00	3.15	2.76	2.53	2.37	2.25	2.17	2.10	2.04	1.99	1.84	1.75	1.65	1.59	1.53	1.39
120	3.92	3.07	2.68	2.45	2.29	2.18	2.09	2.02	1.96	1.91	1.75	1.66	1.55	1.50	1.43	1.25
∞	3.84	3.00	2.60	2.37	2.21	2.10	2.01	1.94	1.88	1.83	1.67	1.57	1.46	1.39	1.32	1.00

Critical values for F for α = .05

*This table gives the critical value for an F test for various numerator degrees of freedom ν_1 and denominator degrees of freedom ν_2. The significance level is α = 0.05. For $\nu_1 = 3$, $\nu_2 = 9$,

$$\int_{3.86}^{\infty} F(3,9;0.05)\, dF = 0.05$$

From "Vital Statistics" by Michael Orkin and Richard Drogin. Copyright 1975, McGraw-Hill Book Company. Used with permission of McGraw-Hill Book Company.

Table A.5 CRITICAL VALUES FOR F TEST WITH α = 0.01*

ν_1 / ν_2	1	2	3	4	5	6	7	8	9	10	15	20	30	40	60	∞
1	4052	5000	5403	5625	5764	5859	5928	5982	6023	6056	6157	6209	6261	6287	6313	6366
2	98.5	99.0	99.2	99.2	99.3	99.3	99.4	99.4	99.4	99.4	99.4	99.4	99.5	99.5	99.5	99.5
3	34.1	30.8	29.5	28.7	28.2	27.9	27.7	27.5	27.3	27.2	26.9	26.7	26.5	26.4	26.3	26.1
4	21.2	18.0	16.7	16.0	15.5	15.2	15.0	14.8	14.7	14.5	14.2	14.0	13.8	13.7	13.7	13.5
5	16.3	13.3	12.1	11.4	11.0	10.7	10.5	10.3	10.2	10.1	9.72	9.55	9.38	9.27	9.20	9.02
6	13.7	10.9	9.78	9.15	8.75	8.47	8.26	8.10	7.98	7.87	7.56	7.40	7.23	7.14	7.06	6.88
7	12.2	9.55	8.45	7.85	7.46	7.19	6.99	6.84	6.72	6.62	6.31	6.16	5.99	5.91	5.82	5.65
8	11.3	8.65	7.59	7.01	6.63	6.37	6.18	6.03	5.91	5.81	5.52	5.36	5.20	5.12	5.03	4.86
9	10.6	8.02	6.99	6.42	6.06	5.80	5.61	5.47	5.35	5.26	4.96	4.81	4.65	4.57	4.48	4.31
10	10.0	7.56	6.55	5.99	5.64	5.39	5.20	5.06	4.94	4.85	4.56	4.41	4.25	4.17	4.08	3.91
11	9.65	7.21	6.22	5.67	5.32	5.07	4.89	4.74	4.63	4.54	4.25	4.10	3.94	3.86	3.78	3.60
12	9.33	6.93	5.95	5.41	5.06	4.82	4.64	4.50	4.39	4.30	4.01	3.86	3.70	3.62	3.54	3.36
13	9.07	6.70	5.74	5.21	4.86	4.62	4.44	4.30	4.19	4.10	3.82	3.66	3.51	3.43	3.34	3.17
14	8.86	6.51	5.56	5.04	4.70	4.46	4.28	4.14	4.03	3.94	3.66	3.51	3.35	3.27	3.18	3.00
15	8.68	6.36	5.42	4.89	4.56	4.32	4.14	4.00	3.89	3.80	3.52	3.37	3.21	3.13	3.05	2.87
16	8.53	6.23	5.29	4.77	4.44	4.20	4.03	3.89	3.78	3.69	3.41	3.26	3.10	3.02	2.93	2.75
17	8.40	6.11	5.19	4.67	4.34	4.10	3.93	3.79	3.68	3.59	3.31	3.16	3.00	2.92	2.83	2.65
18	8.29	6.01	5.09	4.58	4.25	4.01	3.84	3.71	3.60	3.51	3.23	3.08	2.92	2.84	2.75	2.57
19	8.19	5.93	5.01	4.50	4.17	3.94	3.77	3.63	3.52	3.43	3.15	3.00	2.84	2.76	2.67	2.49
20	8.10	5.85	4.94	4.43	4.10	3.87	3.70	3.56	3.46	3.37	3.09	2.94	2.78	2.69	2.61	2.42
21	8.02	5.78	4.87	4.37	4.04	3.81	3.64	3.51	3.40	3.31	3.03	2.88	2.72	2.64	2.55	2.36
22	7.95	5.72	4.82	4.31	3.99	3.76	3.59	3.45	3.35	3.26	2.98	2.83	2.67	2.58	2.50	2.31
23	7.88	5.66	4.78	4.26	3.94	3.71	3.54	3.41	3.30	3.21	2.93	2.78	2.62	2.54	2.45	2.26
24	7.82	5.61	4.72	4.22	3.90	3.67	3.50	3.36	3.26	3.17	2.89	2.74	2.58	2.49	2.40	2.21
25	7.77	5.57	4.68	4.18	3.86	3.63	3.46	3.32	3.22	3.13	2.85	2.70	2.53	2.45	2.36	2.17
30	7.56	5.39	4.50	4.02	3.70	3.47	3.30	3.17	3.07	2.98	2.70	2.55	2.39	2.30	2.21	2.01
40	7.31	5.18	4.31	3.83	3.51	3.29	3.12	2.99	2.89	2.80	2.52	2.37	2.20	2.11	2.02	1.80
60	7.08	4.98	4.13	3.65	3.34	3.12	2.95	2.82	2.72	2.63	2.35	2.20	2.03	1.94	1.84	1.60
120	6.85	4.79	3.95	3.48	3.17	2.96	2.79	2.66	2.56	2.47	2.10	2.03	1.86	1.76	1.66	1.38
∞	6.63	4.61	3.78	3.32	3.02	2.80	2.64	2.51	2.41	2.32	2.04	1.88	1.70	1.59	1.47	1.00

Critical values for F for $\alpha = .01$

*This table gives the critical value for an F test for various numerator degrees of freedom ν_1 and denominator degrees of freedom ν_2. The significance level is $\alpha = 0.01$. For $\nu_1 = 3$, $\nu_2 = 9$,

$$\int_{6.99}^{\infty} F(3,9;0.01)\,dF = 0.01$$

From "Vital Statistics" by Michael Orkin and Richard Drogin. Copyright 1975, McGraw-Hill. Used with permission.

APPENDIX B

DERIVATION OF QUEUEING FORMULAS

B.1 DERIVATION OF EQUATIONS (13.3) AND (13.4)

Based on the assumptions and notation in Sections 13.2 and 13.3, we want to derive the difference equations

$$\lambda_{n-1}P_{n-1} + \mu_{n+1}P_{n+1} - (\lambda_n + \mu_n)P_n = 0 \quad n > 0$$

$$-\lambda_0 P_0 + \mu_1 P_1 = 0 \quad n = 0$$

Arrivals and departures occur completely at random, but the average arrival and departure rates are dependent upon the number in the system.

Equations (13.3) and (13.4) arise as a consequence of trying to determine $P_n(t)$, the probability of n customers in the system at time t. However, to determine $P_n(t)$, we need to determine the probability of n customers in the system at time $t + \Delta t$, where $\Delta t > 0$.

Assume

(a) $\lambda_n \Delta t$ is the probability of an arrival in the interval t to $t + \Delta t$ for Δt sufficiently small, when the system is in state S_n at time t

(b) $\mu_n \Delta t$ is the probability of a departure in the interval t to $t + \Delta t$ for Δt sufficiently small, when the system is in state S_n at time t

(c) Δt is sufficiently small so the probability of more than one arrival and/or departure in the interval t to $t + \Delta t$ is negligible

The system can be in state S_n at time $t + \Delta t$ in exactly four distinct ways:

1 System is in state S_n at time t, and no arrivals or departures occur during the interval Δt

2 System is in state S_{n-1} at time t, and one arrival and no departures occur during the interval Δt

3 System is in state S_{n+1} at time t, and no arrivals and one departure occur during the interval Δt

4 One arrival and one departure, or more than one arrival and/or departure occur in the interval Δt

Since these four ways are all mutually exclusive, the probability of n customers in the system at time $t + \Delta t$, with $n > 0$, may be expressed as the sum of three independent compound probabilities (the probability of way 4 above is assumed to be negligible); namely,

1 The product of the probability
    (*a*) The system is in state S_n at time t: $P_n(t)$
    (*b*) There are no arrivals during the time Δt: $1 - \lambda_n \Delta t$
    (*c*) There are no departures during the time Δt: $1 - \mu_n \Delta t$

2 The product of the probability
    (*a*) The system is in state S_{n-1} at time t: $P_{n-1}(t)$
    (*b*) There is one arrival during the time Δt: $\lambda_{n-1} \Delta t$
    (*c*) There are no departures during the time Δt: $1 - \mu_{n-1} \Delta t$

3 The product of the probability
    (*a*) The system is in state S_{n+1} at time t: $P_{n+1}(t)$
    (*b*) There are no arrivals during the time Δt: $1 - \lambda_{n+1} \Delta t$
    (*c*) There is one departure during the time Δt: $\mu_{n+1} \Delta t$

Thus,

$$P_n(t + \Delta t) = P_n(t)(1 - \lambda_n \Delta t)(1 - \mu_n \Delta t) + P_{n-1}(t)\lambda_{n-1}\Delta t(1 - \mu_{n-1}\Delta t)$$
$$+ P_{n+1}(t)\mu_{n+1}\Delta t(1 - \lambda_{n+1}\Delta t)$$
$$= P_{n-1}(t)\lambda_{n-1}\Delta t - P_n(t)(\lambda_n + \mu_n) + P_{n+1}(t)\mu_{n+1}\Delta t$$
$$+ \text{higher-order terms in } \Delta t$$

All higher-order terms in Δt are assumed to be negligible compared to Δt. If $P_n(t)$ is subtracted from both sides of the last equation above and the resulting equation is divided by Δt, we get

$$\frac{P_n(t + \Delta t) - P_n(t)}{\Delta t} = P_{n-1}(t)\lambda_{n-1} - P_n(t)(\lambda_n + \mu_n) + P_{n+1}(t)\mu_{n+1}$$
$$+ \text{terms in } \Delta t$$

$$\lim_{\Delta t \to 0} \frac{P_n(t + \Delta t) - P_n(t)}{\Delta t} = \frac{dP_n(t)}{dt} = P_{n-1}(t)\lambda_{n-1} - P_n(t)(\lambda_n + \mu_n)$$
$$+ P_{n+1}(t)\mu_{n+1} \quad \text{for } n > 0$$

$$\frac{dP_0(t)}{dt} = -\lambda_0 P_0(t) + \mu_1 P_1(t) \qquad \text{for } n = 0$$

Here we have a set of differential equations, which, if we could solve them, would yield $P_n(t)$ for all n.

Instead of solving for $P_n(t)$, we assume $P_n(t)$ is independent of time, that is,

$$\lim_{t \to \infty} P_n(t) = P_n$$

then the rate of change of P_n with respect to time is zero. That is,

$$\lim_{t \to \infty} \frac{dP_n(t)}{dt} = \frac{dP_n}{dt} = 0$$

Thus, we have the difference equations

$$\lambda_{n-1} P_{n-1} + \mu_{n+1} P_{n+1} - (\lambda_n + \mu_n) P_n = 0 \qquad n > 0$$
$$-\lambda_0 P_0 + \mu_1 P_1 = 0 \qquad n = 0$$

which we set out to obtain.

B.2 DERIVATION OF $L = \dfrac{\lambda}{\mu - \lambda}$ [EQUATION (13.9)]

Let $\theta = \dfrac{\lambda}{\mu}$,

$L = $ expected number in the system

$$= \sum_{k=0}^{\infty} k P_k$$

$$= \sum_{k=0}^{\infty} k\theta^k (1 - \theta)$$

$$= (1 - \theta)(\theta + 2\theta^2 + 3\theta^3 + 4\theta^4 + \cdots)$$

$$= (1 - \theta)(\theta)(1 + 2\theta + 3\theta^2 + 4\theta^3 + \cdots)$$

$$= (1 - \theta)(\theta) \frac{d \int_0^\theta (1 + 2\theta + 3\theta^2 + 4\theta^3 + \cdots)\, d\theta}{d\theta}$$

$$= (1 - \theta)(\theta) \frac{d(\theta + \theta^2 + \theta^3 + \cdots)}{d\theta}$$

$$= (1 - \theta)(\theta) \frac{d\left(\dfrac{\theta}{1 - \theta}\right)}{d\theta}$$

$$= (1 - \theta)(\theta) \frac{1}{(1 - \theta)^2}$$

$$= \frac{\theta}{1 - \theta}$$

$$= \frac{\lambda/\mu}{1 - (\lambda/\mu)}$$

$$= \frac{\lambda}{\mu - \lambda} \quad \text{for } \frac{\lambda}{\mu} < 1$$

B.3 DERIVATION OF $L_q = \dfrac{\lambda^2}{\mu(\mu - \lambda)}$ [EQUATION (13.10)]

L_q = expected number in the queue
= expected number in the system *minus* the expected number in the service facility

The expected number in the service facility would be

(*a*) The number of customers in the service facility when it is busy times the probability it is busy, plus,

(*b*) The number of customers in the service facility when it is not busy times the probability it is not busy

Thus, the expected number in the service facility L_s is

$$L_s = 1(1 - P_0) + 0P_0$$
$$= 1 - P_0$$

Therefore,

$$L_q = L - L_s$$

$$= \frac{\lambda}{\mu - \lambda} - (1 - P_0)$$

$$= \frac{\lambda}{\mu - \lambda} - \frac{\lambda}{\mu}$$

$$= \frac{\lambda^2}{\mu(\mu - \lambda)}$$

B.4 DISTRIBUTION OF INTERARRIVAL TIME FOR A POISSON INPUT

Assume customers arrive at a service facility according to a Poisson process. That is, arrivals occur completely at random. Let

X = number of arrivals in the interval $(0,t)$

then

$$f(x) = \frac{e^{-\lambda t}(\lambda t)^x}{x!} \qquad \begin{array}{l} x = 0, 1, 2, \ldots \\ \lambda > 0 \end{array}$$

= probability of x arrivals in time t

Let $T =$ time between consecutive arrivals

If an arrival occurs at base time zero, the time to the next arrival is less than t if and only if there is one or more arrival in the interval $[0,t]$. Thus,

$$G(t) = P(T < t) = \sum_{x=1}^{\infty} \frac{e^{-\lambda t}(\lambda t)^x}{x!}$$

But,

$$\sum_{x=0}^{\infty} \frac{e^{-\lambda t}(\lambda t)^x}{x!} = 1$$

Therefore,

$$\sum_{x=1}^{\infty} \frac{e^{-\lambda t}(\lambda t)^x}{x!} = 1 - e^{-\lambda t}$$

$$G(t) = P(T < t) = 1 - e^{-\lambda t}$$

Since $G(t)$ is the cumulative distribution of T, the distribution of T is given by

$$g(t) = \frac{dG(t)}{dt} = \frac{d(1 - e^{-\lambda t})}{dt} = \lambda e^{-\lambda t}$$

Thus, $g(t)$, the distribution of the time between consecutive arrivals, is an exponential distribution with parameter λ. We have shown that if the number of arrivals per unit of time has a Poisson distribution with parameter λ, then the time between consecutive arrivals has an exponential distribution with the same parameter λ.

GAUSS–JORDAN METHOD FOR SOLVING A SYSTEM OF LINEAR EQUATIONS

The Gauss-Jordan method can be used to solve a system of n linear equations in n unknowns for the unique values of the unknowns. It is basically a procedure that multiplies an equation by a constant, and adds a multiple of one equation to another until $x_2, \ldots, x_n$ are eliminated from the first equation, $x_1, x_3, x_4, \ldots, x_n$ are eliminated from the second equation, and so on until $x_1, \ldots, x_{n-1}$ are eliminated from the nth equation. For example, given the system

$$2x_1 + 3x_2 + x_3 = 9 \tag{C.1}$$

$$x_1 + x_2 + x_3 = 4 \tag{C.2}$$

$$x_1 - x_2 - x_3 = -2 \tag{C.3}$$

the Gauss-Jordan method for solving the system is:

Step 1
Multiple Equation (C.1) by $\frac{1}{2}$ to give

$$x_1 + \frac{3}{2}x_2 + \frac{1}{2}x_3 = \frac{9}{2} \tag{C.4}$$

Step 2
Multiply Equation (C.4) by -1 and add to Equation (C.2) to give

$$-\frac{1}{2}x_2 + \frac{1}{2}x_3 = -\frac{1}{2} \qquad \text{(C.5)}$$

Step 3
Multiply Equation (C.4) by -1 and add to Equation (C.3) to give

$$-\frac{5}{2}x_2 - \frac{3}{2}x_3 = -\frac{13}{2} \qquad \text{(C.6)}$$

Step 4
The system now has the form

$$x_1 + \frac{3}{2}x_2 + \frac{1}{2}x_3 = \frac{9}{2} \qquad \text{(C.7)}$$

$$-\frac{1}{2}x_2 + \frac{1}{2}x_3 = -\frac{1}{2} \qquad \text{(C.8)}$$

$$-\frac{5}{2}x_2 - \frac{3}{2}x_3 = -\frac{13}{2} \qquad \text{(C.9)}$$

Note that x_1 has been eliminated from Equations (C.8) and (C.9).

Step 5
Multiply Equation (C.8) by -2 to give

$$x_2 - x_3 = 1 \qquad \text{(C.10)}$$

Step 6
Multiply Equation (C.10) by $-\frac{3}{2}$ and add to Equation (C.7) to give

$$x_1 + \frac{4}{2}x_3 = 3 \qquad \text{(C.11)}$$

Step 7
Multiply Equation (C.10) by $\frac{5}{2}$ and add to Equation (C.9) to give

$$-\frac{8}{2}x_3 = -\frac{8}{2} \qquad \text{(C.12)}$$

The system now has the form

$$x_1 \quad + \frac{4}{2}x_3 = 3 \qquad \text{(C.13)}$$

$$x_2 - \quad x_3 = 1 \qquad \text{(C.14)}$$

$$-\frac{8}{2}x_3 = -\frac{8}{2} \qquad \text{(C.15)}$$

Note that x_2 has been eliminated from Equations (C.13) and (C.15).

Step 8
Multiply Equation (C.15) by $-\frac{2}{8}$ to give

$$x_3 = 1 \qquad \text{(C.16)}$$

Step 9
Add Equation (C.16) to (C.14). Multiply Equation (C.16) by -2 and add to Equation (C.13).

The resulting solution is

$$x_1 = 1$$
$$x_2 = 2$$
$$x_3 = 1$$

Consider the general Gauss-Jordan method for solving a system of n linear equations in n unknowns given by

$$a_{11}x_1 + a_{12}x_2 + \cdots + a_{1n}x_n = a_{1,n+1}|$$
$$a_{21}x_1 + a_{22}x_2 + \cdots + a_{2n}x_n = a_{2,n+1}$$
$$\cdots \cdots \cdots \cdots \cdots \cdots \cdots \cdots \cdots \cdots \cdots$$
$$a_{n1}x_1 + a_{n2}x_2 + \cdots + a_{nn}x_n = a_{n,n+1}$$

The basic idea is to perform elementary transformations on the system until it is reduced to the form

$$x_1 \qquad\qquad = a^*_{1,n+1}$$
$$x_2 \qquad\qquad = a^*_{2,n+1}$$
$$\cdots \cdots \cdots \cdots \cdots \cdots$$
$$x_n = a^*_{n,n+1}$$

Write the system of n linear equations in n unknowns as

$$a_{11}^{(k)}x_1 + a_{12}^{(k)}x_2 + \cdots + a_{1n}^{(k)}x_n = a_{1,n+1}^{(k)}$$
$$a_{21}^{(k)}x_1 + a_{22}^{(k)}x_2 + \cdots + a_{2n}^{(k)}x_n = a_{2,n+1}^{(k)}$$
$$\cdots \cdots \cdots \cdots \cdots \cdots \cdots \cdots \cdots \cdots \cdots \cdots$$
$$a_{n1}^{(k)}x_1 + a_{n2}^{(k)}x_2 + \cdots + a_{nn}^{(k)}x_n = a_{n,n+1}^{(k)}$$

where $k = 0$ originally. Then for $k = 1, 2, \ldots, n$, let

$$a_{kj}^{(k)} = \frac{a_{kj}^{(k-1)}}{a_{kk}^{(k-1)}} \qquad\qquad j = k, k+1, \ldots, n+1$$

$$a_{ij}^{(k)} = a_{ij}^{(k-1)} - a_{ik}^{(k-1)}a_{kj}^{(k)} \qquad i = 1, 2, \ldots, k-1, k+1, \ldots, n$$
$$j = k, k+1, \ldots, n+1$$

After n steps, the solution is given by

$$x_1 = a_{1,n+1}^{(n)}$$
$$x_2 = a_{2,n+1}^{(n)}$$
$$\cdots \cdots \cdots \cdots$$
$$x_n = a_{n,n+1}^{(n)}$$

The computer program that follows is a subroutine that solves a system of N linear equations in N unknowns using the Gauss-Jordan method. The user must supply

N = the number of equations
M = the number of equations plus 1
A = the N X M matrix of coefficients

$$
= \begin{bmatrix}
a_{11} & a_{12} & \cdots & a_{1N} & a_{1,N+1} \\
a_{21} & a_{22} & \cdots & a_{2N} & a_{2,N+1} \\
\cdots\cdots\cdots\cdots\cdots\cdots\cdots\cdots \\
a_{N1} & a_{N2} & \cdots & a_{NN} & a_{N,N+1}
\end{bmatrix}
$$

The last column of A consists of the constants from the right side of the equations. The matrix A must be dimensioned as

DIMENSION A(11,12)

in the mainline program. When the program returns to the mainline program from the subroutine, the solution will be in the $(N + 1)st$ column of A.

```
C       ********************************************************************
C       *                                                                *
C       *                 ***  GAUSS JORDAN METHOD  ***                   *
C       *                                                                *
C       *  THIS SUBROUTINE SOLVES A SYSTEM OF N LINEAR EQUATIONS IN N UNKNOWNS.  *
C       *  THE USER SUPPLIES THE ARGUMENTS:                              *
C       *       N    THE NUMBER OF LINEAR EQUATIONS                       *
C       *       M    N+1                                                  *
C       *       A    THE COEFFICIENTS OF THE SYSTEM OF LINEAR EQUATIONS   *
C       *            WHEN THE SUBROUTINE IS CALLED, THE LAST COLUMN CONTAINS *
C       *            THE CONSTANTS FROM THE RIGHT SIDE OF THE EQUATIONS.  *
C       *            THE SOLUTION IS IN THE LAST COLUMN WHEN THE SUBROUTINE *
C       *            RETURNS CONTROL TO THE MAINLINE PROGRAM.            *
C       *               THE USER MUST MAKE SURE THAT THE DIMENSIONS OF A IN *
C       *               THE SUBROUTINE MATCH THE DIMENSIONS OF THE CORRESPONDING *
C       *               MATRIX IN THE MAINLINE PROGRAM.                   *
C       *                                                                *
C       ********************************************************************
        SUBROUTINE GSJOR(N,M,A)
        DIMENSION A(11,12)
        DO 16 K=1,N
        KP1=K+1
        DO 9 J=KP1,M
        A(K,J)=A(K,J)/A(K,K)
      9 CONTINUE
        DO 12 I=1,N
        IF(I.EQ.K) GO TO 12
        DO 14 J=KP1,M
        A(I,J)=A(I,J)-A(I,K)*A(K,J)
     14 CONTINUE
     12 CONTINUE
     16 CONTINUE
     13 RETURN
        END
```

INDEX

INDEX